Oxford Starter French Dictionary

Revised edition

Edited by
Marie-Hélène Corréard
and Mary O'Neill

UNIVERSITY PRESS

OXFORD

UNIVERSITY PRESS

Great Clarendon Street, Oxford OX2 6DP

Oxford University Press is a department of the University of Oxford.
It furthers the University's objective of excellence in research, scholarship,
and education by publishing worldwide in

Oxford New York

Auckland Bangkok Buenos Aires Cape Town Chennai
Dar es Salaam Delhi Hong Kong Istanbul Karachi Kolkata
Kuala Lumpur Madrid Melbourne Mexico City Mumbai Nairobi
São Paulo Shanghai Taipei Tokyo Toronto

Oxford is a registered trade mark of Oxford University Press
in the UK and in certain other countries

Published in the United States
by Oxford University Press Inc., New York

British Library Cataloguing in Publication Data

Data available

Library of Congress Cataloging in Publication Data

Data available

ISBN 0-19-860715-6

10 9 8 7 6 5 4 3 2 1

Typeset in Swift and Arial by Latimer Trend & Company Ltd.
Printed in Italy by
«La Tipografica Varese S.p.A.» Varese

Contents

Contributors

Chief Editor
Marie-Hélène Corréard

Associate Editor
Mary O'Neill

Editors
Gearóid Cronin
Françoise de Peretti
Natalie Pomier

Lexical usage notes
Henri Béjoint
Richard Wakely

Data-capture
Alison Curr
Diane Diffley

Administration
Isabelle Lemoine

Proofreading
Alison Curr
Isabelle Lemoine

North American English
Tim Horner
Carol Petersen

Introduction
Glossary of grammatical terms
Graham Bishop
Mary O'Neill

Dictionary know-how
A guide to French grammar
Martyn Bird

Design
Information Design Unit
Jane Stevenson

Introduction

A fresh approach

Created to meet the specific needs of English speakers who are starting to learn French, the *Oxford Starter French Dictionary* takes a completely fresh approach to helping you make sense of the new language. We have changed the design of the entries to make them different from entries in traditional dictionaries. What exactly is it that makes the entries so different?

- they have a new, clearer layout
- they are designed to provide the information you need in a helpful, readable way with the minimum of clutter
- since you will be using the English–French and the French–English sides of the dictionary for different tasks, each side works differently and it shows in the way the information is presented.

Because of these major changes, you will find that the *Oxford Starter French Dictionary* is a far more efficient language-learning tool for you as a beginner. Finding the right information quickly and easily will make French more satisfying to learn.

A clearer layout

Each page of the dictionary presents the information you will need in entries which are well-spaced, easy to read, and which have a consistent layout both in English and French. The main features of the new design are:

- bullet points and numbers to indicate the various uses of each word
- different typefaces as well as the symbol = to indicate the switch from one language to the other
- use of the symbol ! to indicate important grammar points
- use of the symbol ✷ to indicate informal or colloquial words
- use of the symbol ☞ to indicate words which should be used with care.

More helpful and easy to use

The entries have been designed so that you can find the information you need quickly. Many of the conventions in traditional dictionaries which you may find confusing or offputting have been avoided, so:

- PARTS OF SPEECH and grammatical terms are written out in full for you. A separate section explains all the terms used if you should need to find out more about them
- explanations of specific grammar points and notes on how a word is actually used are provided in short paragraphs at appropriate places in the dictionary text
- groups of words which behave in a similar way, or which present similar difficulties, are treated in a consistent manner which you will quickly

Words in capital letters are found in the glossary

come to recognize. In many entries, you are guided to other parts of the dictionary, to VERB tables, for instance, where you will find all the forms of the main French verbs. You will also find handy language notes which deal with such concepts as colours, countries, and dates.

• the language used in the examples and in the signposts to the right translation has been carefully chosen to ensure that it is clear and up to date.

This dictionary, with its precise and lively examples, contains all the words you will need as a beginner and includes plenty of examples of British as well as American English in both the English–French and French–English texts.

Using the two sides of the dictionary to do different things

Each side of the dictionary has been separately designed to take account of the different ways in which you will use it.

The English–French side is longer. Since you are moving from your own language into French, you will need more detailed guidance. We have provided regular reminders about essential grammar rules. The signposts which pinpoint the precise context in which a word is used are there to help you choose the right translation. These 'sense indicators' are also supported with a wide selection of useful examples.

The French–English side makes the most of what you already know about your own language. The presentation of translations from French is therefore more streamlined. There is detailed treatment of the more irregular and unpredictable features of French which you may come across in newspapers and magazines, for example. A particularly useful feature is that the variations in spelling of IRREGULAR VERBS, ADJECTIVES and PLURAL NOUNS are all listed as separate entries in the WORD LIST. These words then send you to the main dictionary form where you will find the translation you are looking for.

Special features

To help you make the most of your Starter Dictionary, we have provided in this introductory section the following features:

A Guide to Pronunciation
Definitions of Grammatical Terms
A Key to the Design of the Entries
A Guide to Using the Dictionary
A Word Games section

Words in capital letters are found in the glossary

The structure of French–English entries

HEADWORD ········ **bête**
.··**1** *adjective*
numbers indicating ····· = stupid, silly
grammatical ·······**2** *noun, feminine*
categories   **une bête** = an animal ······················· translation clearly
                                                      indicated by =

champion/championne *noun,*
masculine/feminine
    un champion/une championne = a ········· FEMININE form
    champion   of HEADWORD

ABBREVIATION ········ **DOM-TOM** *noun, masculine plural*
(*abbreviation of* **départements et**
territoires d'outre-mer)
explanation of a ········ *French overseas departments and*
feature of French   *territories*
culture

eau *noun, feminine* ································· PART OF SPEECH plus
(*plural*) **eaux**   GENDER
l'eau = water
compounds ··········**l'eau gazeuse** = fizzy water, sparkling
presented in ··.,   water
block at end ···..··**l'eau minérale** = mineral water
of ENTRY   ···**l'eau potable** = drinking water

                                    ··························· number of the
                                                        spelling pattern this
informer *verb* 1   verb follows (tables
1 (**!** + *avoir*)   on pages 380–413)
    = to inform ·······
2 s'informer (**!** + *être*)························· information
• **s'informer** = to keep oneself informed   on correct
• **s'informer de** = to enquire about   grammatical usage

pleut ▶ pleuvoir ······························· cross-reference to
                                                     HEADWORD

rattraper *verb* 1
bullet points ········ • = to catch up with
indicating a ·.,   **rattraper un concurrent** = to catch up
separate meaning of·.,.   with a competitor ·························
the HEADWORD `.,.` • = to make up for ······················· examples
                    rattraper le temps perdu = to make up
                        for lost time
              `.` • = to recapture, to catch

symbol drawing ··········.,
attention to   **zut*** *exclamation*
REGISTER   = blast!
                      = oh dear!

Words in capital letters are found in the glossary

The structure of English–French entries

HEADWORD ········ **circus** *noun*
a circus = un cirque

········ GENDER of French NOUNS made clear

delicious *adjective*
= délicieux/délicieuse ·············· FEMININE form of ADJECTIVES made clear

PART OF SPEECH ·············
made clear

fed up *adjective*
to be fed up = en avoir marre✖ ·············· symbol drawing attention to REGISTER

fire
numbers indicating ········· **1** *noun*
grammatical   fire = le feu ·············· indicators which
categories   a fire (*for heat*) = un feu ·············· spell out the
                     (*causing damage*) = un incendie   different meanings
                     to catch fire = prendre feu   of the HEADWORD
                     to be on fire = être en feu
bullet points ········· **2** *verb*
indicating a ········· • (*to shoot*) = tirer
separate meaning   • (*to dismiss*) = renvoyer
of the HEADWORD

fireman *noun* ▶ **315**⌋ ·············· page number
a fireman = un pompier   where more
separate entries for ········ **fire station** *noun*   information is given
COMPOUND NOUNS   a fire station = une caserne de pompiers

·············· translation clearly
kick *verb*   indicated by =
to kick someone = donner un coup de
pied à quelqu'un
he kicked the ball = il a donné un coup de
pied dans le ballon
PHRASAL VERBS ········ **kick off** = donner le coup d'envoi
presented in ········ **kick out**
separate
blocks   to kick someone out = mettre
                 quelqu'un à la porte

need *verb*
• (*to have to*) ··············· basic structure to
you don't need to ask permission = tu   use as a model
n'es pas obligé de demander la
permission
they'll need to come early = il va falloir
qu'ils viennent de bonne heure

information on
correct grammatical ·········
usage

! *Note that the subjunctive is used after
falloir que.*

• (*to want*) = avoir besoin de
example of a model ·····   they need [money | help | friends...] = ils ont
structure which can   besoin [d'argent | d'aide | d'amis...]
be imitated   we need to see the doctor = nous avons
                              besoin de voir le médecin
                              everything you need = tout ce qu'il
                              vous faut

Words in capital letters are found in the glossary

How to use the dictionary

Where to look for a word

Bilingual dictionaries are divided into two sections. The first section gives you a list of French words followed by their English equivalents as well as information about the contexts in which they are used.

The second section gives you a list of English words followed by the French words which match their exact meaning according to the contexts in which they are used.

- *Decide first which section you need to look at.*

Your Starter Dictionary is particularly good at listing as HEADWORDS the various forms that VERBS, NOUNS, and ADJECTIVES may take in French when they are being used to indicate TENSE, GENDER, or NUMBER. From these more unpredictable forms, you will be referred to the main entry of the BASE FORM for the meaning and any further information.

What information does the dictionary provide you with?

Your dictionary gives you information which falls into three broad categories:

1. information about meaning
2. information about the grammatical characteristics of the words
3. information about the circumstances in which a word may be safely used – either from the point of view of CONTEXT (e.g. medical, sport, school contexts) or REGISTER (e.g. formal, polite, informal registers)

How to recognize the information given in the dictionary

Study carefully the diagrams given on pages x–xi **The Structure of French–English and English–French entries**. There you will see how the three categories of information mentioned above are displayed to help you. If you need help finding out what PART OF SPEECH you are dealing with, have a look at the **Definitions of Grammatical Terms** on page xv.

Finding meanings and translating

When you are looking up words for meaning in order to translate them either from your own language or from French, dictionaries can only give you lists of choices. You must look carefully at the information provided to help you choose the right translation in English or in French for the CONTEXT you are in.

If you look up the French word for '**right**', you need to be clear whether you mean '**right**' as opposed to '**left**' or whether you mean '**right** 'as opposed to '**wrong**'.

Scan the whole entry to find the word in French which matches the meaning you need. The context indicators or 'signposts' will help you to pinpoint this meaning. This will be easier to select when you are looking up English words to translate into French since you will know what each of the choices given in English means and how it is used.

If the entry is a long one, first identify the PART OF SPEECH of the word you want to translate. When you have found the right section of the entry, check the range of meanings covered in that section to find the appropriate one. For example:

- '**ring**' could be a verb, in which case the correct French translation may be '**sonner**' which is also a verb;

Words in capital letters are found in the glossary

- **'ring'** could be a noun, in which case the correct French equivalent might be **'une bague'** (*a piece of jewellery*) or **'la piste'** (*in a circus*) or **'un cercle'** (*a circle*).

Your Starter Dictionary will give you the context clearly so that you can decide on the appropriate word.

Using the entries to find information about a word other than the meaning

- Sometimes you will want to use your dictionary simply to check the spelling of the FEMININE or PLURAL form of a NOUN or ADJECTIVE.
- You may wish to check to see if the word has ACCENTS.
- You may wish to check the GENDER of a noun.
- You may wish to find out how a verb is spelled in a particular TENSE.
- The entry will often tell you which pattern of CONJUGATION the VERB follows by referring you to the tables at the back of the book (see pages 381–397).

How to use the verb tables

Where you see a French verb followed by a number in a box, look at the back of the dictionary where you will find tables of verbs. The number given against the verb indicates the spelling pattern that the verb follows.

For example: **'arriver'** and **'informer'** are both followed by the number 1. In the verb tables this spelling pattern is represented by the verb **'chanter'**.

Verbs can be split into two parts: the *stem* and the *ending*.

e.g. **arriv + er; inform + er**

The endings of **'chant + er'** should be used with the stems of **arriv + er** and **inform + er** to form the tenses you need.

Where the verb is REGULAR the stem does not change, only the endings.

Where the verb is IRREGULAR the stem may alter as well. Just follow the pattern indicated.

e.g.	19 **rappeler**	[rappel + *er*]	note the change from **'l'** to double **'ll'**
	52 **comprendre**	[comprend + *re*]	note how the **'d'** is not always there
	56 **joindre**	[joind + *re*]	note how the **'d'** is not always there and the change to **'gn'** from **'nd'** in certain TENSES

Getting to know your dictionary

In the central section of this dictionary (pages 171–184) you will find a short section of games and exercises which will help you get to know your dictionary better and to use it more effectively. Your dictionary is a very important study aid which can greatly help you to find out how the French language works and how to expand your vocabulary.

Proprietary terms

This dictionary contains some words which are, or are asserted to be, proprietary names or trademarks. Their inclusion does not imply that they have acquired for legal purposes a non-proprietary or general significance, nor is any other judgement implied concerning their legal status. In cases where the editors have some evidence that a word is used as a proprietary name or trademark, this is indicated by the symbol ®, but no judgement concerning the legal status of such words is made or implied thereby.

Glossary of grammatical terms

The list of words and definitions below contains most of the words which you will come across when learning a language and its grammar. Some are used in this dictionary; others you will see in grammars and textbooks.

Abbreviation
a shortened form of a word or phrase, e.g. (English) exam ▶ examination; (French) imper ▶ imperméable

Accent
1. (in writing) a mark associated with a letter, usually showing how the letter is pronounced, e.g. grave accent (è); acute accent (é); circumflex (â)
2. (in speech) a person's way of speaking

Adjective
a word describing a noun, e.g. a *green* shirt = une chemise *verte*; a *small* girl = une *petite* fille

Adverb
a word that describes or modifies the meaning of a verb, an adjective or another adverb, e.g. he speaks *quickly* = il parle *vite*; fairly big = *assez* grand; very slowly = *très* lentement

Agree, Agreement
when a word agrees with another, its spelling changes to match the number of that other word, e.g. one child = un enfant; two children = deux enfant**s**; it must also match it for gender, e.g. the **big** dog = **le grand** chien; the **big** house = **la grande** maison

Article
the definite article 'the'; the indefinite article 'a' or 'an'; the partitive articles 'some', 'any' are all used before a noun (see grammar box on page 352 and also the glossary entry DETERMINER)

Auxiliary, Auxiliary verb
either of the verbs être or *avoir* which are used to form the perfect, pluperfect, or future perfect tenses, e.g. j'*ai* mangé = I have eaten; je *suis* revenu = I came back; ils *avaient* vu Bob = they had seen Bob

Base form
see DICTIONARY FORM

Clause
a self-contained section of a sentence which contains a subject and a verb

Cognates
words which resemble each other in more than one language and which historically have the same origin, e.g. republic, république. They do not always retain the same meaning. See FAUX AMI

Colloquial
refers to a word or an expression used in relaxed, everyday situations. Colloquial language is usually spoken, or used in personal letters or informal writing

Comparative
the form of the adjective or adverb which allows a comparison to be made, e.g. big*ger* = *plus* grand; *more* intelligent = *plus* intelligent; clever*er* = *plus* malin

Compound noun
A noun formed from two or more separate words: an airport = un aéroport

Conditional	the form of the verb that expresses what might happen IF something else occurred first, e.g. *if* it tasted good, I **would eat** it = **si** c'était bon, je le **mangerais**
Conjunction	a word used to join clauses together, e.g. *and*, *but*, *because*
Consonant	a letter representing a sound such as b, c, d, p, t, s, z, etc. Consonants cannot form a complete sound unit or syllable without a vowel. See VOWEL
Construction	the way the words in a phrase or sentence work together grammatically
Context	the environment or surroundings within which a word occurs and which affect its meaning. Compare *the **tank** fired first* with *he filled the petrol **tank***. Information about the context of a word helps to pinpoint its exact sense. Knowing the sense and then using the dictionary signposts will guide you to the right translation
Definite Article	See ARTICLE
Determiner	a word which is used before a noun to make clear what is being referred to. It describes the function of definite and indefinite articles as well as words like *this*, *my*, and *certain*, e.g. *this* money = *cet* argent; *my* room = *ma* chambre; *certain* people = *certaines* personnes. In French, the determiner will match the gender and the number of the noun it is referring to
Dictionary form	the form of a word given in the dictionary WORD LIST. For verbs, it is the spelling of the infinitive in English and French; for French nouns, the spelling of the masculine singular form (or the feminine singular form if there is no masculine form); for French adjectives, the spelling of the masculine singular form
Direct object	the noun or pronoun directly affected by the verb, e.g. she bought *the book* = elle a acheté *le livre*; he carried *it* = il *l'*a porté; help *me* = aidez-*moi*
Ending	that part of a noun or an adjective which can be changed to show gender or number and of a verb to show number or tense. The ending doesn't change the basic meaning of the word
Entry	the information given in a dictionary about the word you have looked up; also the word itself. See HEADWORD
Exclamation	a sound, word or remark expressing a strong feeling such as anger, fear, or joy, e.g. ouch! = aïe!
Faux ami	one of a pair of words from two different languages which look alike but which do not have the same meaning, e.g. *sensible* (English) = *having good sense* and *sensible* (French) = *sensitive*
Feminine	one of the two genders for nouns in French, which is most clearly indicated by the article used with the noun, e.g. *the* girl = *la* fille; *a* table = *une* table. Pronouns and adjectives also carry gender information e.g., *she* eats = *elle* mange; a black dress = une robe noire (because the noun *robe* is feminine)

Gender
marks words in French as being either masculine or feminine (whether they refer to persons *or things*) whereas English does not make the distinction. The gender of a French noun is important because it will affect the form of adjectives which describe it, e.g. a white cow = **une** vache blan**che**; a white horse = **un** cheval blanc. Gender will also affect the form of pronouns which replace a French noun, e.g. the boy laughed ▶ he laughed = **il** a ri; the beach (feminine) is clean ▶ it is clean = **elle** est propre

Headword
the word which is used in the dictionary word list to begin each separate entry.

Imperative
a verb form for expressing commands, e.g. *close* the door = *ferme* la porte; *be quiet! = taisez-vous!; let's go! = allons-y!*

Imperfect tense
the tense of the verb which refers to a continuous action or state in the past, e.g. I *was singing* = je *chantais;* or to something that used to happen regularly, e.g. he *used to eat* meat = il *mangeait* la viande; I *took* the bus every day = je *prenais* le bus tous les jours

Impersonal verb
a verb whose action is not performed by a person or a thing, e.g. *it* is raining = *il* pleut; *it's* going to snow = *il* va neiger

Indefinite article
See ARTICLE

Indefinite pronoun
a pronoun that does not identify a specific person or object, e.g. *you* never know = *on* ne sait jamais; *one* wonders why = *on* se demande pourquoi; *it's* raining = *il* pleut

Indicative
a verb form which is used when indicating or stating a fact, e.g. I don't understand = je ne comprends pas; it was true = c'était vrai. See SUBJUNCTIVE

Indirect object
the noun or pronoun indirectly affected by the verb and often following a preposition, e.g. I wrote *to him* = je *lui* ai écrit. The direct object also has an effect on the indirect object, e.g. she gave the book *to the boy* = elle a donné le livre *au garçon*; he tells *us* stories = il *nous* raconte des histoires

Infinitive
the basic part or 'name' of a verb before it is altered to indicate tense or number, e.g. to sing = chanter; to drive = conduire. See DICTIONARY FORM

Interrogative
a form of wording used to ask questions

Intonation
the quality in a human voice which indicates an emotion (surprise, shock) or which shows that a speaker is asking a question, stating a fact or giving an order

Inverted commas
punctuation marks used to indicate direct speech, e.g. "come here," she said. They are also referred to as quotation marks.

Irregular verb
a verb whose spelling is not predictable or does not follow a regular pattern when it changes to express tense. See REGULAR VERB

Masculine   one of the two genders for nouns in French, which is most clearly indicated by the article used with the noun, e.g. *the* boy = *le* garçon; *a* dog = *un* chien. Pronouns and adjectives also carry gender information e.g., *he* eats = *il* mange; a black hat = un chapeau *noir* (because the noun *chapeau* is masculine)

Noun   a word which names a person, an animal, an object, a feeling or an event, e.g. a student = un étudiant; a dog = un chien; a house = une maison; envy = l'envie; the storm = l'orage

Number   a form of the word indicating whether it is singular, e.g. a boy = un garçon, or plural, e.g. two boys = deux garçons

Object   the person, thing or idea affected by or referred to by a verb, e.g. he walked *the dog* = il a promené *le chien*; we crossed *the road* = nous avons traversé *la rue*. See also DIRECT OBJECT, INDIRECT OBJECT

Part of speech   the grammatical term which describes the function of a word and categorizes it as *noun, verb, adjective, adverb*, etc. All the entries in this dictionary carry information about the part of speech of the word you look up.

Past participle   the part of the verb used to form compound tenses in combination with an auxiliary verb, e.g. I have *sung* = j'ai *chanté*; we had *stayed* = nous étions *restés*; she's *gone* to bed = elle s'est *couchée*

Past simple   the tense of the verb which refers to past events which have been completed. In French, it is a verb form which is mostly used in written language

Perfect tense   the tense of the verb which refers to past events which have been completed, e.g. we *have finished* the work = nous *avons terminé* le travail. She *left* yesterday = elle *est partie* hier. It is also called the *passé composé* in French and is used in spoken language as well as in print

Person   the 'person' of a verb shows you **who** or **what** is carrying out the action referred to by the verb. There are six persons in the singular: *I, you, he, she, it, one* and three in the plural: *we, you, they*

Phonetics   the system of sounds of a language. The word can also refer to the symbols used to represent these sounds. The most common system of symbols is the International Phonetic Alphabet

Phrasal verb   a form of the English verb which combines with a preposition or an adverb to produce a particular meaning, e.g. to *turn up* = *arriver*; to *carry on* working = *continuer* à travailler

Phrase   1. a self-contained section of a sentence which does not contain a full verb
2. an expression which has a particular meaning which can make it more difficult to translate word for word, e.g. to lay the table = mettre la table; to hang around = traîner

Pluperfect tense   the tense of the verb referring to (1) past events which precede (2) other events taking place in a more recent past, e.g. he (1) *had sold* the car when (2) he *told me* about it = il (1) *avait vendu* la voiture quand (2) il *m'en a parlé*

Plural	the form of nouns and pronouns which refers to more than one of something, e.g. *boys, we, they.* French ADJECTIVES also have plural forms, e.g. red shoes = des chaussures rouge**s** to agree with the noun they are describing
Preposition	a word which stands in front of a noun or pronoun, connecting it to the rest of a sentence, e.g. *between* the chairs = *entre* les chaises; *with* us = *avec* nous; *to* Paris = *à* Paris; *from* Bob = *de* Bob
Present tense	the tense of the verb referring to something that is happening now, e.g. I *am watching* television = je *regarde* la télévision; she *understands* = elle *comprend*
Pronoun	a word which takes the place of a noun, e.g. is it *your dog*? ▶ is it *yours*?; I sold *the car* ▶ I sold *it*
Reflexive verb	a verb whose object is the same as its subject, e.g. *he* washed *himself* = *il s'*est lavé; *I* hurt *myself* = *je me* suis blessé
Register	the style of language used in speech and writing which is suited (and which you can adapt) to the circumstances. These may range from very formal situations to very relaxed or informal contexts
Regular verb	a verb which follows a set pattern in its different forms and tenses and can be classified in a fixed group of verbs. In French, there are many verbs ending in, for example, -er (*aim**er**, chant**er**, tourn**er***) which behave regularly. See IRREGULAR VERB
Sentence	a set of words usually containing a subject and a verb, which can stand alone and make sense, e.g. she's gone = elle est partie; who is it? = qui est-ce?; (you) leave me alone! = laisse-moi tranquille!
Singular	the form of nouns and pronouns which refers to just one of something, e.g. *boy, I, it.* See PLURAL
Stem	the part of the verb to which endings which indicate tense, number and gender are added, e.g. the regular verb *chanter* is made up of the stem *chant-* and the ending *-er.* When a verb is regular, the stem doesn't change. When it is irregular, the stem as well as the endings change
Subject	the noun or pronoun which causes the action of a verb and can usually be identified by asking **who..?** or **what..?**, e.g. *he* wants to leave = *il* veut partir; *the computer's* broken down = *l'ordinateur* est en panne
Subjunctive	a verb form that is used to express a desire, doubt or unlikelihood, e.g. I'm not sure he'll come = je ne suis pas sûr *qu'il vienne.* It often indicates how the speaker feels about something rather than the fact itself, e.g. I'm happy *that you are back* = je suis content *que tu sois rentré*
Superlative	the form of the adjective which makes it 'the most', e.g. *the biggest* = *le plus* grand; *the smallest* = *le plus* petit; *the most* intelligent = *le plus* intelligent
Syllable	part of a word which can form a spoken unit built around the VOWEL it contains, e.g. the word **in-tel-li-gent** has four syllables
Synonym	a word which has the same (or almost the same) meaning as another, e.g. *enormous* and *gigantic, sure* and *certain*

Tense	the form of the verb which indicates a particular time frame – past: I *had* = j'*avais*; present: I *have* = j'*ai*; future: I *will have* = j'*aurai*
Verb	a word which indicates what is being done or which describes a situation, e.g. he *left* the house = il *a quitté* la maison; you *seem* happy = tu *as* l'air heureux; I *am* tired = je *suis* fatigué
Vowel	a sound which forms the basis of the syllable and which can be spoken by itself, e.g. *a, i, e, o, u*. See CONSONANT, SYLLABLE
Word list	the list of headwords or vocabulary items which is found in a dictionary

A guide to French pronunciation

While phonetics have not been given for entries in the present dictionary, a simplified, user-friendly table summarizing the main features of French pronunciation and spelling follows.

This table is designed
(a) to help English speakers to bridge the gap between the sound systems of English and French
(b) to connect French sounds to the most frequent written representations of those sounds, illustrating the link by means of examples from basic French vocabulary.

Learners will find in it a useful point of departure for a more advanced study of French phonetics at a later stage. It is not, however, meant to take the place of either a human model—a teacher, for example—or a recording of the same sounds produced by a native speaker.

The table is subdivided into three main categories of phonetic sounds: *vowels*, *semi-vowels*, and *consonants*. The French sounds are presented in order of increasing complexity when compared with the English sound system. In many cases, the sounds are broadly similar, if not actually the same. In others, however, it is only possible in the present format to give an approximation in English terms of the French sound. This is indicated by the symbol ≈. This is particularly true of the French vowels which are nasalized (represented by ɛ̃, ɑ̃, ɔ̃, and œ̃ in the International Phonetic Alphabet) and those which require a marked degree of lip rounding (represented by ø, œ, y, and ɥ).

A major distinguishing feature of written French is the mute h, as in **homme, hôtel**. It functions in the same way as a vowel and spelling or pronunciation adjust accordingly l'homme, **cet** homme, **les** hommes [lezɔm]. We have systematically included the mute h in the column dealing with French spelling forms while notes throughout the dictionary text regularly draw users' attention to this important feature.

M. O'N.

Vowels

phonetic symbol	sounds like English	written in French as	examples
a	c*a*t, fl*a*t	a, à, ha-	**a**cheter, basse, patte, **à**, voil**à**, **ha**meau (*note also* femme)
ɑ	*a*rm, c*a*r	â, as	**â**gé, g**â**teau, p**â**te, bas, las
e	h*ay*, tr*ay* but *shorter*	-er, -es, -ez, -é, -ée, é-, hé-	all**er**, d**es**, n**ez**, âg**é**, ann**ée**, **é**tage, **hé**las
ɛ	p*e*t, thr*ea*t	è-, ê-, e-, ai, -ais, ait, -ei-, aî-, -ë-, -et	r**è**gle, tr**ès**, **ê**tre, b**ê**te, **e**lle, c**et**, **ai**de, f**ai**ble, fran**çai**s, l**ai**t, **é**t**ait**, pl**ei**ne, conna**î**tre, No**ë**l, secr**et**
i	tr*ea*t, fl*ee*t	i, -ie, -is, î-, hi, y, -ï	**i**l, **i**mmeuble, l**i**bre, p**i**le, v**ie**, pr**is**, **î**le, **hi**bou, elle **y** va, t**y**pe, ma**ï**s
o	h*or*se, c*our*se	au, eau, aux, eaux, o, os, ô, hô-	**au**ssi, g**au**che, tuy**au**, b**eau**, ch**â**teau, chev**aux**, **eaux**, chose, orage, loto, gros, côte, **hô**tel (*note also* trop)
ɔ	h*o*t, wh*a*t	o-, ho-, hô-	**o**bjet, d**o**mmage, rand**o**nnée, b**o**tte, **ho**raire, **hô**pital

Vowels

phonetic symbol	sounds like English	written in French as	examples
u	hoot, flute	ou, où, -oû-, -oo-, hou-, -oux	ouvrir, trou, mourir, amour, où, goûter, football, houx, roux (note also août)
ə	ago, gather (British English)	e (silent at the end of words and may even be left out)	mère, elle, j'aime, même, premier, grenouille, menu, le, ne, de, petit, fera, chemin, médecin
ø	purr, her but shorter	eu, eux	Europe, peu, neveu, bleu, chanteuse, heureux, cheveux, yeux
œ	≈ fun, son	eu, œu-, heu-, œ	peur, déjeuner, meuble, humeur, fauteuil, œuf, sœur, heure, œil
y	ee but with rounded lips	u, û, hu	une, utile, rue, vendu, mûr, sûr, humeur, hurler (note also eu)
ɛ̃	an/am + nasal twang	in, im, ain, -ein, -yn, ym, -en, -aim, hein	intéressant, matin, imbécile, train, copain, plein, peindre, syndicat, sympa, italien, rien, faim, hein
ɑ̃	awn/alm + nasal twang	an, -ant, en, em-, -ent, am-	an, chanter, chant, entrer, ennui, empêcher, tempête, souvent, rampe (note also temps, paon, banc, sang and champ)
ɔ̃	on + nasal twang	on, om, hon-	onze, bon, montrer, jambon, ombre, sombre, tromper, honte
œ̃	fun, son + nasal twang	un, -um	un, brun, lundi, parfum

Semi-Vowels

phonetic symbol	sounds like English	written in French as	examples
j	yes, player	-i-, y, -il, -ill-	bien, ciel, tiède, il y a, yaourt, payer, soleil, travail, feuille, fille, billet
w	≈ was	oi, -oî-, ou, -oê-, w-	oiseau, voir, besoin, quoi, oui, jouet, boîte, poêle, K-way
ɥ	≈ we, tweet but with rounded lips	-ui-, hui, -uî-, huî-	nuit, lui, aujourd'hui, huit, huître

French pronunciation

Consonants

phonetic symbol	sounds like English	written in French as	examples
b	as English	b, -bb-	bain, robe, abbaye
d	as English	d, -dd-	devoir, aide, addition
f	as English	f, -ff-, ph	fête, neuf, affaires, photo, téléphone
k	as English	c, qu-, -q, -cc-, k, -ck-, -ch-	café, sac, quartier, marquer, coq, occupé, kilomètre, kayak, ticket, orchestre
l	as English	l, -ll-	lettre, pile, mal, ville, salle
m	as English	m, -mm-	mère, madame, femme, sommeil
n	as English	n, -nn-	non, animal, panne, donner
p	as English	p, -pp-, -bs-	pomme, chapeau, hop, appuyer, observer
s	as English	s, -ss-, c, ç-, sc-	son, festival, assiette, poisson, chasse, cette, tracer, cil, garçon, ça, reçu, scène, piscine (note also six, dix)
t	as English	t, -tt-, th	tour, auto, patte, thé, bibliothèque
v	as English	v, w	venir, lever, grave, wagon, W-C
z	as English	-s-, z, -x-	maison, loisirs, brise, zoo, bizarre, dix-huit, sixième
g	as English	g, gu-, -gg-	goût, bagarre, gai, guitare, blague, aggressif
ʒ	leisure, seizure	j, g-, ge-	j'ai, jeune, déjeuner, plage, geler, gifler, gîte, nageons
ʃ	rash, shoe	ch, sh	château, achats, riche, poche, short
ɲ	new, onion	gn	ignorer, vignoble, soigner, champignon (note also oignon)
ŋ	sing, wrong	-ng	camping, parking
R	≈ a very soft loch sound produced at the back of the throat	r, -rr-, rh-	rouge, partir, arrêter, marre, rhume

French–English

a ▶ avoir 8

à *preposition*
(**!** à + le *becomes* au; à + les *becomes* aux)

> **!** *You will find translations for phrases with* à *such as* à côté de, à l'étranger, penser à, *etc. under the entries* côté, étranger, penser, *etc.*

- (*showing destination*) = to
  se rendre [à Nice | à l'école | aux courses …]
  = to go [to Nice | to school | to the races …]
- (*showing location*) = in
  = at
  = on
  habiter [à la campagne | au Portugal | aux États-Unis …] = to live [in the country | in Portugal | in the United States …]
- (*in a description*) = with
  la maison aux volets verts = the house with the green shutters
- (*showing ownership*)
  le livre est [à moi | à eux | à Isabelle …] = the book is [mine | theirs | Isabelle's …]
- (*indicating a time, a speed, a price*) = at
  à minuit = at midnight
  un timbre à trois euros = a three-euro stamp
- (*meaning during a period of time*) = in
  au printemps = in (the) spring
- (*indicating a distance*)
  à cinq kilomètres = five kilometres away
- (*showing how something is done*)
  écrire au crayon = to write in pencil
  à pied = on foot

abandonner *verb* 1
- = to abandon
- = to give up

abeille *noun, feminine*
une abeille = a bee

abîmer *verb* 1
1 (**!** + *avoir*)
= to damage, to spoil
2 s'abîmer (**!** + *être*)
s'abîmer = to get damaged

abonné/abonnée *noun,*
masculine/feminine
un abonné/une abonnée = a subscriber

abonnement *noun, masculine*
un abonnement = a subscription

abonner: s'abonner à *verb* 1 (**!** + *être*)
s'abonner à = to subscribe to

abord: d'abord *adverb*
d'abord = first, at first
tout d'abord = first of all

abri *noun, masculine*
un abri = (a) shelter

abricot *noun, masculine*
un abricot = an apricot

abriter *verb* 1
1 (**!** + *avoir*)
= to shelter
2 s'abriter (**!** + *être*)
s'abriter = to shelter, to take shelter

absent/absente *adjective*
= absent, missing

absolument *adverb*
= absolutely

accélérer *verb* 14
= to accelerate

accepter *verb* 1
- = to accept
- = to agree to

accès *noun, masculine* (**!** *never changes*)
l'accès = access
'accès interdit' = 'no entrance', 'do not enter'

accident *noun, masculine*
un accident = an accident

accompagner *verb* 1
- = to accompany, to go with
- = to take

accomplir *verb* 3
= to carry out, to accomplish

accord *noun, masculine*
- **un accord** = an agreement
- **d'accord!** = OK!, all right!
  je suis d'accord avec toi = I agree with you

accorder *verb* 1
= to give, to grant

accotement *noun, masculine*
un accotement = a verge, a shoulder
accotement non stabilisé = soft verge, soft shoulder

accroc *noun, masculine*
un accroc (*in material*) = a tear, a rip

accrocher *verb* 1
1 (**!** + *avoir*)
= to hang
2 s'accrocher (**!** + *être*)
s'accrocher = to hang on, to cling
accroche-toi à la branche = hang on to the branch

accueil *noun, masculine*
un accueil = a welcome, a reception
ils nous ont fait bon accueil = they made us welcome, they made us feel at home
la famille d'accueil = the host family

accueillir verb 27
- (*if it's a host*) = to welcome
- (*if it's a stadium, a hotel*) = to accommodate

achat noun, masculine
un achat = a purchase
faire des achats = to do some shopping

acheter verb 18
= to buy

acheteur/acheteuse noun,
masculine/feminine
un acheteur/une acheteuse = a buyer, a
purchaser

acteur/actrice noun,
masculine/feminine
un acteur/une actrice = an actor/an actress

actif/active adjective
= active

activité noun, feminine
une activité = an activity

actrice ▶ acteur

actualité
1 noun, feminine
l'actualité = current affairs, current events
2 actualités noun, feminine plural
les actualités = the news

actuel/actuelle adjective
= present, current

actuellement adverb
= currently, at the moment

addition noun, feminine
- (*in a restaurant, a café*)
l'addition = the bill, the check
- (*in arithmetic*)
une addition = an addition

additionner verb 1
= to add

adhérent/adhérente noun,
masculine/feminine
un adhérent/une adhérente = a member

adhésion noun, feminine
l'adhésion = membership

adieu noun, masculine
(*plural*) **adieux**
= goodbye, farewell
faire ses adieux = to say goodbye

adjectif noun, masculine
un adjectif = an adjective

admettre verb 60
- = to admit
- = to allow
- être admis à un examen = to pass an
exam, to pass a test
- admettons qu'il vienne = (let's) suppose he
comes

admis/admise ▶ admettre 60

admission noun, feminine
l'admission = admission

adolescent/adolescente noun,
masculine/feminine
un adolescent/une adolescente = a
teenager, an adolescent

adorer verb 1
= to love, to adore

adresse noun, feminine
une adresse = an address
changer d'adresse = to move
une adresse électronique = an email
address

adresser verb 1
1 (**!** + *avoir*)
- = to send
- = to address
2 s'adresser (**!** + *être*)
- s'adresser à un employé = to talk to an
employee
- s'adresser à la banque = to contact the
bank

adroit/adroite adjective
- = skil(l)ful
- = clever, smart

adversaire noun, masculine/feminine
un adversaire/une adversaire = an
opponent

aérer verb 14
= to air

aérien/aérienne adjective
= air

aérobic noun, masculine
l'aérobic = aerobics

aérogare noun, feminine
une aérogare = an air terminal

aéroglisseur noun, masculine
un aéroglisseur = a hovercraft

aéroport noun, masculine
un aéroport = an airport

affaire
1 noun, feminine
une affaire = a bargain
2 affaires noun, feminine plural
- les affaires = business
- mes affaires = my things, my belongings

affairer: s'affairer verb 1 (**!** + *être*)
s'affairer = to bustle about

affectueusement adverb
= affectionately
(*ending a letter*) = love

affectueux/affectueuse adjective
= affectionate

affiche noun, feminine
une affiche = a poster
= a notice

afficher verb [1]
- = to put up, to hang up
- = to display
  afficher complet = to be fully booked

affoler verb [1]
1 (**!** + avoir)
  = to throw into a panic
2 s'affoler (**!** + être)
  s'affoler = to get into a panic

affreux/affreuse adjective
  = awful

afin
1 afin de preposition
  afin de = in order to
2 afin que conjunction
  afin que = so that

africain/africaine adjective
  = African

Afrique noun, feminine
  l'Afrique = Africa

agacer verb [12]
  = to annoy, to irritate

âge noun, masculine
  l'âge = age
  quel âge as-tu? = how old are you?

âgé/âgée adjective
- = old, elderly
- être âgé de 18 ans = to be 18 years old

agence noun, feminine
  une agence = an agency
  une agence immobilière = an estate
  agent's, a real estate agency
  une agence de voyages = a travel
  agency

agenda noun, masculine
  un agenda = a diary, a date book

agent noun, masculine
  un agent = an agent
  un agent de la circulation = a traffic
  policeman
  un agent de police = a policeman, a
  police officer

agglomération noun, feminine
  une agglomération = a town
  = a village

agile adjective
  = agile

agir verb [3]
1 (**!** + avoir)
  = to act
2 s'agir de (**!** + être)
  s'agir de = to be about
  de quoi s'agit-il? = what's it about?

agitation noun, feminine
- l'agitation = (the) bustle
- l'agitation = (the) excitement

agité/agitée adjective
  (describing the sea) = rough, choppy

agiter verb [1]
1 (**!** + avoir)
- agiter un mouchoir = to wave a
  handkerchief
- agiter un flacon = to shake a bottle
2 s'agiter (**!** + être)
- s'agiter = to fidget
- s'agiter = to become restless

agneau noun, masculine
(plural) **agneaux**
- (the animal)
  un agneau = a lamb
- (the meat)
  l'agneau = lamb

agréable adjective
  = pleasant

agressif/agressive adjective
  = aggressive

agression noun, feminine
- une agression = an attack
- une agression = a mugging

agricole adjective
  = agricultural

agriculteur/agricultrice noun,
masculine/feminine
  un agriculteur/une agricultrice = a farmer

ai ▶ avoir [8]

aide
1 noun, feminine
  l'aide = help
  = assistance
2 noun, masculine/feminine
  un aide/une aide = an assistant

aider verb [1]
1 (**!** + avoir)
  = to help
2 s'aider de (**!** + être)
  s'aider de = to use

aïe exclamation
  = ouch!

aigle noun, masculine
  un aigle = an eagle

aigre adjective
- (tasting unpleasant) = sour
- (sounding unpleasant) = sharp

aiguille noun, feminine
- une aiguille = a needle
  une aiguille à tricoter = a knitting needle
- les aiguilles d'une montre = the hands on
  a watch

ail noun, masculine
  l'ail = garlic

aile noun, feminine
  une aile = a wing

aille ▶ aller 1 [9]

ailleurs
1 *adverb*
ailleurs = elsewhere, somewhere else
2 d'ailleurs = besides

aimable *adjective*
= kind, friendly

aimer *verb* 1
• = to love
aimer ses enfants = to love one's children
• = to like, to be fond of
j'aime mieux le vin = I prefer wine

aîné/aînée *adjective*
= eldest, oldest
= elder, older

ainsi
1 *adverb*
• = in this way
et ainsi de suite = and so on
• = so
ainsi tu t'en vas? = so you're leaving?
2 ainsi que = and, as well as

air *noun, masculine*
• l'air = (the) air
en plein air = in the open (air), outdoors
allons prendre l'air = let's go and get some
fresh air
• de l'air = a wind, a breeze
• (*appearance*)
un air = a look
avoir l'air heureux = to look happy
il n'a pas l'air de comprendre = he doesn't
seem to understand
• (*for a song*)
un air = a tune

aire *noun, feminine*
une aire = an area
une aire de jeux = a playground
une aire de loisirs = a recreation area

aise: à l'aise *adverb*
à l'aise = at ease

ajouter *verb* 1
1 (**!** + *avoir*)
= to add
2 s'ajouter à (**!** + *être*)
s'ajouter à = to be added to

alarme *noun, feminine*
donner l'alarme = to raise the alarm

album *noun, masculine*
un album = an album
un album à colorier = a colo(u)ring book

alcool *noun, masculine*
l'alcool = alcohol
sans alcool = nonalcoholic, alcohol-free

alcoolisé/alcoolisée *adjective*
= alcoholic

alcootest *noun, masculine*
un alcootest = a Breathalyzer   test

algèbre *noun, feminine*
l'algèbre = algebra

Alger *noun*
= Algiers

Algérie *noun, feminine*
l'Algérie = Algeria

algérien/algérienne *adjective*
= Algerian

aliment *noun, masculine*
un aliment = a food

alimentation *noun, feminine*
• (*the foods usually eaten*)
une alimentation saine = a healthy diet
• (*food retailing*)
un magasin d'alimentation = a grocery
store

allais ▶ aller 1 9

allée
1 *noun, feminine*
une allée = a path
(*wider*) = an avenue
(*leading to a garage*) = a drive, a driveway
2 allées *noun, feminine plural*
leurs allées et venues = their comings
and goings

Allemagne *noun, feminine*
l'Allemagne = Germany

allemand/allemande
1 *adjective*
= German
2 allemand *noun, masculine*
l'allemand = German

aller
1 *verb* 9 (**!** + *être*)
• = to go
où vas-tu? = where are you going?
il faut que j'aille les voir = I must go and
see them
allons-y! = let's go!
• (*when talking about the near future*) = to be
going to
= to be about to
attention, tu vas tomber! = careful, you're
going to fall!
j'allais partir quand il est arrivé = I was
about to leave when he arrived
• (*when talking about health, business*)
comment vas-tu?, comment allez-vous?
= how are you?
je vais bien = I'm fine
qu'est-ce qui ne va pas? = what's the
matter?
  ! *For more examples, see* ça.

• (*to be flattering or convenient*) = to suit, to
be good for
le rouge te va bien = red suits you, red is
right for you
• (*to be of the right size*) = to fit
son costume ne lui va plus = his suit
doesn't fit him any more
• (*when urging or encouraging*)
allons, taisez-vous! = come on, be quiet!
allez-y, tirez! = go on, pull!

2 s'en aller verb (**!** + être)
- (if it's a person)
  s'en aller = to leave, to be off, to go (away)
  va-t'en!, allez-vous-en! = go away!
- (if it's a stain)
  s'en aller = to come out
3 noun, masculine
  un aller simple = a single (ticket), a one-way ticket
  un aller retour = a return ticket, a round trip ticket

allô exclamation
  allô! = hello!

allonger verb [13]
1 (**!** + avoir)
- = to lengthen
- = to stretch out
2 s'allonger (**!** + être)
- **s'allonger** = to lie down
- **s'allonger** = to get longer

allumer verb [1]
- = to light
- = to turn on

allumette noun, feminine
  une allumette = a match

allure noun, feminine
- **l'allure** = the speed
  = the pace
  à toute allure = at top speed
- **une allure** = an appearance
  = a look

alors
1 adverb
- = so
  et alors? = so what?
- = then
  alors je prendrai le bleu = I'll take the blue one then, OK I'll take the blue one
- **ça alors!** = my goodness!, oh dear!
2 alors que = while
  = even though

alouette noun, feminine
  une alouette = a lark

alpinisme noun, masculine
  l'alpinisme = climbing, mountaineering

alpiniste noun, masculine/feminine
  un alpiniste/une alpiniste = a mountain-climber

altitude noun, feminine
  l'altitude = the altitude
  = the height

amande noun, feminine
  une amande = an almond

amateur noun, masculine
- (a keen person)
  un amateur = an enthusiast
- (not a professional)
  un amateur = an amateur

ambassade noun, feminine
  une ambassade = an embassy

ambiance noun, feminine
  l'ambiance = the atmosphere
  il y a de l'ambiance = it's pretty lively

ambition noun, feminine
  l'ambition = ambition

âme noun, feminine
  une âme = a soul

amélioration noun, feminine
  une amélioration = an improvement

améliorer verb [1]
  = to improve

aménagé/aménagée adjective
- = fully-equipped
- = converted

aménager verb [13]
- = to equip
  = to fit out
- = to convert
  aménager une grange = to convert a barn

amende noun, feminine
  une amende = a fine

amener verb [16]
  = to bring
  amenez vos amis = bring your friends

amer/amère adjective
  = bitter

américain/américaine
1 adjective
  = American
2 américain noun, masculine
  l'américain = American English

Amérique noun, feminine
  l'Amérique = America
  l'Amérique du Nord = North America

ami/amie noun, masculine/feminine
  un ami/une amie = a (male) friend/a (female) friend
  un petit ami/une petite amie = a boyfriend/a girlfriend

amical/amicale adjective
(plural) **amicaux/amicales**
  = friendly

amicalement adverb
- = in a friendly way
- (ending a letter) = best wishes

amitié noun, feminine
- **l'amitié** = friendship
- (ending a letter)
  amitiés = kindest regards, fondly

amour noun, masculine
  l'amour = love

amoureux/amoureuse adjective
  = in love

ampoule *noun, feminine*
* (*for lighting*)
  une ampoule = a light bulb
* (*on the skin*)
  une ampoule = a blister

amusant/amusante *adjective*
= entertaining
= funny

amuser *verb* $\boxed{1}$
1 (**!** + *avoir*)
= to amuse
2 s'amuser (**!** + *être*)
s'amuser = to enjoy oneself
= to have fun

an *noun, masculine*
un an = one year
avoir seize ans = to be sixteen years old

ananas *noun, masculine* (**!** *never changes*)
un ananas = a pineapple

ancêtre *noun, masculine/feminine*
un ancêtre/une ancêtre = an ancestor

anchois *noun, masculine* (**!** *never changes*)
un anchois = an anchovy

ancien/ancienne *adjective*
* (*if placed before the noun*) = former
  l'ancienne mairie = the former town hall
* (*if placed after the noun*) = old
  = antique

âne *noun, masculine*
un âne = a donkey

ange *noun, masculine*
un ange = an angel

angine *noun, feminine*
une angine = a throat infection, tonsillitis

anglais/anglaise
1 *adjective*
= English
2 anglais *noun, masculine*
l'anglais = English

Anglais/Anglaise *noun, masculine/feminine*
un Anglais/une Anglaise = an Englishman/an Englishwoman
les Anglais = the English

angle *noun, masculine*
* **un angle** = an angle
* **un angle** = a corner
  le magasin qui fait l'angle = the shop on the corner

Angleterre *noun, feminine*
l'Angleterre = England

animal *noun, masculine*
(*plural*) **animaux**
un animal = an animal
un animal de compagnie = a pet

animé/animée *adjective*
= lively

anneau *noun, masculine*
(*plural*) **anneaux**
un anneau = a ring

année *noun, feminine*
une année = a year
Bonne année! = Happy New Year!
les années 60 = the sixties

anniversaire *noun, masculine*
un anniversaire (*of one's birth*) = a birthday
(*of an event*) = an anniversary
Joyeux anniversaire! = Happy birthday!

annonce *noun, feminine*
* **une annonce** = an advertisement
  les petites annonces = classified advertisements
* **une annonce** = an announcement

annoncer *verb* $\boxed{12}$
1 (**!** + *avoir*)
= to announce
2 s'annoncer (**!** + *être*)
ça s'annonce bien = it looks promising

annuaire *noun, masculine*
un annuaire (téléphonique) = a telephone directory, a phone book
l'annuaire électronique = the electronic telephone directory on Minitel

annuler *verb* $\boxed{1}$
= to cancel

antigel *noun, masculine*
l'antigel = antifreeze

antillais/antillaise *adjective*
= West Indian

Antilles *noun, feminine plural*
les Antilles = the West Indies

antipathique *adjective*
= unpleasant

antivol *noun, masculine*
un antivol = an antitheft device

anxieux/anxieuse *adjective*
= anxious

août *noun, masculine*
août = August

apercevoir *verb* $\boxed{5}$
1 (**!** + *avoir*)
= to catch sight of
= to see
2 s'apercevoir (**!** + *être*)
s'apercevoir que = to realize that
= to notice that

aperçu/aperçue
1 ▶ apercevoir $\boxed{5}$
2 aperçu *noun, masculine*
un aperçu = a general idea

aplatir *verb* $\boxed{3}$
= to flatten

appareil noun, masculine
- un appareil = a device, a gadget
  = an appliance
- un appareil = a telephone
  Victor à l'appareil = (this is) Victor
  speaking
- un appareil = an aeroplane, an airplane
- un appareil (photo) = a camera

apparence noun, feminine
l'apparence = appearance

appartement noun, masculine
un appartement = a flat, an apartment

appartenir verb 36
appartenir à = to belong to
à qui appartiennent les clés? = whose keys
are they?

appel noun, masculine
- (in order to attract attention)
  un appel = a call
- (at school)
  l'appel = registration
  faire l'appel = to take the register, to call
  the roll

appeler verb 19
1 (! + avoir)
- = to call
- = to phone
2 s'appeler (! + être)
s'appeler = to be called
comment t'appelles-tu? = what's your
name?

appendicite noun, feminine
l'appendicite = appendicitis

appétissant/appétissante adjective
= appetizing

appétit noun, masculine
l'appétit = appetite
bon appétit! = enjoy your meal!

applaudir verb 3
= to applaud, to clap

applaudissements noun, masculine
plural
des applaudissements = applause

appliquer verb 1
1 (! + avoir)
- (on the skin, on a surface) = to apply
- (to enforce) = to implement
2 s'appliquer (! + être)
- (to do one's best)
  s'appliquer = to apply oneself
- (to be relevant)
  s'appliquer = to apply

apporter verb 1
= to bring

apprécier verb 2
= to like, to appreciate

apprendre verb 52
- (to get knowledge) = to learn
  ils ont appris à lire = they've learned to
  read
- (to give lessons) = to teach
  elle m'apprenait à conduire = she was
  teaching me to drive
  ça t'apprendra! = that'll teach you!
- (to receive information) = to hear
  j'ai appris qu'elle était partie = I heard that
  she'd left
- (to give information) = to tell

apprentissage noun, masculine
- l'apprentissage = training
- l'apprentissage du russe = learning
  Russian

appris/apprise ▶ apprendre 52

approcher verb 1
1 (! + avoir)
- = to get nearer, to get closer
- = to bring nearer, to bring closer
2 approcher de (! + avoir)
approcher de = to be getting close to
3 s'approcher de (! + être)
s'approcher de = to go closer to
= to come closer to

approuver verb 1
= to approve of

approximativement adverb
= approximately

appuyer verb 22
1 (! + avoir)
- = to press, to push
- = to rest
- = to lean
2 s'appuyer (! + être)
s'appuyer = to lean

après
1 preposition
= after
2 adverb
= afterward(s), after
= later
3 d'après
d'après moi = in my opinion
d'après [lui | eux | le journal ...] = according
to [him | them | the newspaper ...]

après-demain adverb
= the day after tomorrow

après-midi noun, masculine or feminine
(! never changes)
un or une après-midi = an afternoon

après-vente adjective (! never changes)
le service après-vente = after-sales service

aquarium noun, masculine
un aquarium = an aquarium, a fish tank

arabe
1 adjective
= Arab
= Arabic

2 noun, masculine
l'arabe = Arabic

Arabe noun, masculine|feminine
un Arabe/une Arabe = an Arab

araignée noun, feminine
une araignée = a spider

arbitre noun, masculine
un arbitre = a referee

arbre noun, masculine
un arbre = a tree
un arbre de Noël = a Christmas tree

arc noun, masculine
un arc (a weapon) = a bow

arc-en-ciel noun, masculine
(plural) **arcs-en-ciel**
un arc-en-ciel = a rainbow

arche noun, feminine
une arche = an arch

ardoise noun, feminine
l'ardoise = slate

arête noun, feminine
• (in a fish)
 une arête = a fishbone
• (of a mountain)
 l'arête = the ridge

argent noun, masculine
• (metal)
 l'argent = silver
• (currency)
 l'argent = money
l'argent liquide = cash
l'argent de poche = pocket money,
 spending money

argot noun, masculine
l'argot = slang

arme noun, feminine
une arme = a weapon
une arme à feu = a firearm

armée noun, feminine
une armée = an army

armoire noun, feminine
une armoire = a wardrobe, a closet
une armoire à pharmacie = a medicine
cupboard, a medicine cabinet

arracher verb [1]
• = to pull out
 = to tear out
• = to snatch

arranger verb [13]
1 (**!** + avoir)
• = to arrange
• = to fix, to repair
• = to tidy, to clean up
• = to suit
 ça m'arrange d'y aller avec eux = it suits
 me to go with them

2 s'arranger (**!** + être)
• s'arranger = to improve
 le temps s'est arrangé = the weather has
 improved
• s'arranger = to sort itself out, to work out
• s'arranger = to come to an agreement

arrestation noun, feminine
une arrestation = an arrest

arrêt noun, masculine
un arrêt = a stop
un arrêt d'autobus = a bus stop

arrêter verb [1]
1 (**!** + avoir)
• = to stop
 arrête de crier = stop shouting
 arrête! = stop it!
• = to arrest
2 s'arrêter (**!** + être)
s'arrêter = to stop

arrhes noun, feminine plural
des arrhes = a deposit

arrière
1 adjective
 = back
 = rear
2 noun, masculine
• (the rear part)
 l'arrière = the back
• (in sport)
 un arrière = a fullback
 = a defender
3 en arrière adverb
• = backward(s)
 se pencher en arrière = to lean back
• = behind
 rester en arrière = to stay behind

arrivée noun, feminine
• (of a plane, a passenger)
 une arrivée = an arrival
 aller chercher un ami à l'arrivée du train
 = to meet a friend off the train, to meet
 a friend from the train
• (of a race)
 l'arrivée = the finish

arriver verb [1] (**!** + être)
• = to arrive
• = to come
 j'arrive! = I'm coming!
 ils sont arrivés en courant = they came up
 running, they ran up
• = to reach
• arriver à faire = to manage to do, to
 succeed in doing
 je n'y arrive pas = I can't manage it, I can't
 do it
• = to happen
 c'est arrivé à mon frère = it happened to
 my brother
 que t'est-il arrivé? = what happened to
 you?
 il m'arrive d'oublier = I sometimes forget

arrondir verb ③
arrondir un chiffre = to round off a figure

arrondissement noun, masculine
un arrondissement = an arrondissement, a district

arroser verb ①
= to water
= to spray

arrosoir noun, masculine
un arrosoir = a watering can

art noun, masculine
l'art = art
les arts ménagers = home economics

artichaut noun, masculine
un artichaut = an artichoke

article noun, masculine
• (in grammar)
un article = an article
• (in a shop)
un article = an item
des articles de sport = sports equipment
des articles de toilette = toiletries

artificiel/artificielle adjective
= artificial
= man-made

artisan noun, masculine
un artisan = a craftsman

artisanal/artisanale adjective
(plural) **artisanaux/artisanales**
une méthode artisanale = a traditional method
de fabrication artisanale = hand-crafted, hand-made
= home-made

artisanat noun, masculine
l'artisanat = the craft industry
magasin d'artisanat = arts and crafts shop

artiste noun, masculine/feminine
un artiste/une artiste = an artist
(in films, plays) = an actor/an actress
un artiste peintre = a painter

as¹ ▶ avoir ⑧

as² noun, masculine (**!** never changes)
un as = an ace

ascenseur noun, masculine
un ascenseur = a lift, an elevator

ascension noun, feminine
une ascension = an ascent

Ascension noun, feminine
l'Ascension = Ascension

asiatique adjective
= from the Far East, Asian

Asie noun, feminine
l'Asie = Asia

asperge noun, feminine
des asperges = asparagus

asphyxier: s'asphyxier verb ②
(**!** + être)
s'asphyxier = to suffocate

aspirateur noun, masculine
un aspirateur = a vacuum cleaner

assassin noun, masculine
un assassin = a murderer

assassinat noun, masculine
un assassinat = a murder

assassiner verb ①
= to murder

asseoir: s'asseoir verb ㉞ (**!** + être)
s'asseoir = to sit (down)
(in bed) = to sit up

assez adverb
= enough
= quite, pretty

assiette noun, feminine
une assiette = a plate
une assiette anglaise = assorted cold meats, cold cuts

assis/assise
1 ▶ asseoir ㉞
2 adjective
= seated

assister verb ①
• assister à = to attend, to be at
• assister à = to witness

association noun, feminine
une association sportive = a sports association, a (sports) club

assorti/assortie adjective
• = matching
• = assorted

assurance noun, feminine
• (a feeling)
l'assurance = (self-)confidence
• (against accidents)
une assurance = insurance
l'assurance maladie = health insurance
l'assurance au tiers = third-party insurance
l'assurance tous risques
= comprehensive insurance

assuré/assurée
1 adjective
• = confident
• = certain
2 noun, masculine/feminine
l'assuré/l'assurée = the insured party

assurer verb ①
1 (**!** + avoir)
• (to tell confidently) = to assure
il m'a assuré que c'était vrai = he assured me that it was true
• (against accidents) = to insure
2 s'assurer (**!** + être)
• s'assurer = to take out insurance
• s'assurer que = to make sure that

astrologue noun, masculine|feminine
un astrologue/une astrologue = an
astrologer

astronaute noun, masculine|feminine
un astronaute/une astronaute = an
astronaut

astuce noun, feminine
• une astuce = a trick
• l'astuce = cleverness
= shrewdness

astucieux/astucieuse adjective
= clever, smart
= shrewd

atelier noun, masculine
un atelier (for a craftsman) = a workshop
(for a painter) = a studio

athlétisme noun, masculine
l'athlétisme = athletics

Atlantique noun, masculine
l'(océan) Atlantique = the Atlantic (Ocean)

atout noun, masculine
• (at cards)
un atout = a trump
atout trèfle! = clubs are trumps!
• (in life)
un atout = an asset, an advantage

attacher verb 1
1 (**!** + avoir)
= to tie
= to fasten
2 s'attacher à (**!** + être)
s'attacher à = to become attached to

attaquer verb 1
1 (**!** + avoir)
= to attack
2 s'attaquer à (**!** + être)
s'attaquer à = to attack

atteindre verb 55
• = to reach
• = to hit
• être atteint d'une maladie = to suffer from
a disease

atteint/atteinte ▶ **atteindre** 55

attendre verb 6
1 (**!** + avoir)
• = to wait
= to wait (for)
• = to expect
j'attends une visite = I'm expecting a visit
2 s'attendre à (**!** + être)
s'attendre à = to expect
il fallait s'y attendre = it was to be expected

attendu/attendue ▶ **attendre** 6

attentat noun, masculine
un attentat (on a person) = an
assassination attempt
(on a group, a building) = an attack

attente noun, feminine
l'attente = wait(ing)

attention noun, feminine
l'attention = attention
faire attention (to take care) = to be careful
(to concentrate) = to pay attention
attention! = careful!, watch out!
attention à la marche! = mind the step!,
watch the step!

attentivement adverb
= attentively

atterrir verb 3
= to land

atterrissage noun, masculine
un atterrissage = a landing

attirer verb 1
1 (**!** + avoir)
= to attract
2 s'attirer (**!** + être)
s'attirer des ennuis = to get into trouble

attraction noun, feminine
• l'attraction = attraction
• des attractions = entertainment
un parc d'attractions = an amusement
park

attraper verb 1
= to catch

au ▶ **à**

auberge noun, feminine
une auberge = an inn
une auberge de jeunesse = a youth
hostel

aucun/aucune
1 adjective
= no, not any
en aucun cas = under no circumstances
aucune idée! = I've no idea!
2 pronoun
= none, not any
aucun d'entre nous = none of us
aucune des deux = neither of them

audace noun, feminine
l'audace (bravery) = boldness
(guts) = audacity, nerve

audacieux/audacieuse adjective
= bold

au-delà de preposition
= beyond
= over

au-dessous de preposition
= below
= under

au-dessus de preposition
= above
= over

auditeur/auditrice noun,
masculine/feminine
un auditeur/une auditrice = a listener

augmenter *verb* [1]
= to increase

aujourd'hui *adverb*
* = today
* = nowadays

aurai ▶ **avoir** [8]

aussi
1 *adverb*
* = also, as well
= too
eux aussi ont faim = they are hungry too
* = so
je ne savais pas que c'était aussi cher = I didn't know it was so expensive
il n'avait jamais vu un aussi gros chien = he'd never seen such a large dog
* = as
aussi [riche | vieux | petit …] que = as [rich | old | small …] as
2 *conjunction*
= so, consequently
aussi sommes-nous partis = (and) so we left

aussitôt
1 *adverb*
= immediately, right away
2 aussitôt que = as soon as

Australie *noun, feminine*
l'Australie = Australia

australien/australienne *adjective*
= Australian

autant *adverb*
1 autant que = as much as
il gagne autant que toi = he earns as much as you
2 autant de = as much
= as many
autant de [valeur | patience | temps …] que = as much [value | patience | time …] as
autant de [fautes | lettres | soucis …] que = as many [mistakes | letters | worries …] as

auteur *noun, masculine*
l'auteur (*of a book*) = the author
(*of a song*) = the composer

auto *noun, feminine*
une auto = a car

autobus *noun, masculine* (**!** *never changes*)
un autobus = a bus

autocar *noun, masculine*
un autocar = a coach, a bus

autocollant/autocollante
1 *adjective*
= self-adhesive
2 autocollant *noun, masculine*
un autocollant = a sticker

auto-école *noun, feminine*
(*plural*) **auto-écoles**
une auto-école = a driving school

automne *noun, masculine*
l'automne = autumn, fall

A

automobile *noun, feminine*
une automobile = a (motor)car, an automobile

automobiliste *noun, masculine/feminine*
un automobiliste/une automobiliste = a motorist

autoritaire *adjective*
= authoritarian

autoroute *noun, feminine*
une autoroute = a motorway, a highway

auto-stop *noun, masculine*
l'auto-stop = hitchhiking
faire de l'auto-stop = to hitchhike

autour de *preposition*
= around

autre
1 *determiner*
= other
l'autre jour = the other day
rien d'autre = nothing else
2 d'autre part = besides
= on the other hand

autrefois *adverb*
= in the past
= before

autrement *adverb*
* = in a different way, differently
autrement dit = in other words
* (*if not*) = otherwise
autrement il ne viendra pas = otherwise he won't come

Autriche *noun, feminine*
l'Autriche = Austria

autrichien/autrichienne *adjective*
= Austrian

autruche *noun, feminine*
une autruche = an ostrich

aux ▶ **à**

avais ▶ **avoir** [8]

avaler *verb* [1]
= to swallow

avance
1 *noun, feminine*
* (*of an army*)
l'avance = the advance
* (*on a competitor*)
une avance = a lead
* (*money*)
une avance = an advance
2 à l'avance = in advance
3 d'avance
* payer d'avance = to pay in advance
* avoir cinq minutes d'avance = to be five minutes early

avoir verb [8]

present	imperfect	future	past participle
j'ai	j'avais	j'aurai	eu / eue
tu as	tu avais	tu auras	
il / elle a	ill / elle avait	il / elle aura	
nous avons	nous avions	nous aurons	
vous avez	vous aviez	vous aurez	
ils / elles ont	ils / elles avaient	ils / elles auront	

● **1 avoir** functions as an ordinary verb:
  = to have (got)
      ils **ont** un chien   = *they have a dog*
● = to get
      réussir à **avoir** des billets = *to manage to get tickets*

2 avoir is used as an auxiliary verb to conjugate most other verbs, except all reflexive verbs and those verbs labelled (**!** + *être*):
      elle **a** bu son lait   = *she drank her milk*
      ils **auraient** aimé te voir = *they would have liked to see you*

3 avoir is used in the phrase **il y a**:
      il y **a**   = *there is or there are*
      il y **aura**   = *there will be*

4 avoir is used in expressions like **avoir faim, avoir soif, avoir l'air, avoir besoin de** etc. You will find translations at **faim, soif, air, besoin** etc.

---

4 en avance
  arriver en avance = to arrive early
  être en avance sur les autres = to be ahead of the others

avancer *verb* [12]
1 (**!** + *avoir*)
• = to move forward
  avancer d'un mètre = to move forward one metre
• = to make progress
  avancer lentement = to make slow progress
• = to be fast
  ta montre avance de cinq minutes = your watch is five minutes fast
• = to bring forward
  avancer une réunion = to bring a meeting forward, to push a meeting up
• = to lend
  avancer de l'argent à un ami = to lend money to a friend
2 s'avancer (**!** + *être*)
  s'avancer = to move forward
  il s'est avancé vers la table = he moved toward(s) the table

avant
1 *noun, masculine*
• (*the front part*)
  l'avant = the front

• (*in sport*)
  un avant = a forward
2 *adjective* (**!** *never changes*)
  = front
  les roues avant = the front wheels
3 *preposition*
  = before
  juste avant de partir = just before leaving
4 *adverb*
  = before
  = first
  que faisait-il avant? = what was he doing before?
  la semaine d'avant = the week before
  la dame était avant = the lady was first
5 en avant = forward(s)
• se pencher en avant = to lean forward(s)
• partir en avant = to go (on) ahead

avantage *noun, masculine*
  un avantage = an advantage

avant-hier *adverb*
  = the day before yesterday

avare *adjective*
  = mean, miserly

avec *preposition*
  = with

avenir *noun, masculine*
  l'avenir = the future
  à l'avenir = in (the) future

✕ in informal situations

aventure *noun, feminine*
une aventure = an adventure
partir à l'aventure = to set off in search of
  adventure

aventurier/aventurière *noun,*
masculine/feminine
un aventurier/une aventurière = an
  adventurer

averse *noun, feminine*
une averse = a shower, a downpour

avertir *verb* 3
• = to warn
• = to inform

aveugle *adjective*
= blind

avez ▶ **avoir** 8

avion *noun, masculine*
un avion = an aeroplane, an airplane
un avion = a jet (plane)

aviron *noun, masculine*
• l'aviron = rowing
• un aviron = an oar

avis *noun, masculine* (*! never changes*)
• (*a belief*)
  un avis = an opinion
  changer d'avis = to change one's mind
• (*an announcement*)
  un avis = a notice, a sign

avocat¹ *noun, masculine*
un avocat = an avocado

avocat²/avocate *noun,*
masculine/feminine
un avocat/une avocate = a lawyer
  = a barrister, an attorney

avoir *verb* 8
▶ *See the boxed note.*

avons ▶ **avoir** 8

avouer *verb* 1
= to confess

avril *noun, masculine*
avril = April

ayant ▶ **avoir** 8

---

baby-foot *noun, masculine* (*! never*
changes)
le baby-foot = table football

bac*, baccalauréat *noun, masculine*
le baccalauréat = the baccalaureate (*a*
  school-leaving diploma taken at 17–18)

badaud *noun, masculine*
un badaud = an onlooker

bagage *noun, masculine*
un bagage = a piece of luggage

bagarre *noun, feminine*
une bagarre = a fight

bagarrer: se bagarrer *verb* 1 (*! + être*)
se bagarrer = to fight

bague *noun, feminine*
une bague = a ring

baguette *noun, feminine*
• (*bread*)
  une baguette = a baguette, a French stick,
  French bread
• (*a thin piece of wood*)
  une baguette = a stick
une baguette magique = a magic wand

baie *noun, feminine*
• (*on the coast*)
  une baie = a bay
• (*fruit*)
  une baie = a berry

baignade *noun, feminine*
la baignade = swimming

baigner: se baigner *verb* 1 (*! + être*)
se baigner = to go for a swim

baignoire *noun, feminine*
une baignoire = a bathtub

bâiller *verb* 1
= to yawn

bain *noun, masculine*
• (*at home*)
  un bain = a bath
  prendre un bain = to have a bath, to take a
  bath
• (*at the swimming pool*)
  le grand bain = the (main) pool
  le petit bain = the shallow pool, the
  learners' pool

baiser *noun, masculine*
un baiser = a kiss

baisser *verb* 1
1 (*! + avoir*)
• = to lower
  baisser le store = to lower the blinds
• = to drop
  la température a baissé = the temperature
  has dropped
2 se baisser (*! + être*)
se baisser = to bend down, to reach down

bal *noun, masculine*
un bal = a dance, a ball

balade *noun, feminine*
une balade (*on foot*) = a walk, a stroll
  (*by car*) = a drive
  (*on a bicycle*) = a ride

balader: **se balader** verb [1] (**!** + être)
se balader (on foot) = to go for a walk
(by car) = to go for a drive
(on a bicycle) = to go for a ride

baladeur noun, masculine
un baladeur = a walkman

balai noun, masculine
un balai = a broom

balance noun, feminine
une balance = scales

Balance noun, feminine
la Balance = Libra

balançoire noun, feminine
une balançoire = a swing
= a see-saw

balayer verb [21]
= to sweep

balcon noun, masculine
un balcon = a balcony

baleine noun, feminine
une baleine = a whale

balle noun, feminine
• (for playing)
une balle = a (small) ball
• (for a gun)
une balle = a bullet

ballerine noun, feminine
• (a person)
une ballerine = a ballerina
• (footwear)
une ballerine (for dancing) = a ballet
pump, a ballet slipper
(for walking) = a flat pump, a slipper

ballon noun, masculine
un ballon = a (large) ball

bambou noun, masculine
le bambou = bamboo

banal/banale adjective
= commonplace, ordinary

banane noun, feminine
• une banane = a banana
• une banane = a bum bag, a fanny pack

banc noun, masculine
un banc = a bench

bancaire adjective
= bank, banking

bande noun, feminine
• (of people)
une bande = a group, a bunch
• (with sound)
une bande = a tape
• (something long and narrow)
une bande = a strip
une bande dessinée = a comic strip

bandeau noun, masculine
(plural) **bandeaux**
un bandeau (holding the hair) = a
hairband, a headband
(over the eyes) = a blindfold

banlieue noun, feminine
la banlieue = the suburbs

banque noun, feminine
une banque = a bank

banquette noun, feminine
une banquette = a seat

banquier noun, masculine
un banquier = a banker

baptême noun, masculine
un baptême = a christening

bar noun, masculine
un bar = a bar

barbant/barbante�֊ adjective
= boring

barbare noun, masculine/feminine
un barbare/une barbare = a barbarian

barbe noun, feminine
• une barbe = a beard
• **quelle barbe✗!** = what a bore!
la barbe à papa = candyfloss, cotton
candy

barber: **se barber✗** [1] (**!** + être)
se barber = to be bored

barboter verb [1]
= to paddle

barbu noun, masculine
un barbu = a bearded man

barque noun, feminine
une barque = a (small) boat

barrage noun, masculine
• (on a river)
un barrage = a dam
• (on a road)
un barrage de police = a police roadblock

barre noun, feminine
• (of metal, chocolate)
une barre = a bar
• (a line)
une barre = a stroke, a mark
• (on a ship)
la barre = the tiller, the helm

barreau noun, masculine
(plural) **barreaux**
un barreau (on a cage) = a bar

barrer verb [1]
• = to cross out
• = to block

barrière noun, feminine
• (enclosing an area)
une barrière = a fence

- *(an obstacle)*
  une barrière = a barrier

bar-tabac *noun, masculine*
(plural) **bars-tabac**
  un bar-tabac = a café *(also selling stamps and cigarettes)*

bas/basse
1 *adjective*
  = low
2 **bas** *adverb*
- = low
  voir plus bas = see below
- = quietly
  parler tout bas = to speak in a whisper
3 **bas** *noun, masculine* (**!** *never changes*)
- *(the lower part)*
  le bas = the bottom
  en bas = downstairs
- à bas les patrons! = down with bosses!
- *(a garment)*
  un bas = a stocking

basculer *verb* [1]
- *(to fall over)* = to topple over
- *(to tilt)* = to tip up

basilic *noun, masculine*
  le basilic = basil

basket
1 *noun, masculine*
  le basket = basketball
2 *noun, feminine*
  des baskets = trainers, sneakers

basse ▶ **bas 1**

bassin *noun, masculine*
  un bassin = a pool

bataille *noun, feminine*
  une bataille = a battle
  la bataille navale = battleships

bateau *noun, masculine*
(plural) **bateaux**
  un bateau = a boat
  faire du bateau = to go boating
  = to go sailing

bateau-mouche *noun, masculine*
(plural) **bateaux-mouches**
  un bateau-mouche *a large river boat for sightseeing*

bâtiment *noun, masculine*
  un bâtiment = a building

bâtir *verb* [3]
  = to build

bâton *noun, masculine*
  un bâton = a stick

batterie *noun, feminine*
- *(in a car)*
  la batterie = the battery
- *(in a band)*
  la batterie = the percussion, the drums

battre *verb* [61]
1 (**!** + *avoir*)
  = to beat
  battre un record = to break a record
- le cœur battant = with a beating heart
- battre des mains = to clap
2 **se battre** (**!** + *être*)
  se battre = to fight

battu/battue ▶ **battre** [61]

baudruche *noun, feminine*
  un ballon en baudruche = a balloon

bavard/bavarde *adjective*
  = talkative

bavarder *verb* [1]
  = to chat

bazar *noun, masculine*
  un bazar *(a shop)* = a general store

BD *noun, feminine*
  une BD = a comic strip

beau/belle *adjective*
(plural) **beaux/belles**

  ! **bel** *is used instead of* **beau** *before masculine nouns beginning with a vowel or a mute h. The plural of* **bel** *is* **beaux**.

  = beautiful, handsome
  = fine
  il fait beau = the weather is fine

beaucoup *adverb*
  = a lot
  = much
  c'est beaucoup trop = it's far too much
  beaucoup de [patience | temps | livres ...] = a lot of [patience | time | books ...]
  il ne me reste plus beaucoup d'argent = I haven't got much money left

beau-frère *noun, masculine*
(plural) **beaux-frères**
  un beau-frère = a brother-in-law

beau-père *noun, masculine*
(plural) **beaux-pères**
  un beau-père = a father-in-law
  = a stepfather

beauté *noun, feminine*
  la beauté = beauty

beaux-arts *noun, masculine plural*
  les beaux-arts = fine arts

bébé *noun, masculine*
  un bébé = a baby

bec *noun, masculine*
  un bec = a beak

bêche *noun, feminine*
  une bêche = a spade, a shovel

beignet *noun, masculine*
  un beignet = a fritter
  = a doughnut, a donut

bel ▶ beau

belge *adjective*
= Belgian

Belgique *noun, feminine*
la Belgique = Belgium

Bélier *noun, masculine*
le Bélier = Aries

belle ▶ beau

belle-fille *noun, feminine*
(*plural*) **belles-filles**
une belle-fille = a daughter-in-law

belle-mère *noun, feminine*
(*plural*) **belles-mères**
une belle-mère = a mother-in-law
= a stepmother

belle-sœur *noun, feminine*
(*plural*) **belles-sœurs**
une belle-sœur = a sister-in-law

bénéfice *noun, masculine*
faire un bénéfice = to make a profit

béquille *noun, feminine*
une béquille = a crutch

berceau *noun, masculine*
(*plural*) **berceaux**
un berceau = a cradle

bercer *verb* 12
= to rock

berge *noun, feminine*
la berge (de la rivière) = the (river)bank

berger/bergère *noun,*
masculine/feminine
un berger/une bergère = a shepherd/a
shepherdess
un berger allemand = a German
shepherd dog, an Alsatian

bermuda *noun, masculine*
un bermuda = bermuda shorts

besoin *noun, masculine*
un besoin = a need
avoir besoin d'argent = to need money

bête
1 *adjective*
= stupid, silly
2 *noun, feminine*
une bête = an animal

bêtise *noun, feminine*
• la bêtise = stupidity
• faire une bêtise = to do something silly
dire des bêtises = to talk nonsense

béton *noun, masculine*
le béton = concrete

betterave *noun, feminine*
une betterave = a beetroot, a beet

beurre *noun, masculine*
le beurre = butter

bibelot *noun, masculine*
un bibelot = an ornament

biberon *noun, masculine*
un biberon = a (baby's) bottle, a (nursing)
bottle

bibliothèque *noun, feminine*
une bibliothèque (*a room or a building*) = a
library
(*a piece of furniture*) = a bookcase

bic *noun, masculine*
un bic = a biro , a ballpoint pen

bicyclette *noun, feminine*
• (*the equipment*)
une bicyclette = a bicycle
• (*the sport*)
faire de la bicyclette = to cycle, to go
cycling

bidon
1 *adjective*✱ (**!** *never changes*)
= bogus, phoney
2 *noun, masculine*
un bidon = a can
= a drum

bidonville *noun, masculine*
un bidonville = a shanty town

bien
1 *adjective* (**!** *never changes*)
• = good
2 *adverb*
• = well
ils vont bien = they're well
ça s'est bien passé = it went well
c'est bien fait pour lui! = it serves him
right!
• = very
c'est bien triste = it's very sad
je l'espère bien = I very much hope so, I
hope so
• = exactly
• = definitely
c'est bien ce que je pensais = that's
(exactly) what I thought
la voiture rouge est bien à eux = the red
car is definitely theirs
je te l'avais bien dit! = I told you so!
3 *noun, masculine*
le bien = good
c'est pour ton bien = it's for your own good
4 bien sûr = of course
5 bien entendu = naturally

bientôt *adverb*
= soon

bienvenu/bienvenue *adjective*
= welcome

bière *noun, feminine*
la bière = beer
la bière (à la) pression = draught beer,
draft beer

✱ in informal situations

la bière blonde = lager, light beer
la bière brune = stout

bifteck *noun, masculine*
le bifteck = steak

bifurquer *verb* $\boxed{1}$
* (*if it's a road*) = to fork
* (*if it's a driver*) = to turn off

bijou *noun, masculine*
(*plural*) **bijoux**
un bijou = a piece of jewellery, a piece of jewelry

bijouterie *noun, feminine*
une bijouterie = a jeweller's, a jewellery shop, a jewelry store

bijoutier/bijoutière *noun,*
masculine/feminine
un bijoutier/une bijoutière = a jeweller, a jeweler

bilingue *adjective*
= bilingual

billard *noun, masculine*
le billard = billiards
le billard américain = pool
le billard anglais = snooker

bille *noun, feminine*
une bille = a marble

billet *noun, masculine*
* (*on a train, at the theatre*)
un billet = a ticket
* (*money*)
un billet (de banque) = a (bank)note, a bill

biscotte *noun, feminine*
une biscotte ≈ a rusk

bise* *noun, feminine*
une bise* = a kiss

bisou* *noun, masculine*
un bisou* = a kiss

bissextile *adjective*
une année bissextile = a leap year

bistro(t)* *noun, masculine*
un bistro(t)* = a bistro, a café

bizarre *adjective*
= strange, peculiar

blague* *noun, feminine*
* une blague* = a funny story
* (*a piece of mischief*)
une blague* = a trick
faire une blague* à un ami = to play a trick on a friend

blanc/blanche
1 *adjective*
* = white
* = blank
2 blanc *noun, masculine*
un blanc (*a space*) = a blank
un blanc d'œuf = an egg white

du blanc de poulet = a piece of chicken breast

blanchisserie *noun, feminine*
une blanchisserie = a laundry, a dry cleaner's

blé *noun, masculine*
le blé = wheat, corn

blessé/blessée
1 *adjective*
= injured
= wounded
2 *noun, masculine/feminine*
un blessé/une blessée = an injured person
= a casualty

blesser *verb* $\boxed{1}$
1 (**!** + *avoir*)
= to hurt
= to wound
2 se blesser (**!** + *être*)
se blesser = to hurt oneself
elle s'est blessée à la jambe – she hurt her leg

blessure *noun, feminine*
une blessure = an injury
= a wound

bleu/bleue
1 *adjective*
= blue
bleu marine = navy blue
2 bleu *noun, masculine*
un bleu = a bruise

bloc
1 *noun, masculine*
(*for writing*)
un bloc = a notepad
2 à bloc = completely
vissé à bloc = tightly screwed
gonflé à bloc = fully inflated

blond/blonde *adjective*
(*describing hair*) = blonde, blond
(*describing tobacco*) = light, Virginia

bloquer *verb* $\boxed{1}$
1 (**!** + *avoir*)
* = to block
* = to jam
* bloquer les salaires = to freeze wages
2 se bloquer (**!** + *être*)
se bloquer = to jam

blouse *noun, feminine*
* (*worn for protection*)
une blouse = an overall
* (*a kind of shirt*)
une blouse = a blouse

blouson *noun, masculine*
un blouson = a blouson, a jacket

bobo* *noun, masculine*
ce n'est qu'un bobo* = it's only a scratch

B

bocal *noun, masculine*
(*plural*) **bocaux**
  un bocal = a jar

bœuf *noun, masculine*
• (*the animal*)
  un bœuf = an ox
• (*the meat*)
  le bœuf = beef

boire *verb* [51]
  = to drink

bois
1 ▶ boire [51]
2 *noun, masculine* (**!** *never changes*)
• (*timber*)
  le bois = wood
• (*a place*)
  un bois = a wood

boisson *noun, feminine*
  une boisson = a drink

boîte *noun, feminine*
  une boîte = a box
une boîte de conserve = a tin, a can
une boîte aux lettres = a postbox, a
  mailbox
  = a letter box, a mailbox
une boîte de nuit = a nightclub
une boîte de vitesses = a gearbox

boiter *verb* [1]
  = to limp

boiteux/boiteuse *adjective*
  = lame

bol *noun, masculine*
  un bol = a bowl

bombe *noun, feminine*
• (*a weapon*)
  une bombe = a bomb
• (*an aerosol*)
  une bombe = a spray

bon/bonne¹
1 *adjective*
• = good
• = right
  la bonne réponse = the right answer
• = valid
  le billet est encore bon = the ticket is still
  valid
• **bon anniversaire!** = happy birthday!
  bonne journée! = have a nice day
2 bon *adverb*
  il fait bon dehors = it's nice outside
  sentir bon = to smell nice
3 bon *noun, masculine*
  un bon = a coupon
  = a voucher
4 bon *exclamation*
  bon! = right!
  ah bon? = really?

bon marché = cheap
le bon sens = common sense

bonbon *noun, masculine*
  un bonbon = a sweet, a candy

bonbonne *noun, feminine*
  une bonbonne (*for wine*) = a demijohn
  (*for gas*) = a cylinder

bond *noun, masculine*
  un bond = a leap

bondé/bondée *adjective*
  = packed

bondir *verb* [3]
  = to leap

bonhomme✶ *noun, masculine*
(*plural*) **bonshommes**
  un bonhomme✶ = a chap, a guy, a fellow
un bonhomme de neige = a snowman

bonjour *noun, masculine*
  bonjour! = hello!, good morning!, good
  afternoon!

bonne² *noun, feminine*
  une bonne = a maid

bonnet *noun, masculine*
  un bonnet = a cap, a hat

bonsoir *noun, masculine*
  bonsoir = good evening!, good night!

bonté *noun, feminine*
  la bonté = kindness

bord
1 *noun, masculine*
  le bord (*of a bed, a cliff*) = the edge
  (*of a road*) = the side
  (*of a river*) = the bank
  des vacances au bord de la mer = seaside
  holidays, a seaside vacation
2 à bord = on board, aboard

bordeaux
1 *adjective* (**!** *never changes*)
  = burgundy
2 *noun, masculine* (**!** *never changes*)
  le Bordeaux = Bordeaux wine

bordure *noun, feminine*
  la bordure (*the limit*) = the edge
  (*ornamental*) = the border

bosse *noun, feminine*
  une bosse (*on the head*) = a lump
  (*on the back*) = a hump
  (*on a car*) = a dent

botte *noun, feminine*
• (*footwear*)
  une botte = a boot
• (*a bundle*)
  une botte = a bunch

bouc *noun, masculine*
• (*an animal*)
  un bouc = a billy goat

- (*a beard*)
  un bouc = a goatee

bouche *noun, feminine*
la bouche = the mouth
une bouche de métro = a tube entrance, a subway entrance

bouchée *noun, feminine*
une bouchée = a mouthful

boucher¹ *verb* 1
- = to plug
  = to fill up
- = to block
  = to clog up
- = to cork

boucher²/bouchère *noun, masculine/feminine*
le boucher/la bouchère = the butcher

boucherie *noun, feminine*
une boucherie = a butcher's (shop)

bouchon *noun, masculine*
- (*on a bottle*)
  un bouchon = a cork
  = a top
- (*on the road*)
  un bouchon = a traffic jam

boucle *noun, feminine*
- (*on a belt*)
  une boucle = a buckle
- (*of hair*)
  une boucle = a curl
- (*a curved shape*)
  une boucle = a loop
une boucle d'oreille = an earring

bouclé/bouclée *adjective*
= curly

boucler *verb* 1
- = to buckle
- = to fasten

boudin *noun, masculine*
le boudin = black pudding, blood pudding

boue *noun, feminine*
la boue = mud

bouffer* *verb* 1
= to eat

bouger *verb* 13
= to move

bougie *noun, feminine*
- (*for lighting*)
  une bougie = a candle
- (*in an engine*)
  une bougie = a sparking plug, a spark plug

bouillir *verb* 31
= to boil

bouilloire *noun, feminine*
une bouilloire = a kettle

bouillotte *noun, feminine*
une bouillotte = a hot-water bottle

boulanger/boulangère *noun, masculine/feminine*
un boulanger/une boulangère = a baker

boulangerie *noun, feminine*
une boulangerie = a baker's (shop)

boule *noun, feminine*
- (*a shape*)
  une boule = a ball
  une boule de neige = a snowball
- (*in games*)
  une boule = a bowl
  = a boule

boulevard *noun, masculine*
un boulevard = an avenue

boulot* *noun, masculine*
- **le boulot*** = work
- **un boulot*** = a job

boum* *noun, feminine*
une boum* = a party

bouquet *noun, masculine*
un bouquet = a bunch

bouquin* *noun, masculine*
un bouquin* = a book

bourgeon *noun, masculine*
un bourgeon = a bud

bousculer *verb* 1
- = to bump into
  = to jostle
- = to rush
  ne me bouscule pas = don't rush me

boussole *noun, feminine*
une boussole = a compass

bout *noun, masculine*
- **un bout** = a piece
- **le bout** = the end
  = the tip

bouteille *noun, feminine*
une bouteille = a bottle
une bouteille de gaz = a gas cylinder

boutique *noun, feminine*
une boutique = a shop

bouton *noun, masculine*
- (*on a coat, for a doorbell*)
  un bouton = a button
- (*on the skin*)
  un bouton = a spot, a pimple
- (*on an appliance*)
  un bouton = a switch
- (*on a plant*)
  un bouton = a bud

boxe *noun, feminine*
la boxe = boxing

bracelet *noun, masculine*
un bracelet = a bracelet
= a bangle

B

un bracelet de montre = a watchstrap, a watchband

branche noun, feminine
* (on a tree)
  une branche = a branch
* (an area of work, study)
  une branche = a field

branché/branchée* adjective
= trendy, cool

brancher verb [1]
= to plug in
= to connect

braquer verb [1]
* **braquer un revolver sur quelqu'un** = to aim a gun at someone
* **braquer le volant à gauche** = to turn the wheel hard (to the) left

bras noun, masculine (**!** never changes)
un bras = an arm
en bras de chemise = in one's shirtsleeves

brasserie noun, feminine
* (for meals)
  une brasserie = a brasserie, a café
* (a factory)
  une brasserie = a brewery

bravo exclamation
= bravo!, well done!

brebis noun, feminine (**!** never changes)
une brebis = a ewe

bref/brève
1 adjective
= brief, short
2 (en) bref adverb
= in short

Bretagne noun, feminine
la Bretagne = Brittany

breton/bretonne
1 adjective
= Breton
2 breton noun, masculine
le breton = Breton

brève ▶ bref 1

brevet noun, masculine
un brevet (a qualification) = a certificate
un brevet des collèges = a certificate of general education
un brevet de pilote = a pilot's licence

bricolage noun, masculine
le bricolage = DIY, do-it-yourself

brillant/brillante adjective
* = shiny
* = brilliant

briller verb [1]
= to shine

brin noun, masculine
un brin (of parsley, mimosa) = a sprig
(of grass) = a blade

brioche noun, feminine
une brioche = a brioche, a (sweet) bun

briquet noun, masculine
un briquet = a cigarette lighter

britannique adjective
= British

brocante noun, feminine
une brocante = a flea market

brocanteur/brocanteuse noun, masculine/feminine
un brocanteur/une brocanteuse = a bric-à-brac dealer

broche noun, feminine
* (an ornament)
  une broche = a brooch, a pin
* (for cooking)
  une broche = a spit

brochette noun, feminine
une brochette = a kebab, a brochette

brochure noun, feminine
une brochure = a brochure

broder verb [1]
= to embroider

bronzage noun, masculine
un bronzage = a (sun)tan

bronzé/bronzée adjective
= tanned, brown

bronzer verb [1]
= to get a tan, to go brown

brosse noun, feminine
une brosse = a brush
avoir les cheveux (taillés) en brosse = to have a crew cut
une brosse à dents = a toothbrush

brosser verb [1]
= to brush

brouillard noun, masculine
le brouillard = fog

brouillé/brouillée adjective
= jumbled, mixed up

brouillon noun, masculine
un brouillon = a rough draft

broussailles noun, feminine plural
les broussailles = the undergrowth

brugnon noun, masculine
un brugnon = a nectarine

bruit noun, masculine
le bruit = noise

brûlant/brûlante adjective
= burning hot

---

* in informal situations

brûlé noun, masculine
ça sent le brûlé = there's a smell of burning

brûler verb ①
1 (**!** + avoir)
• = to burn
• brûler un feu (rouge) = to jump the lights, to run the lights
2 se brûler (**!** + être)
se brûler = to burn oneself

brume noun, feminine
la brume = mist

brumeux/brumeuse adjective
= misty

brun/brune adjective
• = brown, dark
• = dark-haired

brunir verb ③
= to tan

brusque adjective
• = abrupt
• = sudden

Bruxelles noun
= Brussels

bruyant/bruyante adjective
= noisy

bu/bue ▶ boire 51

bûche noun, feminine
une bûche = a log

buffet noun, masculine
• (a piece of furniture)
un buffet = a sideboard
• (a meal, a place)
un buffet = a buffet

buisson noun, masculine
un buisson = a bush
= a shrub

buissonnière adjective, feminine
faire l'école buissonnière = to play truant, to play hooky

bulle noun, feminine
• (of soap)
une bulle = a bubble
faire des bulles = to blow bubbles
• (in a cartoon)
une bulle = a speech bubble

bulletin noun, masculine
un bulletin = a report
= a form
= a certificate
un bulletin météorologique = a weather report
un bulletin scolaire = a school report, a report card

bureau noun, masculine
(plural) **bureaux**

• (a piece of furniture)
un bureau = a desk
• (a room)
un bureau = an office
le bureau de poste = the post office
le bureau des renseignements = the information office, the information desk

bus noun, masculine (**!** never changes)
un bus = a bus

but noun, masculine
• (what one has in mind)
un but = a goal
= an aim, a purpose
= an intention
dans le but de = with the intention of
• (in football)
un but = a goal

buvable adjective
= drinkable
(on a medicine label) = to be taken orally

buveur/buveuse noun, masculine/feminine
un buveur/une buveuse = a drinker

Cc

c' ▶ ce

ça pronoun
• = this
= that
donne-moi ça = give me that
ça, c'est bizarre = that's strange
• = it
ça ne fait rien = it doesn't matter
c'est ça! = that's right!, that's it!
c'est pour ça que ... = that's why ...
et avec ça? = anything else?
• où ça? = where?
• comment ça va? = how are you?
ça va mal = things are bad
ça y est, j'ai fini = that's it, I've finished

cabane noun, feminine
une cabane = a hut, a shack

cabillaud noun, masculine
le cabillaud = cod

cabine noun, feminine
une cabine (for sleeping) = a cabin
(for changing) = a cubicle, a changing room
une cabine d'essayage = a fitting room
une cabine téléphonique = a telephone box, a telephone booth

cabinet *noun, masculine*
- (*a place of work*)
  un cabinet = an office
  (*for a doctor*) = a surgery, an office
- (*a W.C.*)
  le cabinet, les cabinets = the toilet, the bathroom
un cabinet de toilette = washing facilities

câble *noun, masculine*
  un câble = a cable

cacahuète *noun, feminine*
  une cacahuète = a peanut

cacao *noun, masculine*
  le cacao = cocoa

cache-cache *noun, masculine* (**!** *never changes*)
  jouer à cache-cache = to play hide and seek

cacher *verb* ①
  = to hide

cachet *noun, masculine*
- (*a medicine*)
  un cachet = a tablet, a pill
- (*on a form*)
  un cachet = a stamp

cachette *noun, feminine*
  une cachette = a hiding place
  en cachette = secretly

c-à-d *conjunction*
  (*abbreviation of* **c'est-à-dire**)
  c-à-d = i.e.

cadeau *noun, masculine*
  (*plural*) **cadeaux**
  un cadeau = a present, a gift

cadet/cadette *adjective*
  = younger, youngest

cadre *noun, masculine*
- (*for a picture*)
  un cadre = a frame
- (*an employee*)
  un cadre = an executive
- (*the space around a person or a thing*)
  le cadre = the surroundings

cafard *noun, masculine*
- **un cafard** = a cockroach
- **avoir le cafard** = to feel down, to feel blue

café *noun, masculine*
- (*a product*)
  le café = coffee
- (*a place*)
  un café = a café, a diner
un café crème = an espresso with milk
un café au lait = a coffee with milk

cafetière *noun, feminine*
  une cafetière = a coffee maker

---

cage *noun, feminine*
  une cage = a cage

cahier *noun, masculine*
  un cahier = an exercise book
un cahier de brouillon = a rough book, a notebook
un cahier de textes = a homework notebook

caillou *noun, masculine*
  (*plural*) **cailloux**
  un caillou = a stone

Caire *noun, masculine*
  le Caire = Cairo

caisse *noun, feminine*
- (*for goods*)
  une caisse = a crate
- (*for money*)
  une caisse = a till, a cash register
- (*where you pay in a shop*)
  la caisse = the cash desk
  = the checkout

calcul *noun, masculine*
- (*the study of numbers*)
  le calcul = arithmetic
- (*an operation*)
  un calcul = a calculation

calculatrice *noun, feminine*
  une calculatrice = a (pocket) calculator

calculer *verb* ①
  = to calculate, to work out

calé/calée✗ *adjective*
  = clever

caleçon *noun, masculine*
  un caleçon (*for men*) = boxer shorts
  (*for women*) = leggings
un caleçon long = long johns

calendrier *noun, masculine*
  un calendrier = a calendar

caler *verb* ①
- (*in order to fix in a position*) = to wedge
- (*when driving*) = to stall

calmant *noun, masculine*
  un calmant = a sedative

calmar *noun, masculine*
  un calmar = a squid

calme
  1 *adjective*
  = calm, quiet
  2 *noun, masculine*
  le calme = peace (and quiet)

calmer *verb* ①
  1 (**!** + *avoir*)
  = to calm (down)
  2 se calmer (**!** + *être*)
  se calmer = to calm down

camarade *noun, masculine/feminine*
  un camarade/une camarade = a friend

cambriolage noun, masculine
un cambriolage = a burglary

cambrioler verb 1
= to burgle

caméra noun, feminine
une caméra = a (cine-)camera, a movie camera

caméscope noun, masculine
un caméscope = a camcorder

camion noun, masculine
un camion = a lorry, a truck

camionnette noun, feminine
une camionnette = a van

campagne noun, feminine
• (the area around towns)
la campagne = the country
= the countryside
• (for an election, in war)
une campagne = a campaign

camper verb 1
= to camp

campeur/campeuse noun, masculine/feminine
un campeur/une campeuse = a camper

camping noun, masculine
• (the activity)
le camping = camping
• (the place)
un camping = a campsite, a campground

camping-car noun, masculine
(plural) **camping-cars**
un camping-car = a camper-van, an RV

Canada noun, masculine
le Canada = Canada

canadien/canadienne adjective
= Canadian

canal noun, masculine
(plural) **canaux**
• (a waterway)
un canal = a canal
• (in telecommunications)
un canal = a channel

canapé noun, masculine
un canapé = a settee, a sofa

canard noun, masculine
un canard = a duck

Cancer noun, masculine
le Cancer = Cancer

candidat/candidate noun, masculine/feminine
un candidat/une candidate (in an examination, an election) = a candidate
(for a job) = an applicant

caniche noun, masculine
un caniche = a poodle

canif noun, masculine
un canif = a penknife, a pocketknife

canne noun, feminine
une canne = a (walking) stick, a cane
une canne à pêche = a fishing rod

canoë noun, masculine
• (the equipment)
un canoë = a (Canadian) canoe
• (the sport)
le canoë = canoeing

canot noun, masculine
un canot = a (small) boat, a dinghy
un canot de sauvetage = a lifeboat

cantine noun, feminine
une cantine = a canteen

caoutchouc noun, masculine
le caoutchouc = rubber

CAP noun, masculine ▶ **certificat**

capitaine noun, masculine
un capitaine = a captain

capitale noun, feminine
• (a town)
une capitale = a capital (city)
• (a letter)
une capitale = a capital

capot noun, masculine
le capot = the bonnet, the hood

Capricorne noun, masculine
le Capricorne = Capricorn

capuchon noun, masculine
• (for the head)
un capuchon = a hood
• (for a pen)
un capuchon = a cap

car
1 noun, masculine
un car = a coach, a bus
2 conjunction
car = because, for

caractère noun, masculine
• (a personality)
un caractère = a character, a nature
• (in writing)
un caractère = a letter

Caraïbes noun, feminine plural
les Caraïbes = the Caribbean islands

carambolage noun, masculine
un carambolage = a pile-up

caramel noun, masculine
• (on ice cream, custard)
le caramel = caramel
• (a sweet)
un caramel = a toffee

caravane noun, feminine
une caravane = a caravan, a trailer

carburateur noun, masculine
le carburateur = the carburettor

caresser verb ①
= to stroke

carnet noun, masculine
• (in which to write)
un carnet = a notebook
• (a set of tickets, stamps)
un carnet = a book
un carnet d'adresses = an address book
un carnet de chèques = a cheque book,
a checkbook

carotte noun, feminine
une carotte = a carrot

carré/carrée adjective
= square

carreau noun, masculine
(plural) **carreaux**
• (on a window)
un carreau = a window pane
• (on the wall, the floor)
un carreau = a tile
du tissu à carreaux = check(ed) material,
chequered material
• (at cards)
carreau = diamonds

carrefour noun, masculine
le carrefour = the crossroads

carrière noun, feminine
• (a profession)
une carrière = a career
• (a place)
une carrière = a quarry

carrosserie noun, feminine
la carrosserie = bodywork

cartable noun, masculine
un cartable = a satchel, a schoolbag
= a briefcase

carte noun, feminine
• (in games)
une carte = a card
• (of a country)
une carte = a map
• (in a restaurant)
la carte = the menu
une carte bleue = a credit card
une carte grise = a logbook
une carte d'identité = an ID card
une carte orange = a season ticket (in the
Paris area)
une carte postale = a postcard
une carte à puce = a smart card
une carte de visite = a visiting card
= a business card
une carte de vœux = a greeting(s) card

carton noun, masculine
• (the substance)
le carton = cardboard

• (a container)
un carton = a cardboard box

cas noun, masculine (! never changes)
un cas = a case

case noun, feminine
une case = a box

casier noun, masculine
un casier (for messages) = a pigeonhole
(for keeping things organized) = a locker

casque noun, masculine
• (for protection)
un casque = a helmet
= a hard hat
• (for listening to music)
un casque = headphones

casquette noun, feminine
une casquette = a cap

casse-croûte noun, masculine (! never
changes)
un casse-croûte = a snack

casser verb ①
1 (! + avoir)
= to break
2 se casser (! + être)
se casser = to break
je me suis cassé le poignet = I broke my
wrist

casserole noun, feminine
une casserole = a saucepan, a pan

cassis noun, masculine (! never changes)
le cassis = blackcurrants

catastrophe noun, feminine
une catastrophe = a disaster

catch noun, masculine
le catch = wrestling

catéchisme noun, masculine
le catéchisme = catechism

catégorie noun, feminine
une catégorie = a category

cauchemar noun, masculine
un cauchemar = a nightmare

cause noun, feminine
la cause = the cause
à cause de = because of

causer verb ①
• = to cause
causer un accident = to cause an accident
• ✶ = to chat, to talk

caution noun, feminine
une caution = a deposit

cave noun, feminine
une cave = a cellar

✶ in informal situations

ce¹/cette *adjective*
(*plural*) **ces**

> **!** cet *is used instead of* ce *before a masculine noun beginning with a vowel or a mute h. The plural of* cet *is* ces.

= this, that
ce livre(-ci) = this book
cet oiseau(-là) = that bird
ces enfants = these children, those children

ce² *pronoun* (**c'** *before e*)
• (*when the verb* être *is in the singular*)
c'est un cadeau = it's a present
ce serait dommage = it would be a shame
qui est-ce? = who is it?
qu'est-ce que c'est? = what is it?
c'est moi qui l'ai cassé = I was the one who broke it
• (*when the verb* être *is in the plural*)
ce sont des insectes = they're insects
ce sont des détails sans importance = these are unimportant details
• voilà ce que j'ai dit = that's what I said
prenez ce dont vous avez besoin = take what you need
c'est ce qui les inquiète = that's what worries them
ce qui m'ennuie le plus, c'est qu'il faudra se lever tôt = what bothers me most is that we'll have to get up early
il est venu, ce qui est étonnant = he came, which is surprising

> **!** *Look up the verb* être *for translations of* est-ce que.

ceci *pronoun*
= this

céder *verb* 14
• = to give up
• = to give in
céder le passage = to give way, to yield
• = to collapse

cédille *noun, feminine*
une cédille = a cedilla

CEE *noun, feminine* ▶ **communauté**

ceinture *noun, feminine*
une ceinture = a belt
une ceinture de sécurité = a seatbelt

cela *pronoun*
= it, that

célèbre *adjective*
= famous

célébrer *verb* 14
= to celebrate

céleri *noun, masculine*
le céleri = celery

célibataire
1 *adjective*
= single

2 *noun, masculine/feminine*
un célibataire/une célibataire = a single man/woman

celle ▶ **celui**

celle-ci ▶ **celui-ci**

celle-là ▶ **celui-là**

celles-ci ▶ **celui-ci**

celles-là ▶ **celui-là**

celui/celle *pronoun*
(*plural*) **ceux/celles**
celui/celle = the one
ceux/celles = the ones
= those
celle de ma sœur = my sister's

celui-ci/celle-ci *pronoun*
(*plural*) **ceux-ci/celles-ci**
celui-ci/celle-ci = this one
ceux-ci/celles-ci = these

celui-là/celle-là *pronoun*
(*plural*) **ceux-là/celles-là**
celui-là/celle-là = that one
ceux-là/celles-là = those

cendre *noun, feminine*
la cendre = ash

cendrier *noun, masculine*
un cendrier = an ashtray

censé/censée *adjective*
être censé = to be meant to

cent *number*
= hundred
pour cent = per cent

centaine *noun, feminine*
une centaine = about a hundred

centième *number*
= hundredth

centime *noun, masculine*
• (*of euro*)
un centime (d'euro) = a cent
• (*of franc*)
un centime = a centime

centimètre *noun, masculine*
• (*a unit of length*)
un centimètre = a centimetre, a centimeter
• (*a measuring device*)
un centimètre = a tape measure

central/centrale¹
(*plural*) **centraux/centrales**
1 *adjective*
= central
2 central *noun, masculine*
le central (téléphonique) = the (telephone) exchange

centrale² *noun, feminine*
une centrale = a power station

centre noun, masculine
le centre = the centre, the center
un centre aéré = a children's outdoor activity centre
un centre commercial = a shopping centre, a shopping mall

centre-ville noun, masculine
(plural) **centres-villes**
le centre-ville = the town centre, the town center

cependant conjunction
= however

cercle noun, masculine
un cercle = a circle

cercueil noun, masculine
un cercueil = a coffin

céréale noun, feminine
une céréale = a cereal, a grain

cérémonie noun, feminine
une cérémonie = a ceremony

cerf noun, masculine
un cerf = a stag

cerf-volant noun, masculine
(plural) **cerfs-volants**
un cerf-volant = a kite

cerise noun, feminine
une cerise = a cherry

cerisier noun, masculine
un cerisier = a cherry tree

certain/certaine
1 adjective
= certain, sure
2 determiner
= some
3 **certains/certaines** pronoun, plural
= some
certains d'entre vous = some of you

certainement adverb
= most probably
= certainly

certificat noun, masculine
un certificat = a certificate
un certificat d'aptitude professionnelle, un CAP = a vocational training qualification
un certificat médical = a doctor's certificate
un certificat de naissance = a birth certificate

cerveau noun, masculine
(plural) **cerveaux**
le cerveau = the brain

cervelle noun, feminine
la cervelle = the brain

ces ▶ **ce¹**

CES noun, masculine ▶ **collège**

cesser verb ①
= to stop

c'est-à-dire adverb
= that is (to say)

cet ▶ **ce¹**

CET noun, masculine ▶ **collège**

cette ▶ **ce¹**

ceux ▶ **celui**

chacun/chacune pronoun
• = each (one)
chacun d'entre vous = each one of you
• = everybody

chahut noun, masculine
du chahut = a racket

chaîne noun, feminine
• (linked metal rings)
une chaîne = a chain
• (on television)
une chaîne = a channel
• (in a factory)
la chaîne = the assembly line
une chaîne hi-fi = a hi-fi system
une chaîne laser = a CD system
une chaîne de montagnes = a mountain range

chair noun, feminine
la chair = flesh
la chair de poule = goose pimples, goose bumps

chaise noun, feminine
une chaise = a chair
une chaise longue = a deckchair

chaleur noun, feminine
la chaleur = heat, warmth

chambre noun, feminine
une chambre = a room, a bedroom
une chambre pour une personne
= a single room
une chambre pour deux personnes
= a double room
une chambre d'hôte = a room in a B & B
'chambres d'hôte' = 'bed and breakfast'

chameau noun, masculine
(plural) **chameaux**
un chameau = a camel

champ
1 noun, masculine
un champ = a field
2 **à tout bout de champ✖** = all the time

champignon noun, masculine
un champignon = a mushroom

champion/championne noun, masculine/feminine
un champion/une championne
= a champion

✖ in informal situations

championnat noun, masculine
un championnat = a championship

chance noun, feminine
• (good fortune)
la chance = luck
• (possibility)
avoir des chances de gagner = to stand a
chance of winning

change noun, masculine
le taux de change = the exchange rate

changement noun, masculine
un changement = a change

changer verb [13]
= to change
changer d'avis = to change one's mind
changer d'adresse = to move

chanson noun, feminine
une chanson = a song

chant noun, masculine
un chant = a song

chanter verb [1]
= to sing

chanteur/chanteuse noun,
masculine/feminine
un chanteur/une chanteuse = a singer

chantier noun, masculine
un chantier = a building site

chantilly noun, feminine (! never
changes)
la chantilly = whipped cream

chapeau noun, masculine
(plural) **chapeaux**
• un chapeau = a hat
• (when praising)✱
chapeau✱! = well done!, good job!
un chapeau melon = a bowler hat,
a derby hat

chapitre noun, masculine
un chapitre = a chapter

chaque determiner
= each, every

char noun, masculine
• (in a carnival)
un char = a float
• (a military vehicle)
un char = a tank

charcuterie noun, feminine
• (a shop)
une charcuterie = a pork butcher's
• (a type of food)
la charcuterie = cooked pork meats

charcutier/charcutière noun,
masculine/feminine
un charcutier/une charcutière = a pork
butcher

charger verb [13]
1 (! + avoir)

• = to load
charger un camion de légumes = to load a
truck with vegetables
• = to ask
charger quelqu'un [de poster une lettre |
d'arroser les plantes | de transmettre un
message...] = to ask someone [to post a
letter | to water the plants | to pass on a
message...]
• ils sont chargés de surveiller les enfants
= they're responsible for looking after the
children
2 se charger (! + être)
se charger d'une tâche = to take
responsibility for a job, to see to a job
je me charge de le leur dire = I'll tell them

chariot noun, masculine
un chariot = a trolley, a cart

charité noun, feminine
la charité = charity

charmant/charmante adjective
= charming

chasse noun, feminine
la chasse = hunting
la chasse d'eau = the (toilet) flush

chasse-neige noun, masculine (! never
changes)
un chasse-neige = a snowplough,
a snowplow

chasser verb [1]
• = to hunt
• = to shoot
• = to drive away

chasseur noun, masculine
un chasseur = a hunter

chat noun, masculine
un chat = a cat

châtaigne noun, feminine
une châtaigne = a (sweet) chestnut

châtain adjective
= brown

château noun, masculine
(plural) **châteaux**
un château = a castle
un château fort = a fortified castle

chaton noun, masculine
un chaton = a kitten

chatte noun, feminine
une chatte = a (female) cat

chaud/chaude
1 adjective
= hot, warm
2 chaud adverb
il fait chaud ici = it's hot in here
3 chaud noun, masculine
avoir chaud = to be hot

chaudière noun, feminine
une chaudière = a boiler

chauffage *noun, masculine*
le chauffage = the heating

chauffard✗ *noun, masculine*
un chauffard✗ = a reckless driver

chauffer *verb* [1]
• = to heat
• = to overheat
le moteur chauffe = the engine is
overheating
• = to give out heat, to give off heat
le poêle chauffe bien = the stove gives out
a lot of heat
le soleil chauffe aujourd'hui = the sun is
hot today

chauffeur *noun, masculine*
un chauffeur = a driver

chaumière *noun, feminine*
une chaumière = a thatched cottage

chaussée *noun, feminine*
la chaussée = the road, the highway
'chaussée déformée' = 'uneven road
surface'

chausser *verb* [1]
chausser du 39 = to take a size 39 (in
shoes), to take a size 6

chaussette *noun, feminine*
une chaussette = a sock

chausson *noun, masculine*
• (*footwear*)
un chausson = a slipper
• (*a cake*)
un chausson = a turnover

chaussure *noun, feminine*
une chaussure = a shoe
des chaussures de ski = ski boots

chauve *adjective*
= bald

chauve-souris *noun, feminine*
(*plural*) **chauves-souris**
une chauve-souris = a bat

chef
1 *noun, masculine*
• (*the person in charge*)
le chef = the leader
• (*in a restaurant*)
un chef (cuisinier) = a chef
2 en chef
l'ingénieur en chef = the chief engineer
un chef d'entreprise = a company
manager
un chef d'État = a head of state
un chef de gare = a station master
un chef d'orchestre = a conductor

chef-d'œuvre *noun, masculine*
(*plural*) **chefs-d'œuvre**
un chef-d'œuvre = a masterpiece

chemin *noun, masculine*
• un chemin = a country lane, a path
• le chemin = the way
le chemin de fer = the railway, the
railroad

cheminée *noun, feminine*
une cheminée = a chimney
= a fireplace
= a mantelpiece, a mantel

chemise *noun, feminine*
une chemise = a shirt

chemisier *noun, masculine*
un chemisier = a blouse

chêne *noun, masculine*
un chêne = an oak (tree)

chenille *noun, feminine*
une chenille = a caterpillar

chèque *noun, masculine*
un chèque = a cheque, a check
un chèque sans provision = a bad
cheque, a dud check

chèque-voyage *noun, masculine*
(*plural*) **chèques-voyage**
un chèque-voyage = a traveller's cheque, a
traveler's check

chéquier *noun, masculine*
un chéquier = a cheque book, a checkbook

cher/chère *adjective*
• = dear
• = expensive

chercher *verb* [1]
• = to look for
• aller chercher de l'eau = to go and get
some water

chère ▶ cher

chéri/chérie *noun, masculine/feminine*
(mon) chéri/(ma) chérie = (my) darling

cheval *noun, masculine*
(*plural*) **chevaux**
• (*an animal*)
un cheval = a horse
monter à cheval = to ride (a horse)
• (*the sport*)
le cheval = horseriding, horseback riding
• (*meat*)
le cheval = horsemeat

chevalier *noun, masculine*
un chevalier = a knight

chevet *noun, masculine*
une lampe de chevet = a bedside lamp

cheveu *noun, masculine*
(*plural*) **cheveux**
les cheveux = hair

cheville *noun, feminine*
une cheville = an ankle

✗ in informal situations

chèvre *noun, feminine*
une chèvre = a goat

chez *preposition*
• = at
  je serai chez moi = I'll be at home
  il est chez eux ce matin? = is he at their
  place this morning?
• = to
  aller chez le dentiste = to go to the
  dentist's

chic *adjective*
• (*elegant*) = chic, smart
• (*kind, obliging*)✘ = nice

chien *noun, masculine*
• un chien = a dog
  un chien d'aveugle = a guide dog
• il fait un temps de chien✘ = the weather is
  awful

chienne *noun, feminine*
une chienne = a female dog, a bitch

chiffon *noun, masculine*
un chiffon = a rag, a cloth
un chiffon (à poussière) = a duster, a dust
cloth

chiffre *noun, masculine*
un chiffre = a figure

chignon *noun, masculine*
un chignon = a bun, a chignon

chimie *noun, feminine*
la chimie = chemistry

chimique *adjective*
= chemical

chinois/chinoise
1 *adjective*
= Chinese
2 chinois *noun, masculine*
le chinois = Chinese

chiot *noun, masculine*
un chiot = a puppy

chips *noun, feminine* (**!** *never changes*)
une chips = a crisp, a (potato) chip

chirurgien *noun, masculine*
un chirurgien = a surgeon

choc *noun, masculine*
un choc = a shock

chocolat *noun, masculine*
le chocolat = chocolate

choisir *verb* 3
= to choose

choix *noun, masculine* (**!** *never changes*)
un choix = a choice
des produits de choix = choice products
de premier choix = top quality

chômage *noun, masculine*
le chômage = unemployment
être au chômage = to be unemployed

chômeur/chômeuse *noun,*
masculine/feminine
un chômeur/une chômeuse = an
unemployed man/woman

choquer *verb* 1
= to shock

chorale *noun, feminine*
une chorale = a choir

chose *noun, feminine*
une chose = a thing
quelque chose = something
= anything
pas grand chose = not much

chou *noun, masculine*
(*plural*) **choux**
• (*a vegetable*)
  un chou = a cabbage
• (*a cake*)
  un chou = a choux bun, a pastry shell
• (*a person*)
  mon chou = my darling
un chou de Bruxelles = a Brussels sprout
un chou à la crème = a cream puff

choucroute *noun, feminine*
la choucroute = sauerkraut

chouette
1 *adjective*✘
= nice, great
2 *noun, feminine*
une chouette = an owl

chou-fleur *noun, masculine*
(*plural*) **choux-fleurs**
un chou-fleur = a cauliflower

chronométrer *verb* 14
= to time

chrysanthème *noun, masculine*
un chrysanthème = a chrysanthemum

chuchoter *verb* 1
= to whisper

chut *exclamation*
chut! = shh!, hush!

chute *noun, feminine*
une chute = a fall

cicatrice *noun, feminine*
une cicatrice = a scar

ci-contre *adverb*
= opposite

ci-dessous *adverb*
= below

ci-dessus *adverb*
= above

cidre *noun, masculine*
le cidre = cider, hard cider

ciel *noun, masculine*
• le ciel = the sky
• le ciel = heaven

cieux *noun, masculine plural*
les cieux = heaven

cigale *noun, feminine*
une cigale = a cicada

ci-joint/ci-jointe *adjective*
= enclosed

cil *noun, masculine*
un cil = an eyelash

cime *noun, feminine*
la cime = the top

cimetière *noun, masculine*
un cimetière = a graveyard, a cemetery

ciné✱ *noun, masculine*
le ciné✱ = the pictures, the movies

cinéma *noun, masculine*
• un cinéma = a cinema, a movie theater
• le cinéma = the cinema, the movies

cinglé/cinglée✱ *adjective*
= mad, crazy

cinq *number*
= five

cinquantaine *noun, feminine*
une cinquantaine = about fifty

cinquante *number*
= fifty

cinquième
1 *number*
= fifth
2 *noun, feminine*
la cinquième = *the class for secondary school students aged 12 to 13*

cirage *noun, masculine*
le cirage = shoe polish

circuit *noun, masculine*
• (*visiting several places*)
un circuit = a tour
• (*in a race*)
un circuit = a circuit

circulation *noun, feminine*
la circulation = the traffic

circuler *verb* 1
• = to move
• = to run
ce train ne circule pas le dimanche = this train doesn't run on Sundays
• = to circulate

cirque *noun, masculine*
le cirque = the circus

ciseaux *noun, masculine plural*
des ciseaux = scissors

citadelle *noun, feminine*
une citadelle = a fortress

cité *noun, feminine*
• une cité = a city, a town
• une cité = a housing estate, a housing development
une cité universitaire = student halls of residence, dormitories

citoyen/citoyenne *noun, masculine/feminine*
un citoyen/une citoyenne = a citizen

citron *noun, masculine*
un citron = a lemon
un citron pressé = a freshly squeezed lemonade

citronnade *noun, feminine*
la citronnade = lemon squash, (still) lemonade

clair/claire
1 *adjective*
• = clear
• = light
2 clair *noun, masculine*
le clair de lune = moonlight

claqué/claquée✱ *adjective*
= exhausted

claquer *verb* 1
• = to slam
claquer la porte = to slam the door
• = to bang
une porte claquait = a door was banging
• faire claquer ses doigts = to snap one's fingers
il claque des dents = his teeth are chattering

claquettes *noun, feminine plural*
les claquettes = tap dancing

clarinette *noun, feminine*
une clarinette = a clarinet

classe *noun, feminine*
• (*a room*)
une (salle de) classe = a classroom
aller en classe = to go to school
• (*a category*)
une classe = a class
un billet de première classe = a first-class ticket
une classe de mer = a seaside trip (*with a school*)
une classe de neige = a skiing trip (*with a school*)
une classe verte = a field trip (*with a school*)

classeur *noun, masculine*
un classeur = a folder

clavier *noun, masculine*
un clavier = a keyboard

clé *noun, feminine*
• (*for a lock*)
une clé = a key
fermer à clé = to lock

✱ in informal situations

- (a tool)
  une clé = a spanner, a wrench
- **le mot(-)clé** = the key word

clef ▶ clé

client/cliente noun, masculine/feminine
un client/une cliente = a customer, a client

clignotant noun, masculine
un clignotant = an indicator, a turn signal

climat noun, masculine
le climat = the climate

climatisation noun, feminine
la climatisation = air-conditioning

clinique noun, feminine
une clinique = a (private) clinic

clochard/clocharde noun,
masculine/feminine
un clochard/une clocharde = a tramp, a
bum

cloche noun, feminine
- une cloche = a bell
- une cloche* = an idiot

cloche-pied: à cloche-pied adverb
sauter à cloche-pied = to hop

clocher noun, masculine
un clocher = a steeple
= a church tower, a bell tower

clochette noun, feminine
une clochette = a small bell

cloison noun, feminine
une cloison = a partition

cloque noun, feminine
une cloque = a blister

clos/close adjective
- = enclosed
- = closed

clôture noun, feminine
une clôture = a fence

clou
1 noun, masculine
un clou = a nail
2 clous noun, masculine plural
les clous = the pedestrian crossing, the
crosswalk

clouer verb 1
= to nail (down)

clouté adjective, masculine
un passage clouté = a pedestrian crossing,
a crosswalk

clown noun, masculine
un clown = a clown
faire le clown = to clown around

club noun, masculine
un club = a club

cobaye noun, masculine
un cobaye = a guinea pig

coca noun, masculine
un coca = a Coke , a Coca-Cola

cocher verb 1
= to tick, to check (off)

cochon noun, masculine
un cochon = a pig
un cochon d'Inde = a guinea pig

coco noun, masculine
une noix de coco = a coconut

cocotier noun, masculine
un cocotier = a coconut tree

code
1 noun, masculine
un code = a code
2 codes noun, masculine plural
les codes = dipped headlights, dimmed
headlights
se mettre en codes = to dip one's
headlights, to dim one's headlights
un code confidentiel (d'identification)
= a personal identification number
un code postal = a postcode, a zip code
le code de la route = the highway code,
the rules of the road

cœur
1 noun, masculine
- le cœur = the heart
avoir mal au cœur = to feel sick, to feel
nauseous
avoir bon cœur = to be kind-hearted
- (at cards)
cœur = hearts
2 par cœur = by heart

coffre noun, masculine
- un coffre (for storage) = a chest, a trunk
(for valuables) = a safe
- (in a car)
le coffre = the boot, the trunk

coffre-fort noun, masculine
(plural) **coffres-forts**
un coffre-fort = a safe

cognac noun, masculine
le cognac = brandy

coiffer: se coiffer verb 1 (! + être)
se coiffer = to do one's hair

coiffeur/coiffeuse noun,
masculine/feminine
un coiffeur/une coiffeuse = a hairdresser, a
hairstylist

coin noun, masculine
- (an angle)
un coin = a corner
au coin de la rue = on the corner of the
street
au coin du feu = by the fire
- (a place)
un coin = a spot
un petit coin tranquille = a nice quiet spot

- (the surrounding area)
  le coin = the neighbo(u)rhood
  le café du coin = the local café
  dans le coin = in the area

coincer verb 12
= to jam, to wedge

col noun, masculine
- (on a garment)
  un col = a collar
  un col roulé = a polo neck, a turtleneck
- (in the mountain)
  un col = a pass

colère noun, feminine
  la colère = anger

coléreux/coléreuse adjective
= quick-tempered, short-tempered

colique noun, feminine
  la colique = diarrh(o)ea

colis noun, masculine (**!** never changes)
  un colis = a parcel, a package

collant/collante
1 adjective
= sticky
2 collant noun, masculine
  un collant = (a pair of) tights, pantyhose

colle noun, feminine
  la colle = glue

collectionner verb 1
= to collect

collège noun, masculine
  **un collège (d'enseignement secondaire),
  un CES** = a secondary school, ≈ a junior
  high school (for students aged 11 to 14)
  **un collège d'enseignement technique, un
  CET** = a technical secondary school (for
  students aged 11 to 14)

collègue noun, masculine/feminine
  un collègue/une collègue = a colleague

coller verb 1
- = to stick, to glue
- (in an examination)✶
  se faire coller✶ à un examen = to fail an
  examination

collier noun, masculine
  un collier (on a person) = a necklace
  (on an animal) = a collar

colline noun, feminine
  une colline = a hill

colonie noun, feminine
  une colonie = a colony
  une colonie de vacances = a holiday
  camp, a summer camp (for children)

colonne noun, feminine
  une colonne = a column

---

colorier verb 2
= to colo(u)r

coloris noun, masculine (**!** never changes)
  un coloris = a colo(u)r

combien
1 adverb
  combien (de) = how much, how many
2 noun (**!** never changes)
  le combien sommes-nous? = what's the
  date today?
  du combien chaussez-vous? = what size
  shoe do you take?

combinaison noun, feminine
  une combinaison (a fashion garment) = a
  jumpsuit
  (protective clothing) = overalls, coveralls
  une combinaison de plongée = a
  wetsuit
  une combinaison de ski = a ski-suit

combiné noun, masculine
  le combiné = the handset, the receiver

comédie noun, feminine
- (a play)
  une comédie = a comedy
- (pretence)
  de la comédie = an act

comédien/comédienne noun,
masculine/feminine
  un comédien/une comédienne = an
  actor/an actress

comestible adjective
= edible

comique adjective
- = comic
- = funny

commandant noun, masculine
  le commandant = the major
  le commandant de bord = the captain

commande noun, feminine
- (for goods)
  une commande = an order
- (a device)
  une commande = a control
  être aux commandes = to be at the
  controls

commander verb 1
- (in a restaurant) = to order
- (in a group) = to be in command

comme
1 adverb
  comme c'est beau! = it's so beautiful!
2 conjunction
- = like
  il conduit comme un fou = he drives like a
  maniac
- = as
  comme toujours = as always
  gros comme mon poing = as big as my fist

• = as, since
  comme il pleuvait, je ne suis pas sorti = as
  it was raining I didn't go out
• = as a
  travailler comme serveuse = to work as a
  waitress
  comme ci comme ça✱ = so so
3 comme il faut = properly, correctly

commencer verb 12
= to start, to begin

comment adverb
• = how
  comment allez-vous? = how are you?
• = what
  comment s'appelle-t-il? = what's his
  name?
  comment trouves-tu leur jardin? = what do
  you think of their garden?
  c'est comment? = what's it like?
• (when asking someone to repeat)
  comment? = sorry?, pardon?, excuse me?

commentaire noun, masculine
• (on a text, on a match)
  un commentaire = a commentary
• (a remark)
  un commentaire = a comment

commerçant/commerçante noun,
masculine/feminine
  un commerçant/une commerçante = a
  shopkeeper

commerce noun, masculine
• (a place)
  un commerce = a shop, a store
• (an activity)
  le commerce = trade

commettre verb 60
  commettre un meurtre = to commit a
  murder
  commettre une erreur = to make a mistake

commis/commise ▶ **commettre** 60

commissariat noun, masculine
  le commissariat (de police) = the police
  station

commode
1 adjective
  = convenient, handy
2 noun, feminine
  une commode = a chest of drawers, a
  dresser

commun/commune adjective
  = common

communauté noun, feminine
  une communauté = a community
la Communauté Européenne, la CE
  = the European Community, the EC

communication noun, feminine
  une communication (téléphonique) = a
  (phone) call

communiquer verb 1
= to communicate

compagne noun, feminine
  une compagne = a (female) companion

compagnie noun, feminine
• (a firm, a group of actors)
  une compagnie = a company
• (the presence of other people)
  la compagnie = company
une compagnie aérienne = an airline

compagnon noun, masculine
  un compagnon = a (male) companion

comparaison noun, feminine
  une comparaison = a comparison

comparer verb 1
= to compare

compartiment noun, masculine
  un compartiment = a compartment

compétition noun, feminine
• **la compétition** = competition, rivalry
• **une compétition (sportive)** = a sporting
  event

complet/complète adjective
• = complete
• = full

compliment noun, masculine
  un compliment = a compliment
  tous mes compliments! = congratulations!

compliqué/compliquée adjective
= complicated

comporter verb 1
1 (! + avoir)
  = to consist of
2 se comporter (! + être)
  se comporter = to behave

composer verb 1
1 (! + avoir)
• = to dial
  composer un numéro = to dial a number
• = to put together
  composer un menu = to put a menu
  together
• = to make up
  les joueurs qui composent l'équipe = the
  players who make up the team
  composé de = made up of
• = to compose
  qui a composé la musique du film? = who
  composed the score for the film?
2 se composer de (! + être)
  se composer de = to be made up of

compositeur/compositrice noun,
masculine/feminine
  un compositeur/une compositrice = a
  composer

composter verb 1
= to punch

compote noun, feminine
la compote de pommes = stewed apple

comprendre verb 52
1 (**!** + avoir)
• = to understand
• = to include
2 se comprendre (**!** + être)
• se comprendre = to understand each other
• se comprendre = to be understandable

comprimé noun, masculine
un comprimé = a tablet, a pill

compris/comprise
1 ▶ comprendre 52
2 adjective
= included
3 y compris = including

compte noun, masculine
• (in a bank, a post office)
un compte = an account
• se rendre compte = to realize
• tenir compte de = to take into account
• travailler à son compte = to be self-employed

compter verb 1
• = to count
• = to intend
• compter sur = to count on

comptoir noun, masculine
le comptoir (in a shop) = the counter
(in a café) = the bar, the counter

con✷ noun, masculine
un con✷ = a stupid jerk

concerner verb 1
• = to concern
• = to affect

concessionnaire noun, masculine/feminine
un concessionnaire/une concessionnaire = a distributor, an agent

concierge noun, masculine/feminine
un concierge/une concierge = a caretaker, a superintendent

concombre noun, masculine
un concombre = a cucumber

concours noun, masculine (**!** never changes)
• (a game, an event)
un concours = a competition, a contest
• (an examination)
un concours = a competitive examination

concurrence noun, feminine
la concurrence = competition

concurrent/concurrente noun, masculine/feminine
un concurrent/une concurrente = a competitor

condamner verb 1
• (to declare someone guilty) = to convict
• (to punish) = to sentence
être condamné à une amende = to be fined

condition noun, feminine
une condition = a condition
à condition de, à condition que = provided (that), on condition that

condoléances noun, feminine plural
des condoléances = condolences

conducteur/conductrice noun, masculine/feminine
un conducteur/une conductrice = a driver

conduire verb 62
1 (**!** + avoir)
• = to drive
• = to lead
le sentier conduit au village = the path leads to the village
2 se conduire (**!** + être)
se conduire = to behave

conduite noun, feminine
ta conduite = your behavio(u)r
= your conduct

confection noun, feminine
la confection = ready-to-wear clothes

confiance noun, feminine
• (in someone's honesty)
la confiance = trust
faire confiance = to trust
• (in someone's ability)
la confiance = confidence
la confiance en soi = (self-)confidence

confier verb 2
1 (**!** + avoir)
= to entrust
2 se confier (**!** + être)
se confier à quelqu'un = to confide in someone

confiserie noun, feminine
une confiserie = a sweet shop, a candy store

confisquer verb 1
= to confiscate

confiture noun, feminine
la confiture = jam, jelly
la confiture d'orange = marmalade

confort noun, masculine
le confort = comfort

confortable adjective
= comfortable

congé noun, masculine
un congé = a holiday, a vacation
être en congé = to be on holiday, to be on vacation
un congé de maladie = sick leave

congélateur *noun, masculine*
un congélateur = a freezer

conjuguer *verb* $\boxed{1}$
= to conjugate

connaissance *noun, feminine*
• la connaissance = knowledge
• une connaissance = an acquaintance
j'ai fait la connaissance de leur fils = I met
their son
• perdre connaissance = to lose
consciousness
sans connaissance = unconscious

connaître *verb* $\boxed{63}$
1 (! + *avoir*)
= to know
2 se connaître (! + *être*)
• se connaître = to know each other
• se connaître = to know oneself
3 s'y connaître en (! + *être*)
s'y connaître en = to know about
tu t'y connais en voitures? = do you know
about cars?

connu/connue
1 ▶ connaître $\boxed{63}$
2 *adjective*
= well-known

consciencieux/consciencieuse
adjective
= conscientious

conseil *noun, masculine*
• (*an opinion*)
un conseil = a piece of advice
des conseils = advice
• (*a group of people*)
un conseil = a council
un conseil de classe = a staff meeting
(*for those teaching a given class*)
le conseil municipal = the town council

conseiller¹ *verb* $\boxed{1}$
• = to advise
• = to recommend

conseiller²/conseillère *noun,*
masculine/feminine
• (*an expert*)
un conseiller/une conseillère = an adviser,
a consultant
• (*an elected member*)
un conseiller/une conseillère = a
councillor
un conseiller d'éducation = a
supervisor
un conseiller municipal = a town
councillor
un conseiller d'orientation = a careers
adviser

conservatoire *noun, masculine*
un conservatoire = an academy, a
conservatory

conserve *noun, feminine*
les conserves (*in tins*) = canned food

(*in jars*) = preserves
une boîte de conserve = a can (of food)

conserver *verb* $\boxed{1}$
• = to keep
• = to preserve

consigne *noun, feminine*
• la consigne = the left luggage office
• la consigne = orders, instructions
la consigne automatique = the left
luggage lockers, the baggage lockers

consoler *verb* $\boxed{1}$
= to comfort
= to console

consommateur/consommatrice
noun, masculine/feminine
un consommateur/une consommatrice (*of*
goods, services) = a consumer
(*in a café*) = a customer

consommation *noun, feminine*
• (*in a café*)
une consommation = a drink
• (*of gas, food*)
la consommation = consumption

consommer *verb* $\boxed{1}$
= to consume

constater *verb* $\boxed{1}$
= to notice

construire *verb* $\boxed{62}$
= to build

construit ▶ construire $\boxed{62}$

consulat *noun, masculine*
un consulat = a consulate

consulter *verb* $\boxed{1}$
= to consult

contacter *verb* $\boxed{1}$
= to contact, to get in touch with

contagieux/contagieuse *adjective*
= contagious

conte *noun, masculine*
un conte = a story, a tale
un conte de fées = a fairy tale

contenir *verb* $\boxed{36}$
• = to contain
• = to hold

content/contente *adjective*
= happy, pleased, glad
il est content de te voir = he's happy to see
you

contenu/contenue
1 ▶ contenir $\boxed{36}$
2 contenu *noun, masculine*
le contenu = the contents

continuellement *adverb*
= continuously

continuer *verb* $\boxed{1}$
= to continue

contourner verb 1
= to go (a)round
= to bypass

contraire adjective
= opposite

contrarier verb 2
= to upset

contravention noun, feminine
une contravention = a fine

contre
1 preposition
= against
2 noun, masculine
le pour et le contre = the pros and cons
3 par contre = on the other hand

contrebande noun, feminine
la contrebande = smuggling
des produits de contrebande = smuggled
goods

contrebasse noun, feminine
une contrebasse = a double bass, an
upright bass

contribuer verb 1
contribuer à = to contribute to

contrôle noun, masculine
• (a way of checking)
un contrôle = a check
= an inspection
(in class) = a test
un contrôle de qualité = a quality check
un contrôle des billets = a ticket
inspection
• (over a vehicle)
le contrôle = control
le contrôle (continu) des
connaissances = (continuous)
assessment

contrôler verb 1
= to check
= to inspect

contrôleur/contrôleuse noun,
masculine/feminine
un contrôleur/une contrôleuse = an
inspector

convaincre verb 57
= to convince
= to persuade

convaincu/convaincue ▶
convaincre 57

convenable adjective
• = suitable
• = proper

convenir verb 36
convenir à = to suit
= to be suitable for

---

convenu/convenue ▶ **convenir** 36

convoi noun, masculine
un convoi = a convoy

convoquer verb 1
= to summon
= to send for

copain noun, masculine
mon copain = my friend
= my boyfriend

copie noun, feminine
• (of a letter, a painting)
une copie = a copy
• (a piece of schoolwork)
une copie = a paper

copier verb 2
= to copy

copine noun, feminine
ma copine = my friend
= my girlfriend

coq noun, masculine
un coq = a cock, a rooster

coquillage noun, masculine
• un coquillage = a shell
• les coquillages = shellfish

coquille noun, feminine
une coquille = a shell
une coquille Saint-Jacques = a scallop

cor noun, masculine
un cor = a horn

corbeau noun, masculine
(plural) **corbeaux**
un corbeau = a crow

corbeille noun, feminine
une corbeille = a basket
une corbeille à papier = a wastepaper
basket

corde noun, feminine
• une corde = a rope
• (on a violin, a bow, a racket)
une corde = a string
une corde à sauter = a skipping rope, a
jumprope

corne noun, feminine
une corne = a horn

cornet noun, masculine
• (for ice cream)
un cornet = a cornet
• (for fries, sweets)
un cornet = a bag

Cornouailles noun, feminine
la Cornouailles = Cornwall

corps noun, masculine (! never changes)
le corps = the body

correct/correcte adjective
• = correct

• = proper
• = polite

correspondance *noun, feminine*
• (*when travelling*)
  une correspondance = a connection
• (*when writing letters*)
  la correspondance = correspondence

correspondant/correspondante
noun, masculine/feminine
  un correspondant/une correspondante = a penfriend, a penpal

correspondre *verb* [6]
• = to write
• **correspondre à** = to correspond to, to match

corrigé *noun, masculine*
  le corrigé = the correct version

corriger *verb* [13]
• = to correct
• = to mark, to grade

Corse *noun, feminine*
  la Corse = Corsica

cortège *noun, masculine*
  un cortège = a procession

corvée *noun, feminine*
  une corvée = a chore

costaud* *adjective*
  = strong, sturdy

costume *noun, masculine*
• (*a man's outfit*)
  un costume = a suit
• (*worn by actors*)
  un costume = a costume

côte
1 *noun, feminine*
• (*by the sea*)
  la côte = the coast
• (*an incline*)
  une côte = a hill
  = a slope
• (*in the body*)
  une côte = a rib
2 côte à côte = side by side

côté
1 *noun, masculine*
  un côté = a side
2 à côté = nearby
  j'habite à côté = I live nearby
  la maison d'à côté = the house next door
3 à côté de = next to

Côte-d'Ivoire *noun, feminine*
  la Côte-d'Ivoire = the Ivory Coast

côtelette *noun, feminine*
  une côtelette = a chop, a cutlet

cotisation *noun, feminine*
  une cotisation = a subscription

coton *noun, masculine*
• (*a natural fibre*)
  le coton = cotton
• (*fluffy wadding*)
  le coton (hydrophile) = cotton wool, (absorbent) cotton

cou *noun, masculine*
  le cou = the neck

couche *noun, feminine*
• (*a thickness*)
  une couche = a layer
• (*on a baby*)
  une couche = a nappy, a diaper

coucher
1 *verb* [1] (**!** + *avoir*)
• = to put to bed
• = to sleep
2 se coucher *verb* [1] (**!** + *être*)
• **se coucher** = to go to bed
  ils sont couchés = they're in bed
• **se coucher** = to lie (down)
• **se coucher** = to set, to go down
  le soleil se couche vers 8 heures = the sun sets at about 8 o'clock
3 *noun, masculine*
  le coucher du soleil = sunset

couchette *noun, feminine*
  une couchette = a couchette, a berth

coucou *exclamation*
  coucou! = peekaboo!

coude *noun, masculine*
  un coude = an elbow

coudre *verb* [66]
  = to sew

couette *noun, feminine*
• (*on a bed*)
  une couette = a duvet, a comforter
• (*a hairstyle*)
  des couettes = bunches, pigtails

couler *verb* [1]
  = to flow

couleur *noun, feminine*
  une couleur = a colo(u)r

couloir *noun, masculine*
  un couloir = a corridor, a hallway
  = a passage

coup *noun, masculine*
  ! *For translations of phrases such as* **coup de foudre, coup de fil, coup de soleil** *etc look up the entries at* **foudre, fil, soleil** *etc.*

• (*a hard hit*)
  un coup = a blow
  donner un coup de [pied | poing | couteau …]
  à quelqu'un = [to kick | to punch | to stab …]
  someone
  à coups de marteau = with a hammer

• (*a loud noise*)
  un coup = a knock
  frapper trois coups à la porte = to knock
  three times on the door
• (*the firing of a gun*)
  un coup de [**feu** | **fusil** | **revolver** ...] = a shot
  tué d'un coup de fusil = shot dead
• (*an attempt, an occasion*)
  du premier coup = first time
  à chaque coup = every time
  ce coup-ci = this time
  sur le coup = at the time
  = instantly
  tout d'un coup, tout à coup = suddenly, all
  of a sudden

coupable
1 *adjective*
  = guilty
2 *noun, masculine|feminine*
  un coupable|une coupable = a culprit

coupe *noun, feminine*
• (*a trophy*)
  une coupe = a cup
• (*at the hairdresser's*)
  une coupe = a haircut
• (*a container*)
  une coupe = a bowl

couper *verb* $\boxed{1}$
1 (**!** + *avoir*)
  = to cut off
2 se couper (**!** + *être*)
  se couper = to cut oneself
  se couper le doigt = to cut one's finger

cour *noun, feminine*
• (*an enclosed area*)
  une cour = a yard
  = a courtyard
  = a farmyard
• (*a play area at school*)
  une cour (de récréation) = a playground, a
  schoolyard
• (*for royalty, trials*)
  la cour = the court

courageux|courageuse *adjective*
  = courageous, brave

couramment *adverb*
• = fluently
• = widely

courant
1 ▶ courir $\boxed{26}$
2 *noun, masculine*
  un courant = a current
3 au courant
  être au courant de ce qui se passe = to
  know what's going on
  je vous tiendrai au courant = I'll keep you
  informed
un courant d'air = a draught, a draft

coureur|coureuse *noun, masculine|*
feminine
  un coureur|une coureuse = a runner
un coureur cycliste = a racing cyclist
courir *verb* $\boxed{26}$
• = to run
• = to race
• = to rush
couronne *noun, feminine*
• (*on a king's head*)
  une couronne = a crown
• (*on a grave*)
  une couronne = a wreath
courrier *noun, masculine*
  le courrier = the post, the mail
  = letters
  par retour du courrier = by return (post),
  by return mail
le courrier du cœur = the problem page,
  the advice column
cours *noun, masculine* (**!** *never changes*)
• (*a teaching session*)
  un cours = a lesson, a class
  faire cours = to teach
• (*a series of lessons*)
  un cours = a course
• (*on the foreign exchange*)
  le cours du dollar = the (exchange) rate for
  the dollar
• **au cours de la journée** = during the course
  of the day
  en cours de route = along the way
un cours d'eau = a waterway
un cours du soir = an evening class
course
1 *noun, feminine*
• (*a competition*)
  une course = a race
• (*some business to attend to*)
  une course = an errand
2 courses *noun, feminine plural*
  des courses = shopping
coursier|coursière *noun, masculine|*
feminine
  un coursier|une coursière = a messenger, a
  dispatch rider
court|courte *adjective*
  = short
  de courte durée = short-lived
couru|courue ▶ courir $\boxed{26}$
cousin|cousine *noun,*
masculine|feminine
  un cousin|une cousine = a cousin
coussin *noun, masculine*
  un coussin = a cushion
cousu|cousue ▶ coudre $\boxed{66}$
coût *noun, masculine*
  le coût = the cost
couteau *noun, masculine*
(*plural*) **couteaux**
  un couteau = a knife

coûter verb [1]
= to cost

coûteux/coûteuse adjective
= costly

coutume noun, feminine
une coutume = a custom

couture noun, feminine
• (an activity)
la couture = sewing
• (in a garment)
une couture = a seam

couvercle noun, masculine
un couvercle = a lid

couvert[1] noun, masculine
un couvert = a place setting
mettre le couvert = to set the table

couvert[2]/**couverte** ▶ couvrir [32]

couverture noun, feminine
• (on a bed)
une couverture = a blanket
• (on a book)
une couverture = a cover

couvrir verb [32]
= to cover

crabe noun, masculine
un crabe = a crab

cracher verb [1]
• = to spit
• = to spit out

craie noun, feminine
la craie = chalk

craindre verb [54]
• = to fear, to be afraid
ne craignez rien = don't be afraid
• = to be sensitive to

craint/crainte[1] ▶ craindre [54]

crainte[1] noun, feminine
la crainte = fear

cramoisi/cramoisie adjective
= crimson

crampe noun, feminine
une crampe = a cramp

crâne noun, masculine
le crâne = the skull

crapaud noun, masculine
un crapaud = a toad

craquer verb [1]
• = to break
• = to creak
• (emotionally)✗ = to crack up

cravate noun, feminine
une cravate = a tie

crayon noun, masculine
un crayon = a pencil

un crayon à bille = a ballpoint pen
un crayon de couleur = a colo(u)red
pencil
un crayon feutre = a felt-tip pen

crèche noun, feminine
• (for babies)
une crèche = a day-nursery, a nursery
• (a Christmas scene)
une crèche = a crib, a crèche

crédit noun, masculine
le crédit = credit
acheter à crédit = to buy on credit
'la maison ne fait pas de crédit' = 'no
credit'

créer verb [11]
• = to create
• = to set up, to found

crème
1 noun, feminine
la crème = cream
2 noun, masculine
un crème = an espresso with milk

crémerie noun, feminine
une crémerie = a cheese shop, a cheese
store

crêpe noun, feminine
une crêpe = a pancake

crêperie noun, feminine
une crêperie = a pancake restaurant

cresson noun, masculine
le cresson = watercress

crête noun, feminine
• (of a hill, a wave)
la crête = the crest
• (of a roof)
la crête = the ridge
• (on a bird)
la crête = the comb

creuser verb [1]
• = to dig
• l'exercice, ça creuse✗! = exercise gives you
an appetite!

creux/creuse adjective
= hollow

crevaison noun, feminine
une crevaison = a puncture

crevant/crevante✗ adjective
• = exhausting
• = hilarious

crevé/crevée✗ adjective
• = exhausted
• = flat, punctured

crever verb [16]
• = to have a puncture
• = to burst
= to puncture
• = to die
un chat crevé = a dead cat

- (*to exhaust*)✖ = to wear out
  la course m'a crevé✖ = the race wore me
  out

crevette *noun, feminine*
  une crevette grise = a shrimp
  une crevette rose = a prawn

cri *noun, masculine*
- (*by a person*)
  un cri = a cry, a shout
  = a scream
  pousser un cri = to scream
- (*by an animal*)
  un cri = a cry
  = a call

crier *verb* [2]
  = to shout
  = to scream

crime *noun, masculine*
  un crime (*a criminal action*) = a crime
  (*an unlawful killing*) = a murder

criminel/criminelle
1 *adjective*
  = criminal
2 *noun, masculine/feminine*
  un criminel/une criminelle = a criminal
  = a murderer

crise *noun, feminine*
- (*a difficult situation*)
  une crise = a crisis
- (*an outburst*)
  une crise = a fit
- (*a sudden illness*)
  une crise = an attack
une crise cardiaque = a heart attack

critiquer *verb* [1]
  = to criticize

crochet *noun, masculine*
- (*a piece of bent metal*)
  un crochet = a hook
- (*on a journey*)
  un crochet = a detour

croire *verb* [53]
1 (**!** + *avoir*)
- = to believe
  je te crois = I believe you
- = to think
  je ne crois pas = I don't think so
2 se croire (**!** + *être*)
  il se croit malin = he thinks he's smart

croisement *noun, masculine*
  un croisement = a junction, an
  intersection

croiser *verb* [1]
1 (**!** + *avoir*)

- = to cross
  les jambes croisées = legs crossed
  les bras croisés = arms folded
- = to pass
  croiser une voiture = to pass a car (coming
  the other way)
2 se croiser (**!** + *être*)
- **se croiser** = to cross
- **se croiser** = to pass each other

croisière *noun, feminine*
  une croisière = a cruise

croissance *noun, feminine*
  la croissance = growth

croissant *noun, masculine*
- (*a pastry*)
  un croissant = a croissant
- (*a shape*)
  un croissant = a crescent

croix *noun, feminine* (**!** *never changes*)
  une croix = a cross

croque-monsieur *noun, masculine*
(**!** *never changes*)
  un croque-monsieur = a grilled ham and
  cheese sandwich

crotte *noun, feminine*
  de la crotte de chien = dog mess, dog poop

croûte *noun, feminine*
- (*on bread*)
  la croûte = the crust
- (*on cheese*)
  la croûte = the rind
- (*on the skin*)
  une croûte = a scab

croûton *noun, masculine*
  un croûton = a crouton

CRS *noun, masculine* (**!** *never changes*)
  un CRS *a member of the French riot police*

cru/crue
1 ▶ **croire** [53]
2 *adjective*
  = raw

crudités *noun, feminine plural*
  des crudités = raw vegetables

cruel/cruelle *adjective*
  = cruel

cueillir *verb* [27]
  = to pick

cuiller, cuillère *noun, feminine*
  une cuiller, une cuillère = a spoon
**une cuillère à café, une petite
  cuillère** = a teaspoon
une cuillère à soupe = a soup spoon

---

cuillerée *noun, feminine*
une cuillerée = a spoonful

cuir *noun, masculine*
le cuir = leather

cuire *verb* 62
= to cook
= to bake

cuisine *noun, feminine*
• (*a room*)
une cuisine = a kitchen
• (*the preparation of food*)
la cuisine = cooking

cuisinier/cuisinière¹ *noun,*
masculine/feminine
un cuisinier/une cuisinière = a cook

cuisinière² *noun, feminine*
une cuisinière = a cooker, a stove, a range

cuisse *noun, feminine*
une cuisse = a thigh
des cuisses de grenouille = frog's legs

cult/culte ▶ cuire 62

cul* *noun, masculine*
le cul* = the arse, the ass

culot* *noun, masculine*
le culot* = cheek, nerve

culotte *noun, feminine*
une culotte = pants, panties, knickers

cultiver *verb* 1
• = to cultivate
• = to grow

cure *noun, feminine*
une cure = a course of treatment (*in a*
spa)

curé *noun, masculine*
un curé = a (parish) priest

curieux/curieuse
1 *adjective*
• = inquisitive
• = odd, strange
2 curieux *noun, masculine plural*
les curieux = onlookers

curiosité *noun, feminine*
la curiosité = curiosity

cuvette *noun, feminine*
une cuvette = a bowl

CV *noun, masculine*
• (*personal details*)
un CV = a CV, a résumé
• (*a unit of power*)
un CV = one HP

cyclable *adjective*
une piste cyclable = a cycle lane

cycliste *noun, masculine/feminine*
un cycliste/une cycliste = a cyclist

cygne *noun, masculine*
un cygne = a swan

cyprès *noun, masculine* (**!** *never changes*)
un cyprès = a cypress

Dd

d' ▶ de

dactylo *noun, masculine/feminine*
un dactylo/une dactylo = a typist

daim *noun, masculine*
• (*an animal*)
un daim = a deer
• (*a type of leather*)
le daim = suede

dame
1 *noun, feminine*
une dame = a lady
2 dames *noun, feminine plural*
les dames = draughts, checkers

Danemark *noun, masculine*
le Danemark = Denmark

danger *noun, masculine*
le danger = danger
'danger de noyade' = 'unsafe for
swimming'

dangereux/dangereuse *adjective*
= dangerous

danois/danoise
1 *adjective*
= Danish
2 danois *noun, masculine*
le danois = Danish

dans *preposition*
• = in
vivre dans une ville = to live in a town
être dans les affaires = to be in business
aller dans la bonne direction = to go in the
right direction
dans une semaine = in a week's time
• = into
entrer dans une maison = to go into a
house
sortir dans le jardin = to go out into the
garden
• = on
être dans un train = to be on a train
monter dans un avion = to get on a plane
dans l'ensemble = on the whole
• = through
fouiller dans un sac = to rummage
through a bag
• = out of
prendre un verre dans un placard = to take
a glass out of a cupboard

danse noun, feminine
- **la danse** = dancing
- **une danse** = a dance
la danse classique = ballet dancing

danser verb ⓵
= to dance

danseur/danseuse noun,
masculine/feminine
un danseur/une danseuse = a dancer

date noun, feminine
la date = the date
'date limite de consommation' = 'use-by
  date'

dater verb ⓵
= to date
dater de = to date from

datte noun, feminine
une datte = a date

daube noun, feminine
la daube beef stew cooked in wine

dauphin noun, masculine
un dauphin = a dolphin

davantage adverb
- = more
- = longer

de (**d'** before vowel or mute h; de + le
becomes du; de + les becomes des)

> ! You will find translations for phrases with
> de such as d'abord, pomme de terre,
> chemin de fer etc under the words abord,
> pomme, chemin, etc.

1 preposition
- = of
un verre d'eau = a glass of water
la voiture de mon père = my father's car
- = from
le paquet vient de Paris = the package
  comes from Paris
du matin au soir = from morning till night
- = by
un tableau de Picasso = a painting by
  Picasso
il était suivi de son chien = he was
  followed by his dog
- = about
elle parle des voisins = she's talking about
  the neighbo(u)rs
de quoi s'agit-il? = what's it about?
- = than
plus de trois heures après mon arrivée
  = more than three hours after I'd
  arrived
moins de dix pour cent = less than ten per
  cent
2 determiner
  = some
  = any
voulez-vous de la bière? = would you like
  some beer?
il n'a pas de monnaie = he hasn't got any
  change
as-tu des courses à faire? = have you got
  any shopping to do?

dé noun, masculine
- (in games)
un dé = a dice
- (in sewing)
un dé = a thimble

déballer verb ⓵
- = to unpack
- = to display

débarquer verb ⓵
- = to disembark, to get off
- = to unload

débarras noun, masculine (! never
changes)
- (a room)
un débarras = a junk room
- **bon débarras!** = good riddance!

débarrasser verb ⓵
1 (! + avoir)
- = to clear (out)
débarrasser (la table) = to clear the table
débarrasser une pièce = to clear out a
  room
- = to rid
je vous débarrasse de votre manteau?
  = shall I take your coat?
2 se débarrasser de (! + être)
se débarrasser de = to get rid of

débattre: se débattre verb ⓺⓵ (! + être)
se débattre = to struggle

déborder verb ⓵
= to overflow

débouché noun, masculine
un débouché = an opening

déboucher verb ⓵
- = to open
déboucher une bouteille = to open a bottle
- = to unblock, to unclog
déboucher un évier = to unblock a sink
- = to lead to
le sentier débouche sur une route = the
  path leads to a road
- = to come out
la voiture a débouché d'une petite rue
  = the car came out of a side street

debout adverb
- = standing
se mettre debout = to stand up
rester debout = to stand
- = upright
mets la caisse debout = stand the crate in
  an upright position
- = up
être debout à six heures du matin = to be
  up at six in the morning
debout! = get up!

déboutonner verb ⓵
= to unbutton

débraillé/débraillée adjective
= dishevelled

débrancher verb [1]
= to unplug

débrayer verb [21]
= to put the clutch in

débris noun, masculine (**!** never changes)
• (of glass, china)
un débris = a fragment
• (of car, plane)
un débris = a piece of wreckage

débrouiller verb [1]
1 (**!** + avoir)
• = to unscramble
• = to disentangle
2 se débrouiller (**!** + être)
• se débrouiller = to manage
se débrouiller pour avoir des billets = to
manage to get tickets
• se débrouiller = to get by
se débrouiller en anglais = to get by in
English

début noun, masculine
le début = the beginning
au début = at the beginning
début avril = at the beginning of April, in
early April

débutant/débutante noun,
masculine/feminine
un débutant/une débutante = a beginner

décacheter verb [20]
= to unseal

décaféiné/décaféinée adjective
= decaffeinated

décalage noun, masculine
le décalage horaire = the time difference
= jet lag

décapsuleur noun, masculine
un décapsuleur = a bottle-opener

décéder verb [14]
= to die
être décédé = to be dead

décembre noun, masculine
décembre = December

déception noun, feminine
une déception = a disappointment

décès noun, masculine (**!** never changes)
un décès = a death

décevant/décevante adjective
= disappointing

décevoir verb [5]
= to disappoint

déchaîner: se déchaîner verb [1]
(**!** + être)
se déchaîner = to go wild

décharger verb [13]
= to unload

déchets noun, masculine plural
les déchets = waste

déchiffrer verb [1]
= to decipher
= to decode

déchirer verb [1]
1 (**!** + avoir)
= to tear (up)
2 se déchirer (**!** + être)
se déchirer = to tear

décidément adverb
= really

décider verb [1]
1 (**!** + avoir)
• = to decide
elle a décidé de les inviter = she's decided
to invite them
c'est décidé = it's settled
• = to persuade
j'ai décidé mes amis à venir = I persuaded
my friends to come
2 se décider (**!** + être)
se décider = to make up one's mind

déclarer verb [1]
1 (**!** + avoir)
• = to declare
rien à déclarer = nothing to declare
• = to report
déclarer un vol = to report a theft
2 se déclarer (**!** + être)
se déclarer = to break out
un incendie s'est déclaré = a fire broke
out

déclencher verb [1]
= to set off
= to trigger

décollage noun, masculine
le décollage = take-off

décoller verb [1]
1 (**!** + avoir)
• = to peel off
décoller une étiquette = to peel off a label
• = to take off
l'avion va décoller = the plane is about to
take off
2 se décoller (**!** + être)
se décoller = to come off

décolleté/décolletée adjective
= low-cut

décolorer verb [1]
• = to bleach
• = to cause to fade

décombres noun, masculine plural
les décombres = the rubble

décongeler verb [17]
= to defrost

décontracté/décontractée
adjective
• = relaxed, laid-back
• = casual

décorer *verb* [1]
= to decorate

découper *verb* [1]
= to cut out
= to cut up
= to carve

décourager *verb* [13]
= to discourage

découvert/découverte[1]
▶ **découvrir** [32]

découverte[2] *noun, feminine*
une découverte = a discovery

découvrir *verb* [32]
• = to discover
• = to uncover

décrire *verb* [42]
= to describe

décrocher *verb* [1]
• (*to remove from its hook*) = to take down
  décrocher le téléphone = to pick up the
    receiver
  = to take the phone off the hook
• (*in a competition, an exam*)✖ = to pass
  = to get
  décrocher✖ son permis = to pass one's
    driving test

déçu/déçue ▶ **décevoir** [5]

dedans *adverb*
= inside

défaire *verb* [10]
1 (**!** + *avoir*)
  = to undo
  défaire sa valise = to unpack one's
    suitcase
2 se défaire (**!** + *être*)
  se défaire = to come undone

défaut *noun, masculine*
un défaut = a fault

défavorisé/défavorisée *adjective*
• = underprivileged
• = disadvantaged

défectueux/défectueuse *adjective*
= faulty

défendre *verb* [6]
1 (**!** + *avoir*)
• = to forbid
  je vous défends de sortir = I forbid you to
    go out
  c'est défendu = it's forbidden, it's not
    allowed
• = to defend
2 se défendre (**!** + *être*)
  se défendre = to defend oneself

défendu/défendue ▶ **défendre** [6]

défense *noun, feminine*
• (*an order*)
  'défense de fumer' = 'no smoking'
• (*against an attack, an accusation*)
  la défense = the defence, the defense
  prendre la défense d'un ami = to stand up
    for a friend
  sans défense = helpless, defenceless,
    defenseless
• (*of an elephant, a walrus*)
  une défense = a tusk

défilé *noun, masculine*
• (*a military display*)
  un défilé = a parade
• (*people filing past*)
  un défilé = a procession
  = a march
• (*a constant flow of people*)
  un défilé de visiteurs = a stream of visitors

défiler *verb* [1]
= to march past

défoncer *verb* [12]
  défoncer une porte = to break down a
    door

déformé/déformée *adjective*
  = distorted
  = misshapen
  'chaussée déformée' = 'uneven road
    surface'

dégager *verb* [13]
1 (**!** + *avoir*)
• = to clear
  ciel dégagé = clear sky
• = to free
• = to give off
  dégager de la chaleur = to give off heat
2 se dégager (**!** + *être*)
• se dégager = to clear
  le temps s'est dégagé = the weather has
    cleared
• se dégager (de) = to free oneself (from)

dégâts *noun, masculine plural*
  les dégâts = the damage

dégonfler *verb* [1]
1 (**!** + *avoir*)
• = to deflate, to let down
2 se dégonfler (**!** + *être*)
• se dégonfler = to deflate, to go down
• (*when faced with a challenge*)✖
  se dégonfler✖ = to lose one's nerve, to
    chicken out

dégoûtant/dégoûtante *adjective*
• = filthy
• = disgusting

degré *noun, masculine*
• (*a unit of measurement*)
  un degré = one degree

- (a level)
l'enseignement du second degré
= secondary education, high school
education (for students aged 11 to 18)

dégringoler* verb ⟦1⟧
= to take a tumble
= to tumble down

déguiser verb ⟦1⟧
1 (**!** + avoir)
= to disguise
2 se déguiser (**!** + être)
- **se déguiser** = to disguise oneself
- **se déguiser** = to dress up

dégustation noun, feminine
une dégustation de vin = a wine tasting

déguster verb ⟦1⟧
- = to taste, to sample
- = to enjoy

dehors adverb
= outside

déjà adverb
= already

déjeuner
1 noun, masculine
- (in the middle of the day)
le déjeuner = lunch
- (in the morning)
le (petit) déjeuner = breakfast
2 verb
- = to have lunch
- = to have breakfast

delà: **au delà de** preposition
au delà de = beyond

délabré/délabrée adjective
= dilapidated

délai noun, masculine
- (time allowed)
dans un délai de 24 heures = within 24
hours
sans délai = immediately
mardi, dernier délai = Tuesday at the latest
- (additional time)
un délai = an extension

délasser verb ⟦1⟧
= to refresh
= to relax

délicieux/délicieuse adjective
= delicious

délit noun, masculine
un délit = an offence, an offense

délivrer verb ⟦1⟧
- = to free
délivrer un prisonnier = to free a prisoner
- = to issue
délivrer un passeport = to issue a passport

deltaplane noun, masculine
- (the equipment)
un deltaplane = a hang-glider

- (the sport)
le deltaplane = hang-gliding

demain adverb
= tomorrow
à demain = see you tomorrow

demande noun, feminine
- **une demande** = an application
= a request
faire une demande de prêt = to apply for a
loan
'demandes d'emploi' = 'jobs wanted'
- (in business)
l'offre et la demande = supply and
demand

demander verb ⟦1⟧
1 (**!** + avoir)
- = to ask (for)
elle a demandé de l'argent à ses parents
= she's asked her parents for money
- = to require
ça demande trop d'efforts = it requires too
much effort
2 se demander (**!** + être)
se demander = to wonder

démarrer verb ⟦1⟧
- (if it's a vehicle) = to pull away
- (if it's a driver) = to drive off

démarreur noun, masculine
le démarreur = the starter

déménagement noun, masculine
- (going to live elsewhere)
un déménagement = a move
- (transporting furniture)
un déménagement = a removal

déménager verb ⟦13⟧
= to move (house)

demeurer verb ⟦1⟧
- = to live
- = to remain

demi/demie[1]
1 adjective
- **demi-** (**!** comes before the noun, never
changes)
= half
= semi
une demi-heure = half an hour
un demi-tarif = a half-price ticket
une demi-finale = a semi-final
- **et demi/et demie** (**!** comes after the noun,
never plural)
= and a half
deux et demi = two and a half
à cinq heures et demie = at half past five,
at five-thirty
2 demi noun, masculine
- (a drink)
un demi = a glass of beer
- (in rugby)
un demi de mêlée = a scrum half
3 à demi = half
à demi éveillé = half awake

D

demie² *noun, feminine*
 la demie = half past
 il est déjà la demie = it's already half past

demi-frère *noun, masculine*
 (*plural*) **demi-frères**
 un demi-frère = a stepbrother, a half-brother

demi-pension *noun, feminine*
 la demi-pension = half board,
  accommodation with one meal only

demi-sœur *noun, feminine*
 (*plural*) **demi-sœurs**
 une demi-sœur = a stepsister, a half-sister

démissionner *verb* [1]
 = to resign

demi-tour *noun, masculine*
 (*plural*) **demi-tours**
 un demi-tour = a half-turn
 faire demi-tour = to turn back

démodé/démodée *adjective*
 = old-fashioned

demoiselle *noun, feminine*
 une demoiselle = a young lady
 une demoiselle d'honneur = a
  bridesmaid

démolir *verb* [3]
 = to demolish

démonter *verb* [1]
 • = to take apart, to dismantle
 • = to remove, to take off

démontrer *verb* [1]
 = to demonstrate

denrée *noun, feminine*
 une denrée = a product

dent *noun, feminine*
 une dent = a tooth
 avoir mal aux dents = to have (a)
  toothache

dentelle *noun, feminine*
 la dentelle = lace

dentifrice *noun, masculine*
 le dentifrice = toothpaste

dentiste *noun, masculine/feminine*
 un dentiste/une dentiste = a dentist

dépannage *noun, masculine*
 'service de dépannage' = 'breakdown
  service', 'emergency service'

dépanner *verb* [1]
 • = to fix, to repair
 • (*if someone's in difficulty*)✱ = to help out

dépanneur/dépanneuse¹ *noun,
 masculine/feminine*
 un dépanneur/une dépanneuse = an
  engineer

dépanneuse² *noun, feminine*
 une dépanneuse = a breakdown truck, a
  tow truck

dépareillé/dépareillée *adjective*
 = odd

départ *noun, masculine*
 • (*the act of leaving*)
 le départ = the departure
 • (*the beginning*)
 le départ = the start
 au départ = at first

département *noun, masculine*
 un département = a department (*an
  administrative district*)

dépasser *verb* [1]
 • = to overtake, to pass
 • = to exceed
 elle le dépasse de 5 centimètres = she's 5
  centimetres taller than him
 • = to be ahead of, to outstrip
 • = to stick out
 • = to pass, to go past
 nous avons dépassé l'école = we've gone
  past the school

dépêcher: se dépêcher *verb* [1]
 (**!** + *être*)
 se dépêcher = to hurry up
 dépêchez-vous! = hurry up!

dépendre *verb* [6]
 dépendre de = to depend on
 ça dépendra du temps = it'll depend on
  the weather
 ça dépend! = it depends!

dépense *noun, feminine*
 la dépense du ménage = the household
  expenditure
 faire une dépense = to spend some money

dépenser *verb* [1]
 = to spend (money)

déplacer *verb* [12]
 1 (**!** + *avoir*)
 = to move
 2 se déplacer (**!** + *être*)
 • se déplacer = to move
 • se déplacer = to travel

dépliant *noun, masculine*
 un dépliant = a leaflet

déplier *verb* [2]
 = to unfold

déposer *verb* [1]
 1 (**!** + *avoir*)
 • déposer des ordures = to dump rubbish,
  to dump garbage
 • déposer une gerbe = to lay a wreath
 • déposer de l'argent sur un compte = to
  deposit money in an account
 • déposer une valise à la consigne
  automatique = to leave a suitcase in a left-luggage locker

✱ in informal situations

- **déposer un passager** = to drop a passenger off
- **déposer une plainte** = to lodge a complaint, to make a complaint
- **une marque déposée** = a registered trademark

2 se déposer (**!** + *être*)
  se déposer = to settle
  = to collect

dépositaire *noun, masculine/feminine*
  un dépositaire/une dépositaire = an agent, a representative
  un dépositaire de journaux = a newsagent, a newsdealer

dépôt *noun, masculine*
- (*for goods*)
  un dépôt = a warehouse
- (*in a shop*)
  faire dépôt de gaz = to sell bottled gas
- (*in a bottle*)
  un dépôt = a deposit, a residue

déprime✶ *noun, feminine*
  la déprime✶ = depression

déprimer *verb* 1
- (*to cause sadness*) = to depress
- (*to feel sadness*)✶ = to be depressed

déprogrammer *verb* 1
  = to cancel

depuis
1 *preposition*
- = since
  depuis lundi = since Monday
  depuis quand est-il à Paris? = how long has he been in Paris?
- = for
  depuis un an = for a year
  je le connais depuis longtemps = I've known him for a long time
  il pleuvait depuis trois jours = it had been raining for three days
  depuis combien de temps le sais-tu? = how long have you known?
2 *adverb*
  = since
  je n'ai pas de nouvelles depuis = since then I haven't heard any news
3 depuis que = since, ever since

député *noun, masculine*
  un député = a Member of the National Assembly
  un député européen = a member of the European Parliament, a Euro-MP

dérailler *verb* 1
  = to be derailed

déranger *verb* 13
1 (**!** + *avoir*)
- = to bother, to disturb
  excusez-moi de vous déranger = I'm sorry to bother you
  ça vous dérange si je mets la radio? = do you mind if I turn the radio on?
- = to disturb, to upset, to mess up

2 se déranger (**!** + *être*)
- **se déranger** = to get up
  = to move
- **se déranger** = to put oneself out

déraper *verb* 1
  = to skid

dériveur *noun, masculine*
  un dériveur = a dinghy

dernier/dernière
1 *adjective*
  = last
  = latest
  au dernier étage = on the top floor
2 *noun, masculine/feminine*
- **le dernier/la dernière** = the last one
  c'est le dernier qui me reste = it's my last one
  arriver le dernier = to arrive last
  être le dernier de la classe = to be bottom of the class, to be last in the class
- **ce dernier/cette dernière** = the latter
3 en dernier = lastly
  last

dernièrement *adverb*
  = recently, lately

derrière
1 *preposition*
  = behind
2 *adverb*
  = behind
  = at the back, in the back
3 *noun, masculine*
- (*the rear*)
  le derrière = the back
  la porte de derrière = the back door
- (*part of the body*)✶
  le derrière✶ = the behind, the backside

des ▶ de

dès
1 *preposition*
  = from
  dès ce soir = from tonight
  dès mon arrivée = as soon as I arrive(d)
2 dès que = as soon as

désagréable *adjective*
  = unpleasant

désastre *noun, masculine*
  un désastre = a disaster

descendre *verb* 6
1 (**!** + *être*)
- = to go down, to come down
  il est descendu au village = he's gone down to the village
  tu es descendu à pied? = did you walk down?
  nous sommes descendus en courant = we ran down
- = to go downstairs, to come downstairs
- = to get off
  je descendrai à la prochaine gare = I'll get off at the next station

- (*other uses*)
  descendre dans un hôtel = to stop (off) at
  a hotel
2 (**!** + *avoir*)
- = to go down
  descendre la rue = to go down the street
  il a descendu l'escalier en courant = he
  ran down the stairs
- = to take down, to bring down
  je dois descendre mes bagages = I must
  take my luggage down
  peux-tu me descendre mes lunettes?
  = can you bring my glasses down to me?

descente *noun, feminine*
- (*a steep surface*)
  une descente = a slope
- (*in a plane*)
  la descente = the descent
- (*in a skiing competition*)
  la descente = the downhill event

désert/déserte
1 *adjective*
  = deserted
2 désert *noun, masculine*
  le désert = the desert

désespéré/désespérée *adjective*
  (*describing a person*) = in despair
  (*describing a situation*) = hopeless

désespoir *noun, masculine*
  le désespoir = despair
  être au désespoir = to be in despair

déshabiller *verb* ⒈
1 (**!** + *avoir*)
  = to undress
2 se déshabiller (**!** + *être*)
  se déshabiller = to get undressed

désigner *verb* ⒈
- = to point out
- = to choose, to designate

désirer *verb* ⒈
  = to want
  que désirez-vous? = what would you like?

désobéir *verb* ⒊
- = to be disobedient
- = to disobey
  désobéir à son père = to disobey one's
  father

désobéissant/désobéissante
adjective
  = disobedient

désolé/désolée *adjective*
  je suis désolé = I'm sorry

désordre *noun, masculine*
- (*in a room*)
  le désordre = untidiness, messiness
  quel désordre! = what a mess!
  être en désordre = to be untidy
  mettre du désordre dans une pièce = to
  make a room untidy, to make a room
  messy

- (*unrest*)
  le désordre = disorder

désormais *adverb*
  = from now on
  = from then on

dessert *noun, masculine*
  un dessert = a dessert

dessin *noun, masculine*
- (*a picture*)
  un dessin = a drawing
- (*a subject*)
  le dessin = art, drawing
  = design
un dessin animé = a cartoon (film)

dessinateur/dessinatrice *noun,*
masculine/feminine
  un dessinateur/une dessinatrice = a
  draughtsman, a draftsman
  = an illustrator
  = a designer

dessiner *verb* ⒈
  = to draw

dessous
1 *adverb*
  = underneath
2 *noun, masculine* (**!** *never changes*)
  le dessous = the underside
  = the bottom
  le drap de dessous = the bottom sheet
  les voisins du dessous = the people who
  live (on the floor) below
3 en dessous = underneath
  la taille en dessous = the next size down,
  the smaller size
4 en dessous de = below
  en dessous de la moyenne = below
  average

dessus
1 *adverb*
  = on top
  écris ton nom dessus = write your name
  on it
2 *noun, masculine* (**!** *never changes*)
  le dessus = the top
  le drap de dessus = the top sheet
  les voisins du dessus = the people who
  live (on the floor) above

destinataire *noun, masculine/feminine*
  le destinataire/la destinataire = the
  addressee

destination
1 *noun, feminine*
  une destination = a destination
2 à destination de = bound for
  vol 802 à destination de Nice = flight 802
  to Nice

détacher *verb* ⒈
1 (**!** + *avoir*)
- = to undo
  = to untie
  = to unfasten
- = to tear off, to detach

2 se détacher (**!** + *être*)
* se détacher = to come undone
* se détacher = to come off

détail *noun, masculine*
* (*a minor point*)
  un détail = a detail
  des détails supplémentaires = extra information
* (*selling direct to the public*)
  le détail = retail

détendre *verb* 6
1 (**!** + *avoir*)
* = to relax
* = to be relaxing
2 se détendre (**!** + *être*)
  se détendre = to relax

détenu/détenue *noun, masculine/feminine*
  un détenu/une détenue = a prisoner

détester *verb* 1
  = to detest, to hate

détraquer *verb* 1
  = to damage

détresse *noun, feminine*
  la détresse = distress

détroit *noun, masculine*
  un détroit = a strait

détruire *verb* 62
  = to destroy

dette *noun, feminine*
  une dette = a debt

deuil *noun, masculine*
* un deuil = a bereavement
* le deuil = mourning

deux *number*
  = two
  ils iront tous les deux = both of them will go

deuxième *number*
  = second

deux-roues *noun, masculine* (**!** *never changes*)
  un deux-roues = a two-wheeler

devant
1 *preposition*
* = in front of
  le livre est devant toi = the book is in front of you
* = ahead of
  Paul était loin devant nous = Paul was (a long) way ahead of us
* = outside
  attends-moi devant la bibliothèque = wait for me outside the library
* = past
  passer devant un magasin = to walk past a shop

2 *adverb*
  = in front
  = at the front
3 *noun, masculine*
  le devant = the front
  la fenêtre de devant = the front window

devenir *verb* 36 (**!** + *être*)
  = to become

déviation *noun, feminine*
  une déviation = a diversion, a detour

deviner *verb* 1
  = to guess

devinette *noun, feminine*
  une devinette = a riddle

devis *noun, masculine* (**!** *never changes*)
  un devis = an estimate

devise *noun, feminine*
* (*money*)
  une devise = a currency
* (*a short saying*)
  une devise = a motto

devoir
1 *noun, masculine*
* (*work set by a teacher*)
  un devoir = a piece of homework, an assignment
  faire ses devoirs = to do one's homework
* (*responsibility*)
  le devoir = duty
  faire son devoir = to do one's duty
2 *verb* 44
* = to owe
  devoir de l'argent à un ami = to owe a friend money
  je leur dois des excuses = I owe them an apology
* (*to be obliged to*) = to have to
  je dois aller travailler = I have to go to work, I must go to work
  tu aurais dû téléphoner = you should have phoned
  vous devriez les remercier = you ought to thank them
* (*meaning that something is likely*) = must
  il doit être arrivé = he must have arrived
  elle devait avoir 11 ans = she must have been 11
  ils ont dû oublier = they must have forgotten
* (*meaning that something is certain or expected*)
  cela devait arriver = it was bound to happen
  le train doit partir vers neuf heures = the train is due to leave at about nine o'clock

devrai ▶ **devoir 2** 44

diabétique *adjective*
  = diabetic

D

diabolo menthe *noun, masculine*
(*plural*) **diabolos menthe**
  un diabolo menthe = a mint cordial and
    lemonade, a mint cordial and soda

diamètre *noun, masculine*
  le diamètre = the diameter

diapositive *noun, feminine*
  une diapositive = a slide

diarrhée *noun, feminine*
  la diarrhée = diarrh(o)ea

dictée *noun, feminine*
  une dictée = a dictation

dicter *verb* 1
  = to dictate

dictionnaire *noun, masculine*
  un dictionnaire = a dictionary

diète *noun, feminine*
  être à la diète = to be on a restricted diet

diététicien/diététicienne *noun,*
masculine/feminine
  un diététicien/une diététicienne = a
    dietician

dieu *noun, masculine*
(*plural*) **dieux**
  un dieu = a god
  mon Dieu! = my God!

différence *noun, feminine*
  une différence = a difference
  à la différence des animaux = unlike
    animals

difficile *adjective*
• = difficult
• = fussy

difficulté *noun, feminine*
  une difficulté = a difficulty

difforme *adjective*
  = deformed

diffuser *verb* 1
  (*on radio*) = to broadcast

dimanche *noun, masculine*
  dimanche = Sunday

dinde *noun, feminine*
  une dinde = a turkey

dîner
1 *noun, masculine*
  le dîner = dinner
  à l'heure du dîner = at dinner time
2 *verb* 1
  = to have dinner

dingue* *adjective*
  = crazy

---

* in informal situations

diplôme *noun, masculine*
  un diplôme = a diploma
  = a qualification

dire *verb* 40
1 (**!** + *avoir*)
• = to say
  on dit que l'usine va fermer = they say the
    factory is going to close down
• = to tell
  dire des mensonges = to tell lies
  dites-leur de venir = tell them to come
• = to think
  qu'est-ce que tu en dis? = what do you
    think?
  on ne dirait pas qu'elle a 20 ans = you
    wouldn't think she was 20, she doesn't
    look 20
  on dirait qu'il va pleuvoir = it looks like
    rain
• vouloir dire = to mean
  qu'est-ce que ça veut dire? = what does it
    mean?
• ça ne me dit rien = it doesn't appeal to me,
    I don't feel like it
  = it doesn't mean anything to me, it
    doesn't ring a bell
2 se dire (**!** + *être*)
• se dire = to tell oneself
• se dire = to claim to be
  il se dit médecin = he claims to be a doctor
• ça ne se dit pas = you can't say that

direct/directe
1 *adjective*
  = direct
2 direct *noun, masculine*
• (*a train*)
  un direct = an express (train)
• (*on radio, TV*)
  le direct = live broadcasting
  en direct de Rome = live from Rome

directement *adverb*
• = straight
• = directly

directeur/directrice *noun,*
masculine/feminine
• (*in a school*)
  le directeur/la directrice = the headteacher,
    the principal
• (*in an organization, a business*)
  un directeur/une directrice = a director
  = a manager

direction *noun, feminine*
• (*when moving*)
  une direction = a direction
  dans quelle direction? = which way?
  en direction de Calais = toward(s) Calais
• (*in an organization*)
  la direction = (the) management
• (*on a car*)
  la direction = the steering

directrice ▶ directeur

diriger verb [13]
1 (! + avoir)
• diriger une affaire = to manage a business, to run a business
• diriger une opération = to direct an operation
• diriger un orchestre = to conduct an orchestra
2 se diriger (! + être)
• se diriger vers Paris = to make for Paris, to head toward(s) Paris
• se diriger dans le noir = to find one's way in the dark

disco noun, masculine
le disco = disco music

discothèque noun, feminine
• (a library)
une discothèque = a record library
• (a nightclub)
une discothèque = a disco(theque)

discours noun, masculine (! never changes)
un discours = a speech

discuter verb [1]
• = to chat, to talk
• = to argue
• discuter de = to discuss

disparaître verb [63]
• = to disappear
• = to die

disparition noun, feminine
la disparition = the disappearance

disparu/disparue ▶ **disparaître** [63]

disponible adjective
= available

disposer verb [1]
1 (! + avoir)
• = to arrange, to position
• disposer de = to have (at one's disposal)
2 se disposer (! + être)
se disposer à partir = to prepare to leave, to be about to leave

dispute noun, feminine
une dispute = an argument, a quarrel

disputer: se disputer verb [1] (! + être)
se disputer = to argue, to quarrel

disque noun, masculine
• (in music)
un disque = a record, an LP
un disque compact = a compact disc
• (in sport)
le disque = the discus

disquette noun, feminine
une disquette = a diskette, a floppy disk

dissimuler verb [1]
= to conceal, to hide

distance noun, feminine
la distance = distance
à une distance de 25 kilomètres = 25 kilometres away
la ville est à quelle distance? = how far is the town?
commande à distance = remote control

distingué/distinguée adjective
= distinguished

distraction noun, feminine
• (leisure activity)
une distraction = entertainment
• (lack of concentration)
la distraction = absent-mindedness

distraire verb [58]
1 (! + avoir)
• = to entertain, to amuse
• = to distract
2 se distraire (! + être)
se distraire = to amuse oneself

distrait/distraite
1 ▶ **distraire** [58]
2 adjective
= absent-minded

distribuer verb [1]
= to give out, to distribute
distribuer le courrier = to deliver the mail
distribuer les cartes = to deal

distributeur noun, masculine
un distributeur automatique de billets = a cash dispenser

divan noun, masculine
un divan = a sofa

divers/diverse adjective
• = various
• = miscellaneous

diviser verb [1]
= to divide

divorcé/divorcée noun, masculine/feminine
un divorcé/une divorcée = a divorcee

divorcer verb [12]
= to get divorced

dix number
= ten

dix-huit number
= eighteen

dix-huitième number
= eighteenth

dixième number
= tenth

dix-neuf number
= nineteen

dix-neuvième number
= nineteenth

dix-sept *number*
= seventeen

dix-septième *number*
= seventeenth

dizaine *noun, feminine*
une dizaine = about ten
= ten

docteur *noun, masculine*
un docteur = a doctor

documentaire *noun, masculine*
un documentaire = a documentary

documentation *noun, feminine*
de la documentation = brochures,
literature

dodo✱ *noun, masculine*
au dodo✱! = beddy-byes!, bed time!

doigt *noun, masculine*
• (*on the hand*)
un doigt = a finger
montrer du doigt = to point at
un doigt de pied = a toe
• (*small amount*)
un doigt de vin = a drop of wine

dois ▶ devoir 2 44

doive ▶ devoir 2 44

domestique
1 *adjective*
= domestic
2 *noun, masculine|feminine*
un domestique/une domestique = a
servant

domicile
1 *noun, masculine*
un domicile = a (place of) residence
2 à domicile
travailler à domicile = to work from home
livrer à domicile = to deliver, to do home
deliveries

domicilié/domiciliée *adjective*
être domicilié à Londres = to live in
London

dominer *verb* 1
1 (**!** + *avoir*)
• = to dominate
• = to tower over
le monument dominait le village = the
monument towered over the village
• = to control
dominer sa peur = to overcome one's fear
• = to be predominant
2 se dominer (**!** + *être*)
se dominer = to control oneself

domino *noun, masculine*
un domino = a domino

dommage *noun, masculine*
• (*in expressions of regret*)
(quel) dommage! = what a pity!, what a
shame!
• (*harm*)
un dommage = damage
des dommages et intérêts = damages

DOM-TOM *noun, masculine plural*
(*abbreviation of* **départements et
territoires d'outre-mer**)
French overseas departments and territories

don *noun, masculine*
• (*talent*)
un don = a gift
• (*something given*)
un don = a donation

donc *conjunction*
= so, therefore
il est malade, donc il restera au lit = he's
unwell, so he'll stay in bed
taisez-vous donc! = be quiet, will you?
sers-toi donc! = do help yourself!

donjon *noun, masculine*
un donjon = a keep

donner *verb* 1
• = to give
donner un jouet à un enfant = to give a
child a toy
donner des coups à un animal = to hit an
animal
• donner une veste à nettoyer = to take a
jacket to be dry-cleaned
• donner sur = to overlook
la chambre donne sur la baie = the
bedroom overlooks the bay

dont *pronoun*
• = whose
voici le chauffeur dont la voiture a pris feu
= this is the driver whose car caught
fire
• = of which
= of whom
c'est le dessin dont il est si fier = it's the
drawing of which he's so proud
ils ont cinq fils, dont deux sont étudiants
= they've got five sons, two of whom are
students
j'ai lu le livre dont tu m'avais parlé = I read
the book that you'd told me about
il a pris les outils dont il avait besoin = he's
taken the tools that he needed
le pays dont elle vient = the country she
comes from
la façon dont il parle = the way he talks
c'est tout ce dont je me souviens = that's
all I can remember

doré/dorée *adjective*
= gilt
= golden
= gold

dormir *verb* 30
= to sleep

✱ in informal situations

dortoir *noun, masculine*
un dortoir = a dormitory

dos *noun, masculine* (**!** *never changes*)
le dos = the back
avoir mal au dos = to have (a) backache
je l'ai vu de dos = I saw him from behind

dose *noun, feminine*
une dose = a dose

dossier *noun, masculine*
• (*part of a seat*)
le dossier = the back(rest)
• (*documents*)
un dossier = a file

douane *noun, feminine*
la douane = the customs

douanier/douanière *noun,*
masculine/feminine
un douanier/une douanière = a customs
officer

double
1 *adjective*
= double
2 *noun, masculine*
• (*a quantity*)
payer le double = to pay twice as much
le double de la taille normale = twice the
normal size
• (*a duplicate*)
un double = a copy
le double des clés = a spare set of keys

doubler *verb* ①
• (*to increase twofold*) = to double
• (*in a car*) = to overtake, to pass
• (*for a film*) = to dub
• (*in dressmaking*) = to line

douce ▶ doux

doucement *adverb*
• = gently
• = softly
• = slowly

douche *noun, feminine*
une douche = a shower

doucher: se doucher *verb* ① (**!** + *être*)
se doucher = to take a shower

doué/douée *adjective*
= gifted, talented

douleur *noun, feminine*
• une douleur = a pain
• la douleur = grief

douloureux/douloureuse *adjective*
= painful

doute
1 *noun, masculine*
le doute = doubt
ça ne fait aucun doute = there's no doubt
about it
2 sans doute = probably

Douvres *noun*
= Dover

doux/douce
1 *adjective*
• = soft
une voix douce = a soft voice
• = mild
un temps doux = mild weather
• = gentle
une pente douce = a gentle slope
2 doux *adverb*
doux = mild
il fait doux aujourd'hui = it's mild today

douzaine *noun, feminine*
une douzaine = a dozen
= about twelve

douze *number*
= twelve

douzième *number*
= twelfth

dragée *noun, feminine*
une dragée = a sugared almond

draguer* *verb* ①
= to chat up, to come on to

drap *noun, masculine*
un drap = a sheet

drapeau *noun, masculine*
(*plural*) **drapeaux**
un drapeau = a flag

dresser *verb* ①
1 (**!** + *avoir*)
• = to train
dresser un animal = to train an animal
• = to put up
dresser une tente = to put up a tent
• = to raise
dresser la tête = to raise one's head
dresser l'oreille = to prick up one's ears
2 se dresser (**!** + *être*)
se dresser = to stand (up)

drogue *noun, feminine*
la drogue = drugs

drogué/droguée *noun,*
masculine/feminine
un drogué/une droguée = a drug addict

droguer: se droguer *verb* ① (**!** + *être*)
se droguer = to take drugs

droguerie *noun, feminine*
une droguerie = a hardware shop, a
hardware store

droguiste *noun, masculine/feminine*
un droguiste/une droguiste = a hardware
dealer, an ironmonger

droit/droite¹
1 *adjective*
- = straight
  = upright
- = right
  du côté droit = on the right-hand side
2 droit *adverb*
  = straight
  continuez tout droit = carry straight on
3 droit *noun, masculine*
- (*something one is entitled to*)
  un droit = a right
  avoir le droit d'aller où l'on veut = to have
    the right to go wherever one wants
  = to be allowed to go wherever one wants
- (*money that has to be paid*)
  un droit = a fee
  = a tax
- (*a course of study*)
  le droit = law
les droits de douane = customs duties

droite² *noun, feminine*
  la droite = the right

droitier/droitière *noun,*
masculine/feminine
  un droitier/une droitière = a right-handed
    person

drôle *adjective*
  = funny

du ▶ de

dû/due ▶ devoir 2 44

duc *noun, masculine*
  un duc = a duke

dur/dure
1 *adjective*
  = hard, tough
  = harsh
2 dur *adverb*
  travailler dur = to work hard

durée *noun, feminine*
- (*of a reign, of a course*)
  la durée = the length
  = the duration
  un séjour de courte durée = a short stay
- (*of a cassette*)
  la durée = the playing time
- (*of a battery*)
  la durée = the life
  pile longue durée = long-life battery

durer *verb* 1
  = to last

duvet *noun, masculine*
- (*for sleeping in*)
  un duvet = a sleeping bag
- (*feathers*)
  le duvet = down

dynamique *adjective*
  = dynamic

Ee

eau *noun, feminine*
(*plural*) **eaux**
  l'eau = water
  l'eau gazeuse = fizzy water, sparkling
    water
  l'eau minérale = mineral water
  l'eau potable = drinking water

eau-de-vie *noun, feminine*
(*plural*) **eaux-de-vie**
  l'eau-de-vie = brandy

éboueur *noun, masculine*
  un éboueur = a dustman, a garbage
    collector

éboulement *noun, masculine*
  un éboulement (de rochers) = a rockfall

écarlate *adjective*
  = scarlet

écarter *verb* 1
1 (**!** + *avoir*)
- (*to open*) = to spread
  = to part
- (*to remove*) = to push aside
  = to move away
2 s'écarter (**!** + *être*)
  s'écarter = to move out of the way
  = to move away

échafaudage *noun, masculine*
  un échafaudage = scaffolding

échalote *noun, feminine*
  une échalote = a shallot

échange
1 *noun, masculine*
  un échange = an exchange
  faire un échange = to swap
2 en échange (de) = in exchange (for), in
  return (for)

échanger *verb* 13
  = to exchange

échangeur *noun, masculine*
  un échangeur = an interchange, a clover
    junction

échapper: s'échapper *verb* 1
(**!** + *être*)
  s'échapper = to escape

écharpe *noun, feminine*
  une écharpe = a scarf

échasse *noun, feminine*
  une échasse = a stilt

échauffer: s'échauffer *verb* 1
(**!** + *être*)
  s'échauffer = to warm up

échec
1 *noun, masculine*
  un échec = a failure
2 **échecs** *noun, masculine plural*
  les échecs = chess

échelle *noun, feminine*
* (*a piece of equipment*)
  une échelle = a ladder
  faire la courte échelle à Roger = to give
    Roger a leg-up
* (*on a map*)
  l'échelle = the scale

échiquier *noun, masculine*
  un échiquier = a chessboard

échouer *verb* ①
1 (! + *avoir*)
  = to fail
  échouer à un examen = to fail an
    examination
2 **s'échouer** (! + *être*)
  s'échouer = to run aground

éclair *noun, masculine*
  (*in the sky*)
  un éclair = a flash of lightning
* (*a cake*)
  un éclair = an eclair

éclairage *noun, masculine*
  l'éclairage = the lighting

éclaircie *noun, feminine*
  une éclaircie = a sunny spell

éclairer *verb* ①
1 (! + *avoir*)
* = to light
* = to give light
2 **s'éclairer** (! + *être*)
  s'éclairer (*if it's a face, a screen*) = to light
    up

éclater *verb* ①
  (*if it's a tyre, a pipe*) = to burst
  (*if it's a bomb*) = to explode
  (*if it's a storm*) = to break
  (*if it's war*) = to break out
  éclater de rire = to burst out laughing

école *noun, feminine*
  une école = a school
une école libre = an independent school
une école maternelle = a nursery school
  (*for children aged 2 to 6*)
une école primaire = a primary school
  (*for children aged 6 to 11*)
une école secondaire = a secondary
  school (*for students aged 11 to 18*)
une école publique = a state school
  (*in the US*) = a public school

écolier/écolière *noun,*
masculine/feminine
  un écolier/une écolière = a schoolboy/a
    schoolgirl

écologie *noun, feminine*
  l'écologie = ecology

écologiste *noun, masculine/feminine*
* (*a scientist*)
  un écologiste/une écologiste = an
    ecologist
* (*a person who is against pollution*)
  un écologiste/une écologiste = an
    environmentalist

économe *adjective*
  = thrifty

économie *noun, feminine*
  une économie = a saving
  faire des économies = to save up, to save
    money

écorce *noun, feminine*
  l'écorce (*on a tree*) = the bark
  (*on an orange*) = the peel

écossais/écossaise *adjective*
* = Scottish
* une veste écossaise = a tartan jacket, a
  plaid jacket

Écosse *noun, feminine*
  l'Écosse = Scotland

écouter *verb* ①
  = to listen to
  écouter un disque = to listen to a record

écran *noun, masculine*
* (*on a television set*)
  un écran = a screen
* (*protection from the sun*)
  une crème écran total = a sun block

écraser *verb* ①
1 (! + *avoir*)
* = to crush
* = to run over
  se faire écraser = to get run over
2 **s'écraser** (! + *être*)
  s'écraser = to crash

écrevisse *noun, feminine*
  une écrevisse = a crayfish, a crawfish

écrire *verb* ㊷
1 (! + *avoir*)
  = to write
2 **s'écrire** (! + *être*)
* s'écrire = to write (to each other)
* s'écrire = to be spelled

écriture *noun, feminine*
* (*the activity*)
  l'écriture = writing
* (*the way one writes*)
  ton écriture = your handwriting

écrivain *noun, masculine*
  un écrivain = a writer

écrou *noun, masculine*
  un écrou = a nut

écrouler: s'écrouler *verb* ① (! + *être*)
  s'écrouler = to collapse

écurie *noun, feminine*
  une écurie = a stable

écusson noun, masculine
   un écusson (on a garment) = a (cloth)
      badge

éducation noun, feminine
• (teaching)
   l'éducation = education
• (politeness)
   l'éducation = manners
   l'éducation physique = PE, physical
      education

effacer verb [12]
   = to erase
   = to delete
   effacer le tableau = to wipe the board, to
      erase the board

effet
1 noun, masculine
• (result)
   un effet = an effect
   n'avoir aucun effet = to have no effect
   faire de l'effet = to be effective
• (impact)
   un effet = an impression
   faire bon effet = to make a good
      impression
   ça m'a fait un drôle d'effet = it made me
      feel strange
2 en effet = indeed

efficace adjective
• = effective
• = efficient

effondrer: s'effondrer verb [1] (! + être)
   s'effondrer = to collapse

effort noun, masculine
   un effort = an effort

effrayant/effrayante adjective
   = frightening

effrayer verb [21]
   = to frighten, to scare

effronté/effrontée adjective
   = cheeky

égal/égale adjective
(plural) **égaux/égales**
   = equal
   ça m'est égal = I don't mind either way
      = I don't care

égaler verb [1]
   = to be equal to

égalité noun, feminine
   l'égalité = equality

égarer verb [1]
1 (! + avoir)
   = to lose
2 s'égarer (! + être)
   s'égarer = to get lost

église noun, feminine
   une église = a church

égoïste adjective
   = selfish

eh bien exclamation
   eh bien! = well!

électricien/électricienne noun,
masculine/feminine
   un électricien/une électricienne = an
      electrician

électroménager
1 adjective, masculine
   un appareil électroménager = an electrical
      household appliance
2 noun, masculine
   l'électroménager = electrical household
      appliances

électrophone noun, masculine
   un électrophone = a record player

élégant/élégante adjective
   = elegant

éléphant noun, masculine
   un éléphant = an elephant

élève noun, masculine/feminine
   un élève/une élève = a pupil, a student

élevé/élevée adjective
• = high
• bien élevé = well brought-up, well-
      mannered
   mal élevé = ill-mannered

élever verb [16]
1 (! + avoir)
• (if it's children) = to bring up, to raise
• (if it's animals) = to breed
• (if it's a wall, a statue) = to erect, to raise
2 s'élever (! + être)
• s'élever = to rise
• s'élever à 500 euros = to add up to 500
   euros

éliminer verb [1]
• = to eliminate
• = to knock out, to eliminate
   être éliminé en quart de finale = to be
      knocked out in the quarter final
• = to rule out

elle pronoun, feminine
(plural) **elles**
• = she
   = it
   elles n'ont rien dit = they said nothing
   elle est cassée = it's broken
• = her
   à cause d'elle = because of her
   la valise bleue est à elle = the blue
      suitcase is hers
   c'est à elle de jouer = it's her turn to play
   les livres sont pour elles = the books are
      for them

elle-même *pronoun, feminine*
(*plural*) **elles-mêmes**
= herself
= itself
elles-mêmes = themselves

elles ▶ **elle**

éloigné/éloignée *adjective*
= distant
éloigné de = far from

éloigner: s'éloigner *verb* ⬚1 (**!** + *être*)
s'éloigner = to move away

Élysée *noun, masculine*
(le palais de) l'Élysée = the Élysée palace
(*the official residence of the French
President*)

email *noun, masculine*
un email = an email

emballage *noun, masculine*
l'emballage = the packaging
= the wrapping

embarquer *verb* ⬚1
1 (**!** + *avoir*)
• = to load
• = to board
2 s'embarquer (**!** + *être*)
s'embarquer = to board

embêtant/embêtante *adjective*
= annoying

embêter *verb* ⬚1
1 (**!** + *avoir*)
• = to annoy
= to pester
• ça m'embête d'y aller = I don't really want
to go
2 s'embêter (**!** + *être*)
s'embêter = to be bored

emblée: d'emblée *adverb*
d'emblée = right away, straightaway

embouteillage *noun, masculine*
un embouteillage = a traffic jam

embrasser *verb* ⬚1
1 (**!** + *avoir*)
= to kiss
2 s'embrasser (**!** + *être*)
s'embrasser = to kiss (each other)

embrayage *noun, masculine*
l'embrayage = the clutch

émeute *noun, feminine*
une émeute = a riot

émigrer *verb* ⬚1
= to emigrate

émission *noun, feminine*
une émission = a broadcast, a
program(me)

emménager *verb* ⬚13
= to move in

emmener *verb* ⬚16
= to take
= to take away

empêcher *verb* ⬚1
1 (**!** + *avoir*)
• = to prevent
empêcher un enfant de sortir = to prevent
a child from going out
• (il) n'empêche que = nevertheless
2 s'empêcher (**!** + *être*)
je n'ai pas pu m'empêcher de rire
= I couldn't help laughing

empiffrer: s'empiffrer* *verb* ⬚1
(**!** + *être*)
s'empiffrer = to stuff oneself

emplacement *noun, masculine*
un emplacement (*for a building*) = a site
(*for a tent*) = a pitch
(*for a vehicle*) = a parking space

emploi *noun, masculine*
• (*a post*)
un emploi = a job
• (*the job market*)
l'emploi = employment
• (*of a word, a product*)
l'emploi = the use
un emploi du temps = a timetable

employé/employée *noun,
masculine/feminine*
un employé/une employée = an employee
un employé de banque = a bank clerk
un employé de bureau = an office
worker

employer *verb* ⬚23
• = to employ
• = to use

empoisonné/empoisonnée
adjective
= poisoned

emporter *verb* ⬚1
1 (**!** + *avoir*)
• = to take
emporte un parapluie = take an umbrella
• = to take away
'plats à emporter' = 'take away food',
'food to go'
• = to sweep away
le pont a été emporté = the bridge has
been swept away
• l'emporter = to win
l'emporter sur = to get the better of, to
beat
2 s'emporter (**!** + *être*)
s'emporter = to lose one's temper

empreinte *noun, feminine*
une empreinte (*left by a foot*) = a footprint
les empreintes digitales = fingerprints

emprunter *verb* ⬚1
= to borrow
emprunter de l'argent à la banque = to
borrow money from the bank

en

! You will find translations for phrases with en such as en train de, s'en aller etc at the entries train, aller, etc.

1 preposition
- = in
  vivre en France = to live in France
  en mai = in May
  faire le trajet en deux heures = to do the journey in two hours
- = to
  = into
  aller en Espagne = to go to Spain
  aller en ville = to go into town
  monter en voiture = to get into the car
- = by
  voyager en [train | bateau | voiture ...] = to travel by [train | boat | car ...]
- = made of
  c'est en bois = it's (made of) wood
  une chaîne en or = a gold chain
- (showing that two things are done at the same time) = while
  chanter en travaillant = to sing while working
  j'ai lu le journal en attendant = I read the paper while I was waiting
- (showing the manner in which something is done)
  sortir en courant = to run out
  se réveiller en pleurant = to wake up crying
  j'ai fini le travail en me levant tous les jours à six heures = I finished the work by getting up at six every day
- (showing the circumstances in which something occurs)
  il est tombé en traversant la rue = he fell as he was crossing the street
  tu t'es trompé en mesurant la pièce = you made a mistake when you measured the room

2 pronoun
- = of it
  = of them
  il en boit beaucoup = he drinks a lot of it
  il y en a quatre = there are four (of them)
  combien en voulez-vous? (if it's cheese) = how much (of it) would you like?
  (if it's cakes) = how many (of them) would you like?
  je m'en souviens = I remember
- = some/any
  encore un peu de thé? il en reste = a little more tea? there's some left
  des roses? il n'y en a plus = roses? there aren't any left .
- (representing a place)
  j'en arrive à l'instant = I've just got back from there

enchanter verb [1]
= to delight
enchanté (de faire votre connaissance) = pleased to meet you

enchères noun, feminine plural
une vente aux enchères = an auction

encombré/encombrée adjective
(describing a street) = congested
(describing a room, a cupboard) = cluttered

encombrement noun, masculine
l'encombrement (on the road) = traffic congestion

encore adverb
- = still
  tu es encore jeune = you're still young
- = again
  il a encore écrit = he's written again
- = more
  = another
  tu veux encore un peu de thé? = would you like some more tea?
  essaie encore une fois = try again
  encore un gâteau? = another cake?
- pas encore = not yet
  elle n'est pas encore arrivée = she hasn't arrived yet
- encore plus = even more
  c'est encore plus cher = it's even more expensive
  il fait encore plus chaud ici = it's even hotter here

encourager verb [13]
= to encourage

encre noun, feminine
l'encre = ink

endormi/endormie adjective
= asleep

endormir verb [30]
1 (! + avoir)
= to put to sleep
la télévision m'endort = television puts me to sleep
2 s'endormir (! + être)
s'endormir = to fall asleep
= to get to sleep

endroit noun, masculine
- (a spot)
  un endroit = a place
  au bon endroit = in the right place
  par endroits = in places
  à quel endroit? = where?
- (a side)
  l'endroit = the right side
  à l'endroit = the right way round, the right way around

énergie noun, feminine
l'énergie = energy

énergique adjective
= energetic

énervé/énervée adjective
= irritable
= on edge

énerver verb 1
1 (! + *avoir*)
= to irritate
ça m'énerve = it irritates me, it gets on my nerves
2 s'énerver (! + *être*)
s'énerver = to get irritable, to get annoyed

enfance noun, feminine
l'enfance = childhood

enfant noun, masculine/feminine
un enfant/une enfant = a child

enfer noun, masculine
l'enfer = Hell
un bruit d'enfer = a hell of a noise

enfermer verb 1
1 (! + *avoir*)
= to lock up
2 s'enfermer (! + *être*)
s'enfermer = to lock oneself in

enfin adverb
• = finally
= at last
• mais enfin, cesse de crier! = for heaven's sake, stop shouting!

enflammer: **s'enflammer** verb 1
(! + *être*)
s'enflammer = to go up in flames
= to catch fire

enfler verb 1
= to swell (up)

enfoncer verb 12
1 (! + *avoir*)
• = to push in
enfoncer un clou = to drive a nail in
enfoncer une épingle = to stick a pin in
enfoncer ses mains dans ses poches = to dig one's hands into one's pockets
• enfoncer une porte = to break down a door
2 s'enfoncer (! + *être*)
• s'enfoncer = to sink
s'enfoncer dans la boue = to sink in the mud
s'enfoncer dans un fauteuil = to sink back into an armchair
• s'enfoncer une épine dans le doigt = to get a thorn in one's finger

enfreindre verb 55
enfreindre le règlement = to break the rules

enfuir: **s'enfuir** verb 29 (! + *être*)
s'enfuir = to run away
= to escape

engin noun, masculine
• un engin = a device
• un engin = a vehicle

engorger verb 13
= to block
= to clog up

enlever verb 16
1 (! + *avoir*)
• = to remove
• = to kidnap
2 s'enlever (! + *être*)
s'enlever = to come off

enneigé/enneigée adjective
= covered in snow

ennui noun, masculine
• un ennui = a problem
• l'ennui = boredom

ennuyer verb 22
1 (! + *avoir*)
• = to bore
• = to bother
= to annoy
ça t'ennuie qu'il vienne? = do you mind if he comes?
2 s'ennuyer (! + *être*)
s'ennuyer = to be bored

ennuyeux/ennuyeuse adjective
• = boring
= tedious
• = annoying

énorme adjective
= huge, enormous

énormément adverb
= tremendously, immensely

enquête noun, feminine
• (*into a crime*)
une enquête = an inquiry, an investigation
• (*on opinions, lifestyles*)
une enquête = a survey

enquêteur/enquêtrice noun, masculine/feminine
un enquêteur/une enquêtrice = an investigator

enregistrement noun, masculine
• (*for sound*)
un enregistrement = a recording
• (*for air passengers*)
l'enregistrement = checking-in

enregistrer verb 1
• (*if it's sound, statistics*) = to record
• (*if it's luggage*) = to register
(*at an airport*) = to check in

enrhumer: **s'enrhumer** verb 1
(! + *être*)
s'enrhumer = to catch a cold
être enrhumé = to have a cold

enseignant/enseignante noun, masculine/feminine
un enseignant/une enseignante = a teacher

enseigne noun, feminine
une enseigne = a sign

enseignement *noun, masculine*
- (*as a career*)
  l'enseignement = teaching
- (*a system*)
  l'enseignement = education
l'enseignement par correspondance
  = correspondence courses

ensemble
1 *adverb*
  = together
2 *noun, masculine*
- (*clothes*)
  un ensemble = an outfit
  = a lady's suit
- (*the entirety*)
  l'ensemble = the whole
  = all
  une vue d'ensemble = an overall view
- (*a collection*)
  un ensemble = a set
  = a group
  un grand ensemble = a high-density
    housing complex, a high-rise housing
    complex
3 dans l'ensemble = on the whole

ensoleillé/ensoleillée *adjective*
  = sunny

ensuite *adverb*
  = then
  = later
  = next

entendre *verb* 6
1 (**!** + *avoir*)
  = to hear
  j'ai entendu dire qu'il était de retour = I've
    heard that he's back
  as-tu entendu parler de ce film? = have
    you heard about this film?
2 s'entendre (**!** + *être*)
  s'entendre = to get on, to get along
  elles s'entendent bien = they get on well,
    they get along well

entendu/entendue
1 ▶ **entendre** 6
2 *adjective*
  = agreed
  entendu! = OK then!
3 bien entendu = of course

enterrement *noun, masculine*
  un enterrement = a funeral

enterrer *verb* 1
  = to bury

enthousiasmer *verb* 1
1 (**!** + *avoir*)
  = to fill with enthusiasm
2 s'enthousiasmer (**!** + *être*)
  s'enthousiasmer = to get enthusiastic

enthousiaste *adjective*
  = enthusiastic

entier/entière *adjective*
  = whole, entire

entourer *verb* 1
- = to surround
  des collines entourent la ville = the town
    is surrounded by hills
  un jardin entouré d'une haie = a garden
    surrounded by a hedge
- = to circle
  entourer une date en rouge = to circle a
    date in red
- entourer son doigt d'un mouchoir = to put
    a handkerchief round one's finger

entracte *noun, masculine*
  un entracte = an interval, an intermission

entraînement *noun, masculine*
  l'entraînement (*for an athlete*) = training
  (*for a musician*) = practice

entraîner *verb* 1
1 (**!** + *avoir*)
- = to lead to
  entraîner des problèmes = to lead to
    problems, to cause problems
- = to drag along
  entraîner un ami à la plage = to drag a
    friend along to the beach
- = to coach, to train
  entraîner une équipe = to coach a team
2 s'entraîner (**!** + *être*)
  s'entraîner = to train
  = to practise, to practice

entraîneur *noun, masculine*
  un entraîneur = a coach

entre *preposition*
  = between
  l'un d'entre eux = one of them

entrée *noun, feminine*
- (*way in*)
  l'entrée = the entrance
  = the (entrance) hall
- (*access*)
  l'entrée = entry
  = admission
  'entrée interdite' = 'no entry', 'do not
    enter'
  'entrée gratuite' = 'free admission'
- (*on a menu*)
  une entrée = a starter, an appetizer

entreprise *noun, feminine*
  une entreprise = a firm
  = a company

entrer *verb* 1 (**!** + *être*)
  = to enter, to go in
  = to enter, to come in
  entrez! = come in!
  entrer dans la cuisine = to go into the
    kitchen
  = to come into the kitchen

entretien *noun, masculine*
- un entretien (*a conversation*) = a
  discussion
  (*for a job*) = an interview

• **l'entretien** (*of a house, a garden*) = the upkeep, the maintenance
(*of clothes, furniture*) = the care

enveloppe *noun, feminine*
une enveloppe = an envelope

envelopper *verb* 1
= to wrap

envers
1 *preposition*
= toward, towards, to
2 *noun, masculine* (**!** *never changes*)
l'envers = the back
= the wrong side
= the reverse
3 **à l'envers** = the wrong way

envie *noun, feminine*
une envie = a desire
avoir envie de pleurer = to want to cry, to feel like crying

environ *adverb*
= about

environs *noun, masculine plural*
les environs = the surrounding area

envoler: s'envoler *verb* 1 (**!** + *être*)
s'envoler (*if it's a bird*) = to fly away
(*if it's a plane*) = to take off

envoyer *verb* 24
• = to send
• = to throw

épais/épaisse *adjective*
= thick

épaule *noun, feminine*
une épaule = a shoulder

épeler *verb* 19
= to spell

épice *noun, feminine*
une épice – a spice

épicerie *noun, feminine*
une épicerie = a grocer's, a grocery store

épicier/épicière *noun,*
masculine/feminine
un épicier/une épicière = a grocer

épinards *noun, masculine plural*
des épinards = spinach

épine *noun, feminine*
une épine = a thorn

épingle *noun, feminine*
une épingle = a pin
une épingle à nourrice, une épingle
de sûreté = a safety pin

épisode *noun, masculine*
un épisode = an episode
un roman à épisodes = a serialized novel

éplucher *verb* 1
= to peel

épluchure *noun, feminine*
des épluchures = peelings

éponge *noun, feminine*
• (*a type of material*)
l'éponge = (terry-)towelling, terrycloth
• (*a sea creature*)
une éponge = a sponge

époque *noun, feminine*
une époque = a period, an era
à notre époque = nowadays, in our times
à l'époque = at the time

épouse *noun, feminine*
une épouse = a wife

épouser *verb* 1
= to marry

épouvantable *adjective*
= dreadful

épouvante *noun, feminine*
l'épouvante = terror
= horror
un film d'épouvante = a horror film, a horror movie

époux (**!** *never changes*)
1 *noun, masculine singular*
un époux = a husband
2 *noun, masculine plural*
les époux = the (married) couple
les jeunes époux = the newly weds

épreuve *noun, feminine*
une épreuve (*at school*) = an examination
(*in sport*) = an event

éprouver *verb* 1
= to feel

EPS *noun, feminine* (**!** *never changes*)
l'EPS = PE

épuisé/épuisée *adjective*
= exhausted

équateur *noun, masculine*
l'équateur = the equator

équilibre *noun, masculine*
l'équilibre = balance
perdre l'équilibre = to lose one's balance
en équilibre = balanced

équilibrer *verb* 1
= to balance

équipage *noun, masculine*
un équipage = a crew

équipe *noun, feminine*
• (*of players, workers*)
une équipe = a team
• (*in a factory*)
l'équipe de nuit = the night shift

équipement *noun, masculine*
l'équipement = the equipment

équitation *noun, feminine*
l'équitation = (horse-)riding

erreur noun, feminine
une erreur = a mistake

es ▶ être 7

escalade noun, feminine
l'escalade = rock climbing

escalader verb 1
= to climb

escalier noun, masculine
• un escalier = a staircase
= (a flight of) stairs
• les escaliers = the stairs
un escalier roulant = an escalator

escargot noun, masculine
un escargot = a snail

esclave noun, masculine|feminine
un esclave/une esclave = a slave

escrime noun, feminine
l'escrime = fencing

escroc noun, masculine
un escroc = a crook

espace noun, masculine
• l'espace = space
• un espace = a space, a gap
un espace vert = an open space, a green
area, a park

Espagne noun, feminine
l'Espagne = Spain

espagnol/espagnole
1 adjective
= Spanish
2 **espagnol** noun, masculine
l'espagnol = Spanish

espèce noun, feminine
• (a sort)
une espèce de roue = a kind of wheel
• (a group of animals or plants)
une espèce = a species

espérer verb 14
= to hope (for)

espionnage noun, masculine
l'espionnage = espionage, spying

esquimau/esquimaude
(plural) **esquimaux/esquimaudes**
1 adjective
= Eskimo
2 **esquimau** noun, masculine
un esquimau = a choc-ice, an ice cream
bar

essayer verb 21
• = to try
essayer d'ouvrir la porte = to try to open
the door
• = to try on
essayer un chapeau = to try on a hat

essence noun, feminine
l'essence = petrol, gas(oline)

l'essence sans plomb = unleaded petrol,
unleaded gas

essorage noun, masculine
l'essorage = spinning

essuie-glace noun, masculine
(plural) **essuie-glaces**
un essuie-glace = a windscreen wiper, a
windshield wiper

essuyer verb 22
1 (! + avoir)
• = to dry
• = to wipe (up)
2 s'essuyer (! + être)
s'essuyer = to wipe oneself
= to dry oneself
s'essuyer les mains = to wipe one's hands

est¹ ▶ être 7

est²
1 noun, masculine
l'est = the east
2 adjective (! never changes)
= east
= eastern

est-ce que ▶ être 7

estivant/estivante noun,
masculine|feminine
un estivant/une estivante = a summer
visitor

estomac noun, masculine
l'estomac = the stomach

et conjunction
= and
et avec ceci? = anything else?

étage noun, masculine
un étage = a floor, a story
habiter au premier étage (in Britain) = to
live on the first floor
(in the US) = to live on the second floor
à l'étage = upstairs

étagère noun, feminine
une étagère (a flat piece of wood, glass)
= a shelf
(a piece of furniture) = a bookshelf

étais ▶ être 7

étaler verb 1
= to spread (out)

étang noun, masculine
un étang = a pond

étant ▶ être 7

étape noun, feminine
• (a place)
une étape = a stop
faire étape à Nice = to stop in Nice
• (part of a journey)
une étape = a stage
(in a race) = a leg

état noun, masculine
un état = a state

États-Unis noun, masculine plural
les États-Unis = the United States

été
1 ▶ **être** 7
2 noun, masculine
l'été = summer

éteindre verb 55
1 (**!** + avoir)
• = to put out
• = to switch off, to turn off
2 s'éteindre (**!** + être)
• s'éteindre = to go out
• s'éteindre = to go off

éteint/éteinte ▶ **éteindre** 55

étendre verb 6
1 (**!** + avoir)
• (to put down flat)
étendre une nappe = to spread out a tablecloth
• (to put out to dry)
étendre le linge = to hang out the washing, to hang out the laundry
2 s'étendre (**!** + être)
• (if it's a person)
s'étendre = to lie down
• (if it's land)
s'étendre = to stretch
• (if it's a conflict)
s'étendre = to spread

étendu/étendue[1]
1 ▶ **étendre** 6
2 adjective
= extensive

étendue[2] noun, feminine
• (of land, water)
une étendue = an expanse
= a stretch
• (of a disaster)
l'étendue = the scale, the size

éternuer verb 1
= to sneeze

êtes ▶ **être** 7

étiquette noun, feminine
une étiquette = a label
= a tag

étirer: s'étirer verb 1 (**!** + être)
s'étirer = to stretch

étoile noun, feminine
une étoile = a star

étonnant/étonnante adjective
= surprising
= amazing

étonner verb 1
1 (**!** + avoir)
= to surprise
2 s'étonner (**!** + être)
s'étonner = to be surprised

étouffant/étouffante adjective
= stifling

étouffer verb 1
1 (**!** + avoir)
• = to smother
• = to suffocate
on étouffe ici! = it's stifling in here!
2 s'étouffer (**!** + être)
s'étouffer = to choke

étourdi/étourdie adjective
= scatterbrained

étrange adjective
= strange

étranger/étrangère
1 adjective
= foreign
2 noun, masculine/feminine
un étranger/une étrangère (from another country) = a foreigner
(an unknown person) = a stranger
3 à l'étranger = abroad

être verb 7 (**!** + avoir)
▶ **64** | See the boxed note.

étroit/étroite adjective
= narrow

étude
1 noun, feminine
• (an activity)
l'étude = study
• (a room in a school)
l'étude = the study room, the study hall
• (on the school timetable)
'étude' = 'private study', 'study hall'
2 études noun, feminine plural
les études = studies, higher education
faire des études = to study, to be a student

étudiant/étudiante noun, masculine/feminine
un étudiant/une étudiante = a student

étudier verb 2
• = to study
• = to examine

étui noun, masculine
un étui = a case
un étui à lunettes = a glasses case

eu/eue ▶ **avoir** 8

euro noun, masculine
un euro = a euro

Europe noun, feminine
l'Europe = Europe

européen/européenne adjective
= European

eux pronoun
• = them
à cause d'eux = because of them

E

être *verb* 7

present	imperfect	future	past participle
je suis	j'étais	je serai	été
tu es	tu étais	tu seras	
il / elle est	il / elle était	il / elle sera	
nous sommes	nous étions	nous serons	
vous êtes	vous étiez	vous serez	
ils / elles sont	ils / elles étaient	ils / elles seront	

1 être functions as an ordinary verb:

● (*showing a quality or state*)   = to be

je **suis** fatigué	= *I'm tired*
le ciel **est** bleu	= *the sky is blue*
elle **est** fatiguée	= *she is tired*
sois sage!	= *be good!*
ils **ont été** malades	= *they've been ill*

● (*showing ownership*)

la maison **est** à Pierre	= *the house belongs to Pierre, the house is Pierre's*
à qui **sont** ces gants?	= *who do these gloves belong to, whose gloves are they?*
ils **sont** à moi	= *they belong to me, they're mine*

2 être is used as an auxiliary verb to conjugate some verbs, notably reflexive verbs and a few others, all of which are labelled (**!** + *être*):

je **suis** né en Italie	= *I was born in Italy*
elle n'**est** pas encore rentrée	= *she hasn't come home yet*
ils **sont** partis	= *they've left*
tu t'**es** lavé les mains?	= *did you wash your hands?*

3 être is used to form questions in the phrase **est-ce que**:

est-ce que tu aimes le jazz?	= *do you like jazz?*
est-ce qu'il fait froid?	= *is it cold?*
est-ce que tu viendras?	= *will you come?*
est-ce qu'ils ont fini?	= *have they finished?*
est-ce que tu as de l'argent?	= *have you got any money?*

• (*indicating possession, turn*)
le chien est à eux = the dog is theirs
c'est à eux de jouer = it's their turn to play
• (*when used for emphasis*) = they
je suis resté, mais eux sont partis = I stayed but they left

eux-mêmes *pronoun*
= themselves

évaluer *verb* 1
• = to assess
• = to estimate
• = to value

évanouir: **s'évanouir** *verb* 3 (**!** + *être*)
s'évanouir = to faint

évasion *noun, feminine*
une évasion = an escape

événement *noun, masculine*
un événement = an event

éventail *noun, masculine*
un éventail = a fan

éventuellement *adverb*
• = possibly
• = if necessary

évidemment *adverb*
= obviously
= of course

évident/**évidente** *adjective*
= obvious

évier *noun, masculine*
un évier = a (kitchen) sink

éviter *verb* 1
= to avoid

exact/**exacte** *adjective*
• = correct
• = exact

✗ in informal situations

exactement *adverb*
= exactly

exagérer *verb* 14
= to exaggerate

examen *noun, masculine*
* (*for pupils, students*)
  un examen = an examination, an exam, a test
  passer un examen = to take an exam
  réussir à un examen = to pass an exam
* (*by a doctor*)
  un examen = an examination

examiner *verb* 1
= to examine

excursion *noun, feminine*
une excursion = an excursion, a trip
faire une excursion = to go on an excursion

excuse *noun, feminine*
* (*a reason*)
  une excuse = an excuse
* (*when saying that one is sorry*)
  des excuses = an apology
  présenter des excuses = to apologize

excuser *verb* 1
1 (**!** + *avoir*)
= to excuse
excusez-moi (*when apologizing*) = I'm sorry
(*when interrupting*) = excuse me
2 s'excuser (**!** + *être*)
s'excuser = to apologize

exemple *noun, masculine*
un exemple = an example
par exemple = for example, for instance

exercer: **s'exercer** *verb* 12 (**!** + *être*)
s'exercer = to practise, to practice
s'exercer à sauter à la corde = to practise skipping

exercice *noun, masculine*
un exercice = an exercise

exiger *verb* 13
= to demand
= to require

expédier *verb* 2
= to send

expéditeur/expéditrice *noun, masculine/feminine*
un expéditeur/une expéditrice = a sender

expérience *noun, feminine*
* (*skill, knowledge*)
  l'expérience = experience
* (*a test*)
  une expérience = an experiment

expliquer *verb* 1
= to explain

explorateur/exploratrice *noun, masculine/feminine*
un explorateur/une exploratrice = an explorer

exploser *verb* 1
= to explode

exposer *verb* 1
* (*in a shop window*) = to display
* (*in a gallery*) = to exhibit
* (*to the sun, to a danger*) = to expose

exposition *noun, feminine*
une exposition = an exhibition

F

exprès *adverb*
= on purpose

express *noun, masculine* (**!** *never changes*)
un express = an express, a fast train

exprimer *verb* 1
= to express

extérieur/extérieure
1 *adjective*
= outside
2 extérieur *noun, masculine*
l'extérieur = the outside
à l'extérieur de la boîte = outside the box

externe
1 *adjective*
= external
2 *noun, masculine/feminine*
un externe/une externe = a day pupil, a day student

extra *adjective*
= first-class, great

extrait *noun, masculine*
un extrait = an extract

Ff

fabrication *noun, feminine*
la fabrication = manufacture

fabriquer *verb* 1
* = to make, to manufacture
* **qu'est-ce que tu fabriques✶?** = what are you up to?

façade *noun, feminine*
la façade = the front

face
1 *noun, feminine*
la face (*on a box*) = the side
(*of a coin*) = the heads side
pile ou face = heads or tails

2 de face = from the front
3 en face (de) = opposite

fâcher: **se fâcher** verb 1
se fâcher = to get angry

facile adjective
= easy

facilement adverb
= easily

façon noun, feminine
une façon = a way
la façon dont il parle = the way he talks
de toute façon = anyway

façonner verb 1
= to shape, to mould

facteur/factrice noun,
masculine/feminine
un facteur/une factrice = a postman/a
postwoman, a mail carrier

facture noun, feminine
une facture = a bill, an invoice

faible adjective
= weak

faillir verb 28
j'ai failli y aller = I (very) nearly went, I
almost went

faim noun, feminine
la faim = hunger
avoir faim = to be hungry

fainéant/fainéante adjective
= lazy

faire verb 10

! You will find translations for phrases with
faire such as faire attention, faire le clown,
faire pousser etc under the words
attention, clown, pousser etc.

1 (! + avoir)
• = to make
faire [un gâteau | un effort | une faute ...] = to
make [a cake | an effort | a mistake ...]
• = to do
faire [la vaisselle | ses devoirs | un travail ...]
= to do [the dishes | one's homework | a job ...]
que fait-il? (for a living) = what does he do?
(at this very moment) = what's he doing?
• = to go
faire [de l'escalade | du vélo | des courses ...]
= to go [climbing | cycling | shopping ...]
• (when talking about the weather)
il fait [chaud | gris | du vent ...] = it's [hot |
overcast | windy ...]
il faisait 30° à l'ombre = it was 30° in the
shade
il fera beau demain = the weather will be
fine tomorrow

---

* in informal situations

• (when talking about a particular length of
time)
ça fait deux heures que j'attends = I've
been waiting for two hours
ça fait longtemps qu'il est parti = he left a
long time ago
• (when talking about measurements)
faire 1,75 m = to be 1.75 m tall
faire du 42 = to take a size 42
• (to cause something to happen)
il m'a fait [tomber | manquer le train |
travailler ...] = he made me [fall | miss the
train | work ...]
• (to get something done)
faire nettoyer une veste = to have a jacket
cleaned
• (some other uses)
ça ne fait rien = it doesn't matter
qu'est-ce que ça peut bien te faire?
= what's it to you?
fais comme tu veux = do as you like
faites comme chez vous = make yourself
at home
2 se faire (! + être)
• (to do something for oneself)
se faire = to make
elle s'est fait du café = she made herself
some coffee
se faire des amis = to make friends
se faire comprendre = to make oneself
understood
• (to get someone to do something for you)
se faire couper les cheveux = to have one's
hair cut
elle s'est fait faire une robe = she's had a
dress made
• (when something is done to you)
se faire [attraper | menacer | écraser ...] = to be
[caught | threatened | run over ...]
• (other uses)
ça ne se fait pas = it isn't the done thing,
it isn't the thing to do
3 s'en faire (! + être)
s'en faire = to worry
ne t'en fais pas = don't worry

faire-part noun, masculine (! never
changes)
un faire-part = an announcement card

fais ▶ faire 10

faisable adjective
= feasible
c'est faisable = it can be done

faisais ▶ faire 10

faisan noun, masculine
un faisan = a pheasant

faisons ▶ faire 10

fait/faite
1 ▶ faire 10
2 adjective
• = done
un travail bien fait = a job well done
c'est bien fait pour lui! = it serves him
right!

- **tout fait** = ready-made
  des rideaux tout faits = ready-made curtains, store-bought drapes
- **c'est fait pour nettoyer les vitres** = it's meant for cleaning windows

3 fait *noun, masculine*
  un fait = a fact
4 au fait = by the way
5 en fait = in fact
un fait divers = a (short) news item

faites ▶ **faire** ⑩

falaise *noun, feminine*
  une falaise = a cliff

falloir *verb* ⑤⓪
  il faut une clé pour ouvrir la porte = you need a key to open the door
  il me fallait de l'argent = I needed some money
  allons, il faut partir = come on, we've got to go
  il ne faut jamais arriver en retard = one must never be late
  achète ce qu'il faut pour le jardin = buy whatever is necessary for the garden
  il le fallait = it was necessary
  il faudra que tu ailles au garage = you will have to go to the garage
  il va falloir que vous le fassiez = you will have to do it

fallu ▶ **falloir** ⑤⓪

familial/familiale *adjective*
(*plural*) **familiaux/familiales**
  = family

familier/familière *adjective*
  = familiar

famille *noun, feminine*
  une famille = a family
  en famille = with the family
  = as a family

fana* *noun, masculine/feminine*
  un fana*/une fana* = a fanatic

fantastique *adjective*
  = fantastic

fantôme *noun, masculine*
  un fantôme = a ghost

farce *noun, feminine*
- (*a trick*)
  une farce = a practical joke
- (*in cooking*)
  la farce = the stuffing

farci/farcie *adjective*
  = stuffed

fard *noun, masculine*
  le fard = make-up

farfelu/farfelue* *adjective*
- = scatterbrained
- = eccentric

farine *noun, feminine*
  la farine = flour

fasse ▶ **faire** ⑩

fatigant/fatigante *adjective*
  = tiring

fatigue *noun, feminine*
  la fatigue = tiredness

fatigué/fatiguée
  = tired

fauché/fauchée* *adjective*
  = broke

faudra ▶ **falloir** ⑤⓪

faune *noun, feminine*
  la faune = wildlife

fausse ▶ **faux**

faut ▶ **falloir** ⑤⓪

faute *noun, feminine*
- (*an error*)
  une faute = a mistake
- (*responsibility*)
  c'est (de) ta faute = it's your fault

fauteuil *noun, masculine*
  un fauteuil = an armchair
  un fauteuil roulant = a wheelchair

faux/fausse
1 *adjective*
- (*not right*) = wrong
- (*not genuine*) = false
  = fake
2 faux *adverb*
  chanter faux = to sing out of tune

favori/favorite *adjective*
  = favo(u)rite

féculent *noun, masculine*
  un féculent = a starchy food

fêlé/fêlée *adjective*
  = cracked

félicitations *noun, feminine plural*
  des félicitations = congratulations

femme *noun, feminine*
  une femme = a woman
  = a wife
  une femme d'affaires = a business-woman
  une femme de ménage = a cleaning lady

fenêtre *noun, feminine*
  une fenêtre = a window

fente *noun, feminine*
  une fente (*for a coin*) = a slot
  (*in a wall*) = a crack
  (*in a mask*) = a slit

fer *noun, masculine*
  le fer = iron
  un fer à repasser = an iron

F

ferai ▶ **faire** 50

férié/fériée *adjective*
un jour férié = a public holiday, a holiday

ferme *noun, feminine*
une ferme = a farm

fermer *verb* 1
= to close, to shut

fermeture *noun, feminine*
• (*of a shop*)
la fermeture = closing (down)
'fermeture annuelle' = 'annual closing'
• (*a device*)
une fermeture = a fastener
une fermeture éclair = a zip(per)

fermier/fermière *noun,*
masculine/feminine
un fermier/une fermière = a farmer

féroce *adjective*
= fierce

ferroviaire *adjective*
= rail, railroad

fesse *noun, feminine*
une fesse = a buttock

fête *noun, feminine*
• (*a special day in a country*)
une fête = a public holiday, a holiday
• (*a special day for a person*)
ma fête = my (saint's) name-day
bonne fête! = happy saint's day!
• (*an organized event*)
une fête = a festival
• (*at home*) = a celebration
= a party
faire une fête = to have a party
une fête foraine = a funfair, a carnival
la fête des Mères = Mother's day
(*celebrated in France on the last Sunday in
May*)
la fête du travail = May Day

fêter *verb* 1
= to celebrate

feu *noun, masculine*
(*plural*) **feux**
• (*flames*)
un feu = a fire
mettre le feu à une maison = to set fire to
a house
au feu! = fire!
en feu = on fire
• (*the flame from a match or a lighter*)
du feu = a light
demander du feu = to ask for a light
• (*on a car, in the street*)
un feu = a light
les feux = the traffic lights
un feu d'artifice = a fireworks display
les feux de détresse = hazard lights

**les feux de signalisation, les feux
tricolores** = the traffic lights

feuille *noun, feminine*
• (*on a tree*)
une feuille = a leaf
• (*paper*)
une feuille = a sheet

feuilleter *verb* 20
= to flick through

feuilleton *noun, masculine*
un feuilleton = a serial
= a soap opera

feutre *noun, masculine*
un feutre = a felt-tip pen

fève *noun, feminine*
• une fève = a broad bean, a fava bean
• une fève = a lucky charm (*hidden in the
galette des rois*)

février *noun, masculine*
février = February

fiançailles *noun, feminine plural*
des fiançailles = an engagement

fiancer: se fiancer *verb* 12 (**!** + *être*)
se fiancer = to get engaged

ficelle *noun, feminine*
• (*around a parcel*)
de la ficelle = string
• (*bread*)
une ficelle = a thin baguette

fiche *noun, feminine*
une fiche = a form
= card

ficher* *verb* 1
1 (**!** + *avoir*)
• = to do
il n'a rien fiché* *or* fichu* de la journée
= he's done nothing all day
• ficher* à la poubelle = to bin, to throw out
• fiche-moi la paix*! = leave me alone!
2 se ficher* (**!** + *être*)
• se ficher de quelqu'un*
(*to mock*) = to make fun of someone
(*to lack consideration*) = to mess someone
around
• je m'en fiche* = I couldn't care less
je me fiche* de ce qu'on dit = I couldn't
care less what people say

fichu/fichue*
1 ▶ **ficher** 1
2 *adjective*
• = rotten, nasty
avoir un fichu* caractère = to have a nasty
temper
• = done for
ma voiture est fichue* = my car's had it
s'il pleut c'est fichu* = if it rains that's the
end of that
• être fichu* de faire = to be capable of
doing

---

* in informal situations

fidèle *adjective*
= faithful

fier/fière *adjective*
= proud

fièvre *noun, feminine*
une fièvre = a fever
avoir de la fièvre = to have a temperature

fiévreux/fiévreuse *adjective*
= feverish

figue *noun, feminine*
une figue = a fig

figure *noun, feminine*
• la figure = the face
• une figure = a figure
= a diagram

figurer *verb* [1]
1 (! + *avoir*)
= to appear, to feature
figurer sur une liste = to appear on a list
2 se figurer (! + *être*)
se figurer = to think, to imagine

fil *noun, masculine*
• (*for sewing*)
le fil = thread
• (*connecting a telephone*)
un fil = a wire
un coup de fil = a phone call
passe-moi un coup de fil = give me a call
le fil de fer = wire

file *noun, feminine*
• (*a row of people or cars*)
une file = a line
(*at a cinema, a bus stop, a store*)
une file d'attente = a queue, a line
• (*part of a road*)
une file = a lane

filer* *verb* [1]
• (*if it's time*) = to fly by
• (*to leave*)***** = to go off
• (*to escape*)***** = to get away

filet *noun, masculine*
un filet = a net
un filet à provisions = a string bag

fille *noun, feminine*
une fille = a girl
= a daughter

fillette *noun, feminine*
une fillette = a little girl

filleul/filleule *noun, masculine/feminine*
un filleul/une filleule = a godson/a
goddaughter

film *noun, masculine*
un film = a film, a movie
un film d'animation = a cartoon (film)
un film policier = a detective film

fils *noun, masculine* (! *never changes*)
un fils = a son

fin¹ *noun, feminine*
la fin = the end
en fin de matinée = late in the morning
en fin de compte = in the end, finally

fin²/fine *adjective*
= thin
= slender
= fine

finalement *adverb*
= finally, in the end

finir *verb* [3]
• = to finish
j'ai fini d'écrire = I've finished writing
• = to end
il a fini par avoir un accident = he ended
up having an accident
l'histoire finit bien = the story has a happy
ending

fioul *noun, masculine*
le fioul = fuel oil

firme *noun, feminine*
une firme = a firm

fixe *adjective*
un prix fixe = a fixed price
une résidence fixe = a permanent address
manger à heure fixe = to eat at a set time

flamme *noun, feminine*
une flamme = a flame

flan *noun, masculine*
un flan ≈ custard
= a custard tart, a custard flan

flâner *verb* [1]
= to stroll

flaque *noun, feminine*
une flaque = a puddle

flèche *noun, feminine*
une flèche = an arrow

fléchette *noun, feminine*
une fléchette = a dart

fleur *noun, feminine*
une fleur = a flower

fleuriste *noun, masculine/feminine*
un fleuriste/une fleuriste = a florist

fleuve *noun, masculine*
un fleuve = a (large) river

flic* *noun, masculine*
un flic***** = a cop, a policeman

flipper *noun, masculine*
le flipper (*the machine*) = the pinball
machine
(*the device in the machine*) = the flipper
(*the game*) = pinball

flocon *noun, masculine*
un flocon de neige = a snowflake

flotter *verb* [1]
= to float

flotteur *noun, masculine*
un flotteur = a float

fluo *adjective* (**!** *never changes*)
= fluorescent

fluorescent/fluorescente *adjective*
= fluorescent

flûte *noun, feminine*
• (*an instrument*)
une flûte = a flute
une flûte à bec = a recorder
• (*bread*)
une flûte = a French stick, French bread

foie *noun, masculine*
le foie = (the) liver

foire *noun, feminine*
une foire = a fair
= a trade fair

fois
1 *noun, feminine* (**!** *never changes*)
encore une fois = one more time
une fois = once
deux fois = twice
trois fois = three times
une fois qu'il aura fini = once he's finished
une fois pour toutes = once and for all
2 à la fois = at the same time
= at once
3 des fois✗ = sometimes

folklorique *adjective*
= folk

folle ▶ fou

foncé/foncée *adjective*
= dark

foncer *verb* 12
foncer sur quelqu'un = to charge at
someone

fonctionnaire *noun, masculine/feminine*
un fonctionnaire/une fonctionnaire = a
civil servant

fonctionner *verb* 1
= to work

fond
1 *noun, masculine*
• (*the deepest part*)
le fond = the bottom
au fond du verre = at the bottom of the
glass
• (*the furthest part*)
le fond (*of a cupboard, a shop*) = the back
(*of a room, a yard*) = the far end
(*on a picture*) = the background
2 à fond
respirer à fond = to breathe deeply
appuyer à fond = to press hard

3 au fond, dans le fond
au fond, ce n'est pas bête = it's a rather
good idea
dans le fond, il a raison = he's right, really
un fond de teint = a foundation, a make-
up base

fonder *verb* 1
= to found

fondre *verb* 6
= to melt
faire fondre = to melt

fondu/fondue *adjective*
= melted

font ▶ faire 10

fontaine *noun, feminine*
une fontaine = a fountain

foot✗ *noun, masculine*
le foot✗ = football, soccer

football *noun, masculine*
le football = football, soccer

footing *noun, masculine*
le footing = jogging

force
1 *noun, feminine*
• (*energy*)
la force = strength
avoir de la force = to be strong
• (*violence*)
la force = force
de force = by force
2 à force de
réussir à force de travailler = to succeed by
dint of hard work
j'ai mal au bras à force d'écrire = I've done
so much writing that my arm hurts

forcer *verb* 12
1 (**!** + *avoir*)
= to force
forcer un enfant à manger = to force a
child to eat
2 se forcer (**!** + *être*)
se forcer = to force oneself

forêt *noun, feminine*
une forêt = a forest

forfaitaire *adjective*
= inclusive

forgeron *noun, masculine*
un forgeron = a blacksmith

formation *noun, feminine*
• (*the learning of skills*)
la formation = training
• (*the process of creating or developing*)
la formation = the formation

---

forme *noun, feminine*
* (*an outline*)
  une forme = a shape
  = a form
  en forme de T = T-shaped
* (*a person's energy*)
  avoir la forme = to be in good form
  être en (pleine) forme = to be in (very)
  good form

former *verb* [1]
* = to form
* = to train

formidable *adjective*
* = tremendous
* = great

formulaire *noun, masculine*
  un formulaire = a form

fort/forte
1 *adjective*
* (*not weak*) = strong
* (*not slim*) = stout
  = broad
* (*not soft*) = loud
* (*not slight*)
  de fortes pluies = heavy rain
  une forte chaleur = intense heat
  une forte pente = a steep slope
* (*gifted*)
  fort en = good at
  être fort en chimie = to be good at
  chemistry
2 fort *adverb*
* = hard
  taper fort = to hit hard
* = loudly
  parler fort = to speak loudly

fortement *adverb*
  = strongly
  = deeply

fortune *noun, feminine*
  une fortune = a fortune
  faire fortune = to make one's fortune

fossé *noun, masculine*
  un fossé = a ditch

fou/folle
1 *adjective*
  = mad, crazy
  être fou*/folle* de quelqu'un = to be mad
  about someone
2 *noun, masculine|feminine*
  un fou/une folle = a madman/a
  madwoman

foudre *noun, feminine*
* **la foudre** = lightning
* **le coup de foudre** = love at first sight

fouiller *verb* [1]
* = to search
* **fouiller dans un tiroir** = to rummage
  around in a drawer

foulard *noun, masculine*
  un foulard = a scarf

foule *noun, feminine*
  la foule = the crowd

fouler: se fouler *verb* [1] (**!** + *être*)
  se fouler la cheville = to sprain one's ankle

four *noun, masculine*
  un four = an oven
  faire cuire au four = to roast
  = to bake
  un four à micro-ondes = a microwave
  (oven)

fourche *noun, feminine*
  une fourche = a garden fork
  = a pitchfork

fourchette *noun, feminine*
  une fourchette = a fork

fourgonnette *noun, feminine*
  une fourgonnette = a (small) van

fourmi *noun, feminine*
  une fourmi = an ant

fournir *verb* [3]
  = to provide, to supply

fourrer* *verb* [1]
1 (**!** + *avoir*)
  = to shove, to put
  fourrer* des lettres dans un sac = to shove
  letters into a bag
2 se fourrer* (**!** + *être*)
  se fourrer = to put oneself

fourrure *noun, feminine*
  la fourrure = fur

foutre: se foutre de* *verb* [6] (**!** + *être*)
  se foutre de* = not to give a damn about
  je m'en fous* = I couldn't care less, I don't
  give a damn

foyer *noun, masculine*
* (*for a large group*)
  un foyer = a hostel
* (*where a family lives*)
  un foyer = a home
* (*in a fireplace*)
  le foyer = the hearth

fracture *noun, feminine*
  une fracture = a fracture

fragile *adjective*
  = fragile
  = delicate

fraîche ▶ frais 1

frais/fraîche
1 *adjective*
* = cool
  = chilled
  des boissons fraîches = cool drinks, cold
  drinks
  'servir frais' = 'serve chilled'

- = fresh
  des légumes frais = fresh vegetables
  des nouvelles fraîches = fresh news
2 frais adverb
- = cool
  = chilly
  il fait frais ce matin = it's cool this morning
  = it's chilly this morning
3 frais noun, masculine (**!** never changes)
  'garder au frais' = 'keep in a cool place'
  prendre le frais = to take a breath of fresh
  air
4 frais noun, masculine plural
  des frais = expenses

fraise noun, feminine
  une fraise = a strawberry

framboise noun, feminine
  une framboise = a raspberry

franc/franche
1 adjective
  = frank
2 franc noun, masculine
  un franc = one franc

français/française
1 adjective
  = French
2 français noun, masculine
  le français = French

Français/Française noun,
masculine/feminine
  un Français/une Française = a
  Frenchman/a Frenchwoman
  les Français = the French

France noun, feminine
  la France = France

franchement adverb
  = frankly

franchir verb ③
- = to cross
  franchir une frontière = to cross a border
- = to get over
  franchir une clôture = to get over a fence
- = to cover
  franchir dix kilomètres = to cover ten
  kilometres

francophone adjective
  = French-speaking

frange noun, feminine
  une frange = a fringe, bangs

frapper verb ①
- = to hit
- = to knock

fraternité noun, feminine
  la fraternité = fraternity

frein noun, masculine
  un frein = a brake
  le frein à main = the handbrake
  donner un coup de frein = to brake

✗ in informal situations

freiner verb ①
  = to brake

fréquenter verb ①
- = to mix with, to associate with
  fréquenter des voyous = to mix with
  hooligans
- = to go to
  = to visit
  = to attend

frère noun, masculine
  un frère = a brother

frigidaire   noun, masculine
  un frigidaire = a refrigerator

frigo✗ noun, masculine
  un frigo✗ = a fridge

frimeur/frimeuse✗ noun,
masculine/feminine
  un frimeur✗/une frimeuse✗ = a show-off

fringues✗ noun, feminine plural
  des fringues✗ = clothes

frire verb ㊴
  = to fry

frisé/frisée adjective
  = curly

frisson noun, masculine
  un frisson = a shiver
  = a shudder

frit/frite adjective
  = fried

frites noun, feminine plural
  les frites = chips, French fries

froid/froide
1 adjective
  = cold
2 froid adverb
  il fait froid = it's cold
3 froid noun, masculine
  le froid = the cold
  avoir froid = to feel cold, to be cold
  prendre froid = to catch (a) cold

fromage noun, masculine
  le fromage = cheese
le fromage blanc ≈ fromage frais

front noun, masculine
  le front = the forehead

frontière noun, feminine
  une frontière = a border, a frontier

frotter verb ①
  = to rub

fruit noun, masculine
  un fruit = a piece of fruit
  des fruits = fruit
des fruits de mer = seafood

fuir verb ㉙
- (if it's a person) = to flee
- (if it's a tap, a hose) = to leak

fuite *noun, feminine*
* (*of a person*)
  la fuite = the flight
  = the escape
* (*in a pipe, a hose*)
  une fuite = a leak

fumée *noun, feminine*
  la fumée = smoke

fumer *verb* 1
  = to smoke

fumeur/fumeuse *noun,*
masculine/feminine
  un fumeur/une fumeuse = a smoker

funiculaire *noun, masculine*
  un funiculaire = a funicular (railway)

fur: au fur et à mesure *adverb*
  au fur et à mesure = as one goes along
  au fur et à mesure que = as
  au fur et à mesure qu'on fait des progrès
  = as one improves

furieux/furieuse *adjective*
  = furious, angry

fuseau *noun, masculine*
(*plural*) **fuseaux**
  un fuseau = ski pants
un fuseau horaire = a time zone

fusée *noun, feminine*
  une fusée = a rocket

fusil *noun, masculine*
  un fusil = a (shot)gun
  = a rifle
  un coup de fusil = a shot

G g

---

gâcher *verb* 1
  = to waste
  = to spoil

gaffe* *noun, feminine*
* une gaffe = a blunder
* faire gaffe* = to watch out

gagnant/gagnante
1 *adjective*
  = winning
2 *noun, masculine/feminine*
  un gagnant/une gagnante = a winner

gagner *verb* 1
* = to win
* = to earn
  il gagne bien sa vie = he makes a good
  living

* = to save
  gagner du temps = to save time
  gagner de la place = to make more room

gai/gaie *adjective*
  = happy
  = cheerful

gain *noun, masculine*
  c'est un gain de temps = it saves time

gala *noun, masculine*
  un gala = a gala, a gala event

galerie *noun, feminine*
* (*a passage*)
  une galerie = a gallery
* (*on a car*)
  la galerie = the roof rack
* une galerie d'art = an art gallery
une galerie marchande = a shopping
  centre, a shopping mall

galet *noun, masculine*
  un galet = a pebble

galette *noun, feminine*
  une galette = a biscuit, a cookie
  = a pancake
la galette des rois = the Twelfth Night
  cake (*eaten on the Epiphany*)

Galles *noun, plural*
  le pays de Galles = Wales

gallois/galloise
1 *adjective*
  = Welsh
2 gallois *noun, masculine*
  le gallois = Welsh

galop *noun, masculine*
  un galop = a gallop
  au galop = at a gallop

galoper *verb* 1
  = to gallop

gamin/gamine* *noun,*
masculine/feminine
  un gamin*/une gamine* = a kid, a child

gamme *noun, feminine*
* (*of products*)
  une gamme = a range
* (*in music*)
  une gamme = a scale

gant *noun, masculine*
  un gant = a glove
un gant de toilette ≈ a face flannel, a
  wash cloth

garage *noun, masculine*
  un garage = a garage
  un garage à vélos = a bicycle shed

garagiste *noun, masculine/feminine*
  un garagiste/une garagiste = a garage
  owner
  = a car mechanic

garantie *noun, feminine*
une garantie = a guarantee
= a warranty
un bon de garantie = a guarantee

garçon *noun, masculine*
• un garçon = a boy
= a young man
• un garçon (de café) = a waiter
un garçon d'honneur = a best man
un garçon manqué = a tomboy

garde
1 *noun, feminine*
• la garde (*of a child*) = the care
(*of a building*) = guarding
• être de garde (*if it's a doctor*) = to be on call
(*if it's a pharmacist*) = to be on duty
2 *noun, masculine*
un garde = a guard
un garde du corps = a bodyguard

garde-chasse *noun, masculine*
(*plural*) **gardes-chasses**
un garde-chasse = a game warden
= a gamekeeper

garde-fou *noun, masculine*
(*plural*) **garde-fous**
un garde-fou = a parapet
= a safeguard

garder *verb* ⓵
• = to keep (on)
• = to look after
• = to guard

gardien/gardienne *noun,*
masculine/feminine
un gardien/une gardienne (*in a prison*) = a
warder, a guard
(*in a museum*) = an attendant, a museum
security guard
(*on work premises*) = a security guard
(*in an apartment block*) = a caretaker, a
janitor
un gardien de but = a goalkeeper
une gardienne d'enfant = a childminder,
a day-care lady

gare
1 *noun, feminine*
une gare = a railway station
2 *exclamation*
gare à toi! = watch it!
une gare maritime = a harbo(u)r station
une gare routière = a coach station, a bus
station

garer *verb* ⓵
1 (**!** + *avoir*)
= to park
2 se garer (**!** + *être*)
se garer = to park
= to pull over

---

garni/garnie *adjective*
= served with vegetables

gars✶ *noun, masculine* (**!** *never changes*)
• un (petit) gars✶ = a (young) lad, a (young)
guy
• un gars✶ = a chap, a guy

gas-oil *noun, masculine*
le gas-oil = diesel oil, fuel oil

gaspiller *verb* ⓵
= to waste

gâteau *noun, masculine*
(*plural*) **gâteaux**
un gâteau = a cake
le gâteau de riz = rice pudding
un gâteau sec = a biscuit, a cookie

gâter *verb* ⓵
1 (**!** + *avoir*)
• = to spoil
un enfant gâté = a spoiled child
2 se gâter (**!** + *être*)
• (*if it's fruit*)
se gâter = to go bad
• (*if it's the weather*)
se gâter = to take a turn for the worse

gauche
1 *adjective*
• = left
• = awkward
= clumsy
2 *noun, feminine*
la gauche = the left
tournez à gauche = turn left
conduire à gauche = to drive on the left-
hand side

gaucher/gauchère *adjective*
= left-handed

gaufre *noun, feminine*
une gaufre = a waffle

Gaulois/Gauloise *noun,*
masculine/feminine
un Gaulois/une Gauloise = a Gaul

gaz *noun, masculine* (**!** *never changes*)
le gaz = gas
se chauffer au gaz = to have gas heating
le gaz carbonique = carbon dioxide
le gaz de ville = mains gas

gazeux/gazeuse *adjective*
= fizzy, sparkling
une boisson gazeuse = a fizzy drink

gazon *noun, masculine*
le gazon = grass, lawn

géant/géante
1 *adjective*
= huge
2 *noun, masculine/feminine*
un géant/une géante = a giant/a giantess

gel *noun, masculine*
• (*in winter*)
le gel = frost

---

* (*for hair*)
 un gel coiffant = a styling gel

gelé/gelée¹ *adjective*
 = frozen

gelée² *noun, feminine*
* (*on the ground*)
 la gelée = frost
* (*in cooking*)
 la gelée de groseilles = redcurrant jelly

geler *verb* [17]
1 (**!** + *avoir*)
 = to freeze
 il gèle = it's freezing
2 se geler* (**!** + *être*)
 se geler* = to be freezing

gélule *noun, feminine*
 une gélule = a capsule

Gémeaux *noun, masculine plural*
 les Gémeaux = Gemini

gémir *verb* [3]
 = to moan
 = to whimper

gênant/gênante *adjective*
 = embarrassing

gendarme *noun, masculine*
 un gendarme = a gendarme, a French
 policeman

gendarmerie *noun, feminine*
* **la gendarmerie (nationale)** = the
 gendarmerie
* **une gendarmerie** ≈ a police station

gendre *noun, masculine*
 un gendre = a son-in-law

généalogique *adjective*
 un arbre généalogique = a family tree

gêner *verb* [1]
1 (**!** + *avoir*)
* = to disturb
 = to bother
 ça te gêne si j'allume? = do you mind if
 I switch the light on?
* = to be in the way
* = to embarrass
2 se gêner (**!** + *être*)
* **se gêner** = to get in each other's way
* **ne te gêne pas pour moi** = don't mind me

général/générale
(*plural*) **généraux/générales**
1 *adjective*
* = general
 de l'avis général = in most people's
 opinion
 dans l'intérêt général = in the public
 interest
* **en général** = generally
 = usually
2 général *noun, masculine*
 un général = a general

généralement *adverb*
 = generally
 = normally

généraliste *adjective*
* = non-specialized
* **un médecin généraliste** = a general
 practitioner, a GP, a family doctor

généreux/généreuse *adjective*
 = generous

génétique *adjective*
 = genetic

Genève *noun*
 = Geneva

génial/géniale* *adjective*
(*plural*) **géniaux/géniales**
 = brilliant

génie *noun, masculine*
 le génie = genius
 une idée de génie = a brainwave

genou *noun, masculine*
(*plural*) **genoux**
 un genou = a knee
 être sur les genoux de sa mère = to be on
 one's mother's lap
 à genoux = on one's knees
 se mettre à genoux = to kneel down

genre *noun, masculine*
* (*a type*)
 un genre = a kind
 ce genre de travail = this kind of work
 un peu dans le genre de ta robe = a little
 bit like your dress
* (*a look*)
 avoir un drôle de genre = to look a bit
 shady
 pour se donner un genre = to make
 oneself look different
* (*in grammar*)
 le genre = gender
* (*in literature, cinema*)
 un genre = a genre

gens *noun, masculine plural*
 les gens = people

gentil/gentille *adjective*
 = kind, nice

gentillesse *noun, feminine*
 la gentillesse = kindness

gentiment *adverb*
 = nicely, kindly

géographie *noun, feminine*
 la géographie = geography

gérant/gérante *noun,*
masculine/feminine
* (*in a shop*)
 un gérant/une gérante = a manager
* (*for a property*)
 un gérant/une gérante = a managing
 agent

G

gerboise noun, feminine
une gerboise = a gerbil

germain/germaine adjective
un cousin germain = a first cousin

geste noun, masculine
un geste = a movement
= a gesture

gibier noun, masculine
le gibier = game

gifle noun, feminine
une gifle = a slap in the face

gigantesque adjective
= huge, gigantic

gigot noun, masculine
un gigot d'agneau = a leg of lamb

gilet noun, masculine
• un gilet = a cardigan
• un gilet = a waistcoat, a vest
un gilet de sauvetage = a lifejacket

girafe noun, feminine
une girafe = a giraffe

gîte noun, masculine
un gîte rural = a self-catering cottage

givrant adjective, masculine
du brouillard givrant = freezing fog

givre noun, masculine
le givre = frost

glace noun, feminine
• (frozen water)
la glace = ice
• (a confection)
la glace = ice cream
une glace à la vanille = a vanilla ice cream
• (a looking glass)
une glace = a mirror

glacé/glacée adjective
• = ice-cold
= frozen
• = glossy

glaçon noun, masculine
un glaçon = an ice cube

glisser verb 1
1 (! + avoir)
• = to slip
= to slide
• = to be slippery
2 se glisser (! + être)
se glisser dans = to slip into
= to sneak into
= to creep into

globe noun, masculine
le globe (terrestre) = the globe, the Earth

gloire noun, feminine
la gloire = glory, fame

goal noun, masculine
un goal = a goalkeeper

gogo: à gogo✶ adverb
à gogo✶ = galore

golfe noun, masculine
un golfe = a gulf

gomme noun, feminine
• une gomme = a rubber, an eraser
• la gomme = gum

gonflé/gonflée adjective
• = inflated
• = swollen
• être gonflé✶ = to have a nerve
= to have guts

gonfler verb 1
• = to inflate
• = to swell (up)

gorge noun, feminine
la gorge = the throat
avoir mal à la gorge = to have a sore throat
avoir la gorge serrée = to have a lump in
one's throat

gorgée noun, feminine
une gorgée = a sip
= a gulp

gorille noun, masculine
• un gorille = a gorilla
• un gorille✶ = a bodyguard

gosse✶ noun, masculine/feminine
un gosse✶/une gosse✶ = a kid, a child

goudron noun, masculine
le goudron = tar

goudronner verb 1
= to tarmac, to blacktop

gourde noun, feminine
une gourde = a gourd
= a flask

gourmand/gourmande adjective
être gourmand = to be fond of good food
(to like sweet things) = to have a sweet
tooth

goût noun, masculine
le goût = taste

goûter
1 verb 1
= to taste
2 noun, masculine
• le goûter = an afternoon snack
• un goûter = a children's party

goutte noun, feminine
une goutte = a drop
goutte à goutte = drop by drop

grâce
1 noun, feminine
la grâce = grace
2 grâce à = thanks to

✶ in informal situations

gradins noun, masculine plural
les gradins = the terraces, the bleachers

graine noun, feminine
une graine = a seed

graisse noun, feminine
la graisse (in food) = fat
(for machinery) = grease

graisser verb [1]
= to grease
= to lubricate

grammaire noun, feminine
la grammaire = grammar

gramme noun, masculine
un gramme = a gram

grand/grande
1 adjective
• = tall
= big, large
= long
Théo est grand = Théo is tall
un grand jardin = a large garden
un grand voyage = a long journey
il n'y avait pas grand monde = there
weren't many people
faire de grands gestes = to wave one's
arms around
• = great
un grand homme = a great man
un train à grande vitesse = a high-speed
train
2 grand adverb
= wide
grand ouvert = wide open
voir grand = to think big
le grand bassin = the main pool
un grand magasin = a department store
le grand public = the general public
une grande personne = a grown-up
une grande surface = a supermarket
les grandes lignes = main train routes
les grandes vacances = the summer
holidays, the summer vacation

grand-chose pronoun
pas grand-chose = not much, not a lot
ça ne sert pas à grand-chose = it's not
much use

Grande-Bretagne noun, feminine
la Grande-Bretagne = Great Britain

grandir verb [3]
= to grow

grand-mère noun, feminine
(plural) **grands-mères**
une grand-mère = a grandmother

grand-père noun, masculine
(plural) **grands-pères**
un grand-père = a grandfather

grands-parents noun, masculine plural
des grands-parents = grandparents

grange noun, feminine
une grange = a barn

granulé noun, masculine
un granulé = a granule

graphique
1 adjective
= graphic
2 noun, masculine
un graphique = a graph

grappe noun, feminine
une grappe = a bunch
= a cluster

gras/grasse
1 adjective
• = greasy
= fatty
= fat
• (if it's a letter) = bold
2 gras noun, masculine (**!** never changes)
le gras (on meat) = fat

gratin noun, masculine
un gratin = a gratin (a dish topped with
browned cheese and breadcrumbs)
un gratin de pommes de terre = potatoes
au gratin

gratis
1 adjective (**!** never changes)
= free
2 adverb
= free, for free

gratter verb [1]
1 (**!** + avoir)
• = to scratch
= to scrape (off)
• ça me gratte partout = I'm itching all over
2 se gratter (**!** + être)
se gratter = to scratch

gratuit/gratuite adjective
= free

gratuitement adverb
= free, for free
travailler gratuitement = to work for
nothing

grave adjective
• = serious
• = grave, solemn
• une voix grave = a deep voice

gravement adverb
• = seriously
• = gravely, solemnly

gravier noun, masculine
du gravier = gravel

gravillon noun, masculine
un gravillon = a bit of grit, some grit

grec/grecque
1 adjective
= Greek
2 grec noun, masculine
le grec = Greek

G

Grèce noun, feminine
la Grèce = Greece

grecque ▶ grec 1

grêle noun, feminine
la grêle = hail
il tombe de la grêle = it's hailing

grêlon noun, masculine
un grêlon = a hailstone

grelotter verb 1
= to shiver

grenier noun, masculine
un grenier = an attic, a loft

grenouille noun, feminine
une grenouille = a frog

grève noun, feminine
* (at work)
une grève = a strike
faire grève = to go on strike
* (by the sea)
la grève = the shore
une grève de la faim = a hunger strike

griffe noun, feminine
une griffe = a claw

griffer verb 1
= to scratch

grignoter verb 1
= to nibble

grillade noun, feminine
une grillade = grilled meat

grillage noun, masculine
le grillage = wire netting

grille noun, feminine
* (in a garden)
une grille = a gate
* (for a crossword)
une grille = a grid

grille-pain noun, masculine (! never changes)
un grille-pain = a toaster

griller verb 1
* (in cooking)
(faire) griller = to grill
= to toast
* griller* un feu = to go through a red light

grimace noun, feminine
une grimace = a (funny) face
faire des grimaces = to make faces
faire la grimace devant un plat = to turn one's nose up at a dish

grimper verb 1
= to climb

grippe noun, feminine
la grippe = flu

gris/grise adjective
* = grey, gray
* = dull, dreary
un temps gris = dull weather

grive noun, feminine
une grive = a thrush

grognon adjective
= grumpy, grouchy

gros/grosse
1 adjective
* = big
* = heavy
un gros fumeur = a heavy smoker
2 gros adverb
* écrire gros = to write in big letters
* perdre gros = to lose a lot
3 gros noun, masculine (! never changes)
* le gros du travail = the bulk of the work
* le prix de gros = the wholesale price
4 en gros
* en gros = roughly
* en gros = wholesale
* en gros = in big letters
le gros lot = the first prize
un gros mot = a swearword
les gros titres = the headlines

groseille noun, feminine
une groseille = a redcurrant
une groseille à maquereau = a gooseberry

grosse ▶ gros 1

grossier/grossière adjective
* = rude
* = coarse

grotte noun, feminine
une grotte = a cave
= a grotto

groupe noun, masculine
un groupe = a group
un groupe scolaire = a school

guépard noun, masculine
un guépard = a cheetah

guêpe noun, feminine
une guêpe = a wasp

guère adverb
= hardly
il n'avait guère le choix = he didn't really have a choice

guérir verb 3
= to cure
= to heal
= to recover

guerre noun, feminine
une guerre = a war

guetter verb 1
= to watch
= to watch out for

---

* in informal situations

gueule *noun, feminine*
une gueule = a mouth
avoir une grande gueule✱ = to have a big
  mouth

gui *noun, masculine*
le gui = mistletoe

guichet *noun, masculine*
un guichet (*in a bank, a post office*) = a
  counter
  = a window
  (*in a museum, a station*) = a ticket office
  (*in a theatre, a cinema*) = a box office
un guichet automatique = an automatic
  cash dispenser

guide *noun, masculine*
un guide = a guide

guidon *noun, masculine*
le guidon = the handlebars

guignol *noun, masculine*
un guignol = a puppet show

guillemets *noun, masculine plural*
des guillemets = inverted commas
  = quotation marks

guitare *noun, feminine*
une guitare = a guitar

gym✱ *noun, feminine*
• (*at school*)
  la gym✱ = physical education
• (*as a sport*)
  la gym✱ = gymnastics

gymnase *noun, masculine*
un gymnase = a gymnasium

gymnastique *noun, feminine*
la gymnastique (*the sport*) = gymnastics
  (*to keep fit*) = exercise

Hh

---

habile *adjective*
  = clever
  = skil(l)ful

habiller *verb* 1
1 (**!** + *avoir*)
  = to dress
2 s'habiller (**!** + *être*)
  s'habiller = to get dressed
  = to dress up

habitant/habitante *noun,*
masculine/feminine
  un habitant/une habitante = an inhabitant

habiter *verb* 1
  = to live (in)
  habiter la campagne = to live in the
    country
  habiter à Paris = to live in Paris

habitude
1 *noun, feminine*
  une habitude = a habit
  avoir l'habitude de se lever tôt = to be in
    the habit of getting up early
    = to be used to getting up early
  avoir l'habitude des enfants = to be used
    to children
2 d'habitude = usually
  comme d'habitude = as usual

habituel/habituelle *adjective*
  = usual

haché/hachée *adjective*
  = minced
  = chopped

hachis *noun, masculine* (**!** *never changes*)
  le hachis = minced, ground meat
le hachis Parmentier = shepherd's pie

haie *noun, feminine*
  une haie = a hedge

haleine *noun, feminine*
  l'haleine = the breath
  hors d'haleine = out of breath

halte *noun, feminine*
  une halte (*a pause*) = a stop
    (*a place*) = a stopping place
  faire halte = to stop

haltérophilie *noun, feminine*
  l'haltérophilie = weightlifting

hameau *noun, masculine*
(*plural*) **hameaux**
  un hameau = a hamlet

hameçon *noun, masculine*
  un hameçon = a fish-hook

hanche *noun, feminine*
  une hanche = a hip

handicapé/handicapée
1 *adjective*
  = handicapped
2 *noun, masculine/feminine*
  un handicapé/une handicapée = a
    handicapped person

hanté/hantée *adjective*
  = haunted

hareng *noun, masculine*
  un hareng = a herring

haricot *noun, masculine*
  un haricot = a bean
les haricots verts = French beans

hasard *noun, masculine*
  le hasard = chance
  un hasard = a coincidence

hâte noun, feminine
- la hâte = haste
  à la hâte = hastily
- j'ai hâte de partir = I can't wait to leave

hausse noun, feminine
une hausse = a rise, an increase

hausser verb 1
= to raise
hausser les épaules = to shrug one's shoulders

haut/haute
1 adjective
- = high
  = tall
- à haute voix = aloud
  = loudly
2 **haut** adverb
- = high
  haut les mains! = hands up!
- = loud(ly)
  tout haut = aloud
3 **haut** noun, masculine
- le haut = the top
  les pièces du haut = the upstairs rooms
- faire 15 mètres de haut = to be 15 metres high
4 **en haut** = at the top
  = upstairs

hauteur noun, masculine
la hauteur = the height

Haye noun, feminine
la Haye = the Hague

hebdomadaire adjective
= weekly

hébergement noun, masculine
l'hébergement = accommodation, lodging

héberger verb 13
= to put up

hein* exclamation
- hein*? = what?
- tu n'iras pas, hein*? = you won't go, will you?

hélas exclamation
hélas! = unfortunately!

hélice noun, feminine
une hélice = a propeller

hélicoptère noun, masculine
un hélicoptère = a helicopter

herbe noun, feminine
- de l'herbe = grass
- une herbe = a(n) herb
- une mauvaise herbe = a weed

hérisson noun, masculine
un hérisson = a hedgehog

héritage noun, masculine
un héritage = an inheritance

hériter verb 1
= to inherit

héritier/héritière noun, masculine/feminine
un héritier/une héritière = an heir/an heiress

héros noun, masculine (! never changes)
un héros = a hero

hésiter verb 1
= to hesitate

heure noun, feminine
- l'heure = the time
  quelle heure est-il? = what time is it?
  il est huit heures = it's eight o'clock
  il est huit heures dix = it's ten past eight
  il est huit heures moins dix = it's ten to eight
  l'heure du déjeuner = lunchtime
  être à l'heure = to be on time
  de bonne heure = early
  mettre sa montre à l'heure = to set one's watch
- une heure = an hour
  toutes les trois heures = every three hours
  faire du 100 à l'heure* = to do 100 km per hour
  les heures d'affluence = peak times
  les heures de pointe = the rush hour
  les heures supplémentaires = overtime

heureuse ▶ heureux

heureusement adverb
= fortunately
= luckily

heureux/heureuse adjective
= happy

heurter verb 1
= to bump into
= to hit, to crash into

hibou noun, masculine
(plural) **hiboux**
un hibou = an owl

hier adverb
= yesterday
hier soir = yesterday evening

hippodrome noun, masculine
un hippodrome = a racecourse

hippopotame noun, masculine
un hippopotame = a hippopotamus

hirondelle noun, feminine
une hirondelle = a swallow

histoire noun, feminine
- l'histoire = history
- une histoire = a story
- faire des histoires* = to make trouble

historique adjective
• = historic
• = historical

hit-parade noun, masculine
(plural) **hit-parades**
le hit-parade = the charts

hiver noun, masculine
l'hiver = winter

HLM noun, masculine or feminine
un(e) HLM ≈ a council flat, a low-rent
apartment
= a block of council flats, a low-rent
apartment building

hocher verb [1]
hocher la tête (in agreement) = to nod
(to say no) = to shake one's head

hollandais/hollandaise
1 adjective
= Dutch
2 hollandais noun, masculine
le hollandais = Dutch

Hollande noun, feminine
la Hollande = Holland

homard noun, masculine
un homard = a lobster

homme noun, masculine
un homme = a man
un homme d'affaires = a businessman

Hongrie noun, feminine
la Hongrie = Hungary

hongrois/hongroise
1 adjective
= Hungarian
2 hongrois noun, masculine
le hongrois = Hungarian

honnête adjective
= honest

honoraire
1 adjective
= honorary
2 honoraires noun, masculine plural
les honoraires = the fee(s)

honte noun, feminine
la honte = shame
avoir honte = to be ashamed

hôpital noun, masculine
(plural) **hôpitaux**
un hôpital = a hospital

hoquet noun, masculine
le hoquet = hiccoughs, hiccups

horaire noun, masculine
un horaire = a timetable
les horaires à la carte, les horaires
libres = flexitime, flextime

horizon noun, masculine
l'horizon = the horizon
à l'horizon = on the horizon

horizontal/horizontale adjective
(plural) **horizontaux/horizontales**
= horizontal, flat

horizontalement adverb
• = horizontally
• (in a crossword) = across

horloge noun, feminine
une horloge = a clock

horloger/horlogère noun,
masculine/feminine
un horloger/une horlogère = a
watchmaker

horreur noun, feminine
• l'horreur = horror
quelle horreur! = how horrible!
= it's hideous!
• l'horreur = loathing
avoir horreur de laver la voiture = to loathe
washing the car

horrible adjective
= awful, horrible

hors preposition
hors (de) = outside, out of
hors d'haleine = out of breath
hors jeu = offside
hors de prix = ridiculously expensive
hors (de) saison = out of season
'hors service' = 'out of order'
hors taxes, HT (describing a shop) = duty-
free
(describing a price) = excluding tax
hors d'usage = worn out

hors-d'œuvre noun, masculine (! never
changes)
un hors-d'œuvre = a starter

hospitalité noun, feminine
l'hospitalité = hospitality

hôte
1 noun, masculine
un hôte = a host
2 noun, masculine/feminine
un hôte/une hôte = a guest

hôtel noun, masculine
un hôtel = a hotel
l'hôtel de ville = the town hall

hôtelier/hôtelière noun,
masculine/feminine
un hôtelier/une hôtelière = a hotel-keeper,
a hotel manager

hôtesse noun, feminine
• (a person who has guests)
une hôtesse = a hostess
• (a person who deals with customers)
une hôtesse (in a firm) = a receptionist
(on a train, a boat) = a stewardess
une hôtesse d'accueil = a receptionist
une hôtesse de l'air = a flight attendant,
an air hostess

H

houx *noun, masculine* (**!** *never changes*)
le houx = holly

HT ▶ hors

hublot *noun, masculine*
un hublot = a porthole

huile *noun, feminine*
l'huile = oil

huissier *noun, masculine*
un huissier (de justice) = a bailiff

huit *number*
= eight
huit jours = a week
= eight days
lundi en huit = a week on Monday

huitaine *noun, feminine*
une huitaine = about a week
= about eight

huitante *number*
= eighty

huitième *number*
= eighth

huître *noun, feminine*
une huître = an oyster

humain/humaine *adjective*
• = human
• = humane

humeur *noun, feminine*
une humeur = a mood
être de bonne humeur = to be in a good
mood
être de mauvaise humeur = to be in a bad
mood

humide *adjective*
= damp
= humid

hurlement *noun, masculine*
un hurlement = a howl

hurler *verb* ⨍1⨍
= to howl

hydroglisseur *noun, masculine*
un hydroglisseur = a hydrofoil

hydrophile *adjective*
= absorbent

hygiénique *adjective*
le papier hygiénique = toilet paper

hyper× *adverb*
= extremely

hypermarché *noun, masculine*
un hypermarché = a hypermarket, a large
supermarket

× *in informal situations*

I i

ici *adverb*
= here
venez par ici = come this way

idéal/idéale *adjective*
(*plural*) **idéaux/idéales**
= ideal

idée *noun, feminine*
une idée = an idea

identifier *verb* ⨍2⨍
= to identify

identité *noun, feminine*
l'identité = identity

idiot/idiote
1 *adjective*
= stupid
2 *noun, masculine/feminine*
un idiot/une idiote = an idiot

ignorer *verb* ⨍1⨍
• = not to know
j'ignore où il habite = I don't know where
he lives
• = to ignore

il *pronoun, masculine*
1 (*referring to a person, an animal or a thing*)
= he
= it
ils = they
2 (*impersonal use*)
• = it
il fait froid = it's cold
il est facile d'obtenir des billets = it's easy
to get tickets
• il y a = there is
= there are
il y a une fuite = there is a leak
• (*when talking about time*)
il y a une heure que j'attends = I've been
waiting for an hour
il y a un an qu'il est parti = he left a year
ago

île *noun, feminine*
une île = an island
les îles Anglo-Normandes = the Channel
Islands

illégal/illégale *adjective*
(*plural*) **illégaux/illégales**
= illegal

illettré/illettrée *adjective*
= illiterate

illimité/illimitée *adjective*
= unlimited

illisible adjective
• = illegible
• = unreadable

illuminé/illuminée adjective
= lit up
= illuminated

illustre adjective
= illustrious

illustré noun, masculine
un illustré = an illustrated magazine
= a comic, a comic book

illustrer verb [1]
= to illustrate

ils pronoun, masculine plural
= they

image noun, feminine
une image = a picture
= an image

imaginaire adjective
= imaginary

imaginer verb [1]
= to imagine

imbattable adjective
= unbeatable

imbécile noun, masculine/feminine
un imbécile/une imbécile = an idiot
faire l'imbécile = to be silly

imiter verb [1]
= to imitate

immatriculation noun, feminine
l'immatriculation = registration
= the registration number

immédiatement adverb
= immediately

immense adjective
= huge
= great

immeuble noun, masculine
un immeuble = a building
= a block of flats, an apartment block

immigré/immigrée adjective
= immigrant

immobile adjective
= still

immobilier noun, masculine
l'immobilier = property, real estate

impair/impaire adjective
les nombres impairs = odd numbers

imparfait/imparfaite
1 adjective
= imperfect
2 imparfait noun, masculine
l'imparfait = the imperfect (tense)

impasse noun, feminine
une impasse = a cul-de-sac, a dead end

impatienter: s'impatienter [1]
(**!** + être)
s'impatienter = to get impatient

imper* noun, masculine
un imper* = a mac, a raincoat

imperméable
1 noun, masculine
un imperméable = a raincoat
2 adjective
= waterproof

impoli/impolie adjective
= impolite, rude

important/importante adjective
= important
= considerable
= sizeable

importer verb [1]
• = to import
• = to be important
il importe de [faire | dire | savoir …] = it's
    important to [do | say | know]
n'importe
n'importe lequel = any
n'importe où = anywhere
n'importe quel = any
n'importe qui = anybody
n'importe quoi = anything

impôt noun, masculine
un impôt = a tax

impressionnant/impressionnante
adjective
= impressive

impressionner verb [1]
= to impress

imprévu/imprévue adjective
= unexpected

imprimé/imprimée
1 adjective
= printed
2 imprimé noun, masculine
• (paper)
un imprimé = a leaflet
• (on material)
un imprimé = a print

imprimer verb [1]
= to print

imprimeur noun, masculine
un imprimeur = a printer

improviser verb [1]
= to improvise

improviste: à l'improviste adverb
à l'improviste = unexpectedly

imprudence noun, feminine
• l'imprudence = recklessness
• faire une imprudence = to do something
reckless

imprudent/imprudente adjective
= reckless

inabordable *adjective*
* (*describing a price*) = prohibitive, unaffordable
* (*describing a person*) = unapproachable

inadmissible *adjective*
= unacceptable

inattendu/inattendue *adjective*
= unexpected

incapable *adjective*
= incompetent
être incapable de conduire = to be incapable of driving
= to be unable to drive

incendie *noun, masculine*
un incendie = a fire

incident *noun, masculine*
un incident = an incident

inclus/incluse *adjective*
* = including
* = enclosed

inconnu/inconnue
1 *adjective*
= unknown
2 *noun, masculine/feminine*
un inconnu/une inconnue = a stranger
= an unknown man/woman

inconvénient *noun, masculine*
un inconvénient = a drawback, a disadvantage
si vous n'y voyez pas d'inconvénient = if you have no objection

incroyable *adjective*
= unbelievable

incroyablement *adverb*
= incredibly

inculpé/inculpée *noun, masculine/feminine*
l'inculpé/l'inculpée = the accused

inculper *verb* 1
= to charge
on l'a inculpé de meurtre = he's been charged with murder

Inde *noun, feminine*
l'Inde = India

indemne *adjective*
= unharmed

indépendant/indépendante *adjective*
= independent

index *noun, masculine* (**!** *never changes*)
l'index = the index finger, the forefinger

indicateur *noun, masculine*
* (*a book giving information*)
un indicateur (*for trains*) = a timetable
(*for streets*) = a directory
* (*an instrument*)
un indicateur = a gauge

indicatif *noun, masculine*
* (*when making a phone call*)
l'indicatif = the dialling code, the area code
* (*of a radio or TV programme*)
l'indicatif = the signature tune, the theme music
* (*in grammar*)
l'indicatif = the indicative

indice *noun, masculine*
un indice = a sign, an indication
(*in a police inquiry*) = a clue

indien/indienne *adjective*
= Indian

indigestion *noun, feminine*
une indigestion = a stomach upset

indigner: s'indigner *verb* 1 (**!** + *être*)
s'indigner = to be indignant

indiquer *verb* 1
* (*with one's hand*) = to indicate, to point to
* (*to give information*) = to tell
pouvez-vous m'indiquer la banque la plus proche? = could you tell me where the nearest bank is?
je leur ai indiqué le moyen d'entrer sans payer = I told them how to get in for free
il m'a indiqué un bon restaurant = he recommended a good restaurant
indiquez votre nom et votre adresse = give your name and address
* (*to display information*) = to show
le village n'est pas indiqué sur la carte = the village isn't shown on the map
* (*to be a sign or a clue*) = to suggest
rien n'indique qu'il changera d'avis = there's nothing to suggest that he'll change his mind

individu *noun, masculine*
un individu = an individual
= a person

individuel/individuelle *adjective*
= individual

industrie *noun, feminine*
l'industrie = industry

industriel/industrielle *adjective*
= industrial

inédit/inédite *adjective*
* = (previously) unpublished
* = new

infect/infecte *adjective*
= horrible, revolting

infecter: s'infecter *verb* 1 (**!** + *être*)
s'infecter = to become infected, to go septic

inférieur/inférieure *adjective*
* = lower
* = inferior

infirme
1 *adjective*
= disabled
2 *noun, masculine|feminine*
un infirme/une infirme = a disabled person

infirmerie *noun, feminine*
l'infirmerie = the sick bay

infirmier/infirmière *noun,*
masculine|feminine
un infirmier/une infirmière = a nurse

inflammable *adjective*
= flammable

infliger *verb* 13
= to inflict

informaticien/informaticienne
noun, masculine|feminine
un informaticien/une informaticienne = a
computer scientist

informations *noun, feminine plural*
les informations = the news

informatique *noun, feminine*
l'informatique = computer science,
computing

informer *verb* 1
1 (! + *avoir*)
= to inform
2 **s'informer** (! + *être*)
• s'informer = to keep oneself informed
• s'informer de = to enquire about

ingénieur *noun, masculine*
un ingénieur = an engineer

ingrat/ingrate *adjective*
• (*not thankful*) = ungrateful
• (*not pretty*) = unattractive

inhabité/inhabitée *adjective*
= uninhabited

inhabituel/inhabituelle *adjective*
= unusual

inhumer *verb* 1
= to bury

initiale *noun, feminine*
une initiale = an initial

injure *noun, feminine*
une injure = an insult

injuste *adjective*
= unfair

inquiet/inquiète *adjective*
= worried, anxious

inquiéter *verb* 14
1 (! + *avoir*)
= to worry
2 **s'inquiéter** (! + *être*)
s'inquiéter = to worry

inquiétude *noun, feminine*
l'inquiétude = worry

inscrire *verb* 42
1 (! + *avoir*)
• = to enrol(l), to register
• = to write down
2 **s'inscrire** (! + *être*)
s'inscrire = to register
= to enrol

inscrit/inscrite ▶ **inscrire** 42

insecte *noun, masculine*
un insecte = an insect

insolation *noun, feminine*
une insolation = sunstroke

insolent/insolente *adjective*
= insolent, cheeky

insomniaque *adjective*
= insomniac, unable to sleep

inspecter *verb* 1
= to inspect

inspecteur/inspectrice *noun,*
masculine|feminine
un inspecteur/une inspectrice = an
inspector
un inspecteur de police = a detective
constable, a police detective

inspirer *verb* 1
1 (! + *avoir*)
• = to inspire
• = to breathe in
2 **s'inspirer de** (! + *être*)
s'inspirer de = to be inspired by, to draw
one's inspiration from

installation
1 *noun, feminine*
• (*the fact of fitting*)
l'installation = installing, putting in
• (*going to new premises*)
une installation = a move
2 **installations** *noun, feminine plural*
des installations = facilities
des installations sanitaires = toilets

installer *verb* 1
1 (! + *avoir*)
• (*to fit*) = to install, to put in
(*if it's gas, water, electricity*) = to connect
faire installer le téléphone = to have the
telephone connected
• (*to position*)
installer une tente sous un arbre = to put
up a tent under a tree
installer un invité dans un fauteuil = to sit
a guest in an armchair
2 **s'installer** (! + *être*)
s'installer dans une ville = to settle in a
town
s'installer près du feu = to sit by the fire

instant *noun, masculine*
un instant = a moment
à chaque instant = constantly

instinctivement *adverb*
= instinctively

instituteur/institutrice *noun,*
masculine/feminine
  un instituteur/une institutrice = a (primary
  school) teacher

instruction *noun, feminine*
• des instructions = instructions
• l'instruction = education
l'instruction civique = social studies
l'instruction religieuse = religious
  education

instrument *noun, masculine*
  un instrument = an instrument
un instrument de musique = a musical
  instrument

insuffisant/insuffisante *adjective*
  = insufficient

insulter *verb* [1]
  = to insult

insupportable *adjective*
  = unbearable

intelligent/intelligente *adjective*
  = intelligent, clever

intention *noun, feminine*
  une intention = an intention
  avoir l'intention de voyager = to intend to
  travel

interdire *verb* [40]
  = to forbid
  elle nous a interdit de sortir = she forbade
  us to go out

interdit/interdite *adjective*
  = forbidden, not allowed
  'baignade interdite' = 'no swimming'

intéressant/intéressante *adjective*
  = interesting

intéresser *verb* [1]
1 (**!** + *avoir*)
  = to interest
  ça ne m'intéresse pas = I'm not interested
2 s'intéresser (**!** + *être*)
  s'intéresser à = to be interested in

intérêt *noun, masculine*
  un intérêt = an interest

intérieur/intérieure
1 *adjective*
  = inside
  = inner
2 extérieur *noun, masculine*
  l'intérieur = the inside
  à l'intérieur de la boîte = inside the box

internat *noun, masculine*
  un internat = a boarding school

interne
1 *adjective*
  = internal

2 *noun, masculine/feminine*
  un interne/une interne (*a pupil*) = a
  boarder, a boarding student

Internet *noun, masculine*
  l'Internet = the Internet

interprète *noun, masculine/feminine*
  un interprète/une interprète = an
  interpreter

interro* *noun, feminine*
(*abbreviation of* **interrogation**)
  une interro* = a test

interrogation *noun, feminine*
• (*in class*)
  une interrogation = a test
  une interrogation écrite = a written test
• (*in grammar*)
  une interrogation = a question

interroger *verb* [13]
• = to question
• = to test

interviewer *verb* [1]
  = to interview

intituler *verb* [1]
1 (**!** + *avoir*)
  = to call, to entitle
2 s'intituler (**!** + *être*)
  s'intituler = to be called

intoxication *noun, feminine*
  une intoxication alimentaire = food
  poisoning

introduire *verb* [62]
1 (**!** + *avoir*)
  = to insert
2 s'introduire dans (**!** + *être*)
  s'introduire dans (*to go in*) = to enter

intrus/intruse *noun, masculine/feminine*
(*a person*)
  un intrus/une intruse = an intruder

inutile *adjective*
  = useless
  = pointless

inutilisable *adjective*
  = unusable

inventer *verb* [1]
• = to invent
• = to think up

inverse *noun, masculine*
  l'inverse = the opposite

invité/invitée *noun, masculine/feminine*
  un invité/une invitée = a guest

inviter *verb* [1]
  = to invite

irai ▶ aller 1 [9]

irlandais/irlandaise
1 *adjective*
  = Irish

---

* in informal situations

2 irlandais *noun, masculine*
l'irlandais = Irish

Irlande *noun, feminine*
l'Irlande = Ireland
la République d'Irlande = the Republic of Ireland
l'Irlande du Nord = Northern Ireland

irriter *verb* 1
= to irritate

islamique *adjective*
= Islamic

isolé/isolée *adjective*
= isolated
= lonely

issue *noun, feminine*
une issue = an exit, a way out
une issue de secours = an emergency exit
'voie sans issue' = 'no through road'

Italie *noun, feminine*
l'Italie = Italy

italien/italienne
1 *adjective*
= Italian
2 italien *noun, masculine*
l'italien = Italian

italique *noun, masculine*
en italique(s) = in italics

itinéraire *noun, masculine*
un itinéraire = a route, an itinerary
'itinéraire bis' = 'alternative route'

ivoire *noun, masculine*
l'ivoire = ivory

ivre *adjective*
= drunk

ivresse *noun, feminine*
l'ivresse = drunkenness, intoxication

ivrogne *noun, masculine/feminine*
un ivrogne/une ivrogne = a drunkard

Jj

j' ▶ je

jadis *adverb*
= in the past, a long time ago

jaloux/jalouse *adjective*
= jealous

jamaïcain/jamaïcaine *adjective*
= Jamaican

Jamaïque *noun, feminine*
la Jamaïque = Jamaica

jamais *adverb*
• (*at no time*) = never
= ever
il n'écrit jamais = he never writes
plus jamais = never again
rien n'est jamais certain = nothing is ever certain
• (*at any other time*) = ever
il fait plus froid que jamais = it's colder than ever

jambe *noun, feminine*
une jambe = a leg

jambon *noun, masculine*
le jambon = ham

janvier *noun, masculine*
janvier = January

Japon *noun, masculine*
le Japon = Japan

japonais/japonaise
1 *adjective*
= Japanese
2 japonais *noun, masculine*
le japonais = Japanese

jardin *noun, masculine*
un jardin = a garden, a yard
faire son jardin = to work in one's garden
un jardin potager = a vegetable garden
un jardin public = a park
un jardin zoologique = a zoo

jardinage *noun, masculine*
le jardinage = gardening

jardinier/jardinière *noun,*
masculine/feminine
un jardinier/une jardinière = a gardener

jaune *adjective*
= yellow

javelot *noun, masculine*
un javelot = a javelin

J.-C. (*abbreviation of* **Jésus-Christ**)
avant J.-C. = BC
après J.-C. = AD

je (**j'** *before vowel or mute h*) *pronoun*
= I

jean *noun, masculine*
un jean = (a pair of) jeans

jetable *adjective*
= disposable

jeter *verb* 20
= to throw (away)

jeton *noun, masculine*
un jeton = a counter

jeu *noun, masculine*
(*plural*) **jeux**
• (*the activity*)
un jeu = a game
faire un jeu = to play a game

* (*the equipment*)
  un jeu = a set
  un jeu d'échecs = a chess set
un jeu de mots = a pun
le jeu de l'oie ≈ snakes and ladders,
  chutes and ladders
un jeu de société = a board game
  = a party game
un jeu télévisé = a game show
les jeux Olympiques = the Olympic
  Games

jeudi *noun, masculine*
  jeudi = Thursday

jeun: à jeun *adverb*
  être à jeun = to have had nothing to eat

jeune
1 *adjective*
  = young
2 *noun, masculine*
  un jeune = a youth, a lad
  les jeunes = young people
  une jeune fille = a girl
  un jeune homme = a young man

jeunesse *noun, feminine*
* (*the young years*)
  la jeunesse = youth
* (*young boys and girls*)
  la jeunesse = young people

jf (*abbreviation of* **jeune fille**)
  = young woman

jh (*abbreviation of* **jeune homme**)
  = young man

Joconde *noun, feminine*
  la Joconde = the Mona Lisa

joie *noun, feminine*
  la joie = joy

joindre *verb* 56
1 (! + *avoir*)
* (*to add*) = to attach
  = to enclose
* (*to link, to fasten*) = to join
  = to put together
* (*to make contact*) = to get hold of
  = to get in touch with
2 se joindre à (! + *être*)
  se joindre à = to join

joli/jolie *adjective*
  = pretty, attractive
  = nice

jongler *verb* 1
  = to juggle

jongleur/jongleuse *noun,*
masculine/feminine
  un jongleur/une jongleuse = a juggler

jonquille *noun, feminine*
  une jonquille = a daffodil

joue *noun, feminine*
  une joue = a cheek

jouer *verb* 1
* = to play
  jouer à [cache-cache | la marelle | colin-
    maillard ...] = to play [hide-and-seek |
    hopscotch | blind man's buff ...]
  jouer aux cartes = to play cards
  à quoi jouez-vous? = what are you
    playing?
  jouer de [la guitare | la flûte | la harpe ...] = to
    play [the guitar | the flute | the harp ...]
  jouer du piano = to play the piano
  de quoi joue-t-il? = what does he play?
* = to gamble
* qu'est-ce qu'on joue au théâtre? = what's
  on at the theatre?, what's showing at the
  theater?

jouet *noun, masculine*
  un jouet = a toy

joueur/joueuse *noun,*
masculine/feminine
  un joueur/une joueuse (*in a game, in sport*)
    = a player
  (*at the casino*) = a gambler
  être mauvais joueur = to be a bad loser

jour *noun, masculine*
* (*24 hours*)
  un jour = a day
  tous les jours = every day
  par jour = per day
  un jour de congé = a day off
  il y a quinze jours = a fortnight ago, two
    weeks ago
  de nos jours = nowadays
* (*the light*)
  le jour = daylight
  il fait jour = it's daylight
  en plein jour = in broad daylight
  voyager de jour = to travel by day, to
    travel in the daytime
le jour de l'An = New Year's (Day)
un jour férié = a bank holiday, a legal
  holiday
le jour J = D-day
un jour ouvrable = a working day

journal *noun, masculine*
(*plural*) **journaux**
* (*a publication*)
  un journal = a newspaper
* (*a private record*)
  un journal (intime) = a diary
le journal télévisé = the TV news

journaliste *noun, masculine/feminine*
  un journaliste/une journaliste = a
    journalist

journée *noun, feminine*
  une journée = a day
  dans la journée = during the day

joyeux/joyeuse *adjective*
  = happy

juger *verb* 13
= to judge

juif/juive
1 *adjective*
= Jewish
2 *noun, masculine/feminine*
un juif/une juive = a Jew

juillet *noun, masculine*
juillet = July
le 14 juillet = Bastille Day

juin *noun, masculine*
juin = June

juive ▶ juif

jumeau/jumelle
(*plural*) **jumeaux/jumelles**
1 *adjective*
= twin
2 *noun, masculine/feminine*
un jumeau/une jumelle = a (male) twin/a
(female) twin
des jumeaux/des jumelles = twins ·

jumelage *noun, masculine*
un jumelage = a (town) twinning

jumelé/jumelée *adjective*
= twinned
Oxford est jumelé avec Grenoble = the
city of Oxford is twinned with Grenoble

jumelles *noun, feminine plural*
des jumelles = binoculars

jupe *noun, feminine*
une jupe = a skirt

jurer *verb* 1
= to swear

jus *noun, masculine* (**!** *never changes*)
• (*from fruit*)
du jus = juice
un jus de fruit = a fruit juice
• (*from a roast*)
le jus = the gravy

jusque (**jusqu'** *before vowel*)
1 *preposition*
• = as far as
aller jusqu'à Rome = to go as far as Rome
• = up to
= down to
de l'eau jusqu'à la taille = water up to the
waist
se pencher jusqu'à terre = to bend down
to the ground
• = until, till
jusqu'à lundi = until Monday
jusqu'à l'an 2000 = until the year 2000
jusqu'ici, jusqu'à présent = till now, up to
now
2 jusqu'à ce que = until

juste
1 *adjective*
• = right, correct
une réponse juste = a correct answer
• = fair
ce n'est pas juste = it's not fair, it's unfair
• = tight
2 *adverb*
• chanter juste = to sing in tune
• il est huit heures juste = it's exactly eight
o'clock
• tout juste = only just
il arrive juste = he's (only) just arrived
juste à temps = just in time
3 au juste = exactly

justement *adverb*
= exactly

kaki
1 *adjective* (**!** *never changes*)
= khaki
2 *noun, masculine*
un kaki = a persimmon

kangourou *noun, masculine*
un kangourou = a kangaroo

karting *noun, masculine*
le karting = go-karting

kayak *noun, masculine*
• (*the equipment*)
un kayak = a kayak
• (*the sport*)
le kayak = canoeing

kermesse *noun, feminine*
une kermesse = a fête, a festival

kilo, kilogramme *noun, masculine*
un kilo, un kilogramme = a kilo, a
kilogram

kilomètre *noun, masculine*
un kilomètre = a kilometre, a kilometer

kiosque *noun, masculine*
un kiosque = a kiosk
un kiosque à journaux = a newspaper
kiosk, a newsstand
un kiosque à musique = a bandstand

klaxon   *noun, masculine*
un klaxon = a (car) horn

klaxonner *verb* 1
= to sound one's horn, to honk the horn

KO *adjective* (**!** *never changes*)
(*abbreviation of* **knocked out**)
• = KO'ed
  mettre son adversaire KO = to KO one's
    opponent
• **je suis KO✶** = I'm exhausted

K-way *noun, masculine*
  un K-way = a windcheater, a windbreaker

L l

l' ▶ **le**

la ▶ **le**

là *adverb*
• (*indicating a place*) = there
  j'habitais là = I used to live there
  passez par là = go that way
  c'est là qu'il est né = that's where he was
    born
  là où elle travaille = where she works
• (*indicating a time*) = then
  d'ici là j'aurai fini = by then, I'll have
    finished
  ce jour-là = that day
  en ce temps-là = in those days

là-bas *adverb*
  = over there

laboratoire *noun, masculine*
  un laboratoire = a laboratory

lac *noun, masculine*
  un lac = a lake

lacet *noun, masculine*
• (*for shoes*)
  un lacet = a lace
• (*in a road*)
  un lacet = a hairpin bend, a hairpin turn
  une route en lacets = a twisting road

lâcher *verb* 1
• (*to stop holding*) = to drop
  = to let go of
• (*to collapse*) = to give way
• (*to stop working*) = to fail

là-dedans *adverb*
  = in there

là-dessous *adverb*
  = under there, under it

là-dessus *adverb*
• (*on a surface*) = there, on it
• (*on a subject*) = about it

là-haut *adverb*
  = up there
  = upstairs

laid/laide *adjective*
  = ugly

laine *noun, feminine*
  la laine = wool
  de laine, en laine = wool(l)en, wool

laisse *noun, feminine*
  une laisse = a leash

laisser *verb* 1
1 (**!** + *avoir*)
• = to leave
  laisser sa voiture à l'ombre = to leave one's
    car in the shade
  laissez-moi tranquille! = leave me alone!
• = to let
  laisser couler l'eau = to let the water run
  laisser tomber un verre = to drop a glass
2 se laisser (**!** + *être*)
• **se laisser influencer** = to allow oneself to
  be influenced
• **se laisser tomber sur le sable** = to flop
  down on the sand

lait *noun, masculine*
  le lait = milk
le lait en poudre = powdered milk
le lait solaire = suntan lotion

laitier/laitière
1 *adjective*
  les produits laitiers = dairy products
  une vache laitière = a dairy cow
2 *noun, masculine/feminine*
  un laitier/une laitière = a milkman/a
    milkwoman

laitue *noun, feminine*
  une laitue = a (head of) lettuce

lame *noun, feminine*
  une lame = a blade
une lame de rasoir = a razor blade

lamentable *adjective*
  = pitiful
  = awful

lampadaire *noun, masculine*
  un lampadaire (*in a house*) = a standard
    lamp, a floor lamp
  (*in the street*) = a streetlamp, a streetlight

lampe *noun, feminine*
  une lampe = a lamp
une lampe de chevet = a bedside lamp
une lampe électrique = a torch, a
  flashlight
une lampe de poche = a pocket torch, a
  flashlight

lancer *verb* 12
1 (**!** + *avoir*)
• = to throw
• = to launch
2 se lancer (**!** + *être*)

- (to jump)
  se lancer = to throw oneself
- (to dare)
  se lancer = to take the plunge
- (to start)
  se lancer dans les affaires = to go into business

langage noun, masculine
  un langage = a language

langouste noun, feminine
  une langouste = a rock lobster

langue noun, feminine
- la langue = the tongue
- une langue = a language
la langue maternelle = the mother tongue
les langues vivantes = modern languages

languir verb ③
1 (! + avoir)
  languir de revoir un ami = to be longing to see a friend
2 se languir de (! + être)
  se languir de = to be pining for

lapin noun, masculine
- un lapin = a rabbit
- poser un lapin* à quelqu'un = to stand someone up

laquelle ▶ lequel

large
1 adjective
  = wide
2 noun, masculine
- faire trois mètres de large = to be three metres wide
- le large = the open sea
  au large de la Bretagne = off the coast of Brittany

largement adverb
  avoir largement le temps = to have plenty of time
  c'est largement suffisant = it's more than enough

largeur noun, feminine
  la largeur = the width

larme noun, feminine
  une larme = a tear

las/lasse adjective
  = tired, weary

lassant/lassante adjective
  = tedious
  = tiresome

lasser: se lasser de verb ① (! + être)
  se lasser de = to grow tired of

latin noun, masculine
  le latin = Latin

laurier noun, masculine
  le laurier = laurel
  = bay
  une feuille de laurier = a bay leaf

lavable adjective
  = washable

lavabo noun, masculine
  un lavabo = a washbasin, a wash-hand basin

lavage noun, masculine
  le lavage = washing

lavande noun, feminine
  la lavande = lavender

lave-linge noun, masculine (! never changes)
  un lave-linge = a washing machine

laver verb ①
1 (! + avoir)
  = to wash
2 se laver (! + être)
  se laver = to wash oneself
  se laver les mains = to wash one's hands

laverie noun, feminine
  une laverie (automatique) = a launderette, a laundromat

lave-vaisselle noun, masculine (! never changes)
  un lave-vaisselle = a dishwasher

le/la (l' before vowel or mute h)
(plural) **les**
1 determiner
- = the
  la fenêtre de la cuisine = the kitchen window
  les Martin = the Martins
- (not translated in some cases)
  apprendre le russe = to learn Russian
  aimer le café = to like coffee
  les enfants aiment les animaux = children like animals
- = a
  8 euros le kilo = 8 euros a kilo
  cent kilomètres à l'heure = one hundred kilometres an hour
- (used with nouns relating to a part of the body)
  avoir les yeux bleus = to have blue eyes
  se casser la jambe = to break one's leg
  il m'a serré la main = he shook my hand
- (used with a day of the week)
  travailler le lundi = to work on Mondays
  tous les mardis = every Tuesday
2 pronoun
- (referring to a person, an animal or a thing)
  = him/her
  = it
  (plural) = them
  il l'a invitée = he invited her
  où les as-tu achetés? = where did you buy them?

• (*other cases*)
  comme vous le savez = as you know
  je te l'avais dit = I told you
  il ne peut pas te le dire = he can't tell you
  espérons-le! = let's hope so!

lécher *verb* 1
  = to lick

leçon *noun, feminine*
  une leçon = a lesson

lecteur/lectrice
1 *noun, masculine/feminine*
  un lecteur/une lectrice = a reader
2 lecteur *noun, masculine*
  un lecteur de cassettes = a cassette player
  un lecteur laser = a CD player

lecture *noun, feminine*
  la lecture = reading

légendaire *adjective*
  = legendary

légende *noun, feminine*
• (*a story*)
  une légende = a legend
• (*on a picture, a cartoon*)
  la légende = the caption
• (*on a map*)
  la légende = the key

léger/légère *adjective*
• (*not heavy*) = light
• (*not serious*) = slight
• (*not strong*)
  un café léger = a weak coffee
  une cigarette légère = a mild cigarette
  un vent léger = a light wind

légèrement *adverb*
  = slightly

légume *noun, masculine*
  un légume = a vegetable

lendemain *noun, masculine*
  le lendemain = the next day, the following
    day
  le lendemain matin = the next morning
  le lendemain de mon arrivée = the day
    after I arrived

lent/lente *adjective*
  = slow

lentement *adverb*
  = slowly

lentille *noun, feminine*
• (*food*)
  des lentilles = lentils
• (*optical device*)
  une lentille = a lens
  les lentilles de contact = contact lenses

lequel/laquelle *pronoun*
(*plural*) **lesquels/lesquelles**
• = which one

lequel d'entre eux a payé? = which one of
    them paid?
  lesquelles veux-tu? = which ones do you
    want?
• = which
  la situation dans laquelle je me trouve
    = the situation in which I find myself

les ▶ le

lesquels/lesquelles ▶ lequel

lessive *noun, feminine*
  la lessive = the washing, the laundry

lettre *noun, feminine*
  une lettre = a letter
  en toutes lettres = in full

leur
1 *determiner*
  = their
  leur jardin = their garden
  leurs sacs = their bags
2 *pronoun* (**!** *never changes*)
  = them
  il leur a prêté sa voiture = he lent them his
    car
  je la leur ai envoyée = I sent it to them
3 *pronoun*
  le leur/la leur/les leurs = theirs

levée *noun, feminine*
  une levée (*from a post-box*) = a collection

lever
1 *verb* 16 (**!** + *avoir*)
  = to raise
  levez les bras = raise your arms
  lever le doigt (*in class*) ≈ to put up one's
    hand
2 se lever *verb* 16 (**!** + *être*)
• (*if it's a person*)
  se lever = to get up
  = to stand up
• (*if it's the sun, the wind*)
  se lever = to rise
3 *noun, masculine*
  au lever = when one gets up
  = on getting up
  le lever du soleil = sunrise

lèvre *noun, feminine*
  une lèvre = a lip

levure *noun, feminine*
  la levure = yeast
  la levure chimique = baking powder

lexique *noun, masculine*
  un lexique = a vocabulary list

libérer *verb* 14
  = to release, to free

liberté *noun, feminine*
  la liberté = freedom

libraire *noun, masculine/feminine*
  un libraire/une libraire = a bookseller

librairie noun, feminine
une librairie = a bookshop, a bookstore

libre adjective
* = free
ils sont libres d'y aller = they're free to go
'entrée libre' = 'admission free'
* = clear
la route est libre = the road is clear
* = vacant
une place libre = a vacant seat
* la ligne n'est pas libre = the line is engaged, the line is busy

librement adverb
= freely

libre-service noun, masculine
(plural) **libres-services**
un libre-service = a self-service

licence noun, feminine
une licence (a diploma) = a degree

licencier verb [2]
= to dismiss, to lay off
= to make redundant, to let go

lien noun, masculine
un lien = a tie
= a bond
= a link

lieu noun, masculine
(plural) **lieux**
1 un lieu = a place
un lieu de rencontre = a meeting place
votre lieu de naissance = your place of birth
2 avoir lieu = to take place
3 au lieu de = instead of

lièvre noun, masculine
un lièvre = a hare

ligne noun, feminine
une ligne = a line

lilas noun, masculine (! never changes)
le lilas = lilac

limande noun, feminine
une limande (a fish) = a dab

limonade noun, feminine
la limonade = lemonade

linge noun, masculine
* (sheets, towels)
le linge (de maison) = (household) linen
le linge sale = dirty linen
* (when being laundered)
le linge = the washing, the laundry
avoir du linge à laver = to have some washing to do

lion noun, masculine
un lion = a lion

Lion noun, masculine
le Lion = Leo

liquide noun, masculine
* un liquide = a liquid
* payer en liquide = to pay cash

lire¹ verb [41]
= to read

lire² noun, feminine
la lire = the lira

lisse adjective
= smooth

liste noun, feminine
une liste = a list
une liste d'attente = a waiting list
être sur liste rouge = to be ex-directory, to have an unlisted number

lit noun, masculine
un lit = a bed
un lit de camp = a camp bed
un grand lit = a double bed
des lits superposés = bunk beds

litre noun, masculine
un litre = a litre, a liter

littérature noun, feminine
la littérature = literature

littoral noun, masculine
(plural) **littoraux**
le littoral = the coast

livraison noun, feminine
une livraison = a delivery

livre
1 noun, masculine
un livre = a book
2 noun, feminine
une livre = a pound

livrer verb [1]
= to deliver

livret noun, masculine
un livret = a booklet
un livret de famille = a family record book (of births, marriages and deaths)
un livret scolaire = a school report book

local/locale
(plural) **locaux/locales**
1 adjective
= local
2 local noun, masculine
un local = a place

locataire noun, masculine/feminine
un locataire/une locataire = a tenant

location noun, feminine
la location (of accommodation) = renting
(of equipment) = hiring
(of seats) = booking, reservation
'location de voitures' = 'car hire', 'car rental'

loge noun, feminine
* (for a caretaker)
une loge = a lodge

L

- (*for an actor*)
  une loge = a dressing room

logé/logée *adjective*
= housed
être logé et nourri = to have room and board

logement *noun, masculine*
- **un logement** = accommodation
  = a flat, an apartment
- **le logement** = housing

loger *verb* 13
1 (**!** + *avoir*)
- (*to provide accommodation*) = to house
  (*for a short time*) = to put up
- (*to have accommodation*) = to live
  (*for a short time*) = to stay
2 se loger (**!** + *être*)
trouver à se loger = to find somewhere to live

logique *adjective*
= logical

loi *noun, feminine*
une loi = a law

loin *adverb*
- = a long way, far (away)
  c'est trop loin = it's too far
  c'est encore loin? = is it much further?
- **de loin** = from a distance
- **au loin** = in the distance

lointain/lointaine *adjective*
= distant

loisir *noun, masculine plural*
- (*spare time*)
  le loisir = leisure
- (*activity*)
  un loisir = a leisure activity, a pastime

Londres *noun*
= London

long/longue
1 *adjective*
= long
2 long *noun, masculine*
faire deux mètres de long = to be two metres long
marcher de long en large = to pace up and down
3 le long de = along

longer *verb* 13
= to follow

longtemps *adverb*
= (for) a long time
il y a longtemps qu'il est parti = he left a long time ago
ça fait longtemps que tu attends? = have you been waiting long?

longue ▶ long

longuement *adverb*
= for a long time

longueur *noun, feminine*
la longueur = the length
à longueur de journée = all day long

lorsque (**lorsqu'** *before vowel or mute h*) *conjunction*
= (at the time) when

loterie *noun, feminine*
une loterie = a lottery

lotissement *noun, masculine*
un lotissement = a housing estate, a housing development

loto *noun, masculine*
le loto = lotto
= bingo

louche
1 *adjective*
= shady
2 *noun, feminine*
une louche = a ladle

louer *verb* 1
- (*as the owner*) = to rent out
  '**à louer**' = 'to let', 'for rent'
- (*as the tenant*) = to rent
  (*as the hirer*) = to hire, to rent

loufoque* *adjective*
= crazy

loup *noun, masculine*
un loup = a wolf

loupe *noun, feminine*
une loupe = a magnifying glass

lourd/lourde *adjective*
- (*weighty*) = heavy
- (*describing the weather*) = muggy, sultry
  il fait lourd = it's muggy

loyer *noun, masculine*
le loyer = the rent

lu/lue ▶ lire¹ 41

lucarne *noun, feminine*
une lucarne = a skylight

lueur *noun, feminine*
une lueur = a (faint) light
= a glow
= a gleam, a flash

luge *noun, feminine*
- (*the equipment*)
  une luge = a toboggan, a sled
- (*the sport*)
  la luge = tobogganing

✗ in informal situations

lui
1 *pronoun, masculine*
- = him
  à cause de lui = because of him
  la voiture est à lui = the car belongs to
  him, the car is his
  c'est à lui de jouer = it's his turn to play
- = he
  elle est restée, mais lui est parti = she
  stayed, but he left
2 *pronoun, feminine*
  = her
  je lui ai prêté ma robe = I lent her my dress

lui-même *pronoun, masculine*
  = himself
  = itself

luire *verb* 62
  = to shine, to glow

luisant/luisante *adjective*
  = shining, glowing

lumière *noun, feminine*
  la lumière = light

lunch *noun, masculine*
  un lunch = a buffet lunch

lundi *noun, masculine*
  lundi = Monday

lune *noun, feminine*
  la lune = the moon

lunette
1 *noun, feminine*
  une lunette = a telescope
2 lunettes *noun, feminine plural*
  des lunettes = glasses, spectacles
  des lunettes de soleil = sunglasses

lustrer *verb* 1
  = to polish

lutin *noun, masculine*
  un lutin = an imp

lutte *noun, feminine*
- (*a fight*)
  une lutte = a struggle
- (*the sport*)
  la lutte = wrestling

lutter *verb* 1
  = to fight
  = to struggle

luxe *noun, masculine*
  le luxe = luxury

Luxembourg *noun, masculine*
  le Luxembourg = Luxembourg

lycée *noun, masculine*
  un lycée = a secondary school, ≈ a senior
  high school (*for students aged 15 to 18*)

lycéen/lycéenne *noun,*
masculine/feminine
  un lycéen/une lycéenne = a secondary
  school student, a high school student
  (*aged 15 to 18*)

Mm

m *noun, masculine* (**!** *never changes*)
(*abbreviation of* **mètre**)
  m = m

m' ▶ **me**

M. (*abbreviation of* **Monsieur**)
  M. = Mr

ma ▶ **mon**

macaron *noun, masculine*
  un macaron = a macaroon

macédoine *noun, feminine*
- **une macédoine de légumes** = mixed diced
  vegetables
- **une macédoine de fruits** = a fruit salad

machin *noun, masculine*
  un machin* = a thing, a what's it

machine *noun, feminine*
  une machine = a machine
  une machine à coudre = a sewing
  machine
  une machine à écrire = a typewriter
  une machine à laver = a washing
  machine
  une machine à sous = a one-armed
  bandit

maçon *noun, masculine*
  un maçon = a bricklayer
  = a mason
  = a builder

madame *noun, feminine*
(*plural*) **mesdames**
  Madame Martin = Mrs Martin
  bonjour madame = good morning
  mesdames et messieurs = ladies and
  gentlemen

mademoiselle *noun, feminine*
(*plural*) **mesdemoiselles**
  Mademoiselle Martin = Miss Martin
  bonjour mademoiselle = good morning
  mesdames, mesdemoiselles et messieurs
  = ladies and gentlemen

magasin *noun, masculine*
  un magasin = a shop, a store
  un grand magasin = a department store

magazine *noun, masculine*
  un magazine = a magazine

magique *adjective*
  = magic

magnétophone *noun, masculine*
  un magnétophone = a tape recorder

magnétoscope *noun, masculine*
  un magnétoscope = a video recorder

magnifique *adjective*
 = magnificent
 = wonderful

mai *noun, masculine*
 mai = May
 le 1er Mai = May Day

maigre *adjective*
• = thin
• = lean

maigrir *verb* ③
 = to lose weight

maillot *noun, masculine*
 un maillot (*for a dancer*) = a leotard
 (*in football*) = a shirt, a jersey
 (*for cyclists*) = a jersey
un maillot de corps = a vest, an
 undershirt
un maillot de bain = a swimsuit

main *noun, feminine*
 une main = a hand
 fait (à la) main = handmade
 se donner la main = to hold hands
 se serrer la main = to shake hands
 je vais te donner un coup de main = I'll
  give you a hand
 haut les mains! = hands up!

maintenant *adverb*
 = now
 = nowadays

maire *noun, masculine*
 le maire = the mayor

mairie *noun, feminine*
 la mairie = the town hall

mais *conjunction*
 = but

maïs *noun, masculine* (**!** *never changes*)
 le maïs = maize, corn
  = sweetcorn

maison
1 *adjective* (**!** *never changes*)
 = homemade
2 *noun, feminine*
 la maison = the house
  = home
 rester à la maison = to stay at home
une maison de campagne = a house in
 the country
une maison de la culture = a
 community arts centre
**une maison des jeunes (et de la
 culture)** = a youth club
une maison de retraite = a retirement
 home

maître/maîtresse *noun, masculine/
feminine*

• (*in a school*)
 le maître/la maîtresse = the teacher
• (*of a pet*)
 le maître/la maîtresse = the master/the
  mistress

majeur/majeure *adjective*
• = major, main
 en majeure partie = for the most part
• être majeur = to be over 18 years of age

mal
1 *adjective* (**!** *never changes*)
 = bad
 c'est mal de mentir = it's bad to lie
 les photos ne sont pas mal✱ = the photos
  aren't bad
2 *adverb*
 mal = badly
  = not well
 ils ont mal dormi = they slept badly
 elle va mal = she isn't well at all
 être mal élevé = to be bad mannered
3 faire mal = to hurt
 ça me fait mal = it hurts
 tu me fais mal = you're hurting me
 je me suis fait mal = I hurt myself
4 avoir mal
 avoir mal à la tête = to have a headache
 avoir mal aux dents = to have (a)
  toothache
 avoir mal à la gorge = to have a sore throat
 avoir mal au cœur = to feel sick
 il a mal au genou = his knee hurts
 avoir le mal de mer = to be seasick

malade
1 *adjective*
 = ill, sick
 tomber malade = to fall ill
2 *noun, masculine/feminine*
 un malade/une malade = a patient
  = a sick person

maladie *noun, feminine*
 une maladie = an illness, a disease

maladroit/maladroite *adjective*
 = clumsy

malaise *noun, masculine*
• (*faintness*)
 un malaise = a dizzy turn
 avoir un malaise = to feel faint
• (*nervousness*)
 un malaise = unease

malfaiteur *noun, masculine*
 un malfaiteur = a criminal

malgré *preposition*
 = despite, in spite of

malheur *noun, masculine*
 un malheur = a misfortune

malheureusement *adverb*
 = unfortunately

✱ in informal situations

malheureux/malheureuse *adjective*
= unhappy
= unfortunate

malhonnête *adjective*
= dishonest

malin/maligne *adjective*
= clever
= crafty

malsain/malsaine *adjective*
= unhealthy

maltraiter *verb* [1]
= to ill-treat

maman *noun, feminine*
une maman = a mum, a mom

mamie✶ *noun, feminine*
ma mamie✶ = my gran, my granny

manche
1 *noun, feminine*
une manche = a sleeve
sans manches = sleeveless
2 *noun, masculine*
un manche = a handle
un manche à balai = a broomstick
= a joystick

Manche *noun, feminine*
la Manche = the (English) Channel

mandat *noun, masculine*
un mandat = a money order

manège *noun, masculine*
un manège = a fairground ride

manger *verb* [13]
= to eat
inviter des amis à manger = to invite
friends for a meal
manger au restaurant = to eat out

mangue *noun, feminine*
une mangue = a mango

manière *noun, feminine*
• (*a method*)
la manière = the way
c'est leur manière de remercier = it's their
way of saying thank you
• (*conduct*)
des manières = manners

manif✶ *noun, feminine*
une manif✶ = a demo

manifestation *noun, feminine*
une manifestation = a demonstration
une manifestation sportive = a
sporting event

mannequin *noun, masculine*
un mannequin (*in a shop window*) = a
dummy, a mannequin
(*a person*) = a (fashion) model

manquer *verb* [1]
• (*to fail to catch, hit, reach, see, hear*) = to
miss
manquer le train = to miss the train
• **mes amis me manquent** = I miss my
friends
ça t'a manqué? = did you miss it?
• (*impersonal use*) = to be missing
il manque un bouton = there's a button
missing
je ne peux pas l'acheter, il me manque dix
euros = I can't buy it, I'm ten euros short
il te manque cinq euros pour payer la note
= you need five euros more to pay the
bill
• **manquer de** = to be short of
= to lack
• **manquer à sa promesse** = to break one's
promise

mansarde *noun, feminine*
une mansarde = an attic room

manteau *noun, masculine*
(*plural*) **manteaux**
un manteau = a coat

maquereau *noun, masculine*
(*plural*) **maquereaux**
un maquereau = a mackerel

maquette *noun, feminine*
une maquette = a scale model

maquillage *noun, masculine*
le maquillage = make-up

maquiller: se maquiller *verb* [1]
(**!** + *être*)
se maquiller = to put on make-up
= to wear make-up

marbre *noun, masculine*
le marbre = marble

marchand/marchande *noun,*
masculine/feminine
un marchand/une marchande = a
'shopkeeper
= a stallholder

marchandise *noun, feminine*
de la marchandise = goods

marche *noun, feminine*
• (*stair*)
une marche = a step
les marches = the stairs
• (*the sport*)
la marche = walking
• (*when talking about a machine, a
mechanism*)
être en marche = to be running
mettre le moteur en marche = to start the
engine up
• (*when talking about a vehicle*)
un train en marche = a moving train
faire marche arrière = to reverse
la marche à suivre = the procedure

M

marché *noun, masculine*
• (*a place*)
  un marché = a market
  faire son marché = to go shopping
• (*in business*)
  un marché = a deal
• être bon marché = to be cheap
le Marché Commun = the Common
  Market
un marché aux puces = a flea market

marcher *verb* 1
• = to walk
• = to work
  comment marche la tondeuse? = how
  does the mower work?
• (*if it's an event, a fest*)✘ = to go well
  les affaires marchent✘ bien = business is
  going well
  l'examen a marché✘? = how did the exam
  go?

mardi *noun, masculine*
  mardi = Tuesday
Mardi gras = Shrove Tuesday

mare *noun, feminine*
  une mare = a pond

marée *noun, feminine*
  la marée = the tide
  la marée monte = the tide is coming in
  la marée descend = the tide is going out
une marée noire = an oil slick

marelle *noun, feminine*
  la marelle = hopscotch

marge *noun, feminine*
  la marge = the margin

mari *noun, masculine*
  un mari = a husband

mariage *noun, masculine*
  un mariage = a wedding
  = a marriage

marié/mariée
1 *adjective*
  = married
2 *noun, masculine/feminine*
  le marié/la mariée = the bridegroom/the
  bride

marier *verb* 2
1 (✘ + *avoir*)
  = to marry
  ils ont marié leur fille = they married their
  daughter
2 se marier (✘ + *être*)
  se marier = to get married, to marry
  elle s'est mariée avec son cousin = she
  got married to her cousin, she married
  her cousin

marin/marine[1]
1 *adjective*

• le sel marin = sea salt
• un pull marin = a seaman's jersey
2 marin *noun, masculine*
  un marin = a sailor

marine[2] *noun, feminine*
  la marine = the navy

marionnette *noun, feminine*
  une marionnette = a puppet

Maroc *noun, masculine*
  le Maroc = Morocco

marocain/marocaine *adjective*
  = Moroccan

maroquinerie *noun, feminine*
  une maroquinerie = a leather shop, a
  leather store

marque *noun, feminine*
• (*in commerce*)
  une marque = a brand, a make
  de marque française = French
• (*a trace*)
  une marque = a mark

marquer *verb* 1
• = to note (down), to write
• = to score
• = to mark, to make an impression

marraine *noun, feminine*
  une marraine = a godmother

marrant/marrante✘ *adjective*
  = funny

marre✘ *adverb*
  en avoir marre✘ = to be fed up

marrer: se marrer✘ *verb* 1 (✘ + *être*)
• se marrer✘ = to laugh
• se marrer✘ = to have a good laugh

marron
1 *adjective* (✘ *never changes*)
  = brown
2 *noun, masculine*
  un marron = a chestnut
  un marron (d'Inde) = a horse chestnut
des marrons chauds = roast chestnuts

mars *noun, masculine*
  mars = March

Marseillaise *noun, feminine*
  la Marseillaise = the Marseillaise (*the
  French national anthem*)

marteau *noun, masculine*
(*plural*) **marteaux**
  un marteau = a hammer
un marteau piqueur = a pneumatic drill,
  a jackhammer

mas *noun, masculine* (✘ *never changes*)
  un mas = a farmhouse (*in Provence*)

masque *noun, masculine*
  un masque = a mask

mât *noun, masculine*
un mât = a mast

match *noun, masculine*
un match de football = a football match, a
football game

matelas *noun, masculine* (**!** *never
changes*)
un matelas = a mattress
un matelas pneumatique = an air bed,
an air mattress

matériel *noun, masculine*
le matériel = the equipment

mathématiques *noun, feminine plural*
les mathématiques = mathematics

maths* *noun, feminine plural*
les maths* = math(s)

matière *noun, feminine*
• (*something studied*)
une matière = a subject
• (*a substance*)
une matière = a material
les matières grasses = fats
les matières premières = raw materials

matin *noun, masculine*
un matin = a morning
demain matin = tomorrow morning
de bon matin = early in the morning

matinal/matinale *adjective*
(*plural*) **matinaux/matinales**
= early
être matinal = to be an early riser

matinée *noun, feminine*
la matinée = the morning
faire la grasse matinée = to have a lie-in,
to sleep in

mauvais/mauvaise
1 *adjective*
• = bad
le mauvais temps = bad weather
être mauvais en algèbre = to be bad at
algebra
• = wrong
la mauvaise adresse = the wrong address
2 mauvais *adverb*
• il fait mauvais = the weather is bad
• ça sent mauvais = it smells
une mauvaise herbe = a weed

maximum *noun, masculine*
un maximum = a maximum
100 euros au maximum = 100 euros at
(the) most

mayonnaise *noun, feminine*
la mayonnaise = mayonnaise

me (**m'** *before vowel or mute h*) *pronoun*
• = me
il m'a vu = he saw me
elle ne me parle pas = she won't speak to
me

• = myself
je me suis coupé = I cut myself

mec* *noun, masculine*
un mec* = a bloke, a guy

mécanicien/mécanicienne
un mécanicien/une mécanicienne (*in a
garage*) = a mechanic
(*on a train*) = an engine driver, a
locomotive engineer

mécanique
1 *adjective*
= mechanical
(*describing a toy*) = clockwork
2 *noun, feminine*
la mécanique = mechanics

méchant/méchante *adjective*
= nasty, mean

méchoui *noun, masculine*
un méchoui = a North African style
barbecue

mécontent/mécontente *adjective*
= dissatisfied, displeased

médaille *noun, feminine*
une médaille = a medal

médecin *noun, masculine*
un médecin = a doctor

médical/médicale *adjective*
(*plural*) **médicaux/médicales**
= medical

médicament *noun, masculine*
un médicament = a medicine, a drug

médiéval/médiévale *adjective*
(*plural*) **médiévaux/médiévales**
= medieval

Méditerranée *noun, feminine*
la (mer) Méditerranée = the
Mediterranean (Sea)

méfiant/méfiante *adjective*
= suspicious, mistrustful

méfier: se méfier *verb* [2] (**!** + *être*)
• se méfier = to distrust
je me méfie de ce garçon = I don't trust
that boy
• se méfier = to be careful
méfie-toi! = be careful

meilleur/meilleure
1 *adjective*
• = better
le film est meilleur que le roman = the film
is better than the novel
• = best
le meilleur vin de la région = the best wine
in the area
2 *noun, masculine/feminine*
le meilleur/la meilleure = the best one

M

3 meilleur adverb
= better
il fait meilleur qu'hier = the weather is better than yesterday

mélanger verb 13
- (to combine) = to mix
- (to muddle up) = to mix up

melon noun, masculine
un melon = a melon

membre noun, masculine
- (a person)
un membre = a member
- (an arm, a leg)
un membre = a limb

même
1 adjective
= same
les mêmes bottes que les miennes = the same boots as mine
2 pronoun
le même/la même = the same one
3 adverb
- (used for emphasis) = even
il n'a même pas répondu = he didn't even reply
j'irai, même s'il pleut = I'll go, even if it rains
- (exactly) = very
aujourd'hui même = this very day
ici même = in this very place, right here

mémé✶ noun, feminine
ma mémé✶ = my gran, my granny

mémoire noun, feminine
la mémoire = memory

mémoriser verb 1
= to memorize

menacer verb 12
= to threaten

ménage noun, masculine
- (cleaning)
le ménage = the housework
- (the people)
un ménage = a couple
= a household

ménager/ménagère¹ adjective
= domestic
= household

ménagère² noun, feminine
une ménagère = a housewife

mendiant/mendiante noun, masculine/feminine
un mendiant/une mendiante = a beggar

mener verb 16
- = to lead
- = to take

mensonge noun, masculine
un mensonge = a lie

mensuel/mensuelle adjective
= monthly

menteur/menteuse noun, masculine/feminine
un menteur/une menteuse = a liar

menthe noun, feminine
la menthe = mint
une menthe à l'eau = a mint cordial

mentionner verb 1
= to mention

mentir verb 30
= to lie

menton noun, masculine
le menton = the chin

menu/menue
1 adjective
= small
2 menu adverb
hacher menu = to chop finely
3 menu noun, masculine
le menu = the menu
le menu à prix fixe = the set menu

mer noun, feminine
la mer = the sea

merci noun, masculine (also exclamation)
merci! = thank you!

mercredi noun, masculine
mercredi = Wednesday

merde✶ exclamation
= shit!

mère noun, feminine
une mère = a mother

méridional/méridionale adjective
(plural) **méridionaux/méridionales**
= southern

mériter verb 1
= to deserve

merveille noun, feminine
une merveille = a marvel, a wonder
faire des merveilles = to work wonders

merveilleux/merveilleuse adjective
= marvellous, wonderful

mes ▶ mon

mesdames ▶ madame

mesdemoiselles ▶ mademoiselle

messe noun, feminine
une messe = a mass

messieurs ▶ monsieur

mesure noun, feminine
- (when determining size)
une mesure = a measurement
sur mesure = made to measure

- (*a decision, a step*)
  une mesure = a measure

mesurer *verb* [1]
= to measure
combien mesures-tu? = how tall are you?
Paul mesure 1,80 m = Paul is six foot tall

météo *noun, feminine*
la météo = the weather forecast
la météo marine = the shipping forecast
la météo annonce de la pluie = the
forecast is for rain

méthode *noun, feminine*
- (*a way of doing things*)
  une méthode = a method
- (*a book*)
  une méthode = a handbook
  = a textbook

métier *noun, masculine*
un métier = a job
= a trade

mètre *noun, masculine*
- (*a unit of measurement*)
  un mètre = a metre, a meter
- (*an instrument*)
  un mètre = a tape measure

métro *noun, masculine*
le métro = the underground, the subway

mets ▶ **mettre** [60]

mettre *verb* [60]
1 (**!** + *avoir*)
- = to put
  j'ai mis la lettre sur la table = I put the
  letter on the table
- = to put on
  il a mis son chapeau = he put on his hat
- (*other uses*)
  mettre le couvert = to set the table
  elle met une heure pour aller au bureau
  = it takes her one hour to get to the
  office
2 se mettre (**!** + *être*)
- (*to place oneself*)
  se mettre debout = to stand up
  il s'est mis à table = he sat down at the
  table
- (*to apply, to wear*)
  se mettre = to put on
  se mettre du rouge à lèvres = to put
  lipstick on
- (*to begin*)
  se mettre à [chanter | pleurer | écrire ...] = to
  start [singing | crying | writing ...]
  se mettre en colère = to lose one's temper,
  to get angry
  se mettre en route = to set off

meuble *noun, masculine*
un meuble = a piece of furniture
des meubles = furniture

meubler *verb* [1]
= to furnish

meurtre *noun, masculine*
un meurtre = a murder

micro *noun, masculine*
un micro = a microphone

microbe *noun, masculine*
un microbe = a germ, a microbe

midi *noun, masculine*
- = twelve o'clock, midday, noon
  il est midi et demi = it's half past twelve, it's
  twelve thirty
- = lunchtime

Midi *noun, masculine*
le Midi = the South of France

miel *noun, masculine*
le miel = honey

mien/mienne *pronoun*
le mien/la mienne = mine
les miens/les miennes = mine

miette *noun, feminine*
une miette = a crumb

mieux *adverb, adjective* (**!** *never changes*)
= better

mignon/mignonne *adjective*
= sweet, cute

mijoter *verb* [1]
- = to simmer
- = to prepare

milieu
(*plural*) **milieux**
1 *noun, masculine*
- (*the centre*)
  le milieu = the middle
- (*the world around*)
  le milieu (*nature*) = the environment
  (*family*) = the background
2 au milieu de = in the middle of
= among

militaire
1 *adjective*
= military
2 *noun, masculine*
un militaire = a soldier

mille
1 *number* (**!** *never changes*)
= a thousand, one thousand
2 *noun, masculine*
un mille (marin) = a (nautical) mile

milliard *noun, masculine*
un milliard = a billion

millier *noun, masculine*
un millier = a thousand
= about a thousand

million *noun, masculine*
un million = a million, one million

M

minable* *adjective*
= pathetic
= shabby

mince
1 *adjective*
= slim, thin, slender
2 *exclamation***
mince*! (*expressing annoyance*) = damn!
(*expressing amazement*) = wow!

minéral/minérale *adjective*
(*plural*) **minéraux/minérales**
= mineral

mineur/mineure
1 *adjective*
• (*under 18*) = underage
• (*not important*) = minor
2 *noun, masculine/feminine*
un mineur/une mineure = a minor
3 mineur *noun, masculine*
un mineur = a miner

Minitel *noun, masculine*
le Minitel = Minitel (*a terminal linking
phone users to interactive databases*)

minuit *noun, masculine*
minuit = twelve o'clock, midnight

minuscule *adjective*
= tiny, minute

minute *noun, feminine*
une minute = a minute, one minute

miroir *noun, masculine*
un miroir = a mirror

mis/mise ▶ mettre 60

misérable *adjective*
= poor
= wretched

misère *noun, feminine*
la misère = poverty

mistral *noun, masculine*
le mistral = the mistral (*a cold north wind*)

mite *noun, feminine*
une mite = a (clothes) moth

mixte *adjective*
= mixed
(*describing a school*) = coeducational

Mlle (*abbreviation of* **Mademoiselle**)
Mlle = Miss, Ms

Mme (*abbreviation of* **Madame**)
Mme = Mrs, Ms

mobilier *noun, masculine*
le mobilier = the furniture

mobylette *noun, feminine*
une mobylette = a moped

moche* *adjective*
• = ugly
• = awful

mode
1 *noun, feminine*
une mode = a fashion
être à la mode (*if it's clothes*) = to be
fashionable
(*if it's a singer, an actor*) = to be popular
2 *noun, masculine*
un mode de vie = a lifestyle

modèle *noun, masculine*
un modèle = a model
= a pattern

modéré/modérée *adjective*
= moderate

moi *pronoun*
= me
moi non plus = nor me, me neither
donne-la-moi = give it to me
ce sac est à moi = this bag belongs to me,
this bag is mine
c'est à moi de jouer = it's my turn to play
viens chez moi = come to my house
moi, je reste ici = I'm staying here

moi-même *pronoun*
= myself

moineau *noun, masculine*
(*plural*) **moineaux**
un moineau = a sparrow

moins
1 *preposition*
• = minus
= less
il fait moins cinq (degrés) = it's minus five
(degrees)
550 euros, moins la caution = 550 euros,
minus the deposit
• (*when talking about time*) = to
il est une heure moins le quart = it's a
quarter to one
2 *adverb*
• = less
moins intéressant = less interesting
moins cher que d'habitude = cheaper than
usual
de moins en moins = less and less
deux fois moins cher = twice as cheap
• moins de = less
= fewer
= less than
= under
un peu moins de sucre = a little less sugar
il a moins d'amis maintenant = he has
fewer friends now
moins de la moitié = less than half
• moins... moins... = the less... the less...
moins... plus... = the less... the more...
moins je travaille, moins j'ai envie de
travailler = the less I work, the less I feel
like working

*** in informal situations

- **le moins/la moins** = the least
  = the less
  le coin le moins ensoleillé du jardin = the least sunny spot in the garden
  le moins cher des deux = the cheaper of the two
3 au moins = at least
4 du moins = at least
4 à moins que, à moins de = unless

mois *noun, masculine* (! *never changes*)
un mois = a month
au mois de mai = in May

moisson *noun, feminine*
la moisson = the harvest

moitié *noun, feminine*
une moitié = a half
à moitié prix = half-price

molle ▶ mou

moment *noun, masculine*
un moment = a moment, one moment
en ce moment = at the moment
par moments = at times
juste au moment où il allait partir = just as he was about to leave

mon/ma *determiner*
(*plural*) **mes**
= my

monde *noun, masculine*
- **le monde** = the world
  faire le tour du monde en bateau = to sail around the world
  le monde des affaires = the business world
- **il y a du monde, il y a beaucoup de monde** = there are a lot of people
  tout le monde = everybody

moniteur/monitrice
1 *noun, masculine/feminine*
un moniteur/une monitrice (*for skiers, drivers*) = an instructor
(*in a holiday camp*) = a group leader, a counselor
2 moniteur *noun, masculine*
un moniteur (*a screen*) = a monitor

monnaie *noun, feminine*
- **la monnaie** = change
- **une monnaie** = a currency

monsieur *noun, masculine*
(*plural*) **messieurs**
un monsieur = a gentleman
bonjour messieurs = good morning (gentlemen)
Monsieur Martin = Mr Martin

monstre
1 *adjective*
monstre* = huge
2 *noun, masculine*
un monstre = a monster

montagne *noun, feminine*
une montagne = a mountain

montagneux/montagneuse
adjective
= mountainous

montant/montante
1 *adjective*
- **un col montant** = a high collar
- **la marée montante** = the rising tide
2 montant *noun, masculine*
le montant (*on a bill*) = the total

monter *verb* ⓵
1 (! + *être*)
- = to go up
  elle est montée au village = she's gone up to the village
  tu es monté à pied? = did you walk up?
  nous sommes montés en courant = we ran up
- = to go upstairs
  montez, le bureau est à l'étage au-dessus = go upstairs, the office is on the next floor
- = to come up
  – to come upstairs
  je suis dans le grenier, monte = I'm in the attic, come up
- = to get in(to)
- = to get on
  elle est montée dans la voiture = she got into the car
  monter dans un avion = to get on a plane
- = to climb
  ne monte pas sur la table = don't climb onto the table
- = to rise, to go up
  les prix montent = prices are rising, prices are going up
- (*other uses*)
  monter à bicyclette = to ride a bicycle
  monter à cheval = to ride
2 (! + *avoir*)
- = to go up
  il a monté la colline en vélo = he cycled up the hill
- = to take up(stairs)
  je vais monter les bagages = I'm going to take the luggage up(stairs)
- = to bring up
  peux-tu me monter mes lunettes? = can you bring my glasses up to me?
- = to put up
  monter une tente = to put up a tent

montgolfière *noun, feminine*
une montgolfière = a hot air balloon

montre *noun, feminine*
une montre = a watch

montrer *verb* ⓵
= to show

monument *noun, masculine*
un monument = a monument
un monument historique = a historical building
un monument aux morts = a war memorial

M

moquer: **se moquer de** verb ⬚1⬚
(**!** + être)
* (to mock)
  se moquer de = to make fun of
* (to dismiss)
  se moquer de = not to care about
  je m'en moque = I don't care

moquette noun, feminine
  une moquette = a fitted carpet, wall-to-wall carpeting

moral noun, masculine
  le moral = morale
  avoir le moral, avoir bon moral = to be in good spirits
  avoir le moral à zéro✱ = to feel very down

morceau noun, masculine
(plural) **morceaux**
  un morceau = a piece
un morceau de sucre = a lump of sugar

mordre verb ⬚6⬚
  = to bite

morpion noun, masculine
  le morpion = noughts and crosses

mort¹ noun, feminine
  la mort = death

mort²/morte
1 ▸ mourir ⬚25⬚
2 adjective
  = dead
  être mort de peur = to be scared stiff
3 noun, masculine/feminine
  un mort/une morte = a dead man/a dead woman

mosquée noun, feminine
  une mosquée = a mosque

mot noun, masculine
* **un mot** = a word
* (a message)
  un mot = a note
des mots croisés = a crossword puzzle

motard noun, masculine
  un motard = a motorcyclist, a biker
  = a police motorcyclist

mot-clé noun, masculine
(plural) **mots-clés**
  un mot-clé = a key word

moteur noun, masculine
  un moteur = an engine
  = a motor

moto noun, feminine
  une moto = a motorbike, a motorcycle

mou/molle adjective
* (describing things) = soft
  = limp

* (describing a person) = spineless
  = lethargic

mouche noun, feminine
  une mouche = a fly

mouchoir noun, masculine
  un mouchoir = a handkerchief

mouette noun, feminine
  une mouette = a seagull

mouiller verb ⬚1⬚
1 (**!** + avoir)
  = to wet
2 se mouiller (**!** + être)
  se mouiller = to get wet

moule
1 noun, feminine
  une moule = a mussel
2 noun, masculine
  un moule = a mould
  = a (baking) tin, a pan

mourir verb ⬚25⬚ (**!** + être)
  = to die
  il est mort en avril = he died in April
  je meurs [de faim | de soif | de froid ...]! = I'm [starving | parched | freezing ...]!
  il meurt d'envie de te le dire = he's dying to tell you

mousse noun, feminine
* (a plant)
  la mousse = moss
* (bubbles)
  la mousse = foam
  = lather
  = froth
* (in cooking)
  une mousse au chocolat = a chocolate mousse
* (a material)
  la mousse = foam rubber

moustache noun, feminine
* (on a man)
  une moustache = a moustache
* (on an animal)
  des moustaches = whiskers

moustique noun, masculine
  un moustique = a mosquito

moutarde noun, feminine
  la moutarde = mustard

mouton noun, masculine
  un mouton = a sheep

moyen/moyenne¹
1 adjective
  = average
  = medium
2 moyen noun, masculine
  un moyen = a means
  = a way
  un moyen de transport = a means of transport
  c'est le seul moyen = it's the only way

✱ in informal situations

3 moyens *noun, masculine plural*
des moyens (*money*) = means
je n'ai pas les moyens de voyager = I can't afford to travel
le Moyen Âge = the Middle Ages

moyenne² *noun, feminine*
• (*in statistics*)
la moyenne = the average
en moyenne = on average
• (*in an exam*)
la moyenne = half marks, 50%

moyennement *adverb*
= moderately
= fairly

Moyen-Orient *noun, masculine*
le Moyen-Orient = the Middle East

muet/muette *adjective*
• = dumb
• = silent

muguet *noun, masculine*
le muguet = lily of the valley

multiplier *verb* 2
= to multiply

municipal/municipale *adjective*
(*plural*) **municipaux/municipales**
= municipal

municipalité *noun, feminine*
la municipalité = the (local) council

munir: se munir de *verb* 3 (**!** + *être*)
se munir de = to equip oneself with

mur *noun, masculine*
un mur = a wall
le mur du son = the sound barrier

mûr/mûre¹ *adjective*
• (*describing fruit*) = ripe
• (*describing people*) = mature

muraille *noun, feminine*
une muraille = a great wall

mûre² *noun, feminine*
une mûre = a blackberry

murmurer *verb* 1
• = to murmur
• = to whisper

musclé/musclée *adjective*
= muscular

musculation *noun, feminine*
la musculation = body-building

musée *noun, masculine*
un musée = a museum, a gallery

musicien/musicienne *noun, masculine/feminine*
un musicien/une musicienne = a musician

musique *noun, feminine*
la musique = music

mutinerie *noun, feminine*
une mutinerie = a mutiny

mystère *noun, masculine*
un mystère = a mystery

mystérieux/mystérieuse *adjective*
= mysterious

Nn

n' ▶ ne

nage *noun, feminine*
la nage = swimming
traverser le fleuve à la nage = to swim across the river

nager *verb* 13
= to swim

nain/naine
1 *adjective*
= dwarf
= miniature
2 *noun, masculine/feminine*
un nain/une naine = a dwarf

naissance *noun, feminine*
la naissance = birth
à ma naissance = when I was born

naître *verb* 64 (**!** + *être*)
= to be born
il est né le 10 janvier = he was born on 10 January

nappe *noun, feminine*
une nappe = a tablecloth
une nappe de brouillard = a blanket of fog

narine *noun, feminine*
une narine = a nostril

natal/natale *adjective*
(*plural*) **natals/natales**
= native

natation *noun, feminine*
la natation = swimming

national/nationale¹ *adjective*
(*plural*) **nationaux/nationales**
= national

nationale² *noun, feminine*
une nationale = a trunk road, a highway

nature
1 *adjective* (**!** *never changes*)
= plain
un yaourt nature = a plain yogurt
un thé nature = a black tea

N

2 *noun, feminine*
  la nature = nature
  la protection de la nature = the protection
    of the environment
une nature morte = a still life

naturel/naturelle
1 *adjective*
  = natural
2 naturel *noun, masculine*
• être d'un naturel timide = to be shy by
  nature
• il manque de naturel = he's not very
  natural
• du thon au naturel = tuna in brine

naufrage *noun, masculine*
  un naufrage = a shipwreck
  faire naufrage (*if it's a ship*) = to be
    wrecked
  (*if it's a crew*) = to be shipwrecked

nausée *noun, feminine*
  la nausée = nausea
  avoir la nausée = to feel sick, to feel
    nauseous

nautique *adjective*
  les sports nautiques = water sports

navet *noun, masculine*
  un navet = a turnip

navette *noun, feminine*
  une navette = a shuttle
  = a shuttle service
  faire la navette = to travel back and forth
  = to commute

navire *noun, masculine*
  un navire = a ship

navré/navrée *adjective*
  je suis vraiment navré = I'm terribly sorry
  avoir l'air navré = to look upset

ne (**n'** *before vowel or mute h*) *adverb*
  ! *In cases where* ne *is used with* aucun,
  guère, jamais, pas, personne, plus, rien
  etc, one should consult the
  corresponding entry. ne + verb + que *is*
  treated in the entry below.

  je ne sais pas = I don't know
  je n'ai que 10 euros = I've only got 10
    euros
  tu n'avais qu'à le dire = you only had to
    say so

né/née ▶ naître 64

néanmoins *adverb*
  = nevertheless

nécessaire
1 *adjective*
  = necessary

2 *noun, masculine*
• faire le nécessaire pour les billets = to see
  about the tickets
• le strict nécessaire = the bare essentials

néerlandais/néerlandaise
1 *adjective*
  = Dutch
2 néerlandais *noun, masculine*
  le néerlandais = Dutch

néfaste *adjective*
  = harmful

négatif/négative *adjective*
  = negative

négliger *verb* 13
  = to neglect

neige *noun, feminine*
  la neige = snow
  des blancs d'œufs battus en neige
    = stiffly beaten eggwhites

neiger *verb* 13
  = to snow
  il neige = it's snowing

nénuphar *noun, masculine*
  un nénuphar = a waterlily

nerf *noun, masculine*
  un nerf = a nerve
  il me tape sur les nerfs✱ = he gets on my
    nerves

nerveux/nerveuse *adjective*
  = nervous, tense

n'est-ce pas *adverb*
  c'est grand, n'est-ce pas? = it's big, isn't it?
  tu viendras, n'est-ce pas? = you will
    come, won't you?

net/nette
1 *adjective*
• (*describing prices or weights*) = net
• (*free from stains or clutter*) = clean
• (*easy to see or understand*) = clear
2 net *adverb*
  s'arrêter net = to stop dead
  refuser net = to refuse flatly

nettoyer *verb* 23
  = to clean

neuf¹ *number*
  = nine

neuf²/neuve *adjective*
  = new
  une voiture toute neuve = a brand new car

neuvième *number*
  = ninth

neveu *noun, masculine*
  (*plural*) **neveux**
  un neveu = a nephew

nez *noun, masculine* (**!** *never changes*)
  le nez = the nose

ni *conjunction*
  ni anglais ni espagnol = neither English
    nor Spanish
  elle ne veut pas le voir ni lui parler = she
    doesn't wish to see him or talk to him
  ni l'un ni l'autre = neither of them

niche *noun, feminine*
* (*for a dog*)
  une niche = a kennel, a doghouse
* (*in a wall*)
  une niche = a recess

nid *noun, masculine*
  un nid = a nest

nièce *noun, feminine*
  une nièce = a niece

nier *verb* ②
  = to deny

n'importe ▶ **importer** ①

niveau *noun, masculine*
  (*plural*) **niveaux**
  un niveau = a level
  = a standard
  le niveau de vie = the standard of living

noce *noun, feminine*
  une noce = a wedding
  des noces d'argent = a silver wedding
    anniversary

nocturne *adjective*
  = nocturnal
  = night

Noël *noun, masculine*
  Noël = Christmas

nœud *noun, masculine*
  un nœud = a knot
  un nœud papillon = a bow tie

noir/noire *adjective*
* = black
* = dark

noisette *noun, feminine*
  une noisette = a hazelnut

noix *noun, feminine* (**!** *never changes*)
  une noix = a walnut, an English walnut

nom
  1 *noun, masculine*
* un nom = a name
* un nom = a noun
  2 au nom de = in the name of
  = on behalf of
  un nom de famille = a surname, a last
    name
  un nom de jeune fille = a maiden name

nombre *noun, masculine*
  un nombre = a number
  un certain nombre de personnes = some
    people

nombreux/nombreuse *adjective*
  = large
  = many
  une foule nombreuse = a large crowd
  de nombreuses personnes = many people
  ils sont peu nombreux = there are few of
    them

nommer *verb* ①
  1 (**!** + *avoir*)
* = to name
  = to call
  nommer un enfant Olivier = to name a
    child Olivier
  une plage nommée 'La Salie' = a beach
    called 'La Salie'
* = to appoint
  être nommé à Paris = to be posted to Paris
  2 se nommer (**!** + *être*)
  se nommer = to be called

non
  1 *adverb*
* = no
  ah, ça non! = definitely not
  je pense que non = I don't think so
* = non
  non alcoolisé = nonalcoholic
  2 non plus
  je ne suis pas d'accord non plus = I don't
    agree either
  il n'a pas aimé le film, moi non plus = he
    didn't like the film, neither did I

nonante *number*
  = ninety

nord
  1 *noun, masculine*
  le nord = the north
  2 *adjective* (**!** *never changes*)
  = north
  = northern

normal/normale *adjective*
  (*plural*) **normaux/normales**
  = normal
  il est normal qu'il soit triste = it's natural
    that he should be sad

normalement *adverb*
  = normally

normand/normande *adjective*
  = Norman
  = from Normandy
  la côte normande = the Normandy coast

Normandie *noun, feminine*
  la Normandie = Normandy

Norvège *noun, feminine*
  la Norvège = Norway

norvégien/norvégienne
  1 *adjective*
  = Norwegian
  2 norvégien *noun, masculine*
  le norvégien = Norwegian

N

nos ▶ notre

note *noun, feminine*
* (*in a hotel*)
  la note = the bill, the check
* (*in music*)
  une note = a note
* (*at school*)
  une note = a mark, a grade
* (*words taken down*)
  des notes = notes

noter *verb* [1]
* = to write down
* = to notice
* = to mark, to grade

notre *determiner*
(*plural*) **nos**
  = our

nôtre *pronoun*
  le nôtre/la nôtre/les nôtres = ours

nouille *noun, feminine*
  les nouilles = noodles, pasta

nourrir *verb* [3]
1 (! + *avoir*)
  = to feed
  = to nourish
2 se nourrir (! + *être*)
  se nourrir = to feed
  = to eat

nourriture *noun, feminine*
  la nourriture = food

nous *pronoun*
* = we
  = us
  nous avons froid = we're cold
  donne-nous le livre = give us the book
  la voiture est à nous = the car is ours
  c'est à nous de jouer = it's our turn to play
  il nous l'a prêté = he lent it to us
* = ourselves
  nous nous soignons = we look after
    ourselves
  nous nous levons tôt = we get up early
* = each other
  nous nous aimons = we love each other

nouveau/nouvelle¹
(*plural*) **nouveaux/nouvelles**
1 *adjective*

  ! **nouvel** *is used instead of* **nouveau**
  before masculine nouns that begin with a
  vowel or a mute h. The plural of **nouvel** *is*
  nouveaux.

  = new
  le Nouvel An = the New Year
  c'est tout nouveau = it's brand new
2 *noun, masculine/feminine*
  le nouveau/la nouvelle (*a pupil*) = the new
    boy/the new girl

3 de nouveau = (once) again

nouveau-né *noun, masculine*
(*plural*) **nouveau-nés**
  un nouveau-né = a newborn baby

nouvel ▶ nouveau 1

nouvelle² *noun, feminine*
  une nouvelle = a piece of news
  la nouvelle = the news
  les nouvelles = the news
  tu connais la nouvelle? = have you heard
    the news?

Nouvelle-Zélande *noun, feminine*
  la Nouvelle-Zélande = New Zealand

novembre *noun, masculine*
  novembre = November

noyau *noun, masculine*
(*plural*) **noyaux**
  un noyau = a stone, a pit

noyé/noyée *noun, masculine/feminine*
  un noyé/une noyée = a drowned person

noyer
1 *noun, masculine*
  un noyer = a walnut tree
2 *verb* [23] (! + *avoir*)
  = to drown
3 se noyer (! + *être*)
  se noyer = to drown

nu/nue *adjective*
  = naked, bare

nuage *noun, masculine*
  un nuage = a cloud

nuageux/nuageuse *adjective*
  = cloudy

nuance *noun, feminine*
* (*a colour*)
  une nuance = a shade
* (*between two things*)
  une nuance = a slight difference

nuée *noun, feminine*
  une nuée = a swarm

nuire *verb* [62]
  nuire à = to harm
  = to be harmful to

nuisible *adjective*
  = harmful

nuit *noun, feminine*
  une nuit = a night
  cette nuit = last night
  = tonight
  il fait nuit = it's dark
une nuit blanche = a sleepless night

nul/nulle
1 *adjective*
* (*describing a person*)✗ = hopeless
  (*describing a piece of work*)✗ = worthless
  (*describing a film, a book*)✗ = trashy

✗ in informal situations

- (*in sports*)
  un match nul = a draw, a tie
  faire match nul = to draw, to tie
2 *determiner*
  nul [**homme** | **pays** | **besoin** ...] = no [man | country | need ...]
  nul autre que vous = no-one else but you
3 *pronoun*
  = no-one
4 nulle part = nowhere

numéro *noun, masculine*
- (*for a house, a telephone, a ticket*)
  un numéro = a number
  un numéro de téléphone = a telephone number
- (*a magazine*)
  un numéro = a copy, an issue

nuque *noun, feminine*
  la nuque = the nape (of the neck)

Oo

obéir *verb* ③
  = to obey
  obéir à son maître = to obey one's master

obéissant/obéissante *adjective*
  = obedient

objet *noun, masculine*
  un objet = an object
  des objets de valeur = valuables
objets trouvés = lost property, lost and found

obligatoire *adjective*
  = compulsory

obliger *verb* ⑬
  obliger un enfant à manger = to make a child eat, to force a child to eat
  je suis obligé de partir = I have to go

obscur/obscure *adjective*
- = dark
- = obscure

obscurité *noun, feminine*
  l'obscurité = darkness

obsèques *noun, feminine plural*
  les obsèques = the funeral

observateur/observatrice *noun, masculine/feminine*
  un observateur/une observatrice = an observer

observer *verb* ①
- = to watch
- = to notice
- = to observe

obtenir *verb* ㊱
  = to get, to obtain

occasion *noun, feminine*
- (*a chance*)
  une occasion = an opportunity
- **une voiture d'occasion** = a second-hand car
- (*a circumstance*)
  une occasion = an occasion

occident *noun, masculine*
  l'occident = the west

occidental/occidentale *adjective*
(*plural*) **occidentaux/occidentales**
  = western

occupé/occupée *adjective*
- (*having a lot to do*) = busy
- (*not vacant*) = engaged

occuper *verb* ①
1 (**!** + *avoir*)
- = to occupy
- = to keep busy
  ça m'occupe = it keeps me busy
2 s'occuper (**!** + *être*)
- **s'occuper** = to keep oneself busy, to occupy oneself
- **s'occuper de** = to take care of, to look after

océan *noun, masculine*
  un océan = an ocean

octante *number*
  – eighty

octobre *noun, masculine*
  octobre = October

odeur *noun, feminine*
  une odeur = a smell

odieux/odieuse *adjective*
  = horrible, hateful

œil *noun, masculine*
(*plural*) **yeux**
  un œil = an eye

œillet *noun, masculine*
  un œillet = a carnation

œuf *noun, masculine*
  un œuf = an egg
  un œuf à la coque = a boiled egg
  un œuf dur = a hard-boiled egg
  un œuf sur le plat = a fried egg

œuvre *noun, feminine*
  une œuvre = a work

offense *noun, feminine*
  une offense = an insult

offenser *verb* ①
  = to offend

office *noun, masculine*
- (*in church*)
  un office = a service

O

* (an organization)
  un office = an office
  l'office du tourisme = the tourist office

offre noun, feminine
  une offre = an offer
  'offres d'emploi' = 'situations vacant'

offrir verb 4
1 (**!** + avoir)
* = to offer
* = to give
2 s'offrir (**!** + être)
  s'offrir une croisière = to treat oneself to a cruise

oie noun, feminine
  une oie = a goose

oignon noun, masculine
  un oignon = an onion

oiseau noun, masculine
(plural) **oiseaux**
  un oiseau = a bird

olivier noun, masculine
  un olivier = an olive tree

ombre noun, feminine
* (darkness)
  l'ombre = shade
* (a shape)
  une ombre = a shadow

ombrelle noun, feminine
  une ombrelle = a sunshade, a parasol

omnibus noun, masculine (**!** never changes)
  un (train) omnibus = a slow train, a local train

omoplate noun, feminine
  l'omoplate = the shoulder blade

on pronoun
* = someone
  on t'appelle = someone's calling you
* = we
  on a eu un accident = we had an accident
* = one
  = you
  = they
  on est obligé de payer à l'avance = one has to pay in advance
  = you have to pay in advance
  on vend des fleurs au supermarché = they sell flowers at the supermarket
* = people
  je me moque de ce qu'on dit = I don't care what people say
* (other possible translations)
  on m'a demandé ma carte = I was asked for my card
  on a réparé la route = the road has been repaired

oncle noun, masculine
  un oncle = an uncle

ondulé/ondulée adjective
  = wavy

ongle noun, masculine
  un ongle = a nail

ont ▶ avoir 8

onze number
  = eleven

onzième number
  = eleventh

opération noun, feminine
* (in mathematics)
  une opération = a calculation
* (on a patient)
  une opération = an operation

opérer verb 14
  = to operate
  se faire opérer = to have an operation

opinion noun, feminine
  une opinion = an opinion

opposé/opposée adjective
  = opposite

optimiste adjective
  = optimistic

or noun, masculine
  l'or = gold
  une montre en or = a gold watch

orage noun, masculine
  un orage = a storm

orageux/orageuse adjective
  = stormy

orchestre noun, masculine
  un orchestre = an orchestra
  = a band

ordinaire adjective
  = ordinary

ordinateur noun, masculine
  un ordinateur = a computer

ordonnance noun, feminine
  une ordonnance = a prescription

ordre noun, masculine
* (a command)
  un ordre = an order
* (a way of arranging things)
  dans l'ordre = in order
* (neatness)
  l'ordre = tidiness
  mettre de l'ordre = to tidy up, to clean up

ordures noun, feminine plural
  les ordures = rubbish, garbage, trash

oreille noun, feminine
  une oreille = an ear

oreiller noun, masculine
  un oreiller = a pillow

organisateur/organisatrice *noun,*
masculine/feminine
  un organisateur/une organisatrice = an
  organizer

organiser *verb* [1]
1 (**!** + *avoir*)
  = to organize
2 s'organiser (**!** + *être*)
  s'organiser = to get organized

organisme *noun, masculine*
  un organisme = an organization, a body

orge *noun, feminine*
  l'orge = barley

orgueil *noun, masculine*
  l'orgueil = pride

orgueilleux/orgueilleuse *adjective*
  = proud

orient *noun, masculine*
  l'orient = the east

oriental/orientale *adjective*
(plural) **orientaux/orientales**
  = eastern

originaire *adjective*
  être originaire d'un pays = to come from a
  country, to be a native of a country

original/originale *adjective*
(plural) **originaux/originales**
• = original
• = eccentric, unusual

origine *noun, feminine*
  l'origine = the origin

orner *verb* [1]
  = to decorate

orphelin/orpheline *noun,*
masculine/feminine
  un orphelin/une orpheline = an orphan

orteil *noun, masculine*
  un orteil = a toe

orthographe *noun, feminine*
  l'orthographe = spelling

ortie *noun, feminine*
  une ortie = a (stinging) nettle

os *noun, masculine* (**!** *never changes*)
  un os = a bone

oser *verb* [1]
  = to dare

osier *noun, masculine*
  l'osier = wicker

otage *noun, masculine*
  un otage = a hostage

ôter *verb* [1]
  = to take off, to remove

ou *conjunction*
• = or
  ou bien = or else
• ou (bien)… ou (bien)… = either… or…

où
1 *adverb*
  = where
  d'où vient le bus? = where does the bus
  come from?
2 *pronoun*
• = where
  restez où vous êtes = stay where you are
• = when
  juste au moment où il partait = just as he
  was leaving

oublier *verb* [2]
  = to forget

ouest
1 *noun, masculine*
  l'ouest = the west
2 *adjective* (**!** *never changes*)
  = west, western

ouf *exclamation*
  ouf! = phew!

oui *adverb*
  = yes
  je crois que oui = I think so

ouragan *noun, masculine*
  un ouragan = a hurricane

ourlet *noun, masculine*
  un ourlet = a hem

ours *noun, masculine* (**!** *never changes*)
  un ours = a bear
un ours en peluche = a teddy bear

oursin *noun, masculine*
  un oursin = a sea urchin

outil *noun, masculine*
  un outil = a tool

outre-mer *adverb*
  = overseas

ouvert/ouverte
1 ▶ **ouvrir** [32]
2 *adjective*
  = open

ouverture *noun, feminine*
  une ouverture = an opening

ouvrable *adjective*
  un jour ouvrable = a working day

ouvrage *noun, masculine*
  un ouvrage = a (piece of) work, a project
  = a book, a work

ouvre-boîtes *noun, masculine* (**!** *never
changes*)
  un ouvre-boîtes = a can-opener

ouvreur/ouvreuse *noun,*
masculine/feminine
  un ouvreur/une ouvreuse = an usher/an
  usherette

O

ouvrier/ouvrière
1 *noun, masculine/feminine*
  un ouvrier/une ouvrière = a worker
2 *adjective*
  = working-class

ouvrir *verb* 32
1 (! + *avoir*)
  = to open
2 s'ouvrir (! + *être*)
  s'ouvrir = to open

Pp

pagaille✗
1 *noun, feminine*
  une pagaille✗ = a mess
  mettre la pagaille✗ = to cause chaos
2 en pagaille✗
  il y a du vin en pagaille✗ = there's loads of
  wine, there's lots of wine

page *noun, feminine*
  une page = a page

paille *noun, feminine*
  la paille = straw

pain *noun, masculine*
• le pain = bread
• un pain = a loaf
  le pain grillé = toast
  un petit pain = a bread roll

pair/paire¹
1 *adjective*
  les nombres pairs = even numbers
2 au pair
  une jeune fille au pair = an au pair

paire² *noun, feminine*
  une paire = a pair

paisible *adjective*
  = peaceful

paix *noun, feminine* (! *never changes*)
  la paix = peace
  = peace and quiet

palais *noun, masculine* (! *never changes*)
• un palais = a palace
• le palais = the palate

pâle *adjective*
  = pale

palier *noun, masculine*
  le palier = the landing

palmier *noun, masculine*
  un palmier = a palm tree

---

pamplemousse *noun, masculine*
  un pamplemousse = a grapefruit

panaché *noun, masculine*
  un (demi-)panaché = a shandy, a beer with
  lemonade

pancarte *noun, feminine*
  une pancarte = a notice, a sign
  = a placard

panier *noun, masculine*
  un panier = a basket

paniquer✗ *verb* 1
  = to panic

panne *noun, feminine*
  une panne = a breakdown
  tomber en panne = to break down
  tomber en panne d'essence = to run out
  of petrol, to run out of gas
  une panne de courant = a power failure

panneau *noun, masculine*
(*plural*) **panneaux**
• un panneau = a panel
• un panneau = a sign
  un panneau d'affichage = a noticeboard
  un panneau de signalisation routière
  = a road sign

pansement *noun, masculine*
  un pansement = a dressing, a bandage
  un pansement adhésif = a plaster, a
  Band-Aid

pantalon *noun, masculine*
  un pantalon = (a pair of) trousers, (a pair
  of) pants

pantoufle *noun, feminine*
  une pantoufle = a slipper

paon *noun, masculine*
  un paon = a peacock

papa *noun, masculine*
  un papa = a dad

pape *noun, masculine*
  le pape = the pope

papeterie *noun, feminine*
  une papeterie = a stationer's

papier *noun, masculine*
  le papier = paper
  le papier alu(minium) = aluminium foil,
  aluminum foil
  le papier d'emballage = wrapping paper
  le papier hygiénique = toilet paper
  le papier peint = wallpaper
  les papiers (d'identité) = (identity)
  papers

papillon *noun, masculine*
  un papillon = a butterfly

pâquerette *noun, feminine*
  une pâquerette = a daisy

Pâques *noun, masculine*
  Pâques = Easter

✗ *in informal situations*

paquet noun, masculine
* un paquet = a packet
* un paquet = a parcel, a package

par
1 preposition
* = by
  il a été piqué par une abeille = he was stung by a bee
  payer par carte de crédit = to pay by credit card
* = through
  le chemin passe par la forêt = the path goes through the forest
  par ici = this way, through here
* = per
  = a
  par personne = per person
  trois par [jour | mois | an ...] = three a [day | month | year ...]
* = in
  mettez-vous deux par deux = stand in twos
  sortir par mauvais temps = to go out in bad weather
* = on
  par une froide journée d'hiver = on a cold winter's day
* = out of
  regarder par la fenêtre = to look out (of) the window
  par bêtise = out of stupidity
2 par contre = on the other hand

parachute noun, masculine
* (the equipment)
  un parachute = a parachute
* (the sport)
  le parachute = parachuting

parages noun, masculine plural
  dans les parages – in the area

paraître verb 63
1 (! + avoir)
* (to create an impression) = to seem, to look
* (to be seen) = to appear
  paraître en public = to appear in public
2 (! + être)
  (if it's a book, a record) = to come out
3 il paraît que = apparently
  il paraît que non = apparently not

parapente noun, masculine
* (the equipment)
  un parapente = a paraglider
* (the sport)
  le parapente = paragliding

parapluie noun, masculine
  un parapluie = an umbrella

parasol noun, masculine
  un parasol = a sunshade, a beach umbrella

parc noun, masculine
  un parc = a park
un parc d'attractions = an amusement park

parce que (parce qu' before vowel or mute h) conjunction
  = because

par-ci adverb
  par-ci par-là = here and there

parcmètre noun, masculine
  un parcmètre = a parking meter

parcourir verb 26
* = to cover
  parcourir une distance = to cover a distance
* = to go all over
  parcourir toute la ville = to go all over the town
* = to glance through
  parcourir un article = to glance through an article

parcours noun, masculine (! never changes)
  un parcours = a journey
  = a route

parcouru/parcourue ▶ parcourir 26

pardessus noun, masculine (! never changes)
  un pardessus = an overcoat

pardon noun, masculine
* le pardon = forgiveness
  demander pardon = to apologize
  = to ask for forgiveness
* pardon! = sorry!
  pardon monsieur, je cherche la mairie = excuse me, I'm looking for the town hall

pardonner verb 1
  = to forgive

pare-brise noun, masculine (! never changes)
  un pare-brise = a windscreen, a windshield

pareil/pareille
1 adjective
* = the same
  = similar
  = identical
* = such
  je n'ai jamais vu un luxe pareil = I've never seen such luxury
2 pareil✳ adverb
  = the same
  faisons pareil✳ = let's do the same

parent/parente
1 noun, masculine|feminine
  un parent/une parente = a relative, a relation
2 parents noun, masculine plural
  les parents = parents

parenthèse noun, feminine
  entre parenthèses = between brackets

P

paresse noun, feminine
la paresse = laziness

paresseux/paresseuse adjective
= lazy

parfait/parfaite adjective
= perfect

parfois adverb
= sometimes

parfum noun, masculine
un parfum = a perfume
= a flavo(u)r

parfumé/parfumée adjective
= scented
= flavo(u)red

parier verb [2]
= to bet

parisien/parisienne adjective
= Parisian

parking noun, masculine
un parking = a car park, a parking lot

parler verb [1]
= to talk
= to speak

parmi preposition
= among

paroisse noun, feminine
une paroisse = a parish

parole noun, feminine
une parole = a word
prendre la parole = to speak
à vous la parole! = your turn to speak!

parrain noun, masculine
un parrain = a godfather

part
1 noun, feminine
• (when dividing)
une part (of food) = a portion
(of a legacy) = a share
• (meaning direction, place)
de toutes parts = from all sides, from
everywhere
nulle part = nowhere
quelque part = somewhere
d'une part… d'autre part = on the one
hand… on the other hand
faire part d'une naissance = to announce
a birth
2 de la part de = from
= on behalf of
elle m'a fait part de sa décision = she
informed me of her decision
3 à part = apart (from)

partager verb [13]
= to share

partenaire noun, masculine/feminine
un partenaire/une partenaire = a partner

parterre noun, masculine
• (in a garden)
un parterre = a bed
• (in a theatre)
le parterre = the stalls, the orchestra

participer verb [1]
• participer (à) = to take part (in)
• participer à = to share in

particulier/particulière adjective
= particular
= special

partie
1 noun, feminine
• (not the whole)
une partie = (a) part
• (at cards, in sport)
une partie = a game
2 en partie = partly, in part
3 faire partie de = to be part of
ça fait partie de mon travail = it's part of
my job
faire partie d'un club = to be a member of
a club

partir
1 verb [30] (! + être)
• = to leave
partir en courant = to run off
• = to go
partir à Paris = to go to Paris
• = to start
le sentier part du bois = the path starts in
the wood
2 à partir de = from
à partir de maintenant = from now on

partout adverb
= everywhere

paru ▶ paraître [63]

parvenir verb [36] (! + être)
• parvenir à = to achieve
parvenir à son but = to achieve one's goal
parvenir à faire = to manage to do
• parvenir à = to reach
parvenir à New York = to reach New York

parvenu/parvenue ▶ parvenir [36]

pas
1 adverb
= not
pas du tout = not at all
le film n'est pas mal✶ = the film isn't bad
2 noun, masculine (! never changes)
• (a movement)
un pas = a step
c'est à deux pas d'ici = it's very near here
• (speed)
le pas = the pace
d'un pas lent = slowly

passage noun, masculine
• (a section of a text, a film)
un passage = a passage

---

* (*a means of access*)
un passage = a way
céder le passage = to give way, to yield
'passage interdit' = 'no entry'
* **être de passage** = to be passing through
un passage à niveau = a level crossing, a
grade crossing
un passage pour piétons = a pedestrian
crossing, a crosswalk
un passage souterrain = a subway, a
pedestrian underpass

passager/passagère *noun,*
masculine/feminine
un passager/une passagère = a passenger
un passager clandestin = a stowaway

passant/passante *noun,*
masculine/feminine
un passant/une passante = a passer-by

passé/passée
1 ▶ passer 1
2 *adjective*
* **l'an passé** = last year
* **il est cinq heures passées** = it's past five
o'clock
3 passé *noun, masculine*
le passé = the past

passer *verb* 1
1 (**!** + *avoir*)
* = to spend
passer son temps à lire = to spend one's
time reading
* = to take, to sit
passer un examen = to take an
examination

  ! *Note that* **réussir à un examen** *means to*
  pass an exam.

* = to show
= to play
passer un film = to show a film
passer un disque = to play a record
* = to pass
= to give
peux-tu passer le sel? = can you pass the
salt?
il m'a passé son rhume = he gave me his
cold
je vous la passe (*on the telephone*) = I'll
put her on
* (*to miss*)
passer son tour = to pass
2 (**!** + *être*)
* (*to walk, to drive, to fly past*) = to go past, to
go by
un bus vient de passer = a bus has just
gone past
passer devant l'église = to go past the
church, to pass the church
* (*to go a certain way*)
passer par = to go through, to go by
passer par la porte de derrière = to go
through the back door

* (*to make one's way*) = to get past
je ne peux pas passer = I can't get past
laisser passer les enfants = to let the
children past
* (*to call, to arrive*) = to come
le facteur passe vers dix heures = the
postman comes at about ten o'clock
* (*to pay a visit*) = to drop in
passer voir un ami = to drop in on a friend
* (*to move to a different level*)
passer dans la classe supérieure = to
move up to the next class
* = to pass
le temps passe trop vite = time passes too
quickly
3 se passer (**!** + *être*)
* **se passer** = to happen
qu'est-ce qui se passe? = what's
happening?, what's going on?
* **se passer** = to go
ça s'est bien passé = it went well
* **se passer de** = to do without

passerelle *noun, feminine*
une passerelle = a footbridge
= a gangway

passe-temps *noun, masculine* (**!** *never*
changes)
un passe-temps = a hobby

passion *noun, feminine*
une passion = a passion

passionnant/passionnante
adjective
= fascinating
= exciting

passionné/passionnée
1 ▶ passionner 1
2 *adjective*
= passionate
3 *noun, masculine/feminine*
un passionné/une passionnée de football
= a football enthusiast, a football fan

passionner *verb* 1
1 (**!** + *avoir*)
= to fascinate
2 se passionner pour (**!** + *être*)
se passionner pour = to have a passion for

passoire *noun, feminine*
une passoire = a colander
= a strainer

pastèque *noun, feminine*
une pastèque = a watermelon

pasteur *noun, masculine*
un pasteur = a parson, a minister

pastille *noun, feminine*
une pastille = a lozenge, a cough drop

patate* *noun, feminine*
une patate* = a spud, a potato

patauger *verb* 13
= to splash about

pâte
1 *noun, feminine*
- la pâte = pastry
  = dough
  = batter
- une pâte = a paste
2 pâtes *noun, feminine plural*
  des pâtes (alimentaires) = pasta

pâté *noun, masculine*
- le pâté = pâté
  un pâté (en croûte) = a pie
- un pâté de maisons = a block (of houses)

patience *noun, feminine*
- (*a virtue*)
  la patience = patience
- (*a game of cards*)
  faire une patience = to play patience, to play solitaire

patient/patiente
1 *adjective*
  = patient
2 *noun, masculine/feminine*
  un patient/une patiente = a patient

patienter *verb* [1]
  = to wait

patin *noun, masculine*
  un patin = a skate
des patins de frein = brake blocks
des patins à glace = ice-skates
des patins à roulettes = roller-skates

patinage *noun, masculine*
  le patinage = skating

patinoire *noun, feminine*
  une patinoire = an ice rink

pâtisserie *noun, feminine*
- (*a place*)
  une pâtisserie = a cake shop
- (*a sweet*)
  une pâtisserie = a pastry, a cake

pâtissier/pâtissière *noun, masculine/feminine*
  un pâtissier/une pâtissière = a confectioner

patron/patronne
1 *noun, masculine/feminine*
  le patron/la patronne = the boss
  = the manager
2 patron *noun, masculine*
  un patron = a pattern

patronne ▶ patron 1

patte *noun, feminine*
  une patte = a leg
  = a paw
  = a foot
  à quatre pattes = on all fours

---

paupière *noun, feminine*
  une paupière = an eyelid

pause *noun, feminine*
  une pause = a break
  faire une pause = to take a break

pauvre *adjective*
  = poor

pauvreté *noun, feminine*
  la pauvreté = poverty

pavé/pavée
1 *adjective*
  = cobbled
2 pavé *noun, masculine*
  un pavé = a cobblestone

payant/payante *adjective*
  (*describing a person*) = paying
  (*describing a show*) = not free

payer *verb* [21]
1 (! + *avoir*)
  = to pay
2 se payer✳ (! + *être*)
  se payer✳ un repas = to treat oneself to a meal

pays *noun, masculine* (! *never changes*)
  un pays = a country

paysage *noun, masculine*
  un paysage = a landscape

Pays-Bas *noun, masculine plural*
  les Pays-Bas = the Netherlands, Holland

Pays de Galles *noun, masculine*
  le Pays de Galles = Wales

PCV *noun, masculine*
  appeler en PCV = to make a reverse-charge call, to call collect

péage *noun, masculine*
  le péage = the toll
  = the tollbooth

peau *noun, feminine*
  (*plural*) **peaux**
  la peau = skin

pêche *noun, feminine*
- une pêche = a peach
- la pêche = fishing

péché *noun, masculine*
  un péché = a sin

pêcher
1 *verb* [1]
- = to catch
- = to go fishing
2 *noun, masculine*
  un pêcher = a peach tree

pêcheur *noun, masculine*
  un pêcheur = a fisherman

pédale *noun, feminine*
  une pédale = a pedal

pédaler verb 1
= to pedal

pédestre adjective
une randonnée pédestre = a ramble, a walk

peigne noun, masculine
un peigne = a comb

peignoir noun, masculine
un peignoir = a dressing gown, a robe

peindre verb 55
= to paint

peine
1 noun, feminine
• avoir de la peine à finir un travail = to have difficulty finishing a job
• ce n'est pas la peine d'essayer = it's not worth trying
  ça vaut la peine d'y aller = it's worth going
• (sorrow)
  la peine = grief
  faire de la peine à ses amis = to upset one's friends
  avoir de la peine = to be sad
• (punishment)
  une peine de prison = a prison sentence
  la peine de mort = capital punishment
2 à peine = hardly

peint/peinte ▶ peindre 55

peintre noun, masculine
un peintre = a painter

peinture noun, feminine
• la peinture (substance) = paint
  (the activity) = painting
• une peinture = a painting

pêle-mêle adverb
= higgledy-piggledy, pell-mell

peler verb 17
= to peel

pèlerinage noun, masculine
un pèlerinage = a pilgrimage

pelle noun, feminine
une pelle = a shovel

pellicule
1 noun, feminine
une pellicule = a film
2 pellicules noun, feminine plural
des pellicules = dandruff

pelouse noun, feminine
la pelouse = the lawn

peluche noun, feminine
une peluche = a soft toy
un animal en peluche = a soft toy, a stuffed animal

pencher verb 1
1 (! + avoir)
= to tilt
pencher la tête = to bend one's head

2 **se pencher** (! + être)
se pencher = to lean
= to bend down

pendant
1 preposition
• = for
  pendant des heures = for hours
  pendant tout le voyage = for the whole journey, throughout the journey
• = during
  pendant la nuit = during the night
  pendant ce temps = meanwhile
2 pendant que = while

penderie noun, feminine
une penderie = a wardrobe, a closet

pendre verb 6
• = to hang
• = to dangle

pendu/pendue
1 ▶ pendre 6
2 pendu noun, masculine
jouer au pendu = to play hangman

pendule noun, feminine
une pendule = a clock

pénétrer verb 14
pénétrer dans un bâtiment = to enter a building, to get into a building

pénible adjective
= hard, difficult

péniblement adverb
= with difficulty

péniche noun, feminine
une péniche = a barge

pensée noun, feminine
• (an idea)
  une pensée = a thought
• (a flower)
  une pensée = a pansy

penser verb 1
• = to think
  qu'en pensez-vous? = what do you think (about it)?
• penser à = to think of
  = to remember
  je pense à toi = I'm thinking of you
  j'y ai pensé = I thought about it

pension noun, feminine
• (money)
  une pension = a pension
• (a school)
  une pension = a boarding school
• (a hotel)
  une pension = a boarding house
  la pension complète = full board
  une pension de famille = a family hotel

pensionnaire noun, masculine/feminine
un pensionnaire/une pensionnaire (in a school) = a boarder
(in a hotel) = a resident

P

pensionnat *noun, masculine*
un pensionnat = a boarding school

pente *noun, feminine*
une pente = a slope
en pente = sloping

Pentecôte *noun, feminine*
la Pentecôte = Whitsun, Pentecost

pépé✶ *noun, masculine*
un pépé✶ = a grandad

pépin *noun, masculine*
• un pépin = a pip, a seed
• un pépin✶ = a slight problem

perche *noun, feminine*
une perche = a pole
la saut à la perche = pole vaulting

perdant/perdante
1 *adjective*
= losing
2 *noun, masculine/feminine*
un perdant/une perdante = a loser

perdre *verb* 6
1 (**!** + *avoir*)
= to lose
perdre son temps = to waste one's time
2 se perdre (**!** + *être*)
se perdre = to get lost

perdu/perdue
1 ▶ **perdre** 6
2 *adjective*
• = lost
= stray
• = wasted
c'est du temps perdu = it's a waste of time
• = remote, isolated

père *noun, masculine*
un père = a father
le père Noël = Father Christmas, Santa
Claus

perfectionner *verb* 1
1 (**!** + *avoir*)
= to perfect
= to improve
= to refine
2 se perfectionner (**!** + *être*)
se perfectionner = to improve

périmé/périmée *adjective*
= out-of-date

périphérique *noun, masculine*
le périphérique = the ring road, the
beltway

permanence
1 *noun, feminine*
une permanence = a permanently
manned office
(*in school*) = a (supervised) study room, a
study hall

2 en permanence = permanently

permettre *verb* 60
1 (**!** + *avoir*)
= to allow
permettre à un enfant de sortir = to allow a
child to go out
2 se permettre (**!** + *être*)
• (*to act without asking*)
se permettre de se servir = to take the
liberty of helping oneself
• (*to have money*)
pouvoir se permettre d'aller au restaurant
= to be able to afford to eat out

permis/permise
1 ▶ **permettre** 60
2 *adjective*
= permitted, allowed
3 permis *noun, masculine* (**!** *never
changes*)
un permis = a permit
= a licence, a license
un permis de conduire = a driving
licence, a driver's license

perroquet *noun, masculine*
un perroquet = a parrot

perruche *noun, feminine*
une perruche = a budgerigar, a budgie

perruque *noun, feminine*
une perruque = a wig

persienne *noun, feminine*
une persienne = a shutter

persil *noun, masculine*
le persil = parsley

personnage *noun, masculine*
un personnage = a character

personne
1 *pronoun*
= nobody
= anybody
2 *noun, feminine*
une personne = a person
quelques personnes = a few people

personnel/personnelle
1 *adjective*
= personal
2 personnel *noun, masculine*
le personnel = the staff

perte *noun, feminine*
une perte = a loss
une perte de temps = a waste of time

peser *verb* 16
= to weigh

pétanque *noun, feminine*
la pétanque = pétanque, *French bowls*

pétard *noun, masculine*
un pétard = a banger, a firecracker

pétillant/pétillante *adjective*
= sparkling

---

petit/petite
1 *adjective*
  (*in size or importance*) = small, little
  (*in duration, length*) = short
2 *noun, masculine/feminine*
  un petit/une petite = a child
  (*in school*) = a junior
3 petit *noun, masculine*
  un petit = a little one
  les petits = the young
4 petit à petit = little by little, gradually
les petits chevaux ≈ ludo, Parcheesi

petite-fille *noun, feminine*
(*plural*) **petites-filles**
  une petite-fille = a granddaughter

petit-fils *noun, masculine*
(*plural*) **petits-fils**
  un petit-fils = a grandson

petits-enfants *noun, masculine plural*
  des petits-enfants = grandchildren

pétrole *noun, masculine*
  le pétrole = oil, petroleum

peu
1 *noun, masculine*
  un peu = a little
  un tout petit peu = just a little
2 *adverb*
• = not much
  il mange peu = he doesn't eat very much
• = not very
  peu intelligent = not very intelligent
  peu après = soon afterwards
3 peu de *determiner*
  = few, not many
  = little, not much
  peu de livres = few books
  peu de nourriture = little food
  c'est peu de chose = it's not much
4 peu à peu = gradually
5 à peu près = more or less
  = approximately

peuple *noun, masculine*
  un peuple = a people

peur *noun, feminine*
  la peur = fear
  avoir peur = to be afraid
  faire peur à quelqu'un = to frighten
    someone

peut-être *adverb*
  = perhaps, maybe

peux ▶ pouvoir 2 49

phare *noun, masculine*
  un phare (*on a car*) = a headlight
  (*on the coast*) = a lighthouse

pharmacie *noun, feminine*
  une pharmacie = a chemist's (shop), a
    drugstore

pharmacien/pharmacienne *noun,*
masculine/feminine
  un pharmacien/une pharmacienne = a
    chemist, a pharmacist

philatélie *noun, feminine*
  la philatélie = stamp collecting

phoque *noun, masculine*
  un phoque = a seal

photo *noun, feminine*
• (*a picture*)
  une photo = a photograph
• (*the activity*)
  la photo = photography

photocopie *noun, feminine*
  une photocopie = a photocopy

photocopieuse *noun, feminine*
  une photocopieuse = a photocopier

photographe *noun, masculine/feminine*
  un photographe/une photographe = a
    photographer

photographie *noun, feminine*
• (*a picture*)
  une photographie = a photograph
• (*the activity*)
  la photographie = photography

phrase *noun, feminine*
  une phrase = a sentence

physicien/physicienne *noun,*
masculine/feminine
  un physicien/une physicienne = a
    physicist

physique
1 *adjective*
  = physical
2 *noun, feminine*
  la physique = physics
3 *noun, masculine*
  le physique = physical appearance

P

picorer *verb* 1
  = to peck

pièce *noun, feminine*
• (*in a house, an apartment*)
  une pièce = a room
  un trois-pièces cuisine = a three-roomed
    apartment with kitchen
• (*money*)
  une pièce (de monnaie) = a coin
• (*at the theatre*)
  une pièce (de théâtre) = a play
• (*a component*)
  une pièce = a part
  une pièce de rechange = a spare part
• (*an item*)
  une pièce = a piece
  ils coûtent dix euros pièce = they cost ten
    euros each
  un (maillot) deux-pièces = a two-piece
    swimsuit
• (*in a file*)
  une pièce = a document

une pièce détachée = a spare part
une pièce d'identité = identification

pied *noun, masculine*
- *(part of the body)*
  un pied = a foot
  à pied = on foot
  il va à l'école à pied = he walks to school
  pieds nus = barefoot
  un coup de pied = a kick
- *(the lower end)*
  le pied = the foot, the bottom
  au pied de l'escalier = at the bottom of the stairs
- *(an upright part)*
  un pied *(on a table)* = a leg
  (on a lamp) = a base
  (on a glass) = a stem
- *(a measurement)*
  un pied = a foot

piège *noun, masculine*
  un piège = a trap

pierre *noun, feminine*
  une pierre = a stone

piéton/piétonne *noun,*
masculine/feminine
  un piéton/une piétonne = a pedestrian

pieuvre *noun, feminine*
  une pieuvre = an octopus

pigeon *noun, masculine*
  un pigeon = a pigeon
pigeon vole = Simon says

pile
1 *noun, feminine*
- *(in a flashlight, a toy)*
  une pile = a battery
  à piles = battery-operated
- *(on a coin)*
  pile = tails
  jouer à pile ou face = to play heads or tails
- *(things on top of one another)*
  une pile = a pile, a stack
2 *adverb***✷**
  à trois heures pile✷ = at three o'clock on the dot
  s'arrêter pile✷ = to stop dead
  tu tombes pile✷ = you've come at just the right moment

pilier *noun, masculine*
  un pilier = a pillar

pilote *noun, masculine*
  un pilote = a pilot
pilote automobile = racing driver
pilote de rallye = rally driver

pilule *noun, feminine*
  une pilule = a pill

pin *noun, masculine*
  un pin = a pine (tree)

pinceau *noun, masculine*
(plural) **pinceaux**
  un pinceau = a (paint)brush

pincée *noun, feminine*
  une pincée = a pinch

pincer *verb* 12
  = to pinch

pinède *noun, feminine*
  une pinède = a pine forest

pingouin *noun, masculine*
  un pingouin = a penguin

ping-pong *noun, masculine*
(plural) **ping-pongs**
  le ping-pong = table tennis, ping-pong

pin's *noun, masculine* (**!** *never changes*)
  un pin's = a (lapel) badge, a pin

pioche *noun, feminine*
  une pioche = a pickaxe

pipe *noun, feminine*
  une pipe = a pipe

pipi✷ *noun, masculine*
  faire pipi✷ = to have a pee, to take a pee

pique *noun, masculine*
  pique = spades

pique-nique *noun, masculine*
(plural) **pique-niques**
  un pique-nique = a picnic

piquer *verb* 1
1 (**!** + *avoir*)
- *(if it's a bee, a nettle, smoke)* = to sting
  (if it's a snake, a mosquito) = to bite
  (if it's a thorn) = to prick
- *(to take)*✷ = to pinch, to steal
  = to borrow
2 se piquer (**!** + *être*)
  se piquer = to prick oneself

piqûre *noun, feminine*
  une piqûre *(with a syringe)* = an injection
  (from an insect) = a sting
  = a bite

pire
1 *adjective*
  = worse
  = worst
2 *noun, masculine*
  le pire = the worst (about it)

piscine *noun, feminine*
  une piscine = a swimming pool
  une piscine couverte = an indoor swimming pool

pistache *noun, feminine*
  une pistache = a pistachio nut

piste *noun, feminine*
- *(a clearly marked path)*
  une piste *(in a forest)* = a trail, a track
  (when skiing) = a piste, a run

✷ in informal situations

(*in racing events*)
= a (race)track
= a racecourse
* (*in a circus*)
la **piste** = the ring
* (*in a police investigation*)
une **piste** = a lead
une **piste d'atterrissage** = a runway
une **piste cyclable** = a cycle lane
une **piste de danse** = a dance floor

pistolet *noun, masculine*
un pistolet = a gun

pitre *noun, masculine*
un pitre = a clown, a buffoon

pittoresque *adjective*
= picturesque

placard *noun, masculine*
un placard = a cupboard

place *noun, feminine*
* (*in a town*)
une **place** = a square
* (*for a passenger, a spectator*)
une **place** = a seat
une **place assise** = a seat
une **place debout** = a standing ticket
* (*a position*)
une **place** = a place
remettre un livre à sa place = to put a
  book back in its place
obtenir la première place = to take first
  place
à la place de = instead of
* (*a vacant spot*)
une **place** (*at a table*) = a place
(*for a car*) = a parking space
* (*enough empty space*)
de la place = room, space

plafond *noun, masculine*
le plafond = the ceiling

plage *noun, feminine*
la plage = the beach

plaie *noun, feminine*
une plaie = a wound

plaindre *verb* 54
1 (**!** + *avoir*)
= to feel sorry for
2 se plaindre (**!** + *être*)
se plaindre = to complain

plaint/plainte¹ ▶ **plaindre** 54

plainte² *noun, feminine*
* (*expressing dissatisfaction*)
une **plainte** = a complaint
* (*a sound of pain*)
une **plainte** = a moan, a groan

plaire *verb* 59
* s'il te plaît, s'il vous plaît = please
* Marc plaît aux filles = girls find Marc
  attractive
le film leur a plu = they liked the film

plaisanterie *noun, feminine*
une plaisanterie = a joke

plaisir *noun, masculine*
le plaisir = pleasure
ma visite leur a fait plaisir = they were
  pleased to see me

plaît ▶ **plaire** 59

plan *noun, masculine*
* (*of an area*)
un **plan** = a map
* (*for an essay*)
un **plan** = an outline
* (*for a line of action*)
un **plan** = a plan
* (*in films, photography*)
au premier plan = in the foreground
un gros plan = a close-up

planche *noun, feminine*
une **planche** = a plank
= a board
une **planche à repasser** = an ironing
board
une **planche à roulettes** = a skateboard
une **planche à voile** = a windsurfing
board

plancher *noun, masculine*
le plancher = the floor

planète *noun, feminine*
une planète = a planet

planeur *noun, masculine*
* (*the equipment*)
un **planeur** = a glider
* (*the sport*)
le **planeur** = gliding

planifier *verb* 2
= to plan

plante *noun, feminine*
une **plante** = a plant
une **plante grasse** = a succulent
une **plante verte** = a houseplant

planter *verb* 1
* = to plant
* planter une tente = to pitch a tent

plaque *noun, feminine*
une **plaque** (*of metal, glass*) = a plate
une **plaque d'immatriculation** = a
number plate, a license plate

plastique *noun, masculine*
le plastique = plastic

plat/plate
1 *adjective*
= flat
2 plat *noun, masculine*
un **plat** = a dish
= a course
le plat du jour = today's special

3 à plat
* (*the way something lies*)
  à plat = flat
  poser une carte à plat = to lay a map down
    flat
  à plat ventre = flat on one's stomach
* (*describing a tyre*)
  à plat = flat
* (*describing a person*)
  à plat✶ = run down

plateau *noun, masculine*
(*plural*) **plateaux**
  un plateau (*for serving*) = a tray
  un plateau de fromages = a cheeseboard

platine *noun, feminine*
  une platine = a turntable
  une platine CD = a CD player

plâtre *noun, masculine*
  le plâtre = plaster

plein/pleine
1 *adjective*
* = full
* **en pleine forêt** = (right) in the middle of
    the forest
  en plein jour = in broad daylight
  en plein air = in the open air
  en pleine forme = in great shape, really fit
2 plein *noun, masculine*
  faire le plein (**d'essence**) = to fill up (with
    petrol)

pleurer *verb* [1]
  = to cry, to weep

pleut ▶ pleuvoir [33]

pleuvoir *verb* [33]
  = to rain
  il pleut = it's raining

plier *verb* [2]
  = to fold
  = to bend

plombier *noun, masculine*
  un plombier = a plumber

plongée *noun, feminine*
  la plongée = diving
  la plongée sous-marine = deep-sea diving

plongeoir *noun, masculine*
  un plongeoir = a diving-board

plongeon *noun, masculine*
  un plongeon = a dive

plonger *verb* [13]
* = to dive
* = to plunge

plongeur/plongeuse *noun,*
masculine/feminine
  un plongeur/une plongeuse = a diver

✶ in informal situations

plu
* **▶ plaire** [59]
* **▶ pleuvoir** [33]

pluie *noun, feminine*
  la pluie = rain

plume *noun, feminine*
* (*on a bird*)
  une plume = a feather
* (*on a pen*)
  une plume = a nib

plupart *noun, feminine*
  la plupart de = most of

pluriel *noun, masculine*
  le pluriel = the plural

plus
1 *conjunction*
  = plus
2 *adverb*
* = more
  c'est plus intéressant = it's more
    interesting
  arriver plus tôt que d'habitude = to arrive
    earlier than usual
  de plus en plus prudent = more and more
    careful
  deux fois plus cher = twice as expensive
* **plus de** = more
  = more than, over
  plus de la moitié = more than half
  elle a plus de seize ans = she's over sixteen
  il est plus de minuit = it's past midnight
* **plus... plus...** = the more... the more
  plus... moins... = the more... the less
  plus... mieux... = the more... the better
  plus on lit, plus on apprend = the more
    you read, the more you learn
* **le plus/la plus** = the most
  = the more
  les plus belles fleurs du jardin = the most
    beautiful flowers in the garden
  le plus cher des deux = the more
    expensive of the two
* **en plus** = on top (of that)
  il fait froid et en plus il pleut = it's cold and
    on top of that it's raining
  en plus de mon travail = on top of my
    work
3 ne... plus = no more, not any more
  = no longer
  il n'y a plus de pain = there's no more
    bread, there's no bread left
  elle ne travaille plus = she doesn't work
    any more, she no longer works
  je n'ai plus que dix euros = I've only got
    ten euros left
  il ne te reste plus rien = you've nothing
    left
  plus jamais = never again
  il n'y va pas, et moi non plus = he's not
    going and neither am I

plusieurs *adjective*
  = several

plutôt *adverb*
= rather
= instead

pluvieux/pluvieuse *adjective*
= rainy

pneu *noun, masculine*
un pneu = a tyre, a tire

pneumatique *adjective*
= inflatable

poche *noun, feminine*
une poche = a pocket

poêle
1 *noun, feminine*
une poêle (à frire) = a frying pan
2 *noun, masculine*
un poêle = a stove

poésie *noun, feminine*
* la poésie = poetry
* une poésie = a poem

poids *noun, masculine* (**!** *never changes*)
le poids = the weight
prendre du poids = to put on weight
un poids lourd = a heavy goods vehicle

poignée *noun, feminine*
* (*on a door*)
une poignée = a handle
* (*an amount*)
une poignée = a handful
une poignée de main = a handshake

poignet *noun, masculine*
un poignet = a wrist
= a cuff

poil *noun, masculine*
un poil (*on the body, on an animal*) = a hair
(*on a brush*) = a bristle

poing *noun, masculine*
le poing = the fist
un coup de poing = a punch

point
1 *noun, masculine*
* (*a punctuation mark*)
un point = a full stop, a period
deux points = a colon
* (*when scoring*)
un point = a point
* (*in sewing, in knitting*)
un point = a stitch
* (*a small round mark*)
un point = a dot, a speck
* (*a particular place or position*)
un point de rencontre = a meeting point
2 à point
un bifteck (cuit) à point = a medium rare
steak
un point de départ = a starting point
un point d'exclamation = an
exclamation mark
un point d'interrogation = a question
mark

un point de repère = a landmark
des points de suspension = suspension
points

pointe *noun, feminine*
la pointe = the point, the tip
sur la pointe des pieds = on tiptoe

pointer: se pointer* *verb* [1] (**!** + *être*)
se pointer* = to show up

pointu/pointue *adjective*
= pointed
= with a sharp point

pointure *noun, feminine*
une pointure = a shoe size

point-virgule *noun, masculine*
(*plural*) **points-virgules**
un point-virgule = a semicolon

poire *noun, feminine*
une poire = a pear

poireau *noun, masculine*
(*plural*) **poireaux**
un poireau = a leek

pois *noun, masculine* (**!** *never changes*)
* (*on material*)
un pois = a dot
à pois = polka dot, dotted
* (*in a pod*)
un pois = a pea
des petits pois = garden peas, petits pois

poisson *noun, masculine*
un poisson = a fish
un poisson d'avril = an April fool's joke
un poisson rouge = a goldfish

poissonnerie *noun, feminine*
une poissonnerie = a fishmonger's, a fish
shop

poissonnier/poissonnière *noun,*
masculine/feminine
un poissonnier/une poissonnière = a
fishmonger, a fish dealer

Poissons *noun, masculine plural*
Poissons = Pisces

poitrine *noun, feminine*
la poitrine = the chest
= the bust

poivre *noun, masculine*
le poivre = pepper

poivron *noun, masculine*
un poivron = a sweet pepper, a capsicum

poli/polie *adjective*
* (*well-mannered*) = polite
* (*shiny*) = polished

police *noun, feminine*
la police = the police
police secours ≈ emergency services

policier *noun, masculine*
un policier = a policeman

P

polluer *verb* [1]
= to pollute

Pologne *noun, feminine*
la Pologne = Poland

polonais/polonaise
1 *adjective*
= Polish
2 polonais *noun, masculine*
le polonais = Polish

pommade *noun, feminine*
une pommade = an ointment

pomme *noun, feminine*
une pomme = an apple
une pomme de pin = a pine cone
une pomme de terre = a potato

pommier *noun, masculine*
un pommier = an apple tree

pompe *noun, feminine*
une pompe = a pump

pompier *noun, masculine*
un pompier = a fireman, a firefighter
les pompiers = the fire brigade, the fire
  department

pompiste *noun, masculine|feminine*
un pompiste/une pompiste = a petrol
  pump attendant, a gas station
  attendant

pont *noun, masculine*
• (*over a river*)
  un pont = a bridge
• (*on a ship*)
  un pont = a deck
• (*extra time off*)
  faire le pont *to have the day(s) off between*
  a public holiday and a weekend

populaire *adjective*
• (*describing an area*) = working-class
• (*meaning well-liked*) = popular

porc *noun, masculine*
• (*the animal*)
  un porc = a pig
• (*the meat*)
  le porc = pork

porc-épic *noun, masculine*
(*plural*) **porc-épics**
  un porc-épic = a porcupine

porcherie *noun, feminine*
une porcherie = a pigsty

port *noun, masculine*
un port = a harbo(u)r, a port
un port de pêche = a fishing harbo(u)r
un port de plaisance = a marina

portail *noun, masculine*
un portail = a gate

porte *noun, feminine*
une porte = a door
= a gate
mettre à la porte = to throw out
une porte d'embarquement = a
  departure gate
la porte d'entrée = the front door

porte-clés, **porte-clefs** *noun,*
masculine (**!** *never changes*)
un porte-clés = a key ring

porte-fenêtre *noun, feminine*
(*plural*) **portes-fenêtres**
une porte-fenêtre = a French window

portefeuille *noun, masculine*
un portefeuille = a wallet

portemanteau *noun, masculine*
(*plural*) **portemanteaux**
un portemanteau = a coat rack
= a coat stand

porte-monnaie *noun, masculine*
(**!** *never changes*)
un porte-monnaie = a purse, a coin purse

porter *verb* [1]
1 (**!** + *avoir*)
• = to carry
• = to wear
• porter bonheur = to bring good luck
  porter malheur = to bring bad luck
2 se porter (**!** + *être*)
se porter bien = to be well

porteur *noun, masculine*
un porteur = a porter

portier *noun, masculine*
un portier = a doorman

portière *noun, feminine*
une portière = a door

portillon *noun, masculine*
un portillon = a gate, a barrier

portrait *noun, masculine*
• (*a likeness*)
  un portrait = a portrait
• (*in words*)
  un portrait = a description

portrait-robot *noun, masculine*
(*plural*) **portraits-robots**
  un portrait-robot = a photofit ✕, an
  identikit

portugais/portugaise
1 *adjective*
= Portuguese
2 portugais *noun, masculine*
le portugais = Portuguese

Portugal *noun, masculine*
le Portugal = Portugal

poser *verb* 1
1 (**!** + *avoir*)
* = to put down
  poser un sac sur une table = to put a bag
    down on a table
* = to ask
  poser une question = to ask a question
2 se poser (**!** + *être*)
  se poser (*if it's a bird*) = to settle, to alight
  (*if it's a plane*) = to land, to touch down

posséder *verb* 14
  = to own
  = to possess

possible
1 *adjective*
  = possible
  le plus de temps possible = as much time
    as possible
  le plus tôt possible = as soon as possible
2 *noun, masculine*
  faire tout son possible = to do one's
    utmost

poste
1 *noun, feminine*
  la poste = the post office
2 *noun, masculine*
* (*employment*)
  un poste = a job, a position
* (*a receiver*)
  un poste de télévision = a television set
* (*a place*)
  le poste (de police) = the police station
* (*for telephoning*)
  un poste = an extension

poster *verb* 1
  = to post, to mail

pot *noun, masculine*
* **un pot** = a pot
  = a jar
* **un pot✱** = a drink

potable *adjective*
  l'eau potable = drinking water

potage *noun, masculine*
  le potage = soup

potager *noun, masculine*
  un (jardin) potager = a vegetable garden

poteau *noun, masculine*
(*plural*) **poteaux**
  un poteau = a post
  un poteau indicateur = a signpost

potier/potière *noun, masculine/feminine*
  un potier/une potière = a potter

poubelle *noun, feminine*
  une poubelle = a dustbin, a trash can

pouce *noun, masculine*
* **un pouce** = a thumb
* **un pouce** = an inch

poudre *noun, feminine*
  la poudre = powder

poule *noun, feminine*
  une poule = a hen

poulet *noun, masculine*
  un poulet = a chicken

poulpe *noun, masculine*
  un poulpe = an octopus

pouls *noun, masculine* (**!** *never changes*)
  le pouls = the pulse

poumon *noun, masculine*
  un poumon = a lung

poupée *noun, feminine*
  une poupée = a doll

pour
1 *preposition*
* = for
  c'est pour toi = it's for you
  un produit pour nettoyer les vitres = a
    product for cleaning windows
* = to, in order to, so as to
  j'ai écrit pour les remercier = I've written
    to thank them
  pour ne pas manquer le train = so as not to
    miss the train
* = per
  dix pour cent = ten per cent
2 *noun, masculine*
  le pour et le contre = the pros and the cons

pourboire *noun, masculine*
  un pourboire = a tip

pourpre *adjective*
  = crimson

pourquoi *adverb, conjunction*
  = why

pourrai ▶ **pouvoir 2** 49

pourri/pourrie *adjective*
  = rotten

pourtant *adverb*
  = yet

pousser *verb* 1
1 (**!** + *avoir*)
* = to push
* = to move
* = to let out
  pousser un cri = to let out a cry
* (*if it's a plant, hair*) = to grow
  faire pousser des fleurs = to grow flowers
2 se pousser (**!** + *être*)
  se pousser = to move over

poussette *noun, feminine*
  une poussette = a pushchair, a stroller

poussière *noun, feminine*
  la poussière = dust

poussin *noun, masculine*
  un poussin = a chick

pouvoir
1 *noun, masculine*
  le pouvoir = power

2 *verb* 49
- • = to be able to
  - il ne pourra pas venir = he won't be able to come
  - elle n'a pas pu partir = she wasn't able to leave, she couldn't leave
  - je ne peux pas payer ce prix = I can't pay that sort of price
  - pourriez-vous me dire où se trouve la gare? = could you tell me where the station is?
  - je n'en peux plus! (*after an effort*) = I've had it!
  - (*after a meal*) = I'm full!
- • = to be allowed to
  - puis-je téléphoner? = may I use the phone?
  - tu ne peux pas te garer là = you can't park there
- • (*expressing a possibility*)
  - attention, tu pourrais glisser = careful, you might slip
  - vous auriez pu m'avertir! = you might have warned me!
  - il pouvait avoir dix ans = he would have been about ten
  - il pouvait être dix heures = it was probably about ten o'clock
- **3 il se peut** (! + *être*)
  - il se peut que j'y aille = I might go
  - il se pourrait bien que l'avion ait du retard = the plane might well be delayed
  - ça se peut = it's possible

prairie *noun, feminine*
une prairie = a meadow

pratique *adjective*
= practical
= handy, convenient

pratiquer *verb* 1
pratiquer le tennis = to play tennis
pratiquer le yoga = to do yoga

pré *noun, masculine*
un pré = a meadow

précieux/précieuse *adjective*
= precious

précipiter: se précipiter *verb* 1
(! + *être*)
se précipiter = to rush
se précipiter sur le journal = to pounce on the newspaper

précis/précise *adjective*
= precise
= accurate
à trois heures précises = at exactly three o'clock, at three o'clock sharp

préféré/préférée
1 ▶ **préférer** 14
2 *adjective*
= favo(u)rite

préférence *noun, feminine*
une préférence = a preference
de préférence = preferably

préférer *verb* 14
= to prefer

premier/première¹
1 *adjective*
= first
2 premier *noun, masculine*
habiter au premier (*in Britain*) = to live on the first floor
(*in the US*) = to live on the second floor
le premier de l'an = New Year's Day

première² *noun, feminine*
- • (*in school*)
  - la première *the class for secondary school students aged 16 to 17*
- • (*when travelling*)
  - voyager en première = to travel first class

prendre *verb* 52
1 (! + *avoir*)
- • = to take
- • = to have
  - allons prendre un verre = let's go and have a drink
  - qu'est-ce que tu prends? = what'll you have?
- • = to go
  - prenez à gauche = go left, turn left
- • = to catch
  - prendre froid = to catch a chill
  - prendre feu = to catch fire
- • qu'est-ce qui te prend✶? = what's up with you?
2 se prendre (! + *être*)
- • pour qui se prend-il? = who does he think he is?
- • elle s'y prend mal = she's going about it the wrong way

prénom *noun, masculine*
un prénom = a first name

préparer *verb* 1
1 (! + *avoir*)
- • préparer un repas = to prepare a meal
- • préparer un examen = to prepare for an examination
- • préparer ses affaires = to get one's things ready
2 se préparer (! + *être*)
se préparer = to get ready

près
1 *adverb*
= close, near(by)
tout près du magasin = near the shop
près de trois mètres = nearly three metres
2 de près = closely
3 à peu près = about
= practically

présenter *verb* 1
1 (! + *avoir*)
- • = to present
- • = to show

- = to introduce
  présenter son passeport = to show one's
    passport
  il m'a présenté à ses amis = he introduced
    me to his friends
2 se présenter (**!** + *être*)
- (*to give one's name*)
  se présenter = to introduce oneself
- (*to show up*)
  se présenter = to present oneself
- (*if it's an opportunity*)
  se présenter = to arise

président/présidente *noun,*
masculine/feminine
  un président/une présidente = a president
  = a chairman/a chairwoman, a
    chairperson

presque *adverb*
  = nearly, almost

pressé/pressée *adjective*
  être pressé = to be in a hurry

pressing *noun, masculine*
  un pressing = a dry-cleaner's

pression *noun, feminine*
  la pression = pressure

prêt/prête
1 *adjective*
  = ready
2 prêt *noun, masculine*
  un prêt = a loan

prêt-à-porter *noun, masculine*
  le prêt-à-porter = ready-to-wear (clothes)

prêter *verb* 1
  = to lend

prêtre *noun, masculine*
  un prêtre = a priest

preuve *noun, feminine*
- **une preuve** = a piece of evidence
  des preuves = evidence
- **la preuve** = the proof
  c'est la preuve qu'il est innocent = it's
    proof that he's innocent
- **faire preuve de** = to show

prévenir *verb* 36
- = to warn
- = to prevent

prévenu/prévenue ▶ **prévenir** 36

prévision *noun, feminine*
  une prévision = a forecast
  les prévisions météorologiques = the
    weather forecast

prévoir *verb* 35
- = to predict
  = to anticipate, to expect
- = to plan
  comme prévu = as planned

prévu/prévue ▶ **prévoir** 35

prier *verb* 2
  = to request, to ask
  je vous en prie = don't mention it

primaire *adjective*
  = primary

primeurs *noun, feminine plural*
  les primeurs = early produce

principal/principale *adjective*
(*plural*) **principaux/principales**
  = main

principauté *noun, feminine*
  une principauté = a principality

printemps *noun, masculine* (**!** *never*
changes)
  le printemps = spring

priorité *noun, feminine*
  la priorité = priority
  (*on the road*) = the right of way

pris/prise¹ ▶ **prendre** 52

prise² *noun, feminine*
- (*electrical*)
  une prise = a plug
    = a socket
- (*when fishing*)
  une prise = a catch

prisonnier/prisonnière *adjective*
  être prisonnier = to be a prisoner

privé/privée *adjective*
  = private

P

prix *noun, masculine* (**!** *never changes*)
- (*the cost*)
  le prix = the price
  à tout prix = at all costs
- (*a reward*)
  un prix = a prize

problème *noun, masculine*
  un problème = a problem
  = an issue

procès *noun, masculine* (**!** *never changes*)
  un procès = a trial

prochain/prochaine *adjective*
  = next
  à l'année prochaine! = see you next year!

proche *adjective*
  = nearby
  le garage le plus proche = the nearest
    garage

producteur/productrice *noun,*
masculine/feminine
  un producteur/une productrice = a
    producer

produire *verb* 62
1 (**!** + *avoir*)
- = to produce
- = to cause

2 se produire (! + *être*)
se produire = to happen

produit/produite
1 ▶ produire 62
2 produit *noun, masculine*
un produit = a product
un produit de beauté = a beauty product
un produit chimique = a chemical

prof* *noun, masculine/feminine*
un prof*/une prof* = a teacher, a lecturer

professeur *noun, masculine*
un professeur = a teacher, a lecturer

profiter *verb* 1
profiter de = to take advantage of
= to make the most of

profond/profonde *adjective*
= deep
peu profond = shallow

profondeur *noun, feminine*
la profondeur = the depth
avoir dix mètres de profondeur = to be ten
metres deep

programmateur *noun, masculine*
un programmateur = a timer

programme *noun, masculine*
un programme = a program(me)
(*for an examination*) = a syllabus
(*for a computer*) = a program

programmer *verb* 1
= to program

progrès *noun, masculine* (! *never
changes*)
le progrès = progress

projecteur *noun, masculine*
• (*a light*)
un projecteur = a floodlight
= a searchlight
• (*for slides*)
un projecteur = a projector

projet *noun, masculine*
un projet = a plan
des projets de vacances = holiday plans,
vacation plans

projeter *verb* 20
= to plan

promenade *noun, feminine*
une promenade (*on foot*) = a walk
(*by car*) = a drive
(*on a bike*) = a ride

promener *verb* 16
1 (! + *avoir*)
promener le chien = to take the dog for a
walk
2 se promener (! + *être*)
se promener (*on foot*) = to go for a walk

(*by car*) = to go for a drive
(*on a bike*) = to go for a ride

promesse *noun, feminine*
une promesse = a promise

promettre *verb* 60
= to promise

promis/promise ▶ promettre 60

promotion *noun, feminine*
• (*in a shop*)
une promotion = a special offer
• (*in one's career*)
une promotion = promotion

pronom *noun, masculine*
un pronom = a pronoun

prononcer *verb* 12
• = to pronounce
• = to deliver

propos *noun, masculine plural*
des propos = words
à propos = by the way
à propos, je n'y vais pas = by the way, I'm
not going
à propos de = about

proposer *verb* 1
• = to suggest
• = to offer
elle m'a proposé sa voiture = she offered
me her car

proposition *noun, feminine*
une proposition = a suggestion
= a proposal

propre *adjective*
• = clean
une serviette propre = a clean towel
• = own
avec mon propre argent = with my own
money

propriétaire *noun, masculine/feminine*
le propriétaire/la propriétaire = the owner
(*with tenants*) = the landlord/the landlady

propriété *noun, feminine*
la propriété = property
'propriété privée' = 'private property'

prospère *adjective*
= prosperous

protéger *verb* 15
= to protect

protester *verb* 1
= to protest

prouver *verb* 1
= to prove

provenance *noun, feminine*
la provenance = the origin
le train en provenance de Paris = the train
from Paris

---

* in informal situations

provençal/provençale
(*plural*) **provençaux/provençales**
1 *adjective*
  = of Provence
  = from Provence
2 provençal *noun, masculine*
  le provençal = Provençal

proviseur *noun, masculine*
  le proviseur = the headteacher, the
  principal

provision
1 *noun, feminine*
  une provision de = a stock of, a supply of
  faire une provision de papier = to stock up
  on paper
2 provisions *noun, feminine plural*
  faire des provisions = to go shopping for
  food

provisoire *adjective*
  = provisional, temporary

provoquer *verb* [1]
* = to cause
* = to provoke

proximité: **à proximité** *adverb*
  = near(by)

prudence *noun, feminine*
  la prudence = caution

prudent/prudente *adjective*
  = careful, cautious

prune *noun, feminine*
  une prune = a plum

pruneau *noun, masculine*
(*plural*) **pruneaux**
  un pruneau = a prune

PTT *noun, feminine plural*
  les PTT *formerly the French postal and
  telecommunications service*

pu ▶ pouvoir 2 [49]

pub* *noun, feminine* **▶ publicité**

public/publique
1 *adjective*
  = public
  (*describing a school, education*) = state
  (*in the US*) = public
2 public *noun, masculine*
  le public (*all the people*) = the public
  (*at a meeting, a show*) = the audience

publicitaire
1 *adjective*
  = advertising
2 *noun, masculine/feminine*
  un publicitaire/une publicitaire = an
  advertising executive

publicité *noun, feminine*
* la publicité = advertising
* une publicité = an advertisement, a
  commercial

publier *verb* [2]
  = to publish

puer *verb* [1]
  = to stink
  ça pue le poisson! = it stinks of fish!

puis *adverb*
  = then
  = next

puisque (**puisqu'** *before vowel or mute
h*) *conjunction*
  = as
  = since

puissant/puissante *adjective*
  = powerful

puisse ▶ pouvoir 2 [49]

puits *noun, masculine* (**!** *never changes*)
  un puits = a well

pull *noun, masculine*
  un pull = a jumper, a sweater

punaise *noun, feminine*
* (*for pinning*)
  une punaise = a drawing pin, a
  thumbtack
* (*an insect*)
  une punaise = a bug

punir *verb* [3]
  = to punish

punition *noun, feminine*
  une punition = a punishment

pur/pure *adjective*
  = pure
  (*describing wine or spirits*) = neat

purée *noun, feminine*
* la purée (de pommes de terre) = mashed
  potatoes
* la purée = puree

PV* *noun, masculine*
  un PV* = a fine
  = a parking ticket

pyjama *noun, masculine*
  un pyjama = pyjamas, pajamas

Q

Qq

qu' ▶ que

quai *noun, masculine*
  un quai (*in a station*) = a platform
  (*in a port*) = a quay
  (*along a river*) = a bank
  le navire est à quai = the ship has docked

qualité noun, feminine
• **une qualité** = a quality
• **nom, prénom et qualité** = surname, first name and occupation
en sa qualité de représentant = in his/her capacity as a representative

quand
1 conjunction
= when
quand il sera vieux = when he's old
tu sortiras quand tu auras fini = you'll go out when you've finished
2 adverb
= when
quand est-ce que vous partez? = when are you leaving?
depuis quand est-il malade? = how long has he been ill?
3 quand même = still, even so

quant à preposition
= as for

quantité noun, feminine
une quantité = a quantity, an amount
des quantités de = lots of

quarante number
= forty

quart noun, masculine
un quart = a quarter
un quart d'heure = a quarter of an hour
une heure moins le quart = a quarter to one
une heure et quart = a quarter past one

quartier noun, masculine
• (part of a town)
un quartier = an area, a district
les gens du quartier = the locals
• (a segment)
un quartier = a quarter
le premier quartier de la lune = the moon's first quarter
un quartier général = headquarters

quatorze number
= fourteen

quatorzième number
= fourteenth

quatre number
= quatre

quatre-vingt(s) number
= eighty

quatre-vingt-dix number
= ninety

quatrième
1 number
= fourth
2 noun, feminine
la quatrième the class for secondary school students aged 13 to 14

que (**qu'** before vowel or mute h)
! The construction ne + verb + que is treated under ne.

1 conjunction
• = that
elle a dit qu'elle le ferait = she said that she would do it
je veux que tu m'accompagnes = I want you to come with me
• = than, as
plus gros que moi = fatter than me
aussi fort que mon père = as strong as my father
c'est le même que le mien = it's the same as mine
• = whether
que tu le veuilles ou non = whether you like it or not
2 pronoun
• = what
que dire? = what can you say?
je ne sais pas ce qu'il a dit = I don't know what he said
qu'est-ce que c'est? = what's that?
• = that
= who
la voiture que tu as achetée = the car (that) you've bought
l'ami que j'ai invité = the friend whom I invited
3 adverb
que c'est joli! = it's so pretty!

québécois/québécoise adjective
= of Quebec
= from Quebec

quel/quelle
1 determiner
= what
= which
quelle est la capitale du Togo? = what's the capital of Togo?
2 adjective
• = what
= which
quelle heure est-il? = what time is it?
quels disques as-tu achetés? = which records did you buy?
• **quelle coïncidence!** = what a coincidence!
• **quel que soit le temps** = whatever the weather
quelles que soient leurs habitudes = whatever their habits

quelque determiner
• (in the singular) = some
depuis quelque temps = for some time
• (in the plural) = some, a few
= any
quelques élèves = some pupils, a few pupils

quelquefois adverb
= sometimes

quelques-uns/quelques-unes
pronoun
= some, a few

quelqu'un *pronoun*
= someone, somebody
= anyone, anybody

quenelle *noun, feminine*
une quenelle *a dumpling made of flour and egg, flavo(u)red with meat or fish*

querelle *noun, feminine*
une querelle = a quarrel

question *noun, feminine*
• (*a sentence asking something*)
une question = a question
poser une question à un élève = to ask a pupil a question
• (*something to be examined*)
une question = a matter
= an issue
c'est une question de vie ou de mort = it's a matter of life and death
pas question! = no way!

questionnaire *noun, masculine*
un questionnaire = a questionnaire

questionner *verb* [1]
= to question

quête *noun, feminine*
une quête = a collection
faire la quête = to pass the hat around
= to collect for charity
= to take the collection

queue *noun, feminine*
• (*on an animal*)
une queue = a tail
• (*people or cars waiting*)
une queue = a queue, a line
faire la queue = to stand in a queue, to stand in line

queue-de-cheval *noun, feminine*
(*plural*) **queues-de-cheval**
une queue-de-cheval = a ponytail

qui *pronoun*
• = who
= whom
qui est-ce? = who is it?
l'homme à qui tu as parlé = the man to whom you spoke
à qui sont ces chaussures? = whose shoes are these?
• = who
= that
= which
qui que vous soyez = whoever you are
je n'ai jamais frappé qui que ce soit = I've never hit anybody

quille *noun, feminine*
une quille = a skittle

quincaillerie *noun, feminine*
une quincaillerie = a hardware shop, a hardware store

quinzaine *noun, feminine*
• une quinzaine = about fifteen
• une quinzaine (de jours) = a fortnight, two weeks

quinze *number*
= fifteen
quinze jours = fifteen days
= a fortnight, two weeks

quinzième *number*
= fifteenth

quittance *noun, feminine*
une quittance = a receipt
= a bill

quitter *verb* [1]
1 (**!** + *avoir*)
• = to leave
• ne quittez pas = hold the line please, hold on please
2 se quitter (**!** + *être*)
se quitter = to part

quoi *pronoun*
= what
quoi de neuf? = what's new?
je ne sais pas quoi faire = I don't know what to do
à quoi penses-tu? = what are you thinking about?
à quoi bon? = what's the point?
si je peux faire quoi que ce soit = if there's anything I can do
il n'y a pas de quoi = my pleasure, don't mention it
il n'y a pas de quoi s'inquiéter = there's nothing to worry about

quotidien/quotidienne
1 *adjective*
= daily, everyday
2 quotidien *noun, masculine*
un quotidien = a daily (paper)

R

Rr

rabais *noun, masculine* (**!** *never changes*)
un rabais = a reduction

raccompagner *verb* [1]
raccompagner quelqu'un = to take someone home

raccourci *noun, masculine*
un raccourci = a short cut

raccourcir *verb* [3]
= to shorten

raccrocher *verb* [1]
(*when telephoning*) = to hang up

racine noun, feminine
  une racine = a root

raconter verb [1]
  = to tell

radiateur noun, masculine
  un radiateur = a radiator

radin/radine* adjective
  = mean

radio noun, feminine
* (for broadcasts)
  la radio = (the) radio
  à la radio = on the radio
* (a medical examination)
  une radio = an X-ray

radis noun, masculine (! never changes)
  un radis = a radish

radoucir: se radoucir verb [3] (! + être)
  se radoucir = to turn milder

rafale noun, feminine
  une rafale de vent = a gust of wind

raffiné/raffinée adjective
  = refined

raffinerie noun, feminine
  une raffinerie = a refinery

rafraîchir verb [3]
  1 (! + avoir)
  = to cool (down)
  2 se rafraîchir (! + être)
* (if it's the weather)
  se rafraîchir = to get cooler
* (if it's a person)
  se rafraîchir = to freshen up, to wash up
  = to have a drink

rafraîchissement noun, masculine
  un rafraîchissement = a cold drink

ragoût noun, masculine
  un ragoût = a stew

raide adjective
  (describing a slope) = steep
  (describing hair) = straight
  (describing a collar, a person) = stiff

raie noun, feminine
* (in hair)
  une raie = a parting, a part
* (a narrow band of colour)
  une raie = a stripe

rail noun, masculine
  un rail = a rail
  les rails = the track(s)

raisin noun, masculine
  le raisin = grapes
  un grain de raisin = a grape
  les raisins de Corinthe = currants
  les raisins secs = raisins

raison noun, feminine
* une raison = a reason
* avoir raison = to be right

raisonnable adjective
  = reasonable, moderate
  = sensible

ralenti noun, masculine
  le ralenti = slow motion
  le moteur tourne au ralenti = the engine is
    (just) ticking over

ralentir verb [3]
  = to slow down

ralentisseur noun, masculine
  un ralentisseur = a speed ramp

râler* verb [1]
  = to moan

ramasser verb [1]
  = to pick (up)
  = to collect

rame noun, feminine
* une rame = an oar
* une rame de métro = a (metro) train

ramer verb [1]
  = to row

rampe noun, feminine
  une rampe (on a staircase) = a banister
  une rampe d'accès
    (to a motorway) = a sliproad, an entrance
      ramp
    (to a building) = a ramp

ramper verb [1]
  = to crawl

rance adjective
  = rancid

rançon noun, feminine
  une rançon = a ransom

randonnée noun, feminine
* (a walk)
  une randonnée = a ramble, a hike
* (an activity)
  la randonnée = hiking
  la randonnée à cheval = pony-trekking
  la randonnée pédestre = rambling, hiking

rang noun, masculine
* (a line)
  un rang = a row
  se mettre en rangs = to get into line
* (a position)
  un rang = a rank

rangée noun, feminine
  une rangée = a row

ranger verb [13]
* = to put away
* = to tidy
  = to sort out, to put in order

râper verb [1]
  = to grate

---

rapide
1 *adjective*
= fast, quick
= prompt
2 *noun, masculine*
• (*a train*)
un rapide = an express
• (*in a river*)
un rapide = rapids

rapidement *adverb*
= quickly, fast

rappel *noun, masculine*
un rappel = a reminder

rappeler *verb* 19
1 (**!** + *avoir*)
• = to call back
• = to remind
2 **se rappeler** (**!** + *être*)
se rappeler = to remember

rapport
1 *noun, masculine*
• (*an account*)
un rapport = a report
• (*a link*)
un rapport = a connection
2 **par rapport à** = compared with

rapporter *verb* 1
1 (**!** + *avoir*)
= to take back, to bring back
2 **se rapporter à** (**!** + *être*)
se rapporter à = to relate to

rapprocher *verb* 1
= to move closer
= to bring closer

raquette *noun, feminine*
une raquette (*in tennis*) = a racket
(*in table tennis*) = a bat, a paddle

rare *adjective*
= rare
= scarce

ras/rase *adjective*
• **des cheveux ras** = close-cropped hair,
short hair
• **une cuillère à café rase** = a level
teaspoonful
plein à ras bord = full to the brim
• **en rase campagne** = in (the) open country

raser: **se raser** *verb* 1 (**!** + *être*)
se raser = to shave

rasoir
1 *noun, masculine*
un rasoir = a razor
2 *adjective*✶ (**!** *never changes*)
= boring

rassembler *verb* 1
1 (**!** + *avoir*)
= to gather
= to bring together

2 se rassembler (**!** + *être*)
se rassembler = to gather
= to get together

rassurer *verb* 1
= to reassure

rat *noun, masculine*
un rat = a rat

râteau *noun, masculine*
(*plural*) **râteaux**
un râteau = a rake

rater *verb* 1
• = to miss
• = to fail

rattraper *verb* 1
• = to catch up with
rattraper un concurrent = to catch up with
a competitor
• = to make up for
rattraper le temps perdu = to make up for
lost time
• = to recapture, to catch

ravin *noun, masculine*
un ravin = a ravine

ravissant/ravissante *adjective*
= beautiful, delightful

ravitailler *verb* 1
ravitailler une ville = to provide a town
with fresh supplies
ravitailler un avion = to refuel a plane

rayé/rayée *adjective*
= striped

rayer *verb* 21
• = to cross out
• = to scratch

rayon *noun, masculine*
• (*of light*)
un rayon = a ray, a beam
• (*for books, goods*)
un rayon = a shelf
• (*of a circle*)
le rayon = the radius

rayure *noun, feminine*
• (*on material*)
une rayure = a stripe
• (*on glass, on metal*)
une rayure = a scratch

réaction *noun, feminine*
une réaction = a reaction

réagir *verb* 3
= to react

réaliser *verb* 1
1 (**!** + *avoir*)
• (*to make something happen*)
réaliser son ambition = to achieve one's
ambition
• (*to understand*) = to realize

R

2 se réaliser (**!** + *être*)
se réaliser = to come true
= to be fulfilled

réaliste *adjective*
= realistic

réalité *noun, feminine*
la réalité = reality

réanimation *noun, feminine*
la réanimation = resuscitation

rebord *noun, masculine*
le rebord de la fenêtre = the windowsill

récemment *adverb*
= recently

récent/récente *adjective*
= recent

récepteur *noun, masculine*
un récepteur = a (telephone) receiver

recette *noun, feminine*
• (*a set of instructions*)
une recette = a recipe
• (*money*)
la recette = the takings

recevoir *verb* 5
• = to receive, to get
• = to receive, to welcome
• être reçu à un examen = to pass an exam

rechange *noun, masculine*
une pièce de rechange = a spare part

recharge *noun, feminine*
une recharge = a refill

réchaud *noun, masculine*
un réchaud = a (portable) stove

réchauffer *verb* 1
• (*if it's food*) = to reheat, to heat up
• (*if it's a person, a part of the body*) = to warm up

recherche *noun, feminine*
• (*into a subject*)
la recherche = research
• (*looking for something*)
une recherche = a search

récipient *noun, masculine*
un récipient = a container

récit *noun, masculine*
un récit = a story

réciter *verb* 1
= to recite

réclamation *noun, feminine*
une réclamation = a complaint

réclame *noun, feminine*
• la réclame = publicity
• une réclame = an advertisement
• 'en réclame' = 'on offer', 'on sale'

réclamer *verb* 1
• = to ask for
• = to complain

récolter *verb* 1
= to harvest, to reap

recommandé/recommandée
adjective
une lettre recommandée = a registered letter

recommander *verb* 1
• = to recommend
• = to advise

recommencer *verb* 12
= to start again, to start over

récompense *noun, feminine*
une récompense = a reward

récompenser *verb* 1
= to reward

reconnaissance *noun, feminine*
la reconnaissance = gratitude

reconnaissant/reconnaissante
adjective
= grateful

reconnaître *verb* 63
• = to recognize
• = to admit
= to acknowledge

recopier *verb* 2
= to copy out
= to write out

record *noun, masculine*
le record du monde = the world record

recouvrir *verb* 32
= to cover

récréation *noun, feminine*
la récréation (*in school*) = break, recess

reçu/reçue
1 ▶ recevoir 5
2 reçu *noun, masculine*
un reçu = a receipt

recueillir *verb* 27
= to collect

reculer *verb* 1
• = to move back
= to reverse
• = to postpone

reculons: à reculons *adverb*
à reculons = backwards

récupérer *verb* 14
• (*after an illness*) = to recover
• (*having lost or lent something*) = to get back
= to collect
• (*in order to reuse*) = to salvage

recyclage *noun, masculine*
le recyclage (*of waste*) = recycling
(*of staff*) = retraining

rédaction *noun, feminine*
une rédaction = an essay, a theme

redescendre verb 6
1 (**!** + être)
= to go down again, to come down again
2 (**!** + avoir)
= to take down again, to bring down
again

rediffusion noun, feminine
une rediffusion = a repeat (broadcast)

redoubler verb 1
redoubler (une classe) = to repeat a year

redresser verb 1
• = to put up again
• = to straighten (up)

réduction noun, feminine
une réduction = a reduction, a discount

réduire verb 62
= to reduce

réduit/réduite
1 ▶ réduire 62
2 réduit noun, masculine
un réduit = a cubbyhole

réel/réelle adjective
= real

réexpédier verb 2
• = to forward, to redirect
• = to send back

refaire verb 10
= to do again
= to redo
= to make again

réfectoire noun, masculine
un réfectoire = a refectory, a dining hall

refermer verb 1
= to close

réfléchir verb 3
• = to reflect
réfléchir la lumière = to reflect light
• réfléchir = to think

reflet noun, masculine
• (an image)
un reflet = a reflection
• (a flash of light)
un reflet = a glint
= a shimmer
cheveux châtain à reflets roux = brown
hair with auburn highlights

refléter verb 14
= to reflect

réflexion noun, feminine
• la réflexion = reflection
• une réflexion = a remark

refrain noun, masculine
• le refrain = the chorus
• c'est toujours le même refrain = it's the
same old refrain

refroidir verb 3
• = to cool down
• = to get cold

refus noun, masculine (**!** never changes)
un refus = a refusal

refuser verb 1
= to refuse
= to turn down

regagner verb 1
• = to get back to, to return to
• = to regain

régaler: se régaler verb 1 (**!** + être)
je me suis régalé = I really enjoyed that

regard noun, masculine
un regard = a look

regarder verb 1
• = to look at
• = to watch
• = to concern
ça ne te regarde pas = it's none of your
business

régime noun, masculine
• (what one eats)
un régime = a diet
• (in politics)
un régime = a regime

région noun, feminine
une région = a region, an area

règle
1 noun, feminine
• (for measuring)
une règle = a ruler
• (to be obeyed)
une règle = a rule
2 règles noun, feminine plural
avoir ses règles = to have a period

règlement noun, masculine
le règlement = the regulations, the rules

régler verb 14
• = to pay
• = to settle
• = to adjust

réglisse noun, feminine
la réglisse = liquorice, licorice

règne noun, masculine
un règne = a reign

regretter verb 1
• = to be sorry
• = to regret
• = to miss

régulier/régulière adjective
• = regular
un vol régulier = a scheduled flight
• = steady
= even

rein
1 noun, masculine
un rein = a kidney

R

2 reins noun, masculine plural
les reins = the small of the back
avoir mal aux reins = to have (a) backache

reine noun, feminine
une reine = a queen

rejoindre verb 56
• = to join
• = to meet up with
• = to catch up with

relais noun, masculine (**!** never changes)
• (a place)
un relais = an inn
un relais routier = a roadside café, a truck
stop
• (in sport)
un relais = a relay

relever verb 16
1 (**!** + avoir)
• (after something has fallen) = to pick up
= to put back up
• (to become aware of) = to notice
2 se relever (**!** + être)
se relever (after a fall) = to get up

relier verb 2
• = to connect
• = to bind

religieuse¹ noun, feminine
• ▶ religieux 2
• (a cake)
une religieuse = a round éclair

religieux/religieuse²
1 adjective
= religious
2 noun, masculine/feminine
un religieux/une religieuse = a monk/a
nun

relire verb 41
= to read again
= to read over

reliure noun, feminine
une reliure = a binding

remarier: se remarier verb 2 (**!** + être)
se remarier = to remarry

remarquer verb 1
= to notice
faire remarquer = to point out

rembourser verb 1
= to reimburse, to pay back

remède noun, masculine
un remède = a medicine
= a cure

remerciement noun, masculine
des remerciements = thanks

remercier verb 2
= to thank

remettre verb 60
1 (**!** + avoir)
• = to put back
remettre une lettre dans un tiroir = to put a
letter back in a drawer
remettre son manteau = to put one's coat
back on
• = to hand over, to give
je leur ai remis les clés = I handed the
keys over to them
2 se remettre (**!** + être)
• se remettre = to recover
se remettre d'une maladie = to recover
from an illness, to get over an illness
• se remettre à [travailler | marcher | pleurer ...]
= to start [working | walking | crying ...] again

remonter verb 1
1 (**!** + être)
• = to go back up(stairs), to come back
up(stairs)
• remonter au dix-septième siècle = to go
back to the seventeenth century
2 (**!** + avoir)
• remonter les escaliers = to go back up the
stairs
• remonter ses bagages = to take one's
luggage back up(stairs)

remorque noun, feminine
une remorque = a trailer

remplacer verb 12
= to replace

remplir verb 3
= to fill

remuer verb 1
• = to move
= to wriggle
• = to stir

renard noun, masculine
un renard = a fox

rencontre noun, feminine
• une rencontre = an encounter
= a meeting
faire la rencontre d'un garçon = to meet a
boy
• (in sport)
une rencontre (sportive) = a match, a
game

rencontrer verb 1
= to meet
= to come across

rendez-vous noun, masculine (**!** never
changes)
un rendez-vous = an appointment
= a date

rendre verb 6
1 (**!** + avoir)
• = to give back, to return
• rendre visite à un ami = to visit a friend

2 se rendre (! + *être*)
• se rendre = to surrender
• se rendre à Paris = to go to Paris
• se rendre compte = to realize
  = to notice
• se rendre malade = to make oneself ill

renne *noun, masculine*
un renne = a reindeer

renoncer *verb* 12
renoncer à = to give up

renouveler *verb* 19
• = to renew
• = to replace

rénover *verb* 1
= to renovate

renseignement
1 *noun, masculine*
un renseignement = (a piece of)
information
des renseignements = information
2 renseignements *noun, masculine plural*
les renseignements (*on the telephone*)
= directory enquiries, information
(*an office*) = enquiries, information

renseigner *verb* 1
1 (! + *avoir*)
= to give information
être bien renseigné = to be well-informed
2 se renseigner (! + *être*)
se renseigner = to find out
= to enquire, to make enquiries

rentrée *noun, feminine*
la rentrée (scolaire *or* des classes) = the
start of the school year

rentrer *verb* 1
1 (! + *être*)
• = to go in, to come in
rentrer dans une pièce = to go/come back
into a room
• = to go home, to come home
• = to fit
rentrer dans une boîte = to fit into a box
• rentrer dans un mur = to crash into a wall
2 (! + *avoir*)
= to take in, to bring in

renverser *verb* 1
• = to spill
• = to knock over

renvoyer *verb* 24
• = to return
= to throw back
= to send back
• = to expel
= to dismiss

réparation *noun, feminine*
une réparation = a repair

réparer *verb* 1
= to mend, to repair

repas *noun, masculine* (! *never changes*)
un repas = a meal

repassage *noun, masculine*
le repassage = ironing

repasser *verb* 1
1 (! + *avoir*)
• repasser une jupe = to iron a skirt
• repasser un examen = to resit an exam
2 (! + *être*)
• = to go past again
• = to call again

répéter *verb* 14
• = to repeat
• = to rehearse

répétition *noun, feminine*
• (*in a text*)
une répétition = a repetition
• (*for actors*)
une répétition = a rehearsal

répondre *verb* 6
= to answer, to reply

réponse *noun, feminine*
une réponse = an answer, a reply

reportage *noun, masculine*
un reportage = a report, an article

repos *noun, masculine* (! *never changes*)
le repos = rest
= relaxation
mon jour de repos = my day off

reposer: se reposer *verb* 1 (! + *être*)
se reposer = to rest

reprendre *verb* 52
• reprendre du pain = to have some more
bread
• = to take back
• reprendre le travail = to go back to work
reprendre ses études = to take up one's
studies again
reprendre la conversation = to continue
the conversation
• = to start again
l'école a repris = school has started again

représentant/représentante *noun,*
masculine/feminine
un représentant/une représentante = a
representative

représenter *verb* 1
= to represent

réprimander *verb* 1
= to tell off

repris/reprise ▶ reprendre 52

république *noun, feminine*
une république = a republic

requin *noun, masculine*
un requin = a shark

R

RER *noun, masculine*
le RER *a rapid-transit rail system in the Paris area*

réseau *noun, masculine*
(*plural*) **réseaux**
un réseau = a network

réservation *noun, feminine*
une réservation = a reservation, a booking

réserver *verb* ⬓1⬓
• = to reserve, to book
• = to put aside, to set aside

résidence *noun, feminine*
une résidence = a residence
= a place of residence
une résidence secondaire = a second home

résolu/résolue
1 ▶ **résoudre** ⬓65⬓
2 *adjective*
= resolute, determined

résoudre *verb* ⬓65⬓
= to solve, to resolve

respecter *verb* ⬓1⬓
= to respect
= to treat with respect

respiration *noun, feminine*
la respiration = breathing

respirer *verb* ⬓1⬓
= to breathe

responsable
1 *adjective*
= responsible
2 *noun, masculine|feminine*
• un responsable/une responsable = a person in charge
• le responsable de l'accident = the person responsible for the accident

ressembler *verb* ⬓1⬓
1 (**!** + *avoir*)
ressembler à = to look like, to resemble
= to be like
2 se ressembler (**!** + *être*)
se ressembler = to look alike

ressort *noun, masculine*
un ressort = a spring

reste *noun, masculine*
• (*the remaining part*)
le reste = the rest
• (*the remains of a meal*)
les restes = the leftovers

rester *verb* ⬓1⬓ (**!** + *être*)
• = to stay
= to remain

• il me reste dix euros = I've got ten euros left
il ne reste que quelques personnes = there are only a few people left

restituer *verb* ⬓1⬓
= to return, to hand back

résultat *noun, masculine*
le résultat = the result

résumé *noun, masculine*
un résumé = a summary

rétablir *verb* ⬓3⬓
1 (**!** + *avoir*)
= to restore
2 se rétablir (**!** + *être*)
se rétablir = to recover

retard *noun, masculine*
un retard = a delay
avoir du retard = to be late
être en retard = to be late

retarder *verb* ⬓1⬓
• = to be slow
• = to postpone, to put off
• = to delay, to hold up

retenir *verb* ⬓36⬓
1 (**!** + *avoir*)
• = to reserve
retenir des places = to reserve seats
• = to hold (back)
retenir son souffle = to hold one's breath
• = to remember
2 se retenir (**!** + *être*)
• se retenir à une branche = to hold on to a branch
• se retenir de pleurer = to stop oneself from crying

retenu/retenue¹ ▶ **retenir** ⬓36⬓

retenue² *noun, feminine*
une retenue (*in school*) = a detention

retirer *verb* ⬓1⬓
= to withdraw, to take out

retour *noun, masculine*
• le retour = the return
• le retour = the return journey
au retour = on the way back

retourner *verb* ⬓1⬓
1 (**!** + *avoir*)
• = to turn over
= to turn inside out
= to turn upside down
• = to send back
2 (**!** + *être*)
= to go back, to return
3 se retourner (**!** + *être*)
se retourner = to turn around, to turn over

retraite *noun, feminine*
la retraite = retirement

retraité/retraitée *noun,*
masculine/feminine
  un retraité/une retraitée = a retired person

rétrécir *verb* ③
  = to shrink

retrouver *verb* ①
1 (**!** + *avoir*)
• (*after losing something*) = to find
• (*after arranging to get together*) = to meet
• (*after losing touch*) = to see again
2 se retrouver (**!** + *être*)
• (*by arrangement*)
  se retrouver = to meet
• (*to end up*)
  se retrouver = to find oneself
  se retouver dans une situation difficile = to
    find oneself in a difficult situation

rétroviseur *noun, masculine*
  un rétroviseur = a rearview mirror

réunion *noun, feminine*
  une réunion = a meeting

réunir *verb* ⑨
1 (**!** + *avoir*)
• = to gather together
• = to collect
2 se réunir (**!** + *être*)
  se réunir = to meet
  = to get together

réussir *verb* ③
• = to succeed
  = to be successful
• réussir à ouvrir la porte = to manage to
  open the door
  réussir à un examen = to pass an exam

réussite *noun, feminine*
• (*an achievement*)
  une réussite = success
• (*a game*)
  une réussite = patience, solitaire

rêve *noun, masculine*
  un rêve = a dream

réveil *noun, masculine*
  un réveil = an alarm clock

réveiller *verb* ①
1 (**!** + *avoir*)
  = to wake (up)
2 se réveiller (**!** + *être*)
  se réveiller = to wake up

réveillon *noun, masculine*
  le réveillon de Noël = Christmas Eve
    celebrations
  le réveillon du Nouvel An = New Year's Eve
    celebrations

révéler *verb* ⑭
  = to reveal
  = to show

revenir *verb* ㊱ (**!** + *être*)
  = to come back

revenu/revenue
1 ▶ revenir ㊱
2 revenu *noun, masculine*
  mon revenu = my income

rêver *verb* ①
  = to dream

réverbère *noun, masculine*
  un réverbère = a streetlamp

rêveur/rêveuse *adjective*
  = dreamy

réviser *verb* ①
• = to revise
• réviser un moteur = to overhaul an engine

revoir
1 *verb* ㊻
• = to see again
• = to go over
  revoir un exercice = to go over an exercise
2 au revoir = goodbye

revu/revue[1] **▶ revoir** 1 ㊻

revue[2] *noun, feminine*
• une revue = a magazine
• une revue = a show

rez-de-chaussée *noun, masculine*
(**!** *never changes*)
  au rez-de-chaussée (*in Britain*) = on the
    ground floor
  (*in the US*) = on the first floor

Rhin *noun, masculine*
  le Rhin = the Rhine

rhum *noun, masculine*
  le rhum = rum

rhume *noun, masculine*
  un rhume = a cold
le rhume des foins = hay fever

riant ▶ rire 1 ㊸

riche *adjective*
  = rich, wealthy

ride *noun, feminine*
  une ride = a wrinkle

rideau *noun, masculine*
(*plural*) **rideaux**
  un rideau = a curtain
  des rideaux = curtains, drapes

ridicule *adjective*
  = ridiculous

rien *pronoun*
  = nothing
  je ne veux rien = I don't want anything
  ça ne fait rien = it doesn't matter
  de rien = don't mention it

rigoler* *verb* ①
• = to laugh
• = to have fun
• = to joke

R

rigolo/rigolote✶ *adjective*
= funny

rimer *verb* [1]
= to rhyme

rinçage *noun, masculine*
le rinçage = rinsing

rincer *verb* [12]
= to rinse

rire
1 *verb* [43]
• = to laugh
• = to have fun
il a dit ça pour rire = he said that as a joke
2 *noun, masculine*
un rire = a laugh, laughter

risque *noun, masculine*
un risque = a risk

risquer *verb* [1]
• = to risk
vos bagages ne risquent rien = your
    luggage is quite safe
• = to venture
• tu risques de tomber = you might fall
il risque de faire froid = it might be cold
ça ne risque pas de se produire = there's
    no chance of that happening

rivage *noun, masculine*
le rivage = the shore

rive *noun, feminine*
la rive (*of a river*) = the bank
(*of a lake*) = the shore

rivière *noun, feminine*
une rivière = a river

riz *noun, masculine* (**!** *never changes*)
le riz = rice

robe *noun, feminine*
une robe = a dress
une robe de chambre = a dressing gown,
a robe

robinet *noun, masculine*
un robinet = a tap, a faucet

robuste *adjective*
(*describing a person*) = robust, sturdy

rocher *noun, masculine*
un rocher = a rock

rognon *noun, masculine*
un rognon = a kidney

roi *noun, masculine*
un roi = a king

rôle *noun, masculine*
un rôle = a role
= a part

romain/romaine *adjective*
= Roman

roman *noun, masculine*
un roman = a novel
un roman policier = a detective novel, a
thriller

romarin *noun, masculine*
le romarin = rosemary

ronce *noun, feminine*
une ronce = a bramble

rond/ronde
1 *adjective*
• = round
• = chubby
2 **rond** *noun, masculine*
un rond = a circle
en rond = in a circle

rondelle *noun, feminine*
une rondelle = a slice

rond-point *noun, masculine*
(*plural*) **ronds-points**
un rond-point = a roundabout, a traffic
circle

ronfler *verb* [1]
= to snore

ronger *verb* [13]
1 (**!** + *avoir*)
= to gnaw
= to eat into
2 **se ronger** (**!** + *être*)
se ronger les ongles = to bite one's nails

ronronner *verb* [1]
= to purr

rosbif *noun, masculine*
un rosbif = a joint of beef, a roast of beef
= roast beef

rose
1 *adjective*
= pink
2 *noun, feminine*
une rose = a rose

roseau *noun, masculine*
(*plural*) **roseaux**
un roseau = a reed

rosée *noun, feminine*
la rosée = dew

roseraie *noun, feminine*
une roseraie = a rose garden

rosier *noun, masculine*
un rosier = a rose bush

rossignol *noun, masculine*
un rossignol = a nightingale

rôti *noun, masculine*
un rôti = a joint
= a roast

roue *noun, feminine*
  une roue = a wheel
une roue de secours = a spare wheel, a
  spare tire

rouge
1 *adjective*
  = red
2 *noun, masculine*
  le rouge = red
le rouge à lèvres = lipstick

rouge-gorge *noun, masculine*
(*plural*) **rouges-gorges**
  un rouge-gorge = a robin

rougeole *noun, feminine*
  la rougeole = measles

rouille *noun, feminine*
  la rouille = rust

rouleau *noun, masculine*
(*plural*) **rouleaux**
  un rouleau = a roll

rouler *verb* 1
• (*if it's a ball, a coin*) = to roll
• (*if it's a car*) = to go
• (*if it's a driver*) = to drive
• rouler✱ = to trick

roumain/roumaine
1 *adjective*
  = Romanian
2 roumain *noun, masculine*
  le roumain = Romanian

Roumanie *noun, feminine*
  la Roumanie = Romania

rouspéter✱ *verb* 14
  = to grumble, to complain

rousse *adjective, feminine* ▶ **roux**

route *noun, feminine*
• une route = a road, a highway
• la route = the way
  en (cours de) route = on the way
  se mettre en route = to set off
  en route! = let's go!
  il y a deux heures de route = it's a two-
    hour drive
une route départementale = a
  secondary road
une route nationale = a trunk road, a
  national highway

routier/routière
1 *adjective*
  = road
2 routier *noun, masculine*
  un routier = a lorry driver, a truck driver

roux/rousse
1 *adjective*
  = red
  = red-haired
2 *noun, masculine/feminine*
  un roux/une rousse = a redhead

Royaume-Uni *noun, masculine*
  le Royaume-Uni = the United Kingdom

ruban *noun, masculine*
  un ruban = a ribbon

ruche *noun, feminine*
  une ruche = a beehive

rude *adjective*
  (*describing a task*) = hard, tough
  (*describing a climate, a voice*) = harsh

rue *noun, feminine*
  une rue = a street

ruée *noun, feminine*
  une ruée = a rush
  = a stampede

ruelle *noun, feminine*
  une ruelle = an alley

ruine *noun, feminine*
• (*financial*)
  la ruine = ruin
• (*remains*)
  des ruines = ruins

ruisseau *noun, masculine*
(*plural*) **ruisseaux**
  un ruisseau = a stream, a brook

rumeur *noun, feminine*
  une rumeur (*gossip*) = a rumo(u)r
  (*a noise*) = a rumble

ruse *noun, feminine*
• une ruse = a trick
• la ruse = cunning

rusé/rusée *adjective*
  = cunning, crafty

russe
1 *adjective*
  = Russian
2 *noun, masculine*
  le russe = Russian

Russie *noun, feminine*
  la Russie = Russia

rustine *noun, feminine*
  une rustine = a patch

rythme *noun, masculine*
  le rythme = (the) rhythm
  = the rate, the pace

R

Ss

s'
1 *pronoun* ▶ **se**
2 *conjunction* ▶ **si 2**

sa ▶ **son²**

sable *noun, masculine*
  le sable = sand

sac *noun, masculine*
  un sac = a bag
un sac de couchage = a sleeping bag
un sac à dos = a rucksack, a backpack
un sac à main = a handbag, a purse
un sac à provisions = a shopping bag, a
  carry-all

saccade *noun, feminine*
  une saccade = a jerk

saccager *verb* 13
  = to wreck, to devastate
  = to vandalize

sache ▶ **savoir** 47

sachet *noun, masculine*
  un sachet = a packet
  = a sachet
  = a bag

sacoche *noun, feminine*
  une sacoche = a bag
  (*on a bicycle*) = a pannier, a saddlebag

sacré/sacrée *adjective*
  = sacred, holy

sage *adjective*
• = good, well-behaved
• = wise

Sagittaire *noun, masculine*
  le Sagittaire = Sagittarius

saignant/saignante *adjective*
  (*describing steak*) = rare

saigner *verb* 1
  = to bleed

sain/saine *adjective*
  = healthy

sais ▶ **savoir** 47

saisir *verb* 3
• (*to catch hold of*) = to grab, to seize
  saisir une balle au vol = to catch a ball
• (*to affect deeply*) = to grip
  être saisi de panique = to be panic-
    stricken
• (*to get the meaning*) = to understand

---

saison *noun, feminine*
  une saison = a season
  en cette saison = at this time of year
  en toute saison = all year round

saisonnier/saisonnière *adjective*
  = seasonal

salade *noun, feminine*
  une salade = a (head of) lettuce
  = a salad

salaire *noun, masculine*
  un salaire = a salary, wages

sale *adjective*
  = dirty

salé/salée *adjective*
  = salty, salted
  = savoury

saler *verb* 1
  = to salt

saleté *noun, feminine*
• la saleté = dirtiness
  = dirt, filth
• **ramasser les saletés** = to pick up the
  rubbish, to pick up the trash

salir *verb* 3
1 (**!** + *avoir*)
  = to dirty, to soil
2 se salir (**!** + *être*)
  se salir = to get dirty

salle *noun, feminine*
  une salle = a room
  = a hall
une salle de bains = a bathroom
une salle de classe = a classroom
la salle d'embarquement = the
  departure lounge
une salle à manger = a dining room
une salle de séjour = a living room

salon *noun, masculine*
  un salon = a lounge, a sitting room, a
  parlor

salopette *noun, feminine*
  une salopette = dungarees

saluer *verb* 1
• = to greet
• = to salute

salut✗ *exclamation*
  salut✗! = hi!
  = goodbye!

salutations *noun, feminine plural*
  des salutations = greetings
  'sincères salutations' = 'yours sincerely'
  = 'yours faithfully'

samedi *noun, masculine*
  samedi = Saturday

sang *noun, masculine*
  le sang = blood

sang-froid noun, masculine (**!** never changes)
le sang-froid = calm, composure

sanglier noun, masculine
un sanglier = a wild boar

sangloter verb [1]
= to sob

sans preposition
= without
sans doute = probably

santé noun, feminine
la santé = health
à votre santé! = cheers!

santon noun, masculine
un santon a Christmas crib figure

saoul/saoule adjective
= drunk

sapin noun, masculine
un sapin = a fir tree
un sapin de Noël = a Christmas tree

satisfaire verb [10]
= to satisfy

satisfaisant/satisfaisante adjective
• = satisfactory
• = satisfying

satisfait/satisfaite adjective
= satisfied

sauce noun, feminine
une sauce = a sauce
= gravy

saucisse noun, feminine
une saucisse = a sausage

saucisson noun, masculine
le saucisson ≈ salami

sauf¹ preposition
= except
sauf si = unless

sauf²/sauve adjective
= safe
sain et sauf/saine et sauve = safe and sound

saumon noun, masculine
un saumon = a salmon

saurai ▶ savoir [47]

saut noun, masculine
un saut = a jump
le saut en hauteur = the high jump

saute-mouton noun, masculine
jouer à saute-mouton = to play leapfrog

sauter verb [1]
= to jump
= to skip
sauter à la corde = to skip, to jump rope

sauterelle noun, feminine
une sauterelle = a grasshopper

sauvage adjective
= wild

sauve ▶ sauf 2

sauvegarder verb [1]
= to save

sauver verb [1]
1 (**!** + avoir)
= to save
= to rescue
2 se sauver (**!** + être)
se sauver = to escape
= to run away

sauvetage noun, masculine
un sauvetage = a rescue

sauveteur noun, masculine
un sauveteur = a rescuer

savant/savante
1 adjective
• = learned
• les animaux savants = performing animals
2 noun, masculine/feminine
un savant/une savante = a scholar
= a scientist

saveur noun, feminine
la saveur = the flavo(u)r

savoir verb [47]
• = to know
je n'en sais rien = I've no idea
• = to know how to

savon noun, masculine
le savon = soap

savonnette noun, feminine
une savonnette = a small bar of soap

savoureux/savoureuse adjective
= tasty

scène noun, feminine
• (in a theatre)
la scène = the stage
• (something seen)
une scène = a scene

schéma noun, masculine
un schéma = a diagram

scie noun, feminine
une scie = a saw

science noun, feminine
la science = science
les sciences (as a school subject)
= science

scier verb [2]
= to saw

scintiller verb [1]
= to twinkle, to sparkle, to glisten

scolaire adjective
= school

S

Scorpion noun, masculine
le Scorpion = Scorpion

scotch noun, masculine
(plural) **scotches**
• le scotch   = Sellotape   , Scotch tape
• le scotch = Scotch (whisky)

scout/scoute noun, masculine/feminine
un scout/une scoute = a boy scout/a girl
  scout

se (**s'** before vowel or mute h) pronoun
• = oneself
  = himself/herself
  = itself
  = themselves
  se faire mal = to hurt oneself
  elles se sont fait mal = they hurt
    themselves
• = each other
  ils s'aimaient = they loved each other

séance noun, feminine
une séance = a session
(in a cinema) = a showing

seau noun, masculine
(plural) **seaux**
un seau = a bucket

sec/sèche adjective
• (without moisture) = dry
  des fruits secs = dried fruit
• (abrupt) = sharp

sèche ▶ sec

sèche-cheveux noun, masculine
(! never changes)
un sèche-cheveux = a hairdryer

sèche-linge noun, masculine (! never
changes)
un sèche-linge = a tumble dryer

sécher verb 14
= to dry (up)

sécheresse noun, feminine
la sécheresse = drought

séchoir noun, masculine
• un séchoir = a hairdryer
• un séchoir = a clothes horse, a drying rack
  = a rotary clothes dryer

second/seconde¹ number
= second

secondaire
1 adjective
  = secondary
2 noun, masculine
  le secondaire = secondary-school
    education, high-school education (for
    students aged 11 to 18)

seconde² noun, feminine
• (a unit of time)
  une seconde = a second
• (in school)
  la seconde   the class for secondary school
    students aged 15 to 16
• (when travelling)
  voyager en seconde = to travel second
    class
  un billet de seconde = a second-class
    ticket

secouer verb 1
= to shake

secourir verb 26
= to rescue
= to help

secours
1 noun, masculine (! never changes)
  un secours = help
  au secours! = help!
  une sortie de secours = an emergency exit
2 noun, masculine plural
  des secours = rescuers
  = (relief) supplies

secousse noun, feminine
une secousse = a jolt

secret/secrète
1 adjective
  = secret
2 secret noun, masculine
  un secret = a secret

secrétaire noun, masculine/feminine
un secrétaire/une secrétaire = a secretary

secrétariat noun, masculine
le secrétariat = the secretary's office

secrète ▶ secret 1

sectionner verb 1
= to cut

sécuriser verb 1
= to reassure
= to give a feeling of security

sécurité noun, feminine
la sécurité = security
  = safety
  se sentir en sécurité = to feel safe
la sécurité sociale   the French national
  health and pensions organization

séduisant/séduisante adjective
= attractive

seigneur noun, masculine
un seigneur = a lord

sein noun, masculine
un sein = a breast

seize number
= sixteen

seizième number
= sixteenth

séjour noun, masculine
• (a room)
  un séjour = a living room, a parlor
• (time spent somewhere)
  un séjour = a stay
  faire un séjour à l'étranger = to spend
    some time abroad
un séjour linguistique = a language-
  study holiday, a language-study vacation

sel noun, masculine
  le sel = salt

sélectionner verb [1]
  = to select

selle noun, feminine
  une selle = a saddle

selon preposition
• = according to
  selon moi = in my opinion
• = depending on
  selon le temps = depending on the
    weather

semaine noun, feminine
  une semaine = a week

semblable adjective
  = similar

semblant noun, masculine
  faire semblant [de dormir | d'être malade |
    d'avoir mal ...] = to pretend [to be asleep | to
    be ill | to be in pain ...]

sembler verb [1]
  = to seem
  il me semble que = it seems to me that
  il me semble qu'il pleut = I think it's
    raining

semelle noun, feminine
  une semelle = a sole

semer verb [1]
• = to sow
• = to scatter

semoule noun, feminine
  la semoule = semolina

sens noun, masculine (**!** never changes)
• **un sens** = a meaning
• **le sens** = sense
  le bon sens = common sense
  ça n'a pas de sens = it doesn't make sense
• **le sens** = the way
  = the direction
  plie-le dans l'autre sens = fold it the other
    way
  dans le sens de la flèche = in the
    direction of the arrow
  dans le sens des aiguilles d'une montre
    = clockwise
  une rue à sens unique = a one-way street
  'sens obligatoire' = 'one way'

sensationnel/sensationnelle
adjective
• (causing a stir) = sensational
• (very good)**✘** = fantastic

sensé/sensée adjective
  = sensible

sensible adjective
  = sensitive

senti ▶ **sentir** [30]

sentier noun, masculine
  un sentier = a path
un sentier de grande randonnée = a
  long-distance footpath

sentiment noun, masculine
  un sentiment = a feeling

sentir verb [30]
1 (**!** + avoir)
• = to feel
• = to sense
• = to smell
• = to smell of
  ça sent le brûlé = there's a smell of
    burning
2 se sentir (**!** + être)
  se sentir = to feel

séparer verb [1], **se séparer** (**!** + être)
  = to separate
  = to part
  = to divide

sept number
  = seven

septante number
  = seventy

septembre noun, masculine
  septembre = September

septième number
  = seventh

serai ▶ **être** [7]

série noun, feminine
• (a succession)
  une série = a series
• (a collection)
  une série = a set

sérieux/sérieuse adjective
• = serious
• = reliable

seringue noun, feminine
  une seringue = a syringe

serpent noun, masculine
  un serpent = a snake

serre noun, feminine
  une serre = a greenhouse

serré/serrée adjective
• (not big enough) = tight
• (too close together)
  être serrés = to be packed together

S

serrer verb [1]
1 (**!** + avoir)
* = to grip
  = to squeeze
  serrer la main d'un ami = to shake hands
  with a friend
* = to tighten
  serrer une ceinture = to tighten a belt
* = to be too tight
  ma jupe me serre à la taille = my skirt is
  too tight around the waist
* (on the road)
  '**serrez à droite**' = 'keep to the right'
2 se serrer (**!** + être)
  se serrer = to squeeze up
  je me suis serré contre elle = I huddled up
  against her

serrure noun, feminine
  une serrure = a lock
  le trou de la serrure = the keyhole

serrurier noun, masculine
  un serrurier = a locksmith

serveur/serveuse noun,
masculine/feminine
  un serveur/une serveuse = a waiter/a
  waitress

servi/servie ▶ servir [30]

serviable adjective
  = obliging

service noun, masculine
* **le service** = service
  service compris = service included
* **un service** = a favo(u)r
  rendre service à un ami = to be helpful to
  a friend, to do a friend a favo(u)r

serviette noun, feminine
* (household linen)
  une serviette de toilette = a towel
  une serviette de table = a napkin
* (a kind of bag)
  une serviette = a briefcase

serviette-éponge noun, feminine
(plural) **serviettes-éponges**
  une serviette-éponge = a terry(-cloth) towel

servir verb [30]
1 (**!** + avoir)
* = to serve
  qu'est-ce que je vous sers (à boire)?
  = what would you like to drink?
* = to be of use
  = to come in handy
  garde-le, ça peut servir = keep it, it might
  come in handy
* **servir à quelque chose** = to be used for
  something
  servir à quelqu'un = to be used by
  someone
  à quoi sert cet outil? = what's this tool
  used for?
  ça va me servir pour faire un coussin = I'm
  going to use it to make a cushion
  ça ne sert à rien de se mettre en colère
  = there's no point in losing one's temper
  j'ai écrit, mais ça n'a servi à rien = I wrote,
  but it didn't do any good

* **servir de** = to serve as
  = to be used as
  mon sac m'a servi d'oreiller = I used my
  bag as a pillow
2 se servir (**!** + être)
* **se servir** = to help oneself
* **se servir de** = to use
  il s'est servi d'un dictionnaire = he used a
  dictionary

ses ▶ son[2]

seuil noun, masculine
  le seuil = the threshold

seul/seule adjective
* = alone, by oneself, on one's own
  vivre seul = to live alone
* = lonely
  se sentir seul = to feel lonely
* = single
  pas un seul arbre = not a single tree
  une seule fois = once only

seulement adverb
  = only

sévère adjective
  = strict, harsh
  = severe

shampooing noun, masculine
  un shampooing = a shampoo

short noun, masculine
  un short = shorts

si
1 adverb
* = yes
  '**tu n'y vas pas?**'—'**si!**' = 'aren't you going?'
  —'yes I am!'
* = so
  elle est si jolie! = she's so pretty!
2 conjunction (**s'** before il or ils)
* (introducing a supposition) = if
  si j'étais riche = if I were rich
  si j'avais su = if only I had known, if I'd
  only known
  et s'il ne peut pas le réparer? = and what
  if he can't repair it?
  s'il vous plaît = please
* (introducing a suggestion)
  et si on allait en ville? = how about going
  into town?

sida noun, masculine
  le sida = Aids

siècle noun, masculine
  un siècle = a century
  au vingtième siècle = in the twentieth
  century

siège noun, masculine
* (a piece of furniture)
  un siège = a seat
* (a place)
  le siège (social) = the headquarters, the
  head office

sien/sienne *pronoun*
le sien/la sienne = his/hers
les siens/les siennes = his/hers

sieste *noun, feminine*
une sieste = a siesta, a snooze, a nap

siffler *verb* 1
• = to whistle
• = to blow one's whistle
• = to boo

sifflet *noun, masculine*
un sifflet = a whistle
un coup de sifflet = a whistle blast, a
   whistle blow

sigle *noun, masculine*
un sigle = an acronym

signalement *noun, masculine*
un signalement = a description

signaler *verb* 1
• (*by informing*) = to report
rien à signaler = nothing to report
• (*by drawing attention*) = to point out
je vous signale qu'il est huit heures = may
   I point out that it's eight o'clock
• (*by means of a notice, a sign*) = to indicate
= to signpost

signalisation *noun, feminine*
la signalisation = signs
la signalisation routière = road signs and
   markings

signe *noun, masculine*
un signe = a sign

signer *verb* 1
= to sign

signifier *verb* 2
= to mean

silencieux/silencieuse *adjective*
= silent
= quiet

silhouette *noun, feminine*
• (*a shape*)
une silhouette = a silhouette
= an outline
• (*a person*)
une silhouette = a figure

sillon *noun, masculine*
un sillon = a furrow

simple *adjective*
• = simple
• = ordinary
c'est une simple formalité = it's just a
   formality
• = single
un aller simple = a single (ticket)

singe *noun, masculine*
un singe = a monkey

sinistre
1 *adjective*
= sinister

2 *noun, masculine*
un sinistre = a (natural) disaster
= a fire

sinistré/sinistrée *adjective*
= stricken
une région sinistrée = a disaster area

sinon *conjunction*
= otherwise

sirène *noun, feminine*
une sirène = a siren

sirop *noun, masculine*
un sirop = a syrup
un sirop (de fruits) = a (fruit) cordial
un sirop (pour la toux) = a cough mixture

site *noun, masculine*
un site = a site
• (*a place*)
un site classé = a conservation area
un site pittoresque = a beauty spot
un site touristique = a place of interest
• (*on the Internet*)
un site web = a website

situation *noun, feminine*
• (*a site*)
la situation d'une ville = the location of a
   town
• (*the circumstances*)
la situation est grave = the situation is
   serious
• (*a position*)
une bonne situation = a good job

situé/située *adjective*
= situated, located
la ville est bien située = the town is in a
   good location

situer: se situer *verb* 1 (**!** + *être*)
• (*if it's a building, a town*)
se situer = to be situated
• (*if it's an event*)
se situer = to take place

six *number*
= six

sixième
1 *number*
= sixth
2 *noun, feminine*
la sixième *the class for secondary school
   students aged 11 to 12*

ski *noun, masculine*
• (*the equipment*)
un ski = a ski
• (*the sport*)
le ski = skiing
le ski nautique = water-skiing

skier *verb* 2
= to ski

slip *noun, masculine*
un slip (*for men*) = pants, shorts
(*for women*) = knickers, panties

slovaque
1 *adjective*
= Slovak
2 *noun, masculine*
le slovaque = Slovak

smoking *noun, masculine*
un smoking = a dinner jacket, a tuxedo

SNCF *noun, feminine*
la SNCF the French national railway
company

snob *adjective*
= snobbish

société *noun, feminine*
• la société = society
• une société = a company

soda *noun, masculine*
le soda = soda water

sœur *noun, feminine*
une sœur = a sister

soi *pronoun*
= oneself
= itself

soi-disant
1 *adjective* (**!** *never changes*)
= so-called
2 *adverb*
= supposedly

soie *noun, feminine*
la soie = silk

soif *noun, feminine*
la soif = thirst
avoir soif = to be thirsty

soigné/soignée *adjective*
= meticulous, neat

soigner *verb* 1
1 (**!** + *avoir*)
• = to treat
• = to look after
  = to take care of
• = to take care over
2 se soigner (**!** + *être*)
se soigner = to look after oneself

soigneusement *adverb*
= carefully

soi-même *pronoun*
= oneself

soin
1 *noun, masculine*
le soin = care
avec soin = carefully
2 soins *noun, masculine plural*
les soins = treatment
= care
donner les premiers soins aux blessés
= to give first aid to the injured

soir *noun, masculine*
un soir = an evening
à ce soir = see you tonight

soirée *noun, feminine*
• la soirée = the evening
• une soirée = a party

soit
1 ▶ **être** 7
2 *conjunction*
soit lundi soit mardi = either Monday or
Tuesday

soixante *number*
= sixty

soixante-dix *number*
= seventy

soja *noun, masculine*
le soja = soya

sol *noun, masculine*
le sol = the floor
= the ground
= the soil

solaire *adjective*
= sun
= suntan
= solar

soldat *noun, masculine*
un soldat = a soldier

solde
1 *noun, masculine*
articles en solde = reduced items, sales
bargains, sale items
acheter une veste en solde = to buy a
jacket in a sale, to buy a jacket on sale
2 soldes *noun, masculine plural*
les soldes (*the event*) = the sales
(*the goods*) = sales goods, sale items

soleil *noun, masculine*
le soleil = the sun
au soleil = in the sun
il fait (du) soleil = it's sunny
un coup de soleil = sunburn
attraper un coup de soleil = to get
sunburned

solennel/solennelle *adjective*
= solemn

solide *adjective*
= solid, strong
= sturdy

sombre *adjective*
= dark
il fait sombre = it's dark

sombrer *verb* 1
= to sink

somme
1 *noun, feminine*
une somme = a sum
2 *noun, masculine*
un somme = a nap, a snooze

✱ in informal situations

sommeil *noun, masculine*
le sommeil = sleep
avoir sommeil = to be sleepy

sommes ▶ être 7

sommet *noun, masculine*
le sommet = the summit, the peak, the top

sommier *noun, masculine*
un sommier = a (bed) base

somnifère *noun, masculine*
un somnifère = a sleeping pill

son¹ *noun, masculine*
un son = a sound

son²/sa *determiner*
(*plural*) **ses**
= his/her
= its
son mari = her husband
sa femme = his wife
ses livres = his/her books
ses pattes = its paws

sondage *noun, masculine*
un sondage = a survey
= a(n opinion) poll

sonner *verb* 1
= to ring
(*if it's a clock*) = to strike

sonnerie *noun, feminine*
• (*a noise*)
la sonnerie = the ringing
• (*a mechanism*)
la sonnerie (*on an alarm clock*) = the alarm
(*on a door*) = the bell

sonnette *noun, feminine*
une sonnette = a bell

sonore *adjective*
• (*loud*) = resounding
• effets sonores = sound effects

sont ▶ être 7

sorcier *noun, masculine/feminine*
un sorcier/une sorcière = a wizard/a witch

sordide *adjective*
= squalid
= sordid

sort *noun, masculine*
• le sort = fate
tirer au sort = to draw lots
• son sort = one's lot
être satisfait de son sort = to be satisfied
with one's lot
• un sort = a curse, a spell
jeter un sort à un ennemi = to put a curse
on an enemy

sorte *noun, feminine*
une sorte = a sort, a kind

sortie *noun, feminine*
• (*a way out*)
une sortie = an exit
• (*the action of leaving a place*)
il a été attaqué à sa sortie du bureau = he
was mugged as he left the office
se retrouver à la sortie de l'école = to meet
after school
• (*a trip*)
une sortie = an outing

sortir *verb* 30
1 (**!** + *être*)
• = to go out, to come out
• sortir de = to leave, to come out of
2 (**!** + *avoir*)
= to take out
= to get out
sortir une lettre de sa poche = to take a
letter out of one's pocket
sors ton frère du lit! = get your brother out
of bed!

sou *noun, masculine*
• un sou ≈ a penny, a cent
• avoir des sous✶ = to have money

souci *noun, masculine*
un souci = a worry
se faire du souci = to worry

soucoupe *noun, feminine*
une soucoupe = a saucer

soudain/soudaine
1 *adjective*
= sudden
2 soudain *adverb*
= suddenly

souffler *verb* 1
• = to blow
• = to prompt
on t'a soufflé la réponse = you were
prompted, you were told the answer
• = to breathe out
• = to get one's breath back

souffrant/souffrante *adjective*
= unwell

souffrir *verb* 4
= to suffer
= to be in pain

souhait *noun, masculine*
un souhait = a wish

souhaiter *verb* 1
= to wish
souhaite-moi bonne chance = wish me
luck
souhaiter la bienvenue à un visiteur = to
welcome a visitor
je souhaite qu'il ne fasse pas froid
= I hope that it won't be cold

soûl/soûle *adjective*
= drunk

S

soulager verb 13
= to relieve
le comprimé m'a soulagé = the pill made me feel better

soulever verb 16
= to lift
= to raise

soulier noun, masculine
un soulier = a shoe

souligner verb 1
• = to underline
• = to emphasize, to stress

soupçon noun, masculine
un soupçon = a suspicion

soupçonner verb 1
= to suspect

soupe noun, feminine
la soupe = soup

souper
1 noun, masculine
le souper = supper
2 verb 1
= to have supper

soupir noun, masculine
un soupir = a sigh

soupirer verb 1
= to sigh

souple adjective
• = supple
• = flexible

source noun, feminine
• (water)
une source = a spring
• (the origin or cause of something)
une source = a source

sourcil noun, masculine
un sourcil = an eyebrow

sourd/sourde adjective
• (unable to hear) = deaf
• (describing a noise, a pain) = dull

souriant/souriante adjective
= smiling

sourire
1 verb 43
= to smile
2 noun, masculine
un sourire = a smile

souris noun, feminine (! never changes)
une souris = a mouse

sous
1 preposition
= under, underneath
sous terre = underground
sous la pluie = in the rain
2 ▶ sou

sous-marin/sous-marine
(plural) **sous-marins/sous-marines**
1 adjective
= submarine, underwater
= deep-sea
2 sous-marin noun, masculine
un sous-marin = a submarine

sous-sol noun, masculine
(plural) **sous-sols**
le sous-sol = the basement

sous-titre noun, masculine
(plural) **sous-titres**
un sous-titre = a subtitle

sous-vêtement noun, masculine
(plural) **sous-vêtements**
des sous-vêtements = underwear

soutenir verb 36
= to support

soutenu/soutenue ▶ soutenir 36

souterrain/souterraine
1 adjective
= underground
2 souterrain noun, masculine
un souterrain = a subway, a pedestrian underpass

soutien-gorge noun, masculine
(plural) **soutiens-gorge**
un soutien-gorge = a bra

souvenir
1 noun, masculine
• (something remembered)
un souvenir = a memory
• (an object)
un souvenir = a souvenir
2 se souvenir verb 36 (! + être)
se souvenir de = to remember

souvent adverb
= often
le plus souvent = more often than not

soyons ▶ être 7

spacieux/spacieuse adjective
= spacious

sparadrap noun, masculine
le sparadrap = (sticking) plaster, surgical tape

spatial/spatiale adjective
(plural) **spatiaux/spatiales**
= space

spécial/spéciale adjective
(plural) **spéciaux/spéciales**
• (not ordinary) = special
• (strange) = odd

spécialement adverb
= specially
= especially

spectacle noun, masculine
• (in a theatre, a circus)
un spectacle = a show

- (*something seen*)
  un **spectacle** = a sight

spectateur/spectatrice *noun,*
masculine/feminine
  un **spectateur**/une **spectatrice** = a member
  of the audience
  = a spectator

spéléologie *noun, feminine*
  la **spéléologie** = potholing, spelunking
  = speleology

sponsoriser *verb* 1
  = to sponsor

sport *noun, masculine*
  le **sport** = sport

sportif/sportive
1 *adjective*
- (*describing an event, a magazine*) = sports
- (*describing a person*)
  être **sportif** = to be the sporty type, to be
  athletic
2 *noun, masculine/feminine*
  un **sportif**/une **sportive** = a sportsman/a
  sportswoman

square *noun, masculine*
  un **square** = a small public garden

squelette *noun, masculine*
  le **squelette** = the skeleton

squelettique *adjective*
  = scrawny, thin as a rake

stade *noun, masculine*
  un **stade** = a stadium

stage *noun, masculine*
  un **stage** = a course
  = (a period of) work experience

station *noun, feminine*
- (*in a town*)
  une **station de métro** = a tube station, a
  subway station
  une **station de taxis** = a taxi rank, a taxi
  stand
- (*a town or a village*)
  une **station balnéaire** = a seaside resort
  une **station de ski** = a ski resort
  une **station thermale** = a spa

stationnement *noun, masculine*
  le **stationnement** = parking

station-service *noun, feminine*
(*plural*) **stations-service**
  une **station-service** = a service station, a
  gas station

steak *noun, masculine*
  un **steak** = a steak
  un **steak haché** = a beefburger

sténodactylo
1 *noun, masculine/feminine*
  un **sténodactylo**/une **sténodactylo** = a
  shorthand typist, a stenographer

2 *noun, feminine*
  la **sténodactylo** = shorthand typing,
  stenographing

stop *noun, masculine*
- un **stop** = a stop sign
- le **stop*** = hitch-hiking
  faire du **stop*** = to hitch-hike

store *noun, masculine*
  un **store** = a blind
  = an awning

studio *noun, masculine*
- (*accommodation*)
  un **studio** = a studio flat, a studio
  apartment
- (*a place of work*)
  un **studio** = a studio

stupéfait/stupéfaite *adjective*
  = astounded

stylo *noun, masculine*
  un **stylo** = a (fountain) pen
  un **stylo (à) bille** = a ball-point pen, a bic
  un **stylo feutre** = a felt-tip pen

su/sue ▶ **savoir** 47

subir *verb* 3
  subir une **opération** = to undergo an
  operation
  subir des **dégâts** = to suffer damage

subitement *adverb*
  = suddenly

succès *noun, masculine* (**!** *never*
changes)
  le **succès** = success

sucer *verb* 12
  = to suck

sucette *noun, feminine*
  une **sucette** = a lollipop, a lolly

sucre *noun, masculine*
  le **sucre** = sugar
  un **sucre** = a lump of sugar
  le **sucre d'orge** = barley sugar

sucré/sucrée *adjective*
  = sweet
  = sweetened

sucrer *verb* 1
  = to put sugar in
  = to sweeten

sucreries *noun, feminine plural*
  les **sucreries** = sweets, candies

sud
1 *noun, masculine*
  le **sud** = the south
2 *adjective* (**!** *never changes*)
  = south
  = southern

Suède *noun, feminine*
  la **Suède** = Sweden

S

suédois/suédoise
1 *adjective*
= Swedish
2 suédois *noun, masculine*
le Suédois = Swedish

sueur *noun, feminine*
la sueur = sweat

suffire *verb* 39
• = to be enough
ça me suffit = that's enough for me
• il suffit de demander = all you have to do
is ask
il suffit d'une étincelle = one spark is
enough

suffisamment *adverb*
= enough

suffisant/suffisante *adjective*
= sufficient

suis
• ▶ être 7
• ▶ suivre 37

suisse *adjective*
= Swiss

Suisse *noun, feminine*
la Suisse = Switzerland

suite
1 *noun, feminine*
• la suite = the rest
(*if it's another film or novel*) = the sequel
'suite page 45' = 'continued on page 45'
• une suite de = a succession of, a series of
2 de suite = in a row
à la suite de = following
trois jours de suite = three days in a row
3 tout de suite = straight away, right
away
4 par la suite = subsequently

suivant/suivante
1 *adjective*
= next
= following
2 *noun, masculine/feminine*
le suivant/la suivante = the next (one)
au suivant! = next!
3 suivant = according to

suivi/suivie ▶ suivre 37

suivre *verb* 37
= to follow
'à suivre' = 'to be continued'
faire suivre le courrier = to forward the
mail

sujet *noun, masculine*
un sujet = a subject

super
1 *adjective✱* (**!** *never changes*)
= great

2 *noun, masculine*
le super ≈ 4-star (petrol), super

superficie *noun, feminine*
la superficie = the area

supérieur/supérieure *adjective*
• = upper, top
• = higher
• = superior

supermarché *noun, masculine*
un supermarché = a supermarket

supplémentaire *adjective*
= additional, extra

supportable *adjective*
= bearable

supporter *verb* 1
• = to support, to bear the weight of
• = to put up with, to bear

supprimer *verb* 1
= to remove
= to cancel
= to withdraw
= to do away with
= to cut

sur *preposition*
• = on
sur la table = on the table
• = over
un pont sur la rivière = a bridge over the
river
• = about
un livre sur la guerre = a book about war
• = out of
9 sur 20 = 9 out of 20
• = by
faire 10 mètres sur 15 = to measure 10
metres by 15

sûr/sûre
1 *adjective*
• = sure, certain
c'est sûr = it's certain
j'en suis sûr = I'm sure of it, I'm certain of
it
j'en étais sûr! = I knew it!
être sûr de soi = to be self-confident
• = safe
= reliable
un endroit sûr = a safe place
un homme sûr = a reliable man
2 bien sûr = of course

sûreté *noun, feminine*
la sûreté = safety
= security

surf *noun, masculine*
le surf = surfing

surface *noun, feminine*
la surface = the surface (area)

surgelé/surgelée *adjective*
= (deep-)frozen
les produits surgelés = frozen food

✱ in informal situations

surligneur *noun, masculine*
un surligneur = a highlighter

surnaturel/surnaturelle *adjective*
= supernatural

surnom *noun, masculine*
un surnom = a nickname

surprenant/surprenante *adjective*
= surprising
= amazing

surprise *noun, feminine*
une surprise = a surprise

sursauter *verb* [1]
= to jump, to start

surtout *adverb*
= above all
= especially

surveillant/surveillante *noun,*
masculine/feminine
un surveillant/une surveillante (*in a*
school) = a supervisor
(*in a store*) = a store detective
(*in a prison*) = a warder, a guard

surveiller *verb* [1]
• = to watch, to keep an eye on
• = to supervise

survenir *verb* [36]
= to occur, to happen

survêtement *noun, masculine*
un survêtement = a tracksuit

survivant/survivante *noun,*
masculine/feminine
un survivant/une survivante = a survivor

survoler *verb* [1]
= to fly over

sus: **en sus** *adverb*
en sus = in addition, on top

svelte *adjective*
= slender

SVP (*abbreviation of* **s'il vous plaît**)
SVP = please

sympaˣ *adjective* (**!** *never changes*)
= nice

sympathie *noun, feminine*
avoir de la sympathie pour quelqu'un = to
like someone

sympathique *adjective*
= nice, pleasant

syndicat *noun, masculine*
un syndicat = a trade union
un syndicat d'initiative = a tourist
information office

synthétique *adjective*
= man-made

Tt

t' ▶ **te**

ta ▶ **ton**²

tabac *noun, masculine*
• (*a substance*)
le tabac = tobacco
• (*a shop*)
un tabac = a tobacconist's, a smoke shop

tabagisme *noun, masculine*
le tabagisme = tobacco addiction

table *noun, feminine*
une table = a table
mettre la table = to set the table
se mettre à table = to sit down at the table
à table! = dinner is served!
une table des matières = a table of
contents
une table de nuit = a bedside table, a
night stand

tableau *noun, masculine*
(*plural*) **tableaux**
• (*ornamental*)
un tableau = a painting
= a picture
• (*a surface*)
un tableau = a board
un tableau d'affichage = a noticeboard,
a bulletin board
le tableau de bord = the dashboard
le tableau (noir) = the blackboard

tablier *noun, masculine*
un tablier = an apron

tabouret *noun, masculine*
un tabouret = a stool

tache *noun, feminine*
une tache = a stain

tâche *noun, feminine*
une tâche = a task, a job
les tâches ménagères = household chores

tacher *verb* [1]
= to stain

tâcher *verb* [1]
tâcher de = to try to

taille *noun, feminine*
• (*the middle of the body*)
la taille = the waist, the waistline
• (*overall dimensions*)
la taille = the size
quelle taille faites-vous? = what size do
you take?
taille unique = one size
• (*tallness*)
la taille = the height

T

taille-crayon noun, masculine
(plural) **taille-crayons**
un taille-crayon = a pencil sharpener

tailler verb [1]
= to cut
= to prune
= to carve
= to sharpen

tailleur noun, masculine
• (a garment)
un tailleur = a (woman's) suit
• (a person)
un tailleur = a tailor

taire: se taire verb [59] (**!** + être)
se taire = to stop talking
= to be silent, to fall silent
taisez-vous! = be quiet!

talent noun, masculine
le talent = talent
un acteur de talent = a talented actor

talkie-walkie noun, masculine
(plural) **talkies-walkies**
un talkie-walkie = a walkie-talkie

talon noun, masculine
un talon = a heel

talus noun, masculine (**!** never changes)
un talus = an embankment

tambour noun, masculine
un tambour = a drum

Tamise noun, feminine
la Tamise = the Thames

tampon noun, masculine
un tampon (for documents) = a stamp

tamponner verb [1]
1 (**!** + avoir)
• (to put a mark on) = to stamp
• (to wipe) = to mop, to dab
2 se tamponner (**!** + être)
se tamponner = to collide

tandis que (**tandis qu'** before vowel or
mute h) conjunction
= while, whilst

tant adverb
• = so much
il t'aime tant! = he loves you so much!
tant mieux! = so much the better!
tant mieux pour vous! = good for you!
tant pis! = too bad!
• tant de = so much, so many
• tant que = as much as, as many as
= as long as
mange tant que tu veux = eat as much as
you like
il restera tant qu'il voudra = he'll stay as
long as he likes

tante noun, feminine
une tante = an aunt

tapage noun, masculine
du tapage = a din, a racket

taper verb [1]
• taper sur un clou = to hit a nail
il m'a tapé sur l'épaule = he tapped me on
the shoulder
• taper des mains = to clap one's hands
taper du pied = to tap one's foot
taper à la porte = to knock at the door
• taper (à la machine) = to type

tapis noun, masculine (**!** never changes)
un tapis = a rug
= a carpet

tapisser verb [1]
• = to wallpaper
• = to line

tapisserie noun, feminine
• (woven or embroidered cloth)
une tapisserie = a tapestry
• (paper)
la tapisserie = the wallpaper

taquiner verb [1]
= to tease

tard adverb
= late
plus tard = later
au plus tard = at the latest
pas plus tard qu'hier = only yesterday

tarder verb [1]
• tarder à arriver = to be a long time coming
tes parents ne vont pas tarder = your
parents won't be long
• tarder à répondre à une lettre = to take a
long time replying to a letter
= to put off replying to a letter
• il me tarde de les revoir = I'm longing to
see them again, I can't wait to see them
again

tarif noun, masculine
le tarif = the price
= the price list

tarte noun, feminine
une tarte = a tart, a flan

tartelette noun, feminine
une tartelette = a (small) tart

tartine noun, feminine
une tartine = a slice of bread and butter

tas noun, masculine (**!** never changes)
• un tas = a pile, a heap
en tas = in a pile, in a heap
• un (or des) tas**✶** d'amis = loads of friends

tasse noun, feminine
une tasse = a cup

tâter verb [1]
= to feel

tâtonner verb [1]
= to grope about

tâtons: **à tâtons** adverb
avancer à tâtons = to grope one's way
along

taudis noun, masculine (**!** never changes)
un taudis = a slum

taupe noun, feminine
une taupe = a mole

taureau noun, masculine
(plural) **taureaux**
un taureau = a bull

Taureau noun, masculine
le Taureau = Taurus

taux noun, masculine (**!** never changes)
le taux = the rate
= the level
le taux de change = the exchange rate

tchèque
1 adjective
= Czech
2 noun, masculine
le tchèque = Czech

tchin(-tchin)* exclamation
tchin(-tchin)*! = cheers!

TD noun, masculine plural ▶ **travail**

te (**t'** before vowel or mute h) pronoun
• = you
je te vois = I can see you
elle te l'a donné = she gave it to you
• = yourself
tu t'es fait mal? = did you hurt yourself?

technicien/technicienne noun,
masculine/feminine
un technicien/une technicienne = a
technician

teindre verb [55]
= to dye
= to stain

teint/teinte¹
1 ▶ **teindre** [55]
2 teint noun, masculine
un teint = a complexion

teinte² noun, feminine
une teinte = a shade
= a colo(u)r

teinture noun, feminine
une teinture = a dye

teinturerie noun, feminine
une teinturerie = a dry cleaner's

teinturier/teinturière noun,
masculine/feminine
un teinturier/une teinturière = a dry cleaner

tel/telle adjective
= such
de telle sorte qu'il l'a cassé = in such a
way that he broke it
les pays tels que la France = countries
like France

télé* noun, feminine
la télé* = TV

télécommandé/télécommandée
adjective
= remote control

télécopieur noun, masculine
un télécopieur = a fax (machine)

téléfilm noun, masculine
un téléfilm = a TV film, a TV movie

téléphérique noun, masculine
un téléphérique = a cable car

téléphone noun, masculine
un téléphone = a (tele)phone
un téléphone portable = a mobile phone

téléphoner verb [1]
= to (tele)phone

télésiège noun, masculine
un télésiège = a chair lift

téléski noun, masculine
un téléski = a ski tow

téléspectateur/téléspectatrice
noun, masculine/feminine
un téléspectateur/une téléspectatrice = a
viewer

téléviseur noun, masculine
un téléviseur = a television (set)

télévision noun, feminine
la télévision = television, TV

tellement adverb
• = so (much)
il est tellement riche! = he's so rich!
c'est tellement mieux maintenant! = it's so
much better now!
• tellement de = so much, so many
elle a tellement de temps libre = she has so
much free time
il y avait tellement de monde que je suis
parti = there were so many people that I
left

témoignage noun, masculine
un témoignage = a personal account
(in court) = evidence

témoin noun, masculine
un témoin = a witness
être témoin d'un incident = to witness an
incident

tempérament noun, masculine
un tempérament = a disposition, a
temperament

température noun, feminine
la température = the temperature

T

tempête *noun, feminine*
  une tempête = a storm
  = a gale

temporaire *adjective*
  = temporary

temps *noun, masculine* (**!** *never changes*)
• (*outside conditions*)
  le temps = the weather
  quel temps fait-il? = what's the weather
    like?
  il fait beau temps = the weather is fine
  il a fait mauvais temps = the weather has
    been bad
  quel temps de chien! = what awful
    weather!, it's terrible weather!
• (*as measured in hours*)
  le temps = time
  je n'ai pas le temps de me reposer = I
    haven't got time to rest
  il est grand temps de partir = it's high time
    we left
  ils ont fini à temps = they finished in time
  de temps en temps = from time to time
  pendant ce temps = meanwhile
• (*in grammar*)
  un temps = a tense

tenace *adjective*
  = stubborn, persistent

tenir *verb* 36
1 (**!** + *avoir*)
• = to hold
• tiens!, tenez! (*when giving something*)
    = here!
  (*expressing surprise*) = hey!
2 tenir à (**!** + *avoir*)
  tenir à sa famille = to be fond of one's
    family
3 se tenir (**!** + *être*)
• se tenir = to hold on
  se tenir à la rampe = to hold on to the
    banister
• se tenir = to stand
  se tenir droit (*if standing*) = to stand up
    straight
  se tenir tranquille = to keep still
• se tenir = to behave
  tenez-vous bien! = behave yourselves!
• ils se tenaient par la main = they were
    holding hands
4 si cela ne tenait qu'à moi = if I had my way

tennis *noun, masculine* (**!** *never changes*)
• (*the sport*)
  le tennis = tennis
• (*footwear*)
  un tennis = a tennis shoe

tentation *noun, feminine*
  la tentation = temptation

tentative *noun, feminine*
  une tentative = an attempt

tente *noun, feminine*
  une tente = a tent

tenter *verb* 1
• = to attempt
  = to try
  tenter sa chance = to try one's luck
• = to tempt
  ça ne me tente guère = it doesn't appeal to
    me very much

tenu/tenue¹ ▶ **tenir** 36

tenue² *noun, feminine*
  une tenue = an outfit, clothes
  en tenue de soirée = in evening dress

terminale *noun, feminine*
  la terminale *the class for secondary school
    students aged 17 to 18*

terminer *verb* 1
1 (**!** + *avoir*)
  = to finish, to end
2 se terminer (**!** + *être*)
  se terminer = end
  se terminer par une bagarre = to end in a
    fight

terminus *noun, masculine* (**!** *never
changes*)
  le terminus (*for a train*) = the end of the
    line
  (*for a bus*) = the terminus

terne *adjective*
  = dull

terrain *noun, masculine*
• (*a site*)
  un terrain = a piece of land
  (*used for sport*) = a pitch, a ground
• (*the surface underfoot*)
  le terrain = the ground
  un terrain d'atterrissage = a landing
    strip
  un terrain à bâtir = a building plot
  un terrain de camping = a campsite
  un terrain de jeux = a playground
  un terrain de sports = a sports ground, a
    sports field
  un terrain vague = a piece of wasteland

terrasse *noun, feminine*
  une terrasse = a terrace
  = a flat roof
  s'asseoir à la terrasse d'un café = to sit at
    a table outside a café

terre *noun, feminine*
• (*the surface underfoot*)
  la terre = the ground
  sous terre = underground
  par terre = on the ground, on the floor
• (*the substance*)
  la terre = the earth, the soil
  (*as opposed to the sea*) = land
  aller à terre = to go ashore
• (*a type of clay*)
  un pot en terre = an earthenware pot

✗ in informal situations

- (*an area in private ownership*)
  une terre = a piece of land
  des terres = land

Terre *noun, feminine*
  la Terre = Earth

terrestre *adjective*
  (*describing plants or animals*) = land
  (*relating to the Earth*) = of the Earth

terrible *adjective*
- = terrible
- (*excellent*)✘ = terrific
  le livre n'est pas terrible✘ = it's not a great
  book

tes ▶ ton²

testament *noun, masculine*
  un testament = a will

tester *verb* ⒈
  = to test

tête *noun, feminine*
- (*part of the body*)
  la tête = the head
  se laver la tête = to wash one's hair
- (*the front part of the head*)
  la tête = the face
  tu fais une drôle de tête = you look funny
  faire la tête = to sulk
  n'en faire qu'à sa tête = to get one's way
- (*as opposed to the end*)
  la tête = the front
  = the head
  être en tête = to be at the front
  une tête en l'air = a scatterbrain

têtu/têtue *adjective*
  = stubborn, obstinate

texte *noun, masculine*
  un texte = a text

texto *noun, masculine*
  un texto = a text message

TGV *noun, masculine*
  un TGV = a high speed train

thé *noun, masculine*
- **le thé** = tea
- **un thé** = a cup of tea

théâtre *noun, masculine*
  un théâtre = a theatre, a theater
  faire du théâtre = to be an actor/an actress,
  to act

théière *noun, feminine*
  une théière = a teapot

thème *noun, masculine*
- **le thème** = the theme
- (*a translation*)
  un thème = a prose

thermal/thermale *adjective*
  (*plural*) **thermaux/thermales**
  une source thermale = a thermal spring
  une station thermale = a spa

thermos *noun, masculine* (**!** *never
changes*)
  un thermos = a (vacuum) flask

thon *noun, masculine*
  le thon = tuna

thym *noun, masculine*
  le thym = thyme

tibia *noun, masculine*
  le tibia = the shin

ticket *noun, masculine*
  un ticket = a ticket

tiède *adjective*
  = warm
  = lukewarm, tepid

tien/tienne: *pronoun*
  le tien/la tienne = yours
  les tiens/les tiennes = yours

tiens ▶ tenir ㊱

tiers *noun, masculine* (**!** *never changes*)
  un tiers = one third

tiers-monde *noun, masculine*
  le tiers-monde = the Third World

tige *noun, feminine*
  une tige = a stem

tigre *noun, masculine*
  un tigre = a tiger

tilleul *noun, masculine*
- **un tilleul** = a lime tree
- **le tilleul** = lime tea

timbre *noun, masculine*
  un timbre = a (postage) stamp

timbrer *verb* ⒈
  = to put a stamp on

timide *adjective*
  = shy

timidité *noun, feminine*
  la timidité = shyness

tir *noun, masculine*
- **le tir** (*in an attack*) = firing
  (*as a sport*) = shooting
- **le tir à l'arc** = archery

tirage *noun, masculine*
- (*in a lottery*)
  le tirage (au sort) = the draw
- (*for a newspaper*)
  le tirage = the circulation

tire-bouchon *noun, masculine*
  (*plural*) **tire-bouchons**
  un tire-bouchon = a corkscrew

tirelire *noun, feminine*
  une tirelire = a piggy bank

tirer *verb* ⒈
- = to pull
- = to draw

* = to fire
  = to shoot
* **tirer au sort** = to draw lots

tiroir *noun, masculine*
un tiroir = a drawer

tiroir-caisse *noun, masculine*
(*plural*) **tiroirs-caisses**
un tiroir-caisse = a cash register

tisane *noun, feminine*
la tisane = herbal tea

tisser *verb* [1]
= to weave

tissu *noun, masculine*
le tissu = material, fabric

titre *noun, masculine*
un titre = a title

toc *exclamation*
toc toc! = knock! knock!

toi *pronoun*
= you
plus jeune que toi = younger than you
toi, tu as de la chance = you're lucky, you
  are
ce livre est à toi = this book belongs to
  you, this book is yours
à toi (de jouer)! = it's your turn (to play)!
allons chez toi = let's go to your house
lève-toi! = get up!

toile *noun, feminine*
* (*material*)
  la toile = cloth
  = canvas
* (*in art*)
  une toile = a canvas
une toile d'araignée = a cobweb, a
  spider's web
une toile cirée = an oilcloth

toilette
1 *noun, feminine*
faire sa toilette = to have a wash
2 toilettes *noun, feminine plural*
les toilettes (*in a house*) = the toilet, the
  bathroom
(*in a public place*) = the toilets

toi-même *pronoun*
= yourself

toise *noun, feminine*
une toise = a height gauge

toit *noun, masculine*
un toit = a roof
un toit ouvrant = a sunroof

tôle *noun, feminine*
la tôle = sheet metal
la tôle ondulée = corrugated iron

tomate *noun, feminine*
une tomate = a tomato

tombe *noun, feminine*
une tombe = a grave

tomber *verb* [1] (**!** + *être*)
* = to fall
  = to fall over
  c'est tombé de ma poche = it fell out of
    my pocket
  il est tombé de l'arbre = he fell off the tree
  tomber en panne = to break down
* laisser tomber = to drop
* (*to see or meet by chance*)
  tomber sur = to come across
  = to run into
* (*to happen*)
  ça tombe bien, moi aussi je suis libre
    = that's good, I'm free too

ton¹ *noun, masculine*
* (*a way of speaking*)
  un ton = a tone
  d'un ton sec = drily
* (*a colour*)
  un ton = a shade

ton²/ta *determiner*
(*plural*) **tes**
= your

tonalité *noun, feminine*
la tonalité = the dialling tone, the dial
  tone

tondeuse *noun, feminine*
une tondeuse (à gazon) = a lawnmower

tondre *verb* [6]
tondre le gazon = to mow the grass
tondre un mouton = to shear a sheep
tondre quelqu'un = to shave someone's
  head

tondu/tondue ▶ **tondre** [6]

tonneau *noun, masculine*
(*plural*) **tonneaux**
un tonneau = a barrel

tonnerre
1 *noun, masculine*
le tonnerre = thunder
un coup de tonnerre = a clap of thunder
2 du tonnerre✱ = fabulous

torchon *noun, masculine*
un torchon = a tea towel, a dish towel

tordre *verb* [6]
1 (**!** + *avoir*)
= to twist
= to wring
= to bend
2 se tordre (**!** + *être*)
se tordre la cheville = to twist one's ankle

tordu/tordue *adjective*
1 ▶ **tordre** [6]
2 *adjective*
= crooked
= twisted

✱ in informal situations

tornade noun, feminine
une tornade = a tornado

torrent noun, masculine
un torrent = a torrent
pleuvoir à torrents = to rain very heavily

torse noun, masculine
le torse = the chest

tort noun, masculine
avoir tort = to be wrong

tortue noun, feminine
une tortue = a tortoise, a turtle

tôt adverb
= early
tôt le matin = early in the morning
le plus tôt possible = as soon as possible

toucher verb 1
• = to touch
• = to get
toucher un salaire = to get a wage
• = to cash

touffe noun, feminine
une touffe (of hair, grass) = a tuft

toujours adverb
• (all the time) = always
il est toujours en retard = he's always late
• (showing that something is continuing)
= still
tu habites toujours Paris? = are you still
living in Paris?
il n'est toujours pas levé = he's still not up
elle est toujours aussi jolie = she's as pretty
as ever

tour
1 noun, feminine
• (a building)
une tour = a tower
= a tower block, a high rise
• (in chess)
une tour = a rook, a castle
2 noun, masculine
• (a turning movement)
un tour = a turn
faire un tour de manège = to have a go on
a fairground ride
faire le tour du lac (on foot) = to walk
round the lake
faire le tour du monde en bateau = to sail
round the world
• (in a game, a rota)
un tour = a turn
à tour de rôle = in turn
• (an outing)
(aller) faire un tour = to go for a stroll
aller faire un tour à Rome = to go to Rome
• (a piece of mischief)
un tour = a trick
jouer un tour à un ami = to play a trick on
a friend
• (a size)
un tour = a measurement
mon tour de taille = my waist
measurement

tourbillon noun, masculine
un tourbillon = a whirlpool
un tourbillon (de vent) = a whirlwind
un tourbillon de poussière = a whirl of
dust

tourisme noun, masculine
le tourisme = tourism

touristique adjective
= tourist
un endroit touristique = a popular tourist
spot

tournée noun, feminine
• une tournée (for a postman) = a round
(for a singer, a theatre company) = a tour
• (in a café)
une tournée = a round (of drinks)

tourner verb 1
1 (! + avoir)
• = to turn
tourner un film = to shoot a film
2 se tourner (! + être)
se tourner = to turn around

tournoi noun, masculine
un tournoi = a tournament

tous ▶ tout 1, 2

Toussaint noun, feminine
la Toussaint = All Saints' Day

tousser verb 1
= to cough

tout/toute
(plural) **tous/toutes**
1 adjective
• = all
= every
il a plu toute la journée = it rained all day
(long)
c'est tout ce que tu veux? = is that all you
want?
tout le reste = everything else
tout le monde = everyone
tous les jours = every day
tous les deux ans = every other year
ils sont venus tous les deux = they both
came
• tout un/tout une = a whole
manger tout un pain = to eat a whole loaf
• = any
à toute heure = at any time
de toute façon = in any case
2 pronoun
= everything
= anything
= all
il a tout oublié = he's forgotten everything
tout peut arriver = anything can happen
100 euros en tout = 100 euros in all
tous ensemble = all together

T

3 *adverb*
* = quite
  = very
  c'est tout naturel = it's quite natural
  c'est tout près d'ici = it's very near
  être tout seul = to be all by oneself
  continuer tout droit = to carry straight on
  tout neuf/toute neuve = brand-new
  des rideaux tout faits = ready-made
  curtains
* **tout en** [marchant | travaillant | écoutant la radio …] = while [walking | working | listening to the radio …]
* (*in some phrases*)
  tout à coup = suddenly
  tout à fait = quite
  tout à l'heure = in a moment
  à tout à l'heure! = see you later!
  tout de même = all the same, even so
  tout de suite = at once
4 tout *noun, masculine*
* **le tout** = the lot
* **pas du tout** = not at all

toux *noun, feminine* (! *never changes*)
  une toux = a cough

TP *noun, masculine plural* ▶ **travail**

tracasser *verb* [1]
  = to bother

trace *noun, feminine*
* **une trace** = a trail, a track
* **une trace** = a mark, a trace
  des traces de pas = footprints
  des traces de doigts = fingermarks

tracer *verb* [12]
  = to draw
  = to write

traduire *verb* [62]
  = to translate

trafic *noun, masculine*
  le trafic = traffic

trafiquant/trafiquante *noun,*
masculine/feminine
  un trafiquant/une trafiquante = a
  trafficker, a dealer

train
1 *noun, masculine*
  un train = a train
2 en train de = in the process of
  être en train de [travailler | dormir | se doucher …] = to be [working | sleeping | having a shower …]

traîneau *noun, masculine*
(*plural*) **traîneaux**
  un traîneau = a sledge

traîner *verb* [1]
* = to drag (along)

* **traîner dans les rues** = to hang around
  (on) the streets
* (*to be scattered*) = to be lying around
  laisser traîner ses affaires = to leave one's
  things lying around

trait
1 *noun, masculine*
  un trait = a line
2 traits *noun, masculine plural*
  des traits (*of a face*) = features

traitement *noun, masculine*
  un traitement = a treatment

traiter *verb* [1]
  = to treat

trajet *noun, masculine*
  un trajet = a journey

tranche *noun, feminine*
  une tranche (*of cheese, bread*) = a slice

tranquille *adjective*
  = quiet
  = calm, peaceful

tranquillité *noun, feminine*
  la tranquillité = peace and quiet

transmettre *verb* [60]
* = to broadcast
* = to pass on, to convey
* = to transmit

transpirer *verb* [1]
  = to sweat, to perspire

transport *noun, masculine*
* **le transport** = transport, transportation
* **les transports en commun** = public
  transport

transporter *verb* [1]
  = to carry

travail
(*plural*) **travaux**
1 *noun, masculine*
* **le travail** = work
* **un travail** = a job
2 travaux *noun, masculine plural*
  des travaux = work
  = roadwork(s)
  les travaux ménagers = housework
  les travaux dirigés, TD = practicals
  les travaux manuels = handicrafts
  les travaux pratiques, TP = practical
  work
  les travaux publics = civil engineering

travailler *verb* [1]
  = to work
  = to practise

travailleur/travailleuse
1 *adjective*
  = hardworking
2 *noun, masculine/feminine*
  un travailleur/une travailleuse = a worker

✱ in informal situations

travaux ▶ travail

travers noun, masculine
1 à travers = through
= across
2 de travers
ta cravate est de travers = your tie is
crooked
boutonné de travers = buttoned up
wrongly
j'ai avalé de travers = it went down the
wrong way
3 en travers de
= across

traversée noun, feminine
une traversée = a crossing

traverser verb ①
• = to cross
• = to go through

traversin noun, masculine
un traversin = a bolster

trèfle noun, masculine
• (a plant)
le trèfle = clover
• (at cards)
trèfle = clubs

treille noun, feminine
une treille = a climbing vine

treize number
= thirteen

treizième number
= thirteenth

tremblement noun, masculine
un tremblement = a tremor
un tremblement de terre = an
earthquake

trembler verb ①
= to shake
= to tremble, to quiver

trempé/trempée adjective
= soaked, sodden, soaking wet
trempé jusqu'aux os = soaked to the skin

tremper verb ①
• = to soak
• = to dip

trente number
= thirty

très adverb
= very
avoir très faim = to be very hungry
très volontiers = gladly

trésor noun, masculine
un trésor = a treasure

tresse noun, feminine
une tresse = a plait, a braid

tribu noun, feminine
une tribu = a tribe

tribune noun, feminine
la tribune (in a stadium) = the grandstand

tricher verb ①
= to cheat

tricolore adjective
le drapeau tricolore = the French flag

tricot noun, masculine
• (a craft)
le tricot = knitting
• (a knitted garment)
un tricot = a jumper, a sweater

tricoter verb ①
= to knit

trier verb ②
• = to sort (out)
• = to select

trimestre noun, masculine
un trimestre = a term

triste adjective
= sad

tristesse noun, feminine
la tristesse = sadness

trois number
= three

troisième
1 number
= third
2 noun, feminine
la troisième the class for secondary school
students aged 14 to 15

trombone noun, masculine
• (an instrument)
un trombone = a trombone
• (for fastening papers)
un trombone = a paper clip

trompe noun, feminine
une trompe d'éléphant = an elephant
trunk

tromper verb ①
1 (! + avoir)
= to deceive
2 se tromper (! + être)
• se tromper = to make a mistake
se tromper de bus = to take the wrong bus
se tromper de date = to get the date wrong
• se tromper = to be mistaken

trompette noun, feminine
une trompette = a trumpet

tronc noun, masculine
un tronc = a trunk

trop
1 adverb = too
= too much
c'est trop petit = it's too small
tu parles trop = you talk too much
2 trop de = too much, too many

T

trottoir *noun, masculine*
un trottoir = a pavement, a sidewalk
le bord du trottoir = the kerb, the curb

trou *noun, masculine*
• un trou = a hole
(*in a hedge*) = a gap
• (*a small town*)✱
un trou✱ (perdu) = a dump

troupeau *noun, masculine*
(*plural*) **troupeaux**
un troupeau = a herd
= a flock

trousse *noun, feminine*
une trousse = a (small) case
= a kit
une trousse d'écolier = a pencil case
une trousse de secours = a first-aid kit
une trousse de toilette = a toilet bag

trouver *verb* 1
1 (**!** + *avoir*)
• = to find
• = to think
je trouve qu'il a raison = I think he's right
comment trouves-tu mon copain? = what
   do you think of my friend?
2 se trouver (**!** + *être*)
• se trouver = to be
se trouver à Nice = to be in Nice
• se trouver = to find
se trouver une excuse = to find an excuse
• je me trouve bien ici = I like it here
se trouver mal = to pass out, to faint

truc *noun, masculine*
• (*when referring vaguely to something*)
un truc = a thing
• (*a clever way*)✱
un truc✱ = a trick
= a knack

truffe *noun, feminine*
une truffe = a truffle

truite *noun, feminine*
une truite = a trout

TTC (*abbreviation of* **toutes taxes
comprises**)
TTC = inclusive of tax

tu *pronoun*
= you

tube *noun, masculine*
• un tube = a tube, a pipe
• (*a song*)✱
un tube✱ = a hit

tuer *verb* 1
= to kill

tue-tête: **à tue-tête** *adverb*
chanter à tue-tête = to sing at the top of
   one's voice

tuile *noun, feminine*
une tuile = a tile

Tunisie *noun, feminine*
la Tunisie = Tunisia

tunisien/tunisienne *adjective*
= Tunisian

tunnel *noun, masculine*
un tunnel = a tunnel
le tunnel sous la Manche = the Channel
   Tunnel

turc/turque
1 *adjective*
= Turkish
2 turc *noun, masculine*
le turc = Turkish

Turquie *noun, feminine*
la Turquie = Turkey

tutoyer *verb* 23
tutoyer quelqu'un = to address someone
   using the 'tu' form

tuyau *noun, masculine*
(*plural*) **tuyaux**
un tuyau = a pipe
un tuyau d'arrosage = a hosepipe
le tuyau d'échappement = the exhaust

TVA *noun, feminine*
la TVA = VAT

type *noun, masculine*
• (*a sort*)
un type = a type, a kind
• (*a man*)✱
un type✱ = a bloke, a guy

typique *adjective*
= typical

Uu

ULM *noun, masculine* (**!** *never changes*)
• (*the equipment*)
un ULM = a microlight
• (*the sport*)
l'ULM = microlighting

un/une
1 *number*
= one
trente et un jours = thirty-one days
une fois = once
un jour sur deux = every other day
2 *determiner*
(*plural*) **des**
= a(n)
un chat = a cat
des enfants = children

3 *pronoun*
(*plural*) **uns/unes**
(l')un/(l')une = one
les uns/les unes = some
l'un d'entre vous = one of you
pourquoi les uns et pas les autres? = why
  some and not others?

uni/unie *adjective*
• (*not at odds*) = united
  = close-knit
• (*not patterned*) = plain

unique *adjective*
• = only
  être fils/fille unique = to be an only child
• = unique
  une occasion unique = a unique
   opportunity

uniquement *adverb*
= only

unir *verb* ③
= to unite

unité *noun, feminine*
• une unité = a unit
• l'unité = unity

univers *noun, masculine* (**!** *never
changes*)
  l'univers = the universe

universitaire *adjective*
= university

université *noun, feminine*
  l'université = university, college

uns/unes ▶ **un 3**

urbain/urbaine *adjective*
= urban
la vie urbaine = city life

urbanisme *noun, masculine*
  l'urbanisme = town planning, city
  planning

urgence *noun, feminine*
• l'urgence = the urgency
  téléphonez d'urgence = phone
   immediately
  des mesures d'urgence = emergency
   measures
  on l'a transporté d'urgence à l'hôpital = he
   was rushed to the hospital
• (*in a hospital*)
  une urgence = an emergency
  le service des urgences = the casualty
   department, the accident and
   emergency department

urticaire *noun, feminine*
  l'urticaire = nettle rash

usage *noun, masculine*
  l'usage = the use
  'à usage externe' = 'for external use only'

usager *noun, masculine*
  un usager (*of a service*) = a user
  les usagers de la route = road-users

usé/usée *adjective*
= worn

user *verb* ①
1 (**!** + *avoir*)
  = to wear out
  = to wear down
2 s'user (**!** + *être*)
  s'user = to wear out

usine *noun, feminine*
  une usine = a factory

ustensile *noun, masculine*
  un ustensile = a utensil

utile *adjective*
= useful

utiliser *verb* ①
= to use

Vv

---

va ▶ **aller 1** ⑨

vacances *noun, feminine plural*
  des vacances = holidays, a vacation
  être en vacances = to be on holiday, to be
   on vacation

vacancier/vacancière *noun,
masculine/feminine*
  un vacancier/une vacancière = a
   holidaymaker, a vacationer

vache *noun, feminine*
  une vache = a cow

vagabonder *verb* ①
= to wander

vague
1 *adjective*
  = vague
2 *noun, masculine*
  il regardait dans le vague = he was staring
   into space
3 *noun, feminine*
• une vague = a wave
• une vague de froid = a cold spell

vaincre *verb* ㊼
  = to defeat
  = to overcome

vaincu/vaincue
1 ▶ **vaincre** ㊼
2 *noun, masculine/feminine*
  les vaincus = the losers

vainqueur *noun, masculine*
  un vainqueur = a winner
  = a victor

vais ▶ aller 1 9

vaisselle *noun, feminine*
  la vaisselle = crockery, dishes
  faire la vaisselle = to do the dishes

valable *adjective*
  = valid

valet *noun, masculine*
* (*a person*)
  un valet = a manservant
* (*at cards*)
  un valet = a jack

valeur *noun, feminine*
  la valeur (*in terms of money*) = value
  (*in terms of merit*) = worth
  les objets de valeur = valuables
  sans valeur = worthless

valise *noun, feminine*
  une valise = a suitcase
  faire ses valises = to pack

vallée *noun, feminine*
  une vallée = a valley

valoir *verb* 45
* = to be worth
  = to cost
  ça en vaut la peine = it's worth it
* il vaut mieux partir tôt = it's better to leave
  early
  il vaut mieux que tu y ailles = you'd better
  go

valu ▶ valoir 45

vanille *noun, feminine*
  la vanille = vanilla

vapeur
1 *noun, feminine*
  la vapeur = steam
  un bateau à vapeur = a steamboat
  faire cuire des légumes à la vapeur = to
    steam vegetables
2 vapeurs *noun, feminine plural*
  des vapeurs = fumes

vaporisateur *noun, masculine*
  un vaporisateur = a spray

vaporiser *verb* 1
  = to spray
  = to vaporize

varappe *noun, feminine*
  la varappe = rock-climbing

variable *adjective*
* = variable
* = changeable, unpredictable

variante *noun, feminine*
  une variante = a variation

varié/variée *adjective*
  = varied
  = various
  'sandwichs variés' = 'a selection of
    sandwiches'

variété
1 *noun, feminine*
* la variété = variety
* une variété = a variety
2 variétés *noun, feminine plural*
  un spectacle de variétés = a variety show

vas ▶ aller 1 9

vase
1 *noun, masculine*
  un vase = a vase
2 *noun, feminine*
  la vase = mud

vaste *adjective*
  = vast, huge
  = large

vaudrait ▶ valoir 45

vaut ▶ valoir 45

vautour *noun, masculine*
  un vautour = a vulture

veau *noun, masculine*
(*plural*) **veaux**
* (*the animal*)
  un veau = a calf
* (*the meat*)
  le veau = veal

vécu/vécue
1 ▶ vivre 38
2 *adjective*
  = real-life

vedette *noun, feminine*
* (*a person*)
  une vedette = a star
* (*a boat*)
  une vedette = a motor launch

véhicule *noun, masculine*
  un véhicule = a vehicle

veille *noun, feminine*
  la veille = the day before
  la veille au soir = the night before

veiller *verb* 1
* (*to remain awake*) = to stay up
* (*to be alert*) = to be watchful

veilleur *noun, masculine*
  un veilleur de nuit = a night watchman

veilleuse *noun, feminine*
  une veilleuse = a night light
  = a pilot light

veine *noun, feminine*
* une veine = a vein
* la veine✱ = luck
  avoir de la veine✱ = to be lucky

---

vélo *noun, masculine*
un vélo = a bike
un vélo tout terrain = a mountain bike
faire du vélo = to cycle

vélomoteur *noun, masculine*
un vélomoteur = a moped

velours *noun, masculine* (**!** *never changes*)
le velours = velvet
= corduroy

venais ▶ venir 36

vendanges *noun, feminine plural*
les vendanges = the grape harvest

vendeur/vendeuse *noun, masculine/feminine*
un vendeur/une vendeuse = a seller, a vendor
= a shop assistant
= a salesman/a saleswoman

vendre *verb* 6
1 (**!** + *avoir*)
= to sell
'à vendre' = 'for sale'
2 **se vendre** (**!** + *être*)
se vendre = to be sold
ça se vend bien = it sells well

vendredi *noun, masculine*
vendredi = Friday
le vendredi = on Fridays

vendu/vendue ▶ vendre 6

vénéneux/vénéneuse *adjective*
= poisonous

vengeance *noun, feminine*
la vengeance = revenge

venger *verb* 13
1 (**!** + *avoir*)
= to avenge
2 **se venger** (**!** + *être*)
se venger = to get one's revenge

venir *verb* 36 (**!** + *être*)
• = to come
viens déjeuner = come for lunch
faire venir un plombier = to call a plumber
ça ne m'est jamais venu à l'idée = it never crossed my mind
• venir de faire = to have just done

vent *noun, masculine*
le vent = the wind
il y a du vent, il fait du vent = it's windy

vente *noun, feminine*
une vente = a sale
des médicaments en vente libre = drugs available over the counter
la vente par correspondance = mail-order selling
une vente aux enchères = an auction

ventre *noun, masculine*
le ventre (*a person's*) = the stomach
(*an animal's*) = the (under)belly

venu/venue ▶ venir 36

ver *noun, masculine*
un ver = a worm
= a maggot
un ver de terre = an earthworm

verbe *noun, masculine*
un verbe = a verb

verdure *noun, feminine*
la verdure = greenery

verger *noun, masculine*
un verger = an orchard

verglacé/verglacée *adjective*
= icy

verglas *noun, masculine* (**!** *never changes*)
le verglas = black ice

vérifier *verb* 2
= to check

véritable *adjective*
= real, true, genuine

vérité *noun, feminine*
la vérité = the truth

vernis *noun, masculine* (**!** *never changes*)
le vernis = varnish
= glaze
du vernis à ongles = nail polish

verrai ▶ voir 46

verre *noun, masculine*
• (*a substance*)
le verre = glass
• (*a container*)
un verre = a glass
un verre à vin = a wine glass
un verre de vin = a glass of wine
aller prendre un verre = to go for a drink
• (*on spectacles*)
un verre = a lens
des verres de contact = contact lenses

vers
1 *noun, masculine* (**!** *never changes*)
un vers = a line (of verse)
des vers = poetry
2 *preposition*
• = toward(s)
rouler vers Paris = to go toward(s) Paris
vers le soir = toward(s) evening
• = about
vers six heures = at about six o'clock

Verseau *noun, masculine*
le Verseau = Aquarius

verser *verb* 1
• = to pour
• = to pay

V

version noun, feminine
• (an exercise)
  une version = a translation (into one's own language)
• (an account, an adaptation)
  une version = a version
  un film en version originale = a film in the original language

vert/verte adjective
  = green

vertèbre noun, feminine
  une vertèbre = a vertebra
  se déplacer une vertèbre = to slip a disc

vertical/verticale adjective
(plural) **verticaux/verticales**
  = vertical
  = upright

verticalement adverb
• = vertically
• (in a crossword) = down

vertige noun, masculine
  le vertige = dizziness
  = vertigo
  avoir le vertige = to feel dizzy

veste noun, feminine
  une veste = a jacket

vestiaire noun, masculine
  un vestiaire (in a gym) = a changing room
  (in a theatre, a museum) = a cloakroom

vestibule noun, masculine
  un vestibule = a hall
  = a foyer, a lobby

veston noun, masculine
  un veston = a (man's) jacket

vêtement noun, masculine
  un vêtement = a garment
  des vêtements = clothes, clothing
  'vêtements pour hommes' = 'menswear'

vétérinaire noun, masculine/feminine
  un vétérinaire/une vétérinaire = a veterinary surgeon, a veterinarian

vêtu/vêtue adjective
  = dressed
  elle était vêtue d'une robe noire = she was wearing a black dress

veuf/veuve
1 adjective
  = widowed
2 noun, masculine/feminine
  un veuf/une veuve = a widower/a widow

veuille ▶ vouloir 48

veulent ▶ vouloir 48

veuve ▶ veuf

veux ▶ vouloir 48

vexer verb 1
1 (! + avoir)
  = to offend, to upset

2 se vexer (! + être)
  se vexer = to take offence, to get upset

viande noun, feminine
  la viande = meat
  de la viande de bœuf = beef

victime noun, feminine
  une victime = a victim
  = a casualty

victoire noun, feminine
  une victoire = a victory

vide
1 adjective
  = empty, vacant
  = blank
2 noun, masculine
• (a space)
  un vide = a gap
• (absence of air)
  le vide = a vacuum
  emballé sous vide = vacuum-packed
• **sauter dans le vide** = to jump

vidéothèque noun, feminine
  une vidéothèque = a video library
  = a video collection

vider verb 1
1 (! + avoir)
  = to empty
2 se vider (! + être)
  se vider = to empty

vie noun, feminine
  la vie = life
  être en vie = to be alive
  la vie active = working life
  la vie est chère = the cost of living is high

vieil ▶ vieux 1

vieillard/vieillarde noun, masculine/feminine
  un vieillard/une vieillarde = an old man/an old woman
  les vieillards = old people

vieille ▶ vieux

vieillir verb 3
  = to get old(er)
  = to age

viendrai ▶ venir 36

viens ▶ venir 36

vierge adjective
  = virgin
  = blank
  = new

Vierge noun, feminine
• **la Vierge** = Virgo
• **la (Sainte) Vierge** = the (Blessed) Virgin

vietnamien/vietnamienne
1 adjective
  = Vietnamese

2 vietnamien noun, masculine
le vietnamien = Vietnamese

vieux/vieille
(plural) **vieux/vieilles**
1 adjective
= old

> **!** vieil is used instead of vieux before
> masculine nouns that begin with a vowel
> or a mute h. The plural of vieil is vieux.

un vieil homme = an old man
de vieilles photos = old photographs
2 noun, masculine/feminine
un vieux/une vieille = an old man/an old
woman
les vieux = old people

vif/vive¹ adjective
* (describing a person) = lively
* (describing a pace, a movement) = brisk
rouler à vive allure = to drive at high speed
* (describing a light, a colour) = bright
* (describing the cold, the wind) = biting
* (describing a pain) = sharp

vigne noun, feminine
la vigne = vine
une vigne = a vineyard
la vigne vierge = Virginia creeper

vigneron/vigneronne noun,
masculine/feminine
un vigneron/une vigneronne = a
winegrower

vignette noun, feminine
une vignette = a label
(on a car) = a tax disc

vignoble noun, masculine
un vignoble = a vineyard

vilain/vilaine adjective
* = naughty, nasty
* = ugly

villa noun, feminine
une villa = a detached house
= a villa

village noun, masculine
un village = a village

ville noun, feminine
une ville = a town, a city
aller en ville = to go into town

vin noun, masculine
le vin = wine

vinaigre noun, masculine
le vinaigre = vinegar

vinaigrette noun, feminine
la vinaigrette = vinaigrette, oil and vinegar
dressing

vingt number
= twenty

vingtaine noun, feminine
une vingtaine = about twenty
= twenty

vingt et un/vingt et une number
= twenty-one

vingt et unième number
= twenty-first

vingtième number
= twentieth

violent/violente adjective
= violent

violet/violette¹ adjective
= purple

violette² noun, feminine
une violette = a violet

violon noun, masculine
un violon = a violin

violoncelle noun, masculine
un violoncelle = a cello

vipère noun, feminine
une vipère = an adder, a viper

virage noun, masculine
un virage = a bend

virgule noun, feminine
une virgule = a comma
= a decimal point

vis
1 ▶ vivre 38
2 noun, feminine (**!** never changes)
une vis = a screw

visage noun, masculine
le visage = the face

viser verb 1
* = to aim at
* = to be aimed at

visite noun, feminine
une visite = a visit
= a call
rendre visite à un ami = to pay a visit to a
friend
avoir de la visite = to have visitors
une visite médicale = a medical
examination

visiter verb 1
visiter une ville = to visit a town
visiter un appartement = to view a flat, to
look at an apartment

visser verb 1
= to screw on

vite adverb
= quickly, fast
vite! = quick!
j'ai parlé trop vite = I spoke too hastily

vitesse noun, feminine
* la vitesse = speed
en vitesse = quickly
à toute vitesse = at top speed
* une vitesse = a gear

V

vitre *noun, feminine*
  une vitre = a windowpane
  = a pane of glass
  les vitres d'une voiture = the windows of a
    car

vitrine *noun, feminine*
• (*in a shop*)
  une vitrine = a (shop) window
  faire les vitrines = to go window shopping
• (*in a museum*)
  une vitrine = a display cabinet, a curio
    cabinet

vivant/vivante *adjective*
• = alive, living
  être vivant = to be alive
  les êtres vivants = living creatures
• = lively

vive²
1 *adjective, feminine* ▶ **vif**
2 *verb* ▶ **vivre** 38

vivre *verb* 38
  = to live
  se laisser vivre = to take things easy

vocabulaire *noun, masculine*
  le vocabulaire = vocabulary

vœu *noun, masculine*
(*plural*) **vœux**
  un vœu = a wish
  meilleurs vœux = best wishes
  les vœux du Nouvel An = New Year's
    greetings

voici *preposition*
  = here is, this is
  = here are, these are
  me voici = here I am
  voici un mois = a month ago

voie *noun, feminine*
• (*for traffic*)
  une voie = a road
  = a street
  la voie publique = the public highway
  une voie sans issue = a dead end
• (*part of a road*)
  une voie = a lane
• (*for a train*)
  une voie = a track
• en voie de = in the process of
  un pays en voie de développement = a
    developing country
  une espèce en voie de disparition = an
    endangered species
la voie ferrée = the railway track, the
    railroad track

voilà *preposition*
  = here is, this is
  = here are, these are
  te voilà enfin! = here you are at last!
  voilà tout = that's all
  voilà un mois = a month ago

voile
1 *noun, feminine*
• une voile = a sail
• la voile = sailing
2 *noun, masculine*
  un voile = a veil

voir *verb* 46
1 (**!** + *avoir*)
• = to see
  on verra = we'll see
  un film à voir = a film worth seeing
  faire voir quelque chose à quelqu'un = to
    show someone something
• = to be able to see
  je ne vois rien, je n'y vois rien = I can't see
    a thing
• (*to be connected*)
  ça n'a rien à voir = that's got nothing to do
    with it
• (*when encouraging someone*)
  voyons, soyez sages! = come on, be good!
2 se voir (**!** + *être*)
• (*to be visible*)
  se voir = to show
  ça se voit de loin = it can be seen from a
    distance
• (*to meet*)
  se voir = to see each other

voisin/voisine
1 *adjective*
  = neighbo(u)ring
  = nearby
2 *noun, masculine/feminine*
  un voisin/une voisine = a neighbo(u)r

voiture *noun, feminine*
  une voiture = a car, an automobile
  = a carriage, a car
  en voiture! = all aboard!

voix *noun, feminine* (**!** *never changes*)
• (*the way one speaks*)
  une voix = a voice
  à voix basse = in a low voice
  à haute voix = out loud
• (*in an election*)
  une voix = a vote

vol *noun, masculine*
• (*through the air*)
  un vol = a flight
  à vol d'oiseau = as the crow flies
• (*an offence*)
  un vol = a theft, a robbery
  un vol à main armée = an armed robbery
le vol à voile = gliding

volaille *noun, feminine*
  la volaille = poultry

volant/volante
1 *adjective*
  = flying
2 volant *noun, masculine*
• (*in a car*)
  un volant = a steering wheel
  donner un coup de volant = to turn the
    wheel sharply

- (*in badminton*)
  un volant = a shuttlecock
- (*on a skirt*)
  un volant = a flounce

volcan *noun, masculine*
  un volcan = a volcano

voler *verb* 1
- = to steal
  il s'est fait voler sa voiture = he had his car stolen
- **voler un passant** = to rob a passer-by
- = to fly

volet *noun, masculine*
  un volet (*on a window*) = a shutter

voleur/voleuse *noun, masculine/feminine*
  un voleur/une voleuse = a thief

volontaire
1 *adjective*
  = deliberate
2 *noun, masculine/feminine*
  un volontaire/une volontaire = a volunteer

volonté *noun, feminine*
  la volonté = will
  = will-power

volontiers *adverb*
  = gladly, willingly
  = with pleasure

vomir *verb* 3
- = to vomit, to bring up
- = to be sick, to throw up

vont ▶ **aller 1** 9

vos ▶ **votre**

voter *verb* 1
  = to vote

votre *determiner*
  (*plural*) **vos**
  = your

vôtre *pronoun*
  le vôtre/la vôtre/les vôtres = yours
  à la vôtre! = cheers!

voudrais ▶ **vouloir** 48

vouloir *verb* 48
- (*expressing determination*) = to want
  je veux partir = I want to leave
  il ne voulait pas que tu viennes = he didn't want you to come
- (*expressing a wish, a polite request*)
  que veux-tu boire?, que voulez-vous boire? = what would you like to drink?
  je voudrais des poires = I'd like pears
  comme tu veux = as you wish
  veuillez vous asseoir = please sit down
- **vouloir dire** = to mean
  qu'est-ce que ça veut dire? = what does it mean?

voulu/voulue
1 ▶ **vouloir** 48

2 *adjective*
- = required
- = deliberate, planned

vous *pronoun*
- = you
  vous avez gagné = you've won
  à cause de vous = because of you
  la voiture est à vous = the car is yours
- = yourself
  = yourselves
  soignez-vous = look after yourself
  = look after yourselves
  allez vous laver les mains = go and wash your hands
- = each other
  vous vous aimez? = do you love each other?

vous-même *pronoun*
  (*plural*) **vous-mêmes**
  = yourself
  = yourselves

vouvoyer *verb* 23
  vouvoyer quelqu'un = to address someone using the "vous" form

voyage *noun, masculine*
  un voyage = a trip, a journey
  aimer les voyages = to love travel(l)ing
  un voyage de noces = a honeymoon
  un voyage organisé = a package tour

voyager *verb* 13
  = to travel

voyageur/voyageuse *noun, masculine/feminine*
  un voyageur/une voyageuse = a passenger
  = a travel(l)er

voyant/voyante
1 *adjective*
  = loud
2 *noun, masculine/feminine*
  un voyant/une voyante = a clairvoyant
3 voyant *noun, masculine*
  un voyant lumineux = a warning light

voyelle *noun, feminine*
  une voyelle = a vowel

voyons ▶ **voir** 46

voyou *noun, masculine*
  un voyou = a lout
  = a rascal

vrai/vraie
1 *adjective*
  = true
  = real, genuine
2 vrai *noun, masculine*
  le vrai = the truth
  à vrai dire = to tell the truth
  pour de vrai = for real

vraiment *adverb*
  = really

V

vrombir *verb* ③
= to roar

VTT *noun, masculine*
un VTT = a mountain bike

vu/vue¹
1 ▶ **voir** 46
2 *adjective*
• être bien vu = to be well thought of
  ce serait plutôt mal vu = it wouldn't go
  down well
• bien vu! = good point!
• c'est tout vu = my mind is made up
3 vu = in view of

vue² *noun, feminine*
• la vue = sight
  avoir une bonne vue = to have good
  eyesight
  je la connais de vue = I know her to see
  perdre un ami de vue = to lose touch with
  a friend
  à vue d'œil = visibly
• une vue = a view
  avoir vue sur le lac = to look out onto the
  lake

wagon *noun, masculine*
un wagon = a wagon, a car
= a carriage, a car

wagon-lit *noun, masculine*
(*plural*) **wagons-lits**
un wagon-lit = a sleeper, a sleeping car

wagon-restaurant *noun, masculine*
(*plural*) **wagons-restaurants**
un wagon-restaurant = a restaurant car, a
dining car

WC *noun, masculine plural*
les WC = the toilet, the bathroom

Web *noun, masculine*
le Web = the Web

y *pronoun*
• = it
  j'y pense souvent = I often think about it
  il s'y attendait = he was expecting it
  tu n'y peux rien = you can't do anything
  about it

elle n'y arrivera jamais = she'll never
  manage it
je n'y comprends rien = I don't understand
  a thing
• = there
  j'y mange parfois = I sometimes eat there
  j'y vais = I'm going
• il y a = there is
  = there are
  il n'y en a plus = there's none left
  = there aren't any left

yaourt *noun, masculine*
un yaourt = a yogurt

yeux ▶ **œil**

yoga *noun, masculine*
le yoga = yoga

zapper✱ *verb* ①
= to flick through the TV channels

zèbre *noun, masculine*
un zèbre = a zebra

zéro
1 *number*
= zero
2 *noun, masculine*
zéro (*in school*) = nought, zero
(*in a match*) = nil, nothing
il est zéro heure quinze = it's a quarter
  past midnight
trois (buts) à zéro = three nil, three
  nothing
avoir le moral à zéro✱ = to feel very down
repartir à zéro = to start all over again

zeste *noun, masculine*
un zeste de citron = the zest of a lemon

zigzag *noun, masculine*
un zigzag = a zigzag
une route en zigzag = a winding
  road

zodiaque *noun, masculine*
le zodiaque = the zodiac

zone *noun, feminine*
une zone = a zone, an area
une zone industrielle = an industrial
estate, an industrial park

zoo *noun, masculine*
un zoo = a zoo

zoologique *adjective*
= zoological

zut✱ *exclamation*
= blast!
= oh dear!

Dictionary know-how

This section contains a number of short exercises which will help you to use your dictionary more effectively. You will find answers to all of the exercises at the end of the section p. 182.

1 Identifying French nouns and adjectives

Here is an extract from a French advertisement for a gas oven. See if you can find fourteen different nouns and underline them, and six different adjectives and circle them (or make two lists). If you are not sure of some words, look them up in the French–English half of the dictionary and see if the term 'noun' or 'adjective' is used to describe them.

> ## GAZ DE FRANCE, LE CHOIX DE LA QUALITÉ
>
> Pourquoi les Français préfèrent-ils le gaz naturel?
>
> Si vous venez dîner chez moi, vous verrez un magnifique objet, écran plat, coins carrés, dont la beauté luisante saute aux yeux.
>
> Un poste de télévision? Non, non, ce n'est pas mon téléviseur, c'est mon nouveau four au gaz naturel.

The publishers would like to thank Gaz de France for permission to reproduce copyright material.

2 Checking the gender of French nouns

Here are some English nouns which appear in the English–French half of the dictionary. Find out what their French equivalents are and make two separate lists, masculine nouns and feminine nouns.

bag	**hippopotamus**	**magic**	**saddle**
cake shop	**island**	**oyster**	**thunderstorm**
doorbell	**jumper**	**peach**	**waitress**
felt-tip pen	**library**	**raincoat**	**worm**

3 **Identifying French and English pronouns**

Each of the following phrases appears in the French–English half of this dictionary in entries where a pronoun is the headword. In each one, underline the pronoun(s) and give the English equivalent(s).

ça ne fait rien

c'est un cadeau

ce sont des détails sans importance

il l'a invitée

elle ne me parle pas

donne-la-moi

je lui ai prêté ma robe

elles se sont fait mal

il vous l'a prêté

donne-nous l'adresse

4 **Recognizing French verbs**

Underline the verb in each sentence.

Pierre descend la rue sur son vélo.

Sophie ne connaît pas le nom du magasin.

Les sapeurs pompiers arriveront dans cinq minutes.

Chaque année nous passons nos vacances d'été en France.

Ma sœur a un bassin avec des poissons dans son jardin.

5 **Identifying French adverbs**

Here is a list of twelve French words. Eight of them are adverbs and four are not. Underline the ones which are not, or make a list, and say what they are. If you are not sure of some of them, look them up in the French–English half of the dictionary.

absolument	**enseignement**	**seulement**
certainement	**facilement**	**stationnement**
directement	**heureusement**	**vêtement**
énormément	**médicament**	**vraiment**

6 Identifying subjects and objects

We have left out the subjects and objects from this French newspaper report. Choose suitable words from the list below in order to complete it. When you have finished, list the subjects and objects separately.

> ## L'OURS FÉLIX ATTAQUE
>
> .... a dévoré ....
> depuis son arrivée dans les Pyrénées. Hier, ... ,
> transplanté des forêts de Slovénie, a entièrement dévoré
> .... qui se trouvait près de Portet-d'Aspet en
> Haute-Garonne. .... a aussitôt
> compensé .... de la perte de sa bête.
> .... est de 200 pour l'attaque, qui ne sont versés
> qu'une seule fois, puis de 300 par mouton. Pourtant, ...
> devraient se rassurer: .... sont toujours plus
> prédateurs que les vieux. Avec le temps, ... perdra
> .... pour la chasse.

l'animal	Le département	Félix
le berger	les jeunes ours	sa passion
les bergers	neuf moutons	Le 'tarif'
une brebis	L'ours Félix	

The publishers would like to thank *Libération* for permission to use copyright material.

7 Word search

Here is a grid in which are hidden eleven French words: 3 masculine nouns, 3 feminine nouns, 2 adjectives, 2 verbs and 1 pronoun. They may appear horizontally or vertically, and in either direction. When you have found them, circle them. If you are not sure of any of them, look them up in the French–English section of the dictionary.

B	G	R	A	N	D	K	Y	S	T
H	O	E	P	M	Q	C	E	L	A
S	T	N	D	N	O	R	U	I	V
Z	E	N	X	A	K	E	B	F	C
D	F	O	G	H	J	S	K	L	P
M	R	D	E	N	T	U	A	P	Q
M	O	N	D	E	P	C	O	A	D
P	G	A	W	C	U	X	V	R	N
C	U	B	A	G	U	E	T	T	E
R	H	A	N	F	Q	E	M	T	K

abandonner
baguette
cela
dent
excuser
fils
grand
monde
nez
part
rond

8 **Accents are important!**

Here is part of a letter typed by somebody who does not know how to find the accents on a word processor. Use your dictionary as necessary to help you put them in:

Ma chere Louise,

Merci pour ta lettre que j'ai reçue hier. Ce matin, comme d'habitude, je suis allee faire mes courses au marche ou j'ai rencontre Madame Bonnard, que tu connais tres bien, je crois. Elle m'a dit que sa fille ainee, Sandrine, a fini ses etudes et qu'elle part en Grece faire un stage de six mois dans un hotel. Ça devrait etre amusant, non? Qu'est-ce que tu comptes faire toi-meme cet ete? Est-ce que tu restes en France ou esperes-tu toujours visiter la Norvege? Moi, je vais passer deux semaines dans la maison de campagne de mon frere a Gaillac...

9 **Using page headings**

In order to help you find what you are looking for quickly, every page of the main section of the dictionary has a word at the top which identifies the first entry on that page. In this exercise the left-hand column contains a list of entries and the right-hand column a selection of page headings. Choose the page where you would expect to find the entry you are looking for.

Entry	Page headings
encourager	énerver | enseigne en | énervé
historique	hâte | histoire historique | hôtesse
liquide	librairie | loge logé | luge
mener	mélanger | mesure mesurer | million
renseigner	reine | rendre renne | requin
sérieux	séjour | serré serrer | siège
vieil	version | vietnamien vieux | vitesse

10 **Masculine or feminine?**

Some French nouns can be both masculine and feminine, and change their meaning accordingly. Use your dictionary to find the following nouns and list them with their different meanings in two columns, masculine and feminine, e.g.

un livre = ...   *une* livre = ...
livre
manche
mode
moule
poêle
tour
vase
voile

11 **Which preposition, à or de?**

Many verbs in French take a preposition, either *à* or *de*, before an infinitive e.g. *il m'a demandé de venir demain*; *elle a réussi à ouvrir la porte*. In the following extract, all of the prepositions have been left out. Use your dictionary to check what they should be.

Jean-Pierre a longtemps refusé . . . accepter la proposition de son ami, Michel, mais finalement il a décidé . . . dire oui. Michel avait envie . . . faire une randonnée de plusieurs semaines à vélo à travers l'Europe et avait tout fait pour convaincre son ami . . . venir avec lui. A vrai dire, Jean-Pierre préférait passer son temps . . . se faire bronzer sur la plage, mais il essayait toujours . . . faire plaisir à son copain et c'est pour cette raison que Michel est parvenu . . . le persuader. Bien entendu, c'est Michel qui s'est chargé . . . faire tous les préparatifs du voyage, alors que Jean-Pierre a commencé . . . tracer l'itinéraire sur la carte.

12 **Find the verb**

Some words in English can be both nouns and verbs e.g. race. In this exercise, you have to find the following English words in the English–French half of the dictionary and then give the French for the verb only.

aim	iron	question
block	joke	sail
camp	kiss	train
dance	milk	welcome
finish	paint	yell

13 **Choosing the right word**

Very often you cannot use a word exactly as it is given in the dictionary. In the case of adjectives with an irregular feminine form, for example, you have to make sure that you select the form which is appropriate to the noun you are using. Use your dictionary to find the correct form of the adjective to match the nouns in the following sentences.

Elle a de .... yeux et de .... dents. (*beautiful*)

Notre .... maison était très .... (*former*) (*old*)

C'est une très .... idée. (*good*)

La .... chose à faire est de trouver l'entrée ....
(*first*) (*secret*)

Elles sont si .... (*happy*)

La neige est .... (*white*)

Il a une .... voiture. (*new*)

Mon père est ...., mais ma mère est ....
(*Italian*) (*Norwegian*)

14 Which part of speech?

Use your dictionary to help you arrange these words in separate lists according to their parts of speech (masculine noun, feminine noun, adjective etc). Some words may belong to more than one category and will therefore appear in more than one list.

chasse	**inscrire**	**pâle**
dessous	**juste**	**que**
en	**mouche**	**relire**
facilement	**notre**	**toi-même**
gendre	**ouest**	**vers**

15 Translating phrasal verbs

Use your dictionary to find the correct translation for the following English sentences containing phrasal verbs.

The button's **come off**.

The dustmen have **taken** the rubbish **away**.

She is **bringing up** her children on her own.

They've **given up** smoking.

I'm going to **take** my shoes **off**.

16 Find the plural

Use your dictionary as necessary to find the plural of the following nouns (be careful, some of them are exceptions to the general guidelines):

un bijou, des ....

un cas, des ....

un cheval, deux ....

un cheveu, mes ....

une croix, deux ....

un manteau, deux ....

un pneu, quatre ....

du travail, des ....

un trou, deux ....

un vieux, des ....

17 **Faux amis**

Some French words look the same as, or similar to English words, but in fact have a different meaning. These are known as *faux amis* or false friends. Use your dictionary to find the meanings of the following French words:

actuellement	éventuellement
un bonnet	gentil
un car	le matériel
une cave	le pétrole
une course	un pin
décevoir	sale
délivrer	sensible
un engin	

18 **False friends**

Now use your dictionary to find a French meaning for each of these English 'lookalikes'.

actually	eventually
a bonnet	gentle
a car	material
a cave	petrol
a course	a pin
to deceive	a sale
to deliver	sensible
an engine	

19 **Male or female?**

Some French masculine nouns also have a feminine form. This is particularly true of words denoting an occupation–*un commerçant, une commerçante*. Some simply add -e to the masculine form but many do not. Use your dictionary to find the feminine form of the following nouns:

un astronaute	**un piéton**
un conseiller	**un religieux**
un enquêteur	**un scout**
un jongleur	**un skieur**
un musicien	**un téléspectateur**

20 **Which meaning?**

Some words have more than one meaning and it's important to check that you have chosen the right one. In this dictionary different meanings of a word are marked by a bullet point (•). We have given you one meaning of the French words below. Use your dictionary to find another one.

une baie	• a bay	• ....
blanc	• white	• ....
un centimètre	• a centimetre	• ....
enlever	• to remove	• ....
un gorille	• a gorilla	• ....
le jour	• the day	• ....
mauvais	• bad	• ....
noir	• black	• ....
un pépin	• a pip	• ....
une radio	• a radio	• ....
un tailleur	• a tailor	• ....
voler	• to steal	• ....

21 **Mots croisés**

Across

1 avoid (*verb*) (6)
4 washing (*noun*) (7)
6 stadium (*noun*) (5)
7 him (*pronoun*) (2)
8 studies (*plural noun*) (6)

Down

1 church (*noun*) (6)
2 moment (*noun*) (7)
3 thorn (*noun*) (5)
5 they (*pronoun*) (5)
7 the (*determiner*) (2)

22 **Odd one out**

Hidden in this list of nouns is a verb. See if you can find it, then use your dictionary to check whether you are right.

abattoir	givre
bagarre	injure
colorier	lecture
enfer	ordre
foudre	sentier

23 **Filling in the gaps**

Here is a dialogue between a market stall holder and someone shopping for fruit and vegetables. Use your dictionary to help you fill in the names of the things she buys.

CLIENTE:	Bonjour, monsieur.
MARCHAND:	Bonjour, madame. Que voulez-vous aujourd'hui?
CLIENTE:	Eh bien, nous avons des invités ce soir et j'ai besoin de plusieurs choses. Pour commencer je voudrais un kilo de belles (*tomatoes*), s'il vous plaît, et deux bottes de (*radishes*). C'est tellement bon, les (*radishes*) au beurre.
MARCHAND:	Très bien, et avec ça?
CLIENTE:	J'ai besoin d'une (*lettuce*), une grosse.
MARCHAND:	Voilà. Il y a autre chose?
CLIENTE:	Oui, oui. Je voudrais, deux kilos de (*potatoes*), une livre d'(*onions*), une livre de (*carrots*), un (*cauliflower*) et un (*cucumber*).
MARCHAND:	Et avec ça?
CLIENTE:	Les (*peaches*) sont bonnes aujourd'hui?
MARCHAND:	Oui, elles sont très bonnes.
CLIENTE:	Donnez-m'en un kilo et puis avec ça une livre de (*plums*) et une barquette de (*raspberries*).
MARCHAND:	Bien, madame. Ce sera tout?
CLIENTE:	Oui, merci, c'est tout pour aujourd'hui.

24 **French reflexive verbs**

Use your dictionary to find the French equivalents of the following English sentences:

(a) I'm going to get changed.
(b) We argue about money.
(c) He easily gets bored.
(d) She always parks near the office.
(e) Sometimes I get impatient.
(f) What's happening?
(g) I always wake up at 7 o'clock.
(h) The war's coming to an end.
(i) Stamps are sold in the cafés.
(j) She's great fun.

Answers

1

Nouns: gaz, France, choix, qualité, Français, objet, écran, coins, beauté, yeux, poste, télévision, téléviseur, four.

Adjectives: naturel, magnifique, plat, carrés, luisante, nouveau.

2

Masculine nouns: sac, feutre, hippopotame, pull, imperméable, orage, ver.

Feminine nouns: pâtisserie, sonnette, île, bibliothèque, magie, huître, pêche, selle, serveuse.

3

ça ne fait rien (*it doesn't matter*)

c'est un cadeau (*it's a present*)

ce sont des détails sans importance (*these are unimportant details*)

il **l'**a invitée (*he invited her*)

elle ne **me** parle pas (*she won't speak to me*)

donne-**la-moi** (*give it to me*)

je **lui** ai prêté ma robe (*I lent her my dress*)

elles **se** sont fait mal (*they hurt themselves*)

il **vous l'**a prêté (*he lent it to you*)

donne-**nous** l'adresse (*give us the address*)

4

Pierre **descend** la rue sur son vélo.

Sophie ne **connaît** pas le nom du magasin.

Les sapeurs pompiers **arriveront** dans cinq minutes.

Chaque année nous **passons** nos vacances d'été en France.

Ma sœur **a** un bassin avec des poissons dans son jardin.

5

enseignement, médicament, stationnement, vêtement (*all masculine nouns*).

6

L'ours Félix a dévoré **neuf moutons** depuis son arrivée dans les Pyrénées. Hier, **l'animal** (*or* **Félix**), transplanté des forêts de Slovénie, a entièrement dévoré une brebis qui se trouvait près de Portet-d'Aspet en Haute-Garonne. **Le département** a aussitôt compensé **le berger** de la perte de sa bête. **Le 'tarif'** est de 600F pour l'attaque, qui ne sont versés qu'une seule fois, puis de 800F par mouton. Pourtant, **les bergers** devraient se rassurer: **les jeunes ours** sont toujours plus prédateurs que les vieux. Avec le temps, **Félix** (*or* **l'animal**) perdra **sa passion** pour la chasse.

Subjects: l'ours Félix, l'animal, le département, le 'tarif', les bergers, les jeunes ours, Félix.

Objects: neuf moutons, une brebis, le berger, sa passion.

7

B	G	R	A	N	D	K	Y	S	T
H	O	E	P	M	Q	C	E	L	A
S	T	N	D	N	O	R	U	I	V
Z	E	N	X	A	K	E	B	F	C
D	F	O	G	H	J	S	K	L	P
M	R	D	E	N	T	U	A	P	Q
M	O	N	D	E	P	C	O	A	D
P	G	A	W	C	U	X	V	R	N
C	U	B	A	G	U	E	T	T	E
R	H	A	N	F	Q	E	M	T	K

8

Ma chère Louise,

Merci pour ta lettre que j'ai reçue hier. Ce matin, comme d'habitude, je suis allée faire mes courses au marché où j'ai rencontré Madame Bonnard, que tu connais très bien, je crois. Elle m'a dit que sa fille aînée, Sandrine, a fini ses études et qu'elle part en Grèce faire un stage de six mois dans un hôtel. Ça devrait être amusant, non? Qu'est-ce que tu comptes faire toi-même cet été? Est-ce que tu restes en France ou espères-tu toujours visiter la Norvège? Moi, je vais passer deux semaines dans la maison de campagne de mon frère à Gaillac . . .

9

encourager	**en**	**énerver**
horreur	**historique**	**hôtesse**
liquide	**librairie**	**loge**
mener	**mélanger**	**mesure**
renseigner	**renne**	**requin**
sérieux	**séjour**	**serré**
vieil	**version**	**vietnamien**

10

un livre = *a book*
une livre = *a pound*

un manche = *a handle*
une manche = *a sleeve*

un mode (de vie) = *a (life)style*
une mode = *a fashion*

un moule = *a mould*
une moule = *a mussel*

un poêle = *a stove*
une poêle = *a frying pan*

un tour = *a trick, a turn*
une tour = *a tower*

un vase = *a vase*
la vase = *mud*

un voile = *a veil*
une voile = *a sail*

11

Jean-Pierre a longtemps refusé **d**'accepter la proposition de son ami, Michel, mais finalement il a décidé **de** dire oui. Michel avait envie **de** faire une randonnée de plusieurs semaines à vélo à travers l'Europe et avait tout fait pour convaincre son ami **de** venir avec lui. A vrai dire, Jean-Pierre préférait passer son temps **à** se bronzer sur la plage, mais il essayait toujours **de** faire plaisir à son copain et c'est pour cette raison que Michel est parvenu **à** le persuader. Bien entendu, c'est Michel qui s'est chargé **de** faire tous les préparatifs du voyage, alors que Jean-Pierre a commencé **à** tracer l'itinéraire sur la carte.

12

to aim *viser*; to block *bloquer*; to camp *camper*; to dance *danser*; to finish *finir*; to iron *repasser*; to joke *plaisanter*; to kiss *embrasser*; to milk *traire*; to paint *peindre*; to question *interroger*; to sail *voyager en bateau*; to train *former, entraîner*; to welcome *accueillir*; to yell *crier*.

13

Elle a de **beaux** yeux et de **belles** dents.

Notre **ancienne** maison était très **vieille**.

C'est une très **bonne** idée.

La **première** chose à faire est de trouver l'entrée **secrète**.

Elles sont si **heureuses**.

La neige est **blanche**.

Il a une **nouvelle** voiture.

Mon père est **italien**, mais ma mère est **norvégienne**.

14

Masculine noun: dessous, gendre, ouest, vers.

Feminine noun: chasse, mouche.

Pronoun: en, que, toi-même.

Adjective: juste, ouest, pâle.

Preposition: en, vers.

Verb: inscrire, relire.

Adverb: dessous, facilement, juste, que.

Determiner: notre.

Conjunction: que.

15

Le bouton s'est détaché.
Les éboueurs ont enlevé les déchets.
Elle élève ses enfants toute seule.
Ils ont cessé de fumer.
Je vais enlever mes chaussures.

16

bijoux, cas, chevaux, cheveux, croix, manteaux, pneus, travaux, trous, vieux

17

actuellement currently, at the moment
un bonnet a cap, a hat
un car a coach, bus
une cave a cellar
une course a race, an errand
décevoir to disappoint
délivrer to free, to issue
un engin a device, a vehicle
éventuellement possibly, if necessary
gentil kind, nice
le matériel the equipment
le pétrole oil, petroleum
un pin a pine
sale dirty
sensible sensitive

18

actually *en fait, vraiment, exactement*
a bonnet *un capot*
a cap *une casquette, un capuchon, une capsule*
a car *une voiture*
a cave *une grotte*
a course *un cours, un plat*
to deceive *tromper*
to deliver *livrer*
an engine *un moteur, une locomotive*
eventually *finalement*
gentle *doux*
material *la documentation* (a material *une matière, une substance, un tissu, une étoffe*)
petrol *l'essence*
a pin *une épingle*
a sale *une solde*
sensible *raisonnable, judicieux, pratique*

19

une astronaute
une conseillère
une enquêtrice
une jongleuse
une musicienne
une piétonne
une religieuse
une scoute
une skieuse
une téléspectatrice

20

une baie	• a bay	• a berry
blanc	• white	• blank
un centimètre	• a centimetre	• a tape measure
enlever	• to remove	• to kidnap
un gorille	• a gorilla	• a bodyguard
le jour	• the day	• daylight
mauvais	• bad	• wrong
noir	• black	• dark
un pépin	• a pip	• a slight problem
une radio	• a radio	• an X-ray
un tailleur	• a tailor	• a (woman's) suit
voler	• to steal	• to fly

21

¹É	V	²I	T	³E	R	■
G	■	N	■	P	■	■
⁴L	E	S	S	I	V	⁵E
I	■	T	■	N	■	L
⁶S	T	A	D	E	■	L
E	■	N	■	⁷L	E
■	⁸É	T	U	D	E	S

22
The verb is *colorier*.

23
tomates, radis, salade (*or* laitue), pommes de terre, oignons, carottes, chou-fleur, concombre, pêches, prunes, framboises

24
(a) Je vais **me changer**.
(b) Nous **nous disputons** pour des questions d'argent.
(c) Il **s'ennuie** facilement.
(d) Elle **se gare** toujours près du bureau.
(e) Parfois je **m'impatiente**.
(f) Qu'est-ce qui **se passe**?
(g) Je **me réveille** toujours à sept heures.
(h) La guerre **se termine**.
(i) Les timbres **se vendent** dans les cafés.
(j) On **s'amuse** bien avec elle.

Aa

a, an *determiner*
a, an = un/une
a dog = un chien
an exhibition = une exposition
my mother's a doctor = ma mère est médecin

able *adjective*
* (*having the possibility*)
to be able to [walk | travel | sleep ...]
= pouvoir [marcher | voyager | dormir ...]
* (*having the skill or knowledge*)
to be able to [drive | read | type ...] = savoir
[conduire | lire | taper à la machine ...]

aboard *adverb*
to go aboard = monter à bord

about

> **!** Often **about** occurs in combinations with verbs, for example: bring about, run about etc. To find the correct translations for this type of verb, look up the separate dictionary entries at **bring**, **run** etc.

1 *preposition*
it's a book about France = c'est un livre sur la France
I need some information about the town = j'ai besoin de renseignements sur la ville
2 *adverb*
= environ
I have about 200 euros left = il me reste environ 200 euros
Oxford is about 40 km from here = Oxford est à environ 40 km d'ici
we arrived at about midnight = nous sommes arrivés vers minuit
3 to be about to = être sur le point de
to be about to [leave | cry | fall asleep ...]
= être sur le point de [partir | pleurer | s'endormir ...]

above
1 *preposition*
= au-dessus de
their apartment is above the shop = leur appartement se trouve au-dessus de la boutique
there is a shelf above it = il y a une étagère au-dessus
2 above all = surtout

abroad *adverb*
= à l'étranger
to go abroad = aller à l'étranger

absent *adjective*
= absent/absente

accent *noun*
an accent = un accent

accept *verb*
= accepter

accident *noun*
* (*causing injury or damage*)
an accident = un accident
a car accident = un accident de voiture
* **I heard about it by accident** = je l'ai appris par hasard

accommodation *noun*
to look for accommodation = chercher un logement

accompany *verb*
= accompagner

account *noun*
* (*in a bank or post office*)
an account = un compte
there's money in my account = il y a de l'argent sur mon compte
* **to take travelling expenses into account** = tenir compte des frais de voyage

accountant *noun* ▶ 315 |
an accountant = un comptable/une comptable

accuse *verb*
to accuse someone of cheating = accuser quelqu'un de tricher

across *preposition*
* **to go across the street** = traverser la rue
to run across the street = traverser la rue en courant
to swim across the Channel = traverser la Manche à la nage
a journey across the desert = un voyage à travers le désert
* (*on the other side of*) = de l'autre côté de
he lives across the street = il habite de l'autre côté de la rue

act *verb*
* (*to do something*) = agir
* (*to play a role*) = jouer

activity *noun*
an activity = une activité
sports activities = les activités sportives

actor *noun* ▶ 315 |
an actor = un acteur

actress *noun* ▶ 315 |
an actress = une actrice

actually *adverb*

> **!** Note that **actually** is not translated by actuellement.

actually, she's a very good athlete = en fait, c'est une très bonne athlète
what actually happened? = qu'est-ce qui s'est passé exactement?

adapt verb
= s'adapter (! + être)

add verb
• (to put in) = ajouter
• (in arithmetic) = additionner

address noun
an address = une adresse

admire verb
= admirer

admit verb
• (to recognize as being true) = reconnaître
• (to own up) = avouer
did she admit that she'd stolen the money? = est-ce qu'elle a avoué avoir volé l'argent?
• to be admitted to (the) hospital = être hospitalisé/hospitalisée

adolescent noun
an adolescent = un adolescent/une adolescente

adopt verb
= adopter

adult noun
an adult = un adulte/une adulte

advantage noun
• (a positive point)
an advantage = un avantage
• to take advantage of a situation = profiter d'une situation

adventure noun
an adventure = une aventure

advertisement noun
• (on TV, in the cinema)
an advertisement = une publicité
• (in a newspaper)
an advertisement = une (petite) annonce
to answer job advertisements = répondre aux offres d'emploi

advertising noun
advertising = la publicité

advice noun
a piece of advice = un conseil
advice = des conseils

advise verb
to advise someone to rest = conseiller à quelqu'un de se reposer
I've been advised not to go there = on m'a déconseillé d'y aller

aerial noun
an aerial = une antenne

aerobics noun ▶ 248 |
aerobics = l'aérobic (masculine)

affect verb
the farmers have been affected by the drought = les fermiers ont été touchés par la sécheresse
the war is bound to affect tourism = la guerre va sûrement avoir des conséquences pour le tourisme

afford verb
to be able to afford a car = avoir les moyens d'acheter une voiture

afraid adjective
to be afraid = avoir peur
to be afraid of spiders = avoir peur des araignées
to be afraid to go out = avoir peur de sortir

Africa noun ▶ 218 |
Africa = l'Afrique (feminine)

African ▶ 275 |
1 adjective
= africain/africaine
2 noun
the Africans = les Africains (masculine)

after
1 preposition
= après
we'll leave after breakfast = nous partirons après le petit déjeuner
the day after tomorrow = après-demain
2 conjunction
after we had eaten, we went for a walk = après avoir mangé, nous sommes allés nous promener
they went in after the film had started = ils sont entrés après le début du film
3 after all = après tout

afternoon noun ▶ 211 |, ▶ 356 |
an afternoon = un après-midi, une après-midi

afterwards, afterward (US English) adverb
• (after) = après
• (later) = plus tard

again adverb
= encore
are you going camping again this year? = est-ce que vous allez encore camper cette année?
! Note that there will very often be a specific French verb to translate the idea of doing something again—to start again = recommencer, to do the work again = refaire le travail, to see someone again = revoir quelqu'un.

against preposition
= contre

age noun ▶ 187 |
age = l'âge (masculine)
he's my age, he's the same age as me = il a mon âge

aged adjective
= âgé de/âgée de
a boy aged 13 = un garçon âgé de 13 ans

ago adverb
two weeks ago = il y a deux semaines
long ago = il y a longtemps

Age

Note that, where English says **to be X years old**, French says **avoir X ans** (*to have X years*).

How old?

*how old **are you**?*	= quel âge **as-tu**?
*what age **is she**?*	= quel âge **a-t-elle**?

The word **ans** (*years*) is never dropped:

he is forty-one (years old)	= il a quarante et un **ans**
the house is a hundred years old	= la maison a cent **ans**
a man of fifty	= un homme de cinquante **ans**

Note the use of **de** after **âgé**:

a woman aged thirty	= une femme âgée **de** trente ans

Comparing ages

*I'm older **than** you*	= je suis plus âgé **que** toi
*she's younger **than** him*	= elle est plus jeune **que** lui
*Anne's two years **younger***	= Anne a deux ans **de moins**
*Tom's five years **older than** Jo*	= Tom a cinq ans de plus que Jo

Approximate ages

*he is **about** fifty*	= il a **environ** cinquante ans
*she's **just over** sixty*	= elle **vient** d'avoir soixante ans
*games for **the under** twelves*	= jeux pour **les moins de** douze ans
*only for **the over** eighteens*	= seulement pour **les plus de** dix-huit ans

---

agree *verb*
* (*to have the same opinion*) = être d'accord
  I don't agree with you = je ne suis pas
  d'accord avec toi
* (*to be ready*)
  to agree to come a week later = accepter
  de venir une semaine plus tard
* (*to reach a decision*) = se mettre d'accord
  (**!** + être)

agriculture *noun*
  agriculture = l'agriculture (*feminine*)

ahead *adverb*
  to go on ahead = partir en avant

Aids *noun* ▶ 266 |
  Aids = le sida

aim
  1 *noun*
  an aim = un but
  2 *verb*
* (*to be directed at*)
  to be aimed at young people = viser les
  jeunes
* (*when using a weapon*)
  to aim a rifle at someone = braquer un
  fusil sur quelqu'un

air *noun*
  air = l'air (*masculine*)
  to throw a ball up into the air = lancer un
  ballon en l'air
  to let the air out of a tyre = dégonfler un
  pneu

air force *noun*
  the air force = l'armée de l'air
  ! *Note that* armée *is feminine.*

air hostess *noun* ▶ 315 | (*British English*)
  an air hostess = une hôtesse de l'air

airmail *noun*
  to send a letter by airmail = envoyer une
  lettre par avion

airport *noun*
  an airport = un aéroport

alarm clock *noun*
  an alarm clock = un réveil

alcohol *noun*
  alcohol = l'alcool (*masculine*)

alive *adjective*
  = vivant/vivante

all
  1 *determiner*
  = tout/toute (+ *singular*)
  = tous/toutes (+ *plural*)
  I spent all week working = j'ai passé toute
  la semaine à travailler
  all the men have left = tous les hommes
  sont partis
  2 *pronoun*
  = tout
  that's all = c'est tout
  after all we've done = après tout ce que
  nous avons fait

3 *adverb*
  to be all alone = être tout seul/toute seule
  all along the street = tout le long de la rue

allow *verb*
  to allow someone to [work | play | leave ...]
    = permettre à quelqu'un de [travailler |
    jouer | partir ...]
  they don't allow me to smoke at home
    = on ne me permet pas de fumer à la
    maison
  smoking is not allowed = il est interdit de
    fumer

all right *adjective*
* (*when giving your opinion*) = pas mal✱
  the film was all right = le film n'était pas
    mal✱
* (*when talking about health*)
  are you all right? = ça va?
* (*when asking someone's opinion*)
  is it all right if I come later? = est-ce que ça
    va si je viens plus tard?
  come at about nine, all right? = viens vers
    neuf heures, d'accord?
* (*when agreeing*) = d'accord

almond *noun*
  an almond = une amande

almost *adverb*
  = presque
  we're almost there = nous sommes
    presque arrivés
  I almost forgot = j'ai failli oublier

alone
1 *adjective*
  = seul/seule
  to be all alone = être tout seul/toute seule
  leave me alone! = laisse-moi tranquille!
2 *adverb*
  [to work | to live | to travel ...] alone
    = [travailler | vivre | voyager ...] seul/seule

along *preposition*
  = le long de
  there are seats all along the canal = il y a
    des bancs tout le long du canal

aloud *adverb*
  to read aloud = lire à haute voix

already *adverb*
  = déjà
  it's ten o'clock already = il est déjà dix
    heures
  have you finished already? = tu as déjà
    fini?

also *adverb*
  = aussi

although *conjunction*
  = bien que
  although she's strict, she's fair = bien
    qu'elle soit sévère, elle est juste

! *Note that the subjunctive is used after*
bien que.

always *adverb*
  = toujours
  I always go to France in (the) summer = je
    vais toujours en France en été

amazed *adjective*
  = stupéfait/stupéfaite

amazing *adjective*
  = extraordinaire

ambition *noun*
  an ambition = une ambition

ambitious *adjective*
  = ambitieux/ambitieuse

ambulance *noun*
  an ambulance = une ambulance

America *noun* ▶ 218 |
  America = l'Amérique (*feminine*)

American ▶ 275 |
1 *adjective*
  = américain/américaine
2 *noun*
  the Americans = les Américains
    (*masculine*)

among, amongst *preposition*
* (*in the middle of*) = parmi
  the ruins are hidden among the trees = les
    ruines sont cachées parmi les arbres
* (*in a particular group*) = chez
  unemployment among young people = le
    chômage chez les jeunes

amount *noun*
  an amount = une quantité

amusement arcade *noun*
  an amusement arcade = une salle de jeux
    électroniques

amusement park *noun*
  an amusement park = un parc
    d'attractions

an ▶ **a**

ancestor *noun*
  an ancestor = un ancêtre/une ancêtre

and *conjunction*
* and = et
  a red and white sweater = un pull rouge
    et blanc
  she stood up and went out = elle s'est
    levée et elle est sortie
  to go faster and faster = aller de plus en
    plus vite
* (*in numbers, and is not translated*)
  three hundred and sixty-five = trois cent
    soixante-cinq

anger *noun*
  anger = la colère

angry *adjective*
to be angry = être en colère
to be angry with someone = être en colère
contre quelqu'un

animal *noun*
an animal = un animal
farm animals = les animaux de la ferme

ankle *noun* ▶ **201**
the ankle = la cheville

announcement *noun*
an announcement = une annonce

annoy *verb*
= agacer

annoyed *adjective*
to be annoyed with someone = être
fâché/fâchée contre quelqu'un

another
1 *determiner*
• another = un autre/une autre, encore
un/une
another cup of coffee? = encore un café?
I'll buy another ticket for Alison = je vais
acheter un autre billet pour Alison
• (*different*) = un autre/une autre
there's another way of doing it = il y a une
autre façon de le faire
she's got another boyfriend now = elle a
un nouveau copain maintenant
2 *pronoun*
there are some pears left—would you like
another? = il reste des poires—est-ce que
tu en veux encore une?

! *Note that it is necessary to use* en,
*which might be translated as 'of it' or 'of
them', with pronouns like* another. *See
also* any, a few, a lot *etc for this use of* en.

answer
1 *noun*
an answer = une réponse
did you get an answer? = est-ce que tu as
eu une réponse?
there's no answer (*at the door*) = il n'y a
personne
(*on the phone*) = ça ne répond pas
2 *verb*
= répondre
to answer a question = répondre à une
question
to answer the phone = répondre au
téléphone
answer back = répondre

answering machine *noun*
an answering machine = un répondeur
(téléphonique)

ant *noun*
an ant = une fourmi

antique *noun*
an antique = un objet ancien

antique shop *noun*
an antique shop = un magasin
d'antiquités

anxious *adjective*
= inquiet/inquiète, anxieux/anxieuse
then I started to get anxious = j'ai
commencé à m'inquiéter à ce moment-
là

any
1 *determiner*
• (*in questions*) = du/de la (**!** de l' + *vowel or
mute h*)
= des (+ *plural*)
is there any tea? = est-ce qu'il y a du thé?
is there any tart left? = est-ce qu'il reste de
la tarte?
have you got any money? = est-ce que
vous avez de l'argent?
• (*with the negative*) = de (**!** d' + *vowel or
mute h*)
we don't have any bread = nous n'avons
pas de pain
I didn't have any friends = je n'avais pas
d'amis
• (*whatever*)
take any cup you like = prenez n'importe
quelle tasse
2 *pronoun*
= en
do you have any? = est-ce que vous en
avez?
he doesn't have any = il n'en a pas

! *Note that it is necessary to use* en,
*which might be translated as 'of it' or 'of
them', with pronouns like* any. *See also*
another, a few, a lot *etc for this use of* en.

anyone *pronoun* (*also* **anybody**)
• (*in questions*) = quelqu'un
do you know anyone who could help us?
= est-ce que tu connais quelqu'un qui
pourrait nous aider?
• (*with the negative*) = personne
there isn't anyone in the house = il n'y a
personne dans la maison
• (*everyone*)
anyone could do it = n'importe qui
pourrait le faire

anything *pronoun*
• (*in questions*) = quelque chose
can I do anything to help? = est-ce que je
peux faire quelque chose pour vous
aider?
• (*with the negative*) = rien
she didn't say anything = elle n'a rien dit
there isn't anything to do here = il n'y a
rien à faire ici
• (*everything*) = tout
I like anything to do with sports = j'aime
tout ce qui a rapport au sport

anyway *adverb*
= de toute façon
I didn't want to go there anyway = de
toute façon je ne voulais pas y aller

anywhere *adverb*
- (*in questions*) = quelque part
  can you see a phone booth anywhere? = est-ce que tu vois une cabine téléphonique quelque part?
- (*with the negative*) = nulle part
  you can't go anywhere = on ne peut aller nulle part
- (*any place*)
  we can meet anywhere you like = nous pouvons nous retrouver où tu veux

apart
1 *adjective*
  they don't like being apart = ils n'aiment pas être séparés
2 apart from = à part

apartment *noun*
  an apartment = un appartement

apartment block *noun*
  an apartment block = un immeuble

apologize *verb*
  = s'excuser (**!** + *être*)

apology *noun*
  an apology = des excuses (*feminine plural*)

appear *verb*
- (*to seem*)
  to appear happy = avoir l'air heureux/heureuse
- (*to come into view*) = apparaître (**!** + *être*)

appetite *noun*
  the appetite = l'appétit (*masculine*)
  to have a good appetite = avoir bon appétit

apple *noun*
  an apple = une pomme

apple juice *noun*
  apple juice = le jus de pomme

appliance *noun*
  an appliance = un appareil

application *noun*
  an application = une candidature

apply *verb*
  to apply for a job = poser sa candidature pour un emploi
  to apply for a passport = faire une demande de passeport

appointment *noun*
  an appointment = un rendez-vous
  to make an appointment = prendre rendez-vous

appreciate *verb*

  > **!** *Note that* **apprécier** *usually means to* **like**.

  I'd appreciate it if you could let me know = je vous serais reconnaissant de m'informer

approach *verb*
  = s'approcher de (**!** + *être*)

approve *verb*
  to approve of someone = apprécier quelqu'un

apricot *noun*
  an apricot = un abricot

April *noun* ▶ **222|**
  April = avril (*masculine*)

Aquarius *noun*
  Aquarius = Verseau (*masculine*)

architect *noun* ▶ **315|**
  an architect = un architecte/une architecte

area *noun*
  an area (*of a country*) = une région
  (*of a city*) = un quartier
  in the poorer areas of Paris = dans les quartiers plus défavorisés de Paris

area code *noun* (*US English*)
  an area code = un indicatif

argue *verb*
- (*to quarrel*) = se disputer (**!** + *être*)
  to argue about money = se disputer pour des questions d'argent
- (*to discuss a subject*) = discuter
  to argue about politics = discuter de politique

argument *noun*
  an argument = une dispute
  to have an argument with someone = se disputer avec quelqu'un

Aries *noun*
  Aries = Bélier (*masculine*)

arm *noun* ▶ **201|**
  the arm = le bras
  she's hurt her arm = elle s'est fait mal au bras

armchair *noun*
  an armchair = un fauteuil

armed *adjective*
  = armé/armée

arms *noun*
  arms = les armes (*feminine*)

army *noun*
  an army = une armée
  to join the army = s'engager (**!** + *être*)

around

  > **!** *Often* **around** *occurs in combinations with verbs, for example:* **run around, turn around** *etc. To find the correct translations for this type of verb, look up the separate dictionary entries at* **run, turn** *etc.*

1 *preposition*
= autour de
there are trees all around the garden = il y a des arbres tout autour du jardin
the people around me were speaking French = les gens autour de moi parlaient français
to go around the world = faire le tour du monde
2 *adverb*
= environ
it costs around £200 = ça coûte environ 200 livres sterling
we'll be there at around four o'clock = nous serons là vers quatre heures

arrange *verb*
to arrange a break in Italy = organiser des vacances en Italie
to arrange to have lunch together = s'arranger pour déjeuner ensemble

arrest *verb*
= arrêter

arrive *verb*
= arriver (**!** + *être*)
we arrived at the station at noon = nous sommes arrivés à la gare à midi

arrow *noun*
an arrow = une flèche

art *noun*
• art = l'art (*masculine*)
• (*as a school subject*)
art = le dessin

art gallery *noun*
an art gallery = un musée d'art

artificial *adjective*
= artificiel/artificielle

artist *noun* ▶ 315 |
an artist = un artiste/une artiste

arts and crafts *noun*
arts and crafts = les travaux manuels
| **!** *Note that* **travaux** *is masculine plural.*

as
1 *conjunction*
• **as** = comme
as you know, we're leaving = comme vous le savez, nous partons
• (*at the time when*)
the phone rang as I was getting out of the bath = le téléphone a sonné au moment où je sortais du bain
I used to live there as a child = j'habitais là quand j'étais enfant
• (*British English*) (*because, since*) = comme
as you were out, I left a message = comme tu étais sorti j'ai laissé un message
• (*when used with* **the same**)
my coat is the same as yours = j'ai le même manteau que toi

2 *preposition*
she's got a job as a teacher = elle a trouvé un poste d'enseignante
he was dressed as a sailor = il était habillé en marin
3 *adverb*
as [intelligent | rich | strong ...] **as** = aussi [intelligent | riche | fort ...] que
go there as fast as you can = vas-y aussi vite que possible
I have as much work as you = j'ai autant de travail que toi
he plays the piano as well as his sister = il joue du piano aussi bien que sa sœur
4 as usual = comme d'habitude

ashamed *adjective*
to be ashamed = avoir honte

ashes *noun*
ashes = les cendres (*feminine*)

ashtray *noun*
an ashtray = un cendrier

Asia *noun* ▶ 218 |
Asia = l'Asie (*feminine*)

Asian *adjective* ▶ 275 |
(*from China, Japan*) = asiatique

ask *verb*
• **to ask** = demander
he asked me my name = il m'a demandé mon nom
to ask someone to [phone | take a message | do the shopping ...] = demander à quelqu'un de [téléphoner | prendre un message | faire les courses ...]
I'll ask them if they want to come = je vais leur demander s'ils veulent venir
to ask for money = demander de l'argent
to ask to speak to someone = demander à parler à quelqu'un
to ask a question = poser une question
• (*to invite*) = inviter
to ask some friends to dinner = inviter des amis à dîner
he asked her out = il l'a invitée à sortir avec lui
• (*to look for information*) = se renseigner (**!** + *être*)
did you ask about the tickets? = est-ce que tu t'es renseigné pour les billets?

asleep *adjective*
to be asleep = dormir
to fall asleep = s'endormir (**!** + *être*)

assemble *verb*
= se rassembler (**!** + *être*)

assignment *noun*
a school assignment = un devoir

assistant *noun*
an assistant = un assistant/une assistante

at *preposition*

> **!** *There are many verbs which involve the use of* at, *like* look at, laugh at, point at *etc. For translations, look up the entries at* look, laugh, point *etc.*

- (*when talking about a position or place*) = à
  we met at a concert = nous nous sommes rencontrés à un concert
  she's at an exhibition = elle est allée à une exposition
  he's not at his desk = il n'est pas à son bureau
  at the = au/à la (**!** à l' + *vowel or mute h*) = aux (+ *plural*)
  they're at the clinic = ils sont à la clinique
  I saw her at the races = je l'ai vue aux courses
  to be [at home | at school | at work ...] = être [à la maison | à l'école | au travail ...]
- (*at the house, shop, practice of*) = chez
  we'll be at Nathalie's = nous serons chez Nathalie
  he's got an appointment at the dentist's = il a rendez-vous chez le dentiste
- (*when talking about time*) = à
  the film starts at nine o'clock = le film commence à neuf heures
  I was here at dawn = j'étais ici à l'aube
- (*when talking about age*) = à
  she was able to read at four years of age = elle savait lire à l'âge de quatre ans

athlete *noun* ▶ 315 |
  an athlete = un athlète/une athlète

athletics *noun* ▶ 248 |
  athletics (*in Britain*) = l'athlétisme (*masculine singular*)
  (*in the US*) = les sports (*masculine*)

Atlantic *noun*
  the Atlantic = l'Atlantique (*masculine*)

atmosphere *noun*
- (*the air*)
  the atmosphere = l'atmosphère (*feminine*)
- (*a mood, a feeling*)
  an atmosphere = une ambiance

attach *verb*
  = attacher
  to be attached to the wall = être fixé/fixée au mur

attack *verb*
  to attack a town = attaquer une ville
  to attack someone in the street = agresser quelqu'un dans la rue

attempt
1 *verb*
  to attempt to break the record = tenter de battre le record
2 *noun*
  an attempt = une tentative

attend *verb*
  to attend the village school = fréquenter l'école du village
  to attend evening classes = suivre des cours du soir

attention *noun*
  attention = l'attention (*feminine*)
  to get someone's attention = attirer l'attention de quelqu'un
  to pay attention to the teacher = écouter le professeur

attic *noun*
  an attic = un grenier

attitude *noun*
  an attitude = une attitude
  he has a strange attitude toward(s) people = il a une attitude bizarre envers les gens

attract *verb*
  = attirer

attractive *adjective*
  to be attractive = être séduisant/séduisante

auburn *adjective* ▶ 213 |
  = auburn (**!** *never changes*)

audience *noun*
  an audience = un public

August *noun* ▶ 222 |
  August = août (*masculine*)

aunt *noun*
  an aunt = une tante

au pair *noun*
  an au pair = une jeune fille au pair

Australia *noun* ▶ 218 |
  Australia = l'Australie (*feminine*)

Australian ▶ 275 |
1 *adjective*
  = australien/australienne
2 *noun*
  the Australians = les Australiens (*masculine*)

Austria *noun* ▶ 218 |
  Austria = l'Autriche (*feminine*)

Austrian ▶ 275 |
1 *adjective*
  = autrichien/autrichienne
2 *noun*
  the Austrians = les Autrichiens (*masculine*)

author *noun* ▶ 315 |
  an author = un écrivain

automatic *adjective*
  = automatique

autumn *noun*
  autumn = l'automne (*masculine*)
  in (the) autumn = en automne

available *adjective*
- (*on sale*)
  tickets for the concert are still available = il reste encore des billets pour le concert

* (*free*) = disponible
are you available? = est-ce que vous êtes
disponible?

average *adjective*
= moyen/moyenne
the average teenager = l'adolescent
moyen

avoid *verb*
* (*to prevent*) = éviter
to avoid spending money = éviter de
dépenser de l'argent
* (*to stay away from*) = éviter

awake *adjective*
to be awake (*having slept*) = être
réveillé/réveillée
to stay awake = rester éveillé/éveillée
to keep someone awake = empêcher
quelqu'un de dormir

award *noun*
an award = un prix
she got the award for best actress = elle a
reçu le prix de la meilleure actrice

aware *adjective*
to be aware of the [problem | danger | risk ...]
= être conscient/consciente du [problème |
danger | risque ...]

away *adverb*
* (*absent*)
to be away = être absent/absente
she's away on business = elle est en
voyage d'affaires
* (*when talking about distances*)
to be far away = être loin
London is 40 km away = Londres est à 40
km d'ici

awful *adjective*
* (*no good*) = épouvantable
I thought the film was awful = j'ai trouvé le
film épouvantable
* (*causing shock*) = terrible
* **I feel awful** = je ne me sens pas bien du
tout

awkward *adjective*
(*describing a situation, a problem*)
= délicat/délicate
I feel awkward about telling him = ça me
gêne de le lui dire

axe, **ax** (*US English*) *noun*
an axe = une hache

Bb

baby *noun*
a baby = un bébé

babysit *verb*
= faire du babysitting

back

> **!** Often **back** occurs in combinations with
> verbs, for example: come back, get back,
> give back *etc*. To find the correct
> translations for this type of verb, look up
> the separate dictionary entries at **come**,
> **get**, **give** *etc*.

1 *noun*
* (*part of the body*) ▶ **201**
the back = le dos
I've hurt my back = je me suis fait mal au
dos
* (*the rear*)
at the back of the supermarket = derrière
le supermarché
to sit in the back of the car = s'asseoir à
l'arrière de la voiture
2 *adverb*
* **to be back** = être de retour
I'll be back in five minutes = je serai de
retour dans cinq minutes
* (*before in time*)
back in January = en janvier

back door *noun*
the back door = la porte de derrière

background *noun*
* (*of a person*)
a background = un milieu
* (*of a picture*)
the background = l'arrière-plan
(*masculine*)
in the background = à l'arrière-plan

backpack *noun*
a backpack = un sac à dos

back seat *noun*
the back seat = le siège arrière

back to front *adverb*
= sens devant derrière
to put a sweater on back to front = mettre
un pull sens devant derrière

backwards, **backward** (*US English*)
adverb
= en arrière

bacon *noun*
bacon = le bacon

bad *adjective*
- bad = mauvais/mauvaise (**!** *before the noun*)
  a bad film = un mauvais film
  a bad idea = une mauvaise idée
  I have some bad news = j'ai une mauvaise nouvelle
  to be bad [at maths | at tennis | at chess ...] = être mauvais/mauvaise [en maths | au tennis | aux échecs ...]
  it's a bad time to go on holiday = ce n'est pas le bon moment pour partir en vacances
  'was the film good?'—'not bad' = 'est-ce que le film était bien?'—'pas mal**✱**'
  smoking is bad for you = fumer est mauvais pour ta santé
- (*serious*) = grave
  a bad accident = un accident grave
- (*when talking about food*) = mauvais/mauvaise (**!** *before the noun*)
- (*not kind, not honest*) = méchant/méchante
  to feel bad = culpabiliser
- (*severe*)
  to have a bad cold = avoir un gros rhume

badger *noun*
  a badger = un blaireau

badly *adverb*
- (*not well*) = mal
  she slept badly = elle a mal dormi
- (*seriously*) = gravement
  he was badly injured = il a été gravement blessé

badminton *noun* ▶ 248 |
  badminton = le badminton

bad-tempered *adjective*
  to be bad-tempered = avoir mauvais caractère

bag *noun*
  a bag = un sac

baggage *noun*
  baggage = les bagages (*masculine plural*)

bake *verb*
- (*to prepare bread or cakes*) (*bread*) = faire du pain
  (*cakes*) = faire des gâteaux
- (*to be cooked in the oven*) = cuire (au four)

baker *noun* ▶ 315 |
  a baker = un boulanger/une boulangère

bakery *noun* ▶ 315 |
  a bakery = une boulangerie

balance *noun*
  balance = l'équilibre (*masculine*)
  to lose one's balance = perdre l'équilibre

balcony *noun*
  a balcony = un balcon

bald *adjective*
  = chauve

ball *noun*
  a ball (*in football, rugby or basketball*) = un ballon
  (*in tennis, golf or cricket*) = une balle
  (*in billiards*) = une bille
  to play ball = jouer au ballon

ballet *noun*
  ballet = le ballet

balloon *noun*
  a balloon = un ballon en baudruche

ban *verb*
  = interdire

banana *noun*
  a banana = une banane

band *noun*
  a band = un groupe
  a rock band = un groupe de rock

bandage *noun*
  a bandage = un bandage

bang
1 *noun*
- (*a loud noise*)
  a bang = une détonation
- (*US English*) (*a fringe*)
  bangs = une frange
2 *verb*
- (*to close with a bang*) = claquer
- (*to hurt*)
  to bang one's head on the wall = se cogner la tête contre le mur
- (*to hit*)
  to bang one's fist on the table = taper du poing sur la table

bank *noun*
  a bank = une banque

bank account *noun*
  a bank account = un compte bancaire

bank holiday *noun* (*British English*)
  a bank holiday = un jour férié

bank manager *noun* ▶ 315 |
  a bank manager = un directeur de banque

bar *noun*
- (*a place*)
  a bar = un bar
  to go to a bar = aller dans un bar
- (*a piece of metal*)
  a bar = une barre
- (*on a cage or window*)
  a bar = un barreau
- (*other uses*)
  a bar of soap = une savonnette
  a bar of chocolate = une tablette de chocolat

barbecue *noun*
  a barbecue = un barbecue

barely adverb
= à peine
he was barely able to walk = il pouvait à
   peine marcher

bargain noun
a bargain = une affaire

bark verb
= aboyer

barn noun
a barn = une grange

barrel noun
a barrel = un tonneau

base verb
to be based in London = être basé/basée à
   Londres
to be based on a true story = être
   basé/basée sur une histoire vécue

baseball noun ▶ 248 |
baseball = le base-ball

basement noun
a basement = un sous-sol

basically adverb
= au fond

basin noun
a basin = une cuvette

basket noun
a basket = un panier

basketball noun ▶ 248 |
basketball = le basket

bat noun
• (in cricket or baseball)
   a bat = une batte
• (an animal)
   a bat = une chauve-souris

bath noun
• to have a bath = prendre un bain
   he's in the bath = il est dans son bain
• (a bathtub)
   a bath = une baignoire

bathroom noun
• a bathroom = une salle de bains
• (US English) (the toilet)
   to go to the bathroom = aller aux toilettes

battery noun
a battery (for a torch) = une pile
   (for a car) = une batterie

battle noun
a battle = une bataille

bay noun
a bay = une baie

be verb
▶ 196 | See the boxed note on be for more
information and examples.

• to be = être
   to be intelligent = être
      intelligent/intelligente
   he is tall = il est grand
   we are rich = nous sommes riches
   be polite! = sois poli!
   it's a girl = c'est une fille
   it's Monday = c'est lundi
   it's past midnight = il est minuit passé
   it's late = il est tard
   the house has been sold = la maison a été
      vendue
   he'll be famous = il sera célèbre
• (when talking about jobs) ▶ 315 |
   she is a lawyer = elle est avocat
   he is a good doctor = c'est un bon
      médecin
• (when describing a physical or mental
   state)
   to be [cold | hungry | afraid ...] = avoir [froid |
      faim | peur ...]
   my feet are cold = j'ai froid aux pieds
   I am 18 = j'ai 18 ans
• (when describing the weather)
   the weather is [fine | awful | cold ...] = il fait
      [beau | mauvais | froid ...]
   it's not too hot = il ne fait pas trop chaud
   it's raining = il pleut
• (when talking about travelling)
   I've never been to Spain = je ne suis
      jamais allé en Espagne
   have you ever been to Africa? = est-ce que
      tu es déjà allé en Afrique?
• (when talking about health)
   how are you? = comment allez-vous?,
      comment vas-tu?
   I'm very well = je vais très bien
   how is your mother? = comment va ta
      mère?
• (in continuous tenses)
   I'm coming = j'arrive
   it was snowing = il neigeait
   he is reading = il lit, il est en train de lire
• (in questions and short answers)
   it's a lovely house, isn't it? = c'est une
      belle maison, n'est-ce-pas?
   'he's not here'—'yes he is' = 'il n'est pas
      là'—'si'

beach noun
a beach = une plage

beak noun
a beak = un bec

beam noun
a beam = une poutre

bean noun
a bean = un haricot

bear
1 noun
a bear = un ours
2 verb
= supporter

beard noun
a beard = une barbe

B

be

As an ordinary verb

When **be** is used as a simple verb in *subject* + *verb* sentences, it is generally translated by **être**:

*I **am** tired*	= je **suis** fatigué
*Paul **is** a doctor*	= Paul **est** médecin

As an auxiliary verb in progressive tenses

In English, **be** can be used in combination with another verb to form a progressive tense which allows us to express *an idea of duration, of something happening over a period of time.*

The present
French uses the present tense to translate both forms of the English present tense, the simple and the progressive:

I work in London	= je travaille à Londres
I am working in London	= je travaille à Londres

To emphasize the idea of duration, **être en train de** + *infinitive* can be useful:

I'm working	= je suis **en train de** travailler
he's reading the paper	= il est **en train de** lire le journal

The future
By using the progressive form of the present tense, you can also refer to the future:

we're going to Paris next week	= nous allons à Paris la semaine prochaine

The past
To express the difference between *she watched TV* and *she was watching TV*, French uses the perfect and the imperfect tenses:

*she **watched** TV*	= elle a **regardé** la télévision
*she **was watching** TV*	= elle **regardait** la télévision

Again, to emphasize the idea of an activity happening over a period of time, the phrase **être en train de** + *infinitive* is useful:

*she **was watching** TV when I phoned her*	= elle **était en train de regarder** la télévision quand je lui ai téléphoné

As part of the passive

In French, as in English, the passive is formed in exactly the same way using **être**:

*the rabbit **was killed by** a fox*	= le lapin a **été tué** par un renard
*the window **has been fixed***	= la fenêtre a **été réparée**

However, in spoken French, the impersonal pronoun **on** is often used to translate the passive if there is a person clearly involved:

the window has been fixed	= **on** a réparé la fenêtre

In short questions

With questions like *aren't you?, wasn't she?*, the general French phrase **n'est-ce pas?** can be useful in specific cases:

*you're a doctor, **aren't you?***	= vous êtes médecin, **n'est-ce pas?**

With negative questions, **par hasard** can be useful:

*he's not there, **is he?***	= il n'est pas là **par hasard?**

In short answers

There is no French equivalent for the verb in short answers such as *no, he's not, yes, we were* etc.

'is he around?' — *'no, he's not'*	= 'est-ce qu'il est là?' — 'non'
'are you coming?'— *'yes, I am'*	= 'est-ce que tu viens?' — 'oui'

If answering 'yes' to contradict a negative statement, the most useful translation is **si**:

*'you're **not** coming, are you?'* — ***'yes, I am'***	= 'tu **ne** viens pas?' — '**si**'

beat verb
- (to hit hard) = battre
- (in cooking) = battre
- (to win against) = battre
  Scotland beat England two nil = l'Écosse a
  battu l'Angleterre deux à zéro
beat up = battre

beautiful adjective
= beau/belle (**!** before the noun)

> **!** Note that bel is used instead of beau
> before masculine nouns beginning with a
> vowel (endroit) or a mute h (hôtel). The
> plural of beau and bel is beaux.

a beautiful garden = un beau jardin
a beautiful girl = une belle fille
a beautiful place = un bel endroit
they are beautiful cities = ce sont de belles
villes

beauty noun
beauty = la beauté

because
1 conjunction
= parce que
he did it because it was necessary = il l'a
fait parce que c'était nécessaire
2 **because of** = à cause de
we didn't go out because of the rain
= nous ne sommes pas sortis à cause de
la pluie

become verb
= devenir
to become an adult = devenir adulte

bed noun
a bed = un lit
to go to bed = se coucher (**!** + être)

bedroom noun
a bedroom = une chambre

bee noun
a bee = une abeille

beef noun
beef = le bœuf
roast beef = le rosbif

beer noun
- (the product)
  beer = la bière
- (a glass of beer)
  a beer = une bière

beet, beetroot (British English) noun
a beet(root) = une betterave

before
1 preposition
= avant
before the holidays = avant les vacances
the day before yesterday = avant-hier
the day before the exam = la veille de
l'examen

2 adjective
= précédent/précédente, d'avant
the week before = la semaine précédente,
la semaine d'avant
the day before = la veille
3 adverb
= avant
two months before = deux mois avant
have you been to Paris before? = est-ce
que tu es déjà allé à Paris?
4 conjunction
I'd like to see him before I go = j'aimerais
le voir avant de partir
I'd like to see him before he goes
= j'aimerais le voir avant son départ

beg verb
= mendier

beggar noun
a beggar = un mendiant/une mendiante

begin verb
= commencer
to begin [working | laughing | raining ...]
= commencer à [travailler | rire | pleuvoir ...]

beginner noun
a beginner = un débutant/une débutante

beginning noun
the beginning = le début
in the beginning = au début
at the beginning of May = début mai

behave verb
= se conduire (**!** + être)
he behaved badly = il s'est mal conduit
to be well behaved = être sage
behave yourself! = tiens-toi bien!

behaviour (British English), **behavior**
(US English) noun
behaviour = la conduite

behind preposition
= derrière
I looked behind me = j'ai regardé derrière
moi

Belgian ▶ 275 |
1 adjective
= belge
2 noun
the Belgians = les Belges (masculine)

Belgium noun ▶ 218 |
Belgium = la Belgique

believe verb
= croire

bell noun
- (in a church)
  a bell = une cloche
- (on a door or bicycle)
  a bell = une sonnette

belong *verb*
- (*to be the property of*)
  to belong to someone = appartenir à
  quelqu'un
  that book belongs to me = ce livre
  m'appartient
- (*to be a member of*)
  to belong to a club = faire partie d'un club

belongings *noun*
belongings = les affaires (*feminine*)

below *preposition*
= au-dessous de
the kitchen is below my bedroom = la
  cuisine se trouve au-dessous de ma
  chambre
there's a cupboard below it = il y a un
  placard au-dessous

belt *noun*
a belt = une ceinture

bench *noun*
a bench = un banc

bend
1 *verb*
- (*to lean, to move*) = se pencher (**!** + *être*)
  to bend one's head = pencher la tête
  to bend one's knees = plier les genoux
- (*to make crooked*) = tordre
2 *noun*
a bend = un tournant, un virage
bend down = se pencher (**!** + *être*)

beneath *preposition*
= sous

beside *preposition*
= à côté de
he is sitting beside me = il est assis à côté
  de moi
to live beside the sea = habiter au bord de
  la mer

best
1 *noun*
the best = le meilleur/la meilleure
to be the best at French = être le
  meilleur/la meilleure en français
who is the best at drawing? = qui dessine
  le mieux?
to do one's best = faire de son mieux
2 *adjective*
= meilleur/meilleure
the best hotel in town = le meilleur hôtel
  de la ville
she speaks the best French = c'est elle
  qui parle le mieux français
my best friend = mon meilleur ami/ma
  meilleure amie
the best book I've ever read = le meilleur
  livre que j'aie jamais lu

> **!** Note that the subjunctive is used after
> the superlative le meilleur... que.

the best thing to do would be to phone
  him = le mieux serait de lui téléphoner

3 *adverb*
= le mieux
the best dressed man = l'homme le
  mieux habillé
I like tennis best = le tennis est mon sport
  préféré

bet *verb*
= parier

better
1 *adjective*
= meilleur/meilleure
her new film is better than the others
  = son nouveau film est meilleur que les
  précédents
he is better at sports than me = il est
  meilleur en sport que moi
the weather is going to get better = le
  temps va s'améliorer
he was ill but now he's better = il était
  malade mais maintenant il va mieux
2 *adverb*
= mieux
he speaks French better than I do = il
  parle mieux le français que moi
we'd better go = nous ferions mieux de
  partir
it's better to [phone | write | check ...] = il
  vaut mieux [téléphoner | écrire | vérifier ...]

between
1 *preposition*
= entre
there is a wall between the two gardens
  = il y a un mur entre les deux jardins
between now and next year = d'ici l'année
  prochaine
2 in between = au milieu

beyond *preposition*
= au-delà de
beyond the village = au-delà du village

bicycle *noun*
a bicycle = un vélo

big *adjective*
- (*large*) = grand/grande (**!** *before the noun*)
  a big garden = un grand jardin
  a big party = une grande fête
  they have big houses = ils ont de grandes
    maisons
  a big car = une grosse voiture
- (*heavy, thick*) = gros/grosse (**!** *before the
  noun*)
  a big parcel = un gros paquet
  a big book = un gros livre
- (*important, serious*) = gros/grosse (**!** *before
  the noun*)
  a big salary = un gros salaire
  to make a big mistake = faire une grave
    erreur

bike *noun*
a bike = un vélo

bill *noun*
- (*for gas, electricity, telephone*)
  a bill = une facture

- (*in a restaurant*)
  a bill = une addition
  could we have the bill please?
  = l'addition, s'il vous plaît
- (*in a hotel*)
  a bill = une note
- (*US English*) (*money*)
  a bill = un billet de banque

billiards *noun* ▶ 248 |
  billiards = le billard

bin *noun* (*British English*)
  a bin = une poubelle

biology *noun*
  biology = la biologie

bird *noun*
  a bird = un oiseau

biro *noun* (*British English*)
  a biro = un stylo-bille

birth *noun*
  a birth = une naissance
  a place of birth = un lieu de naissance

birthday *noun*
  a birthday = un anniversaire
  Happy birthday! = Bon anniversaire!

biscuit *noun* (*British English*)
  a biscuit = un gâteau sec, un biscuit

bit
  1 *noun*
  (*of cheese, bread, wood*) = un morceau
  (*of string, paper*) = un bout
  2 a bit (*British English*)
  a bit [early | nasty | odd ...] = un peu [tôt |
  méchant | bizarre ...]

bite *verb*
  = mordre
  to bite one's nails = se ronger les ongles

bitter *adjective*
  = amer/amère

black *adjective* ▶ 213 |
  = noir/noire

blackberry *noun*
  a blackberry = une mûre

blackboard *noun*
  a blackboard = un tableau noir

blackcurrants *noun*
  blackcurrants = le cassis (*singular*)

blade *noun*
- (*of a knife, a sword*)
  a blade = une lame
- **a blade of grass** = un brin d'herbe

blame
  1 *verb*
  to blame someone = en vouloir à
  quelqu'un
  2 *noun*
  to take the blame = prendre la
  responsabilité

blank *adjective*
  (*describing a page*) = blanc/blanche
  (*describing a cassette*) = vierge

blanket *noun*
  a blanket = une couverture

blaze *verb*
  = être en flammes

bleed *verb*
  = saigner
  my nose is bleeding = je saigne du nez

blind
  1 *adjective*
  = aveugle
  2 *verb*
- (*destroy someone's sight*) = aveugler
- (*to dazzle*) = éblouir
  3 *noun*
  a blind = un store

blink *verb*
  = cligner des yeux

blister *noun*
  a blister = une ampoule

block
  1 *noun*
- (*a building*)
  a block of apartments = un immeuble
- (*a group of houses*)
  a block of houses = une pâté de maisons
- (*a large piece*)
  a block = un bloc
  a block of ice = un bloc de glace
  2 *verb*
  = bloquer
  to block a road = bloquer une route

blond, blonde *adjective* ▶ 213 |
  = blond/blonde
  he has blond hair = il a les cheveux blonds
  my sister's blonde = ma sœur est blonde

blood *noun*
  blood = le sang

blouse *noun*
  a blouse = un chemisier

blow
  1 *verb*
- (*if it's the wind*) = souffler
  the wind blew the door shut = un coup de
  vent a fermé la porte
- (*if it's a person*) = souffler
  to blow a whistle = donner un coup de
  sifflet
  to blow one's nose = se moucher
  (**!** + *être*)
  to blow bubbles = faire des bulles
- (*if it's a light bulb*) = sauter
  2 *noun*
  a blow = un coup
blow away
  to be blown away = être
  emporté/emportée par le vent

B

blow down
  to be blown down = être abattu/abattue
    (par le vent)
blow out = souffler
  to blow out a candle = souffler une bougie
blow up
* (*to destroy*) = faire sauter
  to blow up a car = faire sauter une voiture
* (*to be destroyed*) = sauter
* (*to put air into*) = gonfler

blue *adjective* ▶ **213**
  = bleu/bleue

blush *verb*
  = rougir

board
1 *noun*
* (*a piece of wood*)
  a board = une planche
* (*for games*)
  a board (*in chess*) = un échiquier
  (*in draughts, checkers*) = un damier
* (*a blackboard*)
  a board = un tableau noir
2 *verb*
  to board a ship = monter à bord d'un
    navire
3 on board = à bord

boarding school *noun*
  a boarding school = une pension

boast *verb*
  = se vanter (**!** + *être*)

boat *noun*
  a boat = un bateau

body *noun*
  the body = le corps
  a dead body = un cadavre

boil *verb*
* (*if it's a person*)
  to boil water = faire bouillir de l'eau
  to boil an egg = faire cuire un œuf
* (*if it's water, milk*) = bouillir

boiled egg *noun*
  a boiled egg = un œuf à la coque

boiler *noun*
  a boiler = une chaudière

boiling *adjective*
  = bouillant/bouillante

bomb
1 *noun*
  a bomb = une bombe
2 *verb*
  = bombarder

bone *noun* ▶ **201**
  a bone (*in the body, in meat*) = un os
  (*in fish*) = une arête

✕ in informal situations

bonnet *noun* (*British English*)
  the bonnet (*in a car*) = le capot

book
1 *noun*
  a book = un livre
2 *verb*
  = réserver
  to book a room = réserver une chambre
  the flight is fully booked = le vol est
    complet

booking *noun*
  a booking = une réservation

bookshop, bookstore *noun* ▶ **315**
  a bookshop, a bookstore = une librairie

boot *noun*
* (*worn on the feet*)
  a boot = une botte
* (*British English*) (*of a car*)
  the boot = le coffre

border *noun*
  a border = une frontière
  to cross the border = passer la frontière

bore *verb*
  = ennuyer

bored *adjective*
  to be bored, to get bored = s'ennuyer
    (**!** + *être*)

boring *adjective*
  = ennuyeux/ennuyeuse

born *adjective*
  to be born = naître (**!** + *être*)
  he was born in February = il est né au
    mois de février
  she was born in Italy = elle est née en
    Italie

borrow *verb*
  = emprunter
  to borrow some money from someone
    = emprunter de l'argent à quelqu'un

boss *noun*
  the boss = le patron/la patronne

both
1 *determiner*
  both girls are blonde = les deux filles sont
    blondes
  both my sons = mes deux fils
  both Anne and Brian came = Anne et
    Brian sont venus tous les deux
2 *pronoun*
  = tous les deux/toutes les deux
  you are both wrong, both of you are
    wrong = vous avez tort tous les
    deux/toutes les deux

bother *verb*
* (*to take the trouble*)
  don't bother calling back = ce n'est pas la
    peine de rappeler
* (*to worry, to upset*) = tracasser

The human body

Note the use of **le**, **la**, **l'** or **les** in French where English uses a possessive adjective:

> *he raised his hand*   = il a levé **la** main
> *she closed her eyes*   = elle a fermé **les** yeux
> *my eye hurts*   = j'ai mal à **l'**œil

For expressions such as *he hurt his foot* or *she brushed her teeth*, where the action involves more than the simple movement of a body part, use a reflexive verb in French:

> *she has broken her leg*   = **elle s'est cassé** la jambe
> *he was washing his hands* = **il se lavait** les mains

Note also the following:

> *she broke his nose*   = **elle lui a cassé** le nez (literally *she broke to him the nose*)

Describing people

Here are some ways of describing people in French:

> *his hair is long*   = il a les cheveux longs
> *he has long hair*   = il a les cheveux longs
> *a boy with long hair*   = un garçon aux cheveux longs
> *her eyes are blue*   = elle a les yeux bleus
> *she has blue eyes*   = elle a les yeux bleus
> *the girl with blue eyes*   = la fille aux yeux bleus
> *his nose is red*   = il a le nez rouge
> *he has a red nose*   = il a le nez rouge
> *a man with a red nose*   = un homme au nez rouge

▶ For other expressions with terms relating to parts of the body, ▶ **266** .

• (*in polite apologies*) = déranger
I'm sorry to bother you = je suis désolé de vous déranger

bottle *noun*
a bottle = une bouteille

bottle-opener *noun*
a bottle-opener = un décapsuleur

bottom
1 *noun*
• (*the lowest part*)
the bottom of the hill = le pied de la colline
at the bottom of [the page | the stairs | the street ...] = en bas [de la page | de l'escalier | de la rue ...]
at the bottom [of the lake | of the sea | of the garden ...] = au fond [du lac | de la mer | du jardin ...]
• (*at the lowest level*)
to be bottom of the class = être dernier/dernière de la classe
• (*part of the body*) ▶ **201**
the bottom = le derrière✱
2 *adjective*
the bottom [shelf | drawer | cupboard ...] = [l'étagère | le tiroir | le placard ...] du bas

bound: to be bound to *verb*
it's bound to create problems = ça va sûrement créer des problèmes
she's bound to complain = elle va sûrement se plaindre
it was bound to happen = cela devait arriver

bow¹ *noun*
• (*a knot*)
a bow = un nœud
• (*a weapon*)
a bow = un arc

bow² *verb*
= saluer
to bow one's head = baisser la tête

bowl *noun*
a bowl = un bol
(*shallow*) = une assiette

bowling *noun* ▶ **248**
bowling = le bowling

box *noun*
a box = une boîte
(*when moving*) = un carton

boxing *noun* ▶ **248**
boxing = la boxe

boy *noun*
a boy = un garçon

boyfriend *noun*
a boyfriend = un copain

bra *noun*
a bra = un soutien-gorge

bracelet *noun*
a bracelet = un bracelet

braid *noun* (*US English*)
a braid = une natte, une tresse

brain *noun* ▶ 201 |
  the brain = le cerveau

brake *noun*
  a brake = un frein

branch *noun*
  a branch = une branche

brand-new *adjective*
  = tout neuf/toute neuve

brandy *noun*
  brandy = le cognac

brave *adjective*
  = courageux/courageuse

Brazil *noun* ▶ 218 |
  Brazil = le Brésil

bread *noun*
  bread = le pain

break
1 *verb*
* (*to be damaged*) = se casser (**!** + *être*)
  the chair broke = la chaise s'est cassée
* (*to crack, to smash or damage*) = casser
  to break an egg = casser un œuf
* (*to injure*)
  to break one's leg = se casser la jambe
  she broke her arm = elle s'est cassé le bras
* (*not to keep*)
  to break a promise = manquer à une
    promesse
  to break the rules = enfreindre le
    règlement
2 *noun*
* a break (*a short rest*) = une pause
  (*at school*) = une récréation
  to take a break = faire une pause
* (*a holiday*)
  a break = des vacances (*feminine plural*)
break down
* (*if it's a TV, a car*) = tomber en panne
  (**!** + *être*)
* (*to get upset*) = s'effondrer (**!** + *être*)
break into = cambrioler
  to be broken into = être
    cambriolé/cambriolée
break out
  (*if it's a fire*) = se déclarer (**!** + *être*)
  (*if it's violence*) = éclater
break up
* (*if it's a crowd*) = se disperser (**!** + *être*)
* (*if it's a couple*) = se séparer (**!** + *être*)
  to break up with someone = rompre avec
    quelqu'un
* (*to put an end to*) = mettre fin à
  the police broke up the demonstration
  = la police a mis fin à la manifestation

breakfast *noun*
  breakfast = le petit déjeuner
  to have breakfast = prendre le petit
    déjeuner

✳ in informal situations

breast *noun* ▶ 201 |
  a breast = un sein

breath *noun*
  breath = le souffle
  to be out of breath = être hors d'haleine
  to hold one's breath = retenir sa
    respiration

breathe *verb*
  = respirer
breathe in = inspirer
breathe out = expirer, souffler

breeze *noun*
  a breeze = une brise

brick *noun*
  a brick = une brique

bride *noun*
  a bride = une mariée

bridegroom *noun*
  a bridegroom = un marié

bridge *noun*
  a bridge = un pont

brief *adjective*
  = bref/brève (**!** *before the noun*)

bright *adjective*
* (*describing colours, light*) = vif/vive
  a bright yellow dress = une robe jaune vif
* (*having plenty of light, sun*) = clair/claire
  this room is not very bright = cette pièce
    n'est pas très claire
  a bright spell = une belle éclaircie
  to get brighter = s'éclaircir (**!** + *être*)
* (*intelligent*) = intelligent/intelligente

brilliant *adjective*
* (*very intelligent*) = brillant/brillante
* (*British English*) (*used for emphasis*)
  = génial/géniale✳

bring *verb*
* to bring = apporter
  to bring someone a present = apporter un
    cadeau à quelqu'un
  it will bring us good luck = ça va nous
    porter chance
* (*to be accompanied by*) = amener
  he brought his sister to the party = il a
    amené sa sœur à la soirée
bring about
  to bring about a change = provoquer un
    changement
bring back = rapporter
  he brought me back some perfume = il
    m'a rapporté du parfum
bring up = élever
  to bring up a child = élever un enfant

Britain *noun* ▶ 218 |
  Britain = la Grande-Bretagne

British ▶ 275 |
1 *adjective*
  = britannique

B

2 noun
the British = les Britanniques (*masculine plural*)

broad adjective
= large

broadcast verb
= diffuser
to be broadcast live = être diffusé/diffusée en direct

brochure noun
a brochure = une brochure

broke adjective
= fauché/fauchée**✱**

broken adjective
= cassé/cassée

bronze noun
bronze = le bronze

brother noun
a brother = un frère

brother-in-law noun
a brother-in-law = un beau-frère

brown adjective ▶ 213 |
• (*in colour*) = marron (**!** *never changes*)
to have brown eyes = avoir les yeux marron
• (*describing hair*) = châtain (**!** *never changes*)
• to go brown = bronzer

bruise noun ▶ 266 |
a bruise = un bleu

brush
1 noun
• (*for hair, teeth, clothes or shoes*)
a brush = une brosse
• (*for sweeping up*)
a brush = un balai
• (*for painting*)
a brush = un pinceau
2 verb
to brush one's hair = se brosser les cheveux
to brush one's teeth = se brosser les dents

Brussels noun ▶ 218 |
Brussels = Bruxelles

bubble noun
a bubble = une bulle

bucket noun
a bucket = un seau

budgerigar, **budgie** noun
a budgerigar = une perruche

build verb
= construire
to build a house = construire une maison

building noun
a building = un bâtiment

Bulgaria noun ▶ 218 |
Bulgaria = la Bulgarie

bull noun
a bull = un taureau

bullet noun
a bullet = une balle

bulletin noun
a bulletin = un bulletin
a news bulletin = un bulletin d'informations

bully verb
= tyranniser

bump verb
to bump one's head = se cogner la tête
bump into
• (*to hit*) = rentrer dans (**!** + *être*)
• (*to meet*) = tomber sur (**!** + *être*)

bunch noun
a bunch of flowers = un bouquet de fleurs
a bunch of grapes = une grappe de raisins
a bunch of keys = un trousseau de clés

burger noun
a burger = un hamburger

burglar noun
a burglar = un cambrioleur/une cambrioleuse

burglar alarm noun
a burglar alarm = une sirène d'alarme

burglary noun
a burglary = un cambriolage

burn
1 verb
• (*to destroy, to get rid of*) = brûler
to burn rubbish = brûler des ordures
• (*to injure*)
to burn oneself = se brûler (**!** + *être*)
to burn one's finger = se brûler le doigt
• (*to be on fire*) = brûler
• (*when cooking*) = laisser brûler
• (*in the sun*)
to burn easily = attraper facilement des coups de soleil
2 noun
a burn = une brûlure
burn down = brûler

burst verb
• (*if it's a balloon*) = éclater
• (*if it's a pipe*) = éclater
• (*if it's a river*)
to burst its banks = déborder
burst into
to burst into tears = fondre en larmes
burst out
to burst out laughing = éclater de rire

bury verb
= enterrer

bus noun
a bus = un bus

bus conductor *noun* ▶ 315 |
  a bus conductor = un receveur/une receveuse d'autobus

bus driver *noun* ▶ 315 |
  a bus driver = un conducteur/une conductrice d'autobus

bush *noun*
  a bush = un buisson

business *noun*
• (*commercial activities*)
  business = les affaires (*feminine plural*)
  to go to London on business = aller à Londres pour affaires
• (*a company*)
  a business = une entreprise
• (*when protecting one's privacy*)
  that's my business = ça me regarde
  it's none of your business = ça ne te regarde pas

businessman *noun* ▶ 315 |
  a businessman = un homme d'affaires

businesswoman *noun* ▶ 315 |
  a businesswoman = une femme d'affaires

bus station *noun*
  a bus station = une gare routière

bus stop *noun*
  a bus stop = un arrêt d'autobus

busy *adjective*
  = occupé/occupée
  to be busy packing = être occupé à faire ses valises
  to have a busy day = avoir une journée chargée
  to lead a busy life = mener une vie active

but *conjunction*
  = mais
  he understands French but he doesn't speak it = il comprend le français mais il ne le parle pas

butcher *noun* ▶ 315 |
  a butcher = un boucher

butter *noun*
  butter = le beurre

butterfly *noun*
  a butterfly = un papillon

button *noun*
  a button = un bouton

buy *verb*
  = acheter
  to buy a present for someone = acheter un cadeau à quelqu'un
  she bought herself a new coat = elle s'est acheté un nouveau manteau

buzz *verb*
  = bourdonner

by *preposition*

• by = par
  by accident = accidentellement
  by chance = par hasard
  by mistake = par erreur
  one by one = un par un/une par une
  he was bitten by a dog = il a été mordu par un chien
• (*on one's own*)
  by oneself = tout seul/toute seule
• (*using*)
  to travel by bus = voyager en bus
  we went there by bicycle = nous y sommes allés à bicyclette
  to pay by cheque = payer par chèque
  to book by phone = réserver par téléphone
  to come in by the back door = entrer par la porte de derrière
• (*as a result of*)
  he succeeded by working hard = il a réussi en travaillant beaucoup
• (*beside*)
  by the sea = au bord de la mer
  by the side of the road = au bord de la route
• (*indicating the author or painter*) = de
  a book by Charles Dickens = un livre de Charles Dickens
  a painting by Chagall = un tableau de Chagall
• (*when talking about time*)
  by next Thursday = d'ici jeudi prochain
  he should be here by now = il devrait déjà être là
• (*when talking about figures, rates*)
  to increase by 20% = augmenter de 20%
  to be paid by the hour = être payé/payée à l'heure
  8 metres by 4 metres = 8 mètres sur 4

Cc

cab *noun*
  a cab = un taxi

cabbage *noun*
  cabbage = le chou

cable car *noun*
  a cable car = un téléphérique

café *noun*
  a café = un café

cake *noun*
  a cake = un gâteau

cake shop *noun* ▶ 315 |
  a cake shop = une pâtisserie

calculator *noun*
  a calculator = une calculatrice, une calculette

calendar *noun*
a calendar = un calendrier

calf *noun*
* (*the animal*)
a calf = un veau
* (*part of the leg*) ▶ **201** |
the calf = le mollet

call *verb*
* (*to name*) = appeler
he's called **Michael** = il s'appelle Michael
it's called '**un robinet**' in French = en français ça s'appelle 'un robinet'
* (*to describe as*)
to call someone a coward = traiter quelqu'un de lâche
* (*to call out (to)*) = appeler
the teacher is calling us = le professeur nous appelle
to call the register (*British English*) = faire l'appel
* (*to phone*) = appeler
who's calling? = qui est à l'appareil?
* (*to get to come*) = appeler
to call the doctor = faire venir le médecin
* (*to wake*) = réveiller
* (*to pay a visit*) = passer (**!** + *être*)
they called yesterday = ils sont passés hier

call back
* (*to come back*) = repasser (**!** + *être*)
* (*to phone back*) = rappeler
call off = annuler
call out
to call out the numbers for the lottery = annoncer les numéros gagnants du loto
call up = appeler

calm
1 *adjective*
= calme
2 *verb*
= calmer
calm down = se calmer (**!** + *être*)

camcorder *noun*
a camcorder = un caméscope

camel *noun*
a camel = un chameau

camera *noun*
a camera (*for taking photos*) = un appareil photo
(*in a studio, for videos*) = une caméra

camp
1 *noun*
a summer camp = un camp de vacances
2 *verb*
= camper
to go camping = faire du camping

camping *noun*
camping = le camping

campsite *noun*
a campsite = un camping

can[1] *verb*
* (*to have the possibility*)
can you come? = est-ce que tu peux venir?
where can I buy stamps? = où est-ce que je peux acheter des timbres?
he can't sleep when it's hot = il ne peut pas dormir quand il fait chaud
* (*when talking about* seeing, hearing, understanding, *you don't usually translate* can)
I can hear you better now = je t'entends mieux maintenant
can they see us? = est-ce qu'ils nous voient?
he can't understand Japanese = il ne comprend pas le japonais
* (*to be allowed to*)
can I smoke? = est-ce que je peux fumer?
we can't turn right here = nous ne pouvons pas tourner à droite ici
* (*to know how to*)
she can swim = elle sait nager
he can't drive yet = il ne sait pas encore conduire
can you speak French? = est-ce que tu parles français?
* (*when asking, offering or suggesting*)
can we borrow your car? = est-ce que nous pouvons emprunter ta voiture?
can I help you? = est-ce que je peux vous aider?
you can phone back later if you like = vous pouvez rappeler plus tard si vous voulez

can[2] *noun*
a can = une boîte

Canada *noun* ▶ **218** |
Canada = le Canada

Canadian ▶ **275** |
1 *adjective*
= canadien/canadienne
2 *noun*
the Canadians = les Canadiens (*masculine*)

canal *noun*
a canal = un canal

cancel *verb*
= annuler

cancer *noun* ▶ **266** |
cancer = le cancer

candle *noun*
a candle (*in a room, on a cake*) = une bougie
(*in a church*) = un cierge

candy *noun* (*US English*)
* candy = la confiserie
* (*a sweet*)
a candy = un bonbon

canoe *noun*
a canoe = un canoë, un canoë-kayak

canoeing *noun* ▶ 248|
canoeing = le canoë-kayak

can-opener *noun*
a can-opener = un ouvre-boîtes

canteen *noun*
a canteen = une cantine

cap *noun*
a cap = une casquette
a baseball cap = une casquette de base-ball

capable *adjective*
• to be capable of looking after oneself
= être capable de se débrouiller tout seul
• (*having ability, skill*)
= compétent/compétente

capital
1 *noun*
the capital = la capitale
Paris is the capital of France = Paris est la capitale de la France
2 *adjective*
= majuscule
capital P = P majuscule

captain *noun*
a captain = un capitaine

car *noun*
a car = une voiture

caravan *noun* (*British English*)
a caravan = une caravane

card *noun*
• (*for sending to someone*)
a card = une carte
• (*for playing games*)
a card = une carte (à jouer)
to play cards = jouer aux cartes

cardphone *noun*
a cardphone = un téléphone à carte

care
1 *noun*
• (*to take care*) = faire attention
to take care crossing the street = faire attention en traversant la rue
• to take care of someone = s'occuper de quelqu'un
2 *verb*
I don't care = ça m'est égal
to care about the environment
= s'intéresser à l'environnement

career *noun*
a career = une carrière

careful *adjective*
to be careful = faire attention
to be careful crossing the street = faire attention en traversant la rue
to be careful not to make mistakes = faire attention de ne pas faire d'erreurs

careless *adjective*
to be careless = être négligent/négligente

car ferry *noun*
a car ferry = un ferry, un transbordeur

carnival *noun*
• (*British English*) (*a festival*)
a carnival = un carnaval
• (*US English*) (*a fair*)
a carnival = une fête foraine

car park *noun* (*British English*)
a car park = un parking, un parc de stationnement

carpet *noun*
carpet = la moquette

car phone *noun*
a car phone = un téléphone de voiture

carrot *noun*
a carrot = une carotte

carry *verb*
• (*to hold*) = porter
I can't carry the shopping = je ne peux pas porter les courses
• (*to move*)
to carry the baggage upstairs = monter les bagages
to carry the boxes downstairs = descendre les cartons
carry on = continuer

cartoon *noun*
a cartoon (*a comic strip*) = une bande dessinée, une BD
(*a film*) = un dessin animé

case¹: in case *conjunction*
= au cas où
keep the bike in case you need it = garde le vélo au cas où tu en aurais besoin
! *Note that the conditional is used after* au cas où.

case² *noun*
a case = une valise

cash
1 *noun*
cash = l'argent liquide
! *Note that* argent *is masculine.*
I don't have any cash = je n'ai pas d'argent liquide
to pay in cash = payer en espèces
2 *verb*
= encaisser

cash dispenser *noun*
a cash dispenser = un distributeur automatique de billets

cassette *noun*
a cassette = une cassette

cassette player *noun*
a cassette player = un lecteur de cassettes

castle *noun*
a castle = un château

cat *noun*
a cat = un chat/une chatte

catch *verb*
* (*to capture*) = attraper
  to catch a fish = attraper un poisson
* (*to take hold of*) = attraper
* (*to pinch, to stick*)
  he caught his finger in the door = il s'est
    pris le doigt dans la porte
  my shirt got caught in the thorns = ma
    chemise s'est prise dans les ronces
* he was running to catch his train = il
    courait pour attraper son train
* (*to take by surprise*)
  to catch someone stealing = surprendre
    quelqu'un en train de voler
  to get caught = se faire prendre (**!** + *être*)
* (*to become ill with*)
  to catch flu = attraper la grippe
  to catch a cold = s'enrhumer (**!** + *être*),
    attraper un rhume
* to catch fire = prendre feu
catch up
  to catch up with someone = rattraper
    quelqu'un

caterpillar *noun*
a caterpillar = une chenille

cathedral *noun*
a cathedral = une cathédrale

cauliflower *noun*
cauliflower = le chou-fleur

cause *verb*
the storm will cause damage = l'orage va
  causer des dégâts
it has caused us a lot of problems = ça
  nous a causé beaucoup de problèmes
it's going to cause delays = ça va
  provoquer des retards

cautious *adjective*
= prudent/prudente

cave *noun*
a cave = une grotte

CD *noun*
a CD = un disque compact, un CD

CD player *noun*
a CD player = une platine laser

ceiling *noun*
the ceiling = le plafond

celebrate *verb*
= faire la fête

celery *noun*
celery = le céleri

cell *noun*
a cell = une cellule

cellar *noun*
a cellar = une cave

cello *noun* ▶ **290 |**
a cello = un violoncelle

cement *noun*
cement = le ciment

cemetery *noun*
a cemetery = un cimetière

cent *noun*
* (*of euro*)
  a cent = un centime (d'euro)
* (*of dollar*)
  a cent = un cent

centimetre (*British English*),
centimeter (*US English*) *noun* ▶ **285 |**
a centimetre = un centimètre

central heating *noun*
central heating = le chauffage central

centre (*British English*), **center** (*US English*) *noun*
* (*a place for activities, meetings*)
  a centre = un centre
  a leisure centre = un centre de loisirs
* (*the middle*)
  the centre = le centre
  near the centre of London = près du
    centre de Londres

century *noun* ▶ **356 |**
a century = un siècle

certain *adjective*
= certain/certaine

certainly *adverb*
= certainement

chain *noun*
a chain = une chaîne

chair *noun*
a chair = une chaise

chalk *noun*
chalk = la craie

champagne *noun*
champagne = le champagne

champion *noun*
a champion = un champion/une
  championne
a tennis champion = un champion/une
  championne de tennis

chance *noun*
* (*when talking about a possibility*)
  there is a chance that she'll have a job in
    Paris = il est possible qu'elle ait un
    travail à Paris

  ! *Note that the subjunctive is used after* il
  est possible que.

* (*an opportunity*)
  a chance = une occasion
  to have a chance to meet people = avoir
    l'occasion de rencontrer des gens
* by chance = par hasard

change
1 *noun*
* a change = un changement

- (*a different experience*)
  it makes a change from homework = ça
  change des devoirs
  let's go to the beach for a change = allons
  à la plage pour changer
- (*cash*)
  change = la monnaie
  have you got change for 20 euros?
  = pouvez-vous me faire la monnaie de
  20 euros?
2 *verb*
- (*to become different, to make different*)
  = changer
  the town has changed a lot = la ville a
  beaucoup changé
  I've changed my mind = j'ai changé d'avis
- (*to replace*) = changer
  to change a wheel = changer une roue
- (*to exchange in a shop*) = échanger
  change a shirt for a smaller size
  = échanger une chemise pour une taille
  plus petite
- (*to switch*) = changer de
  to change places with someone
  = changer de place avec quelqu'un
  she keeps changing channels = elle
  n'arrête pas de changer de chaîne
- (*when talking about one's clothes*) = se
  changer (**!** + *être*)
  to get changed = se changer (**!** + *être*)
- (*when using transport*) = changer
- **to change dollars into euros** = changer des
  dollars en euros

changing room *noun*
  a changing room = un vestiaire

channel *noun*
  a TV channel = une chaîne de télévision

Channel *noun*
  the (English) Channel = la Manche

chapter *noun*
  a chapter = un chapitre

charge
1 *verb*
  to charge someone for the damage = faire
  payer les dégâts à quelqu'un
  they'll charge you for the electricity = ils
  te feront payer l'électricité
2 *noun*
- (*a price, a fee*)
  a charge = des frais (*masculine plural*)
  there's no charge = c'est gratuit
3 in charge = responsable
  to be in charge of the money = être
  responsable de l'argent

charming *adjective*
  = charmant/charmante

chase *verb*
  (*on foot*) = courir après
  (*in a car*) = poursuivre

chase away = chasser

chat
1 *verb*
  = bavarder, discuter
2 *noun*
  a chat = une conversation
chat up (*British English*) = draguer**✱**

cheap *adjective*
- (*not expensive*) = bon marché (**!** *never
  changes*)
  it's cheap = c'est bon marché, ça ne coûte
  pas cher
  it's cheaper to take the bus = ça coûte
  moins cher de prendre le bus
- (*of poor quality*) = de mauvaise qualité

cheat *verb*
  = tricher

check
1 *verb*
- (*to make sure*) = vérifier
  you should check whether it's true = tu
  devrais vérifier si c'est vrai
- (*to inspect*) = contrôler
  they didn't even check our passports = ils
  n'ont même pas contrôlé nos passeports
2 *noun*
- (*US English*) (*a bill*)
  a check = une addition
- (*US English*) (*a cheque*)
  a check = un chèque
check in = se présenter à l'enregistrement
check out = partir (**!** + *être*)

checkbook *noun* (*US English*)
  a checkbook = un carnet de chèques, un
  chéquier

checkers *noun* ▶ **248** (*US English*)
  checkers = les dames (*feminine*)

check-in *noun*
  the check-in = l'enregistrement
  (*masculine*)

checkout *noun*
  a checkout = une caisse

cheek *noun* ▶ **201**
  the cheek = la joue

cheeky *adjective*
  = effronté/effrontée, insolent/insolente

cheerful *adjective*
  = gai/gaie

cheese *noun*
  cheese = le fromage

chef *noun* ▶ **315**
  a chef = un chef cuisinier

chemist *noun* ▶ **315**
- (*in a shop*)
  a chemist = un pharmacien/une
  pharmacienne
- (*in a laboratory*)
  a chemist = un chimiste/une chimiste

✱ in informal situations

chemistry *noun*
chemistry = la chimie

cheque *noun* (*British English*)
a cheque = un chèque
to write a cheque for £50 = faire un chèque de 50 livres

cheque book *noun* (*British English*)
a cheque book = un carnet de chèques, un chéquier

cherry *noun*
a cherry = une cerise

chess *noun* ▶ **248**
chess = les échecs (*masculine plural*)

chest *noun* ▶ **201**
the chest = la poitrine

chestnut
1 *noun*
a chestnut = un marron, une châtaigne
2 *adjective*
= châtain (**!** *never changes*)
to have chestnut hair = avoir les cheveux châtain

chew *verb*
(*if it's a person*) = mâcher
(*if it's an animal*) = ronger

chewing gum *noun*
chewing gum = le chewing-gum

chicken *noun*
• (*the bird*)
a chicken = une poule
• (*the meat*)
chicken = le poulet

child *noun*
a child = un enfant/une enfant

chilly *adjective*
it's chilly = il fait froid

chimney *noun*
a chimney = une cheminée

chin *noun* ▶ **201**, ▶ **237**
the chin = le menton

China *noun* ▶ **218**
China = la Chine

Chinese ▶ **275**
1 *adjective*
= chinois/chinoise
2 *noun*
• (*the people*)
the Chinese = les Chinois (*masculine plural*)
• (*the language*)
Chinese = le chinois

chips *noun*
• (*British English*) (*French fries*)
chips = les frites (*feminine*)
• (*US English*) (*crisps*)
(potato) chips = les chips (*feminine*)

chocolate *noun*
chocolate = le chocolat
a box of chocolates = une boîte de chocolats

choice *noun*
a choice = un choix
we had no choice = nous n'avions pas le choix

choir *noun*
a choir = une chorale

choke *verb*
= s'étouffer (**!** + *être*)

choose *verb*
= choisir

chore *noun*
a chore = une tâche
to do the chores = faire le ménage

Christian *adjective*
= chrétien/chrétienne

Christian name *noun*
a Christian name = un nom de baptême

Christmas *noun*
Christmas (Day) = (le jour de) Noël
Merry Christmas!, Happy Christmas! = Joyeux Noël!

Christmas carol *noun*
a Christmas carol = un chant de Noël

Christmas cracker *noun* (*British English*)
a Christmas cracker = un diablotin

Christmas Eve *noun*
Christmas Eve = la veille de Noël

Christmas tree *noun*
a Christmas tree = un sapin de Noël

church *noun*
a church (*Catholic or Anglican*) = une église
(*Protestant*) = un temple

cider *noun*
cider = le cidre

cigar *noun*
a cigar = un cigare

cigarette *noun*
a cigarette = une cigarette

cigarette lighter *noun*
a cigarette lighter = un briquet

cinema *noun* (*British English*)
a cinema = un cinéma

circle *noun*
a circle = un cercle
we were sitting in a circle = nous étions assis en cercle

circus *noun*
a circus = un cirque

citizen noun
* (of a country)
  a citizen = un citoyen/une citoyenne
* (of a city or town)
  a citizen = un habitant/une habitante

city noun
  a city = une (grande) ville

city centre (British English), **city center** (US English) noun
  the city centre = le centre-ville

civilized adjective
  = civilisé/civilisée

civil servant noun ▶ 315
  a civil servant = un fonctionnaire/une fonctionnaire

clap verb
  = applaudir

clarinet noun ▶ 290
  a clarinet = une clarinette

class noun
* (a group of students)
  a class = une classe
* (a lesson)
  a class = un cours
  a history class = un cours d'histoire
* (a social group)
  a (social) class = une classe (sociale)

classical music noun
  classical music = la musique classique

classmate noun
  a classmate = un camarade/une camarade de classe

classroom noun
  a classroom = une salle de classe

clean
1 adjective
* (not dirty) = propre
  my hands are clean = j'ai les mains propres
  to keep the house clean = tenir la maison propre
* (not polluted) = pur/pure
2 verb
  = nettoyer
  to have a jacket cleaned = faire nettoyer une veste

clear
1 adjective
* (easy to understand, making sense) = clair/claire
  is that clear? = est-ce que c'est clair?
* (obvious)
  it is clear that no-one is happy = il est clair que personne n'est content
* (easy to see or hear, distinct)
  a clear voice = une voix claire
  your writing must be clear = votre écriture doit être lisible
* (with no rain or cloud) = clair/claire
  on a clear day = par temps clair

2 verb
* (to empty, to remove from)
  to clear the table = débarrasser la table
  to clear the building = évacuer le bâtiment
  to clear the snow off the road = dégager la neige de la route
* (if it's fog, mist) = se dissiper (**!** + être)

clever adjective
* (intelligent) = intelligent/intelligente
  to be clever at mathematics = être doué/douée pour les mathématiques
* (smart) = astucieux/astucieuse

cliff noun
  a cliff = une falaise

climate noun
  a climate = un climat

climb verb
* **to climb (up) a tree** = grimper à un arbre
  to climb a mountain = faire l'ascension d'une montagne
  to climb over a wall = passer par-dessus un mur
* (to rise higher) = monter (**!** + être)

climbing noun ▶ 248
  climbing = l'escalade (feminine)

clinic noun
  a clinic = un centre médical

cloakroom noun
  a cloakroom = un vestiaire

clock noun
  a clock (on a building, in a classroom) = une horloge
  (smaller, as an ornament) = une pendule
  (in sporting events) = un chronomètre

close¹
1 adjective
* (near) = proche
  the station is quite close = la gare est assez proche
  is the house close to the school? = est-ce que la maison est près de l'école?
* (as a friend or relation) = proche
2 adverb
  to live close (by) = habiter tout près
  to come closer = s'approcher (**!** + être)

close² verb
  = fermer
  close your eyes = ferme les yeux
  the shop closes at noon = le magasin ferme à midi
  the door closed suddenly = tout d'un coup, la porte s'est fermée
close down = fermer définitivement

closed adjective
  = fermé/fermée

cloth noun
* (material)
  cloth = le tissu

The clock

What time is it?

what time is it?	= quelle heure est-il?
could you tell me the time?	= pouvez-vous me donner l'heure?
it's exactly four o'clock	= il est exactement quatre heures

It is ...	Il est ...	say
4 o'clock	4 heures	
	4 h	quatre heures
4 o'clock in the morning / 4 am	4 h 00	quatre heures du matin
4 o'clock in the afternoon / 4 pm	16 h 00	quatre heures de l'après-midi
		seize heures*
4.10 / ten past four	4 h 10	quatre heures dix
4.15	4 h 15	quatre heures quinze
a quarter past four	4 h 15	quatre heures et quart
4.20	4 h 20	quatre heures vingt
4.25	4 h 25	quatre heures vingt-cinq
4.30	4 h 30	quatre heures trente
half past four	4 h 30	quatre heures et demie†
4.35	4 h 35	quatre heures trente-cinq
twenty-five to five	4 h 35	cinq heures moins vingt-cinq
4.40	4 h 40	quatre heures quarante
twenty to five	4 h 40	cinq heures moins vingt
4.45 / a quarter to five	4 h 45	cinq heures moins le quart
4.50	4 h 50	quatre heures cinquante
ten to five	4 h 50	cinq heures moins dix
4.55	4 h 55	quatre heures cinquante-cinq
five to five	4 h 55	cinq heures moins cinq
5 o'clock	5 h 00	cinq heures
16.15	16 h 15	seize heures quinze
8 o'clock in the evening	8 h du soir	huit heures du soir
8 pm	20 h 00	vingt heures
12.00	12 h 00	douze heures
noon / 12 noon	12 h 00	midi
midnight / 12 midnight	24 h 00	minuit

* In timetables etc, the twenty-four hour clock is used, so that **4 pm** is **seize heures**. In ordinary usage, one says **quatre heures (de l'après-midi)**.

† Note that **demi** agrees with the noun it follows:

une heure et demie
un jour et demi
minuit et demi
midi et demi

Note also that, when it comes before the noun, **demi** is hyphenated and does not change:

une **demi**-journée
les **demi**-heures.

When?

French never drops the word **heures**: *at five* is **à cinq heures** and so on:

French always uses **à**, whether or not English includes the word *at*. The only exception is when there is another preposition present, as in **vers cinq heures** (*about five o'clock*), **avant cinq heures** (*before five o'clock*) etc:

***what** time did it happen?*	= **à quelle** heure cela s'est-il passé?
***what** time will he come at?*	= **à quelle** heure va-t-il venir?
*it happened **at** two o'clock*	= c'est arrivé **à** deux heures
*he'll come **at** four*	= il viendra **à** quatre heures
***at about** five*	= **vers** cinq heures / **à** cinq heures **environ**
*it must be ready **by** ten*	= il faut que ce soit prêt **avant** dix heures
*closed **from** 1 **to** 2 pm*	= fermé **de** treize **à** quatorze heures
*every hour **on** the hour*	= toutes les heures **à** l'heure juste

- **a cloth** (*for dusting*) = un chiffon
  (*for the floor*) = une serpillière
  (*for dishes*) = un torchon

clothes *noun*
  clothes = les vêtements (*masculine*)
  to put on one's clothes = s'habiller
    (**!** + *être*)
  to take off one's clothes = se déshabiller
    (**!** + *être*)
  to have no clothes on = être tout nu/toute
    nue

cloud *noun*
  a cloud = un nuage

clown *noun*
  a clown = un clown

club *noun*
- a club = un club
  a tennis club = un club de tennis
  to be in a club = faire partie d'un club
- (*a nightclub*)
  a club = une boîte de nuit

clue *noun*
- (*in an investigation*)
  a clue = un indice
- (*in a crossword*)
  a clue = une définition

clumsy *adjective*
  = maladroit/maladroite

coach
1 *noun* (*British English*)
- (*a bus*)
  a coach = un car
- (*of a train*)
  a coach = un wagon
2 *verb*
  = entraîner

coach station *noun*
  a coach station = une gare routière

coal *noun*
  coal = le charbon

coast *noun*
  the coast = la côte

coat *noun*
- a coat = un manteau
- (*of an animal*)
  the coat (*of a dog*) = le poil
  (*of a cat*) = la fourrure

coat hanger *noun*
  a coat hanger = un cintre

cobweb *noun*
  a cobweb = une toile d'araignée

cock *noun*
  a cock = un coq

---

cocoa *noun*
- (*the drink*)
  cocoa = le chocolat
- (*the product*)
  cocoa = le cacao

coconut *noun*
  a coconut = une noix de coco

cod *noun*
  cod = le cabillaud

coffee *noun*
- (*the product*)
  coffee = le café
- (*a cup of coffee*)
  a coffee = un café

coffee machine *noun*
  a coffee machine (*an appliance*) = une
    cafetière électrique
  (*a machine*) = une machine à café

coin *noun*
  a coin = une pièce
  a two-euro coin = une pièce de deux euros

coincidence *noun*
  a coincidence = une coïncidence

cold
1 *adjective*
  = froid/froide
  to be cold, to feel cold = avoir froid
  I'm very cold = j'ai très froid
  it's cold in the classroom = il fait froid
    dans la salle de classe
  you'll get cold = tu vas prendre froid
  to go cold = refroidir
  a cold meal = un repas froid
2 *noun*
- (*the lack of heat*)
  the cold = le froid
- (*a common illness*)
  a cold = un rhume

collapse *verb*
  (*if it's a building, a chair*) = s'effondrer
    (**!** + *être*)
  (*if it's a wall*) = s'écrouler (**!** + *être*)

collar *noun*
- (*on a shirt or jacket*)
  a collar = un col
- (*for a pet*)
  a collar = un collier

colleague *noun*
  a colleague = un collègue/une collègue

collect *verb*
- (*to gather*) = ramasser
  to collect the exercise books = ramasser
    les cahiers
- (*to make a collection of*) = collectionner
  he collects stamps = il collectionne les
    timbres
- (*to take away*)
  to collect the post = faire la levée du
    courrier
  to collect the rubbish = ramasser les
    ordures

Colours

Most colour adjectives agree with the noun they are describing:

a blue coat	= un manteau bleu
a blue dress	= une robe bleue

There are exceptions, labelled (**!** *never changes*) in the dictionary. Even with a plural noun, this type of adjective remains the same:

brown shoes	= des chaussures marron
orange curtains	= des rideaux orange

This rule also applies to shades of colour:

a dark blue dress	= une robe bleu foncé
pale blue curtains	= des rideaux bleu pâle

Describing the colour of something

what colour is your car?	= ta voiture est de quelle couleur?
	(*more formally*) de quelle couleur est ta voiture?
it's green	= elle est verte
to paint something green	= peindre quelque chose en vert

Describing people

Note the use of **les**:

to have brown eyes	= avoir **les** yeux marron

Note the use of **à**:

the girl with the blond hair = la fille **aux** cheveux blonds

---

collection *noun*
* (*a set*)
  a collection = une collection
  she has a great collection of posters
  = elle a une super* collection d'affiches
* (*money collected*)
  a collection = une collecte

college *noun*
  a college = un établissement
  d'enseignement supérieur
  to go to college, to be at college = faire
  des études supérieures

colour (*British English*), **color** (*US English*)
1 *noun*
  a colour = une couleur
  what colour is the car? = de quelle
  couleur est la voiture?
2 *verb*
  to colour the drawings (in) = colorier les
  dessins

colourful (*British English*), **colorful** (*US English*) *adjective*
  a colourful shirt = une chemise aux
  couleurs vives

colour television (*British English*),
color television (*US English*) *noun*
  a colour television = une télévision (en)
  couleur

comb
1 *noun*
  a comb = un peigne
2 *verb*
  to comb one's hair = se peigner (**!** + *être*)

come *verb*
* **to come** = venir (**!** + *être*)
  she's coming today = elle vient
  aujourd'hui
  come to Paris with us = viens avec nous à
  Paris
  we came by bike = nous sommes venus à
  bicyclette
  come and see! = venez voir!
  I'm coming! = j'arrive!
  is the bus coming? = est-ce que le bus
  arrive?
  **be careful when you come down the
  stairs** = faites attention en descendant
  l'escalier
  he won't come into the house = il ne veut
  pas entrer dans la maison
  to come through the city centre = passer
  par le centre-ville
* (*to call around*) = passer (**!** + *être*)
* (*to reach*)
  **turn left when you come to the traffic
  lights** = tournez à gauche quand vous
  arriverez aux feux
* (*to attend*) = venir (**!** + *être*)
  will you be able to come to the meeting?
  = est-ce que tu pourras venir à la
  réunion?

* (to be a native or a product of)
  she comes from Italy = elle est italienne
  the strawberries all come from Spain
  = toutes les fraises viennent d'Espagne
* (in a contest)
  to come first = arriver premier/première
come around ▶ come round
come back = revenir (! + être)
  to come back home = rentrer (! + être)
come in
* (to enter) = entrer (! + être)
* (if it's a plane, a train) = arriver (! + être)
* the tide's coming in = la marée monte
come off
  (if it's a cover, a lid) = s'enlever (! + être)
  (if it's a button, a label) = se détacher
  (! + être)
come on
* (to start to work) (if it's heating) = se mettre
  en marche
  (if it's a light) = s'allumer (! + être)
* (when encouraging someone)
  come on, hurry up! = allez, dépêchez-
  vous!
  come on, you can do better than that!
  = allez, tu peux faire mieux!
come on to (US English)
  to come on to someone = draguer
  quelqu'un✱
come out
* (to leave a place) = sortir (! + être)
  I saw him as I was coming out of the shop
  = je l'ai vu en sortant du magasin
* (to become available)
  (if it's a film) = sortir (! + être)
  (if it's a book) = paraître (! + être)
* (to wash out) = s'en aller (! + être)
* (if it's a photo)
  the photo didn't come out = la photo est
  ratée
* (if it's smoke, fire)
  there are flames coming out of the
  windows = il y a des flammes qui
  sortent par les fenêtres
come round
* (to visit) = venir (! + être)
* (after a faint) = reprendre connaissance
come to
  the meal came to 25 euros = le repas a
  coûté 25 euros
  how much does it come to? = ça fait
  combien?
come up
* (to be discussed)
  to come up in conversation = être
  abordé/abordée dans la conversation
* (if it's the sun) = se lever (! + être)

comfortable adjective
* (if it's a chair, a bed) = confortable
  are you comfortable? = êtes-vous bien
  installés?
* (relaxed) = à l'aise
* (having enough money) = aisé/aisée

comforter noun (US English)
  a comforter = une couette

comic strip noun
  a comic strip = une bande dessinée, une
  BD

commercial
1 adjective
  = commercial/commerciale
2 noun
  a commercial = une publicité

commit verb
  to commit a crime = commettre un crime

common adjective
  = courant/courante

communicate verb
  = communiquer

community noun
  a community = une communauté

company noun
* (a business)
  a company = une société
* (a group of actors)
  a theatre company = une troupe de
  théâtre
* (other people)
  company = la compagnie
  to keep someone company = tenir
  compagnie à quelqu'un
  to keep bad company = avoir de
  mauvaises fréquentations

company secretary noun ▶ 315 |
  a company secretary = un secrétaire
  général

compare verb
  = comparer
  to compare France with Italy = comparer
  la France à l'Italie
  she compares herself to her older sister
  = elle se compare à sa sœur aînée

compass noun
  a compass = une boussole

competition noun
* competition = la concurrence
  there's a lot of competition between the
  schools = il y a beaucoup de
  concurrence entre les écoles
* (a contest)
  a competition = un concours
  a drawing competition = un concours de
  dessin

competitive adjective
  to be competitive = avoir l'esprit de la
  compétition

complain verb
  = se plaindre (! + être)
  to complain about the food = se plaindre
  de la nourriture

complete
1 *adjective*
it was a complete disaster = c'était un désastre total
this is a complete waste of time = c'est vraiment du temps perdu
2 *verb*
= terminer
to complete a training course = terminer un stage de formation

completely *adverb*
= complètement

complicate *verb*
= compliquer

complicated *adjective*
= compliqué/compliquée

compliment
1 *noun*
a compliment = un compliment
2 *verb*
to compliment someone = faire des compliments à quelqu'un

comprehensive *noun* (*British English*)
a comprehensive = une école (publique) secondaire

compulsory *adjective*
= obligatoire

computer *noun*
a computer = un ordinateur

computer game *noun*
a computer game (*the game*) = un jeu électronique
(*the software*) = un logiciel de jeu

computer programmer *noun* ▶ 315|
a computer programmer = un programmeur/une programmeuse

computer scientist *noun* ▶ 315|
a computer scientist = un informaticien/une informaticienne

computer studies *noun*
computer studies = l'informatique (*feminine*)

concentrate *verb*
= se concentrer (**!** + *être*)

concert *noun*
a concert = un concert
in concert at Wembley = en concert à Wembley

concert hall *noun*
a concert hall = une salle de concert

concrete *noun*
concrete = le béton

condemn *verb*
to condemn someone to death = condamner quelqu'un à mort

condition
1 *noun*
a condition = un état
in a terrible condition = dans un état lamentable
the car is in good condition = la voiture est en bon état
2 on condition that = à condition que
you can go on condition that her parents drive you home = tu peux y aller à condition que ses parents te ramènent
! *Note that the subjunctive is used after* à condition que.

condom *noun*
a condom = un préservatif

conductor *noun* ▶ 315|
a conductor = un chef d'orchestre

cone *noun*
a cone = un cornet

conference *noun*
a conference = une conférence

confidence *noun*
• confidence = l'assurance (*feminine*)
• (*trust*)
to have confidence in someone = avoir confiance en quelqu'un

confident *adjective*
= sûr de soi
she's a confident girl = c'est une fille sûre d'elle

confidential *adjective*
= confidentiel/confidentielle

confiscate *verb*
= confisquer

conflict *noun*
a conflict = un conflit

confused *adjective*
to get confused = s'embrouiller (**!** + *être*)

congratulate *verb*
= féliciter

congratulations *noun* (also *exclamation*)
congratulations! = félicitations!

connection *noun*
a connection = un rapport
it has no connection with the strike = cela n'a aucun rapport avec la grève

conscientious *adjective*
= consciencieux/consciencieuse

conscious *adjective*
• (*aware*) = conscient/consciente
• (*after an operation*) = réveillé/réveillée

construct *verb*
= construire

consult *verb*
= consulter

contact
1 noun
  to be in contact with someone = être en contact avec quelqu'un
  to lose contact = perdre contact
2 verb
  = contacter

contact lens noun
  a contact lens = une lentille de contact

contain verb
  = contenir

content adjective
  = content/contente

contest noun
  a contest = un concours
  the Eurovision song contest = le concours Eurovision de la chanson

continent noun
• (a large mass of land)
  a continent = un continent
• (British English) (Europe)
  the Continent = l'Europe continentale

continental quilt noun (British English)
  a continental quilt = une couette

continue verb
  = continuer
  to continue to talk, to continue talking = continuer à parler
  to continue down the street = continuer à descendre la rue

continuous adjective
  = incessant/incessante
  the continuous noise of the traffic = le bruit incessant de la circulation

contraception noun
  contraception = la contraception

contract noun
  a contract = un contrat
  to have a two-year contract = avoir un contrat de deux ans

contradict verb
  = contredire

contradiction noun
  a contradiction = une contradiction

contrast noun
  a contrast = un contraste

contribute verb
• (to give money) = donner (de l'argent)
• **to contribute to a discussion** = participer à une discussion

control
1 noun
  to take control of a situation = prendre une situation en main
  to lose control of a car = perdre le contrôle d'une voiture

2 verb
  to control a region = contrôler une région
  to control traffic = diriger la circulation

convenient adjective
• (useful, practical) = pratique
  it's more convenient to take the bus = il est plus pratique de prendre le bus
• (suitable) = pratique
  it's a convenient place to meet = c'est un endroit pratique pour se retrouver
  it's not convenient for me = ça ne me convient pas

conversation noun
  a conversation = une conversation
  to make conversation = faire la conversation

convince verb
  = convaincre

cook
1 verb
• (to prepare food) = faire la cuisine, cuisiner
  to cook a meal = préparer un repas
  to cook vegetables = faire cuire des légumes
• (to be cooked in the oven) = cuire
2 noun ▶ 315 |
  a cook = un cuisinier/une cuisinière

cooker noun (British English)
  a cooker = une cuisinière

cookie noun (US English)
  a cookie = un gâteau sec, un biscuit

cooking noun
  cooking = la cuisine
  to do the cooking = faire la cuisine

cool adjective
• (fresh, not hot) = frais/fraîche
  a cool drink = une boisson fraîche
  it's much cooler today = il fait beaucoup plus frais aujourd'hui
• (calm) = calme
• (fashionable) = branché/branchée✕
• (relaxed) = décontracté/décontractée
cool down
• (to get colder) = refroidir
• (to calm down) = se calmer (**!** + être)

cooperate verb
  = coopérer

cope verb
• (to manage) = se débrouiller (**!** + être)
• **to cope with pain** = supporter la douleur

copper noun
  copper = le cuivre

copy
1 noun
  a copy = une copie
2 verb
  = copier
  to copy in an exam = copier à un examen

copy down, copy out = recopier

cork *noun*
* a cork = un bouchon
* cork = le liège

corkscrew *noun*
a corkscrew = un tire-bouchon

corner *noun*
* (*of a street, a building*)
the corner = l'angle (*masculine*)
= le coin
the shop on the corner = le magasin qui fait l'angle
to go around the corner = tourner au coin de la rue
* (*in football, hockey*)
a corner = un corner

correct
1 *adjective*
= bon/bonne (**!** *before the noun*), correct/correcte
the correct answer = la bonne réponse, la réponse correcte
that is correct = c'est exact
2 *verb*
= corriger

correction *noun*
a correction = une correction

corridor *noun*
a corridor = un couloir

cost *verb*
= coûter
how much does it cost? = ça coûte combien?
it costs a lot of money = ça coûte très cher

costume *noun*
a costume = un costume

cosy *adjective* (*British English*)
a cosy room = une pièce confortable

cot *noun* (*British English*)
a cot = un lit de bébé

cottage *noun*
a cottage = une petite maison

cotton *noun*
* (*the material*)
cotton = le coton
* (*the thread*)
cotton = le fil de coton

cotton wool *noun* (*British English*)
cotton wool = le coton hydrophile

couch *noun*
a couch = un canapé

cough *verb*
= tousser

could *verb*
* (*had the possibility*)
I couldn't move = je ne pouvais pas bouger
he couldn't sleep for weeks = il n'a pas pu dormir pendant des semaines
* (*knew how to*)
she could read at the age of three = elle savait lire à l'âge de trois ans
he couldn't type = il ne savait pas taper à la machine
I couldn't speak any German = je ne parlais pas allemand
* (*when talking about* seeing, hearing, understanding, *you don't translate* could)
I couldn't see a thing = je n'y voyais rien
he could hear them = il les entendait
they couldn't understand me = ils ne me comprenaient pas
* (*when implying that something did not happen*)
she could have become a doctor = elle aurait pu devenir médecin
you could have apologized! = tu aurais pu t'excuser!
* (*when indicating a possibility*)
they could be wrong = ils se trompent peut-être
a bike could be useful = un vélo pourrait être utile
* (*when asking, offering or suggesting*)
could I speak to Annie? = est-ce que je pourrais parler à Annie?
could you take a message? = est-ce que vous pourriez prendre un message?
we could ask Gary = nous pourrions demander à Gary

count *verb*
= compter
count on
to count on someone = compter sur quelqu'un

counter *noun*
a counter (*in a shop*) = un comptoir
(*in a bank, a post office*) = un guichet
(*in a bar*) = un bar, un comptoir

country *noun*
* (*a state*)
a country = un pays
* (*the countryside*)
the country = la campagne
to live in the country = vivre à la campagne

countryside *noun*
the countryside = la campagne

couple *noun*
* a couple of days (*two days*) = deux jours
(*a few days*) = deux ou trois jours
* (*two people*)
a couple = un couple

courage *noun*
courage = le courage

courageous *adjective*
= courageux/courageuse

course
1 *noun*
* (*a series of lessons or lectures*)
a course = un cours

Countries, cities, and continents

Countries and continents

Most countries and all continents are used with the definite article in French:

I like France | Canada   = j'aime **la** France | **le** Canada
to visit the United States   = visiter **les** États-Unis

All the continent names are feminine in French. Generally, the names of countries ending in **e** are feminine and the rest are mostly masculine. Some names of countries are plural, eg **les États-Unis**.

In, to, and from somewhere

With continent names and feminine singular names of countries, for **in** and **to** use **en**, and for **from** use **de** (or **d'** before a vowel or mute 'h'):

*to go **to** Europe | **to** France*   = aller **en** Europe | **en** France
*to come **from** France | **from** Germany*   = venir **d'**Europe | **d'**Allemagne

With masculine names of countries beginning with a consonant, use **au** for **in** and **to**, and **du** for **from** and with masculine names of countries beginning with a vowel use **en** for **in** and **to**, and **d'** for from

*to live **in** Canada | **in** Iraq*   = vivre **au** Canada | **en** Irak
*to come **from** Japan | **from** Iraq*   = venir **du** Japon | **d'**Irak

With plurals, use **aux** for **in** and **to**, and **des** for **from**

*to live **in the** United States*   = vivre **aux** États-Unis
*to come **from the** United States*   = venir **des** États-Unis

Towns and cities

For **in** and **to** with the name of a town, use **à** in French; if the French name includes the definite article, **à** will become **au**, **à la**, **à l'** or **aux**.

*to live **in** Toulouse | **in le** Havre |*   = vivre **à** Toulouse | **au** Havre |
***in la** Rochelle | **in les** Arcs*   **à la** Rochelle | **aux** Arcs

Similarly, **from** is **de**, becoming **du**, **de la**, **de l'** or **des** when it combines with the definite article in town names:

*to come **from** Toulouse | **from le** Havre |* = venir **de** Toulouse | **du** Havre |
***from la** Rochelle | **from les** Arc*   **de la** Rochelle | **des** Arcs

---

a language course = un cours de langue
* (*part of a meal*)
  a course = un plat
  what's the main course? = qu'est-ce qu'il y
  a comme plat principal?
2 of course = bien sûr
  of course not! = bien sûr que non!

court *noun*
* (*of law*)
  a court = une cour, un tribunal
  to go to court = aller devant les tribunaux
* (*for playing sports*)
  a tennis court = un court de tennis
  a basketball court = un terrain de basket

court case *noun*
  a court case = un procès

cousin *noun*
  a cousin = un cousin/une cousine

cover
1 *verb*
* **to cover** = couvrir
  to be covered in spots = être
  couvert/couverte de boutons
* (*to decorate*)
  to cover a cake with chocolate = recouvrir
  un gâteau de chocolat
2 *noun*
* (*a lid*)
  a cover = un couvercle
* (*for a cushion, a quilt*)
  a cover = une housse
* (*a blanket*)
  a cover = une couverture
* (*on a book, a magazine, an exercise book*)
  the cover = la couverture

cow *noun*
  a cow = une vache

coward *noun*
  a coward = un lâche/une lâche

cowboy noun
  a cowboy = un cowboy

cozy adjective (US English)
  a cozy room = une pièce confortable

crab noun
  a crab = un crabe

crack verb
• (to damage) = fêler
• (to get damaged) = se fêler (**!** + être)
• (to get broken) = se casser (**!** + être)

cradle noun
  a cradle = un berceau

cramp noun
  a cramp = une crampe

crash
1 noun
  a crash = un accident
  a car crash = un accident de voiture
2 verb
  to crash into a tree = rentrer dans un
    arbre
  the plane crashed = l'avion s'est écrasé

crayon noun
  a crayon = une craie grasse

crazy adjective
  = fou/folle

cream noun
  cream = la crème

create verb
  = créer
  to create employment = créer des emplois

credit noun
  credit = le crédit
  they don't give credit = ils ne font pas
    crédit

credit card noun
  a credit card = une carte de crédit

cricket noun ▶ 248|
  cricket = le cricket

crime noun
• (a criminal act)
  a crime (serious) = un crime
  (minor) = un délit
• (in general)
  crime = la criminalité

criminal
1 noun
  a criminal = un criminel/une criminelle
2 adjective
  = criminel/criminelle

crisis noun
  a crisis = une crise

crisps noun (British English)
  crisps = les chips (feminine)

critical adjective
  = critique

criticize verb
  = critiquer

crocodile noun
  a crocodile = un crocodile

crooked adjective
  a crooked line = une ligne brisée
  the picture is crooked = le tableau est de
    travers

cross
1 verb
• (to go across)
  to cross the road = traverser la rue
  to cross the Channel = traverser la
    Manche
  to cross the border = passer la frontière
  to cross into Italy = passer en Italie
• (other uses)
  to cross one's legs = croiser les jambes
  our letters crossed = nos lettres se sont
    croisées
2 noun
  a cross = une croix
3 adjective
  = fâché/fâchée
  to get cross = se fâcher (**!** + être)
cross out = rayer

crossroads noun
  a crossroads = un carrefour

crossword puzzle noun
  a crossword puzzle = des mots croisés
  | **!** Note that mots is masculine plural.

crow noun
  a crow = un corbeau

crowd noun
• (a large number of people)
  a crowd = une foule
  crowds of people = une foule de gens
• (watching a game)
  the crowd = les spectateurs (masculine
    plural)

crown noun
  a crown = une couronne

cruel adjective
  = cruel/cruelle

cruelty noun
  cruelty = la cruauté

cruise noun
  a cruise = une croisière

crush verb
  = écraser

crutch noun
  a crutch = une béquille

cry
1 verb
  = pleurer
2 noun
  a cry = un cri

cub *noun*
  a cub = un petit

cuckoo *noun*
  a cuckoo = un coucou

cucumber *noun*
  a cucumber = un concombre

cuddle *noun*
  a cuddle = un câlin
  to give someone a cuddle = faire un câlin
    à quelqu'un

culprit *noun*
  a culprit = un coupable/une coupable

cultural *adjective*
  = culturel/culturelle

culture *noun*
  culture = la culture

cunning *adjective*
  (*describing a person*) = rusé/rusée
  (*describing a plan*) = habile

cup *noun*
• a cup = une tasse
  a cup of coffee = une tasse de café
• (*in sport*)
  a cup = une coupe

cupboard *noun*
  a cupboard = un placard

curb *noun* (*US English*)
  the curb = le bord du trottoir

cure
1 *verb*
  = guérir
2 *noun*
  a cure = un traitement

curious *adjective*
  = curieux/curieuse

curly *adjective*
  = frisé/frisée
  to have curly hair = avoir les cheveux
    frisés

currency *noun*
  a currency = une monnaie
  foreign currency = les devises étrangères
  ! *Note that* devises *is feminine plural.*

curry *noun*
  a curry = un curry

curtain *noun*
  a curtain = un rideau
  to draw the curtains = tirer les rideaux

cushion *noun*
  a cushion = un coussin

custard *noun* (*British English*)
  custard ≈ la crème anglaise

custom *noun*
  a custom = une coutume

customer *noun*
  a customer = un client/une cliente

customs *noun*
  customs = la douane
  to go through customs = passer à la
    douane

customs officer *noun* ▶ 315
  a customs officer = un douanier/une
    douanière

cut
1 *verb*
  = couper
  to cut an apple in half = couper une
    pomme en deux
  to cut [one's fingers | one's knee | one's foot ...]
    = se couper [les doigts | le genou | le pied ...]
  she cut herself = elle s'est coupée
  to have one's hair cut = se faire couper les
    cheveux
  I got my hair cut = je me suis fait couper
    les cheveux
2 *noun*
  a cut = une coupure
cut down = abattre
cut out
  to cut a photo out of a magazine
    = découper une photo dans un
    magazine
cut up = couper

cute *adjective*
  = mignon/mignonne

CV *noun*
  a CV = un CV, un curriculum vitae

cycle *verb*
  to cycle to school = aller à l'école à vélo
  to go cycling = faire du vélo

cycle lane, **cycle path** *noun*
  a cycle lane = une piste cyclable

cycling *noun* ▶ 248
  cycling = le cyclisme

cyclist *noun*
  a cyclist = un cycliste/une cycliste

cynical *adjective*
  = cynique

Czech Republic *noun* ▶ 218
  the Czech Republic = la République
    tchèque

Dd

dad, **Dad** noun
    a dad = un papa

daffodil noun
    a daffodil = une jonquille

daisy noun
    a daisy = une pâquerette

damage
1 verb
    to damage = abîmer
    the building was damaged by the fire = le
        bâtiment a été endommagé par
        l'incendie
    (to harm) = nuire à
    it can damage your health = cela nuit à la
        santé
2 noun
    damage = les dégâts (masculine plural)
    to cause damage = faire des dégâts

damp adjective
    = humide

dance
1 verb
    = danser
2 noun
    a dance = une danse

dancer noun ▶ 315 |
    a dancer = un danseur/une danseuse

dancing noun
    dancing = la danse

danger noun
    danger = le danger
    to be in danger = être en danger

dangerous adjective
    = dangereux/dangereuse

Danish ▶ 275 |
1 adjective
    = danois/danoise
2 noun
    Danish = le danois

dare verb
    (to have the courage) = oser
    (when testing someone)
    to dare someone to play a trick = défier
        quelqu'un de jouer un tour
    (when expressing anger)
    don't dare speak to me like that! = je
        t'interdis de me parler sur ce ton!

dark
1 adjective
    (lacking light) = sombre
    it's getting dark = il commence à faire
        nuit

(describing a colour, clothes) ▶ 213 |
    = sombre
    he always wears dark clothes = il porte
        toujours des vêtements sombres
    a dark blue dress = une robe bleu foncé
    (describing a person) = brun/brune
2 noun
    the dark = le noir, l'obscurité (feminine)

darts noun ▶ 248 |
    darts = les fléchettes (feminine)

date noun ▶ 222 |
    (in a calendar)
    a date = une date
    what date is today? = quelle est la date
        aujourd'hui?
    (with a friend)
    a date = un rendez-vous
    to go out on a date with someone = sortir
        avec quelqu'un

daughter noun
    a daughter = une fille

daughter-in-law noun
    a daughter-in-law = une belle-fille

dawn noun
    dawn = l'aube (feminine)
    at dawn = à l'aube

day noun ▶ 356 |

> **!** Note that day is usually translated by
> jour in French. However it is sometimes
> translated by journée, when there is an
> emphasis on the idea of duration.

    a day = un jour
    what day is it today? = quel jour sommes-
        nous aujourd'hui?
    during the day = pendant la journée
    we had a very nice day = nous avons
        passé une journée très agréable
    the next day, the day after = le lendemain
    the day before = la veille

daylight noun
    daylight = le jour, la lumière du jour

dazzle verb
    = éblouir

dead adjective
    = mort/morte
    he is dead = il est mort

deaf adjective
    = sourd/sourde

deal
1 noun
    a deal (in business) = une affaire
    (with a friend) = un marché
    a great deal [of money | of time | of energy ...]
        = beaucoup [d'argent | de temps | d'énergie ...]
2 verb
    to deal the cards = distribuer les cartes
deal with = s'occuper de (**!** + être)
    to deal with a problem = s'occuper d'un
        problème

Dates, days, and months

The days of the week

Note that French uses lower-case letters for the names of days.

Write the names of days in full; do not abbreviate as in English (*Tues*, *Sat* and so on).

Monday	= lundi
Tuesday	= mardi
Wednesday	= mercredi
Thursday	= jeudi
Friday	= vendredi
Saturday	= samedi
Sunday	= dimanche

lundi in the notes below stands for any day; they all work the same way. Note the use of **le** for regular occurrences, and no article for single ones. (*Remember: do not translate* **on**.)

on Monday	= lundi
on Mondays	= le lundi
Monday afternoon	= lundi après-midi
last / next Monday	= lundi dernier / prochain
last Monday night	= la nuit de lundi dernier
	(*if evening*) lundi dernier dans la soirée
early on Monday	= lundi matin de bonne heure
late on Monday	= lundi soir tard
a month from Monday	= dans un mois lundi
from Monday on	= à partir de lundi

The months of the year

As with the days of the week, do not use capitals to spell the names of the months in French, and do not abbreviate as in English (*Jan*, *Feb* and so on).

January	= janvier	*July*	= juillet
February	= février	*August*	= août
March	= mars	*September*	= septembre
April	= avril	*October*	= octobre
May	= mai	*November*	= novembre
June	= juin	*December*	= décembre

May in the notes below stands for any month; they all work the same way.

in May	= en mai / au mois de mai
next May	= en mai prochain
last May	= l'année dernière en mai
in early / late May	= début / fin mai

Dates

French has only one generally accepted way of writing dates: **le 10 mai** (say **le dix mai**).

If the days of the week is included, put it after the **le**:

Monday, May 1st 1901	= le lundi 1er mai 1901
what's the date?	= quel jour sommes-nous?
it's the tenth of May	= nous sommes le 10 mai / on est le 10 mai
in 1968	= en 1968
in the year 2000	= en l'an 2000
in the seventeenth century	= au dix-septième siècle

	Write	**Say**
May 1	le 1er mai	le premier mai
May 2	le 2 mai	le deux mai
from 4th to 16th May	du 4 au 16 mai	du quatre au seize mai
May 6 1968	le 6 mai 1968	le six mai mille neuf cent soixante-huit
in the 1980s	dans les années 80	dans les années quatre-vingt
the 16th century	le XVIe siècle	le seizième siècle

dear
1 *adjective*
(*in letters*) = cher/chère
Dear Anne = Chère Anne
Dear Anne and Paul = Chers Anne et Paul
Dear Sir/Madam = Monsieur, Madame
(*expensive*) = cher/chère
2 *exclamation* ▶ 237 |
oh dear! = oh mon Dieu!

death *noun*
death = la mort

death penalty *noun*
the death penalty = la peine de mort

debate *noun*
a debate = un débat

debt *noun*
a debt = une dette
to be in debt = avoir des dettes

decade *noun*
a decade = une décennie

decaffeinated *adjective*
= décaféiné/décaféinée

deceive *verb*
= tromper

December *noun* ▶ 222 |
December = décembre (*masculine*)

decide *verb*
= décider
he decided [to accept | to stay | to get
married ...] = il a décidé [d'accepter | de
rester | de se marier ...]

decision *noun*
a decision = une décision
to make a decision = prendre une
décision

deck *noun*
a deck = un pont
on deck = sur le pont

deckchair *noun*
a deckchair = une chaise longue

decorate *verb*
(*with ornaments*) = décorer
(*with wallpaper*) = tapisser
(*to paint*) = peindre

decoration *noun*
a decoration = une décoration

deep *adjective* ▶ 285 |
= profond/profonde
how deep is the lake? = quelle est la
profondeur du lac?
the hole is three metres deep = le trou fait
trois mètres de profondeur

deer *noun*
a deer (*male*) = un cerf
(*female*) = une biche

defeat
1 *verb*
to defeat an enemy = vaincre un ennemi
the team was defeated = l'équipe a été
battue
2 *noun*
a defeat = une défaite

defence (*British English*), **defense** (*US
English*) *noun*
defence = la défense

D

defend *verb*
= défendre

definite *adjective*
(*describing a decision*) = ferme
(*describing a plan*) = précis/précise
nothing is definite = rien n'est sûr
(*obvious, visible*) = net/nette
a definite improvement = une nette
amélioration

definitely *adverb*
= sans aucun doute
they're definitely lying = ils mentent sans
aucun doute
I'm definitely coming = c'est décidé, je
viens
'definitely!' = 'absolument!'

defy *verb*
= défier

degree *noun*
(*from a university*)
a degree = un diplôme universitaire
(*in measurements*)
a degree = un degré

delay
1 *verb*
= retarder
2 *noun*
a delay = un retard

deliberate *adjective*
= délibéré/délibérée

deliberately *adverb*
= exprès
he did it deliberately = il l'a fait exprès

delicious *adjective*
= délicieux/délicieuse

delighted *adjective*
= ravi/ravie
to be delighted with a present = être
ravi/ravie d'un cadeau

deliver *verb*
= livrer
to deliver goods = livrer des marchandises
to deliver mail = distribuer le courrier

demand *verb*
= exiger

demolish *verb*
= démolir

demonstration *noun*
a demonstration = une manifestation

denim jacket *adjective*
a denim jacket = un blouson en jean

Denmark *noun* ▶ 218 |
Denmark = le Danemark

dentist *noun* ▶ 315 |
a dentist = un dentiste/une dentiste

deny *verb*
= nier

department *noun*
a department (*in a firm*) = un service
(*in a large store*) = un rayon
(*in a school*) = une section
(*in a university*) = un département

department store *noun*
a department store = un grand magasin

depend *verb*
= dépendre
to depend on someone = dépendre de
  quelqu'un
it depends on you = cela dépend de toi
it depends = ça dépend

depressed *adjective*
= déprimé/déprimée

depressing *adjective*
= déprimant/déprimante

deprive *verb*
= priver

depth *noun* ▶ 285 |
depth = la profondeur

describe *verb*
= décrire

description *noun*
a description = une description

desert *noun*
a desert = un désert

deserve *verb*
= mériter
he deserves to be punished = il mérite
  d'être puni

design
1 *verb*
(*to plan*) = concevoir
the house was designed for a hot climate
  = la maison a été conçue pour un climat
  chaud
(*in fashion*)
to design clothes = créer des vêtements
2 *noun*
(*a subject of study*)
(fashion) design = le stylisme
(*a pattern*)
a design = un motif

desk *noun*
a desk = un bureau

desperate *adjective*
= désespéré/désespérée

dessert *noun*
a dessert = un dessert

destroy *verb*
= détruire

detail *noun*
a detail = un détail
to go into details = entrer dans les détails

detective *noun* ▶ 315 |
a detective = un inspecteur de police
a private detective = un détective

detective story *noun*
a detective story = un roman policier

determined *adjective*
= déterminé/déterminée
to be determined to go = être
  décidé/décidée à y aller

develop *verb*
= développer

development *noun*
a development = un développement

diagram *noun*
a diagram = un schéma

dial *verb*
to dial a number = composer un numéro

dialling code *noun* (*British English*)
a dialling code = un indicatif

dialling tone (*British English*), **dial
tone** (*US English*) *noun*
a dialling tone = une tonalité

diamond *noun*
a diamond = un diamant

diary *noun*
(*for personal thoughts*)
a diary = un journal
(*for appointments*)
a diary = un agenda

dice *noun*
a dice = un dé

dictionary *noun*
a dictionary = un dictionnaire

die *verb*
to die = mourir (**!** + *être*)
he died in the war = il est mort à la guerre
to be dying of cancer = être
  atteint/atteinte d'un cancer incurable
(*used for emphasis*)
I'm dying to go on holiday = je meurs
  d'envie de partir en vacances

diet *noun*
a diet = un régime
to go on a diet = se mettre au régime

difference *noun*
  a difference = une différence
  I can't tell the difference = je ne vois pas la différence
  it won't make any difference = ça ne changera rien
  what difference does it make? = qu'est-ce que ça change?

different *adjective*
  = différent/différente

difficult *adjective*
  = difficile
  Spanish is not difficult to learn = l'espagnol n'est pas difficile à apprendre
  to be difficult to get along with = être difficile à vivre

difficulty *noun*
  a difficulty = une difficulté, un problème
  to have difficulty concentrating = avoir du mal à se concentrer

dig *verb*
  = creuser
dig up
  (*when gardening*) = bêcher
  (*to find what was buried*) = déterrer

dim *adjective*
  (*describing a light*) = faible
  (*describing a room*) = sombre

diner *noun* (*US English*)
  a diner = un café-restaurant

dinghy *noun*
  a dinghy = un dériveur

dining room *noun*
  a dining room = une salle à manger

dinner *noun*
  a dinner = un dîner
  dinner's ready! = à table!

dip *verb*
  = tremper

direct
1 *adjective*
  = direct/directe
2 *verb*
  (*when talking about directions*)
  could you direct me to the station? = pourriez-vous m'indiquer le chemin pour aller à la gare?
  (*in cinema or theatre*)
  to direct a film = réaliser un film
  to direct a play = mettre en scène une pièce

direction *noun*
  a direction = une direction, un sens
  is this the right direction? = est-ce que c'est la bonne direction?
  they were going in the other direction = ils allaient dans l'autre sens

directions *noun*
  directions = les indications (*feminine*)
  to give someone directions = donner des indications à quelqu'un
  to ask someone for directions = demander le chemin à quelqu'un

director *noun* ▶ 315|
  (*of a film or play*)
  a director = un metteur en scène
  (*of a company*)
  a director = un directeur/une directrice

D

dirt *noun*
  dirt = la saleté

dirty
1 *adjective*
  = sale
  to get dirty = se salir (**!** + *être*)
2 *verb*
  = salir

disabled *adjective*
  = handicapé/handicapée

disadvantage *noun*
  a disadvantage = un désavantage

disagree *verb*
  = ne pas être d'accord
  I disagree with you = je ne suis pas d'accord avec toi

disappear *verb*
  = disparaître

disappoint *verb*
  = décevoir

disappointed *adjective*
  = déçu/déçue

disappointing *adjective*
  = décevant/décevante

disappointment *noun*
  disappointment = la déception

disapprove *verb*
  to disapprove of someone = ne pas apprécier quelqu'un

disaster *noun*
  a disaster = une catastrophe, un désastre

discipline *noun*
  discipline = la discipline

disco *noun*
  a disco = une discothèque

disconnect *verb*
  (*to pull out a plug*) = débrancher
  (*to cut off*) = couper

discourage *verb*
  = décourager

discover *verb*
  = découvrir

discovery *noun*
  a discovery = une découverte

discreet *adjective*
= discret/discrète

discrimination *noun*
discrimination = la discrimination

discuss *verb*
= discuter de
to discuss politics = discuter de politique

discussion *noun*
a discussion = une discussion

disease *noun* ▶ **266**
a disease = une maladie

disguise
1 *noun*
a disguise = un déguisement
to wear a disguise = être déguisé/déguisée
2 *verb*
to disguise oneself as a woman = se
déguiser en femme

disgusting *adjective*
= dégoûtant/dégoûtante

dish *noun*
(*food*)
a dish = un plat
the dishes = la vaisselle (*singular*)
to wash the dishes = faire la vaisselle

dishonest *adjective*
= malhonnête

dishwasher *noun*
a dishwasher = un lave-vaisselle

dislike *verb*
= ne pas aimer
I dislike him = je ne l'aime pas

dismiss *verb*
= renvoyer

disobedient *adjective*
= désobéissant/désobéissante

disobey *verb*
to disobey someone = désobéir à
quelqu'un

display *noun*
a display = un étalage
a window display = une vitrine

dispute *noun*
a dispute (*between individuals*) = une
dispute
(*between groups*) = un conflit

disqualify *verb*
= disqualifier

disrupt *verb*
= perturber

dissatisfied *adjective*
= mécontent/mécontente

distance *noun*
a distance = une distance
in the distance = au loin
to keep one's distance = garder ses
distances

distinct *adjective*
(*easy to see, to hear*) = distinct/distincte
(*definite*) = net/nette (**!** *before the noun*)

distinguish *verb*
= distinguer
to distinguish between truth and lies
= faire la distinction entre la vérité et les
mensonges

distract *verb*
= distraire
to distract someone from working
= empêcher quelqu'un de travailler

distressed *adjective*
= bouleversé/bouleversée

distribute *verb*
= distribuer

disturb *verb*
= déranger

disturbing *adjective*
= troublant/troublante

dive *verb* ▶ **248**
= plonger
to go diving = faire de la plongée

divide *verb*
(*in arithmetic*) = diviser
(*to share*) = partager

diving board *noun*
a diving board = un plongeoir

divorce
1 *noun*
a divorce = un divorce
2 *verb*
= divorcer

DIY *noun* (*British English*)
DIY = le bricolage

dizzy *adjective*
to feel dizzy = avoir la tête qui tourne

do *verb* ▶ **237**
▶ **227** *See the boxed note on* do *for more
information and examples.*
to do = faire
to do the cooking = faire la cuisine
to do one's homework = faire ses devoirs
what has he done with the newspaper?
= qu'est-ce qu'il a fait du journal?
what has she done to her hair? = qu'est-ce
qu'elle a fait à ses cheveux?
do as you're told = fais ce qu'on te dit
(*in questions, negatives*)
do you like cats? = est-ce que tu aimes les
chats?
I don't like cats = je n'aime pas les chats
I didn't do anything = je n'ai rien fait
don't shout! = ne crie pas!

do

As an ordinary verb

Usually, the French equivalent of the verb **to do** is **faire**:

*she is **doing** her homework*	= elle **fait** ses devoirs
*what **has** he **done** with the newspaper?*	= qu'est-ce qu'il **a fait** du journal?

As an auxiliary verb

In questions

In French there is no auxiliary verb in questions equivalent to **do** in English.

When the subject is a pronoun, use either of these structures: *verb + hyphen + subject* or, less formally, **est-ce que** + *subject* + *verb*:

***do** you like Mozart?*	= aimes-tu Mozart?
	= **est-ce que** tu aimes Mozart?

When the subject is a noun, there are again two possibilities:

***did** your sister ring?*	= **est-ce que** ta sœur a téléphoné?
	= ta sœur a-t-elle téléphoné?

In negatives

Equally, auxiliaries are not used in negatives in French:

*I **don't** like Mozart*	= je n'aime pas Mozart.

In emphatic uses

There is no verbal equivalent for the use of **do** in such expressions as *I do like your dress*. In emphatic uses, French may use an adverb like *beaucoup, vraiment*:

*I **do** like your dress*	= j'aime **beaucoup** ta robe
*I **do** think you should go*	= je pense **vraiment** que tu devrais y aller

When referring back to another verb

In this case the verb **to do** is not translated at all:

*I live in Oxford and so **does** Lily*	= j'habite à Oxford et Lily aussi
*she gets paid more than I **do***	= elle est payée plus que moi
*'I don't like carrots' — 'neither **do** I'*	= 'je n'aime pas les carottes' — 'moi non plus'

In polite requests

In polite requests the phrase *je vous en prie* or *je t'en prie* is useful:

***do** sit down*	= asseyez-vous, **je vous en prie**

In imperatives

In French there is no use of an auxiliary verb in imperatives:

***don't** shut the door*	= ne ferme pas la porte
***do** be quiet*	= tais-toi!

In short questions

With questions like **doesn't he?** or **didn't he?**, there is a general French phrase question **n'est-ce pas?** which will work in many cases:

*you like fish, **don't** you?*	= tu aimes les poisson, **n'est-ce pas?**

With positive tag questions, **par hasard** can often be used as a translation:

Lola didn't phone, did she?	= Lola n'a pas téléphoné **par hasard?**

In short answers

There is no direct French equivalent for the verb such as *no, he doesn't, yes, we did* etc.

*'does he play tennis?' — '**no, he doesn't**'*	= 'est-ce qu'il joue au tennis?' — '**non**'
*'do you like strawberries?' —'**yes I do**'*	= 'aimez-vous les fraises?' — '**oui**'

If answering 'yes' to contradict a negative statement, the most useful translation is **si**:

*'Marion didn't say that' —'**yes she did**'*	= 'Marion n'a pas dit ça' — '**si**'

▶ For more examples, see the entry **do**.

(*in short answers and tag questions*)
'do you like strawberries?'—'yes, I do'
= 'est-ce que tu aimes les fraises?'—'oui'
'I never said I liked him'—'yes, you did'
= 'je n'ai jamais dit que je l'aimais'—'si,
tu l'as dit'
'I love chocolate'—'so do I!' = 'j'adore le
chocolat'—'moi aussi!'
'who wrote it?'—'I did' = 'qui l'a écrit?'
—'moi'
he lives in London, doesn't he? = il habite
à Londres, n'est-ce-pas?
Martine didn't phone, did she? = Martine
n'a pas téléphoné, par hasard?
'may I sit down?'—'yes, please do'
= 'puis-je m'asseoir?'—'je t'en prie'
(*to be enough*) = suffire
ten pounds will do = dix livres suffiront
that box will do = cette boîte fera l'affaire
(*to perform*)
he did well = il s'est bien débrouillé
he did badly = il s'est mal débrouillé
do up (*British English*)
to do up one's buttons = se boutonner
(**!** + *être*)
to do up a house = refaire une maison
do with
it's got something to do with computers
= ça a quelque chose à voir avec
l'informatique
it has nothing to do with him = ça n'a rien
à voir avec lui
do without = se passer de (**!** + *être*)
I can do without a television = je peux me
passer de télévision

dock *noun*
a dock = un dock

doctor *noun* ▶ 315 |
a doctor = un médecin

document *noun*
a document = un document

documentary *noun*
a documentary = un documentaire

dog *noun*
a dog = un chien

doll *noun*
a doll = une poupée

dollar *noun*
a dollar = un dollar

dolphin *noun*
a dolphin = un dauphin

dominoes *noun* ▶ 248 |
dominoes = les dominos (*masculine*)

donkey *noun*
a donkey = un âne

door *noun*
a door = une porte

doorbell *noun*
a doorbell = une sonnette

dormitory *noun*
a dormitory = un dortoir

dose *noun*
a dose = une dose

double
1 *adjective*
(*of an amount*) = double
a double helping of strawberries = une
double portion de fraises
(*when spelling or giving a number*)
Annie is spelled with a double 'n' = Annie
s'écrit avec deux 'n'
three double five (*British English*) = trois
cent cinquante cinq
2 *verb*
= doubler

double bass *noun* ▶ 290 |
a double bass = une contrebasse

double bed *noun*
a double bed = un grand lit

double-decker *noun*
a double-decker = un autobus à impériale

double room *noun*
a double room = une chambre pour deux
personnes

doubt
1 *noun*
a doubt = un doute
there's no doubt that he is innocent = son
innocence ne fait aucun doute
I've no doubt that it's true = je suis certain
que c'est vrai
2 *verb*
= douter
I doubt if she'll come = je doute qu'elle
vienne

! *Note that the subjunctive is used after*
douter que.

dough *noun*
dough = la pâte

doughnut, donut (*US English*) *noun*
a doughnut = un beignet

down

! *Often* down *occurs in combinations with
verbs, for example:* calm down, let down,
slow down *etc. To find the correct
translations for this type of verb, look up
the separate dictionary entries at* calm,
let, slow *etc.*

1 *preposition*
to go down the street = descendre la rue
he walked down the corridor = il a
descendu le couloir
he ran down the hill = il a descendu la
colline en courant
the kitchen is down those stairs = la
cuisine est en bas de cet escalier

2 adverb
she's **down** in the cellar = elle est dans la cave
down in Brighton = à Brighton
to go **down** to the country = aller à la campagne
to go **down** = descendre (**!** + être)
to fall **down** = tomber (**!** + être)
down there = là-bas

downstairs adverb
= en bas
to go **downstairs** = descendre (l'escalier)
to bring the boxes **downstairs** = descendre les cartons

dozen noun ▶ 317 |
a **dozen** = une douzaine
a **dozen** eggs = une douzaine d'œufs

draft noun (US English)
a **draft** = un courant d'air

drag verb
= traîner

drain verb
(when cooking) = égoutter
(if it's water)
to **drain** (away) = s'écouler (**!** + être)

drama noun
(a play, an event)
a **drama** = un drame
(theatre)
drama = le théâtre

dramatic adjective
= spectaculaire

drapes noun (US English)
drapes = les rideaux (masculine)

draught noun (British English)
a **draught** = un courant d'air

draughts noun ▶ 248 | (British English)
draughts = les dames (feminine)

draw
1 verb
(with a pen or pencil) = dessiner
to **draw** a rabbit = dessiner un lapin
to **draw** a picture = faire un dessin
to **draw** a line = tracer une ligne
she **drew** his portrait = elle a fait son portrait
(to pull) = tirer
to **draw** the curtains = tirer les rideaux
(to take out) = sortir
to **draw** a knife = sortir un couteau
(in a lottery)
to **draw** a ticket = tirer un ticket au sort
(to attract) = attirer
the circus **drew** a large crowd = le cirque a attiré beaucoup de monde
(British English) (in sport) = faire match nul
Christmas is **drawing** near = Noël approche

2 noun
(in sport)
a **draw** = un match nul
(in a lottery)
a **draw** = un tirage au sort

draw aside
to **draw** someone aside = prendre quelqu'un à part

draw back
to **draw** back the curtains = ouvrir les rideaux

draw up
to **draw** up a list = dresser une liste

drawer noun
a **drawer** = un tiroir

drawing noun
drawing = le dessin

dread verb
= appréhender

dreadful adjective
= épouvantable

dream
1 noun ▶ 237 |
a **dream** = un rêve
to have a **dream** = faire un rêve
2 verb
= rêver
to **dream** of going to Japan = rêver d'aller au Japon

dress
1 noun
a **dress** = une robe
2 verb
(to put one's own clothes on) = s'habiller (**!** + être)
(to put clothes on someone) = habiller

dress up
(in good clothes) = s'habiller (**!** + être)
(in a disguise) = se déguiser (**!** + être)
she **dressed** up as a clown = elle s'est déguisée en clown

dressing gown noun
a **dressing gown** = une robe de chambre

drill
1 noun
a **drill** = une perceuse
2 verb
to **drill** a hole = percer un trou
to **drill** through the wall = percer un trou dans le mur

drink
1 verb
= boire
2 noun
a **drink** = une boisson
a **drink** of water = un verre d'eau

drive
1 *verb*
(*in a car*) = conduire
to learn to drive = apprendre à conduire
he drives to work = il va au travail en voiture
to drive someone home = ramener quelqu'un en voiture
(*to make*)
to drive someone mad = rendre quelqu'un fou/folle
2 *noun*
a drive = un tour (en voiture)
to go for a drive = aller faire un tour (en voiture)
drive away
(*in a car*) = démarrer
(*to chase away*) = chasser
drive back = rentrer (en voiture) (**!** + *être*)

driver *noun*
a driver = un conducteur/une conductrice

driver's license (*US English*), driving licence (*British English*) *noun*
a driver's license = un permis de conduire

drizzle *verb*
= bruiner

drop
1 *verb*
(*to come down*) = baisser
the temperature has dropped = la température a baissé
(*to let fall*) = laisser tomber
she dropped her suitcase = elle a laissé tomber sa valise
(*to fall*) = tomber (**!** + *être*)
2 *noun*
(*a fall*)
a drop = une baisse
a drop in temperature = une baisse de température
(*of liquid*)
a drop = une goutte
drop in = passer (**!** + *être*)
he dropped in to see me = il est passé me voir
drop off = déposer
could you drop me off at the station? = est-ce que tu pourrais me déposer à la gare?
drop out
to drop out of school = abandonner ses études
to drop out of a race = se retirer d'une course

drought *noun*
a drought = une sécheresse

drown *verb*
= se noyer (**!** + *être*)

drug
1 *noun*
(*for illegal use*)
a drug = une drogue

to be on drugs = se droguer (**!** + *être*)
(*for medical use*)
a drug = un médicament
2 *verb*
to drug someone = droguer quelqu'un

drug addict *noun*
a drug addict = un toxicomane/une toxicomane

drum *noun* ▶ 290 |
a drum = un tambour
to play drums = jouer de la batterie

drunk *adjective*
= ivre

dry
1 *adjective*
= sec/sèche
a dry day = une journée sans pluie
2 *verb*
to dry clothes = faire sécher des vêtements
to dry oneself = se sécher (**!** + *être*)
he dried his hands = il s'est séché les mains
to dry the dishes = essuyer la vaisselle

duck
1 *noun*
a duck = un canard
2 *verb*
= baisser la tête

due
1 due to = à cause de
the game was cancelled due to bad weather = le match a été annulé à cause du mauvais temps
2 *adjective*
(*expected*)
the train is due (in) at two o'clock = le train doit arriver à deux heures
(*owed*) = dû/due
the amount due = la somme due

dull *adjective*
(*describing a person or book*) = terne
(*describing a colour*) = terne
(*describing the weather or a landscape*) = morne

dumb *adjective*
(*unable to speak*) = muet/muette
(*stupid*) = bête

dump
1 *verb*
= jeter
2 *noun*
a dump = une décharge

during *preposition*
= pendant
during the summer = pendant l'été

dust
1 *noun*
dust = la poussière

2 *verb*
= épousseter

dustbin *noun* (*British English*)
a **dustbin** = une poubelle

dustman *noun* (*British English*)
a **dustman** = un éboueur

dustpan *noun*
a **dustpan** = une pelle (à poussière)

Dutch ▶ 275 |
1 *adjective*
= hollandais/hollandaise
2 *noun*
the **Dutch** = les Hollandais (*masculine plural*)

duty *noun*
• (*a task, part of one's job*)
a **duty** = une fonction
to take up one's **duties** = prendre ses fonctions
(*of a soldier, a nurse*)
to be on **duty** = être de service
• (*what one must do*)
duty = le devoir
it's my **duty** to go = il est de mon devoir d'y aller
• (*a tax*)
customs **duties** = les droits de douane
! *Note that* **droits** *is masculine.*

dye *verb*
= teindre
to **dye** one's hair = se teindre les cheveux

Ee

each
1 *determiner*
= chaque
each time I see him = chaque fois que je le vois
2 *pronoun*
= chacun/chacune
each of the boys = chacun des garçons
each of them has a car, they **each** have a car = ils ont chacun/elles ont chacune une voiture

each other *pronoun*
! *Note that* **each other** *is very often translated by using a reflexive pronoun like* **se, s', nous** *or* **vous**.

they know **each other** already = ils se connaissent déjà
we write to **each other** every year = nous nous écrivons tous les ans

eager *adjective*
= enthousiaste

eagle *noun*
an **eagle** = un aigle

ear *noun* **▶ 201 |**
an **ear** = une oreille

early *adverb*
• **early** = tôt
to get up **early** = se lever tôt
early in the afternoon = en début d'après-midi
• (*ahead of time*) = en avance
to arrive **early** = arriver en avance

earn *verb*
to **earn** lots of money = gagner beaucoup d'argent

earring *noun*
an **earring** = une boucle d'oreille

earth *noun*
• (*the planet*)
the **earth** = la terre
• (*soil*)
earth = la terre

easily *adverb*
= facilement

east
1 *noun*
the **east** = l'est (*masculine*)
in the **east** of France = dans l'est de la France
2 *adverb*
to go **east** = aller vers l'est
to live **east** of Paris = vivre à l'est de Paris
3 *adjective*
= est (! *never changes*)
to work in **east** London = travailler dans l'est de Londres

Easter *noun*
Easter = Pâques (*feminine plural*)
Happy **Easter**! = Joyeuses Pâques!

Easter egg *noun*
an **Easter egg** = un œuf de Pâques

easy *adjective*
= facile
it's **easy** to fix = c'est facile à réparer
it's not **easy** to find work there = il n'est pas facile d'y trouver du travail

eat *verb*
= manger
eat out = manger au restaurant

EC *noun*
the **EC** = la Communauté Européenne

echo *noun*
an **echo** = un écho

economic *adjective*
= économique

economics noun
economics = les sciences économiques
| ! Note that sciences is feminine plural.

economy noun
the economy = l'économie (feminine)

edge noun
• (of a road, table, an object)
the edge = le bord
the edge of the lake = le bord du lac
at the edge of the town = aux abords de la ville
• (of a forest, a wood or field)
the edge = la lisière
• (of a blade or knife)
the edge = le tranchant

educate verb
= instruire
he was educated in Paris = il a fait ses études à Paris

education noun
education = l'instruction (feminine)
to get a good education = recevoir une bonne instruction

effect noun
an effect = un effet

effective adjective
= efficace

efficient adjective
= efficace

effort noun
an effort = un effort
to make an effort = faire un effort

egg noun
an egg = un œuf

eggcup noun
an eggcup = un coquetier

eight number ▶ 187 |, ▶ 211 |
eight = huit
eight apples = huit pommes
I've got eight (of them) = j'en ai huit

eighteen number ▶ 187 |, ▶ 211 |
eighteen = dix-huit

eighteenth number
• (in a series) = dix-huitième
• (in dates) ▶ 222 |
the eighteenth of August = le dix-huit août

eighth number
• (in a series) = huitième
• (in dates) ▶ 222 |
the eighth of August = le huit août

eighty number ▶ 187 |
eighty = quatre-vingts

either
1 conjunction
they're coming on either Tuesday or Wednesday = ils viendront soit mardi, soit mercredi
he didn't contact either Helen or Paul = il n'a contacté ni Helen ni Paul
2 pronoun
take either (of them) = prends l'un ou l'autre/l'une ou l'autre
I don't know either (of them) = je ne connais ni l'un ni l'autre/l'une ni l'autre
3 determiner
take either road = prenez l'une ou l'autre route
I don't want to live in either country = je ne veux habiter dans aucun des deux pays
4 adverb
= non plus
she can't do it either = elle ne peut pas le faire non plus

elbow noun ▶ 201 |
the elbow = le coude

elder adjective
= aîné/aînée

elderly adjective
= âgé/âgée

eldest adjective
= aîné/aînée
the eldest daughter = l'aînée

elect verb
= élire

election noun
an election = une élection
to win an election = remporter les élections

electric adjective
= électrique

electrician noun ▶ 315 |
an electrician = un électricien/une électricienne

electricity noun
electricity = l'électricité (feminine)

elegant adjective
= élégant/élégante

elephant noun
an elephant = un éléphant

elevator noun (US English)
an elevator = un ascenseur

eleven number ▶ 187 |, ▶ 211 |
eleven = onze
eleven apples = onze pommes
I've got eleven (of them) = j'en ai onze

eleventh number
• (in a series) = onzième
• (in dates) ▶ 222 |
the eleventh of May = le onze mai

else
1 *adverb*
= d'autre
someone else = quelqu'un d'autre
nothing else = rien d'autre
what else did he say? = qu'est-ce qu'il a
dit d'autre?
something else = autre chose
everything else = tout le reste
2 or else = sinon
be quiet or else! = taisez-vous sinon!

elsewhere *adverb*
= ailleurs

email *noun*
an email = un email, un mél
an email address = une adresse
électronique

embarrassed *adjective*
= gêné/gênée

embarrassing *adjective*
= gênant/gênante

embassy *noun*
an embassy = une ambassade

emergency *noun*
an emergency = une urgence
in an emergency = en cas d'urgence

emergency exit *noun*
an emergency exit = une sortie de secours

emigrate *verb*
= émigrer

emotion *noun*
an emotion = une émotion

emotional *adjective*
• (*describing a scene or moment*)
= émouvant/émouvante
• (*describing a person*) = émotif/émotive

emperor *noun*
an emperor = un empereur

employ *verb*
= employer

employed *adjective*
to be employed = avoir un emploi

employee *noun*
an employee = un employé/une employée

employer *noun*
an employer = un employeur

employment *noun*
employment = le travail, l'emploi
(*masculine*)

empty
1 *adjective*
= vide
2 *verb*
= vider

encourage *verb*
= encourager

end
1 *noun*
• (*the final part*)
the end = la fin
at the end of May = fin mai
in the end = finalement
• (*the furthest part*)
the end = le bout
at the end of the street = au bout de la rue
2 *verb*
• (*to come to an end*) = se terminer
(**!** + *être*)
• (*to put an end to*) = mettre fin à
• (*to finish*) = terminer

end up
to end up in London = se retrouver à
Londres
to end up going abroad = finir par aller à
l'étranger

ending *noun*
the ending = la fin

enemy *noun*
an enemy = un ennemi/une ennemie

energetic *adjective*
= énergique

energy *noun*
energy = l'énergie (*feminine*)

engaged *adjective*
• **to get engaged** = se fiancer (**!** + *être*)
to be engaged = être fiancé/fiancée
• (*British English*) (*describing a phone, toilet*)
= occupé/occupée

engine *noun*
• (*of a car*)
an engine = un moteur
• (*for a train*)
an engine = une locomotive

engineer *noun* ▶ 315 |
an engineer = un ingénieur

England *noun* ▶ 218 |
England = l'Angleterre (*feminine*)

English ▶ 275 |
1 *adjective*
= anglais/anglaise
2 *noun*
• (*the people*)
the English = les Anglais (*masculine
plural*)
• (*the language*)
English = l'anglais (*masculine*)

enjoy *verb*
• (*to like*) = aimer
he enjoys fishing = il aime la pêche
did you enjoy your holiday? = est-ce que
tu as passé de bonnes vacances?
• (*to have a good time*) ▶ 237 |
to enjoy oneself = s'amuser (**!** + *être*)

enjoyable *adjective*
= agréable

enormous *adjective*
= énorme

enough
1 *determiner*
= assez de
I don't have enough [time | friends …] = je n'ai pas assez [de temps | d'amis …]
there's enough room for everyone = il y a assez de place pour tout le monde
2 *adverb*
= assez
is it big enough? = est-ce que c'est assez grand?
you're not old enough = tu n'es pas assez grand
3 *pronoun*
= assez
we have enough to eat = nous avons assez à manger
I've had enough = j'en ai assez
that's enough = ça suffit

enquire *verb*
= se renseigner (**!** + *être*)
I'll enquire about the price = je vais me renseigner sur le prix

enter *verb*
• (*to go into*) = entrer dans (**!** + *être*)
• (*to take part in*) = participer à

entertain *verb*
= divertir

entertaining *adjective*
= divertissant/divertissante

entertainment *noun*
entertainment = le divertissement, les distractions (*feminine plural*)

enthusiasm *noun*
enthusiasm = l'enthousiasme (*masculine*)

enthusiastic *adjective*
= enthousiaste

entrance *noun*
an entrance = une entrée
the entrance to the castle = l'entrée du château

envelope *noun*
an envelope = une enveloppe

environment *noun*
the environment = l'environnement (*masculine*)

envy
1 *noun*
envy = l'envie (*feminine*)
2 *verb*
= envier

episode *noun*
an episode = un épisode

equal
1 *adjective*
= égal/égale
to fight for equal rights = lutter pour l'égalité des droits

2 *verb*
= égaler
six and four equals ten = six et quatre égalent dix

equality *noun*
equality = l'égalité (*feminine*)

equator *noun*
the equator = l'équateur (*masculine*)

equipment *noun*
equipment (*in an office, a laboratory, a factory*) = le matériel
(*for an activity*) = l'équipement (*masculine*)

eraser *noun*
an eraser = une gomme

escalator *noun*
an escalator = un escalier mécanique

escape *verb*
• (*to get away*) = s'échapper (**!** + *être*)
he escaped from prison = il s'est échappé de prison
• (*to avoid*) = échapper à
to escape death = échapper à la mort

especially *adverb*
= surtout

essay *noun*
an essay (*by a pupil*) = une rédaction
(*by a student*) = une dissertation

essential *adjective*
= essentiel/essentielle

ethnic *adjective*
= ethnique

euro *noun*
a euro = un euro

eurocheque *noun*
a eurocheque = un Eurochèque

Europe *noun* ▶ 218 |
Europe = l'Europe (*feminine*)

European *adjective* ▶ 275 |
= européen/européenne

European Union *noun*
the European Union = l'Union européenne
! *Note that* **Union** *is feminine.*

evacuate *verb*
= évacuer

even¹
1 *adverb*
• (*when expressing surprise*) = même
he didn't even try = il n'a même pas essayé
she even works on weekends = elle travaille même le week-end
• (*in comparisons*) = encore
it's even colder today = il fait encore plus froid aujourd'hui

2 even though = bien que
he's bored even though he's with other
people = bien qu'il soit avec d'autres
personnes, il s'ennuie

! *Note that the subjunctive is used after*
bien que.

even² *adjective*
* (*flat, smooth*) = régulier/régulière
* (*when talking about numbers*)
an even number = un nombre pair

evening *noun* ▶ 211 |, ▶ 356 |

! *Note that evening is usually translated*
by soir in French. However it is sometimes
translated by soirée, when there is an
emphasis on the idea of duration.

an evening = un soir
at eight o'clock in the evening = à huit
heures du soir
to spend the evening at home = passer la
soirée à la maison

event *noun*
an event = un événement

eventually *adverb*

! *Note that eventually is never translated*
by éventuellement.

= finalement

ever *adverb*
* (*at any time*)
nothing ever happens here = il ne se
passe jamais rien ici
no-one will ever know = personne ne le
saura jamais
have you ever been to Greece? = est-ce
que tu es déjà allé en Grèce?
I hardly ever go there = je n'y vais presque
jamais
* (*always*)
he's as lazy as ever = il est toujours aussi
paresseux

every *determiner* ▶ 356 |
= tous les/toutes les
every time I meet her = toutes les fois que
je la rencontre
every day = tous les jours
every second day, every other day = tous
les deux jours
two out of every three people = deux
personnes sur trois

everyone *pronoun* (*also* **everybody**)
= tout le monde
everyone else = tous les autres

everything *pronoun*
= tout

everywhere *adverb*
= partout
everywhere else = partout ailleurs

evidence *noun*
a piece of evidence = une preuve
to give evidence = témoigner

evil *noun*
evil = le mal

exact *adjective*
= exact/exacte

exactly *adverb*
= exactement

exaggerate *verb*
= exagérer

exam *noun*
an exam = un examen
to pass an exam = réussir à un examen
to take an exam = passer un examen

examine *verb*
= examiner

example *noun*
an example = un exemple
for example = par exemple

excellent *adjective*
= excellent/excellente

except *preposition*
= sauf

exchange *verb*
= échanger
to exchange a hat for a scarf = échanger
un chapeau contre une écharpe

exchange rate *noun*
the exchange rate = le taux de change

excited *adjective*
= excité/excitée

exciting *adjective*
= passionnant/passionnante

exclude *verb*
= exclure

excuse
1 *noun*
an excuse = une excuse
to make excuses = trouver des excuses
2 *verb*
= excuser
excuse me! = excusez-moi!

exercise *noun*
* (*to keep fit*)
an exercise = un exercice
to take exercise, to do exercise = faire de
l'exercice
* (*a piece of work*)
an exercise = un exercice

exercise book *noun*
an exercise book = un cahier

exhausted *adjective*
= épuisé/épuisée

exhibition *noun*
an exhibition = une exposition

exit *noun*
an exit = une sortie

expect verb
* (to be prepared for) = s'attendre à (**!** + être)
  to expect bad news = s'attendre à de mauvaises nouvelles
  they expect to win = ils s'attendent à gagner
* (to wait for) = attendre
* (to want) = vouloir
  they expect us to do the work = ils veulent que nous fassions le travail

  | **!** Note that the subjunctive is used after vouloir que.

expenses noun
  expenses = les frais (masculine)

expensive adjective
  = cher/chère

experience noun
  an experience = une expérience

experienced adjective
  = expérimenté/expérimentée

experiment
1 noun
  an experiment = une expérience
2 verb
  = expérimenter

expert noun
  an expert = un spécialiste/une spécialiste
  a computer expert = un spécialiste/une spécialiste en informatique

explain verb
  = expliquer
  to explain a rule to someone = expliquer une règle à quelqu'un

explanation noun
  an explanation = une explication

explode verb
  = exploser

exploit verb
  = exploiter

explosion noun
  an explosion = une explosion

export verb
  = exporter

express
1 verb
  to express oneself = s'exprimer (**!** + être)
2 adverb
  to send a letter express = envoyer une lettre en exprès

expression noun
  an expression = une expression

express train noun
  an express train = un rapide

extinct adjective
  (describing an animal) = disparu/disparue
  (describing a volcano) = éteint/éteinte

extra
1 adjective
  = supplémentaire
  an extra bed = un lit supplémentaire
  to pay an extra ten pounds = payer dix livres de plus
2 adverb
  to pay extra = payer un supplément

extraordinary adjective
  = extraordinaire

extreme adjective
  = extrême

extremely adverb
  = extrêmement

eye noun ▶ **201** |
  an eye = un œil
  to have green eyes = avoir les yeux verts

eyebrow noun ▶ **201** |
  an eyebrow = un sourcil

eyelash noun ▶ **201** |
  an eyelash = un cil

eyelid noun ▶ **201** |
  an eyelid = une paupière

eye shadow noun
  eye shadow = le fard à paupières

eyesight noun
  eyesight = la vue
  to have good eyesight = avoir une bonne vue

Ff

face
1 noun
  the face = le visage, la figure
  to make a face = faire une grimace
2 verb
  (to be opposite) = être face à
  she was facing me = elle était face à moi
  (to have to deal with) = confronter
  I can't face seeing them again = je n'ai pas le courage de les revoir
  (to look toward(s))
  my room faces the sea = ma chambre donne sur la mer
face up to = faire face à

fact
1 noun
  a fact = un fait
2 in fact = en fait

factory noun
  a factory = une usine

Useful everyday expressions in spoken French

When things are going well

well done!	= bravo!	congratulations!	= félicitations!
	= chapeau✱!	good luck!	= bonne chance!
	(I take my hat	way to go! (US English)	= bravo!
	off to him / you etc)	wow!	= super✱!, génial✱!

When things are not so good

hard luck!	= pas de chance!	good luck! (you'll need it)	= bon courage!
too bad !	= tant pis!	ouch!	= aïe!, ouïlle!
cheer up!, chin up!	= courage!	shit!	= merde☛!
oh dear!	= oh là là✱!	yuck!, ugh!	= beurk✱!
	= ça alors!	phew! (that was close)	= ouf!
damn!	= ah, mince✱!	get well soon!	= bon rétablissement!,
blast!	= zut✱!		remets-toi vite!

Coming

welcome!	= bienvenue!
nice to meet you, pleased to meet you	= enchanté/enchantée de faire votre connaissance
hello!	= bonjour! (face to face)
	= allô, bonjour! (on the phone)
hi!	= salut✱!
hi again!	= rebonjour✱!

Going

goodbye!	= au revoir!
bye!	= salut✱! tchao✱!
cheers! (British English)	= salut✱!
see you soon / later / next week!	= à bientôt! / plus tard! / la semaine prochaine!
see you around!	= à un de ces jours!
(have a) safe journey!	= bon voyage!
all the best!	= bonne continuation!

Wishing someone well

have a nice day!	= bonne journée!
have a good weekend!	= bon week-end!
have a great holiday or vacation!	= bonnes vacances!
have a good time!, enjoy yourself!	= amuse-toi bien!, amusez-vous bien!
have a good trip!	= bon voyage!

Special greetings

Happy birthday!	= Bon anniversaire!	Happy New Year!	= Bonne année!
Happy Christmas!	= Joyeux Noël!	April fool!	= poisson d'avril!

In reply to: 'Would you like ... ?'

yes, please	= volontiers
	= oui, je veux bien!
	= pourquoi pas?

In reply to: 'Thank you'

you're very welcome	= je t'en prie, je vous en prie
don't mention it	= (il n'y a) pas de quoi
no problem, not at all	= de rien

Eating and drinking

enjoy your meal!	= bon appétit!
cheers!	= santé!, à la tienne!, à la vôtre!, tchin! tchin!

Sleeping

good night!	= bonne nuit!	sweet dreams!	= fais de beaux rêves!
sleep well!	= dors bien!		

✱ in informal situations   ☛ may be considered offensive

fade verb
(if it's a material) = se décolorer (! + être)
(if it's a colour) = passer (! + être)

fail verb
= échouer
to fail an exam = échouer à un examen

failure noun
a failure (an event, an attempt) = un échec
(a person) = un raté/une ratée

faint verb
= s'évanouir (! + être)

fair
1 adjective
(just) = juste
it's not fair = ce n'est pas juste
(in colour)
to have fair hair = avoir les cheveux
blonds
to have fair skin = avoir le teint clair
2 noun
(British English) (a funfair)
a fair = une fête foraine
(a display of goods)
a (trade) fair = une foire

fairly adverb
= assez

faith noun
to have faith in someone = avoir
confiance en quelqu'un

faithful adjective
= fidèle

fall
1 verb
(if it's a person) = tomber (! + être)
she fell to the ground = elle est tombée
par terre
(to come down, to be reduced) = baisser
(other uses)
to fall asleep = s'endormir (! + être)
to fall ill = tomber malade (! + être)
to fall in love with someone = tomber
amoureux/amoureuse de quelqu'un
2 noun
(in prices, temperature)
a fall = une baisse
a fall in prices = une baisse des prix
(US English) (autumn)
fall = l'automne (masculine)
fall down
(if it's a person) = tomber (! + être)
(if it's a building) = s'effondrer (! + être)
fall off = tomber (! + être)
to fall off a chair = tomber d'une chaise
fall out
(from somewhere) = tomber (! + être)
the letter fell out of his pocket = la lettre
est tombée de sa poche
(to quarrel) = se brouiller (! + être)

fall over = tomber (par terre) (! + être)
fall through = tomber à l'eau

false adjective
= faux/fausse

false teeth noun
false teeth = un dentier (singular)

familiar adjective
= familier/familière

family noun
a family = une famille

famous adjective
= célèbre

fan noun
(of a pop star, an actor, a sport)
a fan = un fan/une fan
(for cooling)
a fan (electric) = un ventilateur
(hand-held) = un éventail

fancy dress party noun (British
English)
a fancy dress party = une soirée costumée

fantastic adjective
= formidable, super✶

far
1 adverb
▶ 285
far (away) = loin
how far is it to London? = Londres est à
combien de kilomètres?
how far is Oxford from London? = Oxford
est à quelle distance de Londres?
we went as far as the coast = nous
sommes allés jusqu'à la côte
(in time)
as far back as 1950 = déjà en 1950
(very much) = beaucoup
you're eating far too much bread = tu
manges beaucoup trop de pain
we know far fewer people here = on
connaît beaucoup moins de monde ici
2 adjective
= autre (! before the noun)
at the far side of the room = de l'autre côté
de la pièce
3 so far = jusqu'ici

fare noun
the fare (on a bus or the underground) = le
prix du ticket
(on a train or plane) = le prix du billet

farm noun
a farm = une ferme

farmer noun ▶ 315
a farmer = un fermier

fascinating adjective
= fascinant/fascinante

fashion noun
fashion = la mode
to be in fashion = être à la mode
to go out of fashion = se démoder
(! + être)

fashionable *adjective*
= à la mode

fast
1 *adjective*
(*describing movement*) = rapide
to be fast = avancer
my watch is ten minutes fast = ma montre
avance de dix minutes
2 *adverb*
= vite, rapidement

fasten *verb*
to fasten a seatbelt = attacher une
ceinture de sécurité

fast-forward *verb*
to fast-forward a cassette = faire avancer
rapidement une cassette

fat *adjective*
= gros/grosse (**!** *before the noun*)
to get fat = grossir

fatal *adjective*
= mortel/mortelle

father *noun*
a father = un père

Father Christmas *noun* (*British
English*)
Father Christmas = le père Noël

father-in-law *noun*
a father-in-law = un beau-père

faucet *noun* (*US English*)
a faucet = un robinet

fault *noun*
to be someone's fault = être (de) la faute
de quelqu'un
it's not my fault = ce n'est pas (de) ma
faute
whose fault was it? = à qui la faute?

favour (*British English*), **favor** (*US
English*)
1 *noun*
a favour = un service
to do someone a favour = rendre (un)
service à quelqu'un
to ask someone a favour = demander un
service à quelqu'un
2 in favour of
to be in favour of a change in the law
= être pour un changement de la loi

favourite (*British English*), **favorite** (*US
English*) *adjective*
= préféré/préférée
it's my favourite film = c'est mon film
préféré

fax *noun*
a fax = un fax

fear *noun*
fear = la peur

feather *noun*
a feather = une plume

February *noun* ▶ **222**
February = février (*masculine*)

fed up *adjective*
to be fed up = en avoir marre✸

fee *noun*
a fee (*to attend an event, a show*) = un
droit d'entrée
(*to join a club, a union*) = une cotisation

feeble *adjective*
= faible

feed *verb*
= nourrir
I must feed the children = je dois donner à
manger aux enfants

feel *verb*
(*referring to an emotion, an impression*)
to feel happy = être heureux/heureuse
he's feeling uncomfortable = il se sent
mal à l'aise
to feel afraid = avoir peur
I feel as if I'm being followed = j'ai
l'impression qu'on me suit
it feels like winter = on se croirait en hiver
it feels good to be back home = ça fait du
bien d'être chez soi
(*referring to a physical feeling*)
to feel [hot | cold | sleepy …] = avoir [chaud |
froid | sommeil …]
to feel ill = se sentir malade
to feel a draught = sentir un courant d'air
I don't feel a thing = je ne sens rien
(*describing how something seems*)
the box felt very heavy = la boîte était
lourde
the room feels very cold = la pièce est très
froide
(*to touch*) = tâter, toucher
to feel like [going out | eating | dancing …]
= avoir envie de [sortir | manger | danser …]
I don't feel like it = je n'en ai pas envie

feeling *noun*
(*emotional*)
a feeling = un sentiment
to hurt someone's feelings = blesser
quelqu'un
(*physical*)
a feeling = une sensation
I have a feeling he's right = j'ai
l'impression qu'il a raison

felt-tip pen *noun*
a felt-tip pen = un crayon feutre

female *adjective*
(*in biology*) = femelle
(*relating to women*) = féminin/féminine

feminine *adjective*
= féminin/féminine

fence *noun*
a fence = une clôture

fencing *noun* ▶ **248**
fencing = l'escrime (*feminine*)

F

festival *noun*
a festival = une fête

fetch *verb*
= aller chercher
go and fetch some water = va chercher de l'eau

fever *noun*
to have a fever = avoir de la fièvre

few ▶ 317 |
1 a few
a few [people | houses | books ...] = quelques [personnes | maisons | livres ...]
a few of the houses were burned down = quelques-unes des maisons ont été brûlées
a few of them speak Greek = quelques-uns d'entre eux parlent grec
I would like a few more = j'en voudrais quelques-uns/quelques-unes de plus

! Note that it is necessary to use en, which may be translated as 'of them', with phrases like a few. See also another, a lot, none etc for this use of en.

2 *determiner*
(*not many*) = peu de
few [visitors | letters | meals ...] = peu de [visiteurs | lettres | repas ...]
(*several*)
the first few weeks = les premières semaines
3 *pronoun*
= peu
few of us succeeded = peu d'entre nous ont réussi
there are so few of them (*of people*) = ils sont si peu nombreux
(*of things*) = il y en a tellement peu

fewer ▶ 317 |
1 *determiner*
= moins de
fewer shops = moins de magasins
2 *pronoun*
= moins
fewer than ten people = moins de dix personnes

fewest
1 *determiner*
the fewest = le moins de
they have the fewest advantages = ce sont eux qui ont le moins d'avantages
2 *pronoun*
the fewest = le moins

field *noun*
a field = un champ

fifteen *number* **▶ 187 |, ▶ 211 |**
fifteen = quinze

fifteenth *number*
(*in a series*) = quinzième
(*in dates*) **▶ 222 |**
the fifteenth of May = le quinze mai

fifth *number*
(*in a series*) = cinquième
(*in dates*) **▶ 222 |**
the fifth of June = le cinq juin

fifty *number* **▶ 187 |, ▶ 211 |**
fifty = cinquante

fight
1 *verb*
to fight (against) prejudice = lutter contre les préjugés
to fight for justice = lutter pour la justice
(*in war*) = se battre (! + *être*)
to fight the enemy = combattre l'ennemi
(*physically*) = se battre (! + *être*)
(*to quarrel*) = se disputer (! + *être*)
2 *noun*
(*a campaign*)
a fight = une lutte
(*physical*)
a fight = une bagarre
fight back = se défendre (! + *être*)

figure *noun*
(*a number*)
a figure = un chiffre
to have a good figure = être bien fait/bien faite

file *noun*
a file (*for documents*) = un dossier
(*in a computer*) = un fichier
in single file = en file indienne

fill *verb*
(*to make full*) = remplir
(*to become full*) = se remplir (! + *être*)
fill in = remplir

film
1 *noun*
(*in cinema or on TV*)
a film = un film
(*for a camera*)
a film = une pellicule
2 *verb*
= filmer

filthy *adjective*
= sale

final
1 *adjective*
= dernier/dernière (! *before the noun*)
2 *noun*
a final = une finale

finally *adverb*
= finalement

find *verb*
= trouver
find out
to find out the truth = découvrir la vérité
if he ever finds out he'll be furious = si jamais il l'apprend il sera furieux

fine
1 *adjective*
(*very good, excellent*) = beau/belle
(! *before the noun*)
the weather is fine = il fait beau

(*in good health*)
I feel fine = je me sens très bien
(*expressing agreement*)
(that's) fine = d'accord
2 *noun*
a fine = une amende

finger *noun* ▶ **201**
a finger = un doigt

finish
1 *verb*
(*to end*) = finir
to finish writing a letter = finir d'écrire
    une lettre
(*to come to an end*) = finir
2 *noun*
the finish (*in a race*) = l'arrivée (*feminine*)

Finland *noun* ▶ **218**
Finland = la Finlande

fire
1 *noun*
fire = le feu
a fire (*for heat*) = un feu
(*causing damage*) = un incendie
to catch fire = prendre feu
to be on fire = être en feu
2 *verb*
(*to shoot*) = tirer
(*to dismiss*) = renvoyer

fire alarm *noun*
a fire alarm = une sonnerie d'alarme
    incendie

fire brigade (*British English*), **fire
department** (*US English*) *noun*
the fire brigade = les pompiers (*masculine
    plural*)

fire engine *noun*
a fire engine = une voiture de pompiers

fireman *noun* ▶ **315**
a fireman = un pompier

fire station *noun*
a fire station = une caserne de pompiers

fireworks display *noun*
a fireworks display = un feu d'artifice

firm
1 *noun*
a firm = une entreprise
2 *adjective*
= ferme

first
1 *adjective*
= premier/première (**!** *before the noun*)
the first time = la première fois
the first three weeks = les trois premières
    semaines
2 *adverb*
(*to begin with*) = d'abord
first of all = tout d'abord
(*for the first time*) = pour la première fois

to arrive first = arriver le premier/la
première
3 *noun*
(*in a series or group*)
the first = le premier/la première
he was the first to congratulate us = il a
    été le premier à nous féliciter
(*in dates*) ▶ **222**
the first of June = le premier juin
4 at first = au début

first aid *noun*
first aid = les premiers soins

> **!** Note that **soins** is masculine plural.

first class *adverb*
to travel first class = voyager en première
    classe

first floor *noun*
the first floor (*in Britain*) = le premier étage
(*in the US*) = le rez-de-chaussée

first name *noun*
a first name = un prénom

fish
1 *noun*
a fish = un poisson
2 *verb*
to go fishing = aller à la pêche

fisherman *noun* ▶ **315**
a fisherman = un pêcheur

fishing *noun* ▶ **248**
fishing = la pêche

fishing rod *noun*
a fishing rod = une canne à pêche

fist *noun* ▶ **201**
the fist = le poing

fit
1 *verb*
the shoes don't fit me = les chaussures ne
    me vont pas
the photo won't fit into the envelope = la
    photo ne rentre pas dans l'enveloppe
will the table fit here? = est-ce qu'il y a de
    la place pour la table ici?
2 *adjective*
(*suitable, capable*)
the house isn't fit to live in = la maison
    n'est pas habitable
to be fit to drive = être en état de conduire
he's not fit to be a minister = il n'est pas
    capable d'être ministre
(*healthy*)
to be fit = être en forme
fit in
(*in a room or car*)
can you all fit in? = est-ce qu'il y a de la
    place pour vous tous?
(*in a group or team*) = s'intégrer (**!** + *être*)

fitness *noun*
(physical) fitness = la forme (physique)

F

five *number* ▶ **187** ▶ **211**
  five = cinq
  five apples = cinq pommes
  I've got five (of them) = j'en ai cinq

fix *verb*
  (*to decide on, to set*) = fixer
  (*to repair*) = réparer
  to get a watch fixed = faire réparer une
    montre
  (*to prepare*) = préparer

flag *noun*
  a flag = un drapeau

flame *noun*
  a flame = une flamme
  to go up in flames = s'enflammer
    (**!** + *être*)

flash
1 *noun*
  a flash (*for a camera*) = un flash
2 *verb*
  to flash (on and off) = clignoter

flashlight *noun*
  a flashlight = une lampe de poche

flask *noun*
  a flask = un thermos

flat
1 *noun* (*British English*)
  a flat = un appartement
2 *adjective*
  = plat/plate
  to have a flat tyre = avoir un pneu à plat

flavour (*British English*), **flavor** (*US English*) *noun*
  a flavour (*of food*) = une saveur, un goût
  (*of ice cream, yogurt*) = un parfum

flea *noun*
  a flea = une puce

flight *noun*
  a flight = un vol

flight attendant *noun* ▶ **315**
  a flight attendant = un steward/une
    hôtesse de l'air

float *verb*
  = flotter
  to float up into the air = s'envoler (**!** + *être*)

flock *noun*
  (*of sheep, goats, geese*)
  a flock = un troupeau
  (*of birds*)
  a flock = une volée

flood *noun*
  a flood = une inondation

floor *noun*
  (*a surface*)
  a floor = un plancher
  to sit on the floor = s'asseoir par terre
  (*a storey*)
  a floor = un étage

florist *noun* ▶ **315**
  a florist = un fleuriste/une fleuriste

flour *noun*
  flour = la farine

flow *verb*
  (*if it's a liquid*) = couler
  (*if it's traffic*) = circuler

flower
1 *noun*
  a flower = une fleur
2 *verb*
  = fleurir

flu *noun* ▶ **266**
  flu = la grippe

fluently *adverb*
  = couramment

flush *verb*
  to flush the toilet = tirer la chasse d'eau

flute *noun* ▶ **290**
  a flute = une flûte

fly
1 *noun*
  a fly = une mouche
2 *verb*
  (*if it's a bird, a kite, a plane, an insect*)
    = voler
  (*if it's a passenger*) = prendre l'avion
  to fly from London to Paris = aller de
    Londres à Paris en avion
  to fly a plane = piloter un avion
  (*if it's a flag*) = flotter
  fly away = s'envoler (**!** + *être*)

fog *noun*
  fog = le brouillard

fold *verb*
  to fold a shirt = plier une chemise
  to fold one's arms = croiser les bras

folder *noun*
  a folder (*for work*) = une chemise
  (*in computing*) = un dossier

follow *verb*
  (*to go or come after*) = suivre
  (*to use, to look at*) = suivre
  I followed the signposts = j'ai suivi les
    panneaux indicateurs

following *adjective*
  = suivant/suivante

fond *adjective*
  I'm very fond of you = je t'aime beaucoup

food *noun*
  food = la nourriture

fool *verb*
  = tromper, duper

foot *noun*
  (*part of the leg*) ▶ **201**
  the foot = le pied
  on foot = à pied

(*of a rabbit, a cat, a dog, a cow*)
the foot = la patte
(*in measurements*) ▶ **285**
a foot = un pied
| ! *Note that a* **foot** = *30.48 cm.*

football *noun* ▶ **248**
football (*soccer*) = le football
(*American football*) = le football américain
(*a ball*)
a football = un football

footballer (*British English*), **football player** (*US English*) *noun* ▶ **315**
a footballer = un joueur/une joueuse de football

footprint *noun*
a footprint = une trace de pas

footstep *noun*
a footstep = un pas

for *preposition*
▶ **244** *See the boxed note on* for *for more information and examples.*
for = pour
the letter is for you = la lettre est pour toi
to work for a company = travailler pour une entreprise
he cooked dinner for us = il nous a préparé à manger
(*when talking about time*)
we've been living here for two years = on habite ici depuis deux ans, ça fait deux ans qu'on habite ici
he's going to Paris for a year = il va à Paris pour un an
she read for two hours = elle a lu pendant deux heures
I've been waiting for three hours = ça fait trois heures que j'attends
he won't arrive for another two weeks = il ne va pas arriver avant deux semaines
(*when talking about distance*) = pendant
we drove for 80 kilometres = nous avons roulé pendant 80 kilomètres
(*when talking about money*)
he bought it for £50 = il l'a acheté pour 50 livres
a cheque for £20 = un chèque de 20 livres
(*in favour of*) = pour
say hello to her for me = donne-lui le bonjour de ma part
(*other uses*)
T for Tom = T comme Tom
the Minister for Education = le ministre de l'éducation
what is the French for 'badger'? = comment dit-on 'badger' en français?
we went [for a swim | for a run | for a walk ...] = nous sommes allés [nager | courir | nous promener ...]

forbid *verb*
= interdire
to forbid someone to go out = interdire à quelqu'un de sortir
smoking is forbidden = il est interdit de fumer

force
1 *verb*
= forcer
to force someone to leave = forcer quelqu'un à partir
2 *noun*
force = la force
by force = de force

forecast *noun*
the forecast = les prévisions (*feminine plural*)
the forecast is for rain = la météo prévoit de la pluie

forehead *noun* ▶ **201**
the forehead = le front

foreign *adjective*
= étranger/étrangère

foreigner *noun*
a foreigner = un étranger/une étrangère

forest *noun*
a forest = une forêt

forever, for ever *adverb*
= pour toujours

forget *verb*
= oublier
to forget about someone = oublier quelqu'un
to forget [to do the shopping | to eat | to call ...] = oublier [de faire les courses | de manger | de téléphoner ...]

forgive *verb*
to forgive someone = pardonner à quelqu'un

fork *noun*
a fork = une fourchette

form
1 *noun* ▶ **245**
(*a shape*)
a form = une forme
(*a document*)
a form = un formulaire
(*referring to mood or fitness*)
to be in good form = être en bonne forme
(*British English*) (*a class*)
a form = une classe
to be in the sixth form = être en terminale
2 *verb*
(*to create, to make*) = former
to form a circle = former un cercle
(*to start, to set up*) = créer

formal *adjective*
(*describing language*) = soutenu/soutenue
to wear formal clothes (*for the evening*) = être en tenue de soirée
(*official*) = officiel/officielle

former *adjective*
= ancien/ancienne (! *before the noun*)

fortnight *noun* ▶ **356** (*British English*)
a fortnight = quinze jours (*masculine plural*)

for

Some general uses

for is generally translated by **pour**:

    for my sister   = **pour** ma sœur
    for me   = **pour** moi

When **for** followed by a verb is used to explain the purpose of something, it is translated by **pour** + *infinitive*:

    a product for losing weight   = un produit **pour** maigrir

When talking about time

for in time expressions may be translated by **depuis**, **pendant** or **pour**. The following examples are designed to show you which translation to choose. Note that tense is very important in distinguishing between them.

- When **for** is used to express the time period of something that started in the past and is still going on, French uses either *present tense* + **depuis** or **ça fait�** + **que** + *present tense*:

    I have been waiting for three hours = j'attends **depuis** trois heures
    (and I am still waiting)   = **ça fait✱** trois heures **que** j'attends

    we've been together for two years = nous sommes ensemble **depuis** deux ans
    (and we're still together)   = **ça fait✱** deux ans **que** nous sommes ensemble

When **for** is used after a verb in the past perfect tense placing an event even further back in time, French uses either *imperfect* + **depuis** or **ça faisait✱** ... **que** + *imperfect*:

    I had been waiting for two hours = j'attendais **depuis** deux heures
    (and was still waiting)   = **ça faisait✱** deux heures **que** j'attendais

- When **for** is used in negative sentences with the present perfect tense to express the time that has elapsed since something has happened, French uses the same tense as English, either *perfect* + **depuis** or **ça fait✱** ... **que** + *perfect*:

    I haven't seen him for ten years = je ne l'ai pas vu **depuis** dix ans
    (and I still haven't seen him)   = **ça fait✱** dix ans que je ne l'ai pas vu

When **for** is used in negative sentences after a verb in the past perfect tense, again placing events further back in time, French uses either *past perfect* + **depuis** or **ça faisait✱** ... **que** + *past perfect*:

    I hadn't seen him for ten years = je ne l'avais pas vu **depuis** dix ans
                         = **ça faisait✱** dix ans que je ne l'avais pas vu

- When **for** is used to express the time period of something that happened in the past and is no longer going on, French uses *present perfect* + **pendant**:

    last Sunday I read for two hours = dimanche dernier j'ai lu **pendant** deux heures

- When **for** is used to express a time period in the future, French uses *present* or *future* + **pour**:

    I'm going to Montreal for six weeks = je vais à Montréal **pour** six semaines
    I will go to Montreal for six weeks = j'irai à Montréal **pour** six semaines

- When the verb **to be** is used in the future with **for** to emphasize the period of time, French uses *future* + **pendant**:

    I will be in Brussels for six weeks = je serai à Bruxelles **pendant** six semaines

    ✱ in informal situations

---

fortunately *adverb*
  = heureusement

fortune *noun*
  a fortune = une fortune
  to make a fortune = faire fortune
  to tell someone's fortune = dire la bonne
  aventure à quelqu'un

forty *number* ▶ **187** |, ▶ **211** |
  forty = quarante

forward
  1 *adverb*
    = en avant
    to step forward = faire un pas en
    avant

Forms of address (Miss, Mr, Mrs)

When speaking to someone

Where English puts the surname after the title, French normally uses the title alone:

Good morning, **Miss Jones**	= bonjour, **Mademoiselle**
Good evening, **Mr Halpin**	= bonsoir, **Monsieur**
Good morning, **Mrs Davies**	= bonjour, **Madame**

When speaking about someone

In this case, French and English behave the same:

*Miss Jones	Mr Halpin	Mrs Davies*	= Mademoiselle Jones / Monsieur Halpin /
is here	Madame Davies est là

When writing to someone

When starting a letter, translations will differ according to the degree of formality involved:

	formal	less formal
Dear Miss Jones	= Mademoiselle	= Chère Mademoiselle
Dear Mr Halpin	= Monsieur	= Cher Monsieur
Dear Mrs Davies	= Madame	= Chère Madame

▶ There is no French equivalent of **Ms** but one can use **Madame** in similar circumstances.

---

2 *verb*
  to forward a letter to someone = faire
  suivre une lettre à quelqu'un

found *verb*
  = fonder

fountain *noun*
  a fountain = une fontaine

four *number* ▶ **187** , ▶ **211**
  four = quatre
  four apples = quatre pommes
  I've got four (of them) = j'en ai quatre

fourteen *number* ▶ **187** , ▶ **211**
  fourteen = quatorze

fourteenth *number*
  (*in a series*) = quatorzième
  (*in dates*) ▶ **222**
  the fourteenth of July = le quatorze juillet

fourth *number*
  (*in a series*) = quatrième
  (*in dates*) ▶ **222**
  the fourth of July = le quatre juillet

fox *noun*
  a fox = un renard

fragile *adjective*
  = fragile

frame *noun*
  a frame = un cadre

France *noun* ▶ **218**
  France = la France

frank *adjective*
  = franc/franche

freckle *noun*
  a freckle = une tache de rousseur

free
1 *adjective*
  (*costing nothing*) = gratuit/gratuite
  (*independent, able to come and go*) = libre
  he is free to do what he likes = il est libre
  de faire ce qu'il veut
  (*not occupied, available*) = libre
  are you free on Monday? = est-ce que tu
  es libre lundi?
2 *verb*
  = libérer
3 *adverb*
  = gratuitement

freedom *noun*
  freedom = la liberté

freeway *noun* (*US English*)
  a freeway = une autoroute

freeze *verb*
  (*in cold weather*) = geler
  the river froze = la rivière a gelé
  the ground was frozen = le sol était gelé
  (*in a freezer*) = congeler
  to freeze to death = mourir de froid

freezer *noun*
  a freezer = un congélateur

F

freezing *adjective*
  it's freezing = il fait un temps glacial
  this room is freezing = cette pièce est
    glaciale
  to be freezing (*if it's a person*) = être
    gelé/gelée

French ▶ 275 |
  1 *adjective*
  = français/française
  2 *noun*
  (*the people*)
  the French = les Français (*masculine
    plural*)
  (*the language*)
  French = le français

French fries *noun*
  French fries = les frites (*feminine*)

fresh *adjective*
  = frais/fraîche

Friday *noun* ▶ 222 |
  Friday = vendredi (*masculine*)

fridge *noun*
  a fridge = un frigo✶

fried *adjective*
  = frit/frite

fried egg *noun*
  a fried egg = un œuf sur le plat

friend *noun*
  a friend = un ami/une amie
  to make friends = se faire des amis
  to make friends with someone = devenir
    ami/amie avec quelqu'un

friendly *adjective*
  = gentil/gentille

fright *noun*
  to get a fright = avoir peur
  to give someone a fright = faire peur à
    quelqu'un

frightened *adjective*
  to be frightened = avoir peur

fringe *noun* (*British English*)
  a fringe = une frange

frog *noun*
  a frog = une grenouille

from *preposition*

  ! *There are many verbs which involve the
  use of* from, *like* borrow from, escape from
  etc. For translations, look up the entries at
  borrow, escape *etc.*

from = de (**!** d' + *vowel or mute h*)
  the boy from London = le garçon (qui
    vient) de Londres
  where is she from? = d'où vient-elle?
  to come back from the office = rentrer du
    bureau
  to return from a holiday = rentrer de
    vacances
  there's a message from Paul = il y a un
    message de Paul
  the train from Oxford is late = le train en
    provenance d'Oxford est en retard
  we live ten minutes from the city centre
    = nous habitons à dix minutes du
    centre-ville
  (*when talking about time*) = de, à partir de
  the shop is open from eight to six = le
    magasin est ouvert de huit heures à
    dix-huit heures
  from Monday to Saturday = du lundi au
    samedi
  from April on = à partir du mois d'avril
  from then on = à partir de ce moment-là
  fifty years from now = d'ici cinquante ans
  (*British English*) (*in arithmetic*)
  5 from 8 leaves 3 = 5 ôté de 8, il reste 3

front
  1 *noun*
  (*of a building*)
  the front of a house = la façade d'une
    maison
  the front of a shop = la devanture d'un
    magasin
  my room is at the front of the house = ma
    chambre est sur le devant de la maison
  (*of a car, a train or queue*)
  at the front of the bus = à l'avant du bus
  at the front of the queue = au début de la
    queue
  2 in front of = devant

front door *noun*
  the front door = la porte d'entrée

front page *noun*
  the front page = la première page

front seat *noun*
  the front seat = le siège avant

frost *noun*
  frost = le givre, la gelée

frozen *adjective*
  = congelé/congelée

fruit *noun*
  a piece of fruit = un fruit
  he likes fruit = il aime les fruits

frustrated *adjective*
  = frustré/frustrée

fry *verb*
  to fry potatoes = faire frire des pommes de
    terre

frying pan *noun* (*British English*)
  a frying pan = une poêle

full *adjective*
  (*not empty*) = plein/pleine
  the streets were full of people = les rues
    étaient pleines de monde
  (*describing a flight, a hotel*)
  = complet/complète
  (*maximum*)
  to travel at full speed = rouler à toute
    vitesse
  to get full marks = obtenir la note
    maximale
  (*complete*)
  to pay the full fare = payer plein tarif
  his full name = ses nom et prénom

full-time *adverb*
  = à plein temps
  to work full-time = travailler à plein temps

fumes *noun*
  fumes = les fumées (*feminine*)

fun *noun*
  it's fun = c'est amusant
  skiing is fun = c'est amusant de faire du
    ski
  to have fun = s'amuser (**!** + *être*)
  she's fun = on s'amuse bien avec elle

function *verb*
  = fonctionner

funeral *noun*
  a funeral = un enterrement

funfair *noun* (*British English*)
  a funfair = une fête foraine

funny *adjective*
  (*amusing*) = drôle, amusant/amusante
  (*odd*) = drôle, bizarre

fur *noun*
  fur (*an animal's coat*) = les poils (*masculine
    plural*)
  (*on a garment*) = la fourrure

furious *adjective*
  = furieux/furieuse

furniture *noun*
  a piece of furniture = un meuble
  furniture = les meubles

further *adverb*
  = plus loin
  he lives further away from the school = il
    habite plus loin de l'école
  how much further is it? = c'est encore
    loin?

fuss *noun*
  a fuss = des histoires (*feminine plural*)

future
1 *noun*
  the future = l'avenir (*masculine*)
  in the future = dans l'avenir
  in future, let us know = à l'avenir, préviens-
    nous
2 *adjective*
  = futur/future

gallery *noun*
  a gallery = un musée

game *noun*
  a game = un jeu
  a game of football = un match de football
  a game of tennis = une partie de tennis

games *noun* (*British English*)
  games = le sport

G

game show *noun*
  a game show = un jeu télévisé

gang *noun*
  a gang (*a group of friends, young people*)
    = une bande
  (*of criminals*) = un gang

gap *noun*
  a gap (*in a fence or hedge*) = un trou
  (*between buildings, cars*) = un espace
  (*a period of time*)
  a gap = un intervalle

garage *noun*
  a garage = un garage

garbage *noun* (*US English*)
  garbage = les ordures (*feminine plural*)

garden
1 *noun*
  a garden = un jardin
2 *verb*
  = faire du jardinage

gardener *noun* ▶ 315
  a gardener = un jardinier/une jardinière

gardening *noun*
  gardening = le jardinage

garlic *noun*
  garlic = l'ail (*masculine*)

gas *noun*
  (*for cooking, heating*)
  gas = le gaz
  (*US English*) (*gasoline*)
  gas = l'essence (*feminine*)

gas station *noun* (*US English*)
  a gas station = une station-service

gate *noun*
  a gate (*to a garden, a town, a prison*) = une
    porte
  (*to a field*) = une barrière

gather *verb*
  (*to come together*) = se rassembler
  (**!** + *être*)

Games and sports

With or without the definite article?

French normally uses **le, la, l'** or **les** with names of games and sports:

football	= le football
chess	= les échecs (*masculine plural*)
to play football	= jouer au football
to play tennis	= jouer au tennis
to play chess	= jouer aux échecs
to go climbing	= faire de l'escalade
to beat somebody at tennis	= battre quelqu'un au tennis
to win at chess	= gagner aux échecs
to lose at marbles	= perdre aux billes

Players and events

a tennis player	= un joueur de tennis

but

I'm not a tennis player	= je ne joue pas au tennis
he's a good tennis player	= il joue bien au tennis
a game of tennis	= une partie de tennis
a tennis champion	= un champion de tennis
the French tennis champion	= le champion de France de tennis
a tennis championship	= un championnat de tennis
the rules of tennis	= les règles du tennis

- (*to collect*)
  to gather wood = ramasser du bois
  to gather fruit = cueillir des fruits

gay *adjective*
= homosexuel/homosexuelle

gear *noun*
- (*in a car or bus, on a bike*)
  a gear = une vitesse
- (*equipment*)
  gear = le matériel
  fishing gear = le matériel de pêche
- (*clothes*)
  my football gear = ma tenue de football
  your swimming gear = tes affaires pour la
  piscine

Gemini *noun*
  Gemini = Gémeaux (*masculine*)

general
1 *noun*
  a general = un général
2 *adjective*
  = général/générale
3 in general = en général

generation *noun*
  a generation = une génération

generous *adjective*
  = généreux/généreuse

Geneva *noun* ▶ 218 |
  Geneva = Genève

genius *noun*
  a genius = un génie

gentle *adjective*
  = doux/douce

gentleman *noun*
  a gentleman = un monsieur

geography *noun*
  geography = la géographie

germ *noun*
  a germ = un microbe

German ▶ 275 |
1 *adjective*
  = allemand/allemande
2 *noun*
- (*the people*)
  the Germans = les Allemands (*masculine*)
- (*the language*)
  German = l'allemand (*masculine*)

Germany *noun* ▶ 218 |
  Germany = l'Allemagne (*feminine*)

get *verb*
▶ *See the boxed note on* **get** *for more
information and examples.*
get away
- (*to escape*) = s'échapper (**!** + *être*)
- **he won't get away with it** = il ne va pas s'en
  tirer comme ça
get back
- (*to return*) = revenir (**!** + *être*)
- (*to have back*) = récupérer
  I got my bike back = j'ai récupéré mon
  vélo
  he'll get his money back = il va être
  remboursé

get

A multi-purpose verb

The word **get** is extremely common in English and does not have a multi-purpose French equivalent.

However, it is helpful to try to find a synonym (a word which has the same sense) and from there, a suitable translation:

*he's gone to **get** (or **fetch**) help*	= il est parti **chercher** de l'aide
*I'll call when **we get** (or **arrive**) there*	= j'appellerai quand **nous arriverons**

Main senses

When changing from one state (of mind) to another

French very often has a specific verb for the various combinations of **to get** + *adjective*:

*to get old	angry	worried*	= vieillir / se fâcher / s'inquiéter

devenir + *adjective* is also useful:

*to **get** jealous*	= **devenir** jaloux / jalouse

When asking, telling or persuading

The translations **dire** (à **quelqu'un**) and **demander** (à **quelqu'un**) are helpful:

***get him** to call me*	= **dis-lui** de m'appeler
*I'll **get her** to help me*	= je **lui demanderai** de m'aider

When getting things done by someone else

The construction **faire** + *infinitive verb* is useful here:

*to **get** the car **cleaned***	= **faire nettoyer** la voiture
*to **get** a TV **repaired***	= **faire réparer** une télévision
*to **get** one's hair **cut***	= **se faire couper** les cheveux

When *to get* means *to obtain*

*to **get** (or **buy**)someone a present*	= **acheter** un cadeau à quelqu'un
*I **got** (or **found**) a job in Paris*	= j'**ai trouvé** un travail à Paris

When *to get* means *to receive*

The best translation is **recevoir**:

*we **got** a letter from Mark*	= nous **avons reçu** une lettre de Mark

but

*to **get** good grades*	= **avoir** de bonnes notes

When cooking

A translation which will work well is **préparer**:

*to **get** dinner*	= **préparer** le déjeuner

With illnesses:

In this context **attraper** is useful:

*to **get** measles*	= **attraper** la rougeole
*to **get** a cold*	= s'enrhumer (+ *être*)

When using transport

The most reliable translation is **prendre**:

*we can **get** the bus*	= on peut **prendre** le bus
*to **get** a taxi to the station*	= **prendre** un taxi pour aller à la gare

▶ To find translations for other expressions using **get**—to get sick, to get a surprise, to get better, etc. —look up the entries at **sick**, **surprise**, **better**, etc.

▶ You will also find translations for *phrasal verbs* using **get** (**get down**, **get away**, **get on**, **get up**) listed separately in the dictionary.

get down
* (to come or go down) = descendre
  (**!** + être)
  can he get down from the tree? = est-ce qu'il peut descendre de l'arbre?
* (to take down) = descendre (**!** + avoir)
  I got the box down from the shelf = j'ai descendu la boîte de l'étagère
* (to depress) = déprimer
  it gets him down = ça le déprime

get in = entrer (**!** + être)

get off
* (to leave a bus or train) = descendre
  (**!** + être)
  I'm getting off at the next stop = je descends au prochain arrêt
  he fell as he was getting off the train = il est tombé en descendant du train
* (to remove) = enlever
  to get a stain off = enlever une tache

get on
* (to climb on board a bus or train) = monter
  (**!** + être)
  to get on the bus = monter dans le bus
* (to get on well) = bien s'entendre (**!** + être)
  I get on well with her = je m'entends bien avec elle
* (in polite enquiries)
  how did you get on? = comment est-ce que ça s'est passé?
  how is she getting on at school? = et ses études, ça marche✗?

get out
* (to leave) = sortir (**!** + être)
  she got out of the building = elle est sortie du bâtiment
* (to take out) = sortir (**!** + avoir)
  to get the furniture out of the house = sortir les meubles de la maison

get over
  to get over a shock = se remettre d'un choc

get through to
  to get through to someone = avoir quelqu'un au téléphone

get together = se réunir (**!** + être)

get up = se lever (**!** + être)

ghost *noun*
  a ghost = un fantôme

gift *noun*
* (a present)
  a gift = un cadeau
* (an ability)
  a gift = un don
  to have a gift for languages = avoir le don des langues

ginger *adjective* ▶ **213**
  = roux/rousse
  to have ginger hair (British English) = avoir les cheveux roux

girl *noun*
  a girl = une fille

girlfriend *noun*
  a girlfriend (in a couple) = une (petite) amie
  (a female friend) = une amie

give *verb*
  ! For translations of expressions like to give someone a lift, to give someone an injection, to give someone a fright etc, look up the entries **lift**, **injection**, **fright**.

* **to give** = donner
  to give someone a book = donner un livre à quelqu'un
  I gave him the photos = je lui ai donné les photos
  give me the newspapers = donne-moi les journaux
  give them to me = donne-les-moi
  to give someone a drink = donner à boire à quelqu'un
  to give one's seat to someone = laisser sa place à quelqu'un
* (to offer) = offrir
  he gave us one of his pictures = il nous a offert un de ses tableaux
  to give someone a present = faire un cadeau à quelqu'un
* **to give someone a message** = transmettre un message à quelqu'un

give away
* (to make a present of) = donner
* **to give away a secret** = révéler un secret

give back = rendre

give in = céder

give off
  to give off fumes = dégager des vapeurs

give out
  to give out the exercise books = distribuer les cahiers

give up
* (to stop)
  to give up smoking = cesser de fumer
  to give up the idea of working abroad = renoncer à l'idée de travailler à l'étranger
* **to give oneself up to the police** = se livrer à la police

glad *adjective*
  = content/contente

glass *noun*
  a glass = un verre

glasses *noun*
  glasses = les lunettes (feminine)

glove *noun*
  a glove = un gant

glow *verb*
  = luire

glue
1 *noun*
  glue = la colle

✗ in informal situations

2 *verb*
= coller

go *verb*
▶ **253**| *See the boxed note on* go *for more information and examples.*
go across = traverser
go after = poursuivre
go ahead
* (*if it's an event*) = avoir lieu
  the concert's going ahead after all = le concert aura finalement lieu
* (*if it's a person*)
  go ahead, there's no-one there = vas-y, il n'y a personne
go around ▶ **go round**
go around with ▶ **go round with**
go away = partir (**!** + *être*)
  go away! = allez-vous-en!, va-t'en!
go back = retourner (**!** + *être*)
  Gary went back to Paris = Gary est retourné à Paris
  to go back to school = reprendre les cours
  to go back to work = reprendre le travail
  to go back to sleep = se rendormir (**!** + *être*)
go by = passer (**!** + *être*)
go down
* (*if it's quality, a price, a salary*) = baisser
* (*if it's a person*) = descendre
  she went down into the basement = elle est descendue au sous-sol
  we went down the hill = nous avons descendu la pente
* (*if it's the sun*) = se coucher (**!** + *être*)
* (*if it's a computer*) = tomber en panne (**!** + *être*)
go in
* (*to enter*) = entrer (**!** + *être*)
* (*to return inside*) = rentrer (**!** + *être*)
go off
* (*to explode*) = exploser
* (*to ring*) (*if it's an alarm clock*) = sonner
  (*if it's an alarm*) = se déclencher (**!** + *être*)
* (*to leave*) = partir (**!** + *être*)
* the milk will go off = le lait va tourner
* (*to be switched off*) = s'éteindre (**!** + *être*)
go on
* (*to continue*) = continuer
  to go on talking = continuer à parler
* (*to happen*)
  what's going on? = qu'est-ce qui se passe?
* (*to keep talking*)
  he goes on (and on) about his work = il n'arrête pas de parler de son travail
* (*to be switched on*) (*if it's a light*) = s'allumer (**!** + *être*)
  (*if it's heating, a machine*) = se mettre en marche (**!** + *être*)
go out
* (*to leave the house*) = sortir (**!** + *être*)
  are you going out this evening? = est-ce que tu sors ce soir?
* (*as a boyfriend, a girlfriend*)
  to go out with someone = sortir avec quelqu'un

* (*to be switched off, to stop burning*) = s'éteindre (**!** + *être*)
* the tide's going out = la marée descend
go over
* (*to check*)
  to go over some grammar = vérifier quelques points de grammaire
* (*to revise*) = revoir
go round
* (*British English*) (*to call on*) = passer (**!** + *être*)
  to go round to see someone = passer voir quelqu'un
* (*to walk around, to visit*) = visiter
  to go round the museums = visiter les musées
  to go round the shops = faire les magasins
* (*to be enough*)
  is there enough bread to go round? = est-ce qu'il y a assez de pain pour tout le monde?
go round with
  (*British English*) (*to spend time with*) = fréquenter
go through
* (*to have, to live through*)
  to go through a difficult time = traverser une période difficile
  I don't want to go through that again = je ne voudrais pas revivre ça
* (*to search*) = fouiller
* (*to check*) = examiner
go together = aller ensemble
  the skirt and blouse go well together = la jupe et la chemise vont bien ensemble
go up
* (*if it's a person*) = monter
  he went up to bed = il est monté se coucher
  he went up the stairs = il a monté l'escalier
  to go up to the top of the hill = monter jusqu'en haut de la colline
  to go up to the top floor = monter jusqu'au dernier étage
* (*if it's a price, a salary*) = augmenter
go with = aller avec (**!** + *être*)
  the trousers don't really go with your jacket = le pantalon ne va pas très bien avec ta veste

goal *noun*
  a goal = un but

goalkeeper *noun*
  a goalkeeper = un gardien de but

goat *noun*
  a goat = une chèvre

god *noun*
  a god = un dieu
  God = Dieu

goddaughter *noun*
  a goddaughter = une filleule

godfather *noun*
  a godfather = un parrain

G

godmother *noun*
a godmother = une marraine

godson *noun*
a godson = un filleul

going: to be going to
= aller
I'm going to [leave | go to Ireland | learn to
drive …] = je vais [partir | aller en Irlande |
apprendre à conduire …]
we were going to phone you = on allait te
téléphoner

gold
1 *noun*
gold = l'or (*masculine*)
2 *adjective*
= en or
a gold ring = une bague en or

goldfish *noun*
a goldfish = un poisson rouge

golf *noun* ▶ 248 |
golf = le golf

golf course *noun*
a golf course = un terrain de golf

good
1 *adjective*
• good = bon/bonne (**!** *before the noun*)
a good book = un bon livre
a good party = une bonne soirée
we've got some good news = nous avons
de bonnes nouvelles
to have good eyesight = avoir une bonne
vue
to be good [at chemistry | at drawing | at
chess …] = être bon/bonne [en chimie | en
dessin | aux échecs …]
it's a good time to visit Paris = c'est le bon
moment pour visiter Paris
exercise is good for you = ça fait du bien
de faire de l'exercice
to look good (*healthy*) = avoir bonne mine
I don't feel too good = je ne me sens pas
très bien
I had a good time = je me suis bien amusé
• (*talking about food*) = bon/bonne (**!** *before
the noun*)
• (*obedient*) = sage
• (*kind*) = gentil/gentille
it's very good of you to let me know = c'est
très gentil de votre part de me prévenir
2 *noun*
it's no good shouting = ça ne sert à rien
de crier
to be no good at Latin = être nul/nulle✶ en
latin
the change will do you good = le
changement te fera du bien
3 *exclamation*
• (*when pleased*)
good = c'est bien

• (*when relieved*)
'he's much better'—'good' = 'il va
beaucoup mieux'—'tant mieux'
• (*when praising*)
good! = très bien!
4 for good = pour toujours

good afternoon *noun* (*also
exclamation*)
good afternoon (*when meeting*) = bonjour
(*when leaving*) = au revoir

goodbye *noun* (*also exclamation*)
goodbye = au revoir

good evening *noun* (*also exclamation*)
good evening = bonsoir

good-looking *adjective*
= beau/belle (**!** *before the noun*)

good morning *noun* (*also exclamation*)
good morning (*when meeting*) = bonjour
(*when leaving*) = au revoir

goodnight *noun* (*also exclamation*)
goodnight = bonne nuit

goods *noun*
goods = la marchandise (*singular*)

goose *noun*
a goose = une oie

gooseberry *noun*
a gooseberry = une groseille à maquereau

gorilla *noun*
a gorilla = un gorille

gossip *verb*
• (*to chat*) = bavarder
• (*to talk in a harmful way*) = faire des
commérages

got: to have got *verb*
▶ See the boxed note on **got** for more
information and examples.
• (*to have*) = avoir
I've got work to do = j'ai du travail
have you got a cold? = est-ce que tu as un
rhume?
• (*to be obliged to*)
to have got to = devoir
I've got to [go | work | get dressed …] = je
dois [partir | travailler | m'habiller …], il faut
que [je parte | je travaille | je m'habille …]
! *Note that the subjunctive is used after* il
faut que.

government *noun*
a government = un gouvernement

GP *noun* ▶ 315 | (*British English*)
a GP = un médecin, un généraliste

grab *verb*
to grab someone by the arm = saisir
quelqu'un par le bras
he tried to grab my handbag = il a essayé
d'arracher mon sac à main

✶ *in informal situations*

go

▶ You will find translations for phrasal verbs like **go away**, **go back**, **go round**, etc listed separately in the dictionary.

▶ For translations of expressions like **I'm going to leave** / **go to London** / **learn to drive**, see the entry **going**.

Getting from A to B

Generally **go** is translated by **aller** (**!** + *être*):

we went to the cinema	= nous sommes allés au cinéma
to go to town / *to school* / *to the market*	= aller en ville / à l'école / au marché
to go to Brussels / *to Germany* / *to Japan*	= aller à Bruxelles / en Allemagne / au Japon
to go to the dentist's / *the doctor's* / *the chemist's*	= aller chez le dentiste / le médecin / le pharmacien
to go for a swim / *for a coffee* / *for a walk*	= aller nager / prendre un café / se promener

G

Translating verbs of movement in French

Moving in, out, back away etc is usually translated using a single verb in French which takes **être**:

to go into a room	= entrer dans une pièce
to go away on vacation	= partir en vacances
to go back to work in France	= retourner travailler en France
to go home	= rentrer
to go outside	= sortir
to go upstairs	= monter

See also the phrasal verbs listed separately for further translations.

go meaning *to become*

There is often a single French verb to translate the structure **to go** + *adjective*:

to go pale	= pâlir
to go red	= rougir

but

the light went red	= le feu est passé au rouge

devenir + *adjective* is a useful alternative:

to go crazy	= devenir fou / folle
to go blind	= devenir aveugle

In polite inquiries

how's it going?	= comment ça va?
everything's going very well	= tout va très bien
how did the exam go?	= comment s'est passé l'examen?

Talking about time, money, food ...

the time goes so quickly	= le temps passe si vite
50 euros won't go far here	= on n'ira pas loin avec 50 euros ici
the money's / *bread's* / *petrol's gone*	= il n'y a plus d'argent / de pain / d'essence

Describing how (and if) something works

is the car going?	= est-ce que la voiture marche?
it's still not going	= ça ne marche toujours pas
to get the heating going	= mettre le chauffage en marche

grade *noun*
* (*a mark*)
  a grade = une note
* (*US English*) (*a class*)
  a grade = une classe
  he's in the eighth grade = il est en
    quatrième

grade school *noun* (*US English*)
  grade school = l'école primaire
  | **!** *Note that* école *is feminine.*

gradually *adverb*
  = peu à peu

gram(me) *noun* ▶ 285 |
  a gram = un gramme

grammar *noun*
  grammar = la grammaire

grandchild *noun*
  a grandchild = un petit-fils/une petite-
    fille
  the grandchildren = les petits-enfants

granddaughter *noun*
  a granddaughter = une petite-fille

grandfather *noun*
  a grandfather = un grand-père

grandmother *noun*
  a grandmother = une grand-mère

grandparents *noun*
  grandparents = les grands-parents
    (*masculine*)

grandson *noun*
  a grandson = un petit-fils

grapefruit *noun*
  a grapefruit = un pamplemousse

grapes *noun*
  grapes = le raisin (*singular*)
  a bunch of grapes = une grappe de raisin

grass *noun*
  grass = l'herbe (*feminine*)
  (*in gardens*) = la pelouse
  to cut the grass = tondre la pelouse

grasshopper *noun*
  a grasshopper = une sauterelle

grateful *adjective*
  = reconnaissant/reconnaissante
  **I would be grateful if you could let me
    know** = je vous serais reconnaissant de
    me prévenir

grave *noun*
  a grave = une tombe

gray (*US English*) ▶**grey**

grease *noun*
  grease = la graisse

greasy *adjective*
  = gras/grasse

great *adjective*
* (*stressing size, amount, importance*)
  = grand/grande (**!** *before the noun*)
  a great improvement = une grande
    amélioration
  to have great difficulty reading = avoir
    beaucoup de mal à lire
  the guide book was a great help = le
    guide a été très utile
* (*showing enthusiasm*)
  that's great! = c'est formidable!, c'est
    génial**✗**!
  I had a great time = je me suis bien amusé

Great Britain *noun* ▶ 218 |
  Great Britain = la Grande-Bretagne

great grandfather *noun*
  a great grandfather = un arrière-grand-
    père

great grandmother *noun*
  a great grandmother = une arrière-grand-
    mère

Greece *noun* ▶ 218 |
  Greece = la Grèce

greedy *adjective*
  = gourmand/gourmande

Greek ▶ 275 |
1 *adjective*
  = grec/grecque
2 *noun*
* (*the people*)
  the Greeks = les Grecs (*masculine*)
* (*the language*)
  Greek = le grec

green *adjective* ▶ 213 |
  = vert/verte

greenhouse *noun*
  a greenhouse = une serre

grey (*British English*), **gray** (*US English*)
adjective ▶ 213 |
  = gris/grise
  to have grey hair = avoir les cheveux gris

grill *verb*
  = faire griller

grin *verb*
  = sourire

grocer *noun* ▶ 315 |
  a grocer = un épicier/une épicière

grocery *noun* ▶ 315 |
  a grocery = une épicerie

ground *noun*
* **the ground** = le sol
  the ground is hard in winter = le sol est
    dur en hiver
  to throw papers on the ground = jeter des
    papiers par terre
  to get up off the ground = se lever
    (**!** + *être*)

✗ *in informal situations*

- (*land used for sports*)
  a **sports ground** = un terrain de sport

ground floor *noun* (*British English*)
  the **ground floor** = le rez-de-chaussée

group *noun*
- (*a number of people*)
  a **group** = un groupe
- (*a band*)
  a (**rock**) **group** = un groupe (de rock)

grow *verb*
- (*to get big, strong*) (*if it's a person, an animal*) = grandir
  (*if it's a plant*) = pousser
- (*as a gardener, a farmer*) = cultiver
  to **grow vegetables** = cultiver des légumes
- (*to get long*) = pousser
  she's decided to let her hair **grow** = elle a décidé de se laisser pousser les cheveux
- (*to let grow*)
  to **grow a beard** = se laisser pousser la barbe
- (*to become*) = devenir (**!** + *être*)
  she's **grown** more cynical = elle est devenue plus cynique
  to **grow old** = vieillir
- (*to increase in size*)
  the population will **grow** = la population va augmenter
grow up = grandir
  when I **grow up**, I want to be a doctor = je veux être médecin quand je serai grand

grumble *verb*
  = ronchonner

guard *noun*
- (*in a prison, at a bank*)
  a **guard** = un gardien/une gardienne
- (*in the army*)
  a **guard** = un garde
  to be on **guard** = être de garde

guard dog *noun*
  a **guard dog** = un chien de garde

guess *verb*
  = deviner

guest *noun*
- (*a person invited to stay*)
  a **guest** = un invité/une invitée
- (*at a hotel*)
  a **guest** = un client/une cliente

guesthouse *noun*
  a **guesthouse** = une pension de famille

guide
1 *noun*
- (*a person*)
  a (**tour**) **guide** = un guide
- (*British English*) (*a Girl Guide*)
  a **guide** = une guide
2 *verb*
  = guider

guide book *noun*
  a **guide book** = un guide

guided tour *noun*
  a **guided tour** = une visite guidée

guilty *adjective*
  = coupable
  to feel **guilty** = culpabiliser

guinea pig *noun*
  a **guinea pig** = un cochon d'Inde

guitar *noun* ▶ **290**
  a **guitar** = une guitare

gum *noun*
  the **gum** = la gencive

gun *noun*
  a **gun** (*a weapon*) = une arme à feu
  (*a rifle*) = un fusil
  (*a revolver*) = un revolver

gym *noun*
  a **gym** = une salle de gym✱

gymnasium *noun*
  a **gymnasium** = un gymnase

gymnastics *noun* ▶ **248**
  gymnastics = la gymnastique

gypsy *noun*
  a **gypsy** = un gitan/une gitane

H

Hh

habit *noun*
  a **habit** = une habitude

hail *noun*
  hail = la grêle

hair *noun*
  hair (*on the head*) = les cheveux
  (*masculine plural*)
  (*on the body*) = les poils (*masculine plural*)

hairbrush *noun*
  a **hairbrush** = une brosse à cheveux

hairdresser *noun* ▶ **315**
  a **hairdresser** = un coiffeur/une coiffeuse

hairdryer *noun*
  a **hairdryer** = un sèche-cheveux

hairstyle *noun*
  a **hairstyle** = une coiffure

half ▶ **317**
1 *noun*
- a **half** = une moitié
  to cut a melon in **half** = couper un melon en deux
- (*in a game*)
  the first **half** = la première mi-temps

2 *adjective*
  a half-litre of milk, half a litre of milk = un demi-litre de lait
3 *pronoun*
• (*when talking about quantities, numbers*)
  to spend half of one's pocket money = dépenser la moitié de son argent de poche
  half the pupils speak French = la moitié des élèves parlent français
• (*when talking about time, age*) ▶ **211** , ▶ **187**
  an hour and a half = une heure et demie
  he's three and a half = il a trois ans et demi
  it's half (past) three (*British English*) = il est trois heures et demie
4 *adverb*
  Sam's half French half Irish = Sam est moitié français moitié irlandais

half hour *noun* ▶ **356**
  a half hour = une demi-heure

half term *noun* (*British English*)
  half term = les vacances de la mi-trimestre
  | **!** Note that **vacances** is feminine plural.

hall *noun*
• (*in a house, an apartment*)
  a hall = une entrée
• (*for public events*)
  a hall = une grande salle

ham *noun*
  ham = le jambon

hamburger *noun*
  a hamburger = un hamburger

hammer *noun*
  a hammer = un marteau

hamster *noun*
  a hamster = un hamster

hand *noun*
• (*the part of the body*) ▶ **201**
  the hand = la main
  he had a pencil in his hand = il avait un crayon à la main
  to hold someone's hand = tenir quelqu'un par la main
• (*help*)
  a hand = un coup de main
• (*on a clock or watch*)
  a hand = une aiguille
• (*when judging a situation or subject*)
  on the one hand…, on the other… = d'un côté…, d'un autre côté…

handbag *noun*
  a handbag = un sac à main

handball *noun* ▶ **248**
  handball = le handball

handicapped *adjective*
  = handicapé/handicapée

handkerchief *noun*
  a handkerchief = un mouchoir

handle *noun*
  a handle = une poignée

handsome *adjective*
  = beau/belle (**!** *before the noun*)
  a handsome man = un bel homme

handwriting *noun*
  handwriting = l'écriture (*feminine*)

handy *adjective*
• (*practical*) = pratique
• (*helpful*) = utile

hang *verb*
• (*on a hook, a coat hanger, a line*)
  to hang a picture (up) on the wall = accrocher un tableau au mur
  to hang clothes (up) in a wardrobe = suspendre des vêtements dans une armoire
  to hang clothes on a line = étendre du linge
• (*to be attached*)
  the portrait hangs over the piano = le portrait est accroché au-dessus du piano
  to be hanging from the ceiling = être suspendu/suspendue au plafond
• (*to kill*) = pendre
hang around
• (*to wait*) = attendre
• (*to waste time, to do nothing*) = traîner
hang on to = s'agripper à (**!** + *être*)
  she was hanging on to the rope = elle s'agrippait à la corde
hang up
• (*on a hook, a coat hanger, a line*)
  to hang up one's coat = accrocher son manteau
  to hang clothes up to dry = mettre des vêtements à sécher
• **your coat's hanging up in the hall** = ton manteau est suspendu dans l'entrée
• (*when phoning*) = raccrocher

hang-gliding *noun* ▶ **248**
  hang-gliding = le deltaplane

happen *verb*
• (*to occur*) = se passer (**!** + *être*), arriver (**!** + *être*)
  what happened? = qu'est-ce qui s'est passé?, qu'est-ce qui est arrivé?
  the accident happened last week = l'accident est arrivé la semaine dernière
  to happen again = se reproduire (**!** + *être*)
• (*to affect someone*)
  what happened to you? = qu'est-ce qui t'est arrivé?
  something odd happened to me = il m'est arrivé quelque chose de bizarre

happy *adjective*
- (*content*) = heureux/heureuse
  to make someone happy = rendre quelqu'un heureux
  they were happy to hear from you = ils ont été heureux d'avoir de tes nouvelles
  he's happy with the language course = le cours de langue lui plaît
- (*in greetings*)
  Happy birthday! = Bon anniversaire!
  Happy New Year! = Bonne année!

hard
1 *adjective*
- (*firm, stiff*) = dur/dure
  the ground is hard = le sol est dur
- (*difficult*) = difficile
  a hard question = une question difficile
  it's not hard to change a light bulb = ce n'est pas difficile de changer une ampoule
  it's hard to understand = c'est difficile à comprendre
  I find it hard to concentrate = j'ai du mal à me concentrer
- (*harsh, tough*)
  a hard winter = un hiver rude
  to be having a hard time = traverser une période difficile
- (*severe*) = dur/dure, sévère
2 *adverb*
  to work hard = travailler dur
  they hit him hard = ils l'ont frappé fort
  to try hard to concentrate = faire beaucoup d'efforts pour se concentrer

hardly *adverb*
  = à peine
  I hardly know them = je les connais à peine

hardware *noun*
  hardware (*for computers*) = le matériel (informatique)

hard-working *adjective*
  = travailleur/travailleuse

hare *noun*
  a hare = un lièvre

harm *verb*
  to harm someone = faire du mal à quelqu'un
  to harm the environment = nuire à l'environnement

harmful *adjective*
  = nocif/nocive

harmless *adjective*
  = inoffensif/inoffensive

harp *noun* ▶ **290** |
  a harp = une harpe

harvest *noun*
  the harvest (*of wheat*) = la moisson
  (*of fruit*) = la récolte
  (*of grapes*) = la vendange

hat *noun*
  a hat = un chapeau

hate *verb*
- (*to feel a strong dislike for*)
  to hate someone = détester quelqu'un
- (*to feel hatred for*) = haïr

hatred *noun*
  hatred = la haine

have
1 *verb*
▶ **258** | *See the boxed note on* **have** *for more information and examples.*
- (*to eat, to drink*)
  to have a sandwich = manger un sandwich
  to have a glass of wine = boire un verre de vin
  to have dinner = dîner
- (*to get*)
  I had a letter from Bob yesterday = j'ai reçu une lettre de Bob hier
  I'll let you have the money soon = je te donnerai l'argent bientôt
- (*to hold or organize*)
  to have a party = faire une fête
  to have a competition = organiser un concours
- (*to spend*) ▶ **237** |
  we had a nice day at the beach = nous avons passé une journée agréable à la plage
  I'll have a good time in Paris = je m'amuserai bien à Paris
- (*to suffer*)
  to have [flu | a headache | a toothache …] = avoir [la grippe | mal à la tête | mal aux dents …]
- (*to get something done*)
  to have the house painted = faire peindre la maison
  she had her hair cut = elle s'est fait couper les cheveux
- **to have a baby** = avoir un enfant
2 *auxiliary verb*

  ! *For a detailed note on the use of* **have** *as an auxiliary verb, see the boxed note on* **have**. *All verbs which don't take* **avoir** *as an auxiliary verb are marked* (**!** + **être**) *in this dictionary.*

  you've seen her, haven't you? = tu l'as vue, n'est-ce pas?
  he hasn't called, has he? = il n'a pas téléphoné, par hasard?
  'I've no money'—'yes you have!' = 'je n'ai pas d'argent'—'mais si tu en as!'
3 to have to = devoir
  I have to [study | pay | go home …] = je dois [étudier | payer | rentrer …]
  you don't have to go back to France = tu n'es pas obligé de retourner en France

hay *noun*
  hay = le foin

H

have

As an ordinary verb

● When **have** or **have got** is used as a verb meaning *possess*, it can generally be translated by **avoir**:

I have (got) a car	= j'ai une voiture
she has (got) a good memory	= elle **a** une bonne mémoire
they have (got) problems	= ils **ont** des problèmes

For examples and particular usages see the entry **have**; see also the entry **got**.

● **have** is also used with certain noun objects where the whole expression is equivalent to a verb:
to have dinner = to dine; *to have a walk* = to walk; *to have a swim* = to swim. In such cases, the phrase is very often translated by the equivalent verb in French (*dîner, se promener, se baigner*).

As an auxiliary verb

● When used as an auxiliary in present perfect and past perfect tenses, **have** is normally translated by **avoir**:

I have seen	= j'**ai** vu
I had seen	= j'**avais** vu

● However, some verbs in French, especially verbs of movement and change of state (*aller, venir, descendre, mourir*), always take **être** in these tenses:

he has left	= il **est** parti
she's fallen	= elle **est** tombée

In this case, remember the past participle agrees with the subject of the verb:

she has gone	= elle **est** allée
they had come back	= ils **étaient** revenus
we had stayed at home	= nous **étions** restés chez nous

If you are in doubt as to whether a verb conjugates with **être** or **avoir**, consult the French entry, where verbs taking **être** will be indicated like this: (**!** + *être*).

● Reflexive verbs (*se lever, se coucher*) always conjugate with **être**:

she has fainted	= elle **s'est** évanouie
have you had a rest?	= est-ce que tu **t'es** reposé?
he had fallen asleep	= il **s'était** endormi
I had changed my clothes	= je **m'étais** changé

In this case, the past participle agrees with the reflexive pronoun only when the pronoun is a direct object. Otherwise there is no agreement:

she has hurt herself	= elle **s'est** fait mal
I've washed my hair	= je **me suis** lavé les cheveux
he's broken his leg	= il **s'est** cassé la jambe

to have (got) to

● **to have (got) to** meaning *must* is translated by either **devoir** or the impersonal construction **il faut que** + *subjunctive*:

I have to leave now	= je **dois** partir maintenant
	= **il faut que** je parte maintenant
you've got to understand	= tu **dois** comprendre
	= **il faut que** tu comprennes

● In negative sentences, **not to have to** is usually translated by **ne pas être obligé / obligée de**:

you don't have to go	= tu **n'es pas obligé** d'y aller
we don't have to accept	= nous **ne sommes pas obligés** d'accepter

▶ For **have** used with illnesses, see usage note **Illnesses, aches, and pains ▶ 266**.

hazel *adjective* ▶ 213 |
= noisette (**!** *never changes*)

hazelnut *noun*
a hazelnut = une noisette

he *pronoun*
he = il
he's coming next week = il vient la
semaine prochaine
there he is = le voilà!
HE didn't write the letter = ce n'est pas lui
qui a écrit la lettre
I work in London but he doesn't = je
travaille à Londres mais lui non
he's a strange man = c'est un homme
bizarre

head
1 *noun*
• (*the part of the body*) ▶ 201 |
the head = la tête
• (*the mind*)
he's got it into his head that he's ugly = il
s'est mis dans la tête qu'il était laid
• a head of cabbage = un chou
a head of lettuce = une laitue
• (*the person in charge*)
the head = le responsable/la responsable,
le directeur/la directrice
a head of State = un chef d'État
2 *verb*
• (*to be in charge of*)
to head a team = être à la tête d'une
équipe
• (*in soccer*)
to head the ball = faire une tête
head for = se diriger vers (**!** + *être*)

headache *noun* ▶ 266 |
to have a headache = avoir mal à la tête
my headache's gone = mon mal de tête
est passé

headlamp, **headlight** *noun*
a headlamp = un phare

headline *noun*
a headline = un gros titre
to hit the headlines = faire la une des
journaux
the news headlines = les grands titres de
l'actualité

headquarters *noun*
the headquarters (*of a company, a
business*) = le siège social
(*of an army*) = le quartier général

headteacher *noun* ▶ 315 |
a headteacher = un directeur/une
directrice

health *noun*
health = la santé

healthy *adjective*
• (*in good health*) = en bonne santé
• (*good for the health*) = sain/saine

hear *verb*
• to hear = entendre
he can't hear anything = il n'entend rien
I heard someone coming in = j'ai entendu
quelqu'un entrer
you can hear him practising the piano
= on l'entend qui travaille le piano
• (*to learn, to discover*)
to hear the news = apprendre la nouvelle
I've heard about that school = j'ai
entendu parler de cette école
we've heard a lot about you = nous avons
beaucoup entendu parler de vous
• (*to listen to*) = écouter
hear from = avoir des nouvelles de
have you heard from Cathy? = est-ce que
tu as eu des nouvelles de Cathy?
hear of = entendre parler de
I've never heard of the place = je n'ai
jamais entendu parler de cet endroit

heart *noun*
• (*part of the body*) ▶ 201 |
the heart = le cœur
• (*the centre*)
right in the heart of London = en plein
cœur de Londres
• by heart = par cœur

heart attack *noun* ▶ 266 |
a heart attack = une crise cardiaque

heat
1 *verb*
= chauffer
2 *noun*
• the heat = la chaleur
I can't stand the heat = je ne supporte pas
la chaleur
• (*on a cooker*)
to cook at a low heat = faire cuire à feu
doux
• (*in a sporting contest*)
a heat = une épreuve éliminatoire
heat up
• (*to cook*) = faire chauffer
• (*to warm up again*) = réchauffer

heater *noun*
a heater = un appareil de chauffage

heating *noun*
heating = le chauffage

heatwave *noun*
a heatwave = une vague de chaleur

heaven *noun*
heaven = le paradis

heavy *adjective*
• (*in weight*) ▶ 285 | = lourd/lourde
• (*in quantity, intensity*)
the traffic is very heavy = il y a beaucoup
de circulation
to be a heavy smoker = beaucoup fumer
to have a heavy cold = avoir un gros
rhume
• (*describing food*) = lourd/lourde

H

• **it's very heavy today** = il fait très lourd aujourd'hui

hedge *noun*
a hedge = une haie

hedgehog *noun*
a hedgehog = un hérisson

heel *noun* ▶ **201** |
the heel = le talon

height *noun* ▶ **285** |
height (*of a person*) = la taille
(*of a building, a tree*) = la hauteur
to be afraid of heights = avoir le vertige

helicopter *noun*
a helicopter = un hélicoptère

hell *noun*
hell = l'enfer

hello *noun* (*also exclamation*) ▶ **237** |
hello! (*when greeting someone*) = bonjour!
(*on the phone*) = allô!

helmet *noun*
a helmet = un casque

help
1 *verb*
• to help = aider
to help someone to [walk | do the housework | escape …] = aider quelqu'un à [marcher | faire le ménage | s'échapper …]
the medicine helps to cure the illness = le médicament aide à guérir la maladie
to help each other = s'aider, s'entraider
(**!** + *être*)
• (*at a meal*)
to help oneself = se servir (**!** + *être*)
help yourselves! = servez-vous!
• I can't help thinking about it = je ne peux pas m'empêcher d'y penser
2 *exclamation*
help! = au secours!
3 *noun*
help (*a helping hand*) = l'aide (*feminine*)
(*urgent assistance*) = le secours
to ask someone for help = demander de l'aide à quelqu'un
to shout for help = crier au secours
help out = donner un coup de main

helpful *adjective*
• (*ready to help*) = serviable, aimable
• (*useful*) = utile

helping *noun*
a helping = une portion

helpless *adjective*
• (*having no power*)
= impuissant/impuissante
• (*because of weakness, ill health*)
= impotent/impotente

hen *noun*
a hen = une poule

her
1 *pronoun*

> **!** *Note that there is a boxed usage note at* **them**. *The entries* **me, him, her** *and* **us** *are modelled on this note where you will find detailed grammatical information and fuller explanations.*

• her = la (**!** l' + *vowel or mute h*)
I know her = je la connais
I don't know her = je ne la connais pas
do I know her? = est-ce que je la connais?
• he's seen her = il l'a vue
he hasn't seen her = il ne l'a pas vue
has he seen her? = est-ce qu'il l'a vue?
• catch her! = attrape-la!
help her! = aide-la!
don't help her! = ne l'aide pas!
don't hit her! = ne la frappe pas!
• I gave the book to her = je lui ai donné le livre
I didn't give the book to her = je ne lui ai pas donné le livre
did I give the book to her? = est-ce que je lui ai donné le livre?
• her = lui
write to her! = écris-lui!
say it to her! = dis-le-lui!
don't show it to her! = ne le lui montre pas!
• her = elle
he did it for her = il l'a fait pour elle
it's her = c'est elle
stand in front of her = mets-toi devant elle
2 *determiner*
her = son/sa (+ *singular*)
= ses (+ *plural*)

> **!** *Note that* **sa** *becomes* **son** *before a vowel or mute h.*

I hate her dog = je déteste son chien
what do you think of her house? = qu'est-ce que tu penses de sa maison?
she licked her plate = elle a léché son assiette
did you see all her CDs? = est-ce que tu as vu tous ses disques compacts?
she broke her leg = elle s'est cassé la jambe

> **!** *Note that, when talking about parts of the body,* **son, sa, ses** *are not used. See the usage note on* **The human body** ▶ **201** | *for further examples.*

herd *noun*
a herd = un troupeau

here *adverb*
• (*when talking about location*) = ici
is it far from here? = est-ce que c'est loin d'ici?
I'm up here = je suis là

- *(when drawing attention)*
  here's the post office = voici la poste
  here they are = les voici
  here's my telephone number = voici mon
    numéro de téléphone
  here comes the train = voilà le train
  here—take my pencil = tiens—prends mon
    crayon
- *(in general statements)* = là
  tell him I'm not here = dis-lui que je ne
    suis pas là
  we're here to help you = nous sommes là
    pour vous aider

hers *pronoun*
  the green pen is hers = le stylo vert est à
    elle
  which bag is hers? = lequel de ces sacs est
    le sien?
  my jacket is red but hers is green = ma
    veste est rouge mais la sienne est verte
  my parents are younger than hers = mes
    parents sont plus jeunes que les siens

  ! *Note that, when comparing objects,
  people, etc, one of the following
  translations—**le sien, la sienne, les siens**
  or **les siennes**—will be used. To know
  which one to use, find out whether the
  object, person, etc being described is
  masculine or feminine, singular or plural.*

herself *pronoun*
- *(when used as a reflexive pronoun)*
  she wants to enjoy herself = elle veut
    s'amuser
  she's cut herself with a knife = elle s'est
    coupée avec un couteau
- *(when used for emphasis)*
  she said it herself = elle l'a dit elle-même
  she did it all by herself = elle l'a fait toute
    seule

hesitate *verb*
  = hésiter

hi *exclamation*
  hi! = salut✶!

hiccups *noun*
  to have hiccups = avoir le hoquet

hidden *adjective*
  = caché/cachée

hide *verb*
- *(to avoid showing)* = cacher
  to hide documents from the police
    = cacher des documents à la police
- *(to avoid being seen)* = se cacher (**!** + *être*)

hi-fi *noun*
  a hi-fi = une chaîne hi-fi

high
1 *adjective* ▶ **285**⏐
- *(having a great height)* = haut/haute
  the mountains are high = les montagnes
    sont hautes
- *(describing a level, a price, a speed)*
  = élevé/élevée
  prices are high = les prix sont élevés
  the train travels at high speed = le train
    roule très vite

- *(describing a standard, grades)*
  the standard is high = le niveau est élevé
  to get high grades = avoir de très bonnes
    notes
- *(describing a voice)* = aigu/aiguë
2 *adverb*
  don't go any higher = ne montez pas plus
    haut

high rise block *noun*
  a high rise block = une tour d'habitation

high school *noun*
  a high school *(in the US)* = un
    établissement secondaire
  (in Britain) = un lycée

hijack *verb*
  = détourner

hike *verb*
  to go hiking = faire de la randonnée

hiking *noun* ▶ **248**⏐
  hiking = la randonnée

hill *noun*
  a hill = une colline
  (a rise in the road) = une pente

him *pronoun*

  ! *Note that there is a boxed usage note at
  them. The entries **me, him, her** and **us** are
  modelled on this note where you will find
  detailed grammatical information and
  fuller explanations.*

- **him** = le (**!** l' + *vowel or mute h*)
  I know him = je le connais
  I don't know him = je ne le connais pas
  do I know him? = est-ce que je le connais?
- **she's seen him** = elle l'a vu
  she hasn't seen him = elle ne l'a pas vu
  has she seen him? = est-ce qu'elle l'a vu?
- **catch him!** = attrape-le!
  help him! = aide-le!
  don't help him! = ne l'aide pas!
  don't hit him! = ne le frappe pas!
- **I gave the book to him** = je lui ai donné le
    livre
  I didn't give the book to him = je ne lui ai
    pas donné le livre
  did I give the book to him? = est-ce que je
    lui ai donné le livre?
- **him** = lui
  write to him! = écris-lui!
  say it to him! = dis-le-lui!
  don't show it to him! = ne le lui montre
    pas!
- **him** = lui
  he did it for him = il l'a fait pour lui
  it's him = c'est lui
  stand in front of him = mets-toi devant lui

himself *pronoun*
- *(when used as a reflexive pronoun)*
  he wants to enjoy himself = il veut
    s'amuser
  he's cut himself with a knife = il s'est
    coupé avec un couteau

H

- *(when used for emphasis)*
  he said it himself = il l'a dit lui-même
  he did it all by himself = il l'a fait tout seul

hip *noun* ▶ 201 |
  the hip = la hanche

hippopotamus, hippo *noun*
  a hippopotamus = un hippopotame

hire *verb*
- *(to employ)* = embaucher
- *(British English)* *(to rent)* = louer
  to hire a car = louer une voiture
- *(to lend for a fee)* = louer
  they hire (out) the skates = ils louent les
  patins

his
1 *determiner*
  his = son/sa *(+ singular)*
  = ses *(+ plural)*

  ! *Note that* **sa** *becomes* **son** *before a*
  vowel or mute h.

  I hate his dog = je déteste son chien
  what do you think of his house? = qu'est-
  ce que tu penses de sa maison?
  he licked his plate = il a léché son assiette
  did you see all his CDs? = est-ce que tu as
  vu tous ses disques compacts?
  he broke his arm = il s'est cassé le bras

  ! *Note that, when talking about parts of*
  the body, **son, sa, ses** *are not used. See*
  the usage note on **The human body**
  ▶ 201 | *for further examples.*

2 *pronoun*
  the blue pen is his = le stylo bleu est à lui
  which house is his? = laquelle de ces
  maisons est la sienne?
  my shirt is white but his is yellow = ma
  chemise est blanche mais la sienne est
  jaune
  my brother is taller than his = mon frère
  est plus grand que le sien

  ! *Note that, when comparing objects,*
  people, etc, one of the following
  translations—le sien, la sienne, les siens
  or les siennes—will be used. To know
  which one to use, find out whether the
  object, person, etc which is being
  described is masculine or feminine,
  singular or plural.

history *noun*
  history = l'histoire *(feminine)*

hit
1 *verb*
- *(to strike)* = frapper
  to hit someone on the head = frapper
  quelqu'un à la tête
  to hit one's head on a chair = se cogner la
  tête contre une chaise

- *(to crash into)*
  to hit a wall = heurter un mur
  to hit a pedestrian = renverser un piéton
2 *noun*
  a hit *(a song)* = un tube✶
  (a film, a play) = un succès
hit back = riposter
  to hit someone back = rendre un coup à
  quelqu'un

hitchhike *verb*
  = faire de l'auto-stop, faire du stop✶

hitchhiker *noun*
  a hitchhiker = un auto-stoppeur/une auto-
  stoppeuse

hoarse *adjective*
  to be hoarse = être enroué/enrouée

hobby *noun*
  a hobby = un passe-temps

hockey *noun* ▶ 248 |
  hockey = le hockey

hold
1 *verb*
- **to hold** = tenir
  he held some coins in his hand = il avait
  quelques pièces dans la main
- *(to arrange)*
  to hold a competition = organiser un
  concours
  the party will be held in the school = la
  fête aura lieu dans l'école
- *(to keep or hide)* = détenir
  to hold someone hostage = garder
  quelqu'un en otage
- *(to keep back)* = garder
  to hold a seat for someone = garder une
  place pour quelqu'un
- *(other uses)*
  to hold the world record = détenir le
  record mondial
  to hold someone responsible = tenir
  quelqu'un pour responsable
  to hold, to hold the line = patienter
2 *noun*
- **to get hold of the ball** = attraper le ballon
- **to get hold of someone** *(to find)* = trouver
  quelqu'un
  (by phone) = joindre quelqu'un
hold on
- *(to wait)* = attendre
- **hold on tight!** = tiens-toi bien!
hold on to = s'agripper à *(! + être)*
hold up
- *(to raise)* = lever
  to hold up one's hand ≈ lever le doigt
- *(to delay)*
  to hold someone up = retarder quelqu'un
  to hold up the traffic = ralentir la
  circulation
- *(to rob)* = attaquer

hole *noun*
  a hole = un trou

✶ in informal situations

holiday *noun*
- (*British English*) (*a vacation*)
  a holiday = des vacances (*feminine plural*)
  to go on holiday = partir en vacances
- (*a national or religious festival*)
  a (public) holiday = un jour férié
- (*British English*) (*time taken off work*)
  a day's holiday = un jour de congé
  to take two weeks' holiday = prendre quinze jours de congé

Holland *noun* ▶ **218** |
  Holland = la Hollande

holly *noun*
  holly = le houx

home
1 *noun*
- **a home** (*a place to live*) = un logement
  (*a house*) = une maison
  to leave home = quitter la maison
  to work from home = travailler à domicile
- (*for elderly, ill or disabled people*)
  a home for handicapped children = un établissement pour enfants handicapés
  an old people's home = une maison de retraite
2 *adverb*

  ! Note that **chez soi** *changes to* **chez moi, chez lui, chez eux,** *etc depending on the person whose home is being talked about.*

  to go home (*to one's house*) = retourner à la maison, rentrer (chez soi)
  (*to one's home country*) = rentrer (dans son pays)
  on my way home = en rentrant chez moi
  to be home (*from school, work*) = être rentré/rentrée
  I can take you home = je peux te raccompagner chez toi
3 **at home**
- (*in one's house*) = à la maison, chez soi
  she's working at home = elle travaille à la maison, elle travaille chez elle
  he lives at home = il habite chez ses parents
- **to feel at home** = se sentir à l'aise
  make yourselves at home = faites comme chez vous
- (*when talking about a sports team*) = à domicile

homeless *adjective*
  to be homeless = être sans abri, être sans logement

homesick *adjective*
  to be homesick (*when abroad*) = avoir le mal du pays

homework *noun*
  homework = les devoirs (*masculine plural*)

homosexual *noun*
  a homosexual = un homosexuel/une homosexuelle

honest *adjective*
- **honest** = honnête
- (*frank, sincere*) = franc/franche
  to be honest, I'd rather stay here = à vrai dire, je préfère rester ici

honestly *adverb*
  = franchement, honnêtement

honey *noun*
  honey = le miel

honeymoon *noun*
  a honeymoon = un voyage de noces

hood *noun*
- (*to cover the head*)
  a hood = un capuchon
- (*US English*) (*of a car*)
  the hood = le capot

hoof *noun*
  a hoof = un sabot

hook *noun*
- (*for hanging clothes, pictures*)
  a hook = un crochet
- (*for fishing*)
  a hook = un hameçon

hooligan *noun*
  a hooligan = un voyou, un vandale
  a football hooligan = un hooligan

hoover *verb* (*British English*)
  to hoover the house = passer l'aspirateur dans la maison

hop *verb*
  = sauter à cloche-pied

hope
1 *verb*
  = espérer
  I hope you don't mind = j'espère que cela ne vous dérange pas
  I hope she remembers to come = j'espère qu'elle pensera à venir

  ! Note that, when talking about the future, **espérer que** *is followed by the future tense.*

  we hope to meet lots of people = nous espérons rencontrer beaucoup de monde
  I hope so = j'espère que oui
2 *noun*
  hope = l'espoir (*masculine*)
  to give up hope = abandonner tout espoir

hopeless *adjective*
- (*without hope of success*)
  = désespéré/désespérée
- (*without any ability*) = nul/nulle
  to be hopeless at cooking = être incapable de faire la cuisine

horn *noun*
- (*on a car, a bus*)
  a horn = un klaxon
  to blow a horn = klaxonner

- (*of an animal*)
  a horn = une corne
- (*an instrument*) **▶ 290 |**
  a horn = un cor

horoscope *noun*
  the horoscope = l'horoscope (*masculine*)

horrible *adjective*
  = affreux/affreuse

horror film *noun*
  a horror film = un film d'épouvante

horse *noun*
  a horse = un cheval
  he likes horses = il aime les chevaux

horseracing *noun* **▶ 248 |**
  horseracing = les courses (*feminine plural*)

horseriding *noun* **▶ 248 |**
  horseriding = l'équitation (*feminine*)

hospital *noun*
  a hospital = un hôpital
  he's still in (the) hospital = il est toujours
    à l'hôpital
  to be taken to (the) hospital = être
    hospitalisé/hospitalisée

host *noun*
  a host = un hôte

hostage *noun*
  a hostage = un otage

hostel *noun*
  a hostel = un foyer

hostess *noun*
  a hostess = une hôtesse

hot *adjective*
- (*very warm*) = chaud/chaude
  to be hot, to feel hot = avoir chaud
  I'm very hot = j'ai très chaud
  it's too hot in the office = il fait trop chaud
    au bureau
  a hot meal = un repas chaud
- (*strong, with a lot of spices*)
  a hot mustard = une moutarde forte
  a very hot dish = un plat très épicé

hot air balloon *noun*
  a hot air balloon = une montgolfière

hot dog *noun*
  a hot dog = un hot dog

hotel *noun*
  a hotel = un hôtel

hour *noun* **▶ 211 |**, **▶ 356 |**
  an hour = une heure
  I earn two pounds an hour = je gagne
    deux livres (de) l'heure

house *noun*
  a house = une maison
  to go to someone's house = aller chez
    quelqu'un
  the bike is at my house = le vélo est chez
    moi

housewife *noun* **▶ 315 |**
  a housewife = une femme au foyer

housework *noun*
  to do the housework = faire le ménage

housing estate (*British English*),
housing development (*US English*)
noun
  a housing estate = une cité (ouvrière)

hovercraft *noun*
  a hovercraft = un aéroglisseur

how *adverb*
- (*in what way*) = comment
  how did you find us? = comment est-ce
    que tu nous as trouvés?
  I know how [to swim | to ride a horse | to cook
    a curry …] = je sais [nager | monter à cheval |
    préparer un curry …]
- (*in polite questions*)
  how are you? = comment allez-vous?,
    comment vas-tu?
  how is your sister? = comment va ta sœur?
  how was your holiday? = est-ce que tes
    vacances se sont bien passées?
- (*in questions requiring specific information*)
  how long will it take? = combien de temps
    faudra-t-il?
  how tall are you? = combien mesures-tu?
  how old is he? = quel âge a-t-il?
- (*when making a suggestion*)
  how would you like to eat out? = est-ce
    que ça te dirait d'aller au restaurant?
  how about going to the cinema tonight?
    = et si on allait au cinéma ce soir?

however *adverb*
- (*nevertheless*) = toutefois, cependant
- **however hard I try, I can't understand
  grammar** = j'ai beau essayer, je ne
  comprends pas la grammaire

how many ▶ 317 |
1 *pronoun*
  = combien
  how many do you want? = combien en
    voulez-vous?
  how many of you are there? = combien
    êtes-vous?
2 *determiner*
  = combien de
  how many children are going on the trip?
    = combien d'enfants vont participer à
    l'excursion?

how much ▶ 317 |
1 *pronoun*
  = combien
  how much does it come to? = ça fait
    combien?
  how much is the jacket? = combien coûte
    la veste?
2 *determiner*
  = combien de
  how much money do you have left?
    = combien d'argent est-ce qu'il te reste?

huge *adjective*
= énorme

human being *noun*
a human being = un être humain

humour (*British English*), **humor** (*US English*) *noun*
humour = l'humour (*masculine*)
to have a sense of humour = avoir le sens de l'humour

hundred *number* ▶ **187** |
one hundred, a hundred = cent
three hundred = trois cents
five hundred and fifty euros = cinq cent cinquante euros
about a hundred people = une centaine de personnes

Hungary *noun* ▶ **218** |
Hungary = la Hongrie

hungry *adjective*
to be hungry = avoir faim
I'm very hungry = j'ai très faim

hunt *verb* ▶ **248** |
= chasser
to go hunting = aller à la chasse

hurdles *noun* ▶ **248** |
the hurdles = la course de haies

hurrah, **hurray** *noun* (also *exclamation*)
hurrah! = hourra!

hurry
1 *verb*
• = se dépêcher (**!** + *être*)
hurry home! = dépêche-toi de rentrer!
• to hurry someone = bousculer quelqu'un
2 *noun*
to be in a hurry = être pressé/pressée
there's no hurry = ça ne presse pas
hurry up = se dépêcher (**!** + *être*)

hurt *verb*
• (*to injure*)
to hurt oneself = se faire mal (**!** + *être*)
to hurt one's leg = se faire mal à la jambe
• (*to be painful*)
my throat hurts = j'ai mal à la gorge
that hurts = ça fait mal
• (*to upset*) = blesser
to hurt someone's feelings = blesser quelqu'un

husband *noun*
a husband = un mari

I i

I *pronoun*
I = je (**!** *j'* + vowel or mute h)
I've got to go = je dois m'en aller
here I am = me voilà
I didn't do it = ce n'est pas moi qui l'ai fait
I'M the one who does all the work = c'est moi qui fais tout le travail
she drives but I don't = elle conduit mais moi non

ice *noun*
• (*frozen water*)
ice = la glace
• (*on roads*)
ice = le verglas
• (*in a drink*)
ice = des glaçons (*masculine plural*)

ice cream *noun*
ice cream = la glace
an ice cream = une glace

ice hockey *noun* ▶ **248** |
ice hockey = le hockey sur glace

ice rink *noun*
an ice rink = une patinoire

ice-skate *noun*
an ice-skate = un patin à glace

ice-skating *noun* ▶ **248** |
ice-skating = le patin à glace

icing *noun*
icing = le glaçage

idea *noun*
an idea = une idée
what a good idea! = quelle bonne idée!
I've no idea how much it costs = je ne sais pas du tout combien ça coûte

identity card *noun*
an identity card = une carte d'identité

idiot *noun*
an idiot = un idiot/une idiote

if *conjunction*
= si
if you like = si tu veux
if it rains, we won't go = s'il pleut, nous n'irons pas
if I were rich, I would travel = si j'étais riche, je voyagerais
I wonder if they'll come = je me demande s'ils vont venir
if I were you, I'd refuse = à ta place, je refuserais

Illnesses, aches, and pains

Where does it hurt?

where does it hurt?	= où est-ce que ça vous fait mal?
his leg hurts	= il a mal à la jambe

(Do not confuse, **faire mal à quelqu'un** with **faire du mal à quelqu'un**, which means *to harm somebody*.)

Note that with **avoir mal à** French uses the definite article (**le, la, les,** or **l'**) with the part of the body, where English has a possessive, hence:

*he **has a pain in his** leg*	= il **a mal à la** jambe
*his head **was hurting***	= il **avait mal à la** tête

Accidents

*she broke **her** leg*	= elle s'est cassé **la** jambe
*I twisted **my** ankle*	= je me suis foulé **la** cheville

Being ill

French mostly uses the definite article with the name of an illness:

*to have flu	measles*	= avoir **la** grippe / **la** rougeole

but

to have cancer	= avoir **un** cancer

Falling ill

French has no general equivalent of **to get**. However, where English can use **catch**, French can use **attraper**:

*to **catch** measles*	= **attraper** la rougeole
*to **catch** a cold*	= **attraper** un rhume

Treatment

to be treated for rabies	= **se faire soigner contre** la rage
to take tablets for indigestion	= **prendre des comprimés contre** l'indigestion
to be operated on for cancer	= **être opéré d'**un cancer

---

ignore *verb*
 to ignore a person = faire semblant de ne
  pas voir quelqu'un
 to ignore a problem = ne prêter aucune
  attention à un problème

ill *adjective*
 = malade

illegal *adjective*
 = illégal/illégale

illness *noun*
 an illness = une maladie

imagination *noun*
 imagination = l'imagination (*feminine*)
 to have imagination = avoir de
  l'imagination

imagine *verb*
 = imaginer

imitate *verb*
 = imiter

immediately *adverb*
 = immédiatement

impatient *adjective*
 = impatient/impatiente
 to get impatient = s'impatienter (**!** + *être*)

import *verb*
 = importer

important *adjective*
 = important/importante
 it is important to eat well = il est
  important de bien manger

impossible *adjective*
 = impossible
 it's impossible to argue with him = c'est
  impossible de discuter avec lui

impress *verb*
 = impressionner

impression *noun*
 an impression = une impression
 to make a good impression = faire bonne
  impression

improve *verb*
* (*to make better*) = améliorer
  to improve living conditions = améliorer les conditions de vie
  to improve one's French = se perfectionner en français
* (*to get better*) = s'améliorer (**!** + *être*)

improvement *noun*
  an improvement = une amélioration

in

> **!** *Often* in *occurs in combinations with verbs, for example:* **drop in, fit in, move in** *etc. To find the correct translations for this type of verb, look up the separate dictionary entries at* **drop, fit, move** *etc.*

1 *preposition*
* (*inside*) = dans
  in the house = dans la maison
  I read it in the newspaper = je l'ai lu dans le journal
  there's a letter in the envelope = il y a une lettre dans l'enveloppe
  there's a letter in it = il y a une lettre dedans
  the woman in the photograph = la femme sur la photo
* (*at*) = à
  I learned German in school = j'ai fait de l'allemand à l'école
  in the countryside = à la campagne
* (*when talking about countries or cities*)
  to live [in Ireland | in Japan | in Paris ...]
  = vivre [en Irlande | au Japon | à Paris ...]
* (*dressed in*) = en
  in a skirt = en jupe
  to be dressed in black = être habillé/habillée en noir
* (*showing the way in which something is done*) = en
  written in French = écrit en français
  we paid in cash = nous avons payé en espèces
  they were sitting in a circle = ils étaient assis en cercle
  in ink = à l'encre
* (*during*)
  in October = en octobre
  in the night = pendant la nuit
  in the morning = le matin
* (*within*)
  I'll be ready in ten minutes = je serai prêt en dix minutes
  she'll be back in half an hour = elle sera de retour dans une demi-heure
* (*other uses*)
  to stay in the rain = rester sous la pluie
  she's in her twenties = elle a entre vingt et trente ans
  one in ten = un sur dix
  to cut an apple in two = couper une pomme en deux

2 *adverb*
* (*at home, available*) = là
  tell her I'm not in = dis-lui que je ne suis pas là
* (*arrived*)
  the train is in = le train est en gare
  the tide is in = c'est la marée haute

inch *noun* ▶ 285 |
  an inch = un pouce
  | **!** *Note that an* inch = *2.54 cm.*

include *verb*
  = comprendre
  service is included in the bill = le service est compris dans la note

including *preposition*
  = y compris
  they were all invited, including the children = ils étaient tous invités, y compris les enfants

income *noun*
  an income = un revenu

income tax *noun*
  income tax = l'impôt sur le revenu
  | **!** *Note that* impôt *is masculine.*

inconvenient *adjective*
  it's an inconvenient place to meet = c'est un endroit peu pratique pour se retrouver
  an inconvenient time = un moment inopportun
  I hope that's not inconvenient for you – j'espère que cela ne vous dérange pas

increase
1 *verb*
  = augmenter
  to increase in value = augmenter de valeur
  to increase by 10% = augmenter de 10%
2 *noun*
  an increase = une augmentation

incredible *adjective*
  = incroyable

independent *adjective*
  = indépendant/indépendante

India *noun* ▶ 218 |
  = l'Inde (*feminine*)

Indian ▶ 275 |
1 *adjective*
  = indien/indienne
2 *noun*
* (*from India*)
  the Indians = les Indiens (*masculine*)
* (*from North America*)
  the Indians = les Indiens d'Amérique

indicate *verb*
  = indiquer

indifferent *adjective*
  = indifférent/indifférente

indigestion noun ▶ **266**
  to have indigestion = avoir mal à
    l'estomac

individual
  1 adjective
    = individuel/individuelle
  2 noun
    an individual = un individu

indoor adjective
  = couvert/couverte
  an indoor swimming pool = une piscine
    couverte

indoors adverb
  = à l'intérieur

industrial adjective
  = industriel/industrielle

industry noun
  industry = l'industrie (feminine)

inevitable adjective
  = inévitable

infant school noun (British English)
  an infant school = une école maternelle

infection noun
  an infection = une infection

influence
  1 noun
    an influence = une influence
    to have influence = avoir de l'influence
  2 verb
  • (to persuade) = influencer
  • (to make a strong impression on)
    to influence someone = avoir une
      influence sur quelqu'un
    to be too influenced by someone = se
      laisser trop influencer par quelqu'un

inform verb
  to inform the police of an accident
    = signaler un accident à la police
  to keep someone informed = tenir
    quelqu'un au courant

informal adjective
  • (describing a person, a person's manner)
    = simple
  • (describing a word, a language)
    = familier/familière
  • (describing a discussion or an interview)
    = informel/informelle

information noun
  a piece of information = un
    renseignement
  information = des renseignements

information desk noun
  the information desk = l'accueil
    (masculine)

information technology noun
  information technology = l'informatique
    (feminine)

ingredient noun
  an ingredient = un ingrédient

inhabitant noun
  an inhabitant = un habitant/une habitante

injection noun
  an injection = une piqûre
  to give someone an injection = faire une
    piqûre à quelqu'un

injured adjective
  = blessé/blessée

injury noun
  an injury = une blessure

ink noun
  ink = l'encre (feminine)

innocent adjective
  = innocent/innocente

inquiry noun
  an inquiry = une enquête

insect noun
  an insect = un insecte

inside
  1 preposition
    = à l'intérieur de
    inside the house = à l'intérieur de la
      maison
  2 adverb
    = à l'intérieur
    he's inside = il est à l'intérieur
    I looked inside = j'ai regardé à l'intérieur
    let's bring the chairs inside = rentrons les
      chaises
  3 noun
    the inside = l'intérieur (masculine)
    the inside of the palace = l'intérieur du
      palais
  4 adjective
    = intérieur/intérieure
  5 inside out = à l'envers
    to put one's shirt on inside out = mettre sa
      chemise à l'envers

inspect verb
  • (if it's an official) = inspecter
  • (if it's a conductor) = contrôler

inspector noun
  • (of a school)
    an inspector = un inspecteur/une
      inspectrice
  • (on a bus, a train)
    an inspector = un contrôleur/une
      contrôleuse
  • (in the police)
    a police inspector = un inspecteur de
      police

instantly adverb
  = immédiatement

instead
1 instead of
- (*rather than*) = au lieu de
  he hired a van instead of a car = il a loué une camionnette au lieu d'une voiture
  instead of working he watched TV = au lieu de travailler il a regardé la télévision
- (*in place of*) = à la place de
  use oil instead of butter = utilisez de l'huile à la place du beurre
  his wife came instead of him = sa femme est venue à sa place
2 *adverb*
  I don't feel like going to the cinema—let's stay at home instead = je n'ai pas envie d'aller au cinéma—restons plutôt à la maison

instruction *noun*
an instruction = une instruction
to give someone instructions to check the baggage = donner l'ordre à quelqu'un de vérifier les bagages
the instructions for use = le mode d'emploi

instrument *noun* ▶ 290 |
an instrument = un instrument
to play an instrument = jouer d'un instrument

insult *verb*
= insulter

insurance *noun*
insurance = l'assurance (*feminine*)

insure *verb*
= assurer
to insure a car against theft = assurer une voiture contre le vol

intelligent *adjective*
= intelligent/intelligente

intend *verb*
he intends [to leave | to learn Spanish ...] = il a l'intention [de partir | d'apprendre l'espagnol ...]

intense *adjective*
= intense

intensive care *noun*
to be in intensive care = être en soins intensifs

interest
1 *noun*
- (*enthusiasm*)
  interest = l'intérêt (*masculine*)
  to have an interest in music = s'intéresser à la musique
- (*financial*)
  interest = l'intérêt (*masculine*)
2 *verb*
= intéresser

interested *adjective*
= intéressé/intéressée
to be interested [in politics | in sport | in painting ...] = s'intéresser [à la politique | au sport | à la peinture ...]
are you interested? = ça t'intéresse?

interesting *adjective*
= intéressant/intéressante

interfere *verb*
- (*to get involved in*)
  to interfere in someone's business = se mêler des affaires de quelqu'un
- (*to have a bad effect on*)
  it's going to interfere with his work = ça va l'empêcher de travailler

intermission *noun*
an intermission = un entracte

international *adjective*
= international/internationale

Internet *noun*
the Internet = l'Internet, le Net

interpreter *noun* ▶ 315 |
an interpreter = un interprète/une interprète

interrupt *verb*
= interrompre

interval *noun*
- (*in time or at a location*)
  an interval = un intervalle
  at regular intervals = à intervalles réguliers
- (*British English*) (*during a play, a show*)
  an interval = un entracte

interview
1 *noun*
  an interview (*for a job*) = un entretien
  (*with a journalist*) = une interview
2 *verb*
  to interview someone (*if it's an employer*) = faire passer un entretien à quelqu'un
  (*if it's a journalist*) = interviewer quelqu'un
  (*if it's the police*) = interroger quelqu'un

intimidate *verb*
= intimider

into *preposition*
- (*when talking about a location*) = dans
  to go into the garden = aller dans le jardin
  to get into bed = se mettre au lit
- (*indicating a change*) = en
  to translate a letter into French = traduire une lettre en français
  to turn someone into a frog = transformer quelqu'un en grenouille

introduce *verb*
- (*to bring in*) = introduire
  to introduce a law = introduire une loi
- (*when people meet*) = présenter
  he introduced me to Peter = il m'a présenté à Peter

it

● When **it** is used as a subject pronoun to stand for a specific object (or animal), **il** or **elle** is used in French depending on whether the object referred to is masculine or feminine:

> *'where is the book | chair?' — 'it's* = 'où est le livre | la chaise?' — 'il | **elle** est
> *in the kitchen'* dans la cuisine'

● When **it** is used as an object pronoun, it is translated by **le** or **la** (**l'** before a vowel or mute h) depending on whether the object referred to is masculine or feminine:

> *it's my book | my chair and I want it* = c'est mon livre | ma chaise et je **le** | **la** veux

Note that the object pronoun normally comes before the verb in French and that in tenses like the perfect and the past perfect, the past participle agrees with it:

> *I liked his shirt, did you notice it?* = sa chemise m'a plu, est-ce que tu **l'**as remarquée?
> sa chemise m'a plu, **l'**as-tu remarquée?

In imperatives the pronoun comes after the verb:

> *it's my book, give it to me* = c'est mon livre, donne-**le**-moi*
> * Note the hyphens.

However, in negative commands, the pronoun comes before the verb:

> *it's my book, don't give it to him!* = c'est mon livre, ne **le** lui donne pas!

● When **it** is used after a preposition in English, the two words (*preposition* + **it**) are often translated by one word in French. If the preposition would normally be translated by **de** in French (**of**, **about**, **from** etc), the preposition + **it** = **en**:

> *we talked a lot about it* = on **en** a beaucoup parlé
> *have you heard of it?* = est-ce que tu **en** as entendu parler?

If the preposition would normally be translated by **à** in French (**to**, **in**, **at** etc), the preposition + **it** = **y**:

> *they went to it* = ils **y** sont allés

For translations of **it** following prepositions not normally translated by **de** or **à** (*above, under, over, etc*) consult the entry for the preposition.

● When **it** is used in expressions like *it's raining, it will snow* etc, the translation will always be **il**: **il** pleut, **il** va neiger. See the entry for the verb in question.

▶ For translations of *it's Friday, it's five o'clock* etc, consult the usage notes on **Dates, days, and months** and **The clock**.

● (*on radio or television*) = présenter
  to introduce a programme = présenter
  une émission

invade *verb*
  = envahir

invent *verb*
  = inventer

invention *noun*
  an invention = une invention

investigate *verb*
  to investigate a crime = enquêter sur un
  crime

investigation *noun*
  an investigation = une enquête

invisible *adjective*
  = invisible

invitation *noun*
  an invitation = une invitation

invite *verb*
  = inviter
  to invite someone to a party = inviter
  quelqu'un à une fête

involved *adjective*
  to be involved in an accident = avoir un
  accident
  to get involved in someone's problems
  = se mêler des problèmes de quelqu'un

Ireland *noun* ▶ **218**|
  Ireland = l'Irlande (*feminine*)

Irish ▶ **275**|
  1 *adjective*
  = irlandais/irlandaise
  2 *noun*
  ● (*the people*)
  the Irish = les Irlandais (*masculine
  plural*)
  ● (*the language*)
  Irish = l'irlandais (*masculine*)

iron
1 *noun*
- iron = le fer
- an iron = un fer à repasser

2 *verb*
= repasser

island *noun*
an island = une île

it *pronoun*
▶ **270** See the boxed note on it for more information and examples.
where is it? (*if it's an object*) = où est-il/elle?
(*if it's a place*) = où est-ce?
who is it? = qui est-ce?
it's me = c'est moi
it's a nice house = c'est une jolie maison
it is [difficult | easy | complicated ...] = c'est [difficile | facile | compliqué ...]
it doesn't matter = ça ne fait rien
it's easy to make a mistake = il est facile de se tromper
it's [cold | warm | mild ...] = il fait [froid | chaud | doux ...]
I've heard about it = j'en ai entendu parler
did you go to it? = est-ce que tu y es allé?

Italian ▶ **275**
1 *adjective*
= italien/italienne
2 *noun*
- (*the people*)
the Italians = les Italiens (*masculine*)
- (*the language*)
Italian = l'italien (*masculine*)

Italy *noun* ▶ **218**
Italy = l'Italie (*feminine*)

itchy *adjective*
my leg is itchy = j'ai la jambe qui me démange

its *determiner*
its = son/sa (+ *singular*)
= ses (+ *plural*)

> **!** Note that **sa** becomes **son** before a vowel or mute h.

its nose = son nez
its tail = sa queue
its ear = son oreille
its eyes = ses yeux

itself *pronoun*
- (*when used as a reflexive pronoun*)
the cat's going to hurt itself = le chat va se faire mal
- (*when used for emphasis*)
the car itself was not damaged = la voiture elle-même n'a pas été endommagée
the heating comes on by itself = le chauffage se met en marche tout seul

Jj

jacket *noun*
a jacket = une veste
(*gathered at the waist*) = un blouson

jail *noun*
a jail = une prison

jam *noun* (*British English*)
jam = la confiture

Jamaica *noun* ▶ **218**
Jamaica = la Jamaïque

January *noun* ▶ **222**
January = janvier (*masculine*)

Japan *noun* ▶ **210**
Japan = le Japon

Japanese ▶ **275**
1 *adjective*
= japonais/japonaise
2 *noun*
(*the people*)
the Japanese = les Japonais (*masculine plural*)
(*the language*)
japanese = le japonais

jaw *noun* ▶ **201**
the jaw = la mâchoire

jazz *noun*
jazz = le jazz

jealous *adjective*
= jaloux/jalouse
he is jealous of her = il est jaloux d'elle

jeans *noun*
jeans = un jean (*singular*)

jeer *verb*
to jeer someone = se moquer de quelqu'un

jelly *noun*
(*US English*) (*jam*)
jelly = la confiture
(*British English*) (*a dessert*)
jelly = la gelée de fruits

Jesus *noun*
Jesus = Jésus

jet *noun*
a jet = un jet, un avion à réaction

jewellery (*British English*), **jewelry** (*US English*) *noun*
a piece of jewellery = un bijou
jewellery = les bijoux (*plural*)

Jewish *adjective*
= juif/juive

jigsaw puzzle *noun*
a jigsaw puzzle = un puzzle

job *noun*
(*work*)
a job = un emploi
to look for a job = chercher un emploi
(*a task*)
a job = un travail, une tâche

jogging *noun* ▶ 248|
jogging = le jogging

join *verb*
(*meet up with*) = rejoindre
I'll join you in half an hour = je vous
rejoins dans une demi-heure
(*become a member of*)
to join a club = s'inscrire dans un club
to join a company = entrer dans une
entreprise
join in
to join in a game = participer à un jeu

joke
1 *noun*
a joke = une plaisanterie, une blague✶
2 *verb*
= plaisanter

journalist *noun* ▶ 315|
a journalist = un journaliste/une
journaliste

journey *noun*
a journey = un voyage
to go on a journey = partir en voyage

joy *noun*
joy = la joie

judge
1 *noun* ▶ 315|
a judge = un juge
2 *verb*
= juger

judo *noun* ▶ 248|
judo = le judo

jug *noun*
a jug = un pichet

juice *noun*
juice = le jus
fruit juice = le jus de fruits

July *noun* ▶ 222|
July = juillet (*masculine*)

jump *verb*
= sauter
the children were jumping on the bed
= les enfants sautaient sur le lit
to jump across the stream = franchir le
ruisseau d'un bond
to jump rope = sauter à la corde
to jump out of the window = sauter par la
fenêtre

to jump the queue (*British English*) = passer
devant tout le monde

jumper *noun* (*British English*)
a jumper = un pull

June *noun* ▶ 222|
June = juin (*masculine*)

junior high school *noun* (*US English*)
a junior high school ≈ un collège

junior school *noun* (*British English*)
a junior school = une école primaire

jury *noun*
the jury = le jury

just¹ *adverb*
(*very recently*)
I have just [arrived | seen her | received the
letter...] = je viens [d'arriver | de la voir | de
recevoir la lettre...]
I had just turned on the TV = je venais
d'allumer la télévision
(*at this or that very moment*) = juste
I was just about to phone you = j'étais
juste sur le point de t'appeler, j'allais
t'appeler
you've just missed him = il vient juste de
partir
I arrived just as he was leaving = je suis
arrivé juste au moment où il partait
(*only*) = juste
just two days ago = il y a juste deux jours
he's just a child = ce n'est qu'un enfant
(*barely*) = tout juste
I got there just in time = je suis arrivé juste
à temps
she's just 18 = elle a tout juste 18 ans
(*when comparing*)
she is just as intelligent as he is = elle est
tout aussi intelligente que lui
(*immediately*) = juste
just before the weekend = juste avant le
week-end

just² *adjective*
= juste

justice *noun*
justice = la justice

Kk

kangaroo *noun*
a kangaroo = un kangourou

karate *noun* ▶ 248|
karate = le karaté

✶ in informal situations

keen *adjective*
 a keen student = un étudiant/une
  étudiante enthousiaste
 to be keen on swimming = aimer la
  natation

keep *verb*
  = garder
 to keep someone in (the) hospital
  = garder quelqu'un à l'hôpital
 we keep the wine in the cellar = nous
  gardons le vin dans la cave
 this sweater will keep you warm = ce pull
  te tiendra chaud
 to keep someone waiting = faire attendre
  quelqu'un
 (to delay) = retenir
 what kept you? = qu'est-ce qui t'a retenu?
 I won't keep you long = je n'en ai pas pour
  longtemps
 (to put) = ranger
 where do you keep the cups? = où est-ce
  que tu ranges les tasses?
 (not to break, not to reveal)
 to keep a promise = tenir une promesse
 to keep a secret = garder un secret
 (to continue)
 to keep [walking | talking | running ...]
  = continuer à [marcher | parler | courir ...]
 to keep going = continuer
 to keep calm = rester calme
 (if it's food) = se conserver (**!** + *être*)
keep away = ne pas s'approcher (**!** + *être*)
 keep away from the fire! = ne t'approche
  pas du feu!
keep back = retenir
 he kept the children back after school = il
  a retenu les enfants après l'école
keep on
 to keep on [talking | walking | singing ...]
  = continuer à [parler | marcher | chanter ...]
keep out
 to keep out of the sun = ne pas se mettre
  au soleil
 to keep the rain out = empêcher la pluie
  d'entrer
keep up = suivre
 to keep up with the other pupils = suivre
  en classe

kerb *noun (British English)*
 the kerb = le bord du trottoir

kettle *noun*
 a kettle = une bouilloire

key *noun*
 a key = une clé

keyhole *noun*
 a keyhole = un trou de serrure

kick *verb*
 to kick someone = donner un coup de
  pied à quelqu'un
 he kicked the ball = il a donné un coup de
  pied dans le ballon
kick off = donner le coup d'envoi

kick out
 to kick someone out = mettre quelqu'un à
  la porte

kid *noun*
 (a child)
 a kid = un enfant/une enfant, un
  gamin/une gamine*
 (a young goat)
 a kid = un chevreau

kidnap *noun*
  = enlever

kill *verb*
  = tuer
 to kill oneself = se suicider (**!** + *être*)

kilo *noun* ▶ **285**
 a kilo = un kilo

kilogram(me) *noun* ▶ **285**
 a kilogram = un kilogramme

kilometre *(British English)*, **kilometer**
(US English) noun ▶ **285**
 a kilometre = un kilomètre

kind
 1 *noun*
 it's a kind of [fish | novel | hotel ...] = c'est
  une sorte [de poisson | de roman | d'hôtel ...]
 what kind of film is it? = c'est quel genre
  de film?
 what kind of car is it? = qu'est-ce que c'est
  comme voiture?
 2 *adjective*
  = gentil/gentille

king *noun*
 a king = un roi

kingdom *noun*
 a kingdom = un royaume

kiss
 1 *verb*
 to kiss someone = embrasser quelqu'un
 to kiss (each other) = s'embrasser
  (**!** + *être*)
 2 *noun*
 a kiss = un baiser

kitchen *noun*
 a kitchen = une cuisine

kite *noun*
 a kite = un cerf-volant

kitten *noun*
 a kitten = un chaton

knee *noun* ▶ **201**
 the knee = le genou

kneel down *verb*
  = se mettre à genoux (**!** + *être*)

knife *noun*
 a knife = un couteau

knit *verb*
  = tricoter

K

knock
1 *verb*
to knock on the door = frapper à la porte
2 *noun*
a knock = un coup
to get a knock on the head = recevoir un coup sur la tête
knock down
(*in an accident*) = renverser
(*to demolish*) = démolir
knock out
(*to make unconscious*) = assommer
(*in a contest*) = éliminer
knock over = renverser

knot *noun*
a knot = un nœud

know *verb*
(*when talking about facts, information*) = savoir
he thinks he knows everything = il croit tout savoir
I know why he phoned = je sais pourquoi il a téléphoné
she knows how to swim = elle sait nager
I don't know the French word for it = je ne sais pas comment ça se dit en français
let me know = tenez-moi au courant
does he know about the party? = est-ce qu'il est au courant pour la soirée?
to know all about art = s'y connaître en art
(*when talking about people, places*) = connaître
do you know Paris? = est-ce que tu connais Paris?
to get to know someone = faire la connaissance de quelqu'un

knowledge *noun*
knowledge = les connaissances (*feminine plural*)

L1

laboratory *noun*
a laboratory = un laboratoire

lace *noun*
(*the material*)
lace = la dentelle
(*for shoes*)
a lace = un lacet
to tie one's laces = lacer ses chaussures

lack
1 *noun*
a lack [of food | of money | of interest …] = un manque [de nourriture | d'argent | d'intérêt …]

2 *verb*
= manquer de
he lacks confidence = il manque d'assurance

ladder *noun*
a ladder = une échelle

lady *noun*
a lady = une dame

lake *noun*
a lake = un lac

lamb *noun*
a lamb = un agneau

lamp *noun*
a lamp = une lampe

lampshade *noun*
a lampshade = un abat-jour

land
1 *noun*
(*for farming, as opposed to the sea*)
land = la terre
(*property*)
a piece of land = un terrain
to own land = posséder des terres
(*the countryside*)
the land = la campagne
2 *verb*
(*to fall*) = tomber (**!** + *être*)
(*if it's a plane*) = atterrir
(*if it's a passenger*) = débarquer

landscape *noun*
a landscape = un paysage

language *noun*
a language = une langue
foreign languages = les langues étrangères
bad language = le langage grossier

language laboratory *noun*
a language laboratory = un laboratoire de langues

large *adjective*
(*big*) = grand/grande (**!** *before the noun*)
a large garden = un grand jardin
a large house = une grande maison
(*when talking about numbers*) = gros/grosse (**!** *before the noun*)
a large sum of money = une grosse somme
a large population = une forte population
(*bulky*) = gros/grosse (**!** *before the noun*)
a large parcel = un gros paquet

last
1 *adjective*
= dernier/dernière
last week = la semaine dernière
that's the last time I saw her = c'est la dernière fois que je l'ai vue
2 *adverb*
(*most recently*)
when I was last here = la dernière fois que je suis venu ici

Languages and nationalities

Languages

The names of languages in French are always written with a small letter, not a capital as in English. French almost always uses the definite article **le** or **l'** with languages:

    to learn French   = apprendre **le** français

except after **en**:

    to translate a word **into** French = traduire un mot **en** français

and it may be omitted with **parler**:

    to speak French   = parler français / parler le français

but

    to speak **in** French   = parler **en** français

When **French** means **in French** or **of the French**, it is translated by **français**:

    the **French** language   = la langue **française**

If you want to make it clear you mean **in French** and not **from France**, use **en français**:

    a **French** book   = un livre **en français**

When **French** means **relating to French** or **about French**, it is translated by **de français**.

    a **French** class   = une classe **de français**

Nationalities

Adjectives indicating nationality **never** have capitals in French:

    a **French** student   = un étudiant **français** / une étudiante **française**

Nouns have capitals in French when they mean *a person of a specific nationality*:

    a **Frenchman** / a **Frenchwoman** = un **Français** / une **Française**
    French people or the **French** = les **Français** (*masculine plural*)

English sometimes has a special word for a person *of a specific nationality*; in French, the same word is almost always either an adjective (no capitals) or a noun (with capitals):

    Spanish   = espagnol
    a **Spaniard**   = un **Espagnol** / une **Espagnole**
    the **Spaniards**   = les **Espagnols** (*masculine plural*)

You can use either the adjective or the noun to refer to nationality:

    he / she is **French**   = il est **français** / elle est **française**
                                         = c'est un **Français** / c'est une **Française**

(*at the end*) = en dernier
I'll do the dishes last (of all) = je ferai la vaisselle en dernier
(*in final position*)
he came last in the race = il est arrivé dernier dans la course
3 *pronoun*
  the last = le dernier/la dernière
  they were the last to arrive = ils ont été les derniers à arriver
  the night before last = avant-hier soir
4 *verb*
  = durer
  the film lasts two hours = le film dure deux heures

late
1 *adverb*
  (*far into the day or night*) = tard
  late in the afternoon = tard dans l'après-midi
  it's getting late = il se fait tard

(*not on time*) = en retard
  to arrive half an hour late = arriver avec une demi-heure de retard
2 *adjective*
  = en retard
  to be late for work = arriver en retard au travail
  the train was two hours late = le train a eu deux heures de retard
  to make someone late = retarder quelqu'un

later *adverb*
  = plus tard
  I'll call back later = je rappellerai plus tard
  see you later! = à plus tard!

latest
1 *adjective*
  = dernier/dernière (**!** *before the noun*)
  the latest news = les dernières nouvelles
2 at the latest = au plus tard

Latin *noun*
Latin = le latin

laugh
1 *verb*
= rire
to laugh at a joke = rire d'une plaisanterie
to make someone laugh = faire rire
quelqu'un
to laugh at someone = se moquer de
quelqu'un
2 *noun*
a laugh = un rire

laundry *noun*
the laundry = le linge (sale)
to do the laundry = faire la lessive

law *noun*
(*a set of rules in a country*)
the law = la loi
to obey the law = respecter la loi
it's against the law = c'est interdit par la
loi
(*a rule*)
a law = une loi
(*as a subject*)
law = le droit

lawn *noun*
a lawn = une pelouse

lawnmower *noun*
a lawnmower = une tondeuse à gazon

lawyer *noun* ▶ 315
a lawyer = un avocat/une avocate

lay *verb*
(*to put*) = poser, mettre
lay some newspapers on the floor = mets
des journaux par terre
to lay the table = mettre le couvert
(*of a chicken*)
to lay an egg = pondre un œuf
lay down = poser, mettre
he laid the tray down on the table = il a
posé le plateau sur la table
lay off = licencier

lazy *adjective*
= paresseux/paresseuse

lead¹ *verb*
(*to guide*) = mener, conduire
this road will lead you to the village
= cette route vous mènera au village
(*in a match*) = mener
(*in a race*) = être en tête
to lead a busy life = mener une vie active
(*to have as a result*)
to lead to an accident = entraîner un
accident

lead² *noun*
lead = le plomb

leader *noun*
a leader (*of a political party*) = un leader,
un dirigeant
(*of a state*) = un chef d'État

leaf *noun*
a leaf = une feuille

leak *verb*
(*if it's a container*) = fuir
the pipe leaks = il y a une fuite dans le
tuyau
(*if it's a boat, shoes*) = prendre l'eau

lean
1 *verb*
(*to support oneself*)
to lean against the wall = s'appuyer contre
le mur
(*to put*)
to lean a bicycle against the wall
= appuyer un vélo contre le mur
to lean out of the window = se pencher par
la fenêtre
2 *adjective*
= maigre
lean back = se pencher en arrière
(**!** + *être*)
lean forward = se pencher en avant
(**!** + *être*)
lean on = s'appuyer sur (**!** + *être*)

learn *verb*
= apprendre
to learn how to drive = apprendre à
conduire

leash *noun*
a leash = une laisse

least
1 *determiner*
the least
= le moins de
they have the least money = ce sont eux
qui ont le moins d'argent
2 *pronoun*
it was the least I could do! = c'était la
moindre des choses!
3 *adverb*
the least = le moins/la moins (+ *singular*)
= les moins (+ *plural*)
the least expensive shop = le magasin le
moins cher
the least difficult question = la question la
moins difficile
4 at least
(*at the minimum*) = au moins
he's at least thirty = il a au moins trente
ans
(*when expressing some doubt*) = du moins
he's gone out—at least, I think so = il est
sorti—du moins, il me semble

leather *noun*
leather = le cuir

leave *verb*
(*to go away from*) = quitter
to leave school = quitter l'école
she left her husband = elle a quitté son
mari

(*to go away*) = partir (**!** + *être*)
he left the next day = il est parti le
　lendemain
(*to go out of*) = sortir de (**!** + *être*)
she left the room = elle est sortie de la
　pièce
(*to allow to remain*) = laisser
leave your coat here = laisse ton manteau
　ici
she left the window open = elle a laissé la
　fenêtre ouverte
(*to put, to give*) = laisser
he didn't leave a message = il n'a pas
　laissé de message
she left him some money = elle lui a laissé
　de l'argent
(*to put off*) = laisser
leave it until tomorrow = laisse ça pour
　demain
(*to remain*)
there's nothing left = il ne reste rien
we've got ten minutes left = il nous reste
　dix minutes
(*other uses*)
I left them to clean the windows = je les ai
　laissés nettoyer les fenêtres
leave behind = laisser
he left his belongings behind = il a laissé
　ses affaires
leave out
　(*not to show or talk about*) (*by accident*)
　= oublier
　(*deliberately*) = omettre
　(*to exclude*) = exclure
to feel left out = se sentir exclu/exclue
leave over
　there was not much left over = il ne restait
　plus grand-chose
　there is some food left over = il reste un
　peu de nourriture

lecture *noun*
　a lecture (*to students*) = un cours
　magistral
　(*to the public*) = une conférence

left
1 *noun*
　the left = la gauche
　the first street on the left = la première rue
　à gauche
2 *adjective*
　= gauche
　his left hand = sa main gauche
3 *adverb*
　= à gauche
　to turn left = tourner à gauche

leg *noun*
　(*of a person*) ▶ **201** |
　the leg = la jambe
　(*of animals*)
　the leg = la patte
　(*of meat*)
　a leg of lamb = un gigot d'agneau

legal *adjective*
　= légal/légale

leisure *noun*
　leisure = les loisirs (*masculine plural*)

leisure centre (*British English*),
leisure center (*US English*) *noun*
　a leisure centre = un centre de loisirs

lemon *noun*
　a lemon = un citron

lemonade *noun*
　lemonade = la limonade

lend *verb*
　= prêter
　to lend someone money = prêter de
　l'argent à quelqu'un

length *noun* ▶ **285** |
　(*in measurements*)
　length = la longueur
　length (*of a book, a film, a list*) = la
　longueur
　(*of an event*) = la durée

leopard *noun*
　a leopard = un léopard

less ▶ **317** |
1 *determiner*
　= moins de
　less [money | food | time …] = moins
　[d'argent | de nourriture | de temps …]
　I have less work than he does = j'ai moins
　de travail que lui
2 *pronoun*
　= moins
　to cost less = coûter moins cher
　he reads less than she does = il lit moins
　qu'elle
　they have less than you = ils en ont
　moins que toi

　! *Note that it is necessary to use* **en**,
　which might be translated as 'of it', *with
　pronouns like* **less**. *See also* **another, a
　few, a lot** *etc for this use of* **en**.

3 *adverb*
　= moins
　we travel less in winter = nous voyageons
　moins l'hiver
4 *preposition*
　(*minus*) = moins
5 less and less = de moins en moins
　less and less often = de moins en moins
　souvent
6 less than = moins de
　in less than half an hour = en moins d'une
　demi-heure

lesson *noun*
　a lesson = un cours
　a riding lesson = une leçon d'équitation

let¹ *verb*
　(*when making suggestions*)
　let's go home = rentrons
　let's go! = allons-y!

L

(*to allow*) = laisser
to let someone in = laisser entrer
    quelqu'un
he let me help him = il m'a laissé l'aider
she lets him do what he likes = elle le
    laisse faire ce qu'il veut
he's letting his hair grow = il se laisse
    pousser les cheveux
let down = décevoir
let go
(*to stop holding*) = lâcher prise
he let go of me = il m'a lâché
(*to release*) = relâcher
he let the prisoners go = il a relâché les
    prisonniers
let in
(*to a room or house*) = faire entrer
he let me in = il m'a fait entrer
to let in the rain = laisser entrer la pluie
let out
(*to allow to go out*) = laisser sortir
let me out! = laisse-moi sortir!
to let out a scream = laisser échapper un
    cri
let through
to let someone through = laisser passer
    quelqu'un

let² *verb* (*British English*)
= louer

letter *noun*
a letter = une lettre

letter box *noun* (*British English*)
a letter box = une boîte aux lettres

lettuce *noun*
a lettuce = une laitue

level
1 *noun*
a level = un niveau
2 *adjective*
= plat/plate

library *noun*
a library = une bibliothèque

licence (*British English*), **license** (*US English*) *noun*
a licence = un permis

license plate *noun* (*US English*)
a license plate = une plaque
    minéralogique

lick *verb*
= lécher

lid *noun*
a lid = un couvercle

lie
1 *verb*
(*on the ground, on a bed*) = s'allonger
(**!** + *être*)
he lay down on the sofa = il s'est allongé
    sur le canapé
he was lying on the sofa = il était allongé
    sur le canapé

(*to be situated*) = se trouver (**!** + *être*)
(*not to tell the truth*) = mentir
2 *noun*
a lie = un mensonge
to tell a lie = mentir
lie around = traîner
he always leaves his keys lying around
    = il laisse toujours traîner ses clés
lie down = s'allonger (**!** + *être*)

life *noun*
life = la vie
a way of life = un mode de vie

lifestyle *noun*
a lifestyle = un style de vie

lift
1 *verb*
to lift one's arm = lever le bras
to lift a lid = soulever un couvercle
2 *noun*
(*British English*) (*an elevator*)
a lift = un ascenseur
(*in a car*)
to give someone a lift to the station
    = conduire quelqu'un à la gare
lift up = soulever

light
1 *noun*
(*from the sun, moon*)
light = la lumière
(*in a room, on a machine*)
a light = une lumière
to switch on a light = allumer
(*for traffic*)
the lights are green = le feu est au vert
(*in a street*)
a light = un réverbère
have you got a light? = est-ce que vous
    avez du feu?
2 *adjective*
(*not dark*) ▶ **213** = clair/claire
it's still light outside = il fait encore jour
    dehors
a light blue dress = une robe bleu clair
(*not heavy*) = léger/légère
3 *verb*
= allumer
he lit a cigarette = il a allumé une
    cigarette
to light a fire = faire un feu

light bulb *noun*
a light bulb = une ampoule

lighthouse *noun*
a lighthouse = un phare

lightning *noun*
a flash of lightning = un éclair

like¹ *preposition*
= comme
people like you and me = des gens comme
    toi et moi
what's it like? = c'est comment?

like² *verb*
(*when expressing an interest*) = aimer
I like [swimming | reading | dancing …]
= j'aime (bien) [nager | lire | danser …]
I like it! = ça me plaît!
how do you like America? = est-ce que
l'Amérique te plaît?
(*when expressing a wish*) = vouloir, aimer
I'd like coffee please = je voudrais un café
s'il vous plaît
I'd like to live here = j'aimerais vivre ici

limit *noun*
a limit = une limite

line
1 *noun*
a line = une ligne
a straight line = une ligne droite
(*US English*) (*a queue*)
a line = une queue
to stand in line = faire la queue
(*a row*)
a line = une rangée
the line is bad = la ligne est mauvaise
2 *verb*
to be lined with trees = être bordé/bordée
d'arbres

link *verb*
(*by train*) = relier
to link Paris to Brussels = relier Paris à
Bruxelles
(*to make a connection between*) = lier
the two murders are linked = les deux
meurtres sont liés

lion *noun*
a lion = un lion

lip *noun*
a lip = une lèvre

lipstick *noun*
lipstick = le rouge à lèvres

list *noun*
a list = une liste

listen *verb*
= écouter
to listen to someone = écouter quelqu'un

litre (*British English*), **liter** (*US English*)
noun
a litre = un litre

little¹
1 *determiner*
= peu de
little [food | wine | money …] = peu [de
nourriture | de vin | d'argent …]
there is very little time = il y a très peu de
temps
2 *pronoun*
a little = un peu
I only ate a little = je n'en ai mangé qu'un
peu

! *Note that it is necessary to use* en,
which might be translated as 'of it', *with
pronouns like* a little. *See also* **a lot, more,
none,** *etc for this use of* en.

3 *adverb*
= peu
4 a little (bit) = un peu
5 little by little = peu à peu

little² *adjective*
= petit/petite (! *before the noun*)

live¹ *verb*
(*to have one's home*) = vivre, habiter
he lives in London = il habite à Londres, il
vit à Londres
(*to be alive*) = vivre
that's not enough to live on = ça ne suffit
pas pour vivre

live² *adjective*
(*alive*) = vivant/vivante
(*of a match, a show*) = en direct

lively *adjective*
= vivant/vivante

living room *noun*
a living room = une salle de séjour

load *noun*
(*on a truck, being carried*)
a load = un chargement
loads of money = beaucoup d'argent

loaf *noun*
a loaf (of bread) = un pain

loan *noun*
a loan (*money lent*) = un prêt
(*money borrowed*) = un emprunt

lobster *noun*
a lobster = un homard

local *adjective*
a local newspaper = un journal local
the local people = les gens du coin

lock
1 *verb*
= fermer à clé
she locked the door = elle a fermé la porte
à clé
2 *noun*
a lock = une serrure
a bicycle lock = un antivol
lock in
to lock someone in = enfermer quelqu'un
to lock oneself in = s'enfermer (! + *être*)

locker *noun*
a locker = un casier

logical *adjective*
= logique

London *noun* ▶ 218
= Londres

lonely *adjective*
= seul/seule

L

long

1 *adjective* **▶ 285**
= long/longue
a long letter = une longue lettre
to have long hair = avoir les cheveux longs
the film is two hours long = le film dure
  deux heures
I haven't seen him for a long time = ça fait
  longtemps que je ne l'ai pas vu
2 *adverb*
= longtemps
long ago = il y a longtemps
you can stay as long as you like = tu peux
  rester aussi longtemps que tu veux
I won't be long = je n'en ai pas pour
  longtemps
3 as long as = à condition que
as long as the weather is nice = à
  condition qu'il fasse beau

| **!** *Note that the subjunctive is used after* à
| condition que.

look

1 *verb*
= regarder
to look at a picture = regarder un tableau
to look out of the window = regarder par
  la fenêtre
(*to appear*)
to look tired = avoir l'air fatigué/fatiguée
to look well = avoir bonne mine
he looks young = il fait jeune
she looks like her mother = elle ressemble
  à sa mère
what does he look like? = il est comment?
2 *noun*
a look = un regard
look after = s'occuper de (**!** + *être*)
to look after a child = s'occuper d'un
  enfant
look down
(*to lower one's eyes*) = baisser les yeux
to look down on someone = regarder
  quelqu'un de haut
look for = chercher
he is looking for a job = il cherche un
  emploi
look forward to
I am looking forward to meeting her
  = j'attends avec impatience le plaisir de
  faire sa connaissance
look onto = donner sur
my bedroom looks onto the garden = ma
  chambre donne sur le jardin
look out = faire attention
look through
to look through a book = feuilleter un
  livre
look up
to look up a word in a dictionary
  = chercher un mot dans un dictionnaire
(*to raise one's eyes*) = lever les yeux

loose *adjective*
(*describing clothes*) = ample
(*describing a screw*) = desserré/desserrée

lorry *noun* (*British English*)
a lorry = un camion

lose *verb*
= perdre

lost *adjective*
= perdu/perdue
to get lost = se perdre (**!** + *être*)

lot *pronoun* **▶ 317**
a lot = beaucoup
he eats a lot = il mange beaucoup
a lot [of money | of time | of books ...]
  = beaucoup [d'argent | de temps | de livres ...]
there's not a lot left = il n'en reste pas
  beaucoup

| **!** *Note that it is necessary to use* en,
| *which may be translated as* 'of it' *or* 'of
| them', *with pronouns like* a lot. *See also*
| another, a few, any *etc for this use of* en.

lottery *noun*
a lottery = une loterie

loud *adjective*
= fort/forte
to talk in a loud voice = parler fort

loudspeaker *noun*
a loudspeaker = un haut-parleur

lounge *noun*
a lounge = un salon

love

1 *verb*
(*when talking about people*) = aimer
to love each other = s'aimer (**!** + *être*)
(*when talking about things, activities*)
  = adorer
2 *noun*
love = l'amour (*masculine*)
to be in love = être amoureux/amoureuse
to make love = faire l'amour

lovely *adjective*
(*beautiful*) = beau/belle (**!** *before the noun*)
a lovely apartment = un bel appartement
you've got lovely eyes = tu as de beaux
  yeux
(*very nice, kind*) = charmant/charmante

low

1 *adjective*
= bas/basse
to speak in a low voice = parler à voix
  basse
2 *adverb*
= bas
to turn the lights down low = baisser les
  lumières

lower *verb*
= baisser

loyal *adjective*
= loyal/loyale

✗ in informal situations

luck *noun* ▶ **237** |
luck = la chance
good luck! = bonne chance!
to bring someone (good) luck = porter
bonheur à quelqu'un

lucky *adjective*
to be lucky = avoir de la chance

lunch *noun*
lunch = le déjeuner

lung *noun*
the lung = le poumon

Luxembourg *noun* ▶ **218** |
Luxembourg = le Luxembourg

luxury
1 *noun*
luxury = le luxe
2 *adjective*
a luxury hotel = un hôtel de luxe

Mm

machine *noun*
a machine = une machine

mad *adjective*
• (*crazy*) = fou/folle
to go mad = devenir fou/folle
• (*very angry*) = furieux/furieuse
• to be mad about someone = être fou/folle*
de quelqu'un

magazine *noun*
a magazine = un magazine

magic *adjective*
= magique

maiden name *noun*
a maiden name = un nom de jeune fille

mail
1 *noun*
• (*the postal system*)
the mail = la poste
• (*letters*)
mail = le courrier
2 *verb* (*US English*)
to mail a letter to someone = envoyer une
lettre à quelqu'un

mailbox *noun* (*US English*)
a mailbox = une boîte aux lettres

mailman *noun* ▶ **315** | (*US English*)
a mailman = un facteur

main *adjective*
= principal/principale

main course *noun*
a main course = un plat principal

major
1 *adjective*
= majeur/majeure
a major event = un événement majeur
2 *noun*
a major = un commandant

majority *noun*
a majority = une majorité

make *verb*

> **!** Note that the word make can often be
> translated by faire. This entry covers the
> most frequent uses of make but to find
> translations for other expressions like to
> make a mess, to make a mistake, to make
> sure etc, look up the entries at mess,
> mistake, sure etc.

• to make = faire
to make [the bed | a film | some coffee …]
= faire [le lit | un film | du café …]
to make room = faire de la place
to make a phone call = passer un coup de
fil
to make friends = se faire des amis
(**!** + *être*)
to make breakfast = préparer le petit
déjeuner
to be made of [gold | metal | wood …] = être
en [or | métal | bois …]
to be made in France = être
fabriqué/fabriquée en France
• (*to cause a particular reaction*)
to make someone [happy | ill | jealous …]
= rendre quelqu'un [heureux | malade |
jaloux …]
to make someone [annoyed | tired |
sleepy …] = [agacer | fatiguer | endormir …]
quelqu'un
to make someone [cry | laugh | eat …]
= faire [pleurer | rire | manger …] quelqu'un
• to make someone wait = faire attendre
quelqu'un
• (*to earn*)
to make a lot of money = gagner
beaucoup d'argent
to make a living = gagner sa vie
to make a profit = faire un bénéfice
make do = faire avec
make out = faire
to make out a list = faire une liste
to make a cheque out to someone = faire
un chèque à quelqu'un
make up
• (*to be friends again*) = se réconcilier
(**!** + *être*)
• to make up an excuse = inventer un
prétexte
• to make up a parcel = faire un paquet

make-up *noun*
make-up = le maquillage
to wear make-up = se maquiller (**!** + *être*)

male *adjective*
• (*in biology*) = mâle
• (*relating to men*) = masculin/masculine

M

man noun
- **a man** = un homme
  a single man = un célibataire
- **man** = l'homme

manage verb
- (to run) = gérer
- **to manage to finish one's homework** = réussir à finir ses devoirs

manager noun ▶ 315 |
  a manager (of a company, a bank, a project) = un directeur/une directrice
  (of a shop) = un gérant/une gérante
  (of a football team) = un manager

manner noun
  a manner = une attitude

manners noun
  manners = les manières (feminine)
  it's bad manners not to say hello = c'est impoli de ne pas dire bonjour

manufacture verb
  = fabriquer

many ▶ 317 |
1 determiner
- (a lot of) = beaucoup de
  were there many tourists? = est-ce qu'il y avait beaucoup de touristes?
  there weren't many people there = il n'y avait pas beaucoup de monde
- (when used with how, too, so, as)
  how many cases have you got? = combien de valises avez-vous?
  you eat too many chips = tu manges trop de frites
  there are so many things to do here = il y a tant de choses à faire ici
  I got as many presents as you did = j'ai reçu autant de cadeaux que toi
2 pronoun
  are there many left? = est-ce qu'il en reste beaucoup?
  I've got too many = j'en ai trop
  take as many as you like = prends-en autant que tu veux

  ! Note that it is necessary to use **en**, which might be translated as 'of them', with pronouns like **many**. See also **another, a few, a lot** etc for this use of **en**.

  many (of them) speak English = beaucoup (d'entre eux) parlent anglais

map noun
  a map (of a country or region) = une carte
  (of a town or a transport system) = un plan

marble noun
  marble = le marbre

marbles noun ▶ 248 |
  marbles = les billes (feminine)

march verb
- (in the army) = marcher au pas
- (in a demonstration) = manifester

March noun ▶ 222 |
  March = mars (masculine)

margarine noun
  margarine = la margarine

mark
1 noun
- **a mark** (on a surface) = une tache
  (on a person's body) = une marque
  to leave marks on the table = laisser des taches sur la table
- (British English) (a grade)
  a mark = une note
  to get good marks = avoir de bonnes notes
2 verb
- (to stain) = tacher
- **to mark the homework** = corriger les devoirs
- (to indicate) = indiquer

marker noun
  a marker (a pen) = un marqueur
  (a felt-tip pen) = un feutre

market noun
- (the place)
  a market = un marché
  a flea market = un marché aux puces
- (the system)
  the market = le marché
  the job market = le marché du travail

marmalade noun
  marmalade = la confiture d'oranges

marriage noun
  marriage = le mariage

married adjective
  = marié/mariée
  to be married to someone = être marié/mariée à quelqu'un

marry verb
  to marry someone = se marier avec quelqu'un (**!** + être)

marsh noun
  a marsh = un marécage

masculine adjective
  = masculin/masculine

mashed potatoes noun
  mashed potatoes = la purée de pommes de terre

mask noun
  a mask = un masque

mat noun
  a mat = un (petit) tapis

match

1 *noun*
- (*British English*) (*a game*)
  a match = un match
  a football match = un match de football
- (*a matchstick*)
  a match = une allumette

2 *verb*
  the shoes match the belt = les chaussures sont assorties à la ceinture

mate *noun* (*British English*)
  a mate = un copain/une copine

material *noun*
  a material = un tissu, une étoffe

math (*US English*), maths (*British English*) *noun*
  math(s) = les maths (*feminine plural*)

mathematics *noun*
  mathematics = les mathématiques (*feminine plural*)

matter

1 *noun*
  what's the matter? = qu'est-ce qu'il y a?
  what's the matter with her? = qu'est-ce qu'elle a?

2 *verb*
  does it really matter? = est-ce que c'est vraiment important?
  it doesn't matter = ça ne fait rien, ça n'a pas d'importance

maximum

1 *adjective*
  the maximum price = le prix maximum
  a maximum temperature of 80 degrees = une température maximale de 80 degrés

2 *noun*
  the maximum = le maximum

may *verb*
- (*when talking about a possibility*)
  they may be able to come = ils pourront peut-être venir
  she may not have seen him = elle ne l'a peut-être pas vu
  it may rain = il risque de pleuvoir
- (*when asking for or giving permission*)
  may I come in? = est-ce que je peux entrer?, puis-je entrer?
  you may sit down = vous pouvez vous asseoir

May *noun* ▶ 222 |
  May = mai (*masculine*)

maybe *adverb*
  = peut-être

mayor *noun* ▶ 315 |
  a mayor = un maire

me *pronoun*

  ! *Note that there is a boxed usage note at* **them**. *The entries* **me, him, her** *and* **us** *are modelled on this note where you will find detailed grammatical information and fuller explanations.*

- **me** = me (**!** m' + *vowel or mute h*)
  they know me = ils me connaissent
  they don't know me = ils ne me connaissent pas
  do they know me? = est-ce qu'ils me connaissent?
- **he's seen me** = il m'a vu
  he hasn't seen me = il ne m'a pas vu
  has he seen me? = est-ce qu'il m'a vu?
- **help me!** = aide-moi!
  hold me! = tiens-moi!
  don't bother me! = ne m'embête pas!
  don't hit me! = ne me frappe pas!
- **she gave the book to me** = elle m'a donné le livre
  she didn't give the book to me = elle ne m'a pas donné le livre
  did she give the book to me? = est-ce qu'elle m'a donné le livre?
- **write to me!** = écris-moi!
  say it to me! = dis-le-moi!
  don't show it to me! = ne me le montre pas!
- **me** = moi
  he did it for me = il l'a fait pour moi
  it's me = c'est moi
  stand in front of me = mets-toi devant moi

meal *noun*
  a meal = un repas

mean

1 *verb*
- **to mean** = vouloir dire
  what does that mean? = qu'est-ce que ça veut dire?
  what does the word 'bête' mean? = que veut dire le mot 'bête'?
- (*to have as a result*)
  it means giving up my job = ça veut dire que je dois abandonner mon travail
- (*to intend*)
  I meant to order a pizza = je voulais commander une pizza
  she didn't mean to upset you = elle ne voulait pas te faire de la peine
  he meant it as a joke = il voulait plaisanter
- (*to intend to say*) = vouloir dire
  what do you mean? = qu'est-ce que tu veux dire?
- **her work means a lot to her** = son travail compte beaucoup pour elle
  money doesn't mean much to him = l'argent n'a pas beaucoup d'importance pour lui

2 *adjective*
- (*British English*) (*not generous*) = avare, radin/radine*

M

• to be mean to someone = être
méchant/méchante avec quelqu'un

meaning noun
a meaning = un sens

means noun
a means = un moyen
a means of transport = un moyen de
transport
a means of earning money = un moyen de
gagner de l'argent

meant: to be meant to verb
to be meant to = être censé/censée
I'm meant to be at my parents' house = je
suis censé être chez mes parents

meanwhile adverb
= pendant ce temps

measles noun ▶ 266 |
measles = la rougeole

measure verb
= mesurer

meat noun
meat = la viande

mechanic noun ▶ 315 |
a mechanic = un mécanicien/une
mécanicienne

medal noun
a medal = une médaille
the gold medal = la médaille d'or

media noun
the media = les médias (masculine)

medical adjective
= médical/médicale
to have medical treatment = suivre un
traitement médical

medicine noun
a medicine = un médicament

Mediterranean noun
the Mediterranean = la (mer)
Méditerranée

medium adjective
= moyen/moyenne

meet verb
• (by accident or appointment) = rencontrer
she met him at the butcher's = elle l'a
rencontré à la boucherie
can we meet (up) next week? = est-ce
qu'on peut se voir la semaine
prochaine?
to meet again = se revoir (**!** + être)
• (to be introduced to) ▶ 237 | = faire la
connaissance de
she met him at a wedding = elle a fait sa
connaissance à un mariage
have you met Tom? = est-ce que vous
connaissez Tom?

• (to fetch)
I can meet you at the station = je peux
aller te chercher à la gare
can you meet me at the station? = peux-tu
venir me chercher à la gare?
• (to have a meeting) = se réunir (**!** + être)

meeting noun
a meeting = une réunion

melon noun
a melon = un melon

melt verb
• the snow is starting to melt = la neige
commence à fondre
• the salt will melt the ice = le sel fera fondre
le verglas

member noun ▶ 315 |
a member = un membre
a member of staff (in a school) = un
enseignant/une enseignante
(in a bank, a firm) = un membre du
personnel

memory noun
• memory = la mémoire
to have a good memory = avoir bonne
mémoire
he's got a bad memory = il n'a pas de
mémoire
• (of a person, a place or time)
a memory = un souvenir

mend verb
• (to fix) = réparer
• (by sewing) = raccommoder

mental adjective
= mental/mentale

menu noun
a menu = un menu

mess noun
a mess = le désordre
your room is in a mess = ta chambre est
en désordre
to make a mess in the kitchen = mettre du
désordre dans la cuisine

message noun
a message = un message

metal noun
a metal = un métal

method noun
a method = une méthode

metre (British English), **meter** (US
English) noun ▶ 285 |
a metre = un mètre

Mexico noun ▶ 218 |
Mexico = le Mexique

microphone noun
a microphone = un microphone

microwave noun
a microwave = un four à micro-ondes

Length and weight measurements

Length measurements

Note that French has a *comma* where English has a *decimal point*:

1 inch	= 2,54 cm	*1 yard*	= 91,44 cm
1 foot	= 30,48 cm	*1 mile*	= 1,61 km (kilomètres)

Length

how long is the rope?	= quelle est la longueur de la corde?
it's ten metres long	= elle fait dix mètres
the rope is three metres too short	= la corde est trop courte de trois mètres

Height

People	*how tall is he?*	= combien mesure-t-il?
	he's six feet tall	= il mesure un mètre quatre-vingts
	Tom is taller / smaller than Jane	= Tom est plus grand / plus petit que Jane
Things	*how high is the tower?*	= quelle est la hauteur de la tour?
	it's 100 metres high	= elle fait cent mètres de† haut / de† hauteur
	A is higher / lower than B	= A est plus haut / moins haut que B

Distance

how far is it from Paris to Nice?	= quelle distance y a-t-il entre Paris et Nice?
it's about 800 kilometres	= il y a environ 800 kilomètres

Width / breadth

how wide is the river?	= quelle est la largeur de la rivière?
it's seven metres wide	= elle fait sept mètres de† large / de† largeur

Depth

how deep is the lake	= quelle est la profondeur du lac?
it's four metres deep	= il fait quatre mètres de† profondeur

Note the French construction with **de**, coming after the noun it describes:

a street two kilometres long	= une rue **de** deux kilomètres de† long
a 100-metre-high tower	= une tour **de** cent mètres de† haut
a ten-kilometre walk	= une promenade **de** dix kilomètres
a river 50 metres wide	= une rivière **de** 50 mètres de† largeur

Weight measurements

Again, note that French has a *comma* where English has a *decimal point*:

1 ounce	= 28,35 g (grammes)	*1 stone*	= 6,35 kg (kilos)
1 pound *	= 453,60 g	*1 ton*	= 1 014,60 kg

* **a pound** (£1) is translated by **une livre** in French, but the French **livre** = 500 grammes (half a kilo).

People	*how much does he weigh?*	= combien pèse-t-il?
	he weighs 10st / 140 lbs	= il pèse 63 kg 500 (soixante-trois kilos cinq cents)
Things	*what does the parcel weigh?*	= combien pèse le colis?
	how heavy is it?	= quel est son poids?
	it weighs 10 kilos	= il pèse 10 kilos
	A weighs more than B	= A pèse plus lourd que B
	sold by the kilo	= vendu au kilo

† The use of **de** is obligatory in these constructions.

midday noun ▶ 211 |, ▶ 356 |
   midday = midi (*masculine*)
   at midday = à midi

middle noun
   the middle = le milieu
   in the middle of the road = au milieu de la
      route
   to be in the middle of cooking a meal
      = être en train de préparer un repas

middle-aged adjective
   = d'âge mûr (**!** *never changes*)

midnight noun ▶ 211 |, ▶ 356 |
   midnight = minuit (*masculine*)
   at midnight = à minuit

might verb
• (*when talking about a possibility*)
   she might be right = elle a peut-être raison
   they might have got lost = ils se sont peut-
      être perdus
   'will you come?'—'I might' = 'est-ce tu
      viendras?'—'peut-être'
   we might miss the plane = nous risquons
      de rater l'avion
   he said he might not come = il a dit qu'il
      ne viendrait peut-être pas
• (*when implying something didn't happen*)
   you might have been killed! = tu aurais pu
      te faire tuer!
   she might have warned us = elle aurait pu
      nous prévenir
• (*when making suggestions*)
   you might try leaving a message = vous
      pourriez laisser un message
   it might be better to wait = ce serait peut-
      être mieux d'attendre

mild adjective
   = doux/douce
   the weather's mild, it's mild = il fait doux

mile noun ▶ 285 |
   a mile = un mile
   | **!** *Note that a* mile = *1609 m.*

military adjective
   = militaire

milk
1 noun
   milk = le lait
2 verb
   = traire

milkman noun ▶ 315 |
   a milkman = un laitier

million number
   one million, a million = un million
   three million dollars = trois millions de
      dollars
   a million inhabitants = un million
      d'habitants

mind
1 noun
• the mind = l'esprit (*masculine*)
   to have a logical mind = avoir l'esprit
      logique
   I have a lot on my mind = j'ai beaucoup de
      soucis
• to make up one's mind to change jobs = se
   décider à changer de travail
   to change one's mind = changer d'avis
2 verb
• (*when expressing an opinion*)
   'where shall we go?'—'I don't mind' = 'où
      irons-nous?'—'ça m'est égal'
   she doesn't mind the heat = la chaleur ne
      la dérange pas
   I wouldn't mind some cake = je prendrais
      volontiers du gâteau
• (*in polite questions or requests*)
   do you mind if I smoke? = est-ce que cela
      vous dérange si je fume?
   would you mind coming? = est-ce que ça
      vous ennuierait de venir?
• (*to be careful*)
   mind the steps! = fais attention aux
      marches!
   mind you don't break the plates = fais
      attention de ne pas casser les assiettes
• (*to take care of*) = s'occuper de (**!** + *être*)
• never mind, she'll get the next train = ne
   t'en fais pas, elle prendra le train suivant

mine[1] pronoun
   the green pen is mine = le stylo vert est à
      moi
   guess which house is mine = devine
      laquelle de ces maisons est la mienne
   her coat is brown but mine is dark green
      = son manteau est marron mais le mien
      est vert foncé
   his sister's the same age as mine = sa
      sœur a le même âge que la mienne
   | **!** *Note that, when comparing objects,*
   | *people, etc, one of the following*
   | *translations*—le mien, la mienne, les
   | miens *or* les miennes—*will be used. To*
   | *know which one to use, find out whether*
   | *the object, person, etc which is being*
   | *described is masculine or feminine,*
   | *singular or plural.*

mine[2] noun
   a mine = une mine

miner noun ▶ 315 |
   a miner = un mineur

mineral water noun
   a mineral water = une eau minérale

minimum
1 adjective
   the minimum price = le prix minimum
   a minimum temperature of 15 degrees
      = une température minimale de 15
      degrés
2 noun
   the minimum = le minimum

minister noun ▶ 315 |
- (in government)
  a minister = un ministre
  the minister for Education = le ministre de
    l'Éducation
- (in religion)
  a minister = un ministre du culte

minor adjective
= mineur/mineure
a minor injury = une blessure légère

minority noun
a minority = une minorité

minus preposition
= moins
it's minus four outside = il fait moins
  quatre dehors

minute noun ▶ 211 |, ▶ 356 |
a minute = une minute
they'll be here any minute now = ils vont
  arriver d'une minute à l'autre

mirror noun
a mirror (on a wall) = un miroir, une glace
  (on a car) = un rétroviseur

miserable adjective
= malheureux/malheureuse
to feel miserable = avoir le cafard

miss verb
- to miss the target = manquer la cible
  the stone just missed his head = la pierre
    lui a frôlé la tête
- (to fail to see) = rater
  you can't miss it = tu ne peux pas le rater
- to miss an opportunity = laisser passer une
    occasion
- (to feel sad not to see)
  I miss you = tu me manques
  we'll miss Oxford = Oxford va nous
    manquer
- (other uses)
  don't miss this film = ne rate pas ce film
  she missed her plane = elle a raté son
    avion
  to miss school (due to illness) = manquer
    l'école
  (by skipping classes) = sauter les cours

Miss noun
▶ See the boxed note on Forms of address.
Miss = mademoiselle (feminine)

missing adjective
to be missing = manquer
there's a book missing = il manque un
  livre

mist noun
mist = la brume

mistake noun
a mistake = une erreur

a spelling mistake = une faute
  d'orthographe
to make a mistake = se tromper (**!** + être)

mistletoe noun
mistletoe = le gui

mix verb
- (to put together) = mélanger
- (to go together) = se mélanger (**!** + être)
- to mix with the other students = fréquenter
    les autres étudiants
mix up = confondre
  to get the two languages mixed up
    = confondre les deux langues
  I'm always mixing him up with his brother
    = je le confonds toujours avec son frère

mixture noun
a mixture = un mélange

mobile phone noun
a mobile phone = un téléphone portable
  un portable

model noun
- (of a train, a car, a building)
  a model = un modèle réduit, une
    maquette
- ▶ 315 |
  a (fashion) model = un mannequin

modern adjective
= moderne

Mohammed noun
Mohammed = Mahomet

mom, Mom noun (US English)
a mom = une maman

moment noun
a moment = un instant
there's no-one there at the moment = il
  n'y a personne en ce moment

Monday noun ▶ 222 |
Monday = lundi (masculine)

money noun
money = l'argent (masculine)

monkey noun
a monkey = un singe

month noun ▶ 356 |
a month = un mois
he'll be back in two months' time = il sera
  de retour dans deux mois

Montreal noun ▶ 218 |
Montreal = Montréal

monument noun
a monument = un monument

mood noun
to be in a good mood = être de bonne
  humeur
I'm in a very bad mood = je suis de très
  mauvaise humeur

M

moon *noun*
the moon = la lune

moped *noun*
a moped = un vélomoteur

moral *adjective*
= moral/morale

more ▶ 317 |
1 *determiner*
= plus de
more [friends | books | CDs ...] = plus [d'amis | de livres | de disques compacts ...]
more [money | food | time ...] = plus [d'argent | de nourriture | de temps ...]
I have more work than him = j'ai plus de travail que lui
there's no more bread = il n'y a plus de pain
there's more tea = il y a encore du thé
would you like more coffee? = voulez-vous encore du café?
he bought two more tickets = il a acheté deux billets de plus
2 *pronoun*
= plus
to cost more = coûter plus cher
I did more than you = j'en ai fait plus que toi
I can't tell you any more = je ne peux pas t'en dire plus
we need more (of them) = il nous en faut plus
we need more (of it) = il nous en faut davantage

> **!** *Note that it is necessary to use* en, *which might be translated as* 'of it' *or* 'of them', *with pronouns like* more. *See also* another, a few, a lot *etc for this use of* en.

3 *adverb*
• (*when comparing*) = plus
it's more complicated than that = c'est plus compliqué que ça
• (*when talking about time*)
he doesn't live there any more = il n'habite plus là
4 more and more = de plus en plus
more and more expensive = de plus en plus cher
5 more or less = plus ou moins
6 more than = plus de
there were more than 20 people there = il y avait plus de 20 personnes

morning *noun* **▶ 211 |**, **▶ 356 |**

> **!** *Note that* morning *is usually translated by* matin *in French. However it is sometimes translated by* matinée, *when there is an emphasis on the idea of duration.*

a morning = un matin
at three o'clock in the morning = à trois heures du matin
to spend the morning reading the paper = passer la matinée à lire le journal

mosquito *noun*
a mosquito = un moustique

most
1 *determiner*
• (*the majority of*) = la plupart de
most schools will be closed = la plupart des écoles seront fermées
• (*in superlatives*)
the most = le plus de
who has the most money? = qui a le plus d'argent?
2 *pronoun*
= la plupart de
most of the time they phone each other = la plupart du temps ils se téléphonent
most (of them) speak Greek = la plupart (d'entre eux) parlent grec
3 *adverb*
the most
= le plus/la plus (+ *singular*)
= les plus (+ *plural*)
the most expensive shop in London = le magasin le plus cher de Londres
the most beautiful town in France = la plus belle ville de France
4 at (the) most = au maximum, au plus
5 most of all = par-dessus tout

mostly *adverb*
= pour la plupart

mother *noun*
a mother = une mère

mother-in-law *noun*
a mother-in-law = une belle-mère

motor *noun*
a motor = un moteur

motorbike *noun*
a motorbike = une moto

motorcyclist *noun*
a motorcyclist = un motocycliste/une motocycliste

motorist *noun*
a motorist = un automobiliste/une automobiliste

motor racing *noun* **▶ 248 |**
motor racing = la course automobile

motorway *noun* (*British English*)
a motorway = une autoroute

mountain *noun*
a mountain = une montagne
to go camping in the mountains = faire du camping en montagne

mountain bike *noun*
a mountain bike = un vélo tout terrain, un VTT

mountain climbing *noun* **▶ 248 |**
mountain climbing = l'alpinisme (*masculine*)

mouse *noun*
a mouse = une souris

✱ in informal situations

moustache, mustache (*US English*)
noun
  a moustache = une moustache

mouth *noun* ▶ **201**
- (*of a person*)
  the mouth = la bouche
  to have a big mouth = avoir une grande
    gueule**✗**
- (*of an animal*)
  the mouth = la gueule
- (*of a river*)
  the mouth = l'embouchure (*feminine*)

move *verb*
- (*to make a movement*) = bouger
  don't move! = ne bouge pas!
  the train's starting to move = le train
    démarre
- (*to put elsewhere*) = déplacer
  to move the car = déplacer la voiture
  to move a chair (out of the way)
    = déplacer une chaise
- (*to make a movement with*) = bouger
  I couldn't move my leg = je n'arrivais pas à
    bouger la jambe
  don't move the camera = ne bouge pas
    l'appareil photo
- (*to act*) = agir
- to move (house) = déménager
  to move to Paris = déménager à Paris
move away
- (*to live elsewhere*) = déménager
- (*to make a movement away*) = s'éloigner
  (**!** + *être*)
  to move away from the window
    = s'éloigner de la fenêtre
move back = reculer
move forward = s'avancer (**!** + *être*)
move in = emménager
  to move in with friends = s'installer avec
    des amis
move out = déménager
move over = se pousser (**!** + *être*)
  move over please = pousse-toi s'il te plaît

movement *noun*
  a movement = un mouvement

movie *noun* (*US English*)
  a movie = un film

movies *noun* (*US English*)
  the movies = le cinéma

movie theater *noun* (*US English*)
  a movie theater = un cinéma

moving *adjective*
  = émouvant/émouvante

mow *verb*
  to mow the lawn = tondre le gazon

MP *noun* ▶ **315** (*British English*)
  an MP = un député

Mr *noun*
▶ *See the boxed note on* Forms of address.
  Mr = monsieur (*masculine*)

Mrs *noun*
▶ *See the boxed note on* Forms of address.
  Mrs = madame (*feminine*)

much ▶ **317**
1 *adverb*
- (*a lot*) = beaucoup
  her work is much more tiring = son travail
    est beaucoup plus fatigant
  he doesn't read much = il ne lit pas
    beaucoup
- (*often*) = beaucoup
  they don't go out much = ils ne sortent
    pas beaucoup
- (*when used with* very, too *or* so)
  he misses her very much = elle lui
    manque beaucoup
  you talk too much = tu parles trop
  she loves him so much = elle l'aime
    tellement
2 *pronoun*
- (*in questions*) = beaucoup
  (*in negative statements*) = grand-chose
  is there much to be done? = est-ce qu'il y a
    beaucoup à faire?
  he didn't eat much = il n'a pas mangé
    grand-chose
3 *determiner*
- (*a lot of*) = beaucoup de
  I haven't got much time = je n'ai pas
    beaucoup de temps
  do you have much work? = est-ce que
    vous avez beaucoup de travail?
- (*when used with* how, very, too, so *or* as)
  how much money have you got?
    = combien d'argent as-tu?
  she doesn't eat very much meat = elle ne
    mange pas beaucoup de viande
  I spent too much money = j'ai dépensé
    trop d'argent
  don't use so much salt = ne mets pas tant
    de sel
  she has as much work as me = elle a
    autant de travail que moi

mud *noun*
  mud = la boue

mug
1 *noun*
  a mug = une grande tasse
2 *verb*
  to be mugged = se faire agresser (**!** + *être*)

multiply *verb*
  = multiplier

mum, Mum *noun* (*British English*)
  a mum = une maman

mumps *noun* ▶ **266**
  mumps = les oreillons (*masculine plural*)

murder
1 *noun*
  a murder = un meurtre

M

Musical instruments

Playing an instrument

Note the use of **de** with **jouer**:

to play the piano	= **jouer du** piano
to play the flute	= **jouer de la** flûte

but

to learn the piano	= **apprendre le** piano
to learn the guitar	= **apprendre la** guitare

Players

English **-ist** is very often French **-iste**. The gender will reflect the sex of the player:

a pianist	= **un** pianiste / **une** pianiste
a violonist	= **un** violoniste / **une** violoniste

But note the French when these words are used with **good** and **bad** like this:

he's a good pianist	= **il joue bien du** piano
he's a bad pianist	= **il joue mal du** piano

Use with another noun

de is usually correct:

to take piano lessons	= prendre des leçons **de** piano
a guitar solo	= un solo **de** guitare
a piano teacher	= un professeur **de** piano

---

2 *verb*
= assassiner

murderer *noun*
a murderer = un meurtrier

muscle *noun*
a muscle = un muscle

museum *noun*
a museum = un musée

mushroom *noun*
a mushroom = un champignon

music *noun*
music = la musique

musical *noun*
a musical = une comédie musicale

musical instrument *noun*
a musical instrument = un instrument de
musique

musician *noun* ▶ 315 |
a musician = un musicien/une
musicienne

Muslim *adjective*
= musulman/musulmane

mussel *noun*
a mussel = une moule

must *verb*

> **!** *The verbs* devoir *and* falloir *are used to
> translate* must. *Note that the subjunctive
> is used after* il faut que.

- (*when stressing the importance of
  something*)
  you must go to the doctor = il faut que tu
  ailles chez le médecin
  we mustn't tell anyone = il ne faut en
  parler à personne
- (*when talking about a rule*)
  she must take the exam in June = elle
  doit passer l'examen au mois de
  juin
  visitors must go to (the) reception = les
  visiteurs doivent se présenter au bureau
  d'accueil
- (*when assuming that something is
  true*)
  it must be nice to live there = ça doit être
  agréable de vivre là-bas
  you must be David's sister = tu dois être
  la sœur de David
  they must have been bored = ils ont dû
  s'ennuyer

mustard *noun*
mustard = la moutarde

mutton *noun*
mutton = le mouton

Using the subjunctive

There are a number of examples in this dictionary which use the subjunctive. They are highlighted in the text with a note. The type of examples generating the subjunctive fall into three main categories. They are examples which contain:

- certain verbs, mainly:
  falloir
  vouloir

- certain conjunctions:
  bien que . . .
  jusqu'à ce que . . .
  à condition que . . .
  pour que . . .
  à moins que . . .

- certain phrases, often expressing a personal opinion:
  il est bizarre que . . .
  c'est dommage que . . .
  je suis content que . . .
  je doute que . . .

Verbs

- *falloir* is by far the most common verb requiring the subjunctive in this dictionary. The impersonal form **il faut que** is most often used to translate **must**.

I **must** go	= il **faut que** je m'en aille
you **must** come	= il **faut que** tu viennes

- *vouloir*, meaning **to want**, requires the subjunctive in specific cases. Compare:

I want to come	= je veux **venir**
I want you **to come**	= je veux que **tu viennes**

  The second example uses the subjunctive because there are two 'subjects' involved, I and you. In the first example, there is only one subject, which means that no subjunctive is required.

Conjunctions

The most common conjunctions requiring the subjunctive in French in this dictionary are:

M

- **bien que** (= *although, even though, though*)
although she's quite old, she has lots of energy	= **bien qu'**elle soit assez âgée, elle a beaucoup d'énergie

- **jusqu'à ce que** (= *until*)
let's watch television **until** they arrive	= regardons la télévision **jusqu'à ce qu'**ils arrivent

- **à condition que** (= *provided, on condition that, as long as*)
you can go out with them **provided** they bring you home	= tu peux sortir avec eux **à condition qu'**ils te ramènent

- **pour que** (= *so that*)
be quiet **so that** I can sleep	= tais-toi **pour que** je puisse dormir!

- **à moins que** (= *unless*)
I am not going **unless** you come with me	= je n'y vais pas **à moins que** tu viennes avec moi

Phrases

When stating an opinion, the subjunctive is always used with the following phrases:

it's strange that she's never there	= il est bizarre qu'elle ne soit jamais là
it's a pity we can't go there	= c'est dommage qu'on ne puisse pas y aller
I'm glad he has lots of friends	= je suis content qu'il ait beaucoup d'amis
I doubt if he'll come	= je doute qu'il vienne

Superlatives

it's the best book (that) I have ever read	= c'est le meilleur livre **que j'aie jamais lu**
it's the most expensive watch (that) he's seen	= c'est la montre la plus chère **qu'il ait vue**

In French, the subjunctive is always used in clauses with **que** following a superlative adjective like *le meilleur* | *la meilleure, le plus mauvais* | *la plus mauvaise* etc.

▶ For more information on the subjunctive forms of French verbs, see the **verb tables ▶ 381**.

▶ For information on grammar terms used in this note, see the **glossary page x**.

my *determiner*
my = mon/ma (+ *singular*)
= mes (+ *plural*)
> ! *Note that* ma *becomes* mon *before a vowel or mute h.*

they hate my dog = ils détestent mon chien
what do you think of my house? = qu'est-ce que tu penses de ma maison?
he's my age = il a mon âge
I sold all my CDs = j'ai vendu tous mes disques compacts
I broke my leg = je me suis cassé la jambe
> ! *Note that, when talking about parts of the body,* mon, ma *and* mes *are not used. See the usage note on* The human body ▶ 201 *for further examples.*

myself *pronoun*
* (*when used as a reflexive pronoun*)
I want to enjoy myself = je veux m'amuser
I didn't hurt myself = je ne me suis pas fait mal
* (*when used for emphasis*)
I told them myself = je le leur ai dit moi-même
I did it all by myself = je l'ai fait tout seul

mystery *noun*
a mystery = un mystère

Nn

nail *noun* ▶ 201
* (*for use in attaching, repairing*)
a nail = un clou
* (*on the fingers or toes*)
a nail = un ongle

nail polish *noun*
nail polish = le vernis à ongles

naked *adjective*
= nu/nue

name *noun*
* (*of a person*)
a name = un nom
what's your name? = comment t'appelles-tu?, comment vous appelez-vous?
my name is Louis = je m'appelle Louis
* (*of a book, a play or film*)
a name = un titre

narrow *adjective*
= étroit/étroite

nasty *adjective*
* (*mean, unkind*) = méchant/méchante
* (*unpleasant*) = désagréable

national *adjective*
= national/nationale

native *adjective*
a native language = une langue maternelle
a native French speaker = une personne de langue maternelle française

natural *adjective*
= naturel/naturelle
it's natural to be disappointed = c'est normal d'être déçu

naturally *adverb*
= naturellement

nature *noun*
nature = la nature

naughty *adjective*
= vilain/vilaine

navy *noun*
the navy = la marine

navy blue *adjective* ▶ 213
= bleu marine (! *never changes*)

near
1 *preposition*
= près de
he was sitting near us = il était assis près de nous
2 *adverb*
they live quite near = ils habitent tout près

3 *adjective*
= proche
the school is quite near = l'école est assez proche
the nearest shops are several miles away = les magasins les plus proches sont à plusieurs kilomètres d'ici

nearby *adverb*
= à proximité

nearly *adverb*
= presque
we're nearly there = nous sommes presque arrivés
I nearly [forgot | gave up | fell asleep ...] = j'ai failli [oublier | abandonner | m'endormir ...]

neat *adjective*
(*in one's habits*) = ordonné/ordonnée
(*in how one looks*) = net/nette
(*describing work, handwriting*) – soigné/soignée

necessary *adjective*
= nécessaire

neck *noun* ▶ 201 |
the neck = le cou

necklace *noun*
a necklace = un collier

need *verb*
• (*(to) have to*)
you don't need to ask permission = tu n'es pas obligé de demander la permission
they'll need to come early = il va falloir qu'ils viennent de bonne heure
! *Note that the subjunctive is used after falloir que.*

• (*to want*) = avoir besoin de
they need [money | help | friends ...] = ils ont besoin [d'argent | d'aide | d'amis ...]
we need to see the doctor = nous avons besoin de voir le médecin
everything you need = tout ce qu'il vous faut

needle *noun*
a needle = une aiguille

negative
1 *adjective*
• (*pessimistic*) = négatif/négative
• (*harmful*) = néfaste
2 *noun*
a negative = un négatif

neighbour (*British English*), **neighbor** (*US English*) *noun*
a neighbour = un voisin/une voisine

neither
1 *conjunction*
• (*in* neither... nor *sentences*) = ni... ni

she speaks neither French nor English = elle ne parle ni français ni anglais
I have neither the time nor the energy to argue = je n'ai ni le temps ni la force de discuter
• (*nor*)
'I can't sleep'—'neither can I' = 'je n'arrive pas à dormir'—'moi non plus'
2 *determiner*
= aucun des deux/aucune des deux
neither girl answered = aucune des deux filles n'a répondu
3 *pronoun*
= ni l'un/l'une ni l'autre
neither of them is coming = ni l'un ni l'autre ne vient
! *Note that, in sentences with a verb, the negative* ne *or* n' *(before a vowel or mute h) is used together with* ni... ni, aucun/aucune des deux *and* ni l'un/l'une ni l'autre *to translate* neither. *Remember that* ne *comes before the verb or the auxiliary verb.*

nephew *noun*
a nephew = un neveu

nerves *noun*
nerves = les nerfs (*masculine*)
to get on someone's nerves = énerver quelqu'un

nervous *adjective*
• (*frightened*)
to be nervous = avoir peur
• (*anxious*) = angoissé/angoissée
to feel nervous = être angoissé/angoissée

nest *noun*
a nest = un nid

net *noun*
• (*for fishing*)
a net = un filet
• (*in sport*)
the net (*in football*) = les filets (*masculine plural*)
(*in tennis*) = le filet

Netherlands *noun* ▶ 218 |
the Netherlands = les Pays-Bas (*masculine plural*)

network *noun*
a network = un réseau

neutral *adjective*
= neutre

never *adverb*
! *Note that, in sentences with a verb, the negative* ne *or* n' *(before a vowel or mute h) is used together with* jamais *to translate* never. *Remember that* ne *comes before the verb or the auxiliary verb.*

- (*not ever*) = jamais
  they never come to see us = ils ne
  viennent jamais nous voir
  she has never been to the opera = elle
  n'est jamais allée à l'opéra
  I'll never go back there again = je n'y
  retournerai plus jamais
- (*when used for emphasis*)
  she never even apologized = elle ne s'est
  même pas excusée

nevertheless *adverb*
= pourtant, néanmoins

new *adjective*
= nouveau/nouvelle (**!** *before the noun*)

> **!** *Note that* nouvel *is used instead of*
> nouveau *before masculine nouns*
> *beginning with a vowel* (endroit, ordina-
> teur) *or a mute h* (hôtel). *The plural of*
> nouveau *and* nouvel *is* nouveaux.

a new bike = un nouveau vélo
a new car = une nouvelle voiture
a new computer = un nouvel ordinateur
new dresses = de nouvelles robes

newborn baby *noun*
a newborn baby = un nouveau-né

news *noun*
- **a piece of news** = une nouvelle
  have you heard the news? = est-ce que tu
  connais la nouvelle?
  that's good news = c'est une bonne
  nouvelle
  have you any news of John? = est-ce que
  tu as des nouvelles de John?
- (*on radio, TV*)
  the news = le journal (*singular*)= , les
  informations (*feminine*)

newsagent's *noun* ▶ 315 | (*British English*)
a newsagent's = un magasin de journaux

newspaper *noun*
a newspaper = un journal

New Year *noun*
the New Year = le nouvel an
Happy New Year! = Bonne année!

New Year's Day, New Year's (*US English*) *noun*
New Year's (Day) = le jour de l'an

New Year's Eve *noun*
New Year's Eve = la Saint-Sylvestre

New Zealand *noun* ▶ 218 |
New Zealand = la Nouvelle-Zélande

next
1 *adjective*
- (*when talking about what is still to come*)
  = prochain/prochaine

I'll take the next train to London = je
prendrai le prochain train pour Londres
he'll be here next week = il sera là la
semaine prochaine
- (*when talking about what followed*)
  = suivant/suivante
  I took the next train = j'ai pris le train
  suivant
  they arrived the next day = ils sont arrivés
  le lendemain
- (*in a queue*)
  'who's next?' = 'à qui le tour?'
  'I'm next' = 'c'est mon tour'
2 *adverb*
- (*in the past*) = ensuite
  what happened next? = qu'est-ce qui s'est
  passé ensuite?
- (*now*) = maintenant
  what'll we do next? = qu'est-ce qu'on fait
  maintenant?
- (*in the future*)
  **when you next go to Paris, give Gary a
  call** = la prochaine fois que tu iras à
  Paris, passe un coup de fil à Gary
3 next to = à côté de

next door *adverb*
= à côté

nice *adjective*
- (*enjoyable*) = agréable
  it's nice to be able to relax = c'est agréable
  de pouvoir se détendre
- (*kind, friendly*) = sympathique, sympa✱
  to be nice to someone = être
  gentil/gentille avec quelqu'un
- (*attractive*) = beau/belle (**!** *before the noun*)

nickname *noun*
a nickname = un surnom

niece *noun*
a niece = une nièce

night *noun* ▶ 356 |
- (*as opposed to day*)
  a night = une nuit
  I didn't sleep last night = je n'ai pas dormi
  cette nuit
  he stayed out all night = il n'est pas rentré
  de la nuit
- (*evening*)
  a night = un soir
  last night = hier soir
  a night at the cinema = une soirée au
  cinéma

> **!** *See the note at* evening *for information
> on* soir *and* soirée.

nightclub *noun*
a nightclub = une boîte de nuit

nightdress *noun*
a nightdress = une chemise de nuit

nightmare *noun*
a nightmare = un cauchemar
to have a nightmare = faire un cauchemar

nil *noun*
nil = zéro

nine *number* ▶ **187** |, ▶ **211** |
nine = neuf
nine books = neuf livres
I have nine (of them) = j'en ai neuf

nineteen *number* ▶ **187** |, ▶ **211** |
nineteen = dix-neuf

nineteenth *number*
• (*in a series*) = dix-neuvième
• (*in dates*) ▶ **222** |
the nineteenth of July = le dix-neuf juillet

ninety *number* ▶ **187** |
ninety = quatre-vingt-dix

ninth *number*
• (*in a series*) = neuvième
• (*in dates*) ▶ **222** |
the ninth of December = le neuf décembre

no
1 *adverb*
• no = non
no thanks = non merci
• he no longer works here = il ne travaille
plus ici
2 *determiner*
• (*not any*)
we have no money = nous n'avons pas
d'argent
there are no trains = il n'y a pas de trains
• (*when refusing permission*)
no smoking = défense de fumer
no talking! = silence!
• (*when used for emphasis*)
this is no time to argue = ce n'est pas le
moment de discuter
it's no problem = ce n'est pas du tout un
problème

nobody ▶ **no-one**

noise *noun*
noise = le bruit
to make noise = faire du bruit

noisy *adjective*
= bruyant/bruyante

none *pronoun*

> ! Note that, when there is a verb in the
> sentence, the negative ne or n' (before a
> vowel or mute h) is used together with
> aucun/aucune to translate none.
> Remember that ne comes before the verb
> or the auxiliary verb.

none = aucun/aucune
none of the girls went to the class
= aucune des filles n'est allée au cours
none of [us | you | them ...] can speak
German = aucun [de nous | de vous | d'entre
eux ...] ne parle allemand
there's none left = il n'y en a plus
I've got none, I have none = je n'en ai pas

> ! Note that it is necessary to use en which
> might be translated as 'of it' or 'of them',
> with pronouns like none. See also another,
> a few, a lot etc for this use of en.

nonsense *noun*
that's nonsense! = c'est absurde!

noon *noun* ▶ **211** |, ▶ **356** |
noon = midi (*masculine*)
at noon = à midi

no-one *pronoun* (*also* **nobody**)

> ! Note that, when there is a verb in the
> sentence, the negative ne or n' (before a
> vowel or mute h) is used together with
> personne to translate no-one. Remember
> that ne comes before the verb or the
> auxiliary verb.

no-one = personne
no-one tells me anything = personne ne
me dit rien
no-one saw him = personne ne l'a vu
there's no-one else in the office = il n'y a
personne d'autre au bureau

nor *conjunction*

> ! For translations of nor when used in
> combination with neither, look at the entry
> for neither in this dictionary.

'I don't like him'—'nor do I' = 'je ne l'aime
pas'—'moi non plus'

normal *adjective*
= normal/normale

normally *adverb*
= normalement

north
1 *noun*
the north = le nord
in the north of France = dans le nord de la
France
2 *adverb*
to go north = aller vers le nord
to live north of Paris = vivre au nord de
Paris
3 *adjective*
= nord (! *never changes*)
to work in north London = travailler dans
le nord de Londres

North America *noun* ▶ **218** |
North America = l'Amérique du Nord
! *Note that* **Amérique** *is feminine.*

northeast *noun*
the northeast = le nord-est

Northern Ireland *noun* ▶ **218** |
Northern Ireland = l'Irlande du Nord
! *Note that* **Irlande** *is feminine.*

northwest *noun*
the northwest = le nord-ouest

Norway *noun* ▶ **218** |
Norway = la Norvège

not

Used without a verb

When **not** is used without a verb before an adjective, a noun, an adverb, a verb or a pronoun it is translated by **pas**:

not at all	= **pas** du tout
not bad	= **pas** mal
*it's a cat **not** a dog*	= c'est un chat **pas** un chien
*you should walk, **not** run*	= il faut marcher, **pas** courir
*she should apologise, **not** me*	= c'est elle qui devrait s'excuser, **pas** moi

Used with a verb

When **not** is used with the verbs *be, do, have, will* and *would,* the translation is **ne ... pas** (**n'** before a vowel or mute h): **ne** comes before the verb or the auxiliary, and **pas** comes after the verb or auxiliary:

*it's **not** a cat*	= ce n'est **pas** un chat
he doesn't like oranges	= il n'aime **pas** les oranges
I haven't seen him	= je ne l'ai **pas** vu
she hasn't arrived yet	= elle n'est **pas** encore arrivée
she won't come by car	= elle ne viendra **pas** en voiture
it wouldn't matter	= ce ne serait **pas** grave

When used with a verb in the infinitive, **ne** and **pas** are placed together before the verb:

*he decided **not** to go*	= il a décidé de **ne pas** y aller
*you were wrong **not** to tell her*	= tu as eu tort de **ne pas** le lui dire

Used in short questions

When **not** is used in short questions, the whole question can usually be translated by the French **n'est-ce pas**:

*she bought it, **didn't she**?*	= elle l'a acheté, **n'est-ce pas**?
*you were there too, **weren't you**?*	= tu y étais aussi, **n'est-ce pas**?
*they're living in Germany, **aren't they**?*	= ils habitent en Allemagne, **n'est-ce pas**?
*he's got a lot of money, **hasn't he**?*	= il a beaucoup d'argent, **n'est-ce pas**?
*you'll come too, **won't you**?*	= vous viendrez vous aussi, **n'est-ce pas**?
*he likes fish, **doesn't he**?*	= il aime le poisson, **n'est-ce pas**?

▶ For more examples, see the entry **not**.

Norwegian ▶ 275 |
1 *adjective*
= norvégien/norvégienne
2 *noun*
the Norwegians = les Norvégiens

nose *noun* ▶ 201 |
the nose = le nez

not
▶ *See the boxed note on* not *for more information and examples*
1 *adverb*
= ne... pas (**!** n' + *vowel or mute h...* pas)
> **!** *Remember that* ne *or* n' *(before a vowel or mute h) comes before the verb or auxiliary verb and* pas *after.*

she's not at home = elle n'est pas chez elle
hasn't he phoned you? = il ne t'a pas
téléphoné?
I hope not = j'espère que non

we're going to go out whether it rains or
not = qu'il pleuve ou non, nous allons
sortir
not everyone likes football = le football ne
plaît pas à tout le monde
2 not at all
• (*in no way*) = pas du tout
he's not at all worried = il n'est pas du
tout inquiet
• 'thanks a lot'—'not at all' = 'merci
beaucoup'—'de rien'

note
1 *noun*
• (*to remind oneself*)
a note = une note
• (*a message*)
a note = un mot
I left you a note = je t'ai laissé un mot
• (*British English*) (*money*)
a note = un billet
a 50-euro note = un billet de 50 euros

* *(in music)*
  a note = une note
2 *verb*
  to note (down) = noter

notebook *noun*
  a notebook = un carnet

nothing *pronoun*
  nothing = rien

  > **!** *Note that, when there is a verb in the sentence, the negative* ne *or* n' *(before a vowel or mute* h*) is used together with* rien *to translate* nothing. *Remember that* ne *or* n' *comes before the verb or the auxiliary verb.*

  nothing has changed = rien n'a changé
  there's nothing left = il ne reste rien
  she said nothing = elle n'a rien dit
  I knew nothing about it = je n'en savais rien
  there's nothing we can do about it = nous n'y pouvons rien
  I had nothing to do with it! = je n'y étais pour rien!
  it's nothing to do with us = ça ne nous regarde pas

notice
1 *verb*
  = remarquer
2 *noun*
* *(a written sign)*
  a notice = une pancarte
* *(warning people)*
  notice = le préavis
  a month's notice = un mois de préavis
  to be cancelled at short notice = être annulé/annulée à la dernière minute
* **don't take any notice, take no notice** = ne fais pas attention

novel *noun*
  a novel = un roman

November *noun* ▶ 222 |
  November = novembre *(masculine)*

now
1 *adverb*
  = maintenant
  we have to do it now = il faut le faire maintenant
  I'm phoning her now = je suis en train de lui téléphoner
  do it right now = fais-le tout de suite
  now is the time to contact them = c'est le moment de les contacter
  I should have told you before now = j'aurais dû te le dire avant
  it hasn't been a problem until now = ça n'a pas posé de problème jusqu'à présent
  between now and next Monday = d'ici lundi prochain
  from now on = à partir de maintenant
2 now and again, now and then = de temps en temps

nowhere *adverb*
  = nulle part
  I go nowhere without my dog = je ne vais nulle part sans mon chien
  there's nowhere to sit = il n'y a pas d'endroit pour s'asseoir

nuclear *adjective*
  = nucléaire

nuisance *noun*
  to be a nuisance = être pénible
  it's a nuisance having to pay in cash = c'est agaçant de devoir payer en espèces

numb *adjective*
* **to go numb** = s'engourdir (**!** + *être*)
  my hands are numb = j'ai les mains engourdies
* *(before an operation)* = insensible

number
1 *noun*
* **a number** *(a figure)* = un chiffre
  (of a house, a bus, a telephone, a passport) = un numéro
  to dial the wrong number = faire un faux numéro
* *(when talking about quantities)* ▶ 317 |
  a number of [demonstrations | people | times ...] = un certain nombre de [manifestations | personnes | fois ...]
  a small number of tourists = quelques touristes
2 *verb*
  = numéroter

numberplate *noun* *(British English)*
  a numberplate = une plaque minéralogique

nun *noun* ▶ 315 |
  a nun = une religieuse

nurse *noun* ▶ 315 |
  a nurse = un infirmier/une infirmière

nursery *noun*
  a nursery = une crèche

nursery school *noun*
  a nursery school = une école maternelle

nut *noun*
  a nut *(a walnut)* = une noix

nylon *noun*
  nylon = le nylon

N

Oo

oak *noun*
   an oak = un chêne

oar *noun*
   an oar = une rame

obedient *adjective*
   = obéissant/obéissante

obey *verb*
   = obéir
   to obey someone = obéir à quelqu'un
   to obey the law = se conformer à la loi

object
1 *noun*
   an object = un objet
2 *verb*
   = soulever des objections

oblige *verb*
   to be obliged to leave = être obligé/obligée
   de partir
   to oblige someone = rendre service à
   quelqu'un

obtain *verb*
   = obtenir

obvious *adjective*
   = évident/évidente

obviously *adverb*
   = manifestement

occasion *noun*
   an occasion = une occasion
   on special occasions = dans les grandes
   occasions

occasionally *adverb*
   = de temps à autre

occupy *verb*
   (*to take over*) = occuper
   (*to keep busy*)
   to keep oneself occupied = s'occuper
   (**!** + *être*)
   to keep the children occupied = occuper
   les enfants

occur *verb*
   = se produire (**!** + *être*)

ocean *noun*
   the ocean = l'océan (*masculine*)

o'clock *adverb* ▶ 211 |
   it's five o'clock = il est cinq heures
   at one o'clock = à une heure

October *noun* ▶ 222 |
   October = octobre (*masculine*)

octopus *noun*
   an octopus = une pieuvre

odd *adjective*
   (*strange*) = bizarre
   (*not matching*) = dépareillé/dépareillée
   (*when talking about numbers*)
   an odd number = un nombre impair

odour (*British English*), **odor** (*US English*)
noun
   an odour = une odeur

of *preposition*
   of = de (**!** d' + *vowel or mute h*)
   the sound of an engine = le bruit d'un
   moteur
   it's in the centre of Paris = c'est au centre
   de Paris
   a photo of the dog = une photo du chien
   half of the salad = la moitié de la salade
   at the top of the stairs = en haut de
   l'escalier
   the names of the pupils = le nom des
   élèves
   (*when talking about quantities*) ▶ 317 |
   of = de (**!** d' + *vowel or mute h*)
   a kilo of potatoes = un kilo de pommes
   de terre
   a bottle of mineral water = une bouteille
   d'eau minérale
   two cans of beer = deux cannettes de
   bière
   the flowers are lovely so we bought some
   of them = les fleurs sont belles alors
   nous en avons acheté
   have you heard of it? = est-ce que tu en as
   entendu parler?
   there are six of them in the family = ils
   sont six dans la famille
   there were too many of them = ils étaient
   trop nombreux
   ! *Note that* en *is used to translate* 'of it' *or*
   'of them' *when talking about things, but*
   not usually when referring to people.

off

   ! *Often* off *occurs in combinations with*
   verbs, for example: get off, go off, take off
   etc. To find the correct translations for this
   type of verb, look up the separate
   dictionary entries at get, go, take *etc.*

1 *adverb*
   (*leaving*)
   I'm off (*British English*) = je m'en vais
   they're off to Italy tomorrow = ils partent
   pour l'Italie demain
   (*away*)
   the coast is a long way off = la côte est
   loin d'ici
   we could see them from a long way off
   = on les voyait de loin
   (*free*)
   to take a day off = prendre un jour de
   congé
   today's her day off = elle ne travaille pas
   aujourd'hui

(*not working, switched off*)
the lights are all off = toutes les lumières
sont éteintes
2 *adjective*
the milk is off = le lait a tourné

offence (*British English*), **offense** (*US English*) *noun*
(*a crime*)
an offence = un délit
to take offence = s'offenser (**!** + *être*)

offend *verb*
= vexer

offer *verb*
to offer someone a job = offrir un emploi
à quelqu'un
to offer to water the plants = se proposer
pour arroser les plantes

office *noun*
an office = un bureau

office block *noun* (*British English*)
an office block = un immeuble de
bureaux

officer *noun*
an officer (*in the army or navy*) = un
officier
(*in the police*) = un policier

office worker *noun* ▶ 315 |
an office worker = un employé/une
employée de bureau

official *adjective*
= officiel/officielle

often *adverb*
= souvent

oil *noun*
(*for heating, energy*)
oil = le pétrole
(*for a car*)
oil = l'huile (*feminine*)
(*for cooking, for health*)
oil = l'huile (*feminine*)

okay, OK
1 *adjective*
(*when asking or giving opinions*)
is it okay if I come later? = est-ce que je
peux venir plus tard?
it's okay to invite them = on peut les
inviter
(*when talking about health*)
to feel okay = aller bien
are you okay? = ça va?
2 *adverb*
okay = d'accord

old *adjective*
(*not new, not young*) = vieux/vieille
(**!** *before the noun*)

! *Note that* vieil *is used instead of* vieux
*before masculine nouns beginning with a
vowel (*ordinateur*) or a mute h (*hôtel*). The
plural of* vieux *and* vieil *is* vieux.

an old oak = un vieux chêne
an old woman = une vieille femme
an old man = un vieil homme
old houses = de vieilles maisons
old people = les personnes âgées
(*when talking about a person's age*) ▶ 187 |
how old are you? = quel âge as-tu?
a three-year old girl = une fillette de trois
ans
I'm as old as he is = j'ai le même âge que
lui
she's eight years older than her brother
= elle a huit ans de plus que son frère
to be the oldest = être l'aîné/l'aînée
to be old enough to go out at night = être
en âge de sortir le soir
(*previous*) = ancien/ancienne (**!** *before the
noun*)
that's my old address = c'est mon
ancienne adresse
in the old days = autrefois

old-fashioned *adjective*
(*describing attitudes, ideas*)
= démodé/démodée
(*describing people*) = vieux jeu (**!** *never
changes*)

olive
1 *noun*
an olive = une olive
2 *adjective* ▶ 213 |
= vert olive (**!** *never changes*)

olive oil *noun*
olive oil = l'huile d'olive
! *Note that* huile *is feminine.*

Olympics *noun*
the Olympics – les jeux Olympiques
! *Note that* jeux *is masculine plural.*

omelette *noun*
an omelette = une omelette

on
! *Often* on *occurs in combinations with
verbs, for example:* count on, get on, keep
on *etc. To find the correct translations for
this type of verb, look up the separate
dictionary entries for* count, get, keep *etc.*

1 *preposition*
on = sur
it's on the table = c'est sur la table
it's on top of the wardrobe = c'est sur
l'armoire
you've got a spot on your nose = tu as un
bouton sur le nez
there's a stain on it = il y a une tache
dessus
to fall on the floor = tomber par terre
I like the picture on the wall = j'aime le
tableau qui est au mur
to live on Park Avenue = habiter Park
Avenue

O

(*when talking about transport*)
to travel on the bus = voyager en bus
I'm on my bike today = je suis à vélo
  aujourd'hui
(*about*) = sur
it's a book on Africa = c'est un livre sur
  l'Afrique
a programme on primary schools = une
  émission sur les écoles primaires
(*when talking about time*)
she was born on the sixth of December
  = elle est née le six décembre
I'll be there on Saturday = j'y serai samedi
we went there on my birthday = nous y
  sommes allés le jour de mon
  anniversaire
(*when talking about the media*)
on television = à la télévision
I saw it on the news = je l'ai vu aux
  informations
is the film out on video? = est-ce que le
  film est sorti en vidéo?
(*using*)
to be on drugs = se droguer (**!** + *être*)
2 *adverb*
(*when talking about what one wears*)
to have a sweater on = porter un pull
to have make-up on = être
  maquillé/maquillée
(*working, switched on*)
why are all the lights on? = pourquoi est-
  ce que toutes les lumières sont
  allumées?
the radio was on all evening = la radio a
  marché toute la soirée
(*showing*)
what's on? (*on TV*) = qu'est-ce qu'il y a à la
  télévision?
(*in the cinema*) = qu'est-ce qu'on joue (au
  cinéma)?
(*when talking about time*)
from Tuesday on, I'll be here = à partir de
  mardi, je serai là
a little later on = un peu plus tard

once
1 *adverb*
(*one time*) = une fois
once a day = une fois par jour
(*in the old days*) = autrefois
2 *conjunction*
  = une fois que
it'll be easier once we've found a house
  = ce sera plus facile une fois que nous
  aurons trouvé une maison
3 at once = tout de suite

one
1 *number* ▶ **187** |, ▶ **211** |
  one = un/une
  one child = un enfant/une enfant
  one of my colleagues = un/une de mes
    collègues
  one hundred = cent

2 *determiner*
(*the only*)
  she's the one person who can help him
    = c'est la seule personne capable de
    l'aider
  it's the one thing that annoys me = c'est la
    seule chose qui m'agace
(*the same*)
  to take three exams in the one day
    = passer trois examens dans la même
    journée
3 *pronoun*
(*when referring to something generally*)
  I need an umbrella—have you got one?
    = j'ai besoin d'un parapluie—est-ce que
    tu en as un?

  ! *Note that it is necessary to use* en,
  which might be translated as 'of them',
  with pronouns like one. *See also* any, a
  few, many *etc for this use of* en.

(*when referring to a specific person or
thing*)
  **I like the new house but she prefers the
    old one** = j'aime la nouvelle maison
    mais elle préfère l'ancienne
  he's the one who told me to be quiet
    = c'est lui qui m'a dit de me taire
  which one? = lequel/laquelle?
  this one = celui-ci/celle-ci
(*when used to mean 'you' or 'people'*)
  one never knows = on ne sait jamais
4 one by one = un par un/une par une

one another *pronoun*
  ! *Note that* one another *is very often
  translated by using a reflexive pronoun
  like* se, s', nous *or* vous.

  to love one another = s'aimer (**!** + *être*)
  **we don't like being apart from one
    another** = nous n'aimons pas être
    séparés (l'un de l'autre)

oneself *pronoun*
  = se (**!** *s'* + *vowel or mute h*)
  to enjoy oneself = s'amuser (**!** + *être*)
  to hurt oneself = se blesser (**!** + *être*)

onion *noun*
  an onion = un oignon

only
1 *adverb*
  ! *Note that in sentences with a verb, the
  negative* ne *is often used together with*
  que *to translate* only. *Remember that* ne
  *comes before the verb or the auxiliary
  verb.*

  only = ne... que
  it's only a game = ce n'est qu'un jeu
  you only have to ask = vous n'avez qu'à
    demander
  they've only met once = ils ne se sont
    rencontrés qu'une fois
  he only hit his elbow = il s'est juste cogné
    le coude

2 *adjective*
= seul/seule (**!** *before the noun*)
she was the only one who didn't speak French = elle était la seule à ne pas parler français
the only problem is that I can't drive = le seul problème c'est que je ne conduis pas
an only daughter = une fille unique
3 only just
I've only just [arrived | heard the news | moved house ...] = je viens juste [d'arriver | d'apprendre la nouvelle | de déménager ...]
she had only just bought a car = elle venait d'acheter une voiture

onto *preposition*
= sur

open
1 *verb*
to open = ouvrir
to open a letter = ouvrir une lettre
what time do you open? = à quelle heure est-ce que vous ouvrez?
the shop opens at eight = le magasin ouvre à huit heures
the door opens very easily = la porte s'ouvre facilement
(*to start*) (*when talking about a film*) = sortir (**!** + *être*)
(*when talking about a play*) = commencer
2 *adjective*
(*not closed*) = ouvert/ouverte
leave the door open = laisse la porte ouverte
the pool isn't open = la piscine n'est pas ouverte
(*frank*) = franc/franche
3 *noun*
out in the open = dehors, en plein air

opener *noun*
an opener (*for bottles*) = un décapsuleur
(*for cans*) = un ouvre-boîtes

open-minded *adjective*
to be open-minded = avoir l'esprit ouvert

opera *noun*
an opera = un opéra

operate *verb*
(*to make something work*) = faire marcher
(*to carry out an operation*) = opérer
to operate on someone = opérer quelqu'un
to operate on someone's leg = opérer quelqu'un à la jambe

operation *noun*
an operation = une opération
to have an operation = se faire opérer (**!** + *être*)

operator *noun* ▶ **315** |
an operator = un standardiste/une standardiste

opinion *noun*
an opinion (*a point of view*) = un avis
(*when judging a person, a situation*) = une opinion
in my opinion, they're lying = à mon avis, ils mentent

opponent *noun*
an opponent = un adversaire/une adversaire

opportunity *noun*
an opportunity = une occasion
to take the opportunity to visit Paris = profiter de l'occasion pour visiter Paris

oppose *verb*
to oppose a plan = s'opposer à un projet
to be opposed to nuclear weapons = être contre les armes nucléaires

opposite
1 *preposition*
= en face de
she was sitting opposite me = elle était assise en face de moi
2 *adjective*
the opposite sex = le sexe opposé
he was walking in the opposite direction = il allait dans l'autre sens
3 *adverb*
= en face
4 *noun*
the opposite = le contraire
it's the exact opposite = c'est tout le contraire

optician *noun* ▶ **315** |
an optician = un opticien/une opticienne

optimist *noun*
an optimist = un optimiste/une optimiste

optimistic *adjective*
= optimiste

or *conjunction*
or = ou
once or twice a week = une ou deux fois par semaine
we'll stay either here or at Martine's = nous resterons soit ici soit chez Martine
do you have any brothers or sisters? = est-ce que tu as des frères et sœurs?
(*in negative sentences*)
I can't come today or tomorrow = je ne peux venir ni aujourd'hui ni demain
don't tell Mum or Dad = ne le dis ni à maman ni à papa
(*otherwise*) = sinon
be careful or you'll break the cups = fais attention sinon tu vas casser les tasses

oral *adjective*
= oral/orale

orange
1 *noun*
an orange = une orange

O

2 *adjective* ▶ **213** |
= orange (**!** *never changes*)

orange juice *noun*
  orange juice = le jus d'orange

orchard *noun*
  an orchard = un verger

orchestra *noun*
  an orchestra = un orchestre

order
1 *verb*
  (*to tell*)
  to order someone to leave = ordonner à
    quelqu'un de partir
  (*to ask for*) = commander
  to order goods from a magazine
    = commander des articles dans un
    magazine
2 *noun*
  (*an instruction*)
  an order = un ordre
  to give orders = donner des ordres
  the right order = le bon ordre
  the list is in alphabetical order = la liste
    est dans l'ordre alphabétique
3 in order to = pour
  I phoned them in order to change the date
    = je leur ai téléphoné pour changer la
    date

ordinary *adjective*
  (*not unusual*) = ordinaire
  an ordinary family = une famille ordinaire
  (*average*) = moyen/moyenne

organ *noun*
  (*the musical instrument*) ▶ **290** |
  an organ = un orgue
  (*a part of the body*)
  an organ = un organe

organization *noun*
  an organization = une organisation

organize *verb*
  = organiser
  to get organized = s'organiser (**!** + *être*)

original *adjective*
  (*first*) = original/originale
  (*true, real*) = originel/originelle
  (*new, fresh*) = original/originale

ornament *noun*
  an ornament = un bibelot

orphan *noun*
  an orphan = un orphelin/une orpheline

ostrich *noun*
  an ostrich = une autruche

other
1 *adjective*
  = autre (+ *singular*)
  = autres (+ *plural*)
  not that dress, the other one = pas cette
    robe-là, l'autre
  they sold the other car = ils ont vendu
    l'autre voiture
  to annoy the other pupils = embêter les
    autres élèves

  **some people like driving, other people
  hate it** = certains aiment conduire,
    d'autres détestent ça
  every other Saturday = un samedi sur
    deux
2 *pronoun*
  he makes the others laugh = il fait rire les
    autres
  **some students learn French easily,
  others have problems** = certains élèves
    apprennent le français facilement,
    d'autres ont des problèmes
  they came in one after the other = ils sont
    entrés l'un après l'autre

otherwise *conjunction*
  = sinon
  **it's not dangerous, otherwise I wouldn't
  go** = ce n'est pas dangereux, sinon je
    n'irais pas

otter *noun*
  an otter = une loutre

ought *verb*
  (*when talking about what should be done*)
  you ought not to say things like that = tu
    ne devrais pas dire des choses pareilles
  (*when making a polite suggestion*)
  you ought to be in bed = tu devrais être au
    lit
  (*when saying something may happen*)
  they ought to arrive tomorrow = ils
    devraient arriver demain
  (*when saying something didn't happen*)
  someone ought to have gone with them
    = quelqu'un aurait dû les accompagner

our *determiner*
  our = notre (+ *singular*)
  = nos (+ *plural*)
  he ran over our dog = il a écrasé notre
    chien
  what do you think of our house? = qu'est-
    ce que tu penses de notre maison?
  all our CDs have been stolen = on a volé
    tous nos disques compacts

ours *pronoun*
  the grey car is ours = la voiture grise est à
    nous
  which case is ours? = laquelle de ces
    valises est la nôtre?
  their garden is bigger than ours = leur
    jardin est plus grand que le nôtre
  their children are younger than ours
    = leurs enfants sont plus jeunes que les
    nôtres

  ! *Note that, when comparing objects,
  people, etc, one of the following
  translations*—le nôtre, la nôtre *or*
  nôtres—*will be used. To know which one
  to use, find out whether the object,
  person etc which is being described is
  masculine singular, feminine singular or
  just plural.*

ourselves *pronoun*
(*when used as a reflexive pronoun*)
we want to enjoy ourselves = nous
voulons nous amuser, on veut s'amuser
we didn't hurt ourselves = nous ne nous
sommes pas fait mal, on ne s'est pas fait
mal

! *Note that* on *is more usual in spoken
French.*

(*when used for emphasis*)
we organized everything ourselves
= nous avons tout organisé nous-mêmes
we like to be by ourselves = nous aimons
être seuls

out

! *Often* out *occurs in combinations with
verbs, for example:* blow out, come out,
find out, give out *etc. To find the correct
translations for this type of verb, look up
the separate dictionary entries at* blow,
come, find, give *etc.*

1 *adverb*
(*outside*) = dehors
they're out there = ils sont dehors
to stay out in the rain = rester dehors sous
la pluie
she's out in the garden = elle est dans le
jardin
I'm looking for the way out = je cherche la
sortie
(*absent*)
to be out = être sorti/sortie
someone called while you were out
= quelqu'un a téléphoné pendant que tu
étais sorti
(*not lighting, not on*)
to be out = être éteint/éteinte
all the lights were out = toutes les
lumières étaient éteintes
2 out of
to walk out of the building = sortir du
bâtiment
to get out of the city = sortir de la ville
to take a pencil out of the drawer
= prendre un crayon dans le tiroir

outdoor *adjective*
= en plein air
an outdoor swimming pool = une piscine
en plein air

outdoors *adverb*
= dehors

outer space *noun*
outer space = l'espace (*masculine*)

outside
1 *preposition*
(*in front of*) = devant
to wait outside the school = attendre
devant l'école
(*beyond*)
outside the city = en dehors de la ville

2 *adverb*
= dehors
let's go outside = allons dehors
let's bring the chairs outside = sortons les
chaises
3 *noun*
the outside = l'extérieur (*masculine*)
the outside of the building = l'extérieur du
bâtiment
4 *adjective*
= extérieur/extérieure

oven *noun*
an oven = un four

over

! *Often* over *occurs in combinations with
verbs, for example:* get over, move over
*etc. To find the correct translations for this
type of verb, look up the separate
dictionary entries at* get, move *etc.*

1 *preposition*
over = par-dessus
to climb over a wall = passer par-dessus un
mur
we climbed over it = nous sommes passés
par-dessus
(*across*)
it's somewhere over there = c'est quelque
part par là
come over here = viens par ici
(*above*)
the picture over the piano = le tableau au-
dessus du piano
young people over 18 = les jeunes de plus
de 18 ans
(*during*)
we saw them over the weekend = nous les
avons vus pendant le week-end
(*everywhere*)
I've looked all over the house for my keys
= j'ai cherché mes clés partout dans la
maison
2 *adverb*
(*finished*)
the term is over = le trimestre est terminé
is the film over? = est-ce que le film est
fini?
(*to one's home*)
to ask someone over = inviter quelqu'un
to start over again = recommencer à zéro

overdose *noun*
an overdose = une surdose

overtake *verb*
= dépasser

overweight *adjective*
= trop gros/trop grosse

owe *verb*
= devoir
to owe money to someone = devoir de
l'argent à quelqu'un

owl *noun*
an owl = un hibou, une chouette

O

own

1 *adjective*
= propre (**!** *before the noun*)
you should clean your own room = tu devrais ranger ta propre chambre
he'd like his own car = il voudrait une voiture à lui, il voudrait sa propre voiture

2 *pronoun*

> **!** *Note that, when comparing objects, people etc, the translations given for the pronouns* **mine, yours, his, hers, ours** *or* **theirs** *work for* **my own, your own** *etc.*

I didn't use his pencil—I've got my own = je n'ai pas utilisé son crayon—j'ai le mien
they have a house of their own = ils ont une maison à eux, ils ont leur propre maison

3 *verb*
= avoir
he owns a shop in town = il a un magasin en ville
who owns that dog? = à qui est ce chien?

4 on one's own = tout seul/toute seule

own up = avouer

owner *noun*
an owner = un propriétaire/une propriétaire

ox *noun*
an ox = un bœuf

oxygen *noun*
oxygen = l'oxygène (*masculine*)

oyster *noun*
an oyster = une huître

Pp

Pacific *noun*
the Pacific = le Pacifique

pack

1 *verb*
= faire ses bagages
I've got to pack my suitcase = je dois faire ma valise

2 *noun*
a pack = un paquet
a pack of cigarettes = un paquet de cigarettes
a pack of cards = un jeu de cartes

pack up = faire ses bagages
to pack up one's belongings = emballer ses affaires

package *noun*
a package = un paquet, un colis

packed *adjective*
(*describing a room*) = plein/pleine à craquer
(*describing a train, a bus*) = bondé/bondée

packet *noun*
a packet = un paquet

page *noun*
a page = une page
on page six = (à la) page six

pain *noun*
pain = la douleur
I've got a pain in my back = j'ai mal au dos
to be in pain = souffrir

painful *adjective*
= douloureux/douloureuse

paint

1 *noun*
paint = la peinture

2 *verb*
= peindre

paintbrush *noun*
a paintbrush = un pinceau

painter *noun* ▶ 315|
a painter = un peintre

painting *noun*
• (*a picture*)
a painting = un tableau
• (*the activity*)
painting = la peinture

pair *noun*
a pair = une paire
a pair of shoes = une paire de chaussures

pajamas *noun* (*US English*)
pajamas = un pyjama (*singular*)

Pakistan *noun* ▶ 218|
Pakistan = le Pakistan

palace *noun*
a palace = un palais

pale *adjective*
= pâle
to go pale, to turn pale = pâlir

pancake *noun*
a pancake = une crêpe

panic *verb*
= s'affoler (**!** + *être*)

pants *noun*
• (*British English*) (*underwear*)
pants = un slip (*singular*)
• (*US English*) (*trousers*)
pants = un pantalon (*singular*)

pantyhose *noun* (*US English*)
pantyhose = un collant

paper *noun*
• (*for writing or drawing on*)
paper = le papier
a piece of paper = un bout de papier

- (*a newspaper*)
  a paper = un journal

parachuting *noun* ▶ **248**
  parachuting = le parachutisme

parade *noun*
  a parade = un défilé

paragliding *noun* ▶ **248**
  paragliding = le parapente

paralysed (*British English*), **paralyzed**
(*US English*) *adjective*
  = paralysé/paralysée

parcel *noun*
  a parcel = un paquet, un colis

parents *noun*
  parents = les parents (*masculine*)

Paris *noun* ▶ **218**
  Paris = Paris

park
1 *noun*
  a park = un jardin public, un parc
2 *verb*
  to park a car = garer une voiture
  to park near the office = se garer près du
    bureau

parking lot *noun* (*US English*)
  a parking lot = un parking, un parc de
    stationnement

parking meter *noun*
  a parking meter = un parcmètre

parliament *noun*
  a parliament = un parlement

parrot *noun*
  a parrot = un perroquet

part
- **a part** = une partie
  part of the [book | film | time ...] = une partie
    du [livre | film | temps ...]
  it's part of the job = ça fait partie du
    travail
  in this part of the country = dans cette
    région
- (*a piece for a machine, a car*)
  a part = une pièce
- (*a section*)
  a part (*in a programme*) = une partie
  (*in a series*) = un épisode
- (*a role*)
  a part = un rôle
  to play the part of Tommy = jouer le rôle
    de Tommy

participate *verb*
  = participer

particular
1 *adjective*
  = particulier/particulière
2 in particular = en particulier

partner *noun*
- (*in a relationship*)
  a partner = un compagnon/une compagne
- (*in dancing, sport*)
  a partner = un partenaire/une partenaire

part-time *adverb*
  = à temps partiel
  to work part-time = travailler à temps
    partiel

party *noun*
- (*a social event*)
  a party = une fête
  (*held in the evening*) = une soirée
  a birthday party = une fête d'anniversaire,
    un anniversaire
  a children's party = un goûter d'enfants
- **a political party** = un parti politique

pass *verb*
- (*to go past*) = passer (**!** + *être*)
  to let someone pass = laisser passer
    quelqu'un
  to pass the school = passer devant l'école
  to pass a car = dépasser une voiture
  to pass someone in the street = croiser
    quelqu'un dans la rue
- (*to give*) = passer
  pass me the salt, please = passe-moi le
    sel, s'il te plaît
  to pass the ball to someone = passer le
    ballon à quelqu'un
- (*to spend*) = passer
  to pass the time [reading | painting | listening
    to the radio ...] = passer le temps [en lisant |
    en faisant de la peinture | en écoutant la
    radio ...]
- (*to succeed in an exam*) = réussir
  to pass an exam = réussir un examen
pass around
  to pass around the biscuits = faire passer
    les biscuits
pass on = transmettre
  to pass on a message to someone
    = transmettre un message à quelqu'un

passage *noun*
  a passage (*indoors*) = un couloir
  (*outdoors*) = un passage

passenger *noun*
  a passenger = un passager/une passagère

passport *noun*
  a passport = un passeport

past
1 *noun*
  the past = le passé
  in the past = dans le passé
2 *adjective*
  = dernier/dernière (**!** *before the noun*)
  the past few days have been difficult = ces
    derniers jours ont été difficiles
3 *preposition*
- (*when talking about time*) ▶ **211**
  it's twenty past four = il est quatre heures
    vingt
  it's past midnight = il est minuit passé

P

- (*by*)
  to go past someone = passer devant
  quelqu'un
  she ran past me = elle est passée devant
  moi en courant
- (*beyond*) = après
  it's just past the traffic lights = c'est juste
  après les feux
4 adverb
  to go past, to walk past = passer (**!** + *être*)

pasta noun
  pasta = les pâtes (*feminine*)

pastry noun
- (*for baking*)
  pastry = la pâte
  to make pastry = faire de la pâte
- (*a cake*)
  a pastry = une pâtisserie, un gâteau

patch noun
- (*on a garment*)
  a patch = une pièce
- (*on a tyre*)
  a patch = une rustine

path noun
  a path = un chemin
  (*narrower*) = un sentier
  (*in a garden*) = une allée

patience noun
  patience = la patience
  to lose patience with someone = perdre
  patience avec quelqu'un

patient
1 noun
  a patient = un patient/une patiente
2 adjective
  = patient/patiente

patrol car noun
  a patrol car = une voiture de police

pattern noun
- (*a design*)
  a pattern = un dessin, un motif
- (*when making garments*)
  a pattern (*for knitting*) = un modèle
  (*for sewing*) = un patron

pavement noun (*British English*)
  a pavement = un trottoir

paw noun
  a paw = une patte

pay
1 verb
- **to pay** = payer
  to pay the bills = payer les factures
  to pay for the shopping = payer les
  courses
  he paid for my meal = il a payé mon repas
- (*when talking about wages*)
  the work doesn't pay very well = le travail
  est mal payé
  I'm paid eight pounds an hour = je suis
  payé huit livres de l'heure

- (*to give*)
  to pay attention to the teacher = écouter
  le professeur
  to pay someone a visit = rendre visite à
  quelqu'un
  to pay someone a compliment = faire des
  compliments à quelqu'un
2 noun
  pay = le salaire
  the pay is very good = c'est très bien payé
pay back = rembourser

PE noun
  PE = l'éducation physique
  ! *Note that* **éducation** *is feminine.*

pea noun
  a pea = un petit pois

peace noun
  peace = la paix

peach noun
  a peach = une pêche

peacock noun
  a peacock = un paon

peanut noun
  a peanut = une cacahuète

pear noun
  a pear = une poire

pearl noun
  a pearl = une perle

pebble noun
  a pebble (*on a beach*) = un galet

pedestrian noun
  a pedestrian = un piéton

pedestrian crossing noun
  a pedestrian crossing = un passage pour
  piétons

peel verb
  = éplucher

pen noun
  a pen = un stylo

penalty noun
  a penalty (*in soccer*) = un tir de
  réparation, un penalty
  (*in rugby*) = une pénalité

pencil noun
  a pencil = un crayon

pencil case noun
  a pencil case = une trousse à crayons

pencil sharpener noun
  a pencil sharpener = un taille-crayon

penfriend (*British English*), **penpal**
noun
  a penfriend = un correspondant/une
  correspondante

penguin noun
  a penguin = un pingouin

penknife noun
a penknife = un canif

pensioner noun
a pensioner = un retraité/une retraitée

people noun
people (in general) = les gens (masculine plural)
(if counting) = les personnes (feminine plural)
we met very nice people = nous avons fait la connaissance de gens très sympathiques
most people don't know what's going on = la plupart des gens ne savent pas ce qui se passe
there were three people at the meeting = il y avait trois personnes à la réunion
there are too many people here = il y a trop de monde ici
to help other people = aider les autres

pepper noun
• (the spice)
pepper = le poivre
• (the vegetable)
a pepper = un poivron

per preposition
per person = par personne

per cent, percent (US English) noun
per cent = pour cent, %

perfect adjective
= parfait/parfaite
to speak perfect French = parler un français parfait
it's the perfect place for a picnic = c'est l'endroit idéal pour un pique-nique

perform verb
• (to do)
to perform a task = exécuter une tâche
• (to act, to play) = jouer

perfume noun
perfume = le parfum
to wear perfume = mettre du parfum

perhaps adverb
= peut-être

period noun
• (in time)
a period = une période
a trial period = une période d'essai
• (in history)
a period = une époque
• (for women)
a period = des règles (feminine plural)
to have one's period = avoir ses règles
• (a school lesson)
a period = un cours

permanent adjective
= permanent/permanente

permission noun
permission = la permission
to get permission to leave the country = obtenir la permission de quitter le pays

person noun
a person = une personne
an old person = une personne âgée
to be a kind person = être gentil/gentille
he's not a very patient person = il n'est pas très patient

personal adjective
= personnel/personnelle

personality noun
a personality = une personnalité

perspire verb
= transpirer

persuade verb
= persuader
to persuade someone to buy a car = persuader quelqu'un d'acheter une voiture

pessimist noun
a pessimist = un pessimiste/une pessimiste

pessimistic adjective
= pessimiste

pet noun
a pet = un animal de compagnie
do you have any pets? = est-ce que tu as des animaux?

petrol noun (British English)
petrol = l'essence (feminine)
to run out of petrol = tomber en panne d'essence

petrol station noun (British English)
a petrol station = une station d'essence

pet shop noun ▶ 315
a pet shop = une animalerie

phone
1 noun
a phone = un téléphone
the phone's ringing = le téléphone sonne
to answer the phone = répondre au téléphone
he's on the phone = il est au téléphone
2 verb
= téléphoner
to phone someone = téléphoner à quelqu'un, passer un coup de fil à quelqu'un

phone book noun
a phone book = un annuaire téléphonique

phone booth noun
a phone booth = une cabine téléphonique

P

phone call *noun*
  a phone call = un coup de fil, un appel téléphonique
  to receive a phone call = recevoir un appel téléphonique, recevoir un coup de fil
  to make a phone call = téléphoner, passer un coup de fil

phone card *noun*
  a phone card = une télécarte

phone number *noun*
  a phone number = un numéro de téléphone

photo *noun*
  a photo = une photo

photocopier *noun*
  a photocopier = une photocopieuse

photocopy *noun*
  a photocopy = une photocopie

photograph *noun*
  a photograph = une photo
  to take a photograph of someone = prendre quelqu'un en photo

photographer *noun* ▶ 315|
  a photographer = un photographe/une photographe

physical *adjective*
  = physique

physics *noun*
  physics = la physique

piano *noun* ▶ 290|
  a piano = un piano

pick *verb*
• (*to choose*) = choisir
  to pick a number = choisir un chiffre
• (*to collect*) = cueillir
  to pick blackberries = cueillir des mûres
• (*to take*)
  to pick a book off the shelf = prendre un livre sur l'étagère
pick on = s'en prendre à (**!** + *être*)
  he's always picking on me = il s'en prend toujours à moi
pick out = choisir
pick up
• (*to lift*) = ramasser
  to pick the clothes up off the floor = ramasser les vêtements par terre
  to pick a baby up = prendre un bébé dans ses bras
  to pick up the phone = décrocher le téléphone
• (*to collect*)
  to pick up passengers = prendre des passagers
  he's coming to pick me up = il vient me chercher

• (*to buy*) = prendre
  I stopped to pick up some milk = je me suis arrêté pour prendre du lait
• (*to learn*)
  to pick up a little German = apprendre un peu d'allemand

picnic *noun*
  a picnic = un pique-nique
  to go on a picnic = aller faire un pique-nique

picture *noun*
• a picture (*painted*) = une peinture, un tableau
  (*drawn*) = un dessin
  to paint someone's picture = faire le portrait de quelqu'un
• (*a photograph*)
  a picture = une photo
• the pictures = le cinéma (*singular*)

piece *noun*
• (*a bit*)
  a piece = un morceau
  a piece of cheese = un morceau de fromage
  a piece of string = un bout de ficelle
• (*a part of a machine*)
  a piece = une pièce
• (*a broken part*)
  a piece = un morceau
  to fall to pieces = tomber en morceaux
• (*a coin*)
  a 50-pence piece = une pièce de 50 pence
• (*other uses*)
  a piece of furniture = un meuble
  a piece of information = un renseignement
  a piece of advice = un conseil

pierce *verb*
  = percer

pig *noun*
  a pig = un porc, un cochon

pigeon *noun*
  a pigeon = un pigeon

pile
• a pile = une pile
  (*untidy*) = un tas
  a pile of old shoes = un tas de vieilles chaussures
• (*lots*)
  piles of [toys | records | books ...] = des tas✱ de [jouets | disques | livres ...]

pill *noun*
• (*a tablet*)
  a pill = un comprimé
• (*a method of contraception*)
  the pill = la pilule

pillow *noun*
  a pillow = un oreiller

pilot *noun* ▶ 315|
  a pilot = un pilote

✱ in informal situations

pin
1 *noun*
a pin = une épingle
2 *verb*
= accrocher

pinball *noun* ▶ 248 |
pinball = le flipper

pinch *verb*
• to pinch = pincer
he pinched my arm, he pinched me on the arm = il m'a pincé le bras
• (*to hurt by being too tight*) = serrer
my shoes are pinching = mes chaussures me serrent

pineapple *noun*
a pineapple = un ananas

pine tree *noun*
a pine tree = un pin

pink *adjective* ▶ 213 |
= rose

pint *noun*
• (*the quantity*)
a pint ≈ un demi-litre

! Note that a pint = 0.57 l in Britain and 0.47 l in the US.

a pint of milk ≈ un demi-litre de lait
• (*British English*) (*a drink*)
to go for a pint = aller boire une bière

pipe *noun*
• (*for gas, water*)
a pipe = un tuyau
• (*for smoking*)
a pipe = une pipe

pirate *noun*
a pirate = un pirate

Pisces *noun*
Pisces = Poissons (*masculine plural*)

pitch *noun* (*British English*)
a pitch = un terrain
a football pitch = un terrain de football

pity
1 *noun*
• pity = la pitié
• (*when expressing regret*)
what a pity! = quel dommage!
it's a pity you can't come = c'est dommage que tu ne puisses pas venir

! Note that the subjunctive is used after c'est dommage que.

2 *verb*
= plaindre

pizza *noun*
a pizza = une pizza

place *noun*
• a place = un endroit
it's the best place to buy salmon = c'est le meilleur endroit pour acheter du saumon
Oxford is a nice place = Oxford est une belle ville
they come from all over the place = ils viennent de partout
this place is dirty = c'est sale ici
• (*a home*)
at Alison's place = chez Alison
I'd like a place of my own = j'aimerais avoir un chez-moi
• (*in a queue, on a bus, in a car park, at table*)
a place = une place
is this place free? = est-ce que cette place est libre?
to take someone's place = prendre la place de quelqu'un
to find a place to park = trouver une place pour se garer
• (*on a team, a course, in a firm*)
a place = une place
to get a place on a course = obtenir une place dans un cours
• (*in a contest*)
a place = une place
to win first place = gagner la première place

plain
1 *adjective*
• (*simple*) = simple
a plain dress = une robe simple
• (*not good-looking*) = quelconque
2 *noun*
a plain = une plaine

plait *noun* (*British English*)
a plait = une natte, une tresse

plan
1 *noun*
• (*what one intends to do*)
a plan = un plan
we need a plan = il nous faut un plan
• (*what one has arranged to do*)
a plan = un projet
do you have any plans for the future? = est-ce que tu as des projets pour l'avenir?
I don't have any plans for tonight = je n'ai rien de prévu pour ce soir
2 *verb*
• (*to prepare, to organize*)
to plan [a trip | a school timetable | a meeting …] = organiser [un voyage | un emploi du temps | une réunion …]
• (*to intend*) = avoir l'intention de
I'm planning to visit Scotland = j'ai l'intention de visiter l'Écosse

plane *noun*
a plane = un avion

P

planet *noun*
    a planet = une planète

plant
1 *noun*
    a plant = une plante
2 *verb*
    = planter

plaster *noun* (*British English*)
    a plaster = un pansement adhésif

plastic
1 *noun*
    plastic = le plastique
2 *adjective*
    = en plastique

plate *noun*
    a plate = une assiette

platform *noun*
    a platform = un quai
    on platform 4 = au quai numéro 4

play
1 *verb*
* (*to have fun*) = jouer
    to play with friends = jouer avec des amis
    to play a trick on someone = jouer un
        tour à quelqu'un
    to play cards = jouer aux cartes
* (*when talking about sports*) ▶ 248 | = jouer
    to play [football | cricket | tennis ...] = jouer
        [au football | au cricket | au tennis ...]
    France is playing (against) Ireland = la
        France joue contre l'Irlande
* (*when talking about music*) ▶ 290 | = jouer
    to play [the piano | the flute | drums ...] = jouer
        [du piano | de la flûte | de la batterie ...]
* (*to put on*) = mettre
    to play [a video | a CD | a record ...] = mettre
        [une cassette vidéo | un disque compact | un
        disque ...]
* (*when talking about theatre, cinema*)
    to play the role of Richard II = jouer le rôle
        de Richard II
    the film will be playing at the Phoenix = le
        film va passer au Phoenix
2 *noun*
    a play = une pièce
play around = faire l'imbécile
play back
    to play back a tape = repasser une cassette

player *noun* ▶ 248 |
    a player = un joueur/une joueuse
    a tennis player = un joueur/une joueuse
        de tennis

playground *noun*
    a playground = une aire de jeu
    the school playground = la cour de
        récréation

please *adverb*
    (*formal, to several people*) = s'il vous plaît
    (*informal*) = s'il te plaît
    please come in = entrez, je vous en prie
    'more cake?'—'yes please' = 'encore du
        gâteau?'—'oui, je veux bien'

pleased *adjective*
    = content/contente
    I was very pleased with myself = j'étais
        très content de moi
    pleased to meet you = enchanté

plenty *pronoun*
    to have plenty [of time | of money | of
        friends ...] = avoir beaucoup [de temps |
        d'argent | d'amis ...]

plot *noun*
* (*a plan*)
    a plot = un complot
* (*the story in a film, a novel, a play*)
    a plot = une intrigue

plug *noun*
* (*on an appliance*)
    a plug = une prise
    to pull out the plug = débrancher la prise
* (*in a sink or bath*)
    a plug = une bonde
plug in = brancher

plum *noun*
    a plum = une prune

plumber *noun* ▶ 315 |
    a plumber = un plombier

plus *preposition*
    = plus
    three plus three are six = trois plus trois
        font six

pocket *noun*
    a pocket = une poche

pocketbook *noun* (*US English*)
    a pocketbook = un sac à main

pocket money *noun*
    pocket money = l'argent de poche
    ! Note that **argent** is masculine.

poem *noun*
    a poem = un poème

point
1 *noun*
* (*a statement in a discussion*)
    a point = une remarque
    to make a point = faire une remarque
* (*the most important idea*)
    the point = le point essentiel
    that's not the point = là n'est pas la
        question
* (*use*)
    there's no point in shouting = ça ne sert à
        rien de crier
* (*when talking about time*)
    to be on the point of [moving | leaving |
        selling the house ...] = être sur le point de
        [déménager | partir | vendre la maison ...]
* (*the sharp end*)
    the point = la pointe
    the point of a pencil = la pointe d'un
        crayon
* (*in a contest, a game*)
    a point = un point

2 *verb*
- (*to indicate*)
  to point (one's finger) at someone
    = montrer quelqu'un du doigt
  to point at a house = indiquer une maison
  to point the way to the station = indiquer
    la direction de la gare
- (*to aim*)
  to point a gun at someone = braquer un
    pistolet sur quelqu'un
  point out = montrer
  can you point them out to me? = est-ce
    que tu peux me les montrer?

poison
1 *noun*
  poison = le poison
2 *verb*
  = empoisonner

Poland *noun* ▶ 218 |
  Poland = la Pologne

pole *noun*
  a pole = une perche

police *noun*
  the police = la police

policeman *noun* ▶ 315 |
  a policeman = un policier

police station *noun*
  a police station = un poste de police

policewoman *noun* ▶ 315 |
  a policewoman = une femme policier

polish *verb*
  to polish shoes = cirer des chaussures
  to polish the car = lustrer la voiture

polite *adjective*
  = poli/polie

political *adjective*
  = politique

politician *noun* ▶ 315 |
  a politician = un homme/une femme
    politique

politics *noun*
  politics = la politique

pollute *verb*
  = polluer

pollution *noun*
  pollution = la pollution

pond *noun*
  a pond (*large*) = un étang
  (*smaller*) = une mare
  (*in a garden*) = un bassin

pony *noun*
  a pony = un poney

ponytail *noun*
  a ponytail = une queue de cheval

pool *noun*
- (*a swimming pool*)
  a pool = une piscine

- (*on the ground, the floor*)
  a pool of water = une flaque d'eau
- (*the game*) ▶ 248 |
  pool = le billard américain

poor *adjective*
- (*not wealthy*) = pauvre
- (*not satisfactory*) = mauvais/mauvaise
  (**!** *before the noun*)
  to be poor at languages = être faible en
    langues
- (*expressing sympathy*) = pauvre (**!** *before
  the noun*)
  the poor boy is exhausted = le pauvre
    garçon est épuisé

popular *adjective*

  ! *Note that* popular *is not usually
  translated by* populaire.

  a popular hobby = un passe-temps
    répandu
  she's very popular = elle a beaucoup
    d'amis
  to be popular with the girls = avoir du
    succès auprès des filles

population *noun*
  a population = une population

pork *noun*
  pork = le porc

port *noun*
  a port = un port

portrait *noun*
  a portrait = un portrait

Portugal *noun* ▶ 218 |
  Portugal = le Portugal

Portuguese ▶ 275 |
1 *adjective*
  = portugais/portugaise
2 *noun*
- (*the people*)
  the Portuguese = les Portugais (*masculine
    plural*)
- (*the language*)
  Portuguese = le portugais

positive *adjective*
  = positif/positive

possibility *noun*
  a possibility = une possibilité

possible *adjective*
  = possible
  they came as quickly as possible = ils
    sont venus le plus vite possible
  I did as much as possible = j'ai fait tout ce
    que j'ai pu

post (*British English*)
1 *noun*
  the post (*the system*) = la poste
  (*the letters*) = le courrier
  has the post come yet? = est-ce que le
    courrier est arrivé?

P

2 *verb*
to post a letter = poster une lettre

postbox *noun* (*British English*)
a postbox = une boîte aux lettres

postcard *noun*
a postcard = une carte postale

postcode *noun* (*British English*)
a postcode = un code postal

poster *noun*
a poster (*giving information*) = une affiche
(*used as a picture*) = un poster

postman *noun* ▶ 315 | (*British English*)
a postman = un facteur

post office *noun*
a post office = un bureau de poste

postpone *verb*
to postpone a concert = reporter un concert
let's postpone the party until next week = reportons la fête à la semaine prochaine

pot *noun*
• (*a container*)
a pot = un pot
to make a pot of tea = faire du thé
• (*a saucepan*)
a pot = une casserole

potato *noun*
a potato = une pomme de terre

pottery *noun*
pottery = la poterie

pound *noun*
• (*the currency*)
a pound = une livre
• (*the measurement*)
a pound ≈ une livre
| **!** Note that a pound = 453.6 g.

two pounds of apples ≈ un kilo de pommes

pour *verb*
• (*from a container*) = verser
to pour milk into a bowl = verser du lait dans un bol
• (*to serve*) = servir
to pour someone a vodka = servir une vodka à quelqu'un
• (*to flow*) = couler (à flots)
the water was pouring into the kitchen = l'eau coulait dans la cuisine
• (*to escape*)
there is smoke pouring out of the window = il y a de la fumée qui sort par la fenêtre
• (*to rain*)
it's pouring (with rain) = il pleut à verse

• (*to enter or leave in large numbers*)
to pour into the city = affluer dans la ville
to pour out of the stadium = sortir en grand nombre du stade

powder *noun*
a powder = une poudre

power *noun*
• (*control*)
power = le pouvoir
to be in power = être au pouvoir
• (*influence*)
to have great power = avoir une grande influence
• (*electricity*)
power = le courant

practical *adjective*
= pratique

practise (*British English*), **practice** (*US English*) *verb*
(*at the piano, guitar*) = s'exercer (**!** + *être*)
(*at a sport*) = s'entraîner (**!** + *être*)
(*for a play, a concert*) = répéter
to practise [the violin | one's French | a song …] = travailler [le violon | son français | une chanson …]

praise *verb*
to praise someone (*when talking to someone else*) = faire l'éloge de quelqu'un
(*when talking directly to someone*) = féliciter quelqu'un

prawn *noun* (*British English*)
a prawn = une crevette rose

prayer *noun*
a prayer = une prière

precaution *noun*
a precaution = une précaution

precious *adjective*
= précieux/précieuse

precise *adjective*
= précis/précise

prefer *verb*
= préférer, aimer mieux
to prefer chocolate to vanilla = mieux aimer le chocolat que la vanille
I'd prefer to phone = j'aimerais mieux téléphoner

pregnant *adjective*
= enceinte

prejudice *noun*
a prejudice = un préjugé

prepare *verb*
• (*to get something or someone ready*)
= préparer
to prepare pupils for an exam = préparer des élèves à un examen

---

� in informal situations

- (*to get ready*)
  to prepare for [an exam | a trip | a party ...]
  = se préparer pour [un examen | un voyage | une fête ...]

prepared *adjective*
- (*willing*)
  to be prepared to wait = être prêt/prête à attendre
- (*ready*)
  to be prepared for an exam = être prêt/prête pour un examen

prescription *noun*
  a prescription = une ordonnance

present
1 *noun*
- (*a gift*)
  a present = un cadeau
  to give someone a present = offrir un cadeau à quelqu'un
- (*now*)
  the present = le présent
  I'm staying here for the present = je reste ici pour l'instant
2 *verb*
- (*to give*)
  to present a prize to someone = remettre un prix à quelqu'un
- (*on radio or TV*)
  to present a programme = présenter une émission

president *noun* ▶ 315 |
  a president = un président/une présidente

press
1 *verb*
  = appuyer sur
  to press the bell = appuyer sur la sonnette
  to press (oneself) against the wall = se plaquer contre le mur
2 *noun*
  the press = la presse

pressure *noun*
  pressure = la pression
  to put pressure on someone = faire pression sur quelqu'un

pretend *verb*
  = faire semblant
  he's pretending to be annoyed = il fait semblant d'être vexé

pretty
1 *adjective*
  = joli/jolie
2 *adverb*
  = assez
  that's pretty good = ce n'est pas mal du tout**✱**

prevent *verb*
  to prevent a war = éviter une guerre
  to prevent someone from [working | having fun | sleeping ...] = empêcher quelqu'un de [travailler | s'amuser | dormir ...]

previous *adjective*
  = précédent/précédente

price *noun*
  a price = un prix

pride *noun*
- **pride** = la fierté
- (*self-respect*)
  pride = l'amour-propre (*masculine*)

priest *noun* ▶ 315 |
  a priest = un prêtre

primary school *noun*
  a primary school = une école primaire

primary school teacher *noun* ▶ 315 |
  a primary school teacher = un instituteur/une institutrice, un professeur des écoles

prime minister *noun* ▶ 315 |
  the prime minister = le premier ministre

prince *noun*
  a prince = un prince

princess *noun*
  a princess = une princesse

principal *noun*
  a principal (*in a senior school*) = un proviseur
  (*in a junior school*) = un directeur/une directrice

print
1 *verb*
  = imprimer
  to print a book = imprimer un livre
2 *noun*
- (*of a photo*)
  a print = une épreuve
- (*of a finger, a foot*)
  a print = une empreinte

priority *noun*
  a priority = une priorité

prison *noun*
  a prison = une prison
  to put someone in prison = mettre quelqu'un en prison

prisoner *noun*
  a prisoner = un prisonnier/une prisonnière
  to be taken prisoner = être fait prisonnier/faite prisonnière

private
1 *adjective*
- (*personal*) = privé/privée
  my private life = ma vie privée
- (*not run by the state*) = privé/privée
  a private school = une école privée
2 in private = en privé

prize *noun*
  a prize = un prix

probably *adverb*
  = probablement

P

problem *noun*
a problem = un problème
to cause a problem = poser un problème

process *noun*
a process = un processus
to be in the process of writing a letter
= être en train d'écrire une lettre

produce
1 *verb*
• (*to make*) = produire
• (*to create*)
to produce a film = produire un film
to produce a play = mettre en scène une
pièce
2 *noun*
produce = les produits (*masculine plural*)

product *noun*
a product = un produit

production *noun*
production (*of food*) = la production
(*of machinery, cars*) = la fabrication

profession *noun*
a profession = une profession

professional *adjective*
= professionnel/professionnelle

professor *noun* ▶ 315 |
a professor = un professeur d'université

profit *noun*
a profit = un bénéfice

program
1 *noun*
• (*for a computer*)
a program = un programme
• (*US English*) ▶ **programme**
2 *verb*
= programmer

programme (*British English*), **program**
(*US English*)
1 *noun*
• (*on radio, TV*)
a programme = une émission
a programme about China = une émission
sur la Chine
• (*for a play, a concert*)
a programme = un programme
2 *verb*
= programmer

progress *noun*
progress = le progrès
to make progress = faire des progrès

project *noun*
a project (*at school*) = un dossier

promise
1 *verb*
= promettre
to promise [to write | to repay a loan | to say
nothing ...] = promettre [d'écrire | de
rembourser un prêt | de ne rien dire ...]

2 *noun*
a promise = une promesse

pronounce *verb*
= prononcer

proof *noun*
proof = une preuve

properly *adverb*
= correctement

property *noun*
property = la propriété

protect *verb*
= protéger
to protect oneself = se protéger (**!** + *être*)

protest *verb*
• (*to complain*) = protester
• (*to demonstrate*) = manifester

protester *noun*
a protester = un manifestant/une
manifestante

proud *adjective*
= fier/fière
she's proud of her work = elle est fière de
son travail

prove *verb*
= prouver

provide *verb*
to provide meals = fournir des repas
to provide work for people = fournir du
travail aux gens
to provide a transport service = assurer
un service de transport

provided *conjunction*
I'll lend you my car provided you pay me
= je te prête ma voiture à condition que
tu me paies
! *Note that the subjunctive is used after* à
condition que.

psychiatrist *noun* ▶ 315 |
a psychiatrist = un psychiatre/une
psychiatre

psychologist *noun* ▶ 315 |
a psychologist = un psychologue/une
psychologue

pub *noun* (*British English*)
a pub = un pub

public
1 *noun*
the public = le public
2 *adjective*
a public park = un jardin public
a public library = une bibliothèque
municipale
3 in public = en public

public holiday *noun*
a public holiday = un jour férié

Shops, trades, and professions

Work and Jobs

what does she do?	= qu'est-ce qu'elle fait comme métier?
what do you do for a living?	= qu'est-ce que vous faites dans la vie?

- There are various ways of saying what someone works at in French. In this area, the major difference between the two languages is the *absence of article* in French, whereas in the singular English always has **a**.

  Note the following examples:

*he's got a job as **a** mechanic*	= il travaille comme mécanicien
*to work as **a** translator*	= travailler comme traducteur / traductrice
*Paul is **a** dentist*	= Paul est dentiste
*I want to be **a** policeman*	= je voudrais devenir agent de police

- The only case where you would use the article **un / une** or **des** in the plural would be in combination with **c'est** or **ce sont**, so:

she is a teacher	= elle est professeur
but	= **c'est** un professeur*
she's a judge	– elle est juge
but	= **c'est** un juge*
they are all doctors	= ils sont tous médecins
but	= **ce sont** tous **des** médecins*

- When using an adjective to describe what kind of doctor / teacher / worker a person is, you must use **c'est un / une** ...

*she's **a good** journalist*	= **c'est une bonne** journaliste
*he's **a bad** teacher*	= **c'est un mauvais** professeur
*he's **an** excellent chef*	= **c'est un** chef **excellent**

* Note that some professions do not have a feminine form and the article will always be masculine as in the examples using **professeur, juge, médecin, ministre,** ...

Shops

In English you can say *at the baker's* or *at the baker's shop*. French also has this possibility but the translation for **at** will also differ depending on what follows:

at the baker's	= **chez** le boulanger
at the baker's shop	= **à** la boulangerie

chez means *at the house or premises of* and is used with the French word for the particular *tradesman* or *professional*:

*I'm going **to** the chemist's*	= je vais **chez** le pharmacien
*she's gone **to** the hairdresser's*	= elle est allée **chez** le coiffeur
*I've got an appointment **at** the dentist's*	= j'ai rendezvous **chez** le dentiste
*is he **at** the doctor's?*	= est-ce qu'il est **chez** le médecin?

However you can also use **à la / au** (or **à l'** + *vowel* or *mute h*) with the French word for a shop:

*I'm going **to the chemist's***	= je vais **à la pharmacie**
*he's **at the grocer's***	= il est **à l'épicerie**
*they've gone **to the baker's***	= ils sont allés **à la boulangerie**

So in French you could have translations using either **à la** or **chez** in the following example:

*go **to** the butcher's*	= va **à la** boucherie
	= va **chez** le boucher

---

public transport *noun*
public transport = les transports en commun

! *Note that* transports *is masculine plural.*

pudding *noun* (*British English*)
a pudding = un dessert

puddle *noun*
a puddle = une flaque

pull *verb*
* to pull = tirer
  to pull someone's hair = tirer les cheveux
    de quelqu'un
  to pull (on) a rope = tirer sur une corde
* (*to move*)
  to pull the piano into the hall = traîner le
    piano dans l'entrée
  to pull someone away from the door
    = éloigner quelqu'un de la porte
* (*to take out*)
  to pull a handkerchief out of one's pocket
    = tirer un mouchoir de sa poche
  to pull someone out of the river = sortir
    quelqu'un de la rivière
* to pull a face (*British English*) = faire une
    grimace
pull down
* (*to knock down*) = démolir
* (*to lower*) = baisser
pull out
  to pull a tooth out = arracher une dent
pull up
* (*to stop*) = s'arrêter (! + *être*)
* (*to remove*)
  to pull up the flowers = arracher les fleurs
* to pull up one's socks = remonter ses
    chaussettes

pullover *noun*
  a pullover = un pull

pump *noun*
  a pump = une pompe
  a bicycle pump = une pompe à bicyclette
pump up = gonfler

pumpkin *noun*
  a pumpkin = une citrouille

punch *verb*
  = donner des coups de poing
  she punched him in the face = elle lui a
    donné un coup de poing dans la figure

puncture *noun*
  a puncture = une crevaison

punish *verb*
  = punir

pupil *noun*
  a pupil = un élève/une élève

puppet *noun*
  a puppet = une marionnette

puppy *noun*
  a puppy = un chiot

pure *adjective*
  = pur/pure

purple *adjective* ▶ 213
  = violet/violette

purpose
1 *noun*
  a purpose = un but
2 on purpose = exprès
  you did it on purpose! = tu l'as fait exprès!

purse *noun*
* (*for money*)
  a purse = un porte-monnaie
* (*US English*) (*a handbag*)
  a purse = un sac à main

push *verb*
* to push = pousser
  to push a car = pousser une voiture
  to push someone down the stairs
    = pousser quelqu'un dans l'escalier
  to push someone out of the way = écarter
    quelqu'un
  to push past someone = bousculer
    quelqu'un
* (*to sell*) = vendre
  to push drugs = vendre de la drogue

pushchair *noun* (*British English*)
  a pushchair = une poussette

pusher *noun*
  a pusher = un revendeur/une revendeuse
    de drogue

put *verb*
  = mettre
  to put the cards on the table = mettre les
    cartes sur la table
  don't put sugar in my coffee = ne mets pas
    de sucre dans mon café
  to put someone in prison = mettre
    quelqu'un en prison
  to put someone in a bad mood = mettre
    quelqu'un de mauvaise humeur
put away = ranger
put back
* (*to return to its place*) = remettre
  to put a book back on a shelf = remettre
    un livre sur une étagère
* (*to change the time*)
  to put the clocks back = retarder les
    pendules
put down
* (*on a surface*) = poser
  put your cases down here, Laurence
    = pose tes valises ici, Laurence
* (*when phoning*)
  to put the phone down = raccrocher
* (*British English*) (*to give an injection to*)
    = piquer
  our dog had to be put down = on a dû
    faire piquer notre chien
put forward = avancer
  to put the clocks forward = avancer les
    pendules
put off
* (*to delay*)
  we'll have to put the party off till next
    week = il va falloir reporter la fête à la
    semaine prochaine
* (*to switch off*) = éteindre
put on
* (*when dressing*) = mettre
  to put jeans on = mettre un jean

Quantities

Note the use of **en** (*of it* or *of them*) in the following examples. This word must be included when the thing you are talking about is not expressed. However, **en** is not needed when the commodity is specified (*there is a lot of butter* = il y a beaucoup de beurre):

How much?

how much is there?	= combien y **en** a-t-il?
there's a lot	= il y **en** a beaucoup
there's not much	= il n'y **en** a pas beaucoup
there's two kilos	= il y **en** a deux kilos
how much sugar have you?	= combien de sucre as-tu?
I've got a lot	= j'**en** ai beaucoup
I haven't got (very) much	= je n'**en** ai pas beaucoup
I've got two kilos	= j'**en** ai deux kilos

How many?

how many are there?	= combien y **en** a-t-il?*
there are a lot	= il y **en** a beaucoup*
there aren't many	= il n'y **en** a pas beaucoup*
there are twenty	= il y **en** a vingt
how many apples have you?	= combien de pommes as-tu?*
	tu as combien de pommes?
I've got a lot	= j'**en** ai beaucoup
I haven't got many	= je n'**en** ai pas beaucoup

Comparisons

I've got twenty	= j'**en** ai vingt
Tim has got more than Tom	= Tim **en** a plus que Tom
Tim has got more money than Tom	= Tim a plus d'argent que Tom
much more than	= beaucoup plus que
a little more than	= un peu plus que
Tim has got more apples than Tom	= Tim a plus de pommes que Tom
many more apples than Tom	= beaucoup plus de pommes que Tom
a few more apples than Tom	= quelques pommes de plus que Tom
a few more people than yesterday	= quelques personnes de plus qu'hier
Tom has got less than Tim	= Tom **en** a moins que Tim
Tom has got less money than Tim	= Tom a moins d'argent que Tim
much less than	= beaucoup moins que
a little less than	= un peu moins que
Tom has got fewer than Tim	= Tom **en** a moins que Tim
Tom has got fewer apples than Tim	= Tom a moins de pommes que Tim
many fewer than	= beaucoup moins que

Relative quantities

how many are there to the kilo?	= combien y **en** a-t-il au kilo?*
there are ten to the kilo	= il y **en** a dix au kilo*
how many do you get for ten euros?	= combien peut-on **en** avoir pour dix euros?
you get five for ten euros	= il y **en** a cinq pour dix euros
how much does it cost a litre?	= combien coûte le litre?
it costs £5 a litre	= ça coûte cinq livres le litre
how much do apples cost a kilo?	= combien coûte le kilo de pommes?
how many glasses do you get to the bottle?	= combien y a-t-il de verres par bouteille?
you get six glasses to the bottle	= il y a six verres par bouteille

* Note the use of a singular verb in French in these examples.

- (*to switch on*)
  to put the heating on = allumer le chauffage
  to put the kettle on = mettre la bouilloire à chauffer
  to put a CD on = mettre un disque compact
- **to put on weight** = prendre du poids
- (*to organize, to produce*) = monter
  to put on a play = monter une pièce

put out
- **to put out a cigarette** = éteindre une cigarette
- (*to take out*) = sortir
  to put the bins out = sortir les poubelles

put up
- (*to lift*)
  to put one's hair up = remonter ses cheveux
  to put up one's hand (*in class*) ≈ lever le doigt
- (*to attach*)
  to put a sign up = mettre une pancarte
- (*when camping*)
  to put up a tent = planter une tente
- (*British English*) (*to raise*) = augmenter
  to put the rent up = augmenter le loyer
- (*to give someone a place to stay*) = héberger
put up with = supporter

puzzle *noun*
  a puzzle = un casse-tête

pyjamas *noun* (*British English*)
  pyjamas = un pyjama (*singular*)

---

qualified *adjective*
- (*having studied*) = diplômé/diplômée
- (*having experience, skills*) = qualifié/qualifiée

quality *noun*
  quality = la qualité

quantity *noun* ▶ 317 |
  a quantity = une quantité

quarrel
1 *noun*
  a quarrel = une dispute
2 *verb*
  = se disputer (**!** + *être*)

✕ in informal situations

quarter
1 *noun*
  a quarter = un quart
  a quarter of an hour = un quart d'heure
  to cut the tomatoes in quarters = couper les tomates en quatre
2 *pronoun*
- (*when talking about quantities, numbers*) ▶ 317 |
  a quarter of the population can't read = un quart de la population ne sait pas lire
- (*when talking about time*) ▶ 211 |
  an hour and a quarter = une heure et quart
  it's (a) quarter past five = il est cinq heures et quart

quay *noun*
  a quay = un quai

queen *noun*
  a queen = une reine

question
1 *noun*
- (*a request for information*)
  a question = une question
  to ask someone a question = poser une question à quelqu'un
- (*a problem, a matter*)
  a question = un problème
2 *verb*
  = interroger

queue (*British English*)
1 *noun*
  a queue (*of people*) = une queue, une file d'attente
  (*of cars, trucks*) = une file
  to join the queue = se mettre à la queue
2 *verb*
  = faire la queue

quick *adjective*
  = rapide
  a quick answer = une réponse rapide
  it's quicker to go by train = c'est plus rapide d'y aller en train
  it's the quickest way [to get to London | to save money | to make friends ...] = c'est le moyen le plus rapide [d'aller à Londres | de gagner de l'argent | de se faire des amis ...]

quickly *adverb*
  = vite, rapidement

quiet
1 *adjective*
- (*silent*) = silencieux/silencieuse
  to keep quiet = garder le silence
  to go quiet = se taire (**!** + *être*)
  be quiet! = taisez-vous!
- (*not talkative*) = réservé/réservée
- (*calm*) = tranquille
  it's a quiet little village = c'est un petit village tranquille

2 noun
quiet = le silence
quiet please! = silence, s'il vous plaît!

quietly adverb
to speak quietly = parler doucement
to [play | sit | read ...] quietly = [jouer |
s'asseoir | lire ...] en silence

quit verb
• (to resign) = démissionner
• (US English) (to give up)
to quit [smoking | drinking | working ...]
= arrêter de [fumer | boire | travailler ...]

quite adverb
• (rather) = assez
they go back to France quite often = ils
rentrent assez souvent en France
I quite like Chinese food = j'aime assez la
cuisine chinoise
she earns quite a lot of money = elle
gagne pas mal* d'argent
• (completely)
I'm not quite ready yet = je ne suis pas
encore tout à fait prêt
you're quite right = vous avez entièrement
raison
are you quite sure? = en êtes-vous
certain?
• (exactly)
'is it true?'—'not quite' = 'est-ce que c'est
vrai?'—'pas exactement'
I don't quite know what he does = je ne
sais pas exactement ce qu'il fait

quiz noun
a quiz = un jeu de questions-réponses

Rr

rabbit noun
a rabbit = un lapin

rabies noun ▶ 266
rabies = la rage

race
1 noun
(a contest)
a race = une course
to have a race = faire une course
(for horse-racing)
the races = les courses (feminine)
2 verb
(to compete with)
to race (against) someone = faire la
course avec quelqu'un
I'll race you to the car = on fait la course
jusqu'à la voiture
(to take part in a contest) = courir

racehorse noun
a racehorse = un cheval de course

racetrack noun
a racetrack (for horses) = un champ de
courses
(for cars) = un circuit

racism noun
racism = le racisme

racket, racquet noun
a racket = une raquette

radiator noun
a radiator = un radiateur

radio noun
a radio = une radio
on the radio = à la radio

radio station noun
a radio station = une station de radio

rage noun
rage = la rage, la colère
to fly into a rage = se mettre en colère

raid verb
to raid a bank = attaquer une banque
the police raided the building = la police a
fait une descente dans le bâtiment

rail noun
(for holding on to)
a rail = une rampe, une main courante
(for trains)
rails = les rails (masculine)

railway (British English), **railroad** (US
English) noun
(a track)
a railway = une voie ferrée
(the rail system)
the railway = le chemin de fer

railway line noun (British English)
a railway line = une ligne de chemin de
fer

railway station noun (British English)
a railway station = une gare

rain
1 noun
rain = la pluie
to stand in the rain = rester sous la pluie
2 verb
= pleuvoir
it's raining = il pleut

rainbow noun
a rainbow = un arc-en-ciel

raincoat noun
a raincoat = un imperméable

raise verb
(to lift) = lever
(to increase) = augmenter
to raise prices = augmenter les prix
(in anger)
to raise one's voice = hausser le ton

R

(*to talk about*)
to raise a subject = soulever une question
(*to bring up*)
to raise children = élever des enfants

range *noun*
(*a selection*)
a range (*of goods, prices*) = une gamme
(*of activities, school subjects*) = un grand
choix
(*of mountains*)
a range = une chaîne
(*US English*) (*for cooking*)
a range = une cuisinière

rare *adjective*
(*not common*) = rare
(*very slightly cooked*) = saignant/saignante

rarely *adverb*
= rarement

rasher *noun* (*British English*)
a rasher (*of bacon*) = une tranche (de
bacon)

raspberry *noun*
a raspberry = une framboise

rat *noun*
a rat = un rat

rather *adverb*
(*when saying what one would prefer*)
I'd rather [leave | stay here | read the paper ...]
= j'aimerais mieux [partir | rester ici | lire le
journal ...]
I'd rather you came with me = j'aimerais
mieux que tu viennes avec moi

! *Note that the subjunctive is used after*
j'aimerais mieux que.

(*quite*) = plutôt
I think he's rather nice = je le trouve
plutôt sympathique

raw *adjective*
= cru/crue

razor *noun*
a razor = un rasoir

razor blade *noun*
a razor blade = une lame de rasoir

reach *verb*
(*to arrive at*) = atteindre
they reached the town at midnight = ils
ont atteint la ville à minuit
(*to be delivered to*) = parvenir à (! + *être*)
the letter never reached him = la lettre ne
lui est pas parvenue
(*by stretching*)
to reach up = lever le bras
I can't reach the shelf = je n'arrive pas à
atteindre l'étagère
(*to come to*) = arriver à (! + *être*)
to reach a decision = arriver à une
décision
(*to contact by phone*) = joindre
I can be reached at this number = on peut
me joindre à ce numéro

reach out = tendre le bras

react *verb*
= réagir

read *verb*
= lire
the writing is difficult to read = l'écriture
est difficile à lire
to read to someone = faire la lecture à
quelqu'un
read out
to read out the names = lire les noms à
haute voix
read through (*once*) = lire
(*a second time*) = relire

reading *noun*
reading = la lecture

ready *adjective*
(*prepared*) = prêt/prête
are you ready to leave? = est-ce que vous
êtes prêts à partir?
to get ready = se préparer (! + *être*)
to get a meal ready = préparer le repas
(*happy*) = prêt/prête
I'm ready to help them = je suis prêt à les
aider

real *adjective*
(*not imagined*) = réel/réelle
(*not artificial*) = vrai/vraie (! *before the*
noun)
are they real diamonds? = est-ce que ce
sont de vrais diamants?
it's a real shame = c'est vraiment
dommage

reality *noun*
reality = la réalité

realize *verb*
= se rendre compte (! + *être*)
I didn't realize (that) he was your boss
= je ne me suis pas rendu compte que
c'était ton patron

really *adverb*
= vraiment
it's really easy to make = c'est vraiment
facile à faire
what really happened? = qu'est-ce qui
s'est réellement passé?
really? = c'est vrai?

rear
1 *noun*
the rear = l'arrière (*masculine*)
2 *verb*
= élever

reason *noun*
a reason = une raison
that's a good reason to learn French
= c'est une bonne raison d'apprendre le
français
is there any reason why you shouldn't
drive? = pourquoi est-ce que vous ne
devriez pas conduire?
tell me the reason why = dis-moi pourquoi

reassure *verb*
= rassurer

receipt *noun*
a receipt = un reçu
a till receipt = un ticket de caisse

receive *verb*
(*to get*) = recevoir
we received a letter from the teacher
= nous avons reçu une lettre du
professeur
(*to meet*) = accueillir, recevoir
to be well received = être bien reçu/reçue

recent *adjective*
= récent/récente

recently *adverb*
= récemment

reception *noun*
(*in a hotel, a hospital, a company*)
the reception = la réception
ask at (the) reception = adressez-vous à la
réception
(*a formal event*)
a reception = une réception

receptionist *noun* ▶ 315 |
a receptionist = un réceptionniste/une
réceptionniste

recipe *noun*
a recipe = une recette

recognize *verb*
= reconnaître

recommend *verb*
= recommander

record
1 *noun*
(*information*)
the records (*historical, public*) = les
archives (*feminine*)
(*personal, medical*) = le dossier (*singular*)
(*for playing music*)
a record = un disque
(*in sport*)
a record = un record
to break the world record = battre le
record du monde
2 *verb*
= enregistrer

recorder *noun* ▶ 290 |
a recorder = une flûte à bec

record player *noun*
a record player = un électrophone

recover *verb*
= se remettre (**!** + *être*)
to recover from an illness = se remettre
d'une maladie

recycle *verb*
= recycler

red *adjective* ▶ 213 |
= rouge
to go red, to turn red = rougir
to have red hair = avoir les cheveux roux

red-haired *adjective*
= roux/rousse

reduce *verb*
to reduce prices = baisser les prix
to reduce the number of employees
= réduire le nombre d'employés
to reduce speed = ralentir

reduction *noun*
a reduction = une réduction

redundant *adjective* (*British English*)
to be made redundant = être
licencié/licenciée pour raisons
économiques

referee *noun* ▶ 315 |
a referee = un arbitre

reflection *noun*
a reflection = un reflet

refreshing *adjective*
= rafraîchissant/rafraîchissante

refrigerator *noun*
a refrigerator = un réfrigérateur, un
frigidaire

refugee *noun*
a refugee = un réfugié/une réfugiée

refuse¹ *verb*
= refuser
to refuse [to listen | to stop | to pay ...]
= refuser [d'écouter | de s'arrêter | de payer ...]

refuse² *noun* (*British English*)
refuse = les ordures (*feminine plural*)

regards *noun*
give her my regards = transmettez-lui
mes amitiés

region *noun*
a region = une région

regional *adjective*
= régional/régionale

register *noun*
the register = le cahier d'appel
to take the register = faire l'appel

regret *verb*
= regretter
I regret changing my mind = je regrette
d'avoir changé d'avis
he regrets that he can't come = il regrette
de ne pas pouvoir venir
I regret that he can't come = je regrette
qu'il ne puisse pas venir
! *Note that the subjunctive is used after*
regretter que.

regular *adjective*
regular = régulier/régulière

R

regularly adverb
= régulièrement

rehearsal noun
a rehearsal = une répétition

rehearse verb
= répéter

reject verb
to reject someone's advice = rejeter les
conseils de quelqu'un
to reject a candidate = refuser un
candidat

relationship noun
a relationship = une relation, des relations
(plural)
to have a good relationship = bien
s'entendre (**!** + être)
she has a good relationship with her
parents = elle s'entend bien avec ses
parents

relative noun
a relative = un parent/une parente
my relatives = ma famille

relax verb
= se détendre (**!** + être)

relaxed adjective
= détendu/détendue,
décontracté/décontractée

relay race verb
a relay race = une course de relais

release verb
= libérer

reliable adjective
a reliable person = une personne digne de
confiance
a reliable car = une voiture fiable

relieved adjective
= soulagé/soulagée

religion noun
religion = la religion

religious education, RE (British
English) noun
religious education = l'instruction
religieuse
> **!** Note that instruction is feminine.

rely verb
(to depend on) = dépendre de
(to count on) = compter sur
can we rely on you? = est-ce qu'on peut
compter sur toi?

remain verb
= rester

remark noun
a remark = une remarque, une réflexion

remarkable adjective
= remarquable

remember verb
= se souvenir (**!** + être)
do you remember her? = est-ce que tu te
souviens d'elle?
I remember writing down the address = je
me souviens d'avoir noté l'adresse
to remember to [write the letter | water the
plants | turn off the lights …] = penser à
[écrire la lettre | arroser les plantes | éteindre les
lumières …]

remind verb
= rappeler
to remind someone to buy milk = rappeler
à quelqu'un d'acheter du lait
she reminds me of my sister = elle me
rappelle ma sœur

remote control noun
a remote control = une télécommande

remove verb
= enlever
to remove the stains from a carpet
= enlever les taches d'une moquette

rent
1 verb
= louer
to rent an apartment = louer un
appartement
2 noun
a rent = un loyer
rent out = louer

repair verb
= réparer
to have a bicycle repaired = faire réparer
un vélo

repeat verb
(to say again) = répéter
to repeat a year = redoubler une classe

replace verb
= remplacer
they replaced the fence with a wall = ils
ont remplacé la clôture par un mur

reply
1 verb
= répondre
to reply to a letter = répondre à une lettre
2 noun
a reply = une réponse

report
1 verb
(to tell about) = signaler
to report an accident = signaler un
accident
(in the news)
to report on an event = faire un reportage
sur un événement
(to complain about)
to report the noise = se plaindre du bruit
2 noun
(in the news)
a report = un communiqué
(longer) = un reportage

(*an official document*)
a report = un rapport
(*British English*) (*from school*)
a (school) report = un bulletin scolaire

report card *noun* (*US English*)
a report card = un bulletin scolaire

reporter *noun* ▶ 315│
a reporter = un journaliste/une journaliste, un reporter

represent *verb*
= représenter

republic *noun*
a republic = une république

request *noun*
a request = une demande

rescue *verb*
(*from danger*) = sauver

resemble *verb*
= ressembler à
to resemble each other = se ressembler
(**!** + *être*)

resent *verb*
to resent someone = en vouloir à quelqu'un
he resents her for winning = il lui en veut d'avoir gagné

reservation *noun*
a reservation = une réservation

reserve *verb*
= réserver

resign *verb*
= démissionner

resist *verb*
= résister

respect
1 *verb*
= respecter
2 *noun*
respect = le respect
out of respect = par respect

responsibility *noun*
responsibility = la responsabilité

responsible *adjective*
(*the cause of*) = responsable
to be responsible for the damage = être responsable des dégâts
(*in charge*) = responsable
to be responsible for organizing a trip
= être chargé/chargée d'organiser une sortie

rest
1 *noun*
(*what is left*)
the rest = le reste
we spent the rest of the day in the garden
= on a passé le reste de la journée dans le jardin

(*time to recover*)
rest = le repos
to need rest = avoir besoin de repos
(*a break*)
a rest = une pause
to have a rest = se reposer (**!** + *être*)
2 *verb*
= se reposer (**!** + *être*)

restaurant *noun*
a restaurant = un restaurant

result *noun*
a result = un résultat
the exam results = les résultats des examens
as a result of an accident = à la suite d'un accident

résumé *noun* (*US English*)
a résumé = un CV, un curriculum vitae

retire *verb*
= prendre sa retraite

return *verb*
(*to go back*) = retourner (**!** + *être*)
(*to come back*) = revenir (**!** + *être*)
(*from abroad, to one's home*) = rentrer (**!** + *être*)
(*to give back*) = rendre
can you return my book? = est-ce que tu peux me rendre mon livre?
(*to send back*) = renvoyer
to return goods = renvoyer des articles
(*to start again*)
to return to work = reprendre le travail
to return to school = reprendre l'école

return ticket *noun*
a return ticket = un billet aller-retour

reveal *verb*
to reveal a secret = révéler un secret

revenge *noun*
revenge = la vengeance
to get one's revenge = se venger (**!** + *être*)

revolution *noun*
a revolution = une révolution

reward
1 *noun*
a reward = une récompense
2 *verb*
= récompenser

rewind *verb*
= rembobiner

rhinoceros, rhino *noun*
a rhinoceros = un rhinocéros

rhythm *noun*
rhythm = le rythme

rib *noun* ▶ 201│
a rib = une côte

rice *noun*
rice = le riz

rich *adjective*
= riche
to get rich = s'enrichir (**!** + *être*)

rid: **to get rid of** *verb*
= se débarrasser de (**!** + *être*)

ride
1 *verb* **▶ 248 |**
to ride, to go riding = faire du cheval
to ride a horse = monter à cheval
to be riding a bike = rouler à vélo
2 *noun*
to go for a ride (*in a car, on a bike*) = aller faire un tour
(*on a horse*) = aller faire une promenade à cheval

ridiculous *adjective*
= ridicule

rifle *noun*
a rifle = un fusil

right
1 *adjective*
(*not left*) = droit/droite
his right hand = sa main droite
(*honest, good*) = bien
it's not right to steal = ce n'est pas bien de voler
to do the right thing = faire ce qu'il faut
(*correct*) = bon/bonne (**!** *before the noun*)
the right answer = la bonne réponse
is this the right direction? = est-ce que c'est la bonne direction?
what's the right time? = quelle est l'heure exacte?
you're right = tu as raison
that's right = c'est ça
2 *noun*
(*the direction*)
the right = la droite
the first street on the right = la première rue à droite
(*what one is entitled to*)
a right = un droit
to have a right to education = avoir droit à l'instruction
human rights = les droits de l'homme
3 *adverb*
= à droite
to turn right = tourner à droite

ring
1 *verb*
(*British English*) (*to phone*) = appeler
to ring for a taxi = appeler un taxi
(*to make a sound*) = sonner
to ring the bell = sonner
the doorbell rang = on a sonné à la porte
2 *noun*
(*a piece of jewellery*)
a ring = une bague
a wedding ring = une alliance
(*a circle*)
a ring = un cercle
(*in a circus*)
the ring = la piste

ring up (*British English*) = téléphoner

rinse *verb*
= rincer

ripe *adjective*
= mûr/mûre

rise *verb*
(*if it's smoke, water*) = monter (**!** + *être*)
(*if it's a price*) = augmenter
(*if it's a plane*) = s'élever (**!** + *être*)
(*if it's the sun or moon*) = se lever (**!** + *être*)

risk
1 *noun*
a risk = un risque
2 *verb*
= risquer
to risk losing one's job = risquer de perdre son travail

river *noun*
a river = une rivière
(*flowing into the sea*) = un fleuve

riverbank *noun*
a riverbank = une berge

road *noun*
a road = une route
the road to London = la route de Londres

road sign *noun*
a road sign = un panneau de signalisation

roadworks *noun*
roadworks = les travaux (*masculine*)

roar *verb*
(*if it's a lion*) = rugir
(*if it's a person*) = hurler
(*if it's an engine*) = vrombir

roast
1 *verb*
= rôtir
2 *adjective*
= rôti/rôtie
to eat roast beef = manger du rôti de bœuf
3 *noun*
a roast = un rôti

rob *verb*
to rob someone = voler quelqu'un
to rob a bank = dévaliser une banque

robbery *noun*
a robbery = un vol

robin *noun*
a robin = un rouge-gorge

robot *noun*
a robot = un robot

rock *noun*
(*the material*)
rock = la roche
(*a large stone*)
a rock = un rocher
(*music*)
rock = le rock

rock climbing *noun* ▶ **248 |**
  rock climbing = la varappe

rocket *noun*
  a rocket = une fusée

role *noun*
  a role = un rôle

roll
1 *verb*
  = rouler
  the ball rolled under a car = le ballon a
    roulé sous une voiture
  to roll the pastry into a ball = faire une
    boule de la pâte
2 *noun*
  (*of paper, cloth, plastic*)
  a roll = un rouleau
  a roll of film = une pellicule
  (*bread*)
  a roll = un petit pain
  (*US English*) (*at school*)
  to call the roll = faire l'appel
roll about, roll around (*if it's an object*)
  = rouler
roll over = se retourner (**!** + *être*)
roll up = enrouler
  to roll up a newspaper = rouler un journal

roller coaster *noun*
  a roller coaster = des montagnes russes
  ! *Note that* montagnes *is feminine plural.*

roller-skate *noun*
  a roller-skate = un patin à roulettes

roller-skating *noun* ▶ **248 |**
  roller-skating = le patin à roulettes

Romania *noun* ▶ **218 |**
  Romania = la Roumanie

romantic *adjective*
  = romantique

roof *noun*
  a roof = un toit

room *noun*
  a room = une pièce
  (*for sleeping*) = une chambre
  (*for working*) = un bureau
  (*for teaching, holding meetings*) = une salle
  (*space*)
  room = la place
  to make room = faire de la place
  is there room? = est-ce qu'il y a de la
    place?

root *noun*
  a root = une racine

rope *noun*
  a rope = une corde

rose *noun*
  a rose = une rose

rosy *adjective*
  = rose
  to have rosy cheeks = avoir les joues roses

rotten *adjective*
  = pourri/pourrie

rough *adjective*
  (*not smooth*) = rugueux/rugueuse
  to have rough skin = avoir la peau
    rugueuse
  (*not gentle*) = brutal/brutale
  (*tough*) = dur/dure
  to live in a rough area = habiter un
    quartier dur
  (*not exact, precise*)
  a rough figure = un chiffre approximatif
  (*difficult*) = dur/dure, difficile
  to have a rough time = traverser une
    période difficile
  (*caused by bad weather*)
  a rough sea = une mer agitée

round
  ! *Often* round *occurs in combinations with
  verbs. For more information, see the note
  at* **around.**

1 *preposition*
  = autour de
  to be sitting round a table = être
    assis/assises autour d'une table
  to sail round the world = faire le tour du
    monde en bateau
  to go round Oxford = visiter Oxford
2 *adverb*
  to go round and round = tourner en rond
  to go round to John's = passer chez John
  to invite someone round = inviter
    quelqu'un chez soi
3 *noun*
  a round (*in a quiz*) = une manche
  (*in showjumping*) = un parcours
  (*in boxing*) = un round
  (*in an election*) = un tour
4 *adjective*
  = rond/ronde

roundabout *noun*
  (*British English*) (*in a fair*)
  a roundabout = un manège
  (*for traffic*)
  a roundabout = un rond-point

route *noun*
  a route = un itinéraire
  a bus route = une ligne d'autobus

routine *noun*
  a routine = une routine

row¹
1 *noun*
  a row (*of people, trees*) = un rang
  (*of houses, seats*) = une rangée
  (*of cars*) = une file
  the pupils were sitting in rows = les élèves
    étaient assis en rangs
  (*when talking about frequency*)
  to be absent five days in a row = être
    absent/absente cinq jours de suite

R

2 *verb*
(*as an activity*) = ramer
(*as a sport*) ▶ **248** = faire de l'aviron
to row across a lake = traverser un lac à la rame

row² *noun* (*British English*)
a row = une dispute
to have a row with someone = se disputer avec quelqu'un

rowing *noun* ▶ **248**
rowing = l'aviron (*masculine*)

rowing boat (*British English*),
rowboat (*US English*) *noun*
a rowing boat = un bateau à rames

royal *adjective*
= royal/royale

rub *verb*
to rub a stain = frotter une tache
to rub one's eyes = se frotter les yeux
rub out (*British English*) = s'effacer
(**!** + *être*)
to rub out a mistake = effacer une erreur

rubber *noun*
(*the material*)
rubber = le caoutchouc
(*British English*) (*an eraser*)
a rubber = une gomme

rubbish *noun* (*British English*)
(*refuse*)
rubbish (*household*) = les ordures
(*feminine plural*)
(*in the street, in a dump*) = les déchets
(*masculine plural*)
(*poor quality goods*)
rubbish = la camelote**✱**

rubbish bin *noun* (*British English*)
a rubbish bin = une poubelle

rucksack *noun*
a rucksack = un sac à dos

rude *adjective*
(*not polite*) = impoli/impolie
to be rude to someone = être
impoli/impolie envers quelqu'un
(*vulgar*) = grossier/grossière
a rude word = un gros mot

rug *noun*
a rug = un tapis

rugby *noun* ▶ **248**
rugby = le rugby

ruin
1 *verb*
(*to spoil*) = gâcher
to ruin a meal = gâcher un repas
(*to damage*) = abîmer
you'll ruin your shoes = tu vas abîmer tes chaussures

2 *noun*
a ruin = une ruine

rule
1 *noun*
a rule (*of a game, a language*) = une règle
(*in a school, an organization*) = un règlement
it's against the rules = c'est contraire au règlement
2 *verb*
(*if it's a leader*) = gouverner
(*if it's a king, queen*) = régner sur
(*if it's a party*) = diriger

ruler *noun*
a ruler = une règle

rumour (*British English*), **rumor** (*US English*) *noun*
a rumour = une rumeur

run
1 *verb*
to run = courir
to run after someone = courir après quelqu'un
to run across the street = traverser la rue en courant
to run a race = faire une course
(*from danger*) = fuir, s'enfuir (**!** + *être*)
(*to manage*) = diriger
(*to work, to operate*) = marcher
the car runs on unleaded petrol = la voiture marche à l'essence sans plomb
the system is running well = le système marche bien
(*to organize*) = organiser
to run a competition = organiser un concours
(*when talking about transport*) = circuler
the buses don't run after midnight = les bus ne circulent pas après minuit
(*to flow*) = couler
(*to fill with water*)
to run a bath = faire couler un bain
(*to come off*) (*when talking about dyes*) = déteindre
(*when talking about make-up*) = couler
(*in an election*)
to run for president = être candidat/candidate à la présidence
(*other uses*)
to be running late = être en retard
to be running a temperature = avoir de la fièvre
2 *noun*
a run = une course
to go for a run = aller courir
run about, run around = courir
run away = s'enfuir (**!** + *être*)
run off = partir en courant (**!** + *être*)

runner *noun*
a runner = un coureur/une coureuse (à pied)

✱ in informal situations

rush
1 *verb*
- (*to hurry*) = se dépêcher (**!** + *être*)
  to rush to finish one's homework = se dépêcher de finir ses devoirs
  to rush into a shop = se précipiter dans un magasin
  to rush out of the house = se précipiter hors de la maison
  to be rushed to the hospital = être emmené/emmenée d'urgence à l'hôpital
- (*to put pressure on*) = bousculer
2 *noun*
  to be in a rush = être pressé/pressée
  to do one's homework in a rush = faire ses devoirs à la va-vite

rush hour *noun*
the rush hour = les heures de pointe

| **!** Note that **heures** is feminine plural.

Russia *noun* ▶ 218 |
Russia = la Russie

Russian ▶ 275 |
1 *adjective*
= russe
2 *noun*
- (*the people*)
  the Russians = les Russes (*masculine*)
- (*the language*)
  Russian = le russe

rusty *adjective*
= rouillé/rouillée

---

sad *adjective*
= triste

saddle *noun*
a saddle = une selle

safe ▶ 237 |
1 *adjective*
- (*without risk*) = sûr/sûre
  a safe place = un endroit sûr
  it's not safe for children = c'est dangereux pour les enfants
  is it safe to go there? = est-ce qu'on peut y aller sans danger?
- (*free from danger*)
  to feel safe = se sentir en sécurité
  your car is safe here = ici, votre voiture ne risque rien
- (*out of danger*) = sain et sauf/saine et sauve
2 *noun*
  a safe = un coffre-fort

safety *noun*
safety = la sécurité

Sagittarius *noun*
Sagittarius = Sagittaire (*masculine*)

sail
1 *noun*
  a sail = une voile
  to set sail = prendre la mer
2 *verb*
  to sail around the world = faire le tour du monde en bateau
  to go sailing = faire de la voile

sailing *noun* ▶ 248 |
sailing = la voile

sailing boat (*British English*), sailboat
(*US English*) *noun*
  a sailing boat = un bateau à voiles

sailor *noun* ▶ 315 |
a sailor = un marin

saint *noun*
  a saint = un saint/une sainte

salad *noun*
  a salad = une salade

salary *noun*
  a salary = un salaire

sale *noun*
- **to be on sale** (*British English*) = être en vente
  for sale = à vendre
- **the sales** = les soldes (*masculine*)

sales assistant *noun* ▶ 315 | (*British English*)
  a sales assistant = un vendeur/une vendeuse

salmon *noun*
  a salmon = un saumon

salt *noun*
  salt = le sel

same
1 *adjective*
= même
  she's got the same coat as me = elle a le même manteau que moi
  they go to the same school = ils vont à la même école
  it's the same as the car I had before = c'est la même voiture que celle que j'avais avant
  it's all the same to me = ça m'est complètement égal
  the houses all look the same = les maisons sont toutes pareilles
  people are the same everywhere = les gens sont partout pareils
  things aren't the same without them = ce n'est pas la même chose sans eux
  it's the same as ever = c'est toujours la même chose

2 *pronoun*
the same = la même chose
I'll have the same = je prendrai la même chose
to do the same as the others = faire comme les autres
'Happy New Year!'—'the same to you!' = 'Bonne année!'—'à toi de même!'

sand *noun*
sand = le sable

sandal *noun*
a sandal = un nu-pied

sandwich *noun*
a sandwich = un sandwich
a ham sandwich = un sandwich au jambon

Santa (Claus) *noun*
Santa (Claus) = le Père Noël

sardine *noun*
a sardine = une sardine

satellite TV *noun*
satellite TV = la télévision par satellite

satisfactory *adjective*
= satisfaisant/satisfaisante

satisfied *adjective*
= satisfait/satisfaite

Saturday *noun* ▶ **222** |
Saturday = samedi (*masculine*)

sauce *noun*
a sauce = une sauce

saucepan *noun*
a saucepan = une casserole

saucer *noun*
a saucer = une soucoupe

sausage *noun*
a sausage = une saucisse

save *verb*
• (*to rescue*) = sauver
they saved his life = ils lui ont sauvé la vie
• (*to avoid spending*)
to save (up) = faire des économies
to save money = mettre de l'argent de côté
• (*to avoid wasting*)
to save [time | energy | money ...] = économiser [du temps | de l'énergie | de l'argent ...]
• (*to keep*) = garder
to save a piece of cake for someone = garder un morceau de gâteau pour quelqu'un
to save a file = sauvegarder un fichier
• (*to spare*)
to save someone a lot of work = éviter beaucoup de travail à quelqu'un
it will save us from having to drive all night = ça nous évitera de conduire toute la nuit

savings *noun*
savings = les économies (*feminine*)

saw *noun*
a saw = une scie

saxophone *noun* ▶ **290** |
a saxophone = un saxophone

say *verb*
= dire
to say goodbye = dire au revoir
she says (that) she can't go out tonight = elle dit qu'elle ne peut pas sortir ce soir
he said to wait here = il a dit d'attendre ici
they say she's very rich = on dit qu'elle est très riche
I can't say who did it = je ne peux pas dire qui a fait ça
she wouldn't say = elle n'a pas voulu le dire
I said to myself that you'd like that = je me suis dit que ça te ferait plaisir
what does the message say? = que dit le message?
it says here that smoking is not allowed = il est dit ici qu'on n'a pas le droit de fumer
I'd say she was forty = je lui donne quarante ans
let's say there are twenty people at the party = supposons qu'il y ait vingt personnes à la fête

! *Note that the subjunctive is used after* supposer que.

scandal *noun*
a scandal = un scandale

scare *verb*
= faire peur à
you scared me! = tu m'as fait peur!
scare away = faire fuir

scared *adjective*
to be scared = avoir peur

scarf *noun*
a scarf (*long*) = une écharpe
(*square*) = un foulard

scenery *noun*
scenery = le paysage

school
1 *noun*
a school = une école
to be at school = être à l'école
2 *adjective*
= scolaire
a school bus = un car de ramassage scolaire

schoolbag *noun*
a schoolbag = un cartable

schoolboy *noun*
a schoolboy = un élève

schoolgirl *noun*
a schoolgirl = une élève

schoolwork *noun*
schoolwork = le travail de classe

science *noun*
science = la science
to study science = étudier les sciences

scientist *noun* ▶ 315 |
a scientist = un scientifique/une
scientifique

scissors *noun*
scissors = les ciseaux (*masculine*)
a pair of scissors = une paire de ciseaux

score *verb*
to score a goal = marquer un but

Scorpio *noun*
Scorpio = Scorpion (*masculine*)

Scotland *noun* ▶ 218 |
Scotland = l'Écosse

Scottish *adjective* ▶ 275 |
= écossais/écossaise

scratch *verb*
• (*when itchy*) = se gratter (**!** + *être*)
to scratch one's arm = se gratter le bras
• (*if it's a person or an animal*) = griffer
(*if it's a bush, thorns*) = égratigner
• (*to mark, to damage*) = érafler

scream *verb*
= hurler

screen *noun*
a screen = un écran

screw *noun*
a screw = une vis

sea *noun*
a sea = une mer
beside the sea, by the sea = au bord de la
mer

seagull *noun*
a seagull = une mouette

seal *verb*
a seal = un phoque

search *verb*
• to search = chercher
to search for someone = chercher
quelqu'un
• (*to examine a place, a person*) = fouiller
they searched me at the airport = on m'a
fouillé à l'aéroport

seashell *noun*
a seashell = un coquillage

seasick *adjective*
to be seasick, to get seasick = avoir le
mal de mer

seaside *noun*
at the seaside = au bord de la mer
to go to the seaside = aller à la mer

season *noun*
a season = une saison
strawberries are in season = c'est la
saison des fraises

seat *noun*
• (*a chair, a bench*)
a seat = un siège
have a seat = asseyez-vous
• (*on transport, in a theatre*)
a seat = une place

seatbelt *noun*
a seatbelt = une ceinture de sécurité

second
1 *adjective*
= deuxième, second/seconde
it's the second time I've called her = c'est
la deuxième fois que je l'appelle
every second Monday = un lundi sur
deux
2 *noun*
• (*in a series*)
the second = le deuxième/la deuxième, le
second/la seconde
• (*in time*)
a second = une seconde
(*a very short time*) = un instant
• (*in dates*) ▶ 222 |
the second of May = le deux mai
3 *adverb*
= deuxième
to come second = arriver deuxième

secondary school *noun*
a secondary school = une école
secondaire

second-hand *adjective*
a second-hand [car | coat | book ...] = [une
voiture | un manteau | un livre ...] d'occasion

secret
1 *adjective*
= secret/secrète
2 *noun*
a secret = un secret
to tell someone a secret = confier un
secret à quelqu'un
3 in secret = en secret

secretary *noun* ▶ 315 |
a secretary = un secrétaire/une secrétaire

see *verb* ▶ 237 |
• to see = voir
what can you see? = qu'est-ce que tu vois?
I can't see them = je ne les vois pas
he saw the people running = il a vu les
gens qui couraient
do they see each other often? = est-ce
qu'ils se voient souvent?
see you tomorrow! = à demain!
I'll go and see = je vais voir
• (*to accompany*)
I'll see you home = je vais te
raccompagner chez toi

S

seem verb
* (to appear)
  she seems [happy | annoyed | tired …] = elle
  a l'air [contente | vexée | fatiguée …]
  they seem to be looking for someone = on
  dirait qu'ils cherchent quelqu'un
* (when talking about one's impressions)
  = sembler
  it seems (that) there are a lot of problems
  = il semble qu'il y ait beaucoup de
  problèmes
  it seems strange (to me) = ça (me) paraît
  bizarre

seldom adverb
= rarement

self-confident ▶ confident

selfish adjective
= égoïste

sell verb
= vendre
  to sell books to the students = vendre des
  livres aux étudiants
  he sold me his car = il m'a vendu sa
  voiture
  water is sold in bottles = l'eau se vend en
  bouteilles

send verb
= envoyer
  to send help = envoyer des secours
  to send a package to someone = envoyer
  un paquet à quelqu'un
  he sent her a letter = il lui a envoyé une
  lettre
  to send someone to post a letter
  = envoyer quelqu'un mettre une lettre à
  la poste
  to send a pupil home from school
  = renvoyer un élève chez lui/une élève
  chez elle
send away = faire partir
send back = renvoyer
send for = faire venir
  to send for the doctor = faire venir le
  médecin
send off
  to send a player off = expulser un joueur
send on
  to send on baggage = expédier des
  bagages à l'avance
  to send on post = faire suivre du courrier

senior high school (US English),
senior school (British English) noun
  a senior (high) school ≈ un lycée

sense noun
* (common) sense = le bon sens
  to have the sense to go home = avoir le
  bon sens de rentrer chez soi
* (allowing one to see, hear, smell etc)
  a sense = un sens
  the sense of taste = le goût
* (a meaning)
  a sense = un sens
  it doesn't make sense = ça n'a pas de sens
  it makes sense to check first = c'est une
  bonne idée de vérifier d'abord

sensible adjective
  ! Note that sensible in English is never
  translated by sensible in French.

  (describing a person) = raisonnable
  (describing a decision)
  = judicieux/judicieuse
  (describing clothes) = pratique

sensitive adjective
  (describing a person) = sensible
  (describing a situation) = délicat/délicate

sentence
1 noun
* (in grammar)
  a sentence = une phrase
* (for a crime)
  a (prison) sentence = une peine (de
  prison)
2 verb
  to sentence someone to one year in
  prison = condamner quelqu'un à an an
  de prison

separate
1 adjective
  a separate room = une pièce à part
  the children have separate rooms = les
  enfants ont chacun leur chambre
  there are two separate problems = il y a
  deux problèmes différents
2 verb
* to separate = séparer
* (if it's a couple) = se séparer (! + être)

separated adjective
= séparé/séparée

separately adverb
= séparément

September noun ▶ 222
  September = septembre (masculine)

serial noun
  a serial = un feuilleton
  a TV serial = un feuilleton télévisé

series noun
  a series = une série

serious adjective
* (causing worry) = grave
  a serious accident = un accident grave
* (describing a personality)
  = sérieux/sérieuse
* to be serious about football = prendre le
  football au sérieux
  to be serious about going to college
  = avoir vraiment l'intention d'aller à
  l'université

serve verb
* (in a shop) = servir
  are you being served? = est-ce qu'on
  s'occupe de vous?
* (at table) = faire le service
  to serve the soup = servir la soupe
* (in sport) = servir

service noun
* (which people need or find useful)
  a service = un service
* (in a shop, a restaurant)
  service = le service
* (in a church)
  a service = un office

service station noun
  a service station = une station-service

set
1 noun
* (a collection)
  a set of keys = un jeu de clés
  a set of stamps = une série de timbres
* (in tennis)
  a set = un set
2 verb
* (to decide on) = fixer
  to set [a date | a price | a goal ...] = fixer [une
  date | un prix | un but ...]
* (for a particular time)
  to set an alarm clock = mettre un réveil
  to set a video (British English)
  = programmer un magnétoscope
* (in school)
  to set homework = donner des devoirs
  to set an exam = préparer les sujets d'un
  examen
* (to be responsible for)
  to set a record = établir un record
  to set a good example to someone
  = montrer le bon exemple à quelqu'un
* (when talking about a story, a film)
  the film is set in Paris = le film se passe à
  Paris
* (when talking about the sun) = se coucher
  (**!** + être)
* (other uses)
  to set the table = mettre la table
  to set fire to a house = mettre le feu à une
  maison
  to set someone free = libérer quelqu'un
set off
* (to leave) = partir (**!** + être)
* (to cause to go off)
  to set off fireworks = faire partir un feu
  d'artifice
  to set off a bomb = faire exploser une
  bombe
  to set off a burglar alarm = déclencher
  une sirène d'alarme
set up = monter (**!** + avoir)
  to set up a company = monter une
  entreprise

settle verb
* (to end)
  to settle an argument = mettre fin à une
  dispute

* (to decide on) = fixer
  nothing is settled yet = rien n'est encore
  fixé
* (to make one's home) = s'installer
  (**!** + être)
settle down
* (to get comfortable) = s'installer (**!** + être)
* (to marry) = se ranger (**!** + être)
settle in = s'adapter (**!** + être)

seven number ▶ 187 |, ▶ 211 |
  seven = sept
  seven exams = sept examens
  I've got seven (of them) = j'en ai sept

seventeen number ▶ 187 |, ▶ 211 |
  seventeen = dix-sept

seventeenth number
* (in a series) = dix-septième
* (in dates) ▶ 222 |
  the seventeenth of May = le dix-sept mai

seventh number
* (in a series) = septième
* (in dates) ▶ 222 |
  the seventh of July = le sept juillet

seventy number ▶ 187 |
  seventy = soixante-dix

several determiner
  = plusieurs

severe adjective
* (serious) = grave
* (harsh) = sévère

sew verb
  = coudre

sewing noun
  sewing = la couture

sewing machine noun
  a sewing machine = une machine à
  coudre

sex noun
  sex = le sexe
  to have sex = avoir des rapports sexuels

shade noun
* (out of the sun)
  shade = l'ombre (feminine)
  to sit in the shade = s'asseoir à l'ombre
* (a colour)
  a shade = un ton
* (for a lamp)
  a shade = un abat-jour

shadow noun
  a shadow = une ombre

shake verb
* **to shake** = secouer
  the earthquake shook the building = le
  tremblement de terre a ébranlé le
  bâtiment
  to shake a bottle = agiter une bouteille
  to shake hands with someone = serrer la
  main de quelqu'un

S

* (when saying no)
  to shake one's head = faire non de la tête
* (with cold, fear, shock) = trembler
  he was shaking with fear = il tremblait de peur
* (during an explosion, an earthquake) = trembler

shall verb

> **!** Note that, when referring to the future, French uses the future tense of the verb to translate shall + verb: I shall leave = je partirai.

* (when talking about the future)
  I shall see you next Tuesday = je te verrai mardi prochain
* (when making suggestions)
  shall I set the table? = est-ce que je mets la table?
  shall we go to the cinema? = et si nous allions au cinéma?

shame noun
* **shame** = la honte
  shame on you! = tu devrais avoir honte!
* (when expressing regret)
  that's a shame = c'est dommage

shampoo noun
  shampoo = le shampooing

shape noun
* (a form)
  a shape = une forme
  a square shape = une forme carrée
  in the shape of a square = en forme de carré
* (when talking about health)
  to be in good shape = être en forme
  to get in shape = se mettre en forme

share
1 verb
  = partager
  to share a house = partager une maison
2 noun
  a share = une part
  to pay one's fair share = payer sa part
share out (British English) (amongst others) = répartir
  (within a group) = partager

shark noun
  a shark = un requin

sharp adjective
* (used for cutting) = tranchant/tranchante
* (with a point) = pointu/pointue
* (sudden) = brusque
  a sharp bend = un virage serré
* (intelligent) = vif|vive
* (aggressive) = acerbe
* (in taste) = acide

shave verb
  = se raser (**!** + être)

she pronoun
  she = elle
  she'll be there too = elle sera là aussi
  there she is! = la voilà!
  SHE **didn't say it** = ce n'est pas elle qui l'a dit
  he works in London but she doesn't = il travaille à Londres mais elle non
  she's an intelligent girl = c'est une fille intelligente

sheep noun
  a sheep = un mouton
  (female) = une brebis

sheet noun
* (for a bed)
  a sheet = un drap
* (a piece)
  a sheet (of paper) = une feuille
  (of glass) = une plaque

shelf noun
  a shelf (for books, ornaments) = une étagère
  (in a shop) = un rayon
  a set of shelves = une étagère

shell noun
  a shell (of an egg, a nut, a snail) = une coquille
  (of a crab, a tortoise) = une carapace

shelter
1 noun
* (from rain, danger)
  a shelter = un abri
* (for homeless people)
  a shelter = un refuge
2 verb
* (to take shelter) = se mettre à l'abri
* (to help) = donner refuge à

shin noun ▶ **201**|
  the shin = le tibia

shine verb
* (to give out light) = briller
  the light is shining in my eyes = j'ai la lumière dans les yeux
* (to point)
  to shine a torch at someone = braquer une lampe sur quelqu'un
* (to reflect light) = reluire

ship noun
  a ship (large) = un navire
  (smaller) = un bateau
  a passenger ship = un paquebot

shirt noun
  a shirt = une chemise

shiver verb
  (with cold) = grelotter
  (with fear) = trembler

shock
1 *noun*
* (*an upsetting experience*)
  a shock = un choc
  to get a shock = avoir un choc
  to give someone a shock = faire un choc à quelqu'un
* (*the medical state*)
  to be in shock = être en état de choc
* (*from electricity*)
  a shock = une décharge
  to get a shock = recevoir une décharge
2 *verb*
* (*to upset*) = consterner
* (*to cause a scandal*) = choquer

shoe *noun*
a shoe (*for a person*) = une chaussure
(*for a horse*) = un fer

shoot *verb*
* (*using a weapon*) = tirer
  to shoot someone = tirer sur quelqu'un
  they shot him in the leg = ils lui ont tiré dans la jambe
  to shoot someone dead = abattre quelqu'un
* (*to move very fast*)
  to shoot past = passer en trombe
* (*to make*)
  to shoot a film = tourner un film

shop
1 *noun*
  a shop = un magasin
  (*small, fashionable*) = une boutique
2 *verb*
  to go shopping = aller faire des courses

shop assistant *noun* ▶ 315 | (*British English*)
  a shop assistant = un vendeur/une vendeuse

shopkeeper *noun* ▶ 315 |
  a shopkeeper = un commerçant/une commerçante

shopping *noun*
  shopping = les courses (*feminine plural*)
  to do the shopping = faire les courses

shopping cart *noun* (*US English*)
  a shopping cart = un caddie

shopping centre (*British English*), shopping mall (*US English*) *noun*
  a shopping centre, a shopping mall = un centre commercial

shopping trolley *noun* (*British English*)
  a shopping trolley = un caddie

shop window *noun*
  a shop window = une vitrine

shore *noun*
* (*the edge of the sea*)
  the shore = la côte, le rivage
* (*dry land*)
  the shore = la terre

short
1 *adjective*
* (*not lasting long*) = court/courte (**!** *before the noun*)
  to go for a short walk = faire une petite promenade
  a short speech = un bref discours
  the days are getting shorter = les jours diminuent
* (*not long*) = court/courte
  a short skirt = une jupe courte
  to have short hair = avoir les cheveux courts
* (*not tall*) = petit/petite (**!** + *être*)
* **to be short of** [money | food | ideas …] = être à court [d'argent | de nourriture | d'idées …]
2 in short = bref

short cut *noun*
  a short cut = un raccourci

shortly *adverb*
* (*soon*) = bientôt
* (*not long*) = peu de temps
  shortly before we left = peu de temps avant notre départ

shorts *noun*
  shorts = un short (*singular*)

shot *noun*
* (*from a gun*)
  a shot = un coup (de feu)
  to fire a shot at someone = tirer sur quelqu'un
* (*in sports*) ▶ 248 |
  a shot (*in football*) = un tir
  (*in tennis, golf, cricket*) = un coup

should *verb*

> **!** *Note that, in general,* should *is translated by* devoir *in the conditional, either present (*you shouldn't smoke = tu ne devrais pas fumer*) or past (*he shouldn't have left = il n'aurait pas dû partir*).*

* (*when talking about what is right, what one ought to do*)
  she should learn to drive = elle devrait apprendre à conduire
  shouldn't he be at school? = est-ce qu'il ne devrait pas être à l'école?
  you shouldn't have said that! = tu n'aurais pas dû dire ça!
* (*when saying something may happen*)
  we should be there by midday = nous devrions être là vers midi
  it shouldn't be too difficult = cela ne devrait pas être trop difficile
* (*when implying that something, though likely, didn't happen*)
  the letter should have arrived yesterday = la lettre aurait dû arriver hier
* (*when asking for advice or permission*)
  should I call the doctor? = est-ce que je devrais appeler le médecin?

S

shoulder *noun* ▶ **201**
the shoulder = l'épaule
to wear a sweater over one's shoulders
= porter un pull sur les épaules
to have round shoulders = avoir le dos
rond

shout
1 *verb*
= crier
to shout at someone = crier après
quelqu'un
2 *noun*
a shout = un cri
shout out = pousser un cri

shovel *noun*
a shovel = une pelle

show
1 *verb*
• *(to let someone see)* = montrer
to show someone a photo = montrer une
photo à quelqu'un
I'll show you how it works = je vais te
montrer comment ça marche
• *(to go with)*
I'll show you to your room = je vais vous
accompagner à votre chambre
• *(to point to, to indicate)* = indiquer
to show someone where to go = indiquer
à quelqu'un où aller
there's a sign showing the way to the
pool = il y a un panneau qui indique la
direction de la piscine
• *(to be on TV, at the cinema)* = passer
(**!** + *être*)
the film is showing at the Phoenix = le
film passe au Phoenix
to be shown on TV = passer à la télévision
2 *noun*
• a show *(on a stage)* = un spectacle
(on TV, radio) = une émission
• *(an exhibition)*
a show = une exposition
show off = faire le fier/la fière
show round
to show someone around the town = faire
visiter la ville à quelqu'un
show up = se pointer✶ (**!** + *être*)

shower *noun*
• *(for washing)*
a shower = une douche
to have a shower = prendre une douche
• *(rain)*
a shower = une averse

showjumping *noun* ▶ **248**
showjumping = le saut d'obstacles

shrimp *noun*
a shrimp = une crevette grise

shrink *verb*
= rétrécir

✶ in informal situations

shut
1 *adjective*
= fermé/fermée
my eyes were shut = j'avais les yeux
fermés
2 *verb*
= fermer
to shut the windows = fermer les fenêtres
the door doesn't shut properly = la porte
ne ferme pas bien
shut down = fermer
the factory shut down in May = l'usine a
fermé au mois de mai
shut out
to shut someone out = laisser quelqu'un
dehors
shut up
• *(to be quiet)* = se taire (**!** + *être*)
shut up! = tais-toi!
• *(to lock inside)* = enfermer

shy *adjective*
= timide

sick *adjective*
• *(ill)* = malade
to get sick = tomber malade (**!** + *être*)
to feel sick = avoir mal au cœur
to be sick *(British English)* *(to vomit)*
= vomir
• *(fed up)*
he's sick of the neighbours = il en a
marre✶ des voisins

sickness *noun*
a sickness = une maladie

side *noun*
• a side = un côté
it's an apartment block with shops on
either side = c'est un immeuble avec des
magasins de chaque côté
to be driving on the wrong side of the
road = rouler du mauvais côté de la
route
by the side of the river = au bord de la
rivière
the north side of the city = le nord de la
ville
he works on the other side of London = il
travaille à l'autre bout de Londres
• *(of a person's body)*
the side = le côté
to be lying on one's side = être
allongé/allongée sur le côté
on my right side = à ma droite
• *(in a conflict, a contest)*
a side = un camp
• *(a team)*
a side = une équipe
side with = se mettre du côté de

sidewalk *noun* *(US English)*
a sidewalk = un trottoir

sigh *verb*
= soupirer

sight *noun*
  sight = la vue
  to have good sight = avoir une bonne vue
  to catch sight of someone = apercevoir
    quelqu'un
  to be out of sight = être caché/cachée

sightseeing *noun*
  sightseeing = le tourisme

sign
1 *noun*
* (*a mark*)
  a sign = un signe
  the dollar sign = le symbole du dollar
* (*for traffic, for advertising*)
  a sign = un panneau
* (*a notice*)
  a sign = une pancarte
2 *verb*
  = signer
sign on (*British English*) = pointer au
chômage

signal
1 *noun*
  a signal = un signal
2 *verb*
* (*to make signs*) = faire des signes
  to signal to someone to come = faire
    signe à quelqu'un de venir
* (*when driving*) = mettre son clignotant

signature *noun*
  a signature = une signature

signpost *noun*
  a signpost = un panneau indicateur

silence *noun*
  silence = le silence

silent *adjective*
* (*quiet*) = silencieux/silencieuse
* (*without sound or words*) = muet/muette

silk *noun*
  silk = la soie

silly *adjective*
  = idiot/idiote

silver
1 *noun*
  silver = l'argent (*masculine*)
2 *adjective*
  = en argent
  a silver ring = une bague en argent

simple *adjective*
  = simple

since
1 *preposition*
  ! *Note that, when* since *is used to
  describe an event or an action that is still
  going on, rather than an event or an
  action that belongs to the past and has
  finished, the present tense +* depuis *is
  used in French. In the same way, if the
  event or action has its starting point
  further back in the past, in French the
  imperfect tense +* depuis *is used.*

  = depuis
  I haven't seen him since yesterday = je ne
    l'ai pas vu depuis hier
  I haven't been feeling well since Monday
    = je ne me sens pas bien depuis lundi
  she had been living in France since 1988
    = elle vivait en France depuis 1988
2 *conjunction*
* (*from the time when*) = depuis que
  since she left = depuis qu'elle est partie,
    depuis son départ
  I've lived here since I was ten = j'habite
    ici depuis l'âge de dix ans
  it's ten years since she died = cela fait dix
    ans qu'elle est morte
* (*because*) = comme
  since she was ill, she couldn't go
    = comme elle était malade, elle ne
    pouvait pas y aller
3 *adverb*
  = depuis

sincere *adjective*
  = sincère

sincerely *adverb*
  = sincèrement
  Yours sincerely (*British English*),
  Sincerely yours (*US English*) = Veuillez
    agréer, Monsieur/Madame, l'expression
    de mes sentiments les meilleurs
  (*less formal*) = Meilleures salutations

sing *verb*
  = chanter

singer *noun* ▶ **315**
  a singer = un chanteur/une chanteuse

singing *noun*
  singing = le chant

single *adjective*
* (*one*) = seul/seule (**!** *before the noun*)
  we visited three towns in a single day
    = nous avons visité trois villes en une
    seule journée
* (*when used for emphasis*)
  every single day = tous les jours sans
    exception
  I didn't see a single person = je n'ai vu
    absolument personne
* (*without a partner*) = célibataire

single bed *noun*
  a single bed = un lit pour une personne

single room *noun*
  a single room = une chambre à une
    personne

single ticket *noun* (*British English*)
  a single ticket = un aller simple

sink
1 *noun*
  a sink = un évier
2 *verb*
  = couler

S

sister *noun*
  a sister = une sœur

sister-in-law *noun*
  a sister-in-law = une belle-sœur

sit *verb*
• (*to take a seat*) = s'asseoir (**!** + *être*)
  to be sitting on the floor = être assis/assise
    par terre
• (*British English*) (*to take*)
  to sit an exam = passer un examen
sit down = s'asseoir (**!** + *être*)
  to be sitting down = être assis/assise
sit up = se redresser (**!** + *être*)
  sit up straight! = tiens-toi droit!

sitting room *noun*
  a sitting room = un salon

situated *adjective*
  = situé/située
  situated near the town centre
    = situé/située près du centre-ville

situation *noun*
  a situation = une situation

six *number* ▶ 187 |, ▶ 211 |
  six = six
  six weeks = six semaines
  I've got six (of them) = j'en ai six

sixteen *number* ▶ 187 |, ▶ 211 |
  sixteen = seize

sixteenth *number*
• (*in a series*) = seizième
• (*in dates*) ▶ 222 |
  the sixteenth of July = le seize juillet

sixth *number*
• (*in a series*) = sixième
• (*in dates*) ▶ 222 |
  the sixth of February = le six février

sixty *number* ▶ 187 |
  sixty = soixante

size *noun*
• (*when talking about a person*)
  a size = une taille
  she's about your size = elle est à peu près
    de ta taille
• (*when talking about clothes*)
  a size (*of garment*) = une taille
  (*of shoe*) = une pointure
  I'd like this in a smaller size = je voudrais
    ce modèle en plus petit
  what size do you take? (*in clothes*)
    = quelle taille faites-vous?
  (*in shoes*) = vous chaussez du combien?
• (*when talking about how big something is*)
  the size (*of a building, a region*) = la
    grandeur
  (*of an apple, a parcel*) = la grosseur

skateboard *noun* ▶ 248 |
  a skateboard = un skateboard, une
    planche à roulettes

skating *noun* ▶ 248 |
  skating = le patin

skating rink *noun*
  a skating rink (*for ice-skating*) = une
    patinoire
  (*for roller-skating*) = une piste de patin à
    roulettes

sketch *noun*
• (*a drawing*)
  a sketch = un croquis
• (*a funny scene*)
  a sketch = un sketch

ski
1 *noun*
  a ski = un ski
2 *verb*
  to go skiing = faire du ski

skiing *noun* ▶ 248 |
  skiing = le ski

skilful (*British English*), **skillful** (*US
English*) *adjective*
  = habile, adroit/adroite

skill *noun*
• (*the quality*)
  skill (*mental*) = l'habileté (*feminine*)
  (*physical*) = la dextérité
• (*a particular ability*)
  a skill (*learned*) = une compétence
  (*natural*) = une aptitude

skin *noun*
  the skin = la peau

skinny *adjective*
  = maigre

skip *verb*
• (*to give little jumps*) = sautiller
• (*with a rope*) = sauter à la corde
• to skip classes = sauter les cours

ski resort *noun*
  a ski resort = une station de ski

skirt *noun*
  a skirt = une jupe

sky *noun*
  the sky = le ciel
  a clear sky = un ciel dégagé

skydiving *noun* ▶ 248 |
  skydiving = le parachutisme (en chute
    libre)

slap *verb*
  to slap someone = donner une tape à
    quelqu'un
  (*across the face*) = gifler quelqu'un

sled, sledge (*British English*)
1 *noun*
  a sled (*for fun*) = une luge
  (*for transport*) = un traîneau
2 *verb*
  to go sledging (*British English*) = faire de
    la luge

sleep
1 *noun*
sleep = le sommeil
to go to sleep = s'endormir (**!** + *être*)
to go back to sleep = se rendormir
(**!** + *être*)
to put someone to sleep = endormir
quelqu'un
2 *verb*
- (*to be asleep*) = dormir
- to sleep with someone = coucher avec
quelqu'un
sleep in = faire la grasse matinée

sleeping bag *noun*
a sleeping bag = un sac de couchage

sleepy *adjective*
to be sleepy, to feel sleepy = avoir
sommeil, avoir envie de dormir

sleet *noun*
sleet = la neige fondue

sleeve *noun*
a sleeve = une manche
to roll up one's sleeves = retrousser ses
manches

slice
1 *noun*
a slice (*of bread, meat*) = une tranche
(*of lemon, cucumber*) = une rondelle
2 *verb*
to slice bread = couper du pain en
tranches

slide
1 *verb*
= glisser
the plates slid off the table = les assiettes
ont glissé de la table
2 *noun*
- (*an image*)
a slide = une diapositive
- (*in a playground*)
a slide = un toboggan

slim
1 *adjective*
= mince
2 *verb* (*British English*)
= maigrir

slip *verb*
- (*to slide*) = glisser
- the glass slipped out of my hands = le
verre m'a échappé des mains

slipper *noun*
a slipper = une pantoufle

slippery *adjective*
= glissant/glissante

slot machine *noun*
a slot machine = une machine à sous

Slovakia *noun* ▶ 218 |
Slovakia = la Slovaquie

slow *adjective*
- (*not fast*) = lent/lente
to make slow progress = avancer
lentement
- (*not bright*) = lent/lente (d'esprit)
- (*describing a watch, a clock*)
to be slow = retarder
the clock is 20 minutes slow = la pendule
retarde de 20 minutes
slow down = ralentir

slowly *adverb*
= lentement

sly *adjective*
= rusé/rusée

small *adjective*
= petit/petite (**!** *before the noun*)
a small car = une petite voiture
a small quantity = une faible quantité

small ad *noun* (*British English*)
a small ad = une petite annonce

smart *adjective*
- (*British English*) (*elegant*)
= élégant/élégante
- (*intelligent*) = intelligent/intelligente
- (*expensive*) = chic (**!** *never changes*)

smash *verb*
- (*to break*) = briser, fracasser
- (*to get broken*) = se briser, se fracasser
(**!** + *être*)
smash up = démolir

smell
1 *noun*
- (*an odour*)
a smell = une odeur
- (*the sense*)
the sense of smell = l'odorat (*masculine*)
2 *verb*
= sentir
that smells nice = ça sent bon
I can smell burning = ça sent le brûlé

smile
1 *verb*
= sourire
to smile at someone = sourire à quelqu'un
2 *noun*
a smile = un sourire

smoke
1 *noun*
smoke = la fumée
2 *verb*
= fumer

smooth *adjective*
(*not rough*) = lisse
a smooth road = une route plane
a smooth crossing = une traversée sans
heurts

smother *verb*
= étouffer

snack *noun*
a snack = un casse-croûte

S

snail *noun*
a snail = un escargot

snake *noun*
a snake = un serpent

snapshot *noun*
a snapshot = une photo

sneaker *noun*
a sneaker (*high*) = une basket
(*low*) = un tennis

sneeze *verb*
= éternuer

snobbish *adjective*
= snob

snooker *noun* ▶ 248 |
snooker = le billard anglais

snore *verb*
= ronfler

snow
1 *noun*
snow = la neige
2 *verb*
= neiger
it's snowing = il neige

snowball *noun*
a snowball = une boule de neige

snowman *noun*
a snowman = un bonhomme de neige

so
1 *adverb*
• so = si, tellement
he's so [happy | stupid | smart ...] = il est si
[content | bête | malin ...]
they speak so fast = ils parlent si vite, ils
parlent tellement vite
it's so much easier = c'est tellement plus
facile
she has so many clothes = elle a tant de
vêtements
I've so much work to do = j'ai tant de
travail à faire
• (*also*)
I'm fifteen and so is he = j'ai quinze ans et
lui aussi
if you go, so will I = si tu y vas, j'y vais
aussi
• (*other uses*)
I think so = je pense que oui
I'm afraid so = j'ai bien peur que oui
I told you so = je te l'avais bien dit
who says so? = qui dit ça?
so what? = et alors?
and so on = et ainsi de suite
2 **so (that)** = pour que
be quiet so I can work = tais-toi pour que
je puisse travailler

! *Note that the subjunctive is used after
pour que.*

3 **so as** = pour
we left early so as not to miss the train
= nous sommes partis tôt pour ne pas
rater le train

soap *noun*
• (*for washing*)
soap = le savon
• (*on TV*)
a soap = un feuilleton

soccer *noun* ▶ 248 |
soccer = le football
= sociable

social *adjective*
= social/sociale

social studies *noun*
social studies = l'instruction civique
! *Note that* instruction *is feminine.*

social worker *noun* ▶ 315 |
a social worker = un travailleur social/une
travailleuse sociale

sock *noun*
a sock = une chaussette

sofa *noun*
a sofa = un canapé

soft *adjective*
• (*not hard or tough*) = doux/douce
to have soft skin = avoir la peau douce
the ground is soft here = la terre est
meuble ici
a soft toffee = un caramel mou
• (*not harsh or severe*) = doux/douce
• (*not strict*) = indulgent/indulgente

software *noun*
a software = un logiciel

soldier *noun* ▶ 315 |
a soldier = un soldat

sole *noun*
• the sole (of the foot) = la plante du pied
• (*of a shoe*)
a sole = une semelle

solicitor *noun* ▶ 315 | (*British English*)
a solicitor (*for documents*) ≈ un notaire
(*for court work*) ≈ un avocat/une avocate

solution *noun*
a solution = une solution

solve *verb*
= résoudre
to solve a problem = résoudre un
problème

some

1 *determiner*
- (*an amount or a number of*) = du/de la (**!** de l' + *vowel or mute h*)
  = des (+ *plural*)
  I have to buy some bread = je dois acheter du pain
  have some water = prenez de l'eau
  we bought some beer = nous avons acheté de la bière
  she ate some strawberries = elle a mangé des fraises
  we visited some beautiful towns = nous avons visité des villes superbes
- (*certain*) = certains/certaines
  some people don't like travelling by plane = certaines personnes n'aiment pas voyager en avion

2 *pronoun*
- (*an amount or a number of*) = en
  I know where you can find some = je sais où tu peux en trouver
  have some more! = reprenez-en!

  ! Note that it is necessary to use en, which might be translated as 'of it' or 'of them', with pronouns like some. See also any, a few, a lot etc for this use of en.

- (*certain people or things*)
  some are quite expensive = certains sont assez chers/certaines sont assez chères
  some (of them) are French = certains d'entre eux sont français/certaines d'entre elles sont françaises

someone *pronoun* (*also* **somebody**)
= quelqu'un
someone famous = quelqu'un de célèbre

something *pronoun*
= quelque chose
I saw something interesting = j'ai vu quelque chose d'intéressant
there's something odd about him = il a quelque chose de bizarre

sometimes *adverb*
= quelquefois, parfois

somewhere *adverb*
= quelque part
they live somewhere in Ireland = ils habitent quelque part en Irlande
let's go somewhere else = allons ailleurs

son *noun*
a son = un fils

song *noun*
a song = une chanson

son-in-law *noun*
a son-in-law = un gendre

soon *adverb*
- (*in a short time*) = bientôt
  see you soon! = à bientôt!

- (*early*)
  the sooner the better = le plus tôt sera le mieux
  as soon as possible = dès que possible
  come as soon as you can = viens dès que tu pourras

  ! Note that, if talking about future time, the future tense is used after dès que.

sore *adjective*
to have a sore [throat | leg | back ...] = avoir mal [à la gorge | à la jambe | au dos ...]
it's very sore = ça fait très mal

sorry

1 *exclamation*
- (*when apologizing*)
  sorry! = pardon!, désolé/désolée!
- (*when asking someone to repeat*)
  sorry? = pardon?

2 *adjective*
- (*when apologizing*) = désolé/désolée
  I'm sorry I'm late = je suis désolé d'être en retard
  to say sorry = s'excuser (**!** + *être*)
- (*when expressing regret*)
  I'm sorry you can't come = je suis désolé que tu ne puisses pas venir

  ! Note that the subjunctive is used after être désolé que.

- (*to feel pity for*)
  to feel sorry for someone = plaindre quelqu'un
  to feel sorry for oneself = s'apitoyer sur son sort

sort

1 *noun*
it's a sort of [bird | computer | loan ...] = c'est une sorte [d'oiseau | d'ordinateur | de prêt ...]
I don't like that sort of thing = je n'aime pas ce genre de choses
he's not that sort of person = ce n'est pas son genre

2 *verb*
to sort files = classer des dossiers
to sort the books into piles = ranger les livres en piles

sort out
- (*to solve*) = régler
  to sort out a problem = régler un problème
- (*to deal with*) = s'occuper de (**!** + *être*)
  I'll sort it out = je m'en occuperai
- (*to organize*) = classer
  to sort out the documents = classer les documents
- (*to pick out, to choose*)
  to sort out the photos = trier les photos
  to sort out the old clothes from the new = séparer les vieux vêtements des neufs

sound

1 *noun*
- **a sound** (*a noise*) = un bruit
  (*of an instrument, a bell*) = un son

S

I heard the sound of voices = j'ai entendu
  un bruit de voix
• (of a radio, a television)
  the sound = le son
  to turn the sound up = monter le son
2 verb
  it sounds [dangerous | odd | interesting ...]
    = ça a l'air [dangereux | bizarre |
    intéressant ...]
  it sounds like a piano = on dirait un piano

soup noun
  a soup = une soupe, un potage

sour adjective
  = aigre
  to go sour = tourner

south
1 noun
  the south = le sud
  in the south of France = dans le sud de la
    France
2 adverb
  to go south = aller vers le sud
  to live south of Paris = vivre au sud de
    Paris
3 adjective
  = sud (! never changes)
  to work in south London = travailler dans
    le sud de Londres

South Africa noun ▶ 218 |
  South Africa = l'Afrique du Sud
  | ! Note that Afrique is feminine.

South America noun ▶ 218 |
  South America = l'Amérique du Sud
  | ! Note that Amérique is feminine.

southeast noun
  the southeast = le sud-est

southwest noun
  the southwest = le sud-ouest

souvenir noun
  a souvenir = un souvenir

space noun
• (room)
  space = la place
  to take up space = prendre de la place
• (an area of land)
  an open space = un espace libre
• (outer space)
  space = l'espace (masculine)
• (a gap)
  a space = un espace

Spain noun ▶ 218 |
  Spain = l'Espagne (feminine)

Spanish ▶ 275 |
1 adjective
  = espagnol/espagnole
2 noun
  Spanish = l'espagnol (masculine)

spare adjective
• (extra) = en plus
  I've got a spare ticket = j'ai un billet en
    plus
• (available) = disponible
  are there any spare seats? = est-ce qu'il y
    a des places disponibles?

spare part noun
  a spare part = une pièce de rechange

spare room noun
  a spare room = une chambre d'amis

spare time noun
  spare time = les loisirs (masculine plural)

speak verb
  = parler
  to speak German = parler (l')allemand
  they're not speaking (to each other) = ils
    ne se parlent pas
  who's speaking, please? = qui est à
    l'appareil?
  generally speaking = en règle générale
speak up = parler plus fort

special adjective
  = spécial/spéciale
  | ! Note that spécial can also mean odd or
  strange in French: il est assez spécial
  = he's rather strange.

  a special offer = une offre spéciale
  she's a special friend = c'est une amie très
    chère

speciality (British English), **specialty**
(US English) noun
  a speciality = une spécialité

specially adverb
  = spécialement

spectator noun
  a spectator = un spectateur/une
    spectatrice

speech noun
  a speech = un discours

speed
1 noun
  speed = la vitesse
2 verb
• to speed away = s'éloigner à toute allure
• (to drive too fast) = conduire trop vite
speed up = accélérer

speed limit noun
  a speed limit = une limitation de vitesse

spell verb
  (when speaking) = épeler
  (when writing) = écrire
  how do you spell it? = comment ça s'écrit?

spelling noun
  spelling = l'orthographe (feminine)

spend verb
• (to pay money) = dépenser

- (*to pass*)
  to spend (some) time [reading | painting | writing letters …] = passer du temps [à lire | à faire de la peinture | à écrire des lettres …]

spider *noun*
  a spider = une araignée

spill *verb*
- (*if it's a person*) = renverser
  don't spill the milk = ne renverse pas le lait
- (*if it's a liquid*) = se répandre (**!** + *être*)

spinach *noun*
  spinach = les épinards (*masculine plural*)

spit *verb*
  = cracher

spite: **in spite of** *preposition*
  = malgré
  we went out in spite of the weather = nous sommes sortis malgré le temps

spiteful *adjective*
  = méchant/méchante

spoil *verb*
- (*to take away from*) = gâcher
  to spoil the evening = gâcher la soirée
- (*to ruin, to damage*) = abîmer
- (*as a parent*) = gâter
  to spoil a child = gâter un enfant

sponge *noun*
  a sponge = une éponge

spoon *noun*
  a spoon = une cuillère

sport *noun* ▶ **248** |
  a sport = un sport
  to be good at sports = être bon/bonne en sport

sports centre (*British English*), **sports center** (*US English*) *noun*
  a sports centre = un centre sportif

sports club *noun*
  a sports club = un club sportif

spot
1 *noun*
- (*on an animal*)
  a spot = une tache
- (*British English*) (*on the face or body*)
  a spot = un bouton
- (*a place*)
  a spot = un endroit
  on the spot (*there and then*) = sur-le-champ
2 *verb*
- (*to see*) = apercevoir
- (*to recognize*) = repérer

sprain *verb*
  to sprain one's wrist = se fouler le poignet

spring *noun*
  spring = le printemps
  in spring = au printemps

spy *noun*
  a spy = un espion/une espionne

square
1 *noun*
- (*the shape*)
  a square = un carré
- (*in a town*)
  a square = une place
2 *adjective*
  = carré/carrée

squash
1 *noun* ▶ **248** |
  squash = le squash
2 *verb*
  = écraser

squeak *verb*
  (*if it's a door, a wheel*) = grincer
  (*if it's a shoe, a chair*) = craquer

squeeze *verb*
  to squeeze a lemon = presser un citron
  to squeeze someone's hand = serrer la main de quelqu'un

squirrel *noun*
  a squirrel = un écureuil

stable *noun*
  a stable = une écurie

stadium *noun*
  a stadium = un stade

staff *noun*
  the staff (*of a company*) = le personnel
  (*of a school, a college*) = le personnel enseignant

stage *noun*
  a stage = une scène

stain
1 *noun*
  a stain = une tache
2 *verb*
  = tacher

stairs *noun*
  the stairs = l'escalier (*masculine singular*)
  to fall down the stairs = tomber dans l'escalier

stamp *noun*
- (*for an envelope*)
  a stamp = un timbre
  a 0·46 euro stamp = un timbre à 0,46 euros
- (*on a document, a passport*)
  a stamp = un cachet

stamp-collecting *noun*
  stamp-collecting = la philatélie

stand *verb*
- **to be standing** = être debout
  to stay standing, to remain standing = rester debout (**!** + *être*)
  to be able to stand = tenir debout
  you're standing in my way = tu me bloques le passage

S

* (*to put*)
  to stand a vase on a table = mettre un vase sur une table
* (*to step*)
  to stand on a nail = marcher sur un clou
* (*to bear*)
  I can't stand French = je déteste le français
  he can't stand playing football = il déteste jouer au football
* (*other uses*)
  to stand for election (*British English*) = se présenter aux élections
  to stand trial = passer en jugement
stand back = reculer
stand for
* (*to represent*) = représenter
* (*to mean*) = vouloir dire
stand out
  (*if it's a person*) = sortir de l'ordinaire
stand up
* **to stand up** = se lever (**!** + *être*)
* **to stand someone up** = poser un lapin✱ à quelqu'un
stand up for = défendre
  to stand up for oneself = se défendre (**!** + *être*)
stand up to = tenir tête à
  to stand up to someone = tenir tête à quelqu'un

star *noun*
* (*in space*)
  a star = une étoile
* (*a famous person*)
  a star = une vedette, une star

stare *verb*
  to stare at someone = dévisager quelqu'un

start
1 *verb*
* (*to begin*) = commencer
  to start [working | writing | running ...] = commencer à [travailler | écrire | courir ...]
  you should start by phoning them = tu devrais commencer par leur téléphoner
* (*to begin one's working life*)
  to start (out) as a teacher = débuter comme professeur
* (*to set up*) = lancer
  to start a fashion = lancer une mode
* (*to cause*) = déclencher
  to start a war = déclencher une guerre
* (*to begin working*) = démarrer
  the car won't start = la voiture ne veut pas démarrer
* (*to put into action*)
  to start a car = faire démarrer une voiture
  to start a machine = mettre une machine en marche

2 *noun*
  a start = un début
  at the start of the week = au début de la semaine
start off = commencer
start over (*US English*) = recommencer

starter *noun* (*British English*)
  a starter = un hors-d'œuvre

state *noun*
* (*a country, part of a country*)
  a state = un état
* (*a government*)
  the State = l'État
* (*a condition*)
  a state = un état
  to be in a bad state (of repair) = être en mauvais état
  she's in no state to work = elle n'est pas en état de travailler

statement *noun*
  a statement = une déclaration
  (*official*) = un communiqué

station *noun*
* (*for trains*)
  a station = une gare
* (*on TV*)
  a station = une chaîne

statue *noun*
  a statue = une statue

stay
1 *verb*
* (*to remain*) = rester (**!** + *être*)
  we stayed there for a week = nous sommes restés là une semaine
* (*to have accommodation*) = loger
  to stay with friends = loger chez des amis
2 *noun*
  a stay = un séjour
stay away from = éviter
  to stay away from school = ne pas aller à l'école
stay in = rester à la maison
stay out
  to stay out late = rentrer tard
stay up (*to wait*) = veiller
  (*to keep late hours*) = se coucher tard

steady *adjective*
* (*continuous*)
  to make steady progress = faire des progrès réguliers
* (*not likely to move*) = stable

steak *noun*
  a steak = un steak

steal *verb*
  = voler
  to steal from someone = voler quelqu'un
  to steal money from someone = voler de l'argent à quelqu'un

steam *noun*
  steam = la vapeur

✱ in informal situations

steel *noun*
steel = l'acier (*masculine*)

steep *adjective*
= raide

steering wheel *noun*
a steering wheel = un volant

step
1 *noun*
• (*when walking*)
a step = un pas
to take a step = faire un pas
• (*in stairs, at a door*)
a step = une marche
• (*a series of actions*)
to take steps = prendre des mesures
2 *verb*
to step in a puddle = marcher dans une flaque
step aside = s'écarter (**!** + *être*)

stepbrother *noun*
a stepbrother = un demi-frère

stepfather *noun*
a stepfather = un beau-père

stepmother *noun*
a stepmother = une belle-mère

stepsister *noun*
a stepsister = une demi-sœur

stereo *noun*
a stereo = une chaîne stéréo

stewardess *noun* ▶ 315 |
a stewardess = une hôtesse de l'air

stick
1 *verb*
• (*using glue or tape*) = coller
• (*to become attached*) = coller
• (*to get blocked*) = se coincer (**!** + *être*)
the door is stuck = la porte est coincée
2 *noun*
• (*a piece of wood*)
a stick = un bâton
• (*for walking*)
a stick = une canne
stick at
to stick at a task = persévérer dans une tâche
stick out = dépasser
there's a nail sticking out = il y a un clou qui dépasse
his ears stick out = il a les oreilles décollées

sticky tape *noun* (*British English*)
sticky tape = le scotch , le ruban adhésif

stiff *adjective*
• (*not soft, not supple*) = raide
to have stiff legs (*after sport, walking*) = avoir des courbatures dans les jambes
• (*not easy to use*)
to be stiff (*if it's a door, a drawer*) = être dur/dure à ouvrir

(*if it's a handle*) = être dur/dure à tourner

still¹ *adverb*
• (*when there has been no change*) = toujours
does she still play the piano? = est-ce qu'elle joue toujours du piano?
I still don't understand why you left = je ne comprends toujours pas pourquoi tu es parti
• (*when referring to the future*) = encore
she could still win = elle pourrait encore gagner

still²
1 *adverb*
to sit still = se tenir tranquille
2 *adjective*
= calme

sting *verb*
= piquer

stir *verb*
= remuer

stomach *noun* ▶ 201 |, ▶ 266 |
the stomach = l'estomac (*masculine*)
to have a pain in one's stomach = avoir mal au ventre

stone *noun*
a stone = une pierre
(*a pebble*) = un caillou

stop
1 *verb*
• (*to put an end to*) = arrêter
to stop [smoking | laughing | working ...] = arrêter de [fumer | rire | travailler ...]
stop it! = arrête!
• (*to prevent*)
to stop someone from [leaving | winning | talking ...] = empêcher quelqu'un de [partir | gagner | parler ...]
• (*to come to a halt*) = s'arrêter (**!** + *être*)
the bus didn't stop = le bus ne s'est pas arrêté
• (*when talking about machines, noise, weather*) = s'arrêter (**!** + *être*)
suddenly the noise stopped = tout à coup, le bruit s'est arrêté
it's stopped raining = il s'est arrêté de pleuvoir, la pluie s'est arrêtée
2 *noun*
a (bus) stop = un arrêt (de bus)
to miss one's stop = rater son arrêt

store *noun*
a store = un magasin
(*smaller*) = une boutique

storey (*British English*), **story** (*US English*) *noun*
a storey = un étage

storm *noun*
a storm = une tempête
(*with thunder*) = un orage

S

story noun
- a story = une histoire
  a true story = une histoire vécue
  a ghost story = une histoire de fantômes
- (in a newspaper)
  a story = un article
- (a rumour)
  a story = une rumeur
- (US English) ▶ **storey**

stove noun (US English)
  a stove = une cuisinière

straight
1 adjective
- straight = droit/droite
  a straight line = une ligne droite
- (not curly) = raide
  to have straight hair = avoir les cheveux
  raides
- (in the right position) = bien droit/droite
  the picture isn't straight = le tableau est
  de travers
- (honest) = honnête, droit/droite
2 adverb
- straight = droit
  to stand up straight = se tenir droit
  to go straight ahead = aller tout droit
- (without delay) = directement
  to go straight home = rentrer directement

strange adjective
- (odd) = bizarre
  it's strange that she doesn't come any
  more = il est bizarre qu'elle ne vienne
  plus

  ! Note that the subjunctive is used after il
  est bizarre que.

- (unknown) = inconnu/inconnue

stranger noun
  a stranger = un inconnu/une inconnue
  (a foreigner) = un étranger/une étrangère

straw noun
- (for feeding animals)
  straw = la paille
- (for drinking)
  a straw = une paille

strawberry noun
  a strawberry = une fraise

stream noun
  a stream = un ruisseau

street noun
  a street = une rue

streetlamp noun
  a streetlamp = un réverbère

strength noun
  strength = la force

stressful adjective
  = stressant/stressante

---

* in informal situations

stretch verb
  = s'étirer (! + être)
  to stretch one's arms = s'étirer les bras

strict adjective
  = strict/stricte

strike noun
  a strike = une grève
  to go on strike = se mettre en grève

string noun
  string = la ficelle
  a piece of string = un bout de ficelle

striped adjective
  = rayé/rayée

stroke verb
  = caresser

stroller noun (US English)
  a stroller = une poussette

strong adjective
- (having physical, mental strength)
  = fort/forte
  she's strong = elle a de la force, elle est
  forte
- (not easily damaged) = solide
- (having force, power) = fort/forte
  a strong wind = un vent fort
  it's strong tea = c'est du thé fort
- (obvious, noticeable) = fort/forte (! before
  the noun)
  a strong German accent = un fort accent
  allemand
  a strong smell of garlic = une forte odeur
  d'ail
- (having military power)
  = puissant/puissante

stubborn adjective
  = entêté/entêtée

student noun ▶ 315
  a student (at university) = un étudiant/une
  étudiante
  (at school) = un élève/une élève

study
1 verb
  to study history = étudier l'histoire, faire
  des études d'histoire
  to study to be a teacher = faire des études
  pour être professeur
  to study for an exam = réviser pour un
  examen
2 noun
  a study = un bureau

stuff
1 noun
  stuff (things) = les choses (feminine plural)
  (belongings) = les affaires (feminine plural)
2 verb
  to stuff a suitcase with clothes = bourrer
  une valise de vêtements
  to stuff oneself = s'empiffrer* (! + être)

stuffing noun
  a stuffing = une farce

stupid *adjective*
= bête, stupide

style *noun*
• (*a way of dressing, behaving*)
style = la classe
to have style = avoir de la classe
• (*a design, a type*)
a style (*of car, garment*) = un modèle
(*of building*) = un type
• (*a fashion*)
a style = une mode

stylish *adjective*
= élégant/élégante

subject *noun*
• (*of a conversation*)
a subject = un sujet
to change the subject = parler d'autre
chose
• (*being studied*)
a subject (*at school, college*) = une
matière
(*for an essay, a report*) = un sujet

suburb *noun*
the suburbs = la banlieue (*singular*)

subway *noun*
• (*US English*) (*the underground*)
the subway = le métro
• (*British English*) (*an underground passage*)
a subway = un passage souterrain

succeed *verb*
= réussir

success *noun*
success = le succès, la réussite
to be a success (*if it's a party*) = être
réussi/réussie
(*if it's a film, a book*) = avoir du succès

successful *adjective*
to be successful (*in an attempt*) = réussir
(*describing a film, a book*) = avoir du
succès

such
1 *determiner*
there's no such thing = ça n'existe pas
2 *adverb*
they have such a lot of money = ils ont
tant d'argent
she's such a strange person = elle est si
bizarre
I've never seen such a mess = je n'ai
jamais vu une pagaille* pareille

suddenly *adverb*
= tout à coup

suffer *verb* ▶ **266**
= souffrir

sugar *noun*
sugar = le sucre

suggestion *noun*
a suggestion = une suggestion

suicide *noun*
to commit suicide = se suicider (**!** + *être*)

suit
1 *noun*
a suit (*a man's*) = un costume
(*a woman's*) = un tailleur
2 *verb*
• (*to be convenient*) = convenir
to suit someone = convenir à quelqu'un
does Friday suit you? = est-ce que
vendredi te convient?
• (*to look well on*)
the hat suits you = le chapeau te va bien

suitable *adjective*
a suitable present = un cadeau approprié
to be suitable for children = convenir aux
enfants

suitcase *noun*
a suitcase = une valise

sum *noun*
• **a sum of money** = une somme d'argent
• **a sum** = un calcul
to be good at sums = être bon/bonne en
calcul
sum up = récapituler

summer *noun*
summer = l'été (*masculine*)
in summer = en été

summer holiday (*British English*),
summer vacation (*US English*) *noun*
the summer holiday = les vacances d'été
(*from school*) = les grandes vacances
> **!** *Note that* **vacances** *is feminine plural.*

sun *noun*
the sun = le soleil
to sit in the sun = s'asseoir au soleil

sunbathe *verb*
= se faire bronzer (**!** + *être*)

sunburn *noun*
sunburn = un coup de soleil

sunburned *adjective*
to get sunburned = attraper un coup de
soleil

Sunday *noun* ▶ **222**
Sunday = dimanche (*masculine*)

sunglasses *noun*
sunglasses = les lunettes de soleil
> **!** *Note that* **lunettes** *is feminine plural.*

sunny *adjective*
= ensoleillé/ensoleillée
it's going to be sunny = il va faire du soleil

sunset *noun*
sunset = le coucher du soleil

sunshade *noun*
a sunshade = un parasol

sunshine *noun*
sunshine = le soleil

S

suntan *noun*
a suntan = un bronzage
to get a suntan = bronzer

suntan oil *noun*
a suntan oil = une huile solaire

supermarket *noun*
a supermarket = un supermarché

supper *noun*
a supper (*an evening meal*) = un dîner
(*after a show*) = un souper

support *verb*
• (*to agree with, to help*) = soutenir
to support the strike = soutenir la grève
• (*to keep*)
to support a family = subvenir aux besoins
d'une famille
to support oneself = subvenir à ses
propres besoins
• (*to hold, to help physically*) = soutenir

supporter *noun*
a supporter (*of a team*) = un supporter
(*of a party*) = un sympathisant/une
sympathisante

suppose *verb*
• (*to imagine*) = supposer
I don't suppose you know yet? = je
suppose que tu n'es pas encore au
courant?
• (*to be meant to*)
to be supposed to = être censé/censée
I'm supposed to pay for the shopping = je
suis censé payer les courses

sure *adjective*
• (*certain*) = sûr/sûre
I'm sure he said nine o'clock = je suis sûr
qu'il a dit neuf heures
are you sure? = est-ce que tu en es sûr?
I'm not sure if she's coming = je ne sais
pas trop si elle vient
to make sure that the door is closed
= s'assurer que la porte est fermée
• (*bound*)
he's sure to win = il va sûrement gagner
• sure of oneself = sûr/sûre de soi

> **!** *Note that* soi *will change to* moi, lui, elle,
> eux *etc, depending on the person or
> people being described.*

she's sure of herself = elle est sûre d'elle

surf *verb* ▶ 248 |
to go surfing = faire du surf

surface
1 *noun*
a surface = une surface
2 *verb*
= remonter à la surface

surfboard *noun*
a surfboard = une planche de surf

surgeon *noun* ▶ 315 |
a surgeon = un chirurgien

surgery *noun*
• to have surgery = se faire opérer (**!** + *être*)
• (*British English*) (*the place*)
a surgery = un cabinet médical

surname *noun*
a surname = un nom de famille

surprise
1 *noun*
• (*an event, a gift*)
a surprise = une surprise
• (*being amazed*)
surprise = la surprise, l'étonnement
(*masculine*)
to take someone by surprise = prendre
quelqu'un au dépourvu
2 *verb*
= surprendre

surprised *adjective*
= étonné/étonnée
I'm not surprised = ça ne m'étonne pas

surrender *verb*
= se rendre (**!** + *être*)

surround *verb*
= entourer
to be surrounded by trees = être
entouré/entourée d'arbres

surroundings *noun*
the surroundings (*of a town*) = les
environs (*masculine*)

survey *noun*
a survey = un sondage

survive *verb*
= survivre
to survive the winter = survivre à l'hiver
to survive an accident = réchapper d'un
accident

suspect
1 *verb*
= soupçonner
she's suspected of stealing money = elle
est soupçonnée d'avoir volé de l'argent
2 *noun*
a suspect = un suspect/une suspecte

suspicious *adjective*
= méfiant/méfiante
to be suspicious of someone = se méfier
de quelqu'un

swan *noun*
a swan = un cygne

swap *verb*
= échanger

sweat *verb*
= transpirer

sweater *noun*
a sweater = un pull

sweatshirt *noun*
a sweatshirt = un sweatshirt

Sweden noun ▶ 218 |
Sweden = la Suède

Swedish ▶ 275 |
1 adjective
= suédois/suédoise
2 noun
Swedish = le suédois

sweep verb
= balayer

sweet
1 adjective
• sweet (tasting of sugar) = sucré/sucrée
(not bitter or dry) = doux/douce
to have a sweet tooth = aimer les
sucreries
• (describing a smell) = bon/bonne (! before
the noun)
• (kind, gentle) = gentil/gentille
• (cute) = mignon/mignonne
2 noun (British English)
a sweet = un bonbon

swim
1 verb
= nager
to swim across a lake = traverser un lac à
la nage
2 noun
a swim = une baignade
to go for a swim (in the sea) = aller se
baigner (! + être)

swimming noun ▶ 248 |
swimming = la natation

swimming pool noun
a swimming pool = une piscine

swimsuit noun
a swimsuit = un maillot de bain

swing
1 verb
• (to move back and forth) = se balancer
(! + être)
to swing on a gate = se balancer sur un
portillon
• (to move something back and forth)
= balancer
to swing one's legs = balancer les jambes
2 noun
a swing = une balançoire

Swiss ▶ 275 |
1 adjective
= suisse
2 noun
the Swiss = les Suisses (masculine plural)

switch
1 noun
a switch (for a light) = un interrupteur
(on a radio, an appliance) = un bouton
2 verb
= changer
to switch seats = changer de place
to switch from English to French = passer
de l'anglais au français

switch off = éteindre
to switch off the light = éteindre la
lumière
switch on = allumer
to switch the radio on = allumer la radio

Switzerland noun ▶ 218 |
Switzerland = la Suisse

sympathetic adjective
(showing pity)
= compatissant/compatissante
(showing understanding)
= compréhensif/compréhensive

syringe noun
a syringe = une seringue

system noun
a system = un système

Tt

table noun
a table = une table

tablet noun
a tablet = un comprimé

table tennis noun ▶ 248 |
table tennis = le tennis de table, le ping-
pong

tall noun
a tail = une queue

take verb
! See the usage note on Talking about
time ▶ 356 | for more information and
examples.
• (to take hold of) = prendre
to take someone by the hand = prendre
quelqu'un par la main
• (to carry with one) = emporter, prendre
I took my umbrella = j'ai emporté mon
parapluie
I'll take the letters to Jack = je vais porter
les lettres à Jack
• (to accompany, to bring) = emmener
to take the children for a walk = emmener
les enfants faire une promenade
to take someone home = raccompagner
quelqu'un
• (to remove) = prendre
to take a book off the shelf = prendre un
livre sur l'étagère
• (to steal) = prendre, voler
• (to cope with, to bear) = supporter
he can't take the pain = il ne supporte pas
la douleur
I can't take any more = je n'en peux plus

T

- (*when talking about what is necessary*)
  it takes [**time** | **courage** | **patience** ...] = il faut [du temps | du courage | de la patience ...]
  it takes two hours to get to Paris = il faut deux heures pour aller à Paris
  to take a long time to do one's homework = mettre longtemps pour faire ses devoirs
  it won't take long = ça ne prendra pas longtemps
- (*to accept*) = accepter
- (*to react to*) = prendre
  he took the news badly = il a mal pris la nouvelle
- (*to use when travelling*) = prendre
  to take a taxi = prendre un taxi
  take the first turn on the right = prenez la première rue à droite
- (*to do*)
  to take exams = passer des examens
- (*to have*) = prendre
  to take [**a vacation** | **a shower** | **driving lessons** ...] = prendre [des vacances | une douche | des leçons de conduite ...]
  I don't take sugar = je ne prends pas de sucre
- (*to wear*)
  to take a size 10 (*in clothes*) = s'habiller en 38
  to take a size 5 (*in shoes*) = chausser du 38
take apart = démonter
take away
  to take away the rubbish = enlever les déchets
  to take someone away = emmener quelqu'un
take back = rapporter
  I had to take the dress back = j'ai dû rapporter la robe
take down
- (*to remove*)
  to take a poster down = enlever une affiche
  to take down a tent = démonter une tente
- (*to write down*) = noter
take hold of = prendre
take off
- (*from an airport*) = décoller
- (*to remove*) = enlever
  I took off my shoes = j'ai enlevé mes chaussures
  to take off one's clothes = se déshabiller (**!** + *être*)
take out
- (*from a box, a pocket, a bag*) = sortir
  he took a pen out of his pocket = il a sorti un stylo de sa poche
- (*from a bank account*) = retirer
  to take money out = retirer de l'argent
- (*to be nasty to*)
  to take it out on someone = s'en prendre à quelqu'un

take part
  to take part in a game = participer à un jeu
take place = avoir lieu
take up
- (*as a hobby*)
  to take up windsurfing = se mettre à faire de la planche à voile
- (*to use up*) = prendre
  to take up space = prendre de la place

talented *adjective*
= doué/douée

talk
1 *verb*
- (*to speak*) = parler
  to talk on the phone = parler au téléphone
  to talk in French = parler en français
  to talk to someone = parler à quelqu'un
  I talked to them about the trip = je leur ai parlé de la sortie
  they were talking about you = ils parlaient de toi
  to talk to oneself = parler tout seul/toute seule
- (*to chat*) = bavarder
2 *noun*
- (*a conversation*)
  a talk = une conversation
- (*about a special subject*)
  a talk (*in class*) = un exposé
  (*to a club, a group*) = une causerie
- (*discussions*)
  talks = les négociations (*feminine*)

talkative *adjective*
= bavard/bavarde

tall *adjective* ▶ 285 |
  (*describing a person*) = grand/grande
  (**!** *before the noun*)
  (*describing a building, a tree*) = haut/haute
  to be six feet tall ≈ mesurer un mètre quatre-vingts
  to get tall = grandir

tan *noun*
  a tan = un bronzage
  to get a tan = bronzer

tanned *adjective*
= bronzé/bronzée

tap
1 *noun* (*British English*)
  a tap = un robinet
  to turn the tap off = fermer le robinet
2 *verb*
  to tap on the door = frapper à la porte

tape
1 *noun*
- **a tape** (*for a tape recorder*) = une cassette
  (*for a video*) = une cassette vidéo
- (*for repairs, for sticking*)
  tape = le scotch
2 *verb*
= enregistrer

---

tape recorder *noun*
a tape recorder = un magnétophone

target
1 *noun*
a target = une cible
2 *verb*
= viser

tart *noun* (*British English*)
a tart = une tarte
an apple tart = une tarte aux pommes

task *noun*
a task = une tâche

taste
1 *noun*
• (*when eating, drinking*)
a taste = un goût
• (*when talking about preferences*)
taste = le goût
to have good taste = avoir du goût
2 *verb*
• (*when describing a flavour*)
to taste good = être bon/bonne
to taste awful = avoir mauvais goût
it tastes like cabbage = ça a le goût du
chou
• (*when eating, drinking*) = goûter

Taurus *noun*
Taurus = Taureau (*masculine*)

tax *noun*
a tax (*on income, profits*) = un impôt
(*on goods, property*) = une taxe

taxi *noun*
a taxi = un taxi

taxi rank (*British English*), **taxi stand**
(*US English*) *noun*
a taxi rank = une station de taxis

tea *noun*
• (*the product*)
tea = le thé
• (*a cup of tea*)
a tea = un thé
• (*British English*) (*a meal*)
tea (*in the afternoon*) = le thé
(*in the evening*) = le dîner

teach *verb*
• (*to help someone to learn skills*)
to teach someone [to read | to drive | to ride a
horse …] = apprendre à quelqu'un à [lire |
conduire | monter à cheval …]
• (*to work as a teacher*) = enseigner
to teach French to adults = enseigner le
français à des adultes

teacher *noun* ▶ 315 |
a teacher = un enseignant/une
enseignante
(*in a primary school*) = un professeur des
écoles, un instituteur/une institutrice
(*in a secondary school*) = un professeur

team *noun*
a team = une équipe

teapot *noun*
a teapot = une théière

tear¹ *verb*
• (*to cause damage to*) = déchirer
to tear a page out of a book = arracher
une page d'un livre
• (*to get damaged*) = se déchirer (**!** + *être*)
tear off = détacher
tear up = déchirer

tear² *noun*
a tear = une larme
to burst into tears = fondre en larmes

tease *verb*
= taquiner

teaspoon *noun*
a teaspoon = une petite cuillère

technical *adjective*
= technique

teenager *noun*
a teenager = un adolescent/une
adolescente

telephone *noun*
a telephone = un téléphone

telephone directory *noun*
a telephone directory = un annuaire

telescope *noun*
a telescope = un télescope

television *noun*
a television = un téléviseur
I saw the film on television = j'ai vu le
film à la télévision

tell *verb*
• (*to say to*) = dire à
did you tell your parents? = est-ce que tu
l'as dit à tes parents?
to tell someone about a problem = parler
d'un problème à quelqu'un
• (*for interest, fun*) = raconter
to tell jokes = raconter des blagues✶
• (*when giving orders or instructions*)
to tell someone to leave the classroom
= dire à quelqu'un de quitter la salle de
classe
to tell someone not to smoke = interdire à
quelqu'un de fumer
• (*to work out, to know*)
I can tell (that) she's disappointed = je
vois bien qu'elle est déçue
you can tell he's lying = on voit bien qu'il
ment
• (*when making distinctions*)
to tell the twin brothers apart = distinguer
les jumeaux
I can't tell which is which = je n'arrive pas
à les distinguer
• (*to reveal*) = répéter
don't tell anyone = ne le répète pas
tell off
to tell someone off = réprimander
quelqu'un

T

temper *noun*
to be in a temper = être en colère
to lose one's temper = se mettre en colère

temperature *noun* ▶ 266 |
the temperature = la température
to have a temperature = avoir de la
température, avoir de la fièvre

temporary *adjective*
(*describing a job*) = temporaire
(*describing accommodation*) = provisoire

ten *number* ▶ 187 |, ▶ 211 |
ten = dix
ten houses = dix maisons
I've got ten (of them) = j'en ai dix

tennis *noun* ▶ 248 |
tennis = le tennis

tense *adjective*
= tendu/tendue

tent *noun*
a tent = une tente

tenth *number*
• (*in a series*) = dixième
• (*in dates*) ▶ 222 |
the tenth of December = le dix décembre

term *noun*
a term = un trimestre

terrible *adjective*
• (*expressing shock*) = épouvantable
• (*used for emphasis*) = affreux/affreuse

terrified *adjective*
= terrifié/terrifiée

terror *noun*
terror = la terreur

terrorist *noun*
a terrorist = un terroriste/une terroriste

test
1 *verb*
• (*to try out*) = essayer, tester
• (*in exams*) = contrôler
2 *noun*
• a test = un test
  (*in school, college*) (*written*) = un contrôle
  (*oral*) = un contrôle oral
  a driving test = un examen du permis de
  conduire
• to have an eye test = se faire faire un
  examen de la vue

text *noun*
a text = un texte

text message *noun*
a text message = un texto

than
1 *preposition*
• (*in comparisons*) = que
  to be [stronger | more intelligent ...] than
  = être [plus fort | plus intelligent ...] que
  I've got more money than you = j'ai plus
  d'argent que toi

• (*when talking about quantities*) ▶ 317 | = de
  more than half of the pupils are absent
  = plus de la moitié des élèves sont
  absents
  it's worth less than £100 = ça vaut moins
  de 100 livres
2 *conjunction*
  = que
  he's older than Al = il est plus âgé qu'Al

thank *verb*
= remercier

thanks
1 *adverb* = merci
2 thanks to = grâce à

thank you *adverb*
= merci
thank you for coming = merci d'être venu

that *pronoun*
▶ 351 | *See the boxed note on* that *for more
information and examples.*
what's that? = qu'est-ce que c'est?
who's that? = qui est-ce?
is that Louis? = c'est Louis?
that's how they make butter = c'est
  comme ça qu'on fait le beurre
that's not true = ce n'est pas vrai
that's the kitchen = ça, c'est la cuisine

the *determiner*
▶ 352 | *See the boxed note on* the *for
detailed information and examples.*

theatre (*British English*), **theater** (*US
English*) *noun*
a theatre = un théâtre

their *determiner*
their = leur (+ *singular*)
= leurs (+ *plural*)
I don't like their house = je n'aime pas
  leur maison
they're selling their CDs = ils vendent
  leurs disques compacts

theirs *pronoun*
the new house is theirs = la nouvelle
  maison est à eux
which car is theirs? = laquelle est leur
  voiture?
my car is red but theirs is green = ma
  voiture est rouge mais la leur est verte
our parents are younger than theirs = nos
  parents sont plus jeunes que les leurs

! *Note that, when comparing objects,
people etc, one of the following
translations—*le leur, la leur *or* les
leurs—*will be used. To know which one to
use, find out whether the object, person
etc. being described is masculine
singular, feminine singular or just plural.*

that

As a determiner

In French, determiners agree with the noun that follows; so **that** is translated as follows:

ce or **cet**	+	*masculine singular noun*	**ce** monsieur, **cet** homme
cette	+	*feminine singular noun*	**cette** femme
ces	+	*noun plural*	**ces** livres, **ces** histoires

Note, however, that the above translations are also used for the English **this** (plural *these*). So when it is necessary to insist on **that** as opposed to another or others of the same sort, the adverbial tag **-là** is added to the noun:

*I prefer **that** colour* = je préfère **cette** couleur**-là**

As a pronoun

- In French, pronouns reflect the gender and number of the noun they are standing for.

  So **that** (meaning *that one*) is translated by

celui-là	*for a masculine noun*
celle-là	*for a feminine noun*

  and **those** (meaning *those ones*) is translated by

ceux-là	*for a masculine noun*
celles-là	*for a feminine noun*

  all the dresses are nice but = toutes les robes sont jolies mais
  *I like **that** best* je préfère **celle-là**

- When used as a relative pronoun, **that** is translated by **qui** when it is the subject of the verb and by **que** when it is the object:

  *the man **that** stole the car* = l'homme **qui** a volé la voiture
  *the film **that** I saw* = le film **que** j'ai vu

  Remember that in the present perfect and past perfect tenses, the past participle agrees with the noun that **que** is referring back to:

  *the girl **that** I met* = la fille **que** j'ai rencontrée
  *the apples **that** I bought* = les pommes **que** j'ai achetées

- When that is used as a relative pronoun with a preposition, it is translated by **lequel** when standing for a masculine singular noun, by **laquelle** when standing for a feminine singular noun, by **lesquels** when standing for a masculine plural noun, and by **lesquelles** when standing for a feminine plural noun:

  the chair that I was sitting on = la chaise sur **laquelle** j'étais assis
  the children that I bought the = les enfants pour **lesquels** j'ai acheté les livres
  books for

  If the preposition would normally be translated by **à** in French (**to**, **at** etc), the translation of the whole (*preposition + relative pronoun*) will be:

auquel	*for a masculine noun*
à laquelle	*for a feminine noun*
auxquels	*for a masculine plural noun*
auxquelles	*for a feminine plural noun*

  *the girls **that** I was talking to* = les filles **auxquelles** je parlais

  If the preposition used would normally be translated by **de** in French (**of**, **from** etc), the translation of the whole (*preposition + relative pronoun*) will be **dont** in all cases:

  *the people **that** I've talked about* = les personnes **dont** j'ai parlé

As a conjunction

When used as a conjunction, **that** can almost always be translated by **que** (**qu'** before a vowel or mute h):

*she said **that** she would do it* = elle a dit **qu'**elle le ferait

the

- In French the definite article, like determiners, agrees with the noun that follows; so **the** is translated as follows:

le or **l'** +	*masculine singular noun*	**le** chien, **l'**ami
la or **l'** +	*feminine singular noun*	**la** chaise, **l'**amie
les +	*masculine plural noun*	**les** hommes, **les** avions
les +	*feminine plural noun*	**les** femmes, **les** autos

- When **the** is used after a preposition in English, the two words (*preposition* + **the**) are often translated by one word in French. If the preposition would normally be translated by **de** in French (**of, about, from** etc), the *preposition* + **the** is translated according to whether the noun is masculine or feminine, singular or plural:

	le or **l'** + *masculine singular noun*	**du** chien, **de l'**ami
de +	**la** or **l'** + *feminine singular noun*	**de la** chaise, **de l'**amie
	les + *masculine plural noun*	**des** hommes, **des** avions
	les + *feminine plural noun*	**des** femmes, **des** autos

If the preposition would usually be translated by **à** (**at, to** etc) the *preposition* + **the** is translated according to whether the noun is masculine or feminine, singular or plural:

	le or **l'** + *masculine singular noun*	**au** chien, **à l'**ami
à +	**la** or **l'** + *feminine singular noun*	**à la** chaise, **à l'**ami
	les + *masculine plural noun*	**aux** hommes, **aux** avions
	les + *feminine plural noun*	**aux** femmes, **aux** autos

- Other than this, there are few problems in translating **the** into French. The following cases are, however, worth remembering as not following exactly the pattern of the English:

the good, the poor, the unemployed	= **les** bons, **les** pauvres, **les** chômeurs
Charles the First, Elizabeth the Second	= Charles Ier (Premier), Elizabeth II (Deux)
she's the actress of the year	= c'est **la plus grande** actrice de l'année
the Tudors, the Batemans, the Kennedys	= **les** Tudor, **les** Bateman, **les** Kennedy
the sporting event of the year	= **le grand** événement sportif de l'année
it's the film to see	= c'est **le** film à voir

▶ This dictionary contains usage notes on such topics as **days of the week**, **illnesses**, **the human body**, and **musical instruments**, many of which use **the**; for the index to these notes see ▶ **400**.

---

them *pronoun*
▶ **353** See the boxed note on **them** for detailed information and examples.

themselves *pronoun*
- (*when used as a reflexive pronoun*)
  they want to enjoy themselves = ils/elles veulent s'amuser
  they didn't hurt themselves = ils/elles ne se sont pas fait mal
- (*when used for emphasis*)
  they said it themselves = ils l'ont dit eux-mêmes/elles l'ont dit elles-mêmes
  they did it all by themselves = ils l'ont fait tout seuls/elles l'ont fait toutes seules

  ! *Remember that, when talking about mixed groups, the masculine form* **eux-mêmes** *is used to translate* **themselves**.

then *adverb*
- (*at that point in time*) = alors, à ce moment-là
  I was living in Paris then = j'habitais alors Paris

we saw each other a lot then = on se voyait beaucoup à ce moment-là
from then on = à partir de ce moment-là
- (*after, next*) = puis, ensuite
  I went for a drink and then had dinner = je suis allé prendre un pot✷ et puis j'ai dîné

there
1 *pronoun*
  there is a problem = il y a un problème
  there aren't any shops = il n'y a pas de magasins
  there was no room = il n'y avait pas de place
  there will be a lot of people = il y aura beaucoup de monde
2 *adverb*
- (*when talking about location*) = là
  who's there? = qui est là?
  the train wasn't there = le train n'était pas là
  go over there = va là-bas
  when do we get there? = quand est-ce qu'on arrive?
  they don't go there very often = ils n'y vont pas très souvent

---

✷ in informal situations

them

● When used as a direct object pronoun, referring to people, animals or things, **them** is translated by **les**:

I know them	= je **les** connais
I don't know them	= je ne **les** connais pas
do I know them?	= est-ce que je **les** connais?

Note that the object pronoun normally comes before the verb in French and that, in tenses like the present perfect and past perfect, the past participle agrees with the direct object pronoun:

*he's seen **them***	= il **les** a vus
	(***them** being masculine or of mixed gender*)
	= il **les** a vues
	(***them** being all feminine gender*)
*he hasn't seen **them***	= il ne **les** a pas vus
	= il ne **les** a pas vues
*has he seen **them**?*	= est-ce qu'il **les** a vus?
	= est-ce qu'il **les** a vues?

● In imperatives, the direct object pronoun is translated by **les** and comes after the verb:

*catch **them**!*	= attrape **les**!*
*take **them**!*	= prenez-**les**!*

But in negative commands, **les** comes before the verb:

*don't take **them**!*	= ne **les** prenez pas!
*don't hit **them**!*	= ne **les** frappe pas!

● When used as an indirect object pronoun, **them** is translated by **leur**:

*I gave it **to them***	= je le **leur** ai donné
*I didn't give it **to them***	= je ne le **leur** ai pas donné
*did I give it **to them**?*	= est-ce que je le **leur** ai donné?

● In imperatives, the indirect object pronoun is translated by **leur** and comes after the verb:

*write **to them**!*	= écris-**leur**!*
*say it **to them**!*	= dis-le-**leur**!*

But in negative commands, **leur** comes before the verb:

*don't show it **to them**!*	= ne le **leur** montre pas!

● After prepositions and the verb **to be**, the translation is **eux** for masculine or mixed gender and **elles** for feminine gender:

*he did it **for them***	= il l'a fait **pour eux**
	(***them** being masculine or of mixed gender*)
	= il l'a fait pour **elles**
	(***them** being all feminine gender*)
*it's **them***	= ce sont **eux**
	ce sont **elles**

* Note the hyphen(s).

Note that the entries for **her**, **him**, **me** and **us** are modelled in this note.

● (*when drawing attention*)
there's [the sea | my watch | Natalie ...] = voilà [la mer | ma montre | Natalie ...]
there they are = les voilà
there you are, there you go = et voilà

therefore *adverb*
= donc, par conséquent

these
1 *determiner*
these = ces

these books aren't mine = ces livres ne sont pas à moi
2 *pronoun*
what are these? = qu'est-ce que c'est?
these are your things = ce sont tes affaires
these are my friends = ce sont mes amis
I prefer THESE = je préfère ceux-ci/celles-ci
! *See the note on* **this** *for further information about the use of* -**ci**.

they *pronoun*
  they = ils/elles
  they'll be there too = ils/elles seront là
  aussi
  there they are! = les voilà!
  they're intelligent girls = ce sont des filles
  intelligentes
  that's how they make yogurt = c'est
  comme ça qu'on fait le yaourt
  ! *Note that* on *is used to translate* they
  *when talking in an impersonal or vague
  way about people.*

thick *adjective*
  = épais/épaisse

thief *noun*
  a thief = un voleur/une voleuse

thigh *noun* ▶ **201**
  the thigh = la cuisse

thin *adjective*
  = mince
  to get thin = maigrir

thing *noun*
• **a thing** = une chose, un truc
  I've got things to do = j'ai des choses à
  faire
  that was a stupid thing to do = c'était
  stupide de faire ça
  the best thing would be to call him = le
  mieux serait de l'appeler
  I can't hear a thing = je n'entends rien
• (*belongings*)
  things = les affaires (*feminine*)

think *verb*
• (*when talking about opinions*) = penser,
  croire
  what do you think of it? = qu'est-ce que tu
  en penses?
  I think it's unfair = je pense que c'est
  injuste
  'will they come?'—'I don't think so' = 'est-
  ce qu'ils vont venir?'—'je ne crois pas'
  who do you think will win? = qui va
  gagner à ton avis?
• (*to concentrate on an idea*) = réfléchir
  think hard before answering = réfléchis
  bien avant de répondre
• (*to remember*)
  I can't think of his name = je ne me
  rappelle plus son nom
• (*to take into account, to have in mind*)
  to think of someone = penser à quelqu'un
  I thought of you when I saw the dress
  = j'ai pensé à toi quand j'ai vu la robe
  we didn't think of closing the window
  = nous n'avons pas pensé à fermer la
  fenêtre
• (*to have vague plans to*)
  to be thinking of changing jobs
  = envisager de changer de travail
• (*to have an idea about*)
  to think of a solution = trouver une
  solution

third
1 *adjective*
  = troisième
2 *noun*
• (*in a series*)
  the third = le troisième/la troisième
• (*in dates*) ▶ **222**
  the third of June = le trois juin
• (*when talking about quantities*) ▶ **317**
  a third of the population = un tiers de la
  population
3 *adverb*
  = troisième
  to come third = arriver troisième

thirsty *adjective*
  to be thirsty = avoir soif
  I'm very thirsty = j'ai très soif

thirteen *number* ▶ **187**, ▶ **211**
  thirteen = treize

thirteenth *number*
• (*in a series*) = treizième
• (*in dates*) ▶ **222**
  Friday the thirteenth = vendredi treize

thirty *number* ▶ **187**, ▶ **211**
  thirty = trente

this
1 *determiner*
  this = ce/cette (**!** cet + *masculine* + *vowel
  or mute h*)
  I like this garden = j'aime bien ce jardin
  do you know this place? = est-ce que tu
  connais cet endroit?
  who is this woman? = qui est cette
  femme?
  I prefer THIS **hotel to the others** = je préfère
  cet hôtel-ci aux autres
  ! *Note that, since the translations for* this
  and that *are the same, the tag* -ci *must be
  added to the noun and pronoun if a clear
  distinction is to be made.*

2 *pronoun*
  what's this? = qu'est-ce que c'est?
  who's this? = qui est-ce?
  this is the kitchen = voici la cuisine
  this is my sister = voici ma sœur
  this isn't the right address = ce n'est pas la
  bonne adresse
  how much is THIS**?** = combien coûte celui-
  ci/celle-ci?

those
1 *determiner*
  those = ces
  those books are yours = ces livres sont à
  toi
2 *pronoun*
  what are those? = qu'est-ce que c'est?
  those are my letters = ce sont mes lettres
  those are my cousins = ce sont mes
  cousins
  I prefer THOSE = je préfère ceux-là/celles-là
  ▶ **351** *See the boxed note on* that *for further
  information about the use of* -là.

though *conjunction*
= bien que
though it's expensive, it's still a good buy
= bien que ce soit cher, ça reste un bon
achat
! *Note that the subjunctive is used after*
bien que.

thought *noun*
a thought = une pensée

thousand *number*
one thousand, a thousand = mille
four thousand pounds = quatre mille
livres
about a thousand people = un millier de
personnes

thread *noun*
thread = le fil

threat *noun*
a threat = une menace

threaten *verb*
= menacer

three *number* ▶ 187 |, ▶ 211 |
three = trois
three sisters = trois sœurs
I've got three (of them) = j'en ai trois

throat *noun* ▶ 201 |
the throat = la gorge

through
! *Often* through *occurs in combinations*
with verbs, for example: go through, let
through, read through *etc. To find the*
correct translations for this type of verb,
look up the separate dictionary entries at
go, let, read *etc.*

preposition
• (*from one side to the other*) = à travers
to see through the fog = voir à travers le
brouillard
to drive through the desert = traverser le
désert (en voiture)
• (*via, by way of*)
to go through the town centre = passer par
le centre-ville
to look through a window = regarder par
une fenêtre
• (*past*)
to go through a red light = brûler un feu
rouge
to go through customs = passer la douane
• (*when talking about time*)
right through the day = toute la journée
from Friday through to Sunday = de
vendredi jusqu'à dimanche
open April through September (*US*
English) = ouvert d'avril à fin septembre

throw *verb*
= lancer
to throw stones at someone = lancer des
pierres à quelqu'un
throw me the ball = lance-moi le ballon
to throw a book on the floor = jeter un
livre par terre

throw away, throw out = jeter

thumb *noun* ▶ 201 |
the thumb = le pouce

thunder *noun*
thunder = le tonnerre

thunderstorm *noun*
a thunderstorm = un orage

Thursday *noun* ▶ 222 |
Thursday = jeudi (*masculine*)

ticket *noun*
a ticket (*for a plane, a train, a film, an*
event) = un billet
(*for a bus, the underground, a locker*) = un
ticket

tickle *verb*
= chatouiller

tide *noun*
the tide = la maree
the tide is out = c'est la marée basse
the tide is coming in = la marée monte

tidy *adjective*
(*describing a place, a desk*) = bien
rangé/rangée
(*describing a person*) = ordonné/ordonnée
tidy up = ranger

tie
1 *verb*
= attacher
to tie a dog to a tree = attacher un chien à
un arbre
to tie a parcel (up) with string = ficeler un
paquet
2 *noun*
• (*worn with a shirt*)
a tie = une cravate
• (*in sport*)
a tie = un match nul
tie up = ligoter

tiger *noun*
a tiger = un tigre

tight *adjective*
= serré/serrée

tights *noun* (*British English*)
tights = un collant (*singular*)

till¹ ▶ until

till² *noun*
a till = une caisse

timber *noun*
timber = le bois (de construction)

time *noun*
• time = le temps
I don't have time to go there = je n'ai pas
le temps d'y aller
we haven't seen them for some time = ça
fait un moment qu'on ne les a pas vus
a long time ago = il y a longtemps

T

Talking about time

▶ For time by the clock, ▶ **211**]; for days of the week, months, and dates, ▶ **222**].

How long?

Note the various ways of translating **take** into French:

how long does it take?	= combien de temps faut-il?
it took me a week	= il m'a fallu une semaine / cela m'a pris une semaine
it'll take at least a year	= il faudra au moins un an
it'll only take a minute	= ça ne prendra qu'une minute

Use **en** for **in** when expressing the time something took or will take:

*he did it **in** an hour*	= il l'a fait **en** une heure

The commonest translation of **for** in the 'how long' sense is **pendant**:

*I worked in a factory **for** a year*	= j'ai travaillé en usine **pendant** un an

But use **pour** to translate **for** when the length of time is seen as being still to come:

*we're here **for** a month*	= nous sommes là **pour** un mois

And use **depuis** to translate **for** when the action began in the past and is still going on:

*she has been here **for** a week*	= elle est ici **depuis** une semaine
*I haven't seen her **for** years*	= je ne l'ai pas vue **depuis** des années

When?

Use **dans** for **in** when something is seen as happening in the future:

*I'll be there **in** an hour*	= j'y serai **dans** une heure
in *three weeks' time*	= **dans** trois semaines
when did it happen?	= quand est-ce que c'est arrivé?
a month ago	= il y a un mois
a week ago yesterday	= il y a eu huit jours hier
when will you see him?	= quand est-ce que tu le verras?
in *a few days*	= **dans** quelques jours
a month from tomorrow	= **dans** un mois demain
when you see him, tell him to call me	= quand tu le verras,* dis-lui de m'appeler

How often?

how often does it happen?	= cela arrive tous les combien?
every year	= tous les ans
five times a day	= cinq fois par jour
once every three months	= une fois tous les trois mois

How much an hour (etc)?

*how much do you get **an** hour?*	= combien gagnez-vous **de** l'heure?
*to be paid $20 **an** hour*	= être payé 20 dollars **de** l'heure
*to be paid **by the** hour*	= être payé **à** l'heure
*how much do you get **a** week?*	= combien gagnez-vous **par** semaine?
*$3,000 **a** month*	= 3 000 dollars **par** mois

* Note that, when talking about future time, the future tense of the verb is used after **quand**.

• (*when talking about a specific hour or period of time*)
the time = l'heure (*feminine*)
what's the time?, what time is it? = quelle heure est-il?
what time does the film start? = à quelle heure commence le film?

to arrive on time = arriver à l'heure
in [**five days'** | **a week's** | **six months'** ...] **time**
= dans [cinq jours | une semaine | six mois ...]
this time last year = il y a exactement an
by this time next week = d'ici la semaine prochaine
it's time we left = il est temps de partir

- (*a moment*)
  a time = un moment
  at times = par moments
  at the right time = au bon moment
  this is no time to argue = ce n'est pas le
    moment de se disputer
  any time now = d'un moment à l'autre
  for the time being = pour le moment
- (*a period in the past*)
  a time = une époque
  they didn't know each other at the time
    = ils ne se connaissaient pas à l'époque
- (*an experience*)
  to have a good time = bien s'amuser
    (**!** + *être*)
  to have a hard time concentrating = avoir
    du mal à se concentrer
- (*an occasion*)
  the first time we met = la première fois
    que nous nous sommes rencontrés
  from time to time = de temps en temps
- (*when comparing*)
  three times more expensive = trois fois
    plus cher
  ten times quicker = dix fois plus rapide

timetable *noun*
- (*for trains, buses*)
  a timetable = un horaire
- (*in school, at work*)
  a timetable = un emploi du temps

tin *noun*
- (*the metal*)
  tin = l'étain (*masculine*)
- (*British English*) (*a can*)
  a tin = une boîte (de conserve)
  a tin of beans = une boîte de haricots

tin opener *noun* (*British English*)
  a tin opener = un ouvre-boîtes

tiny *adjective*
  = tout petit/toute petite

tip *noun*
- (*the point, the end*)
  the tip (*of a pen, a stick, a shoe*) = la
    pointe
  (*of the finger, nose, tongue*) = le bout
  on the tips of one's toes = sur la pointe
    des pieds
- (*given in a hotel, a restaurant*)
  a tip = un pourboire
- (*a piece of advice*)
  a tip = un conseil

tire *noun* (*US English*)
  a tire = un pneu

tired *adjective*
- (*needing rest*) = fatigué/fatiguée
  to get tired = se fatiguer (**!** + *être*)
- (*needing a change*)
  I'm tired of being a waitress = j'en ai assez
    d'être serveuse

tiring *adjective*
  = fatigant/fatigante

tissue *noun*
  a tissue = un mouchoir en papier

to *preposition* ▶ 211 |
  ▶ 358 | *See the boxed note on* **to**. *There are
  many adjectives like* mean, nice, rude *etc
  and verbs like* belong, write *etc which involve
  the use of* to. *For translations, look up the
  adjective entries at* mean, nice, rude *or the
  verb entries at* belong, write.

toast *noun*
  toast = le pain grillé
  a piece of toast = une tranche de pain
    grillé

toaster *noun*
  a toaster = un grille-pain

today *adverb* ▶ 356 |
  = aujourd'hui

toe *noun* ▶ 201 |
  the toe = l'orteil (*masculine*)

toffee *noun*
  toffee = le caramel

together *adverb*
  = ensemble

toilet *noun*
  a toilet = des toilettes (*feminine plural*)

toilet paper *noun*
  toilet paper = le papier hygiénique

tomato *noun*
  a tomato = une tomate

tomorrow *adverb* ▶ 356 |
  = demain

tongue *noun* ▶ 201 |
  the tongue = la langue

tonight *adverb*
  (*this evening*) = ce soir
  (*during the night*) = cette nuit

too *adverb*
- (*also*) = aussi
  I'm going too = j'y vais aussi
- (*more than is necessary or desirable*)
  = trop
  it's too [big | dear | far ...] = c'est trop [grand |
    cher | loin ...]
  there were too many people = il y avait
    trop de monde
  I ate too much = j'ai trop mangé

tool *noun*
  a tool = un outil

tooth *noun* ▶ 201 |
  a tooth = une dent
  a set of false teeth = un dentier

toothache *noun* ▶ 266 |
  to have a toothache = avoir mal aux dents

toothbrush *noun*
  a toothbrush = une brosse à dents

toothpaste *noun*
  toothpaste = le dentifrice

T

to

▶ This dictionary contains usage notes on such topics as **The clock**, **Length and weight measurements**, **Games and sports** etc. Many of these use the preposition to. For the index to these notes ▶ **400 |**.

As a preposition

● When **to** is used as a preposition with verbs of movement (*go*, *travel* etc), it is often translated by **à** (*à Paris*, *à Londres*), but remember to use **en** with feminine countries (*en France*) and **au** with masculine countries (*au Portugal*).

Remember when using **à** in French that **à** + **le** always becomes **au**:

to the office	= **au** bureau

and **à** + **les** always becomes **aux**:

to the shops	= **aux** magasins

● When **to** is used as a preposition with verbs such as *speak*, *give*, *say* etc, it is usually translated by **à**:

*give the book **to** Jane*	= donne le livre **à** Jane
*I'll speak **to** the headmistress*	= je vais parler **à** la directrice
*she said it **to** my father*	= elle l'a dit **à** mon père
*show it **to** the policeman*	= montre-le **à** l'agent
*I pointed it out **to** the stewardess*	= je l'ai signalé **à** l'hôtesse
*give the ball **to** the little boy*	= donne le ballon **au*** petit garçon
*we gave it **to** the children*	= nous l'avons donné **aux*** enfants

* Remember that à + le = au and à + les = aux

● When **to** is used as a preposition with personal pronouns (*me*, *you*, *him*, *her*, *us*, *them*), the two words (*preposition* + *pronoun*) are translated by **me/te/lui/lui/nous/vous/leur**:

*she gave it **to them***	= elle le **leur** a donné
*I'll say it **to her***	= je vais le **lui** dire
*will you lend it **to me**?*	= est-ce que tu **me** le prêtes?

As part of an infinitive

● When **to** forms the infinitive of a verb taken alone, it needs no translation:

to go	= aller
to sing	= chanter

However, when **to** is used as part of an infinitive giving the meaning **in order to**, it is translated by **pour**:

*he's gone into town **to buy** a shirt*	= il est parti en ville **pour acheter** une chemise
*I need it **to do** my homework*	= j'en ai besoin **pour faire** mes devoirs

● **to** is also used as part of an infinitive after certain adjectives: **easy to read** etc. Here **to** is usually translated by **à**:

*her writing is easy **to read***	= son écriture est facile **à** lire
*his accent is difficult **to understand***	= son accent est dur **à** comprendre

However, when the infinitive has an object, **to** is usually translated by **de**:

*it's easy **to lose** one's way*	= il est facile **de** perdre son chemin
*it's difficult **to work** at night*	= c'est difficile **de** travailler la nuit

▶ **to** is also used as part of an infinitive after certain verbs: *she told me* **to** *wash my hands*, *I'll help him* **to** *tidy the room* etc. Here the translation, usually either **à** or **de**, depends on the verb used in French. To find the correct translation, consult the appropriate verb entry: **tell**, **help** etc.

---

top
1 noun
● (*the highest part*)
   the top of the hill = le sommet de la colline
   the top of the stairs = le haut de l'escalier

at the top of [the page | the stairs | street ...] = en haut [de la page | de l'escalier | de la rue ...]
● (*a cover, a lid*)
   a top (*on a bottle*) = un bouchon
   (*on a pan*) = un couvercle
   (*on a pen*) = un capuchon

- (*the highest level*)
  to get to the top = réussir
  to be at the top of the class = être
  premier/première de la classe
2 *adjective*
  the top [shelf | drawer | button ...] = [l'étagère |
  le tiroir | le bouton ...] du haut

torch *noun* (*British English*)
  a torch = une lampe de poche

torn *adjective*
  = déchiré/déchirée

tortoise *noun*
  a tortoise = une tortue

total
1 *noun*
  a total = un total
2 *adjective*
  = total/totale

touch
1 *verb*
- (*with one's hand*) = toucher
- (*to interfere with*) = toucher à
  don't touch my things = ne touche pas à
  mes affaires
2 *noun*
  to [be | get | stay ...] **in touch with someone**
  = [être | se mettre | rester ...] en contact avec
  quelqu'un

tough *adjective*
- (*not soft, not sensitive*) = coriace
- (*rough*) = dur/dure
  a tough area = un quartier dur
- (*difficult*) = difficile
- (*severe*)
  a tough law = une loi sévère

tour
1 *noun*
- (*by a team, a band, a theatre group*)
  a tour = une tournée
  on tour = en tournée
- (*by tourists, pupils, visitors*)
  a tour = une visite
  to go on a tour of the castle = visiter le
  château
2 *verb*
  to go touring = faire du tourisme
  to tour the United States = visiter les
  États-Unis

tourism *noun*
  tourism = le tourisme

tourist *noun*
  a tourist = un touriste/une touriste

tourist office *noun*
  a tourist office (*local*) = un syndicat
  d'initiative

toward(s) *preposition*
- (*when talking about place, time*) = vers

towards the east = vers l'est
towards evening = vers le soir
- (*when talking about attitudes*) = envers
  to be friendly towards someone = se
  montrer cordial envers quelqu'un

towel *noun*
  a towel = une serviette

tower *noun*
  a tower = une tour

tower block *noun* (*British English*)
  a tower block = une tour d'habitation

town *noun*
  a town = une ville
  to go into town = aller en ville

town hall *noun*
  a town hall = une mairie

toy *noun*
  a toy = un jouet

track *noun*
- (*a path*)
  a track = un sentier, un chemin
- (*for sports*)
  a track = une piste
- (*the rails*)
  the track(s) = la voie ferrée
- (*left by a person, an animal, a car*)
  tracks = des traces (*feminine*)

tracksuit *noun*
  a tracksuit = un survêtement

trade *noun*
- **trade** = le commerce
- **a trade** = un métier

tradition *noun*
  a tradition = une tradition

traffic *noun*
  traffic = la circulation

traffic jam *noun*
  a traffic jam = un embouteillage, un
  bouchon

traffic lights *noun*
  traffic lights = les feux (*masculine*)

train
1 *noun*
  a train = un train
  the train to Paris = le train à destination
  de Paris
2 *verb*
- (*to teach, to prepare*)
  to train employees = former des employés
  to train athletes = entraîner des athlètes
- (*to learn a job*)
  to train as a doctor = suivre une
  formation de médecin
  she trained as a teacher = elle a reçu une
  formation d'enseignante
- (*for a sporting event*) = s'entraîner
  (**!** + *être*)

T

trainer noun (*British English*)
a trainer (*high*) = une basket
(*low*) = un tennis

training course noun
a training course = un stage de formation

tramp noun
a tramp = un clochard/une clocharde

translate verb
= traduire

translator noun ▶ 315 |
a translator = un traducteur/une
traductrice

transport, **transportation** (*US
English*) noun
transport = le transport
a means of transport = un moyen de
transport

trap noun
a trap = un piège
to set a trap for someone = tendre un
piège à quelqu'un

trash noun (*US English*)
trash = les ordures (*feminine plural*)

trash can noun (*US English*)
a trash can = une poubelle

travel verb
= voyager
to travel abroad = aller à l'étranger
to travel a long way = faire beaucoup de
chemin

travel agency noun ▶ 315 |
a travel agency = une agence de voyages

traveller (*British English*), **traveler** (*US
English*) noun
a traveller = un voyageur/une voyageuse

traveller's cheque (*British English*),
traveler's check (*US English*) noun
a traveller's cheque = un chèque-voyage

tray noun
a tray = un plateau

treat verb
• (*to deal with, to behave with*) = traiter
to treat someone badly = mal se conduire
envers quelqu'un
• (*to pay for*)
to treat someone to a glass of wine
= payer un verre de vin à quelqu'un

treatment noun
treatment = le traitement
to receive treatment = être sous
traitement

tree noun
a tree = un arbre

tremble verb
= trembler

trendy adjective
= branché/branchée✱

trial noun
a trial = un procès
to go on trial = passer en jugement

triangle noun
a triangle = un triangle

trick
1 noun
• (*a joke*)
a trick = un tour, une blague✱
to play a trick on someone = jouer un
tour à quelqu'un
• (*a means of deceiving*)
a trick = une combine
• (*to entertain*)
a trick = un tour
2 verb
= duper, rouler✱

trip
1 noun
a trip (*abroad*) = un voyage
(*a day out*) = une excursion, une sortie
to be on a business trip = être en voyage
d'affaires
2 verb
to trip (up) = trébucher
to trip someone (up) = faire trébucher
quelqu'un

trouble noun
• (*difficulties*)
trouble = les ennuis (*masculine plural*)
to be in trouble = avoir des ennuis
to get someone into trouble = créer des
ennuis à quelqu'un
to make trouble = faire des histoires✱
• (*an effort*)
to take the trouble to check = se donner la
peine de vérifier
to go to a lot of trouble = se donner
beaucoup de mal

trousers noun
trousers = un pantalon (*singular*)

trout noun
a trout = une truite

truck noun
a truck = un camion

truck driver noun ▶ 315 |
a truck driver = un routier

true adjective
= vrai/vraie
is it true that he's leaving? = est-ce que
c'est vrai qu'il part?
to come true = se réaliser (**!** + *être*)

trumpet noun ▶ 290 |
a trumpet = une trompette

trunk *noun*
* (*of a tree*)
  a trunk = un tronc
* (*of an elephant*)
  a trunk = une trompe
* (*US English*) (*in a car*)
  the trunk = le coffre

trust *verb*
* (*to believe*) = se fier à (**!** + *être*)
  to trust a friend = se fier à un ami
  I don't trust them = je me méfie d'eux
* (*to rely on*) = faire confiance à
  you can't trust him = on ne peut pas lui
    faire confiance

truth *noun*
  the truth = la vérité

try
1 *verb*
* **to try** = essayer
  to try [to understand | to come | to forget   ]
    = essayer [de comprendre | de venir |
    d'oublier…]
  try phoning him = essaie de lui téléphoner
* (*to test*) = essayer
  to try (out) a recipe = essayer une recette
  to try (on) a pair of jeans = essayer un jean
* (*to taste*) = goûter
* (*in court*) = juger
2 *noun*
  to score a try = marquer un essai

T-shirt *noun*
  a T-shirt = un T-shirt

tube *noun*
* **a tube** = un tube
* (*British English*) (*the underground*)
  the tube = le métro

Tuesday *noun* ▶ **222**❘
  Tuesday = mardi (*masculine*)

tuna *noun*
  tuna = le thon

tunnel *noun*
  a tunnel = un tunnel

turkey *noun*
  a turkey = une dinde

Turkey *noun* ▶ **218**❘
  Turkey = la Turquie

turn
1 *verb*
* (*to move one's body*) = se retourner
  (**!** + *être*)
  to turn one's face toward(s) the sun
    = tourner le visage vers le soleil
* (*to change direction*) = tourner
  to turn right = tourner à droite
  to turn the corner = tourner au coin de la
    rue
* (*to twist*) = tourner
  to turn the handle = tourner la poignée

* (*to change*)
  to turn the bedroom into an office
    = transformer la chambre en bureau
  to turn someone into a criminal = faire un
    criminel de quelqu'un
* (*to become*)
  to turn into a butterfly = se transformer en
    papillon
  to turn red = rougir
2 *noun*
* (*a bend*)
  a turn = un tournant, un virage
* (*in games*)
  a turn = un tour
  whose turn is it? = c'est à qui le tour?
turn around, turn round
* (*to face the other way*) (*if it's a person*) = se
  retourner (**!** + *être*)
  (*if it's a car*) = faire demi-tour
  to turn the table around = tourner la table
    dans l'autre sens
* (*to go round and round*) = tourner
turn away = se détourner (**!** + *être*)
turn back = faire demi-tour
turn down
* (*to lower*) = baisser
  to turn down the radio = baisser la radio
* (*to reject*) = refuser
  to turn someone down = refuser
    quelqu'un
turn off
  to turn the oven off = éteindre le four
  to turn off the light = éteindre la lumière
  to turn the tap off = fermer le robinet
turn on = allumer
  to turn on the TV = allumer la télévision
  to turn the tap on = ouvrir le robinet
turn out
  to turn out all right (in the end)
    = s'arranger (**!** + *être*)
  to turn out to be easy = se révéler facile
turn over
* (*to roll over*) = se retourner (**!** + *être*)
* **to turn over the page** = tourner la page
turn up
* (*to show up*) = arriver
* (*to increase*)
  to turn up the heating = augmenter le
    chauffage
  to turn the music up = mettre la musique
    plus fort

turtle *noun*
* **a (sea) turtle** = une tortue marine
* (*US English*) (*a tortoise*)
  a turtle = une tortue

TV *noun*
  a TV = une télévision, une télé✖

twelfth *number*
* (*in a series*) = douzième
* (*in dates*) ▶ **222**❘
  the twelfth of July = le douze juillet

twelve *number* ▶ **187**❘, ▶ **211**❘
  twelve = douze
  twelve pupils = douze élèves
  I've got twelve (of them) = j'en ai douze

T

twenty number ▶ **187 |**, ▶ **211 |**
  twenty = vingt

twice adverb
  = deux fois
  twice as many people = deux fois plus de
    monde
  twice as much time = deux fois plus de
    temps

twin
1 noun
  a twin = un jumeau/une jumelle
2 adjective
  a twin brother = un frère jumeau
  a twin sister = une sœur jumelle

twist verb
* (to bend out of shape) = tordre
* (to injure) ▶ **266 |**
  to twist one's ankle = se tordre la cheville

two number ▶ **187 |**, ▶ **211 |**
  two = deux
  two brothers = deux frères
  I've got two (of them) = j'en ai deux

type
1 noun
  a type = un type, un genre
  this type of [person | book | building ...] = ce
    genre de [personne | livre | bâtiment ...]
  he's not my type = ce n'est pas mon genre
2 verb
  = taper (à la machine)

typewriter noun
  a typewriter = une machine à écrire

typical adjective
  = typique

typist noun ▶ **315 |**
  a typist = un dactylo/une dactylo

tyre noun (British English)
  a tyre = un pneu

Uu

---

ugly adjective
  = laid/laide

umbrella noun
  an umbrella = un parapluie

unbelievable adjective
  = incroyable

uncle noun
  an uncle = un oncle

uncomfortable adjective
* (awkward) = pénible
  to make someone (feel) uncomfortable
    = mettre quelqu'un mal à l'aise

* (describing shoes, seats) = inconfortable
  (describing heat, conditions) = pénible

unconscious adjective
  = sans connaissance
  to knock someone unconscious
    = assommer quelqu'un

under preposition
* **under** = sous
  to hide under the bed = se cacher sous le
    lit
  I found the newspaper under it = j'ai
    trouvé le journal dessous
* (less than)
  to earn under three pounds an hour
    = gagner moins de trois livres de l'heure
  children under five = les enfants de moins
    de cinq ans

underground noun (British English)
  the underground = le métro

underline verb
  = souligner

underneath
1 adverb
  = en dessous
  I want to see what's underneath = je veux
    voir ce qu'il y a dessous
2 preposition
  = au-dessous de, sous
  underneath the building = au-dessous du
    bâtiment

underpants noun
  underpants = un slip (singular)

understand verb
  = comprendre
  I can't understand what they're saying
    = je ne comprends pas ce qu'ils disent
  to make oneself understood = se faire
    comprendre

understanding adjective
  = compréhensif/compréhensive

underwater adverb
  = sous l'eau

underwear noun
  underwear = les sous-vêtements
    (masculine plural)

undo verb
  = défaire
  to undo a button = défaire un bouton

undress verb
  = se déshabiller (**!** + être)

uneasy adjective
  = inquiet/inquiète

unemployed adjective
  to be unemployed = être au chômage, être
    sans emploi

unemployment noun
  unemployment = le chômage

unfair *adjective*
= injuste

unfortunately *adverb*
= malheureusement

unfriendly *adjective*
(*describing a person*) = peu amical/peu amicale
(*describing a place*)
= inhospitalier/inhospitalière

ungrateful *adjective*
= ingrat/ingrate

unhappy *adjective*
(*sad*) = malheureux/malheureuse
(*not satisfied*) = mécontent/mécontente

unhealthy *adjective*
(*describing a way of life, food*)
= malsain/malsaine
(*describing a person*) = maladif/maladive
(*describing conditions*) = insalubre

uniform *noun*
a uniform = un uniforme

union *noun*
a union = un syndicat

unique *adjective*
= unique

United Kingdom *noun* ▶ 218|
the United Kingdom = le Royaume-Uni

United States (of America) *noun*
▶ 218|
the United States (of America) = les États-Unis (d'Amérique)
| ! Note that États is masculine plural.

universe *noun*
a universe = un univers

university *noun*
a university = une université

unkind *adjective*
to be unkind (*describing a person, an action*) = ne pas être très gentil/gentille
(*describing a remark*) = être désobligeant/désobligeante

unknown *adjective*
= inconnu/inconnue

unless *conjunction*
it won't work unless you plug it in = ça ne marchera pas si tu ne le branches pas
she can't work unless she finds an au pair
= elle ne peut pas travailler à moins de trouver une jeune fille au pair
she can't work unless we find an au pair
= elle ne peut pas travailler à moins qu'on ne lui trouve une jeune fille au pair
| ! Note that the subjunctive is used after à moins que.

unlock *verb*
= ouvrir

unlucky *adjective*
= malchanceux/malchanceuse
you were unlucky = tu n'as pas eu de chance

unpack *verb*
to unpack a suitcase = défaire une valise
to unpack one's belongings = déballer ses affaires

unsuitable *adjective*
= inapproprié/inappropriée

untidy *adjective*
(*in one's habits*)
= désordonné/désordonnée
(*in how one looks*) = peu soigné/peu soignée

until
1 *preposition*
= jusqu'à
I'm staying until Thursday = je reste jusqu'à jeudi
until now = jusqu'à présent
I'm going to wait until after Christmas = je vais attendre que Noël soit passé
she won't get an answer until next week
= elle n'aura pas de réponse avant la semaine prochaine
2 *conjunction*
I'll wait until I get back home = j'attendrai d'être rentré
we'll stay until they come = nous resterons jusqu'à ce qu'ils arrivent
don't look until it's ready = ne regarde pas avant que ce soit prêt
| ! Note that the subjunctive is used after jusqu'à ce que and avant que.

unusual *adjective*
(*rare*) = peu commun/peu commune
it's unusual to see so few people = il est rare de voir si peu de monde
(*different, out of the ordinary*)
= original/originale

up
| ! Often up occurs in combinations with verbs, for example: blow up, give up, own up, etc. To find the correct translations for this type of verb, look up the separate dictionary entries at blow, give, own etc.

1 *preposition*
the cat's up the tree = le chat est dans l'arbre
to go up the street = remonter la rue
she ran up the stairs = elle a monté l'escalier en courant
the library is up those stairs = la bibliothèque se trouve en haut de cet escalier
2 *adverb*
up in the sky = dans le ciel
up on (top of) the wardrobe = sur l'armoire
to go up = monter (! + être)
to go up to Scotland = aller en Écosse
up there = là-haut
put the picture a bit further up = mets le tableau un peu plus haut
to climb all the way up = monter jusqu'en haut

U

3 *adjective*
(*out of bed*)
to be up = être debout
to be up all night = veiller toute la nuit
(*higher in amount, level*)
to be up by 20% = avoir augmenté de 20%
4 up to
(*well enough*)
to be up to going out = avoir la force de
sortir
I'm not up to it = je n'en ai pas la force
(*when talking about who is responsible*)
it's up to [me | you | them ...] to decide
= c'est à [moi | toi | eux ...] de décider
(*until*) = jusqu'à
up to now = jusqu'à présent
up to 1996 = jusqu'en 1996

upset
1 *adjective*
to be upset (*annoyed*) = être
contrarié/contrariée
· (*distressed*) = être très affecté/affectée
to get upset (*annoyed*) = se fâcher
(**!** + *être*)
(*distressed*) = se mettre dans tous ses états
(**!** + *être*)
2 *verb*
(*to make someone unhappy*) (*if it's an
event*) = bouleverser
(*if it's a person*) = faire de la peine à
(*to annoy*) = contrarier

upside down *adverb*
= à l'envers
you're holding the book upside down = tu
tiens le livre à l'envers

upstairs *adverb*
= en haut
to go upstairs = monter (l'escalier)
to bring the cases upstairs = monter les
valises

urgent *adjective*
= urgent/urgente

us *pronoun*

> **!** us *is always translated by* nous. *Note
> that there is a boxed usage note at* them.
> *The entries* me, him, her *and* us *are
> modelled on this note where you will find
> detailed grammatical information and
> fuller explanations.*

they know us = ils nous connaissent
they don't know us = ils ne nous
connaissent pas
do they know us? = est-ce qu'ils nous
connaissent?
he's seen us = il nous a vus
he hasn't seen us = il ne nous a pas vus
has he seen us? = est-ce qu'il nous a vus?
help us! = aide-nous!
catch us! = attrape-nous!
don't bother us! = ne nous embête pas!
don't hit us! = ne nous frappe pas!

she gave the book to us = elle nous a
donné le livre
she didn't give the book to us = elle ne
nous a pas donné le livre
did she give the book to us? = est-ce
qu'elle nous a donné le livre?
write to us! = écris-nous!
say it to us! = dis-le-nous!
don't show it to us! = ne nous le montre
pas!
he did it for us = il l'a fait pour nous
it's us = c'est nous
stand in front of us = mets-toi devant nous

USA *noun* **▶ 218|**
the USA = les USA (*masculine plural*)

use
1 *verb*
(*to make use of*) = se servir de (**!** + *être*)
I use the car to go to work = je me sers de
la voiture pour aller au travail
he uses the room as an office = il se sert
de la pièce comme bureau
what is it used for? = ça sert à quoi?
to use the opportunity to learn French
= profiter de l'occasion pour apprendre
le français
to use a different word = employer un
autre mot
(*to operate on*)
to use petrol = marcher à l'essence
to use water = utiliser de l'eau
(*to go through*) = consommer
it uses a lot of petrol = ça consomme
beaucoup d'essence
(*to take advantage of*)
to use someone = se servir de quelqu'un
2 *noun*
to make use of a room = utiliser une pièce
to have the use of a car = avoir l'usage
d'une voiture
to lose the use of one's legs = perdre
l'usage de ses jambes
(*when talking about what is useful*)
to be of use to someone = être utile à
quelqu'un, servir à quelqu'un
to be no use = ne servir à rien
the bike is no use any more = le vélo est
hors d'usage
what's the use of complaining? = à quoi
bon se plaindre?
use up
to use up all the money = dépenser tout
l'argent
to use up the milk = finir le lait

used
1 *verb*

> **!** *Note that the imperfect tense in French
> is generally used to translate* used to +
> *verb:* she used to live in Toulouse = elle
> habitait Toulouse.

I used to read a lot = je lisais beaucoup
you used not to smoke = tu ne fumais pas
avant
there used to be a castle here = il y avait
un château ici dans le temps

2 *adjective*
to be used to [children | animals | tourists ...]
= avoir l'habitude des [enfants | animaux |
touristes ...]
he's not used to living on his own = il n'a
pas l'habitude de vivre seul
to get used to a new job = s'habituer à un
nouveau travail

useful *adjective*
= utile

useless *adjective*
(*not working, having no use*) = inutilisable
(*having no point or purpose*) = inutile
it's useless complaining = il est inutile de
se plaindre, ça ne sert à rien de se
plaindre
(*describing a person*) = nul/nulle
to be useless at chemistry = être
nul/nulle en chimie

usually *adverb*
– d'habitude, normalement

Vv

vacant *adjective*
= libre

vacation *noun* (*US English*)
a vacation = des vacances (*feminine plural*)
to take a vacation = prendre des vacances

vacuum *verb*
to vacuum a room = passer l'aspirateur
dans une pièce

vacuum cleaner *noun*
a vacuum cleaner = un aspirateur

vague *adjective*
= vague

vain *adjective*
= vaniteux/vaniteuse

valid *adjective*
(*describing a licence, a passport*) = valide
(*describing a ticket, an offer*) = valable

valley *noun*
a valley = une vallée

valuable *adjective*
• (*very useful*) = précieux/précieuse
• (*worth a lot of money*)
to be valuable = avoir de la valeur

van *noun*
a van (*small*) = une camionnette
(*larger*) = un fourgon

vandalize *verb*
= vandaliser

vanilla *noun*
vanilla = la vanille

various *adjective*
= divers/diverses
there are various ways of saying it = on
peut le dire de diverses façons

vary *verb*
= varier
to vary from town to town = varier d'une
ville à l'autre

vase *noun*
a vase = un vase

veal *noun*
veal = le veau

vegetable *noun*
a vegetable = un légume

vegetarian *noun*
a vegetarian = un végétarien/une
végétarienne

vein *noun* ▶ **201|**
a vein = une veine

velvet *noun*
velvet = le velours

versus *preposition*
= contre

very
1 *adverb*
very = très
I don't know him very well = je ne le
connais pas très bien
to eat very little = manger très peu
you haven't said very much = tu n'as pas
dit grand-chose
we like them very much = on les aime
beaucoup
for the very first time = pour la toute
première fois
they called me the very next day = ils
m'ont appelé dès le lendemain
2 *adjective*
at the very beginning = au tout début
to sit at the very front = s'asseoir tout
devant
to stay to the very end = rester jusqu'au
bout
you are the very person I need = tu es
exactement la personne qu'il me faut

vest *noun*
• (*British English*) (*a piece of underwear*)
a vest = un maillot de corps
• (*US English*) (*a waistcoat*)
a vest = un gilet

vet *noun* ▶ **315|**
a vet = un vétérinaire/une vétérinaire

via *preposition*
(*on tickets, timetables*) = via
(*in general*) = en passant par
we came via Paris = nous sommes venus
en passant par Paris

vicious *adjective*
• (*violent*) = brutal/brutale
• (*nasty, meant to hurt*)
  = malveillant/malveillante

victory *noun*
  a victory = une victoire
  to win a victory = remporter une victoire

video
1 *noun*
• (*a recorded film, programme, event*)
  a video = une cassette vidéo
• ▶ **video cassette**, **video recorder**
2 *verb*
• (*to record*) = enregistrer
• (*to film*)
  to video a wedding = filmer un mariage
    en vidéo

video camera *noun*
  a video camera = une caméra vidéo

video cassette *noun*
  a video cassette = une cassette vidéo

video game *noun*
  a video game = un jeu vidéo

video recorder *noun*
  a video recorder = un magnétoscope

view *noun*
• a view = une vue
  you're blocking my view = tu me bouches
    la vue
  if you want to get a better view, come
    here = si tu veux mieux voir, viens ici
• (*an opinion, an attitude*)
  a view = un avis, une opinion
  a point of view = un point de vue

village *noun*
  a village = un village

vinegar *noun*
  vinegar = le vinaigre

vineyard *noun*
  a vineyard = un vignoble

violent *adjective*
  = violent/violente

violin *noun* ▶ **290** ▎
  a violin = un violon

Virgo *noun*
  Virgo = Vierge (*feminine*)

visit
1 *verb*
  to visit Paris (*to see*) = visiter Paris
  (*to stay*) = faire un séjour à Paris
  to visit someone (*to call on*) = aller voir
    quelqu'un
  (*more formally*) = rendre visite à quelqu'un
  (*to stay with*) = aller passer quelques jours
    chez quelqu'un
2 *noun*
  a visit (*a call*) = une visite

(*a stay*) = un séjour
  to pay someone a visit = rendre visite à
    quelqu'un

visitor *noun*
• (*a guest*)
  a visitor = un invité/une invitée
  to have visitors = avoir de la visite
• (*a tourist*)
  a visitor = un visiteur/une visiteuse

vocabulary *noun*
  vocabulary = le vocabulaire

voice *noun*
  a voice = une voix
  to have a good voice = avoir une jolie
    voix
  to speak in a low voice = parler à voix
    basse
  to sing at the top of one's voice = chanter
    à tue-tête

volleyball *noun* ▶ **248** ▎
  volleyball = le volley-ball

vomit *verb*
  = vomir

vote *verb*
  = voter

Ww

wages *noun*
  wages = le salaire (*singular*)

waist *noun* ▶ **201** ▎
  the waist = la taille

waistcoat *noun* (*British English*)
  a waistcoat = un gilet

wait *verb*
• to wait = attendre
  to wait for someone = attendre quelqu'un
  I'm waiting to use the phone = j'attends de
    pouvoir téléphoner
  to wait for someone to leave = attendre
    que quelqu'un s'en aille
  let's have a beer while we're waiting for
    them = allons prendre une bière en
    attendant qu'ils arrivent
  ! *Note that the subjunctive is used after*
  attendre que.

  I can't wait to see them = j'ai hâte de les
    voir
• (*in a restaurant*)
  to wait on table, to wait table (*US English*)
    = travailler comme serveur/serveuse
wait up = veiller
  to wait up for someone = veiller jusqu'au
    retour de quelqu'un

waiter noun ▶ 315 |
a waiter = un serveur

waiting room noun
a waiting room = une salle d'attente

waitress noun ▶ 315 |
a waitress = une serveuse

wake verb
to wake someone = réveiller quelqu'un
wake up = se réveiller (**!** + être)

Wales noun ▶ 218 |
Wales = le pays de Galles

walk
1 verb
(rather than run) = marcher
(rather than drive or ride) = aller à pied
(for pleasure) = se promener (**!** + être)
let's walk to the pool = allons à la piscine
à pied
to walk down the street = descendre la rue
to walk the dog = promener le chien
2 noun
a walk = une promenade
to go for a walk = faire une promenade
it's five minutes' walk from here = c'est à
cinq minutes à pied d'ici
walk around = se promener (**!** + être)
to walk around town = se promener en
ville
to walk around the lake = faire le tour du
lac
walk away = s'éloigner (**!** + être)
walk back = revenir à pied
to walk back home = rentrer à pied
walk by = passer (**!** + être)
walk in = entrer (**!** + être)
walk out = sortir (**!** + être)
to walk out of the room = sortir de la pièce
walk round = faire le tour
to walk round the exhibition = visiter
l'exposition
walk up to = s'approcher de (**!** + être)

walkman noun
a walkman = un baladeur, un walkman

wall noun
a wall = un mur

wallet noun
a wallet = un portefeuille

wallpaper noun
wallpaper = le papier peint

walnut noun
a walnut = une noix

wander verb
to wander around town = se balader en
ville
wander away, wander off = s'éloigner
(**!** + être)

want verb
• to want = vouloir
do you want another coffee? = est-ce que
tu veux un autre café?
he wants [to go out | to go home | to play ...]
= il veut [sortir | rentrer | jouer ...]
she didn't want to stay = elle n'a pas voulu
rester
do you want me to come with you? = est-
ce que tu veux que je vienne avec toi?
! Note that the subjunctive is used after
vouloir que.
• (to need) = avoir besoin de
do you want anything in town? = est-ce
que tu as besoin de quelque chose en
ville?

war noun
a war = une guerre

wardrobe noun
a wardrobe = une armoire

warm
1 adjective
= chaud/chaude
to be warm, to feel warm = avoir chaud
I'm very warm = j'ai très chaud
it's nice and warm in the classroom = il
fait bon dans la salle de classe
to get warm = se réchauffer (**!** + être)
to keep warm = rester au chaud
to keep a meal warm = tenir un repas au
chaud
2 verb
to warm the plates = chauffer les assiettes
to warm one's hands = se réchauffer les
mains
warm up
• (to get warm) = se réchauffer (**!** + être)
• (for a sporting event) = s'échauffer
(**!** + être)
• (to make warm) = réchauffer

warn verb
= avertir, prévenir
to warn someone about the risks = mettre
quelqu'un en garde contre les risques
to warn someone to be careful
= conseiller à quelqu'un de faire
attention
I warned him not to take the car = je lui ai
déconseillé de prendre la voiture

wash verb
• (to clean) = laver
to wash one's clothes = laver ses
vêtements
to wash one's face = se laver le visage
• (to get clean) = se laver (**!** + être)
wash out
to wash out = partir au lavage
to wash a stain out = faire partir une
tache au lavage
wash up
• (British English) (to do the dishes) = faire la
vaisselle

W

- (*US English*) (*to clean oneself*) = se rafraîchir (**!** + *être*)

washbasin (*British English*), **wash-hand basin** *noun*
   a washbasin = un lavabo

washing *noun*
   the washing = le linge
   to do the washing = faire la lessive

washing machine *noun*
   a washing machine = une machine à laver

washing-up *noun* (*British English*)
   the washing-up = la vaisselle
   to do the washing-up = faire la vaisselle

wasp *noun*
   a wasp = une guêpe

waste
1 *verb*
   = gaspiller
   to waste energy = gaspiller de l'énergie
   to waste one's time = perdre son temps
2 *noun*
- it's a waste of money = c'est de l'argent gaspillé
   a waste of time = une perte de temps
   it's a waste of time going there = y aller est une perte de temps
   to let food go to waste = gaspiller de la nourriture
- waste = les déchets (*masculine plural*)

watch
1 *verb*
- (*to look at*) = regarder
   to watch television = regarder la télévision
   she watched me making the meal = elle m'a regardé préparer le repas
- (*to observe, to follow*) = surveiller
   I feel I'm being watched = j'ai l'impression qu'on me surveille
- (*to pay attention to*)
   watch what you're doing = fais attention à ce que tu fais
   watch you don't fall = fais attention de ne pas tomber
2 *noun*
   a watch = une montre
watch out = faire attention

water
1 *noun*
   water = l'eau (*feminine*)
   drinking water = l'eau potable
   to let in water = prendre l'eau
2 *verb*
   = arroser

waterfall *noun*
   a waterfall = une cascade

water-skiing *noun* ▶ **248**
   water-skiing = le ski nautique

wave
1 *verb*
- (*to signal with one's hand*)
   to wave to someone = saluer quelqu'un de la main
   to wave goodbye = faire au revoir de la main
- (*to direct*)
   to wave someone on = faire signe à quelqu'un d'avancer
- to wave flags = agiter des drapeaux
2 *noun*
   a wave = une vague

way
1 *noun*
- (*a means, a method*)
   a way = un moyen
   it's a way of earning money = c'est un moyen de gagner de l'argent
   it's a good way to make friends = c'est un bon moyen de se faire des amis
   he does it the wrong way = il s'y prend mal
   that's not the way to do it = ce n'est pas comme ça qu'on fait
- (*how one does something*)
   a way = une façon
   I like the way she dresses = j'aime sa façon de s'habiller
   I prefer to do it my way = je préfère le faire à ma façon
- (*a route, a road*)
   a way = un chemin
   I can't remember the way to the station = je ne me souviens plus du chemin pour aller à la gare
   we can buy something to eat along the way = on peut acheter quelque chose à manger en chemin
   on the way back = sur le chemin du retour
   I met them on the way back from town = je les ai rencontrés en revenant de la ville
   on the way to Paris = en allant à Paris
   where's the way out? = où est la sortie?
   to make one's way to the stairs = se diriger vers l'escalier
   to lose one's way = se perdre (**!** + *être*)
- (*a direction*)
   which way are you going? = dans quelle direction est-ce que tu vas?
   they went that way = ils sont partis par là
   come this way = venez par ici
- (*someone's route*)
   to be in someone's way = empêcher quelqu'un de passer, bloquer le passage à quelqu'un
   to be in the way = gêner le passage
   to get out of the way = s'écarter (**!** + *être*)
- (*when talking about distances*)
   it's a long way from here = c'est loin d'ici
   to go all the way to Portugal = aller jusqu'au Portugal

- *(what one wants)*
  she always wants her own way = elle ne
  veut en faire qu'à sa tête
  if I had my own way, I'd go alone = si cela
  ne tenait qu'à moi, j'irais tout seul
2 by the way = au fait
  what's his name, by the way? = comment
  s'appelle-t-il, au fait?

we *pronoun*

> **!** *Note that* we *is generally translated by*
> nous *but that, in informal French,* on *is*
> *also very common:* we're going to the
> cinema = nous allons au cinéma, on va au
> cinéma.

  we = nous
  we saw her yesterday = nous l'avons vue
  hier, on l'a vue hier
  we didn't agree = nous, nous n'étions pas
  d'accord
  we all make mistakes = tout le monde
  peut se tromper

weak *adjective*
- *(not healthy)* = faible
  to have a weak heart = avoir le cœur
  fragile
- *(not good or able)* = faible
  to be weak at languages = être faible en
  langues
- *(easily damaged)* = fragile
- *(having very little power)* = faible
- *(describing tea or coffee)* = léger/légère

wealthy *adjective*
  = riche

wear *verb*
- *(to be dressed in)* = porter
  to be wearing jeans = porter un jean
  to wear black = s'habiller en noir
- *(to put on)* = mettre
  what will you wear? = qu'est-ce que tu vas
  mettre?
  I've got nothing to wear = je n'ai rien à me
  mettre
wear out
  to wear out = s'user (**!** + *être*)
  to wear one's shoes out = user ses
  chaussures
  to wear someone out = épuiser quelqu'un

weather *noun*
  the weather = le temps
  what's the weather like? = quel temps
  fait-il?
  the weather is [bad | hot] = il fait [mauvais |
  chaud]
  in [cold | warm | wet …] weather = quand [il
  fait froid | il fait bon | il pleut …]

weather forecast *noun*
  the weather forecast = les prévisions
  météorologiques, la météo

> **!** *Note that* prévisions *is feminine plural.*

Web *noun*
  the Web = le Web

website *noun*
  a website = un site web

wedding *noun*
  a wedding = un mariage

Wednesday *noun* ▶ 222 |
  Wednesday = mercredi *(masculine)*

week *noun* ▶ 356 |
  a week = une semaine
  in two weeks' time = dans quinze jours

weekend *noun* ▶ 356 |
  a weekend = un week-end

weigh *verb* ▶ 285 |
  = peser
  what do you weigh? = combien pèses-tu?
  to weigh oneself = se peser (**!** + *être*)

weight *noun* ▶ 285 |
  weight = le poids
  to lose weight = maigrir

weird *adjective*
  = bizarre

welcome
1 *verb* ▶ 237 |
  to welcome someone = accueillir
  quelqu'un
2 *adjective*
- *(when receiving people)*
  to be welcome = être le bienvenu/la
  bienvenue
  welcome to the United States!
  = bienvenue aux États-Unis!
- *(when acknowledging thanks)*
  'thanks'—'you're welcome' = 'merci'—'de
  rien'

well
1 *adverb* ▶ 237 |
- **well** = bien
  he dresses well = il s'habille bien
  the [exam | interview | class …] went well
  = [l'examen | l'entretien | le cours …] s'est bien
  passé
  the work is well paid = le travail est bien
  payé
  she is well able to defend herself = elle est
  tout à fait capable de se défendre
  he's not eating well = il n'a pas d'appétit
- *(other uses)*
  we may as well go home = on ferait aussi
  bien de rentrer
  you may well be right = il se pourrait bien
  que tu aies raison

> **!** *Note that the subjunctive is used after* il
> se pourrait bien que.

2 *adjective*
  to feel well = se sentir bien
  I hope everyone is well = j'espère que tout
  le monde va bien
  I'm very well = je vais très bien
  to get well = se rétablir (**!** + *être*)
3 as well = aussi

W

4 as well as = ainsi que

well-known *adjective*
= célèbre

Welsh ▶ 275 |
1 *adjective*
= gallois/galloise
2 *noun*
• (*the people*)
the Welsh = les Gallois (*masculine plural*)
• (*the language*)
Welsh = le gallois

west
1 *noun*
the west = l'ouest (*masculine*)
in the west of France = dans l'ouest de la
France
2 *adverb*
to go west = aller vers l'ouest
to live west of Paris = vivre à l'ouest de
Paris
3 *adjective*
= ouest (**!** *never changes*)
to work in west London = travailler dans
l'ouest de Londres

West Indies *noun* ▶ 218 |
the West Indies = les Antilles (*feminine*)

wet
1 *adjective*
• (*damp*) = mouillé/mouillée
your hair is wet = tu as les cheveux
mouillés
to get wet = se faire mouiller (**!** + *être*)
she got her feet wet = elle s'est mouillé les
pieds
• (*when talking about weather*) = humide
in wet weather = par temps humide
on a wet day = quand il pleut
2 *verb*
= mouiller

what
▶ *See the boxed note on* what *for more
information and examples.*
1 *pronoun*
• (*used in questions*)
what's her phone number? = quel est son
numéro de téléphone?
what's that box? = qu'est-ce que c'est que
cette boîte?
what's this button for? = à quoi sert ce
bouton?
what's the French for 'boring'?
= comment dit-on 'boring' en français?
what does he look like? = il est comment?
• (*used as a relative pronoun*)
do what you want = faites ce que vous
voulez
what we need is a timetable = ce qu'il
nous faut c'est un horaire
2 *determiner*
do you know what train to take? = est-ce
que tu sais quel train il faut prendre?
what a great idea! = quelle bonne idée!

3 *exclamation*
= quoi!, comment!
4 what if = et si
what if I don't get there on time? = et si je
n'y suis pas à l'heure?

whatever *pronoun*
• (*when anything is possible*)
take whatever you want = prends tout ce
que tu veux
whatever you think is useful = tout ce qui
vous paraît utile
• (*when it doesn't matter*)
whatever they do, it won't change
anything = quoi qu'ils fassent, ça ne
changera rien
! *Note that the subjunctive is used after* quoi
que *(*quoi qu' *before vowel or mute h).*

wheat *noun*
wheat = le blé

wheel *noun*
a wheel = une roue

wheelchair *noun*
a wheelchair = un fauteuil roulant

when
1 *adverb*
= quand
when did she leave? = quand est-ce
qu'elle est partie?
when is your birthday? = c'est quand ton
anniversaire?
I don't know when the film starts = je ne sais
pas à quelle heure le film commence
! *See the usage note on* The clock ▶ 356 |
for further information on time expressions.

2 *conjunction*
= quand
I was asleep when the phone rang = je
dormais quand le téléphone a sonné
he didn't like French when he was at
school = il n'aimait pas le français
quand il était au collège
when I'm 18 I'll have my own car = quand
j'aurai 18 ans j'aurai ma propre voiture
! *Note that, when talking about future
time, the future tense is used after* quand.

3 *pronoun*
• (*used as a relative pronoun*) = où
in the days when there was no TV = à
l'époque où il n'y avait pas de télévision
• (*used in questions*) = quand

where
1 *adverb*
= où
where are you going? = où vas-tu?
where do they work? = où est-ce qu'ils
travaillent?
do you know where [he is | Tom is | we're
going ...]? = est-ce que tu sais où [il est | est
Tom | nous allons ...]?
I wonder where he lives = je me demande
où il habite
the village where we live = le village où
nous habitons

what

As a pronoun

In questions

- When used in questions as an object pronoun, **what** is translated by **qu'est-ce que** (**qu'est-ce qu'** in front of a vowel or mute h):

what is he doing?	= **qu'est-ce qu'**il fait?
what did you say?	= **qu'est-ce que** tu as dit?
what are we going to do?	= **qu'est-ce que** nous allions faire?

- Alternatively, you can use **que** (**qu'** before a vowel or mute h), but note that, after **que**, the order of subject and verb is reversed and a hyphen is inserted between them if the subject is a pronoun:

what is he doing?	= **que** fait-il?
what did you say?	= **qu'**as-tu dit?
what are we going to do?	= **qu'**allons-nous faire?

- When used in questions as a subject pronoun, what is translated by **qu'est-ce qui**:

what is happening?	= **qu'est ce qui** se passe?
what happened?	= **qu'est-ce qui** s'est passé?
what is going to happen?	= **qu'est-ce qui** va se passer?

Again, if you use **que**, the order of subject and verb is reversed, the subject becomes **il** and a hyphen is inserted between them:

what is happening?	= **que** se passe-t-il?*
what happened?	= **que** s'est-il passé?
what is going to happen?	= **que** va-t-il se passer?

* In this case, an additional -t- is required for the liaison between the two vowels to be made.

To introduce a clause

- When used to introduce a clause as the object of the verb, **what** is translated by **ce que** (**ce qu'** before a vowel or mute h):

*I don't know **what** he wants*	= je ne sais pas **ce qu'**il veut
*did they have **what** you wanted?*	– est-ce qu'ils avaient **ce que** tu voulais?
***what** he said was that he didn't care*	= **ce qu'**il a dit c'est que ça lui était égal

- When **what** is the subject of the verb, it is translated by **ce qui**:

*tell me **what** happened*	= raconte-moi **ce qui** s'est passé
*I want to know **what**'s happening*	= je veux savoir **ce qui** se passe
***what** matters is that we won*	= **ce qui** compte, c'est que nous avons gagné

With prepositions

What, when it is used with a preposition in English, is translated by **quoi**. In French, however, the preposition always comes before **quoi**:

what are you thinking about?	= à **quoi** penses-tu?
*I don't know **what** he is talking about*	= je ne sais pas de **quoi** il parle

As a determiner

When **what** is used as a determiner, it is translated by **quel**, **quelle**, **quels** or **quelles**, according to whether the noun that follows is masculine or feminine, singular or plural:

what train did you catch?	= **quel** train as-tu pris?
what time is it?	= **quelle** heure est-il?
what books do you like?	= **quels** livres aimes-tu?
what colours do you like?	= **quelles** couleurs aimes-tu?

▶ For more examples, see the entry **what**.

W

2 *conjunction*
  that's where she fell = c'est là qu'elle est
    tombée
  I'll leave the key where you can see it = je
    laisserai la clé là où tu peux la voir

whether *conjunction*
  = si
  I don't know whether or not to accept = je
    ne sais pas si je dois accepter

which
▶ *See the boxed note on* which *for more
information and examples.*
1 *pronoun*
  the house which I told you about = la
    maison dont je t'ai parlé
2 *determiner*
  which one of the nurses speaks French?
    = laquelle des infirmières parle
    français?
  ask him which bus leaves first
    = demande-lui quel bus va partir le
    premier

while *conjunction*
  = pendant que
  **I had a party while my parents were in
  Spain** = j'ai fait une fête pendant que
    mes parents étaient en Espagne
  she fell asleep while watching TV = elle
    s'est endormie en regardant la
    télévision

whisper *verb*
  = chuchoter

whistle
1 *verb*
  = siffler
2 *noun*
  a whistle = un sifflet

white *adjective* ▶ 213 |
  = blanc/blanche

who *pronoun*
• *(used in questions)* = qui
  who told you? = qui (est-ce qui) te l'a dit?
  who did you invite? = qui est-ce que tu as
    invité?
  who did he buy the book for? = pour qui
    a-t-il acheté le livre?
• *(used as a relative pronoun)*
  my friend who lives in Paris = mon ami
    qui habite Paris
  those who can't come by car = ceux/celles
    qui ne peuvent pas venir en voiture
  a friend who I see at work = un ami que je
    vois au travail

whole
1 *noun*
  the whole of [the country | London |
    August ...] = tout [le pays | Londres | le mois
    d'août ...]

2 *adjective*
  a whole day = toute une journée, une
    journée entière
  three whole weeks = trois semaines
    entières
  I don't want to spend my whole life here
    = je ne veux pas passer toute ma vie ici

whom *pronoun*
• *(used in questions)* = qui
  whom did you meet? = qui as-tu
    rencontré?
• *(used as a relative pronoun)*
  the person to whom I spoke on the phone
    = la personne à qui j'ai parlé au téléphone

whose
1 *pronoun*
• *(used in questions)* = à qui
  whose is the dog? = à qui est le chien?
• *(used as a relative pronoun)* = dont
  the boy whose bike was stolen = le
    garçon dont le vélo a été volé
  the woman whose house I'm buying = la
    femme dont j'achète la maison
2 *determiner*
  whose car is that? = à qui est cette voiture?
  whose pen did you borrow? = à qui as-tu
    emprunté un stylo?

why
1 *adverb*
• *(used in questions)* = pourquoi
  why did you do that? = pourquoi est-ce
    que tu as fait ça?
  why aren't they coming? = pourquoi est-
    ce qu'ils ne viennent pas?
  why not? = pourquoi pas?
• *(when making suggestions)*
  why don't we eat out tonight? = et si on
    allait au restaurant ce soir?
2 *conjunction*
  = pour ça
  that's why I can't stand him = c'est pour ça
    que je le déteste

wide *adjective* ▶ 285 |
• *(in size)* = large
  a wide garden = un jardin large
  the room is ten metres wide = la pièce a
    dix mètres de large
• *(in range)*
  a wide range of games = un très grand
    choix de jeux

width *noun* ▶ 285 |
  width = la largeur

wife *noun*
  a wife = une femme

wild *adjective*
• *(describing animals, birds)* = sauvage
• *(noisy, out of control)* = fou/folle
  to go wild = se déchaîner (**!** + *être*)

wildlife *noun*
  wildlife = la faune

which

As a pronoun

In questions

When **which** (meaning *which one* or *which ones*) is used as a pronoun in questions, it is translated by **lequel**, **laquelle**, **lesquels** or **lesquelles**, according to whether the noun it is standing for is masculine or feminine, singular or plural:

there are three peaches,	= il y a trois pêches,
which do you want?	**laquelle** veux-tu?

When **which** is followed by a superlative adjective, then the translation is **quel**, **quelle**, **quels** or **quelles**, according to whether the noun it is standing for is masculine or feminine, singular or plural:

(of the apples) **which** *is the biggest?*	= **quelle** est la plus grosse?
(of the books) **which** *is the most useful?*	= **quel** est le plus utile?
(of the cars) **which** *are the fastest?*	= **quelles** sont les plus rapides?
(of the computers) **which** *are the cheapest?*	= **quels** sont les moins chers?

In relative clauses

When used as a pronoun, **which** is translated by **qui** when it is the subject of the verb, and by **que** when it is the object:

the book **which** *is on the table*	= le livre **qui** est sur la table
the book **which** *Tina is reading*	= le livre **que** lit Tina

Note the different word order of subject and verb; this is the case where the subject is a noun but not where the subject is a pronoun:

the book **which** *I am reading*	= le livre **que** je lis
the book **which** *he's writing*	= le livre **qu'**il écrit
the film **which** *we're going to see*	= le film **que** nous allons voir

Remember that in the present perfect and past perfect tenses, the past participle agrees with the noun **que** is referring back to:

the film **which** *we saw*	= le film **que** nous avous vu
the car **which** *they stole*	= la voiture **qu'**ils ont volée
the books **which** *I gave you*	= les livres **que** je t'ai donnés *(masculine plural)*
the dresses **which** *she bought yesterday*	= les robes **qu'**elle a achetées hier *(feminine plural)*

As a determiner

When **which** is used as a determiner in questions, it is translated by **quel**, **quelle**, **quels** or **quelles** according to whether the noun that follows is masculine or feminine, singular or plural:

which *car is yours?*	= **quelle** voiture est la vôtre?
which *dress did she buy?*	= **quelle** robe a-t-elle achetée?*
which *houses are for sale?*	= **quelles** maisons sont à vendre?
which *computer doesn't work?*	= **quel** ordinateur ne marche pas?
which *books did he borrow?*	= **quels** livres a-t-il empruntés?*

Note that, in the second and third examples, the object precedes the verb or auxiliary verb so that the past participle agrees with it.

* In this case, an additional **-t-** is required for the liaison between the two vowels to be made.

W

---

will *verb*

! Note that, when referring to the future, French generally uses the future tense of the verb to translate will + *verb*: I will sing = je chanterai. When talking about something in the near future, the present tense of aller + *verb* is also possible: je vais chanter.

- *(when talking about the future)*
  she won't agree = elle ne sera pas d'accord
  it will be sunny tomorrow = il va faire beau demain
  what will we do? = qu'est-ce que nous allons faire?

- (*when talking about intentions*)
  I'll wait for you at the airport = je t'attendrai à l'aéroport
  we won't stay too long = nous ne resterons pas trop longtemps
- (*in invitations and requests*)
  will you have some coffee? = est-ce que vous voulez du café?, voulez-vous du café?
  will you ask him for me? = est-ce que tu peux lui demander de ma part?
- (*when making assumptions*)
  they won't know what's happened = ils ne doivent pas savoir ce qui s'est passé
- (*in short questions and answers*)
  you'll come again, won't you? = tu reviendras, n'est-ce pas?
  that will be cheaper, won't it? = ça sera moins cher, non?
  'he won't be ready'—'yes he will' = 'il ne sera pas prêt'—'si'

win *verb*
= gagner

wind *noun*
a wind = un vent

window *noun*
a window (*in a house*) = une fenêtre
(*in a shop*) = une vitrine
(*in a car, a bus*) = une vitre

windsurfing *noun* ▶ 248 |
windsurfing = la planche à voile

windy *adjective*
it's windy = il fait du vent

wine *noun*
wine = le vin

wing *noun*
a wing = une aile

winter *noun*
winter = l'hiver (*masculine*)
in winter = en hiver

wipe *verb*
= essuyer
to wipe one's feet = s'essuyer les pieds
to wipe one's nose = se moucher (**!** + *être*)

wise *adjective*
(*describing a person*) = sage
(*describing a decision, a choice*) = judicieux/judicieuse

wish
1 *noun*
- **a wish** = un souhait
  to make a wish = faire un vœu
- (*in greetings*)
  best wishes = meilleurs vœux
  (*in a letter*) = amicalement

2 *verb*
- (*expressing what one would like*)
  I wish they could come = si seulement ils pouvaient venir
  she wished she hadn't lied = elle regrettait d'avoir menti
- (*in greetings*) = souhaiter
  to wish someone a happy birthday = souhaiter un bon anniversaire à quelqu'un

with *preposition*
- **with** = avec
  to go away with friends = partir avec des amis
  I'm living with my parents = j'habite chez mes parents
  to be pleased with the house = être content/contente de la maison
- (*when describing*)
  a girl with black hair = une fille aux cheveux noirs
  the boy with the broken leg = le garçon à la jambe cassée
  his clothes were covered with mud = ses vêtements étaient couverts de boue
  he was walking along with his hands in his pockets = il se promenait les mains dans les poches
  she's married with two children = elle est mariée et mère de deux enfants

without *preposition*
= sans
we got in without paying = on est entré sans payer

wolf *noun*
a wolf = un loup

woman *noun*
a woman = une femme
a single woman = une célibataire

wonder *verb*
- (*to ask oneself*) = se demander (**!** + *être*)
  I wonder [how | why | who ...] = je me demande [comment | pourquoi | qui ...]
  I was wondering when you'd arrive = je me demandais quand tu arriverais
- (*in polite requests*)
  I wonder if you could help me? = pourriez-vous m'aider?

wonderful *adjective*
= merveilleux/merveilleuse

wood *noun*
- (*timber*)
  wood = le bois
  made of wood = en bois
- (*a small forest*)
  a wood = un bois

wool *noun*
wool = la laine

word *noun*
a word = un mot
what's the French word for 'break'? = comment dit-on 'break' en français?
in other words = autrement dit

work
1 *verb*
- (*to have or do a job*) = travailler
  to work at home = travailler à domicile
  to work as a doctor = être médecin
- (*to operate properly*) = marcher
  the TV isn't working = la télévision ne
  marche pas, la télévision est en panne
- (*to be successful*) (*if it's an idea, a trick*)
  = marcher
  (*if it's a plan*) = réussir
  (*if it's a medicine, a treatment*) = agir
- (*to use, to operate*) = se servir de (**!** + *être*)
  do you know how to work the computer?
  = est-ce que tu sais te servir de
  l'ordinateur?
2 *noun*
- **work** = le travail
  I've got work to do = j'ai du travail
  to be out of work = être au chômage
  the students' work = le travail des élèves
  it's hard work learning French = c'est dur
  d'apprendre le français
- (*for building, for repairs*)
  work(s) = les travaux (*masculine plural*)
  there are road works at the moment = il y
  a des travaux en ce moment
- (*by an artist, a musician*)
  a work = une œuvre
work out
- (*to find*) = trouver
  to work out the answer = trouver la
  réponse
- (*to understand*) = comprendre
- (*with figures*) = calculer
- (*to go well*) = marcher
- (*to take exercise*) = s'entraîner (**!** + *être*)
work up
to get worked up = s'énerver (**!** + *être*)

worker *noun*
  a worker (*in a factory*) = un ouvrier/une
  ouvrière
  (*in an office, a bank*) = un employé/une
  employée

world *noun*
  the world = le monde
  all over the world = dans le monde entier
  the biggest city in the world = la plus
  grande ville du monde

World Cup *noun*
  the World Cup = la Coupe du Monde

worm *noun*
  a worm = un ver

worried *adjective*
  = inquiet/inquiète
  to be worried about someone = se faire du
  souci pour quelqu'un

worry *verb*
- (*to be worried*) = s'inquiéter (**!** + *être*)
  there's nothing to worry about = il n'y a
  pas de quoi s'inquiéter
- (*to make someone worried*) = inquiéter
  it's worrying me = ça m'inquiète

worse *adjective*
  = pire
  this book is worse than the others = ce
  livre est pire que les autres
  she's worse than me at sports = elle est
  pire que moi en sport
  the weather is going to get worse = le
  temps va empirer
  he's getting worse (*in health*) = il va plus
  mal

worst
1 *noun*
  the worst = le pire/la pire
  to be the worst at French = être le plus
  mauvais/la plus mauvaise en français
2 *adjective*
  = plus mauvais/plus mauvaise
  the worst hotel in town = le plus mauvais
  hôtel de la ville
  the worst film I've ever seen = le plus
  mauvais film que j'aie jamais vu

  > **!** Note that the subjunctive is used after
  > the superlative **le plus mauvais... que**.

  his worst enemy = son pire ennemi
  the worst thing to do would be to tell him
  = le pire serait de le lui dire

worth *adjective*
  to be worth £100 = valoir 100 livres
  it's not worth the trouble = ça n'en vaut
  pas la peine

would *verb*

  > **!** Note that French usually uses verbs in
  > the conditional to translate **would** + *verb*:
  > **I would buy** = j'achèterais.

- (*when talking about hypothetical rather
  than real situations*)
  if I had more money, I would buy a car = si
  j'avais plus d'argent, j'achèterais une
  voiture
  **we would have missed the train if we'd
  left later** = nous aurions raté le train si
  nous étions partis plus tard
- (*in reported speech*)
  I thought you'd forget to come = je
  pensais que tu oublierais de venir
  we were sure she would like it = nous
  étions sûrs que ça lui plairait
- (*when making an assumption*)
  she'd be 30 now = elle doit avoir 30 ans
  maintenant
  it would have been about midday = il
  devait être à peu près midi
- (*to be prepared to*)
  he wouldn't listen to me = il ne voulait pas
  m'écouter
- (*when talking about one's wishes*)
  I'd like a beer = je voudrais une bière
  we would like to stay another night = nous
  aimerions rester une nuit de plus

W

• (when asking, offering or advising)
would you turn the TV off? = est-ce que tu veux bien éteindre la radio?
would you excuse me? = excusez-moi
would you like something to eat? = voulez-vous manger quelque chose?
you would do well to check = tu ferais mieux de vérifier

wrap verb
= envelopper
to wrap (up) a present = emballer un cadeau

wreck
1 verb
(if it's a person) = détruire
(if it's a fire, a bomb) = dévaster
2 noun
a wreck = une épave

wrestling noun ▶ 248
wrestling = le catch

wrist noun ▶ 201
the wrist = le poignet

write verb
= écrire
to write to someone, to write someone
(US English) = écrire à quelqu'un
to write [an essay | a cheque | a note …]
= faire [une rédaction | un chèque | un mot …]
write back = répondre
write down = noter
write out = écrire

writing noun
writing = l'écriture (feminine)
your writing is good = tu écris bien

writing pad noun
a writing pad = un bloc de papier à lettres

wrong adjective
• (not as it should be)
there's something wrong = il y a quelque chose qui ne va pas
what's wrong? = qu'est-ce qu'il y a?
what's wrong with you? (if ill, in pain)
= qu'est-ce que tu as?
(if behaving oddly) = qu'est-ce qui t'arrive?
• (not proper or suitable)
= mauvais/mauvaise (! before the noun)
I took the wrong key = j'ai pris la mauvaise clé
to say the wrong thing = faire une gaffe
to go the wrong way = se tromper de chemin
• (not correct)
that's wrong = c'est faux
to dial the wrong number = faire un faux numéro, se tromper de numéro
it's the wrong answer = ce n'est pas la bonne réponse
to be wrong (if it's a person) = avoir tort, se tromper (! + être)

• (not honest, not good)
it's wrong to steal = c'est mal de voler
she hasn't done anything wrong = elle n'a rien fait de mal
there's nothing wrong with trying = il n'y a pas de mal à essayer

X-ray
1 noun
an X-ray = une radiographie, une radio
to have an X-ray = se faire radiographier
2 verb
= radiographier

Yy

yacht noun
a yacht = un yacht

yard noun
(when measuring) ▶ 285
a yard ≈ un yard
| ! Note that a yard = 0.9144 m.

(of a building)
a yard = une cour
(US English) (a garden)
a yard = un jardin

yawn verb
= bâiller

year noun
| ! Note that **year** is usually translated by an in French. However it is sometimes translated by **année**, when there is an emphasis on the idea of duration.

(when talking about time) ▶ 356
a year = un an
last year = l'an dernier, l'année dernière
two years ago = il y a deux ans
to work all year round = travailler toute l'année
he's lived there for years = il y habite depuis des années
that'll take years! = ça va prendre une éternité!
(when talking about age) ▶ 187
a year = un an
to be 15 years old, to be 15 years of age = avoir 15 ans
a four-year old = un enfant/une enfant de quatre ans

• (*in a school system*)
first year, year one ≈ la sixième
to be in second year, to be in year two ≈ être en cinquième
a first year ≈ un élève/une élève de sixième

yell
1 *verb*
= hurler
to yell at someone = crier après quelqu'un
2 *noun*
a yell = un hurlement

yellow *adjective* ▶ 213 |
= jaune
to go yellow = jaunir

yes *adverb*
yes = oui
'are you coming with us?'—'yes I am' = 'est-ce que tu viens avec nous?'—'oui'
they don't know each other'—'yes they do' = 'ils ne se connaissent pas'—'(mais) si'
'didn't he tell you?'—'yes he did' = 'il ne te l'a pas dit?'—'si'

yesterday *adverb*
= hier

yet
1 *adverb*
= encore
not yet = pas encore
it's not ready yet = ce n'est pas encore prêt
have they arrived yet? = est-ce qu'ils sont arrivés?
has she met them yet? = est-ce qu'elle les a déjà rencontrés?
2 *conjunction*
= pourtant

yogurt *noun*
yogurt = le yaourt

you *pronoun*
▶ 378 | See the boxed note on **you** for detailed information and examples.

young
1 *adjective*
= jeune
a young lady = une jeune femme
young people = les jeunes (*masculine*)
she is a year younger than me = elle a un an de moins que moi
a younger brother = un frère cadet
a younger sister = une sœur cadette
to look young = faire jeune
2 *noun*
the young (*of an animal*) = les petits (*masculine plural*)

your *determiner*
▶ 379 | See the boxed note on **your** for detailed information and examples. See also the usage note on **The human body** ▶ 201 |.

yours *pronoun*
▶ See also the boxed notes on **you** and **your** for more information.
the red car is yours (*informal*) = la voiture rouge est à toi
(*polite or to several people*) = la voiture rouge est à vous
my garden is bigger than yours (*informal*) = mon jardin est plus grand que le tien
(*polite or to several people*) = mon jardin est plus grand que le vôtre
her children are older than yours (*informal*) = ses enfants sont plus âgés que les tiens
(*polite or to several people*) = ses enfants sont plus âgés que les vôtres

! *Note that, when comparing objects, people, etc, one of the following translations—le tien, la tienne, les tiens/tiennes, le/la vôtre or les vôtres—will be used. To know which one to use, find out whether the object, person, etc being described is masculine or feminine, singular or plural and whether you are using the polite or the informal form of address.*

yourself *pronoun*
• (*when used as a reflexive pronoun*)
you'll enjoy yourself (*informal*) = tu vas t'amuser
(*polite*) = vous allez vous amuser
did you hurt yourself? (*informal*) = est-ce que tu t'es fait mal?
(*polite*) = est-ce que vous vous êtes blessé?
• (*when used for emphasis*)
you did it yourself (*informal*) = tu l'as fait toi-même
(*polite*) = vous l'avez fait vous-même

yourselves *pronoun*
• (*when used as a reflexive pronoun*)
you'll enjoy yourselves = vous allez vous amuser
did you hurt yourselves? = est-ce que vous vous êtes fait mal?
• (*when used for emphasis*)
are you going to organize it yourselves? = est-ce que vous allez l'organiser vous-mêmes?
you want to be by yourselves = vous voulez être seuls

youth *noun*
• (*a young man*)
a youth = un jeune
• (*young people*)
the youth = les jeunes (*masculine plural*)

youth club *noun*
a youth club = un club de jeunes

youth hostel *noun*
a youth hostel = une auberge de jeunesse

youth worker *noun*
a youth worker = un éducateur/une éducatrice

X
Y

you

Used to address people

● In English **you** is used to address everybody, whereas French has two forms: **tu** and **vous**. The usual word to use when you are speaking to anyone you do not know very well is **vous**. This is sometimes called the polite form:

*where are **you** going?*	= où allez-**vous**?
*I'm thinking of **you***	= je pense à **vous**
*would **you** like some coffee?*	= voulez-**vous** du café?
*can I help **you**?*	= est-ce que je peux **vous** aider?
*what can I do for **you**?*	= qu'est-ce que je peux faire pour **vous**?

The more informal pronoun **tu** is used between close friends and family members, within groups of children and young people, by adults when talking to children and always when talking to animals; **tu** is the subject form, the direct and indirect object form is **te** (t' before a vowel or mute h) and the form for emphatic use or use after a preposition is **toi**:

*where are **you** going?*	= où vas-**tu**?
*I'm thinking of **you***	= je pense à **toi**
*would **you** like some coffee?*	= veux-**tu** du café?
*can I help **you**?*	= est-ce que je peux t'aider?
*there's a letter for **you***	= il y a une lettre pour **toi**

As a general rule, when talking to a French person use **vous**, wait to see how they address you and follow suit. It is safer to wait for the French person to suggest using **tu**.

Note that **tu** is only a singular pronoun and **vous** is its plural form.

Remember that in French the object and indirect object pronouns are always placed before the verb:

*she knows **you***	= elle **vous** connaît
	= elle **te** connaît
*I'll give **you** my address*	= je **vous** donnerai mon adresse
	je **te** donnerai mon adresse

● In tenses like the present perfect and the past perfect, the past participle agrees with the direct object:

*I saw **you** on Saturday*	
(to one male: polite form)	= je **vous** ai vu samedi
(to one female: polite form)	= je **vous** ai vue samedi
(to one male: informal form)	= je t'ai vu samedi
(to one female: informal form)	= je t'ai vue samedi
(to two or more people, male or mixed)	= je **vous** ai vus samedi
(to two or more females)	= je **vous** ai vues samedi

Used impersonally

When **you** is used impersonally as the more informal form of **one**, it is translated by **on** for the subject form and by **vous** or **te** for the object form, depending on whether the comment is being made amongst friends or in a more formal context:

***you** can do as **you** like here*	= **on** peut faire ce qu'**on** veut ici
***you** could easily lose your bag here*	= **on** pourrait facilement perdre son sac ici
***you** never know*	= **on** ne sait jamais
*these mushrooms can make **you** ill*	= ces champignons peuvent **vous** rendre malade
	= ces champignons peuvent **te** rendre malade

▶ For a guide to the correct verb forms with **vous**, **tu** and **on**, consult the verb in the French-English part of the dictionary and check the number in the box, which will refer you to the French verb tables at the back of the dictionary.

your

▶ For a full note on the use of the **vous** and **tu** forms in French, see the note on **you** ▶ 378].

● In French, determiners agree with the noun that follows:

your + *masculine singular noun*
(to one person: polite form or to two or more people)   **votre** chien, **votre** ami
(to one person: informal form)   **ton** chien, **ton** ami

your + *feminine singular noun*
(to one person: polite form or to two or more people)   **votre** pomme, **votre** orange
(to one person: informal form)   **ta** pomme, **ton*** orange

* Note that **ton** is used with a feminine noun beginning with a vowel or mute h.

your + *plural noun*
(to one person: polite form or   **vos** chiens, **vos** amis,
to two or more people)   **vos** pommes, **vos** oranges
(to one person: informal form)   **tes** chiens, **tes** amis,
                                                          tes pommes, **tes** oranges

When **your** is stressed, **à vous** or **à toi** is added after the noun:

(to one person: polite form) *your* house   = **votre** maison **à vous**
(to two or more people)   = **vos** maisons **à vous**
(to one person: informal form) *your* house   = **ta** maison **à toi**
(to one person: polite form) *your* parents   = **vos** parents **à vous**
(to two or more people)   = **vos** parents **à vous**
(to one person: informal form) *your* parents   = **tes** parents **à toi**

● When used impersonally to mean **one's**, **your** is translated by **son**, **sa** or **ses**, when **you** is translated by **on**:

you pay your bills at the end of the week   = on paie **ses** factures à la fin de la
                                                         semaine
you get good value for your money   = on en a pour **son** argent

The translation after an impersonal verb in French is **son**, **sa**, **ses**:

you have to buy your tickets at the door   = il faut acheter **ses** billets à l'entrée

Note, however, the following:

smoking is bad for your health   = le tabac est mauvais pour **la** santé
your average student   = **l'**étudiant moyen

▶ For **your** used with parts of the body, see the usage note on **The human body** ▶ 201].

Zz

zap *verb*
• (*to destroy*) = détruire
• (*British English*) (*to switch channels*)
  to zap from channel to channel = zapper**✱**
• (*to remove from a computer screen*)
  = supprimer

zapper *noun* (*British English*)
  a zapper = une télécommande

zebra *noun*
  a zebra = un zèbre

✱ in informal situations

zebra crossing *noun* (*British English*)
  a zebra crossing = un passage pour
  piétons

zero *number*
  zero = zéro

zip (*British English*), **zipper** (*US English*)
noun
  a zip = une fermeture éclair
  to undo a zip = ouvrir une fermeture
  éclair

zip code *noun* (*US English*)
  a zip code = un code postal

zodiac *noun*
  the zodiac = le zodiaque

zone *noun*
  a zone = une zone

zoo *noun*
  a zoo = un zoo

Z

French verbs

Present
je chante = *I sing, I'm singing*

Future
je chanterai = *I will sing*

Imperfect
je chantais = *I was singing*

Perfect
j'ai chanté = *I sang, I have sung*

Past participle
chanté/chantée = *sung*

Present subjunctive
bien que je chante = *although I sing*

Conditional
s'il y avait une chorale, je chanterais = *if there was a choir, I would sing*

Pluperfect
j'avais chanté = *I had sung*

1 chanter

Present		Perfect			Conditional	
je	chante	j'	ai	chanté	je	chanterais
tu	chantes	tu	as	chanté	tu	chanterais
il	chante	il	a	chanté	il	chanterait
nous	chantons	elle	a	chanté	nous	chanterions
vous	chantez				vous	chanteriez
ils	chantent	nous	avons	chanté	ils	chanteraient
		vous	avez	chanté		

Future   ils ont chanté   **Pluperfect**

Future		Perfect (cont.)			Pluperfect	
je	chanterai	ils	ont	chanté	j'	avais	chanté
tu	chanteras	elles	ont	chanté	tu	avais	chanté
il	chantera				il	avait	chanté
nous	chanterons	**Past participle**			elle	avait	chanté
vous	chanterez		chanté/chantée		nous	avions	chanté
ils	chanteront				vous	aviez	chanté

Imperfect		Present subjunctive			Pluperfect (cont.)	
je	chantais	(que) je	chante	ils	avaient	chanté
tu	chantais	(que) tu	chantes	elles	avaient	chanté
il	chantait	(qu') il	chante		
nous	chantions	(que) nous	chantions		
vous	chantiez	(que) vous	chantiez		
ils	chantaient	(qu') ils	chantent		

2 oublier

Present		Perfect			Conditional	
j'	oublie	j'	ai	oublié	j'	oublierais
tu	oublies	tu	as	oublié	tu	oublierais
il	oublie	il	a	oublié	il	oublierait
nous	oublions	elle	a	oublié	nous	oublierions
vous	oubliez				vous	oublieriez
ils	oublient	nous	avons	oublié	ils	oublieraient
		vous	avez	oublié		
		ils	ont	oublié		

Future		Perfect (cont.)			Pluperfect	
j'	oublierai	elles	ont	oublié	j'	avais	oublié
tu	oublieras				tu	avais	oublié
il	oubliera	**Past participle**			il	avait	oublié
nous	oublierons		oublié/oubliée		elle	avait	oublié
vous	oublierez				nous	avions	oublié
ils	oublieront	**Present subjunctive**			vous	aviez	oublié

Imperfect		Present subjunctive			Pluperfect (cont.)	
j'	oubliais	(que) j'	oublie	ils	avaient	oublié
tu	oubliais	(que) tu	oublies	elles	avaient	oublié
il	oubliait	(qu') il	oublie		
nous	oubliions	(que) nous	oubliions		
vous	oubliiez	(que) vous	oubliiez		
ils	oubliaient	(qu') ils	oublient		

3 finir

Present
je	finis
tu	finis
il	finit
nous	finissons
vous	finissez
ils	finissent

Future
je	finirai
tu	finiras
il	finira
nous	finirons
vous	finirez
ils	finiront

Imperfect
je	finissais
tu	finissais
il	finissait
nous	finissions
vous	finissiez
ils	finissaient

Perfect
j'	ai	fini
tu	as	fini
il	a	fini
elle	a	fini
nous	avons	fini
vous	avez	fini
ils	ont	fini
elles	ont	fini

Past participle
fini/finie

Present subjunctive
(que)	je	finisse
(que)	tu	finisses
(qu')	il	finisse
(que)	nous	finissions
(que)	vous	finissiez
(qu')	ils	finissent

Conditional
je	finirais
tu	finirais
il	finirait
nous	finirions
vous	finiriez
ils	finiraient

Pluperfect
j'	avais	fini
tu	avais	fini
il	avait	fini
elle	avait	fini
nous	avions	fini
vous	aviez	fini
ils	avaient	fini
elles	avaient	fini

4 offrir

Present
j'	offre
tu	offres
il	offre
nous	offrons
vous	offrez
ils	offrent

Future
j'	offrirai
tu	offriras
il	offrira
nous	offrirons
vous	offrirez
ils	offriront

Imperfect
j'	offrais
tu	offrais
il	offrait
nous	offrions
vous	offriez
ils	offraient

Perfect
j'	ai	offert
tu	as	offert
il	a	offert
elle	a	offert
nous	avons	offert
vous	avez	offert
ils	ont	offert
elles	ont	offert

Past participle
offert/offerte

Present subjunctive
(que)	j'	offre
(que)	tu	offres
(qu')	il	offre
(que)	nous	offrions
(que)	vous	offriez
(qu')	ils	offrent

Conditional
j'	offrirais
tu	offrirais
il	offrirait
nous	offririons
vous	offririez
ils	offriraient

Pluperfect
j'	avais	offert
tu	avais	offert
il	avait	offert
elle	avait	offert
nous	avions	offert
vous	aviez	offert
ils	avaient	offert
elles	avaient	offert

5 apercevoir

Present	
j'	aperçois
tu	aperçois
il	aperçoit
nous	apercevons
vous	apercevez
ils	aperçoivent

Future	
j'	apercevrai
tu	apercevras
il	apercevra
nous	apercevrons
vous	apercevrez
ils	apercevront

Imperfect	
j'	apercevais
tu	apercevais
il	apercevait
nous	apercevions
vous	aperceviez
ils	apercevaient

Perfect		
j'	ai	aperçu
tu	as	aperçu
il	a	aperçu
elle	a	aperçu
nous	avons	aperçu
vous	avez	aperçu
ils	ont	aperçu
elles	ont	aperçu

Past participle
    aperçu/aperçue

Present subjunctive

(que)	j'	aperçoive
(que)	tu	aperçoives
(qu')	il	aperçoive
(que)	nous	apercevions
(que)	vous	aperceviez
(qu')	ils	aperçoivent

Conditional	
j'	apercevrais
tu	apercevrais
il	apercevrait
nous	apercevrions
vous	apercevriez
ils	apercevraient

Pluperfect

j'	avais	aperçu
tu	avais	aperçu
il	avait	aperçu
elle	avait	aperçu
nous	avions	aperçu
vous	aviez	aperçu
ils	avaient	aperçu
elles	avaient	aperçu

6 attendre

Present	
j'	attends
tu	attends
il	attend
nous	attendons
vous	attendez
ils	attendent

Future	
j'	attendrai
tu	attendras
il	attendra
nous	attendrons
vous	attendrez
ils	attendront

Imperfect	
j'	attendais
tu	attendais
il	attendait
nous	attendions
vous	attendiez
ils	attendaient

Perfect		
j'	ai	attendu
tu	as	attendu
il	a	attendu
elle	a	attendu
nous	avons	attendu
vous	avez	attendu
ils	ont	attendu
elles	ont	attendu

Past participle
    attendu/attendue

Present subjunctive

(que)	j'	attende
(que)	tu	attendes
(qu')	il	attende
(que)	nous	attendions
(que)	vous	attendiez
(qu')	ils	attendent

Conditional	
j'	attendrais
tu	attendrais
il	attendrait
nous	attendrions
vous	attendriez
ils	attendraient

Pluperfect

j'	avais	attendu
tu	avais	attendu
il	avait	attendu
elle	avait	attendu
nous	avions	attendu
vous	aviez	attendu
ils	avaient	attendu
elles	avaient	attendu

7 être

Present	
je	suis
tu	es
il	est
nous	sommes
vous	êtes
ils	sont

Future	
je	serai
tu	seras
il	sera
nous	serons
vous	serez
ils	seront

Imperfect	
j'	étais
tu	étais
il	était
nous	étions
vous	étiez
ils	étaient

Perfect		
j'	ai	été
tu	as	été
il	a	été
elle	a	été
nous	avons	été
vous	avez	été
ils	ont	été
elles	ont	été

Past participle
été (invariable)

Present subjunctive		
(que)	je	sois
(que)	tu	sois
(qu')	il	soit
(que)	nous	soyons
(que)	vous	soyez
(qu')	ils	soient

Conditional	
je	serais
tu	serais
il	serait
nous	serions
vous	seriez
ils	seraient

Pluperfect		
j'	avais	été
tu	avais	été
il	avait	été
elle	avait	été
nous	avions	été
vous	aviez	été
ils	avaient	été
elles	avaient	été

8 avoir

Present	
j'	ai
tu	as
il	a
nous	avons
vous	avez
ils	ont

Future	
j'	aurai
tu	auras
il	aura
nous	aurons
vous	aurez
ils	auront

Imperfect	
j'	avais
tu	avais
il	avait
nous	avions
vous	aviez
ils	avaient

Perfect		
j'	ai	eu
tu	as	eu
il	a	eu
elle	a	eu
nous	avons	eu
vous	avez	eu
ils	ont	eu
elles	ont	eu

Past participle
eu/eue

Present subjunctive		
(que)	j'	aie
(que)	tu	aies
(qu')	il	ait
(que)	nous	ayons
(que)	vous	ayez
(qu')	ils	aient

Conditional	
j'	aurais
tu	aurais
il	aurait
nous	aurions
vous	auriez
ils	auraient

Pluperfect		
j'	avais	eu
tu	avais	eu
il	avait	eu
elle	avait	eu
nous	avions	eu
vous	aviez	eu
ils	avaient	eu
elles	avaient	eu

9 aller

Present		
je	vais	
tu	vas	
il	va	
nous	allons	
vous	allez	
ils	vont	

Future

j'	irai	
tu	iras	
il	ira	
nous	irons	
vous	irez	
ils	iront	

Imperfect

j'	allais	
tu	allais	
il	allait	
nous	allions	
vous	alliez	
ils	allaient	

Perfect

je	suis	allé
tu	es	allé
il	est	allé
elle	est	allée
nous	sommes	allés
vous	êtes	allés
ils	sont	allés
elles	sont	allées

Past participle

allé/allée

Present subjunctive

(que)	j'	aille
(que)	tu	ailles
(qu')	il	aille
(que)	nous	allions
(que)	vous	alliez
(qu')	ils	aillent

Conditional

j'	irais	
tu	irais	
il	irait	
nous	irions	
vous	iriez	
ils	iraient	

Pluperfect

j'	étais	allé
tu	étais	allé
il	était	allé
elle	était	allée
nous	étions	allés
vous	étiez	allés
ils	étaient	allés
elles	étaient	allées

10 faire

Present

je	fais	
tu	fais	
il	fait	
nous	faisons	
vous	faites	
ils	font	

Future

je	ferai	
tu	feras	
il	fera	
nous	ferons	
vous	ferez	
ils	feront	

Imperfect

je	faisais	
tu	faisais	
il	faisait	
nous	faisions	
vous	faisiez	
ils	faisaient	

Perfect

j'	ai	fait
tu	as	fait
il	a	fait
elle	a	fait
nous	avons	fait
vous	avez	fait
ils	ont	fait
elles	ont	fait

Past participle

fait/faite

Present subjunctive

(que)	je	fasse
(que)	tu	fasses
(qu')	il	fasse
(que)	nous	fassions
(que)	vous	fassiez
(qu')	ils	fassent

Conditional

je	ferais	
tu	ferais	
il	ferait	
nous	ferions	
vous	feriez	
ils	feraient	

Pluperfect

j'	avais	fait
tu	avais	fait
il	avait	fait
elle	avait	fait
nous	avions	fait
vous	aviez	fait
ils	avaient	fait
elles	avaient	fait

11 créer

Present		Perfect			Conditional	
je	crée	j'	ai	créé	je	créerais
tu	crées	tu	as	créé	tu	créerais
il	crée	il	a	créé	il	créerait
nous	créons	elle	a	créé		
vous	créez				nous	créerions
ils	créent	nous	avons	créé	vous	créeriez
		vous	avez	créé	ils	créeraient

Future

je	créerai	ils	ont	créé
tu	créeras	elles	ont	créé
il	créera			

Pluperfect

nous	créerons
vous	créerez
ils	créeront

Past participle

créé/créée

j'	avais	créé
tu	avais	créé
il	avait	créé
elle	avait	créé

Imperfect

Present subjunctive

je	créais	(que)	je	crée
tu	créais	(que)	tu	crées
il	créait	(qu')	il	crée
nous	créions	(que)	nous	créions
vous	créiez	(que)	vous	créiez
ils	créaient	(qu')	ils	créent

nous	avions	créé
vous	aviez	créé
ils	avaient	créé
elles	avaient	créé

12 avancer

Present		Perfect			Conditional	
j'	avance	j'	ai	avancé	j'	avancerais
tu	avances	tu	as	avancé	tu	avancerais
il	avance	il	a	avancé	il	avancerait
nous	avançons	elle	a	avancé		
vous	avancez				nous	avancerions
ils	avancent	nous	avons	avancé	vous	avanceriez
		vous	avez	avancé	ils	avanceraient

Future

j'	avancerai	ils	ont	avancé
tu	avanceras	elles	ont	avancé
il	avancera			

Pluperfect

nous	avancerons
vous	avancerez
ils	avanceront

Past participle

avancé/avancée

j'	avais	avancé
tu	avais	avancé
il	avait	avancé
elle	avait	avancé

Imperfect

Present subjunctive

j'	avançais	(que)	j'	avance
tu	avançais	(que)	tu	avances
il	avançait	(qu')	il	avance
nous	avancions	(que)	nous	avancions
vous	avanciez	(que)	vous	avanciez
ils	avançaient	(qu')	ils	avancent

nous	avions	avancé
vous	aviez	avancé
ils	avaient	avancé
elles	avaient	avancé

13 changer

Present				Perfect				Conditional		
je	change			j'	ai	changé		je	changerais	
tu	changes			tu	as	changé		tu	changerais	
il	change			il	a	changé		il	changerait	
nous	changeons			elle	a	changé		nous	changerions	
vous	changez							vous	changeriez	
ils	changent			nous	avons	changé		ils	changeraient	
				vous	avez	changé				

Future

je	changerai
tu	changeras
il	changera
nous	changerons
vous	changerez
ils	changeront

				ils	ont	changé		**Pluperfect**		
				elles	ont	changé		j'	avais	changé

Past participle

changé/changée

Imperfect

je	changeais
tu	changeais
il	changeait
nous	changions
vous	changiez
ils	changeaient

Present subjunctive

(que)	je	change
(que)	tu	changes
(qu')	il	change
(que)	nous	changions
(que)	vous	changiez
(qu')	ils	changent

Pluperfect

j'	avais	changé
tu	avais	changé
il	avait	changé
elle	avait	changé
nous	avions	changé
vous	aviez	changé
ils	avaient	changé
elles	avaient	changé

14 espérer

Present			Perfect				Conditional		
j'	espère		j'	ai	espéré		j'	espérerais	
tu	espères		tu	as	espéré		tu	espérerais	
il	espère		il	a	espéré		il	espérerait	
nous	espérons		elle	a	espéré		nous	espérerions	
vous	espérez						vous	espéreriez	
ils	espèrent		nous	avons	espéré		ils	espéreraient	
			vous	avez	espéré				

Future

j'	espérerai
tu	espéreras
il	espérera
nous	espérerons
vous	espérerez
ils	espéreront

Imperfect

j'	espérais
tu	espérais
il	espérait
nous	espérions
vous	espériez
ils	espéraient

Past participle

espéré/espérée

Present subjunctive

(que)	j'	espère
(que)	tu	espères
(qu')	il	espère
(que)	nous	espérions
(que)	vous	espériez
(qu')	ils	espèrent

Pluperfect

j'	avais	espéré
tu	avais	espéré
il	avait	espéré
elle	avait	espéré
nous	avions	espéré
vous	aviez	espéré
ils	avaient	espéré
elles	avaient	espéré

15 protéger

Present
je	protège
tu	protèges
il	protège
nous	protégeons
vous	protégez
ils	protègent

Future
je	protégerai
tu	protégeras
il	protégera
nous	protégerons
vous	protégerez
ils	protégeront

Imperfect
je	protégeais
tu	protégeais
il	protégeait
nous	protégions
vous	protégiez
ils	protégeaient

Perfect
j'	ai	protégé
tu	as	protégé
il	a	protégé
elle	a	protégé
nous	avons	protégé
vous	avez	protégé
ils	ont	protégé
elles	ont	protégé

Past participle
protégé/protégée

Present subjunctive
(que)	je	protège
(que)	tu	protèges
(qu')	il	protège
(que)	nous	protégions
(que)	vous	protégiez
(qu')	ils	protègent

Conditional
je	protégerais
tu	protégerais
il	protégerait
nous	protégerions
vous	protégeriez
ils	protégeraient

Pluperfect
j'	avais	protégé
tu	avais	protégé
il	avait	protégé
elle	avait	protégé
nous	avions	protégé
vous	aviez	protégé
ils	avaient	protégé

16 mener

Present
je	mène
tu	mènes
il	mène
nous	menons
vous	menez
ils	mènent

Future
je	mènerai
tu	mèneras
il	mènera
nous	mènerons
vous	mènerez
ils	mèneront

Imperfect
je	menais
tu	menais
il	menait
nous	menions
vous	meniez
ils	menaient

Perfect
j'	ai	mené
tu	as	mené
il	a	mené
elle	a	mené
nous	avons	mené
vous	avez	mené
ils	ont	mené
elles	ont	mené

Past participle
mené/menée

Present subjunctive
(que)	je	mène
(que)	tu	mènes
(qu')	il	mène
(que)	nous	menions
(que)	vous	meniez
(qu')	ils	mènent

Conditional
je	mènerais
tu	mènerais
il	mènerait
nous	mènerions
vous	mèneriez
ils	mèneraient

Pluperfect
j'	avais	mené
tu	avais	mené
il	avait	mené
elle	avait	mené
nous	avions	mené
vous	aviez	mené
ils	avaient	mené
elles	avaient	mené

17 peler

Present		Perfect			Conditional	
je	pèle	j'	ai	pelé	je	pèlerais
tu	pèles	tu	as	pelé	tu	pèlerais
il	pèle	il	a	pelé	il	pèlerait
nous	pelons	elle	a	pelé		
vous	pelez				nous	pèlerions
ils	pèlent	nous	avons	pelé	vous	pèleriez
		vous	avez	pelé	ils	pèleraient

Future

		ils	ont	pelé		
je	pèlerai	elles	ont	pelé	**Pluperfect**	
tu	pèleras				j'	avais	pelé
il	pèlera	**Past participle**			tu	avais	pelé
nous	pèlerons		pelé/pelée		il	avait	pelé
vous	pèlerez				elle	avait	pelé
ils	pèleront	**Present subjunctive**				

Imperfect

		(que)	je	pèle	nous	avions	pelé
je	pelais	(que)	tu	pèles	vous	aviez	pelé
tu	pelais	(qu')	il	pèle	ils	avaient	pelé
il	pelait				elles	avaient	pelé
nous	pelions	(que)	nous	pelions			
vous	peliez	(que)	vous	peliez			
ils	pelaient	(qu')	ils	pèlent			

18 acheter

Present		Perfect			Conditional	
j'	achète	j'	ai	acheté	j'	achèterais
tu	achètes	tu	as	acheté	tu	achèterais
il	achète	il	a	acheté	il	achèterait
nous	achetons	elle	a	acheté		
vous	achetez				nous	achèterions
ils	achètent	nous	avons	acheté	vous	achèteriez
		vous	avez	acheté	ils	achèteraient

Future

		ils	ont	acheté		
j'	achèterai	elles	ont	acheté	**Pluperfect**	
tu	achèteras				j'	avais	acheté
il	achètera	**Past participle**			tu	avais	acheté
nous	achèterons		acheté/achetée		il	avait	acheté
vous	achèterez				elle	avait	acheté
ils	achèteront	**Present subjunctive**				

Imperfect

		(que)	j'	achète	nous	avions	acheté
j'	achetais	(que)	tu	achètes	vous	aviez	acheté
tu	achetais	(qu')	il	achète	ils	avaient	acheté
il	achetait				elles	avaient	acheté
nous	achetions	(que)	nous	achetions			
vous	achetiez	(que)	vous	achetiez			
ils	achetaient	(qu')	ils	achètent			

19 rappeler

Present			Perfect			Conditional	
je	rappelle		j'	ai	rappelé	je	rappellerais
tu	rappelles		tu	as	rappelé	tu	rappellerais
il	rappelle		il	a	rappelé	il	rappellerait
			elle	a	rappelé		
nous	rappelons					nous	rappellerions
vous	rappelez		nous	avons	rappelé	vous	rappelleriez
ils	rappellent		vous	avez	rappelé	ils	rappelleraient
			ils	ont	rappelé		

Future				ont	rappelé		
je	rappellerai		elles	ont	rappelé		
tu	rappelleras						
il	rappellera						

Past participle

rappelé/rappelée

Pluperfect

j'	avais	rappelé
tu	avais	rappelé
il	avait	rappelé
elle	avait	rappelé
nous	avions	rappelé
vous	aviez	rappelé
ils	avaient	rappelé
elles	avaient	rappelé

Future		
nous	rappellerons	
vous	rappellerez	
ils	rappelleront	

Present subjunctive

(que)	je	rappelle
(que)	tu	rappelles
(qu')	il	rappelle
(que)	nous	rappelions
(que)	vous	rappeliez
(qu')	ils	rappellent

Imperfect

je	rappelais
tu	rappelais
il	rappelait
nous	rappelions
vous	rappeliez
ils	rappelaient

20 jeter

Present			Perfect			Conditional	
je	jette		j'	ai	jeté	je	jetterais
tu	jettes		tu	as	jeté	tu	jetterais
il	jette		il	a	jeté	il	jetterait
			elle	a	jeté		
nous	jetons					nous	jetterions
vous	jetez		nous	avons	jeté	vous	jetteriez
ils	jettent		vous	avez	jeté	ils	jetteraient
			ils	ont	jeté		
			elles	ont	jeté		

Past participle

jeté/jetée

Pluperfect

j'	avais	jeté
tu	avais	jeté
il	avait	jeté
elle	avait	jeté
nous	avions	jeté
vous	aviez	jeté
ils	avaient	jeté
elles	avaient	jeté

Future	
je	jetterai
tu	jetteras
il	jettera
nous	jetterons
vous	jetterez
ils	jetteront

Present subjunctive

(que)	je	jette
(que)	tu	jettes
(qu')	il	jette
(que)	nous	jetions
(que)	vous	jetiez
(qu')	ils	jettent

Imperfect

je	jetais
tu	jetais
il	jetait
nous	jetions
vous	jetiez
ils	jetaient

21 essayer

Present		Perfect			Conditional	
j'	essaie	j'	ai ·	essayé	j'	essaierais
tu	essaies	tu	as	essayé	tu	essaierais
il	essaie	il	a	essayé	il	essaierait
nous	essayons	elle	a	essayé	nous	essaierions
vous	essayez				vous	essaieriez
ils	essaient	nous	avons	essayé	ils	essaieraient
		vous	avez	essayé		

Future

j'	essaierai
tu	essaieras
il	essaiera
nous	essaierons
vous	essaierez
ils	essaieront

Imperfect

j'	essayais
tu	essayais
il	essayait
nous	essayions
vous	essayiez
ils	essayaient

Perfect (cont.)

ils	ont	essayé
elles	ont	essayé ·

Past participle

essayé/essayée

Present subjunctive

(que)	j'	essaie
(que)	tu	essaies
(qu')	il	essaie
(que)	nous	essayions
(que)	vous	essayiez
(qu')	ils	essaient

Pluperfect

j'	avais	essayé
tu	avais	essayé
il	avait	essayé
elle	avait	essayé
nous	avions	essayé
vous	aviez	essayé
ils	avaient	essayé
elles	avaient	essayé

22 appuyer

Present		Perfect			Conditional	
j'	appuie	j'	ai	appuyé	j'	appuierais
tu	appuies	tu	as	appuyé	tu	appuierais
il	appuie	il	a	appuyé	il	appuierait
nous	appuyons	elle	a	appuyé	nous	appuierions
vous	appuyez				vous	appuieriez
ils	appuient	nous	avons	appuyé	ils	appuieraient
		vous	avez	appuyé		

Future

j'	appuierai
tu	appuieras
il	appuiera
nous	appuierons
vous	appuierez
ils	appuieront

Imperfect

j'	appuyais
tu	appuyais
il	appuyait
nous	appuyions
vous	appuyiez
ils	appuyaient

Perfect (cont.)

ils	ont	appuyé
elles	ont	appuyé

Past participle

appuyé/appuyée

Present subjunctive

(que)	j'	appuie
(que)	tu	appuies
(qu')	il	appuie
(que)	nous	appuyions
(que)	vous	appuyiez
(qu')	ils	appuient

Pluperfect

j'	avais	appuyé
tu	avais	appuyé
il	avait	appuyé
elle	avait	appuyé
nous	avions	appuyé
vous	aviez	appuyé
ils	avaient	appuyé
elles	avaient	appuyé

23 nettoyer

Present		
je	nettoie	
tu	nettoies	
il	nettoie	
nous	nettoyons	
vous	nettoyez	
ils	nettoient	

Future	
je	nettoierai
tu	nettoieras
il	nettoiera
nous	nettoierons
vous	nettoierez
ils	nettoieront

Imperfect	
je	nettoyais
tu	nettoyais
il	nettoyait
nous	nettoyions
vous	nettoyiez
ils	nettoyaient

Perfect		
j'	ai	nettoyé
tu	as	nettoyé
il	a	nettoyé
elle	a	nettoyé
nous	avons	nettoyé
vous	avez	nettoyé
ils	ont	nettoyé
elles	ont	nettoyé

Past participle

nettoyé/nettoyée

Present subjunctive		
(que)	je	nettoie
(que)	tu	nettoies
(qu')	il	nettoie
(que)	nous	nettoyions
(que)	vous	nettoyiez
(qu')	ils	nettoient

Conditional	
je	nettoierais
tu	nettoierais
il	nettoierait
nous	nettoierions
vous	nettoieriez
ils	nettoieraient

Pluperfect		
j'	avais	nettoyé
tu	avais	nettoyé
il	avait	nettoyé
elle	avait	nettoyé
nous	avions	nettoyé
vous	aviez	nettoyé
ils	avaient	nettoyé
elles	avaient	nettoyé

24 envoyer

Present		
j'	envoie	
tu	envoies	
il	envoie	
nous	envoyons	
vous	envoyez	
ils	envoient	

Future	
j'	enverrai
tu	enverras
il	enverra
nous	enverrons
vous	enverrez
ils	enverront

Imperfect	
j'	envoyais
tu	envoyais
il	envoyait
nous	envoyions
vous	envoyiez
ils	envoyaient

Perfect		
j'	ai	envoyé
tu	as	envoyé
il	a	envoyé
elle	a	envoyé
nous	avons	envoyé
vous	avez	envoyé
ils	ont	envoyé
elles	ont	envoyé

Past participle

envoyé/envoyée

Present subjunctive		
(que)	j'	envoie
(que)	tu	envoies
(qu')	il	envoie
(que)	nous	envoyions
(que)	vous	envoyiez
(qu')	ils	envoient

Conditional	
j'	enverrais
tu	enverrais
il	enverrait
nous	enverrions
vous	enverriez
ils	enverraient

Pluperfect		
j'	avais	envoyé
tu	avais	envoyé
il	avait	envoyé
elle	avait	envoyé
nous	avions	envoyé
vous	aviez	envoyé
ils	avaient	envoyé
elles	avaient	envoyé

25 mourir

Present		Perfect			Conditional	
je	meurs	je	suis	mort	je	mourrais
tu	meurs	tu	es	mort	tu	mourrais
il	meurt	il	est	mort	il	mourrait
nous	mourons	elle	est	morte	nous	mourrions
vous	mourez				vous	mourriez
ils	meurent	nous	sommes	morts	ils	mourraient
		vous	êtes	morts		
Future		ils	sont	morts		
je	mourrai	elles	sont	mortes	**Pluperfect**	
tu	mourras				j'	étais	mort
il	mourra	**Past participle**			tu	étais	mort
nous	mourrons		mort/morte		il	était	mort
vous	mourrez				elle	était	morte
ils	mourront	**Present subjunctive**			nous	étions	morts
		(que)	je	meure	vous	étiez	morts
Imperfect		(que)	tu	meures	ils	étaient	morts
je	mourais	(qu')	il	meure	elles	étaient	mortes
tu	mourais					
il	mourait	(que)	nous	mourions		
nous	mourions	(que)	vous	mouriez		
vous	mouriez	(qu')	ils	meurent		
ils	mouraient					

26 courir

Present		Perfect			Conditional	
je	cours	j'	ai	couru	je	courrais
tu	cours	tu	as	couru	tu	courrais
il	court	il	a	couru	il	courrait
nous	courons	elle	a	couru	nous	courrions
vous	courez				vous	courriez
ils	courent	nous	avons	couru	ils	courraient
		vous	avez	couru		
Future		ils	ont	couru		
je	courrai	elles	ont	couru	**Pluperfect**	
tu	courras				j'	avais	couru
il	courra	**Past participle**			tu	avais	couru
nous	courrons		couru/courue		il	avait	couru
vous	courrez				elle	avait	couru
ils	courront	**Present subjunctive**			nous	avions	couru
		(que)	je	coure	vous	aviez	couru
Imperfect		(que)	tu	coures	ils	avaient	couru
je	courais	(qu')	il	coure	elles	avaient	couru
tu	courais					
il	courait	(que)	nous	courions		
nous	courions	(que)	vous	couriez		
vous	couriez	(qu')	ils	courent		
ils	couraient					

27 cueillir

Present	
je	cueille
tu	cueilles
il	cueille
nous	cueillons
vous	cueillez
ils	cueillent

....

Future	
je	cueillerai
tu	cueilleras
il	cueillera
nous	cueillerons
vous	cueillerez
ils	cueilleront

....

Imperfect	
je	cueillais
tu	cueillais
il	cueillait
nous	cueillions
vous	cueilliez
ils	cueillaient

Perfect		
j'	ai	cueilli
tu	as	cueilli
il	a	cueilli
elle	a	cueilli
nous	avons	cueilli
vous	avez	cueilli
ils	ont	cueilli
elles	ont	cueilli

....

Past participle

cueilli/cueillie

....

Present subjunctive		
(que)	je	cueille
(que)	tu	cueilles
(qu')	il	cueille
(que)	nous	cueillions
(que)	vous	cueilliez
(qu')	ils	cueillent

Conditional	
je	cueillerais
tu	cueillerais
il	cueillerait
nous	cueillerions
vous	cueilleriez
ils	cueilleraient

....

Pluperfect		
j'	avais	cueilli
tu	avais	cueilli
il	avait	cueilli
elle	avait	cueilli
nous	avions	cueilli
vous	aviez	cueilli
ils	avaient	cueilli
elles	avaient	cueilli

28 faillir

Perfect		
j'	ai	failli
tu	as	failli
il	a	failli
elle	a	failli
nous	avons	failli
vous	avez	failli
ils	ont	failli
elles	ont	failli

Past participle

failli

Pluperfect		
j'	avais	failli
tu	avais	failli
il	avait	failli
elle	avait	failli
nous	avions	failli
vous	aviez	failli
ils	avaient	failli
elles	avaient	failli

29 fuir

Present	
je	fuis
tu	fuis
il	fuit
nous	fuyons
vous	fuyez
ils	fuient

Future
je	fuirai
tu	fuiras
il	fuira
nous	fuirons
vous	fuirez
ils	fuiront

Imperfect
je	fuyais
tu	fuyais
il	fuyait
nous	fuyions
vous	fuyiez
ils	fuyaient

Perfect
j'	ai	fui
tu	as	fui
il	a	fui
elle	a	fui
nous	avons	fui
vous	avez	fui
ils	ont	fui
elles	ont	fui

Past participle
fui/fuie

Present subjunctive
(que)	je	fuie
(que)	tu	fuies
(qu')	il	fuie
(que)	nous	fuyions
(que)	vous	fuyiez
(qu')	ils	fuient

Conditional
je	fuirais
tu	fuirais
il	fuirait
nous	fuirions
vous	fuiriez
ils	fuiraient

Pluperfect
j'	avais	fui
tu	avais	fui
il	avait	fui
elle	avait	fui
nous	avions	fui
vous	aviez	fui
ils	avaient	fui
elles	avaient	fui

30 sortir

Present	
je	sors
tu	sors
il	sort
nous	sortons
vous	sortez
ils	sortent

Future
je	sortirai
tu	sortiras
il	sortira
nous	sortirons
vous	sortirez
ils	sortiront

Imperfect
je	sortais
tu	sortais
il	sortait
nous	sortions
vous	sortiez
ils	sortaient

Perfect
je	suis	sorti
tu	es	sorti
il	est	sorti
elle	est	sortie
nous	sommes	sortis
vous	êtes	sortis
ils	sont	sortis
elles	sont	sorties

Past participle
sorti/sortie

Present subjunctive
(que)	je	sorte
(que)	tu	sortes
(qu')	il	sorte
(que)	nous	sortions
(que)	vous	sortiez
(qu')	ils	sortent

Conditional
je	sortirais
tu	sortirais
il	sortirait
nous	sortirions
vous	sortiriez
ils	sortiraient

Pluperfect
j'	étais	sorti
tu	étais	sorti
il	était	sorti
elle	était	sortie
nous	étions	sortis
vous	étiez	sortis
ils	étaient	sortis
elles	étaient	sorties

31 bouillir

Present	
je	bous
tu	bous
il	bout
nous	bouillons
vous	bouillez
ils	bouillent

....

Future	
je	bouillirai
tu	bouilliras
il	bouillira
nous	bouillirons
vous	bouillirez
ils	bouilliront

....

Imperfect	
je	bouillais
tu	bouillais
il	bouillait
nous	bouillions
vous	bouilliez
ils	bouillaient

Perfect		
j'	ai	bouilli
tu	as	bouilli
il	a	bouilli
elle	a	bouilli
nous	avons	bouilli
vous	avez	bouilli
ils	ont	bouilli
elles	ont	bouilli

....

Past participle

bouilli/bouillie

....

Present subjunctive		
(que)	je	bouille
(que)	tu	bouilles
(qu')	il	bouille
(que)	nous	bouillions
(que)	vous	bouilliez
(qu')	ils	bouillent

Conditional	
je	bouillirais
tu	bouillirais
il	bouillirait
nous	bouillirions
vous	bouilliriez
ils	bouilliraient

....

Pluperfect

j'	avais	bouilli
tu	avais	bouilli
il	avait	bouilli
elle	avait	bouilli
nous	avions	bouilli
vous	aviez	bouilli
ils	avaient	bouilli
elles	avaient	bouilli

32 découvrir

Present	
je	découvre
tu	découvres
il	découvre
nous	découvrons
vous	découvrez
ils	découvrent

....

Future	
je	découvrirai
tu	découvriras
il	découvrira
nous	découvrirons
vous	découvrirez
ils	découvriront

....

Imperfect	
je	découvrais
tu	découvrais
il	découvrait
nous	découvrions
vous	découvriez
ils	découvraient

Perfect		
j'	ai	découvert
tu	as	découvert
il	a	découvert
elle	a	découvert
nous	avons	découvert
vous	avez	découvert
ils	ont	découvert
elles	ont	découvert

....

Past participle

découvert/
découverte

....

Present subjunctive		
(que)	je	découvre
(que)	tu	découvres
(qu')	il	découvre
(que)	nous	découvrions
(que)	vous	découvriez
(qu')	ils	découvrent

Conditional	
je	découvrirais
tu	découvrirais
il	découvrirait
nous	découvririons
vous	découvririez
ils	découvriraient

....

Pluperfect

j'	avais	découvert
tu	avais	découvert
il	avait	découvert
elle	avait	découvert
nous	avions	découvert
vous	aviez	découvert
ils	avaient	découvert
elles	avaient	découvert

33 pleuvoir

Present

il   pleut
ils   pleuvent

Future

il   pleuvra
ils   pleuvront

Imperfect

il   pleuvait
ils   pleuvaient

Perfect

il   a   plu
ils   ont   plu

Past participle

      piu

Present subjunctive

(qu')   il   pleuve
(qu')   ils   pleuvent

Conditional

il   pleuvrait
ils   pleuvraient

Pluperfect

il   avait   plu
ils   avaient plu

34 asseoir

Present

j'   assieds
tu   assieds
il   assied

nous   asseyons
vous   asseyez
ils   asseyent

Future

j'   assiérai
tu   assiéras
il   assiéra

nous   assiérons
vous   assiérez
ils   assiéront

Imperfect

j'   asseyais
tu   asseyais
il   asseyait

nous   asseyions
vous   asseyiez
ils   asseyaient

Perfect

j'   ai   assis
tu   as   assis
il   a   assis
elle   a   assis

nous   avons   assis
vous   avez   assis
ils   ont   assis
elles   ont   assis

Past participle

      assis/assise

Present subjunctive

(que)   j'   asseye
(que)   tu   asseyes
(qu')   il   asseye

(que)   nous   asseyions
(que)   vous   asseyiez
(qu')   ils   asseyent

Conditional

j'   assiérais
tu   assiérais
il   assiérait

nous   assiérions
vous   assiériez
ils   assiéraient

Pluperfect

j'   avais   assis
tu   avais   assis
il   avait   assis
elle   avait   assis

nous   avons   assis
vous   aviez   assis
ils   avaient assis
elles   avaient assis

35 prévoir

Present		Perfect			Conditional	
je	prévois	j'	ai	prévu	je	prévoirais
tu	prévois	tu	as	prévu	tu	prévoirais
il	prévoit	il	a	prévu	il	prévoirait
nous	prévoyons	elle	a	prévu	nous	prévoirions
vous	prévoyez				vous	prévoiriez
ils	prévoient	nous	avons	prévu	ils	prévoiraient
		vous	avez	prévu		
Future		ils	ont	prévu		
je	prévoirai	elles	ont	prévu	**Pluperfect**	
tu	prévoiras				j'	avais	prévu
il	prévoira	**Past participle**			tu	avais	prévu
nous	prévoirons		prévu/prévue		il	avait	prévu
vous	prévoirez				elle	avait	prévu
ils	prévoiront	**Present subjunctive**			nous	avions	prévu
		(que) je		prévoie	vous	aviez	prévu
Imperfect		(que) tu		prévoies	ils	avaient	prévu
je	prévoyais	(qu') il		prévoie	elles	avaient	prévu
tu	prévoyais					
il	prévoyait	(que) nous		prévoyions		
nous	prévoyions	(que) vous		prévoyiez		
vous	prévoyiez	(qu') ils		prévoient		
ils	prévoyaient					

36 devenir

Present		Perfect			Conditional	
je	deviens	je	suis	devenu	je	deviendrais
tu	deviens	tu	es	devenu	tu	deviendrais
il	devient	il	est	devenu	il	deviendrait
nous	devenons	elle	est	devenue	nous	deviendrions
vous	devenez				vous	deviendriez
ils	deviennent	nous	sommes	devenus	ils	deviendraient
		vous	êtes	devenus		
Future		ils	sont	devenus		
je	deviendrai	elles	sont	devenues	**Pluperfect**	
tu	deviendras				j'	étais	devenu
il	deviendra	**Past participle**			tu	étais	devenu
nous	deviendrons		devenu/devenue		il	était	devenu
vous	deviendrez				elle	était	devenue
ils	deviendront	**Present subjunctive**			nous	étions	devenus
		(que) je		devienne	vous	étiez	devenus
Imperfect		(que) tu		deviennes	ils	étaient	devenus
je	devenais	(qu') il		devienne	elles	étaient	devenues
tu	devenais					
il	devenait	(que) nous		devenions		
nous	devenions	(que) vous		deveniez		
vous	deveniez	(qu') ils		deviennent		
ils	devenaient					

37 suivre

Present		
je	suis	
tu	suis	
il	suit	
nous	suivons	
vous	suivez	
ils	suivent	

Future

je	suivrai
tu	suivras
il	suivra
nous	suivrons
vous	suivrez
ils	suivront

Imperfect

je	suivais
tu	suivais
il	suivait
nous	suivions
vous	suiviez
ils	suivaient

Perfect

j'	ai	suivi
tu	as	suivi
il	a	suivi
elle	a	suivi
nous	avons	suivi
vous	avez	suivi
ils	ont	suivi
elles	ont	suivi

Past participle

suivi/suivie

Present subjunctive

(que)	je	suive
(que)	tu	suives
(qu')	il	suive
(que)	nous	suivions
(que)	vous	suiviez
(qu')	ils	suivent

Conditional

je	suivrais
tu	suivrais
il	suivrait
nous	suivrions
vous	suivriez
ils	suivraient

Pluperfect

j'	avais	suivi
tu	avais	suivi
il	avait	suivi
elle	avait	suivi
nous	avions	suivi
vous	aviez	suivi
ils	avaient	suivi
elles	avaient	suivi

38 vivre

Present		
je	vis	
tu	vis	
il	vit	
nous	vivons	
vous	vivez	
ils	vivent	

Future

je	vivrai
tu	vivras
il	vivra
nous	vivrons
vous	vivrez
ils	vivront

Imperfect

je	vivais
tu	vivais
il	vivait
nous	vivions
vous	viviez
ils	vivaient

Perfect

j'	ai	vécu
tu	as	vécu
il	a	vécu
elle	a	vécu
nous	avons	vécu
vous	avez	vécu
ils	ont	vécu
elles	ont	vécu

Past participle

vécu/vécue

Present subjunctive

(que)	je	vive
(que)	tu	vives
(qu')	il	vive
(que)	nous	vivions
(que)	vous	viviez
(qu')	ils	vivent

Conditional

je	vivrais
tu	vivrais
il	vivrait
nous	vivrions
vous	vivriez
ils	vivraient

Pluperfect

j'	avais	vécu
tu	avais	vécu
il	avait	vécu
elle	avait	vécu
nous	avions	vécu
vous	aviez	vécu
ils	avaient	vécu
elles	avaient	vécu

39 suffire

Present			Perfect			Conditional	
je	suffis		j'	ai	suffi	je	suffirais
tu	suffis		tu	as	suffi	tu	suffirais
il	suffit		il	a	suffi	il	suffirait
nous	suffisons		elle	a	suffi		
vous	suffisez					nous	suffirions
ils	suffisent		nous	avons	suffi	vous	suffiriez
			vous	avez	suffi	ils	suffiraient

....

Future							
je	suffirai		ils	ont	suffi		
tu	suffiras		elles	ont	suffi		
il	suffira						

Pluperfect

....

Past participle

suffi

						j'	avais	suffi
nous	suffirons					tu	avais	suffi
vous	suffirez					il	avait	suffi
ils	suffiront					elle	avait	suffi

....

Present subjunctive

Imperfect								
je	suffisais		(que)	je	suffise	nous	avions	suffi
tu	suffisais		(que)	tu	suffises	vous	aviez	suffi
il	suffisait		(qu')	il	suffise	ils	avaient	suffi
						elles	avaient	suffi
nous	suffisions		(que)	nous	suffisions			
vous	suffisiez		(que)	vous	suffisiez			
ils	suffisaient		(qu')	ils	suffisent			

---

40 dire

Present			Perfect			Conditional	
je	dis		j'	ai	dit	je	dirais
tu	dis		tu	as	dit	tu	dirais
il	dit		il	a	dit	il	dirait
nous	disons		elle	a	dit		
vous	dites*					nous	dirions
ils	disent		nous	avons	dit	vous	diriez
			vous	avez	dit	ils	diraient

....

Future			ils	ont	dit		
je	dirai		elles	ont	dit		
tu	diras						
il	dira						

Pluperfect

....

Past participle

dit/dite

						j'	avais	dit
nous	dirons					tu	avais	dit
vous	direz					il	avait	dit
ils	diront					elle	avait	dit

....

Present subjunctive

Imperfect								
je	disais		(que)	je	dise	nous	avions	dit
tu	disais		(que)	tu	dises	vous	aviez	dit
il	disait		(qu')	il	dise	ils	avaient	dit
						elles	avaient	dit
nous	disions		(que)	nous	disions			
vous	disiez		(que)	vous	disiez			
ils	disaient		(qu')	ils	disent			

....

* vous interdisez

41 lire

Present
je	lis
tu	lis
il	lit
nous	lisons
vous	lisez
ils	lisent

Future
je	lirai
tu	liras
il	lira
nous	lirons
vous	lirez
ils	liront

Imperfect
je	lisais
tu	lisais
il	lisait
nous	lisions
vous	lisiez
ils	lisaient

Perfect
j'	ai	lu
tu	as	lu
il	a	lu
elle	a	lu
nous	avons	lu
vous	avez	lu
ils	ont	lu
elles	ont	lu

Past participle
lu/lue

Present subjunctive
(que)	je	lise
(que)	tu	lises
(qu')	il	lise
(que)	nous	lisions
(que)	vous	lisiez
(qu')	ils	lisent

Conditional
je	lirais
tu	lirais
il	lirait
nous	lirions
vous	liriez
ils	liraient

Pluperfect
j'	avais	lu
tu	avais	lu
il	avait	lu
elle	avait	lu
nous	avions	lu
vous	aviez	lu
ils	avaient	lu
elles	avaient	lu

42 écrire

Present
j'	écris
tu	écris
il	écrit
nous	écrivons
vous	écrivez
ils	écrivent

Future
j'	écrirai
tu	écriras
il	écrira
nous	écrirons
vous	écrirez
ils	écriront

Imperfect
j'	écrivais
tu	écrivais
il	écrivait
nous	écrivions
vous	écriviez
ils	écrivaient

Perfect
j'	ai	écrit
tu	as	écrit
il	a	écrit
elle	a	écrit
nous	avons	écrit
vous	avez	écrit
ils	ont	écrit
elles	ont	écrit

Past participle
écrit/écrite

Present subjunctive
(que)	j'	écrive
(que)	tu	écrives
(qu')	il	écrive
(que)	nous	écrivions
(que)	vous	écriviez
(qu')	ils	écrivent

Conditional
j'	écrirais
tu	écrirais
il	écrirait
nous	écririons
vous	écririez
ils	écriraient

Pluperfect
j'	avais	écrit
tu	avais	écrit
il	avait	écrit
elle	avait	écrit
nous	avions	écrit
vous	aviez	écrit
ils	avaient	écrit
elles	avaient	écrit

43 rire

Present		Perfect			Conditional	
je	ris	j'	ai	ri	je	rirais
tu	ris	tu	as	ri	tu	rirais
il	rit	il	a	ri	il	rirait
nous	rions	elle	a	ri	nous	ririons
vous	riez				vous	ririez
ils	rient	nous	avons	ri	ils	riraient
		vous	avez	ri		
		ils	ont	ri		

Future

je	rirai	elles	ont	ri
tu	riras			
il	rira			

Past participle

ri

Present subjunctive			Pluperfect		
			j'	avais	ri
nous	rirons		tu	avais	ri
vous	rirez		il	avait	ri
ils	riront		elle	avait	ri

Imperfect

(que)	je	rie	nous	avions	ri
(que)	tu	ries	vous	aviez	ri
(qu')	il	rie	ils	avaient	ri
			elles	avaient	ri

je	riais
tu	riais
il	riait

(que)	nous	riions
(que)	vous	riiez
(qu')	ils	rient

nous	riions
vous	riiez
ils	riaient

44 devoir

Present		Perfect			Conditional	
je	dois	j'	ai	dû	je	devrais
tu	dois	tu	as	dû	tu	devrais
il	doit	il	a	dû	il	devrait
nous	devons	elle	a	dû	nous	devrions
vous	devez				vous	devriez
ils	doivent	nous	avons	dû	ils	devraient
		vous	avez	dû		
		ils	ont	dû		

Future

je	devrai	elles	ont	dû
tu	devras			
il	devra			

Past participle

dû/due

			Pluperfect		
nous	devrons		j'	avais	dû
vous	devrez		tu	avais	dû
ils	devront		il	avait	dû
			elle	avait	dû

Present subjunctive

(que)	je	doive	nous	avions	dû
(que)	tu	doives	vous	aviez	dû
(qu')	il	doive	ils	avaient	dû
			elles	avaient	dû

Imperfect

je	devais	(que)	nous	devions
tu	devais	(que)	vous	deviez
il	devait	(qu')	ils	doivent

nous	devions
vous	deviez
ils	devaient

45 valoir

Present		Perfect			Conditional	
je	vaux	j'	ai	valu	je	vaudrais
tu	vaux	tu	as	valu	tu	vaudrais
il	vaut	il	a	valu	il	vaudrait
nous	valons	elle	a	valu	nous	vaudrions
vous	valez				vous	vaudriez
ils	valent	nous	avons	valu	ils	vaudraient
		vous	avez	valu		
		ils	ont	valu		

Future

je	vaudrai
tu	vaudras
il	vaudra
nous	vaudrons
vous	vaudrez
ils	vaudront

Imperfect

je	valais
tu	valais
il	valait
nous	valions
vous	valiez
ils	valaient

Perfect

j'	ai	valu
tu	as	valu
il	a	valu
elle	a	valu
nous	avons	valu
vous	avez	valu
ils	ont	valu
elles	ont	valu

Past participle

valu/value

Present subjunctive

(que)	je	vaille
(que)	tu	vailles
(qu')	il	vaille
(que)	nous	valions
(que)	vous	valiez
(qu')	ils	vaillent

Conditional

je	vaudrais
tu	vaudrais
il	vaudrait
nous	vaudrions
vous	vaudriez
ils	vaudraient

Pluperfect

j'	avais	valu
tu	avais	valu
il	avait	valu
elle	avait	valu
nous	avions	valu
vous	aviez	valu
ils	avaient	valu
elles	avaient	valu

46 voir

Present

je	vois
tu	vois
il	voit
nous	voyons
vous	voyez
ils	voient

Future

je	verrai
tu	verras
il	verra
nous	verrons
vous	verrez
ils	verront

Imperfect

je	voyais
tu	voyais
il	voyait
nous	voyions
vous	voyiez
ils	voyaient

Perfect

j'	ai	vu
tu	as	vu
il	a	vu
elle	a	vu
nous	avons	vu
vous	avez	vu
ils	ont	vu
elles	ont	vu

Past participle

vu/vue

Present subjunctive

(que)	je	voie
(que)	tu	voies
(qu')	il	voie
(que)	nous	voyions
(que)	vous	voyiez
(qu')	ils	voient

Conditional

je	verrais
tu	verrais
il	verrait
nous	verrions
vous	verriez
ils	verraient

Pluperfect

j'	avais	vu
tu	avais	vu
il	avait	vu
elle	avait	vu
nous	avions	vu
vous	aviez	vu
ils	avaient	vu
elles	avaient	vu

47 savoir

Present	
je	sais
tu	sais
il	sait
nous	savons
vous	savez
ils	savent

Future	
je	saurai
tu	sauras
il	saura
nous	saurons
vous	saurez
ils	sauront

Imperfect	
je	savais
tu	savais
il	savait
nous	savions
vous	saviez
ils	savaient

Perfect		
j'	ai	su
tu	as	su
il	a	su
elle	a	su
nous	avons	su
vous	avez	su
ils	ont	su
elles	ont	su

Past participle

su/sue

Present subjunctive

(que)	je	sache
(que)	tu	saches
(qu')	il	sache
(que)	nous	sachions
(que)	vous	sachiez
(qu')	ils	sachent

Conditional	
je	saurais
tu	saurais
il	saurait
nous	saurions
vous	sauriez
ils	sauraient

Pluperfect

j'	avais	su
tu	avais	su
il	avait	su
elle	avait	su
nous	avions	su
vous	aviez	su
ils	avaient	su
elles	avaient	su

48 vouloir

Present	
je	veux
tu	veux
il	veut
nous	voulons
vous	voulez
ils	veulent

Future	
je	voudrai
tu	voudras
il	voudra
nous	voudrons
vous	voudrez
ils	voudront

Imperfect	
je	voulais
tu	voulais
il	voulait
nous	voulions
vous	vouliez
ils	voulaient

Perfect		
j'	ai	voulu
tu	as	voulu
il	a	voulu
elle	a	voulu
nous	avons	voulu
vous	avez	voulu
ils	ont	voulu
elles	ont	voulu

Past participle

voulu/voulue

Present subjunctive

(que)	je	veuille
(que)	tu	veuilles
(qu')	il	veuille
(que)	nous	voulions
(que)	vous	vouliez
(qu')	ils	veuillent

Conditional	
je	voudrais
tu	voudrais
il	voudrait
nous	voudrions
vous	voudriez
ils	voudraient

Pluperfect

j'	avais	voulu
tu	avais	voulu
il	avait	voulu
elle	avait	voulu
nous	avions	voulu
vous	aviez	voulu
ils	avaient	voulu
elles	avaient	voulu

49 pouvoir

Present		Perfect			Conditional	
je	peux	j'	ai	pu	je	pourrais
tu	peux	tu	as	pu	tu	pourrais
il	peut	il	a	pu	il	pourrait
nous	pouvons	elle	a	pu		
vous	pouvez				nous	pourrions
ils	peuvent	nous	avons	pu	vous	pourriez
		vous	avez	pu	ils	pourraient

Future

je	pourrai
tu	pourras
il	pourra
nous	pourrons
vous	pourrez
ils	pourront

Perfect (cont.): ils ont pu; elles ont pu

Past participle: pu

Present subjunctive

(que) je	puisse
(que) tu	puisses
(qu') il	puisse
(que) nous	puissions
(que) vous	puissiez
(qu') ils	puissent

Imperfect

je	pouvais
tu	pouvais
il	pouvait
nous	pouvions
vous	pouviez
ils	pouvaient

Pluperfect

j'	avais	pu
tu	avais	pu
il	avait	pu
elle	avait	pu
nous	avions	pu
vous	aviez	pu
ils	avaient	pu
elles	avaient	pu

50 falloir

Present		Perfect			Conditional	
il	faut	il	a	fallu	il	faudrait

Future: il faudra

Past participle: fallu

Pluperfect: il avait fallu

Imperfect: il fallait

Present subjunctive: (qu') il faille

51 boire

Present		Perfect			Conditional	
je	bois	j'	ai	bu	je	boirais
tu	bois	tu	as	bu	tu	boirais
il	boit	il	a	bu	il	boirait
		elle	a	bu		
nous	buvons				nous	boirions
vous	buvez	nous	avons	bu	vous	boiriez
ils	boivent	vous	avez	bu	ils	boiraient
		ils	ont	bu		

Future

ils ont bu
elles ont bu

Pluperfect

je	boirai
tu	boiras
il	boira

Past participle

bu/bue

j'	avais	bu
tu	avais	bu
il	avait	bu
elle	avait	bu

nous	boirons
vous	boirez
ils	boiront

Present subjunctive

(que)	je	boive
(que)	tu	boives
(qu')	il	boive

nous	avons	bu
vous	aviez	bu
ils	avaient	bu
elles	avaient	bu

Imperfect

je	buvais
tu	buvais
il	buvait

(que)	nous	buvions
(que)	vous	buviez
(qu')	ils	boivent

nous	buvions
vous	buviez
ils	buvaient

52 comprendre

Present		Perfect			Conditional	
je	comprends	j'	ai	compris	je	comprendrais
tu	comprends	tu	as	compris	tu	comprendrais
il	comprend	il	a	compris	il	comprendrait
		elle	a	compris		
nous	comprenons				nous	comprendrions
vous	comprenez	nous	avons	compris	vous	comprendriez
ils	comprennent	vous	avez	compris	ils	comprendraient
		ils	ont	compris		

Future

ils ont compris
elles ont compris

Pluperfect

je	comprendrai
tu	comprendras
il	comprendra

Past participle

compris/comprise

j'	avais	compris
tu	avais	compris
il	avait	compris
elle	avait	compris

nous	comprendrons
vous	comprendrez
ils	comprendront

Present subjunctive

(que)	je	comprenne
(que)	tu	comprennes
(qu')	il	comprenne

nous	avons	compris
vous	aviez	compris
ils	avaient	compris
elles	avaient	compris

Imperfect

je	comprenais
tu	comprenais
il	comprenait

(que)	nous	comprenions
(que)	vous	compreniez
(qu')	ils	comprennent

nous	comprenions
vous	compreniez
ils	comprenaient

53 croire

Present		Perfect			Conditional	
je	crois	j'	ai	cru	je	croirais
tu	crois	tu	as	cru	tu	croirais
il	croit	il	a	cru	il	croirait
nous	croyons	elle	a	cru	nous	croirions
vous	croyez				vous	croiriez
ils	croient	nous	avons	cru	ils	croiraient
		vous	avez	cru		

Future

		ils	ont	cru	
je	croirai	elles	ont	cru	**Pluperfect**
tu	croiras				j'	avais	cru
il	croira	**Past participle**		tu	avais	cru
nous	croirons	cru/crue		il	avait	cru
vous	croirez			elle	avait	cru
ils	croiront	**Present subjunctive**		nous	avions	cru

Imperfect

		(que)	je	croie	vous	aviez	cru
je	croyais	(que)	tu	croies	ils	avaient	cru
tu	croyais	(qu')	il	croie	elles	avaient	cru
il	croyait	(que)	nous	croyions		
nous	croyions	(que)	vous	croyiez		
vous	croyiez	(qu')	ils	croient		
ils	croyaient					

54 plaindre

Present		Perfect			Conditional	
je	plains	j'	ai	plaint	je	plaindrais
tu	plains	tu	as	plaint	tu	plaindrais
il	plaint	il	a	plaint	il	plaindrait
nous	plaignons	elle	a	plaint	nous	plaindrions
vous	plaignez				vous	plaindriez
ils	plaignent	nous	avons	plaint	ils	plaindraient
		vous	avez	plaint		

Future

		ils	ont	plaint	
je	plaindrai	elles	ont	plaint	**Pluperfect**
tu	plaindras				j'	avais	plaint
il	plaindra	**Past participle**		tu	avais	plaint
nous	plaindrons	plaint/plainte		il	avait	plaint
vous	plaindrez			elle	avait	plaint
ils	plaindront	**Present subjunctive**		nous	avions	plaint

Imperfect

		(que)	je	plaigne	vous	aviez	plaint
je	plaignais	(que)	tu	plaignes	ils	avaient	plaint
tu	plaignais	(qu')	il	plaigne	elles	avaient	plaint
il	plaignait	(que)	nous	plaignions		
nous	plaignions	(que)	vous	plaigniez		
vous	plaigniez	(qu')	ils	plaignent		
ils	plaignaient					

55 éteindre

Present

j'	éteins
tu	éteins
il	éteint
nous	éteignons
vous	éteignez
ils	éteignent

Future

j'	éteindrai
tu	éteindras
il	éteindra
nous	éteindrons
vous	éteindrez
ils	éteindront

Imperfect

j'	éteignais
tu	éteignais
il	éteignait
nous	éteignions
vous	éteigniez
ils	éteignaient

Perfect

j'	ai	éteint
tu	as	éteint
il	a	éteint
elle	a	éteint
nous	avons	éteint
vous	avez	éteint
ils	ont	éteint
elles	ont	éteint

Past participle

éteint/éteinte

Present subjunctive

(que)	j'	éteigne
(que)	tu	éteignes
(qu')	il	éteigne
(que)	nous	éteignions
(que)	vous	éteigniez
(qu')	ils	éteignent

Conditional

j'	éteindrais
tu	éteindrais
il	éteindrait
nous	éteindrions
vous	éteindriez
ils	éteindraient

Pluperfect

j'	avais	éteint
tu	avais	éteint
il	avait	éteint
elle	avait	éteint
nous	avions	éteint
vous	aviez	éteint
ils	avaient	éteint
elles	avaient	éteint

56 joindre

Present

je	joins
tu	joins
il	joint
nous	joignons
vous	joignez
ils	joignent

Future

je	joindrai
tu	joindras
il	joindra
nous	joindrons
vous	joindrez
ils	joindront

Imperfect

je	joignais
tu	joignais
il	joignait
nous	joignions
vous	joigniez
ils	joignaient

Perfect

j'	ai	joint
tu	as	joint
il	a	joint
elle	a	joint
nous	avons	joint
vous	avez	joint
ils	ont	joint
elles	ont	joint

Past participle

joint/jointe

Present subjunctive

(que)	je	joigne
(que)	tu	joignes
(qu')	il	joigne
(que)	nous	joignions
(que)	vous	joigniez
(qu')	ils	joignent

Conditional

je	joindrais
tu	joindrais
il	joindrait
nous	joindrions
vous	joindriez
ils	joindraient

Pluperfect

j'	avais	joint
tu	avais	joint
il	avait	joint
elle	avait	joint
nous	avions	joint
vous	aviez	joint
ils	avaient	joint
elles	avaient	joint

57 vaincre

Present

je	vaincs
tu	vaincs
il	vainc
nous	vainquons
vous	vainquez
ils	vainquent

Future

je	vaincrai
tu	vaincras
il	vaincra
nous	vaincrons
vous	vaincrez
ils	vaincront

Imperfect

je	vainquais
tu	vainquais
il	vainquait
nous	vainquions
vous	vainquiez
ils	vainquaient

Perfect

j'	ai	vaincu
tu	as	vaincu
il	a	vaincu
elle	a	vaincu
nous	avons	vaincu
vous	avez	vaincu
ils	ont	vaincu
elles	ont	vaincu

Past participle

vaincu/vaincue

Present subjunctive

(que)	je	vainque
(que)	tu	vainques
(qu')	il	vainque
(que)	nous	vainquions
(que)	vous	vainquiez
(qu')	ils	vainquent

Conditional

je	vaincrais
tu	vaincrais
il	vaincrait
nous	vaincrions
vous	vaincriez
ils	vaincraient

Pluperfect

j'	avais	vaincu
tu	avais	vaincu
il	avait	vaincu
elle	avait	vaincu
nous	avions	vaincu
vous	aviez	vaincu
ils	avaient	vaincu
elles	avaient	vaincu

58 distraire

Present

je	distrais
tu	distrais
il	distrait
nous	distrayons
vous	distrayez
ils	distraient

Future

je	distrairai
tu	distrairas
il	distraira
nous	distrairons
vous	distrairez
ils	distrairont

Imperfect

je	distrayais
tu	distrayais
il	distrayait
nous	distrayions
vous	distrayiez
ils	distrayaient

Perfect

j'	ai	distrait
tu	as	distrait
il	a	distrait
elle	a	distrait
nous	avons	distrait
vous	avez	distrait
ils	ont	distrait
elles	ont	distrait

Past participle

distrait/distraite

Present subjunctive

(que)	je	distraie
(que)	tu	distraies
(qu')	il	distraie
(que)	nous	distrayions
(que)	vous	distrayiez
(qu')	ils	distraient

Conditional

je	distrairais
tu	distrairais
il	distrairait
nous	distrairions
vous	distrairiez
ils	distrairaient

Pluperfect

j'	avais	distrait
tu	avais	distrait
il	avait	distrait
elle	avait	distrait
nous	avions	distrait
vous	aviez	distrait
ils	avaient	distrait
elles	avaient	distrait

59 plaire

Present		
je	plais	
tu	plais	
il	plaît	
nous	plaisons	
vous	plaisez	
ils	plaisent	

Future		
je	plairai	
tu	plairas	
il	plaira	
nous	plairons	
vous	plairez	
ils	plairont	

Imperfect		
je	plaisais	
tu	plaisais	
il	plaisait	
nous	plaisions	
vous	plaisiez	
ils	plaisaient	

Perfect		
j'	ai	plu
tu	as	plu
il	a	plu
elle	a	plu
nous	avons	plu
vous	avez	plu
ils	ont	plu
elles	ont	plu

Past participle

plu/plue

Present subjunctive

(que)	je	plaise
(que)	tu	plaises
(qu')	il	plaise
(que)	nous	plaisions
(que)	vous	plaisiez
(qu')	ils	plaisent

Conditional		
je	plairais	
tu	plairais	
il	plairait	
nous	plairions	
vous	plairiez	
ils	plairaient	

Pluperfect

j'	avais	plu
tu	avais	plu
il	avait	plu
elle	avait	plu
nous	avions	plu
vous	aviez	plu
ils	avaient	plu
elles	avaient	plu

60 mettre

Present		
je	mets	
tu	mets	
il	met	
nous	mettons	
vous	mettez	
ils	mettent	

Future		
je	mettrai	
tu	mettras	
il	mettra	
nous	mettrons	
vous	mettrez	
ils	mettront	

Imperfect		
je	mettais	
tu	mettais	
il	mettait	
nous	mettions	
vous	mettiez	
ils	mettaient	

Perfect		
j'	ai	mis
tu	as	mis
il	a	mis
elle	a	mis
nous	avons	mis
vous	avez	mis
ils	ont	mis
elles	ont	mis

Past participle

mis/mise

Present subjunctive

(que)	je	mette
(que)	tu	mettes
(qu')	il	mette
(que)	nous	mettions
(que)	vous	mettiez
(qu')	ils	mettent

Conditional		
je	mettrais	
tu	mettrais	
il	mettrait	
nous	mettrions	
vous	mettriez	
ils	mettraient	

Pluperfect

j'	avais	mis
tu	avais	mis
il	avait	mis
elle	avait	mis
nous	avions	mis
vous	aviez	mis
ils	avaient	mis
elles	avaient	mis

61 battre

Present		Perfect			Conditional	
je	bats	j'	ai	battu	je	battrais
tu	bats	tu	as	battu	tu	battrais
il	bat	il	a	battu	il	battrait
nous	battons	elle	a	battu	nous	battrions
vous	battez				vous	battriez
ils	battent	nous	avons	battu	ils	battraient
		vous	avez	battu		

Future					Pluperfect		
je	battrai	ils	ont	battu	j'	avais	battu
tu	battras	elles	ont	battu	tu	avais	battu
il	battra				il	avait	battu
nous	battrons	**Past participle**			elle	avait	battu
vous	battrez	battu/battue			nous	avions	battu
ils	battront				vous	aviez	battu

Present subjunctive

Imperfect							
je	battais	(que)	je	batte	ils	avaient	battu
tu	battais	(que)	tu	battes	elles	avaient	battu
il	battait	(qu')	il	batte			
nous	battions	(que)	nous	battions			
vous	battiez	(que)	vous	battiez			
ils	battaient	(qu')	ils	battent			

62 traduire

Present		Perfect			Conditional	
je	traduis	j'	ai	traduit	je	traduirais
tu	traduis	tu	as	traduit	tu	traduirais
il	traduit	il	a	traduit	il	traduirait
nous	traduisons	elle	a	traduit	nous	traduirions
vous	traduisez				vous	traduiriez
ils	traduisent	nous	avons	traduit	ils	traduiraient
		vous	avez	traduit		
		ils	ont	traduit		

Future					Pluperfect		
je	traduirai	elles	ont	traduit	j'	avais	traduit
tu	traduiras				tu	avais	traduit
il	traduira	**Past participle**			il	avait	traduit
nous	traduirons	traduit/traduite			elle	avait	traduit
vous	traduirez				nous	avions	traduit
ils	traduiront				vous	aviez	traduit

Present subjunctive

Imperfect							
je	traduisais	(que)	je	traduise	ils	avaient	traduit
tu	traduisais	(que)	tu	traduises	elles	avaient	traduit
il	traduisait	(qu')	il	traduise			
nous	traduisions	(que)	nous	traduisions			
vous	traduisiez	(que)	vous	traduisiez			
ils	traduisaient	(qu')	ils	traduisent			

63 connaître

Present			Perfect			Conditional		
je	connais		j'	ai	connu	je	connaîtrais	
tu	connais		tu	as	connu	tu	connaîtrais	
il	connaît		il	a	connu	il	connaîtrait	
nous	connaissons		elle	a	connu	nous	connaîtrions	
vous	connaissez					vous	connaîtriez	
ils	connaissent		nous	avons	connu	ils	connaîtraient	
			vous	avez	connu			

Future

je	connaîtrai
tu	connaîtras
il	connaîtra
nous	connaîtrons
vous	connaîtrez
ils	connaîtront

Perfect (continued):

ils	ont	connu
elles	ont	connu

Past participle

connu/connue

Present subjunctive

(que)	je	connaisse
(que)	tu	connaisses
(qu')	il	connaisse
(que)	nous	connaissions
(que)	vous	connaissiez
(qu')	ils	connaissent

Imperfect

je	connaissais
tu	connaissais
il	connaissait
nous	connaissions
vous	connaissiez
ils	connaissaient

Pluperfect

j'	avais	connu
tu	avais	connu
il	avait	connu
elle	avait	connu
nous	avions	connu
vous	aviez	connu
ils	avaient	connu
elles	avaient	connu

64 naître

Present			Perfect			Conditional		
je	nais		je	suis	né	je	naîtrais	
tu	nais		tu	es	né	tu	naîtrais	
il	naît		il	est	né	il	naîtrait	
nous	naissons		elle	est	née	nous	naîtrions	
vous	naissez					vous	naîtriez	
ils	naissent		nous	sommes	nés	ils	naîtraient	
			vous	êtes	nés			

Future

je	naîtrai
tu	naîtras
il	naîtra
nous	naîtrons
vous	naîtrez
ils	naîtront

Perfect (continued):

ils	sont	nés
elles	sont	nées

Past participle

né/née

Present subjunctive

(que)	je	naisse
(que)	tu	naisses
(qu')	il	naisse
(que)	nous	naissions
(que)	vous	naissiez
(qu')	ils	naissent

Imperfect

je	naissais
tu	naissais
il	naissait
nous	naissions
vous	naissiez
ils	naissaient

Pluperfect

j'	étais	né
tu	étais	né
il	était	né
elle	était	née
nous	étions	nés
vous	étiez	nés
ils	étaient	nés
elles	étaient	nées

65 résoudre

Present		Perfect			Conditional	
je	résous	j'	ai	résolu	je	résoudrais
tu	résous	tu	as	résolu	tu	résoudrais
il	résout	il	a	résolu	il	résoudrait
nous	résolvons	elle	a	résolu	nous	résoudrions
vous	résolvez				vous	résoudriez
ils	résolvent	nous	avons	résolu	ils	résoudraient
		vous	avez	résolu		

Future

vous résolvez / ils ont résolu

		ils	ont	résolu	**Pluperfect**	
je	résoudrai	elles	ont	résolu	j'	avais	résolu

Future

je	résoudrai
tu	résoudras
il	résoudra
nous	résoudrons
vous	résoudrez
ils	résoudront

Past participle

résolu/résolue

Present subjunctive

(que)	je	résolve
(que)	tu	résolves
(qu')	il	résolve
(que)	nous	résolvions
(que)	vous	résolviez
(qu')	ils	résolvent

Imperfect

je	résolvais
tu	résolvais
il	résolvait
nous	résolvions
vous	résolviez
ils	résolvaient

Pluperfect

j'	avais	résolu
tu	avais	résolu
il	avait	résolu
elle	avait	résolu
nous	avions	résolu
vous	aviez	résolu
ils	avaient	résolu
elles	avaient	résolu

---

66 coudre

Present		Perfect			Conditional	
je	couds	j'	ai	cousu	je	coudrais
tu	couds	tu	as	cousu	tu	coudrais
il	coud	il	a	cousu	il	coudrait
nous	cousons	elle	a	cousu	nous	coudrions
vous	cousez				vous	coudriez
ils	cousent	nous	avons	cousu	ils	coudraient
		vous	avez	cousu		
		ils	ont	cousu		
		elles	ont	cousu		

Future

je	coudrai
tu	coudras
il	coudra
nous	coudrons
vous	coudrez
ils	coudront

Past participle

cousu/cousue

Present subjunctive

(que)	je	couse
(que)	tu	couses
(qu')	il	couse
(que)	nous	cousions
(que)	vous	cousiez
(qu')	ils	cousent

Imperfect

je	cousais
tu	cousais
il	cousait
nous	cousions
vous	cousiez
ils	cousaient

Pluperfect

j'	avais	cousu
tu	avais	cousu
il	avait	cousu
elle	avait	cousu
nous	avions	cousu
vous	aviez	cousu
ils	avaient	cousu
elles	avaient	cousu

Numbers

Cardinal numbers in French

0	zéro*	80	quatre-vingts‡§
1	un†	81	quatre-vingt-un¶
2	deux	82	quatre-vingt-deux
3	trois	90	quatre-vingt-dix‡
4	quatre	91	quatre-vingt-onze
5	cinq	92	quatre-vingt-douze
6	six	99	quatre-vingt-dix-neuf
7	sept	100	cent
8	huit	101	cent un†
9	neuf	102	cent deux
10	dix	110	cent dix
11	onze	187	cent quatre-vingt-sept
12	douze	200	deux cents
13	treize	250	deux cent◊ cinquante
14	quatorze	1 000□	mille
15	quinze	1 001	mille un†
16	seize	1 002	mille deux
17	dix-sept	1 020	mille vingt
18	dix-huit	1 200	mille** deux cents
19	dix-neuf	2 000	deux mille††
20	vingt	10 000	dix mille
21	vingt et un	100 000	cent mille
22	vingt-deux	100 200	cent deux mille
30	trente	1 000 000	un million‡‡
40	quarante	1 264 932	un million deux cent
50	cinquante		soixante-quatre mille
60	soixante		neuf cent trente-deux
70	soixante-dix‡	1 000 000 000	un milliard‡‡
71	soixante et onze	1 000 000 000 000	un billion‡‡

* In English 0 may be called *nought, zero, nil* or even *nothing*; French is always *zéro*: *a nought = un zéro*.

† *one* is **une** in French when it agrees with a feminine noun, so *un crayon* but *une table, des tables, vingt et une tables*, etc.

‡ (70) Also **septante** in Belgium and Switzerland. (80) Also **octante** in Switzerland and Canada, **huitante** in Switzerland. (90) Also **nonante** in Belgium and Switzerland.

§ Note that when *80* is used as a page number it has no *s*: **page eighty = page quatre-vingt**.

¶ **vingt** has no *s* when it is in the middle of a number. The only exception to this rule is when *quatre-vingts* is followed by *millions, milliards* or *billions*, e.g. **quatre-vingts millions, quatre-vingts billions** etc.

◊ **cent** does not take an *s* when it is in the middle of a number. The only exception to this rule is when it is followed by *millions, milliards* or *billions*, e.g. **trois cents millions, six cents billions** etc. It has a normal plural when it modifies other nouns: **200 inhabitants = deux cents habitants**.

□ Where English would have a comma, French has simply a space. A full stop (period) can be used, e.g. **1.000**. As in English, there is no separation in dates between thousands and hundreds: **in 1995 = en 1995**.

** In dates, the spelling **mil** is preferred to **mille**, i.e. **en 1200 = en mil deux cents**. However, when the year is a round number of thousands, the spelling is always **mille**, so **en l'an mille, en l'an deux mille** etc.

†† **mille** is invariable; it never takes an *s*.

‡‡ The French words **million, milliard** and **billion** are nouns, and when written out in full they take **de** before another noun, e.g. **a million inhabitants = un million d'habitants**. However, when written in figures, **1,000,000 inhabitants = 1 000 000 habitants**, but is still spoken as *un million d'habitants*. When *million* etc. is part of a complex number, *de* is not used before the nouns, e.g. **6,000,210 people = six millions deux cent dix personnes**.

Use of *en*

Note the use of **en** in the following examples:

there are six	= il y **en** a six
I've got a hundred	= j'**en** ai cent

en must be used when the thing you are talking about is not expressed (the French says literally *there of them are six, I of them have a hundred* etc.). However, **en** is not needed when the object is specified:

there are six apples	= il y a six pommes

Approximate numbers

When you want to say *about* ..., remember the French ending **-aine**:

about ten	= une diz**aine**
about ten books	= une diz**aine** de livres
about fifteen	= une quinz**aine**
about fifteen people	= une quinz**aine** de personnes

Similarly *une trentaine, une quarantaine, une cinquantaine, une soixantaine* and *une centaine* (and *une douzaine* means a *dozen*). For other numbers, use **environ** (*about*):

about thirty-five	= **environ** trente-cinq
about four thousand pages	= **environ** quatre mille pages

Note the use of *centaines* and *milliers* to express approximate quantities:

hundreds of books	= **des centaines** de livres
thousands of books	= **des milliers** de livres
I've got thousands	= j'en ai **des milliers**

Phrases

numbers up to ten	= les nombres jusqu'à dix
to count up to ten	= compter jusqu'à dix
almost ten	= presque dix
less than ten	= moins de dix
more than ten	= plus de dix
all ten of them	= tous les dix
all ten boys	= les dix garçons

Note the French word order:

my last ten pounds	= mes dix dernières livres
the next twelve weeks	= les douze prochaines semaines
the other two	= les deux autres
the last four	= les quatre derniers

Calculations in French

$10 + 3 = 13$	dix et trois font *or* égale treize
$10 - 3 = 7$	trois ôté de dix il reste sept *or* dix moins trois égale sept
$10 \times 3 = 30$	dix fois trois égale trente
$30 : 3 = 10$	($30 \div 3 = 10$) trente divisé par trois égale dix

Note how the French division sign differs from the English.

5^2	cinq au carré
5^3	cinq puissance trois
5^{100}	cinq puissance cent
$\sqrt{2}$	racine carrée de deux
$\sqrt{25} = 5$	racine carrée de vingt-cinq égale cinq
$B > A$	B est plus grand que A
$A < B$	A est plus petit que B

Decimals in French

Note that French uses a comma where English has a decimal point.

	say
0,25	zéro virgule vingt-cinq
0,05	zéro virgule zéro cinq
0,75	zéro virgule soixante-quinze
3,45	trois virgule quarante-cinq
8,195	huit virgule cent quatre-vingt-quinze
9,1567	neuf virgule quinze cent soixante-sept *or* neuf virgule mille cinq cent soixante-sept
9,3456	neuf virgule trois mille quatre cent cinquante-six

Percentages in French

	say
25%	vingt-cinq pour cent
50%	cinquante pour cent
100%	cent pour cent
200%	deux cents pour cent
365%	trois cent soixante cinq pour cent
4,25%	quatre virgule vingt-cinq pour cent

Fractions in French

	say
$\frac{1}{2}$	un demi*
$\frac{1}{3}$	un tiers
$\frac{1}{4}$	un quart
$\frac{1}{5}$	un cinquième
$\frac{1}{6}$	un sixième
$\frac{1}{7}$	un septième
$\frac{1}{8}$	un huitième
$\frac{1}{9}$	un neuvième
$\frac{1}{10}$	un dixième
$\frac{1}{11}$	un onzième
$\frac{1}{12}$	un douzième (etc)
$\frac{2}{3}$	deux tiers†
$\frac{2}{5}$	deux cinquièmes
$\frac{2}{10}$	deux dixièmes (etc)
$\frac{3}{4}$	trois quarts
$\frac{3}{5}$	trois cinquièmes
$\frac{3}{10}$	trois dixièmes (etc)
$1\frac{1}{2}$	un et demi
$1\frac{1}{3}$	un (et) un tiers
$1\frac{1}{4}$	un et quart
$1\frac{1}{5}$	un (et) un cinquième
$1\frac{1}{6}$	un (et) un sixième
$1\frac{1}{7}$	un (et) un septième (etc)
$5\frac{2}{3}$	cinq (et) deux tiers
$5\frac{3}{4}$	cinq (et) trois quarts
$5\frac{4}{5}$	cinq (et) quatre cinquièmes
45/100ths of a second	= quarante-cinq centièmes de seconde

Ordinal numbers in French§

1st	1er‡	premier (*fem.* première)
2nd	2e	second *or* deuxième
3rd	3e	troisième
4th	4e	quatrième
5th	5e	cinquième
6th	6e	sixième
7th	7e	septième
8th	8e	huitième
9th	9e	neuvième
10th	10e	dixième
11th	11e	onzième
12th	12e	douzième
13th	13e	treizième
14th	14e	quatorzième
15th	15e	quinzième
16th	16e	seizième
17th	17e	dix-septième
18th	18e	dix-huitième
19th	19e	dix-neuvième
20th	20e	vingtième
21st	21e	vingt et unième
22nd	22e	vingt-deuxième
23rd	23e	vingt-troisième
24th	24e	vingt-quatrième
25th	25e	vingt-cinquième
30th	30e	trentième
31st	31e	trente et unième
40th	40e	quarantième
50th	50e	cinquantième
60th	60e	soixantième
70th	70e	soixante-dixième¶
71st	71e	soixante et onzième
72nd	72e	soixante-douzième
73rd	73e	soixante-treizième
74th	74e	soixante-quartorzième
75th	75e	soixante-quinzième
79th	79e	soixante-dix-neuvième
80th	80e	quatre-vingtième¶
81st	81e	quatre-vingt-unième
90th	90e	quatre-vingt-dixième¶
91st	91e	quatre-vingt-onzième
99th	99e	quatre-vingt-dix-neuvième
100th	100e	centième
101st	101e	cent unième
102nd	102e	cent deuxième
196th	196e	cent quatre-vingt-seizième
200th	200e	deux centième
300th	300e	trois centième
400th	400e	quatre centième
1,000th	1 000e	millième
2,000th	2 000e	deux millième
1,000,000th	1 000 000e	millionième

Like English, French makes nouns by adding the definite article:

the first	= **le** premier (*or* **la** première, *or* **les** premiers *m pl or* **les** premières *f pl*)
the second	= **le** second (*or* **la** seconde etc)
the first three	= **les** trois premiers *or* **les** trois premières

Note the French word order in:

the third richest country in the world	= **le** troisième pays **le** plus riche du monde

* Note that **half**, when not a fraction, is translated by the noun **moitié** or the adjective **demi**; see the dictionary entry.

† Note the use of **les** and **d'entre** when these fractions are used about a group of people or things: **two-thirds of them** = **les deux tiers d'entre eux**.

§ All the ordinal numbers in French behave like ordinary adjectives and take normal plural endings where appropriate.

‡ This is the masculine form; the feminine is **1re** and the plural **1ers** (*m*) or **1res** (*f*). All the other abbreviations of ordinal numbers are invariable.

¶ (70e) Also **septantième** in Belgium and Switzerland. (80e) Also **huitantième** in Switzerland. (90e) Also **nonantième** in Belgium and Switzerland.

Index of lexical and grammar notes

Lexical notes

English grammar notes

French grammar notes

A guide to French grammar

This section expands on many of the terms found in the glossary and used in this dictionary to help you to find the information that you need. The numbers in brackets refer to the appropriate exercises in the Dictionary know-how section p. 171.

Adjective (1, 14) An adjective is used to add extra information to a noun—*a **worried** farmer*, *a **black** cat*, *a **thick** book*. In French: *un fermier **inquiet**, un chat **noir**, un livre **épais***. Note that in English, the adjective usually comes before the noun, whereas in French it usually comes after the noun.

Sometimes, of course, the adjective is separated from its noun:

> *Your garden is **beautiful**.*
> *Votre jardin est **beau**.*

Adverb (5, 16) An adverb is used to add extra information to a verb, an adjective or another adverb—*to walk **slowly**, **extremely** satisfied, **quite** often*. In French: *marcher **lentement**, **extrêmement** satisfait, **assez** souvent*.

Agreement There are two kinds of agreement in French which you must be careful about.

The first is the agreement of nouns and adjectives. All nouns in French have a gender, and most can also be either singular or plural. Any adjective which describes a noun must 'agree' with it in both gender (masculine or feminine) and number (singular or plural). In other words, the adjective must also be masculine or feminine, singular or plural: *un garçon intelligent, une fille intelligente, deux garçons intelligents, deux filles intelligentes*.

The other kind of agreement is that between a verb and its subject. You must always ensure that the ending of the verb is the one which matches the subject. If the subject is a pronoun, this is fairly straightforward since we usually learn the various forms of a verb together with the appropriate pronoun: ***je** vais, **tu** vas, **il/elle** va, **nous** allons, **vous** allez, **ils/elles** vont*.

If the subject of the verb is a noun, or a pronoun like *moi, toi* etc, you have to be more careful to get the form of the verb right.

> *Pierre et son ami vont au cinéma.*
> *(Pierre + son ami = **ils**)*
> *La banque ouvre à neuf heures.*
> *(la banque = **elle**)*
> *Hélène et moi avons deux enfants.*
> *(Hélène + moi = **nous**)*
> *C'est toi qui as acheté ces carottes?*
> *(c'est toi qui = **tu**)*

Auxiliary verbs An auxiliary verb is a verb which is combined with another verb in order to form the so-called compound tenses of that verb (the main compound tenses in French are the perfect, the pluperfect and the future perfect). There are two auxiliary verbs in French, *avoir* and *être*, and each is used with a particular group of verbs.

The auxiliary verb *être* is used first of all to form the compound tenses of all reflexive verbs:

> *Vous vous **êtes** levé à quelle heure?*
> *(What time did you get up?)*
> *Je m'**étais** couché tard.*
> *(I had gone to bed late).*

It is also used to form the compound tenses of a small group of verbs. These verbs are:

aller	to go
arriver	to arrive
descendre	to go|come down
entrer	to enter
monter	to go|come up
mourir	to die
naître	to be born
partir	to leave, to set out
passer	to go past, to drop in on
rester	to remain, to stay
retourner	to return
sortir	to go|come out
tomber	to fall
venir	to come

> *il est allé au marché.*
> *(he went to the market.)*
> *je suis descendu.*
> *(I went down.)*

The auxiliary verb *avoir* is used to form the compound tenses of all other verbs:

> *j'ai fait le ménage.*
> *(I've done the housework.)*
> *elle a fini son travail.*
> *(she has finished her work.)*
> *nous avions déjà mangé.*
> *(we had already eaten.)*

Comparative The comparative, as its name indicates, is the form of the adjective or adverb which enables us to compare two or more nouns or pronouns. In English, this is usually done by putting *more*, *less* or *as* before the appropriate adjective or adverb:

> *Anne is **more** sensitive (than her sister).*
> *Louise is **less** tired (than Jacqueline).*
> *Léa is **as** intelligent (as Louise).*

In French, the equivalent comparatives are *plus*, *moins* and *aussi*:

> *Anne est **plus** sensible (que sa sœur).*
> *Louise est **moins** fatiguée (que Jacqueline).*
> *Léa est **aussi** intelligente (que Louise).*

Note that the French for both *than* and *as* is *que*.

In English, a few adjectives have an irregular comparative form (*good*/**better**, *bad*/**worse**, *little*/**less**, *much* or *many*/**more**) and some shorter English adjectives have a special comparative form ending in *-er* (for example, *bigger, smaller, happier, slower*). In French, there are only three adjectives with a special form: *bon*/**meilleur** (*good*/*better*); *mauvais*/**pire** (*bad*/*worse*); *petit*/**moindre** (*small*/*less*). However, note that *plus petit* is used instead of *moindre* when referring to size: *ma voiture est* **plus petite** *que la tienne* (*my car is smaller than yours*). The only irregular form which is always used is *meilleur*—don't forget that, like all comparative adjectives, it must agree with its noun: *une* **meilleure** *chanson* (*a better song*), *de* **meilleurs** *chanteurs* (*better singers*).

The comparative of adverbs is formed in much the same way:

> Paul walks **more** slowly (than his brother).
> Peter speaks **less** quickly (than Paul).
> Paul goes to Paris **as** often (as Peter).

> Paul marche **plus** lentement (que son frère).
> Peter parle **moins** vite (que Paul).
> Paul va à Paris **aussi** souvent (que Peter).

In both English and French, there are four irregular forms: *beaucoup*/**plus** (*much* or *a lot*/*more*); *bien*/**mieux** (*well*/*better*); *peu*/**moins** (*little*/*less*); *mal*/**pis** or *plus mal* (*badly*/*worse*). However, *pis* is only found in a few fixed expressions and the usual comparative of *mal* is *plus mal*: *je chante* **plus mal** *que lui* (*I sing worse than he does*).

Conditional A conditional sentence is one in which the statement contained in the main clause can only be fulfilled if the condition stated in the subordinate clause is also fulfilled. This condition is usually introduced by *if* in English and by *si* in French.

> If it's fine tomorrow, we'll go to the beach.
> I would be surprised if he came today.

> S'il fait beau demain, nous irons à la plage.
> Je serais surpris s'il venait aujourd'hui.

Conjunction (14) A conjunction can be either (i) a word like *and* or *but* which is used to join words or simple sentences together, or (ii) a word like *when, although, if, where,* which is used to form a complex sentence. Look at these examples:

> (i) John **and** Sarah
> Tired **but** happy
> They came down the steps **and** got into the car.

> Sophie **et** Pierre
> Fatigué **mais** heureux
> Ils ont descendu les marches **et** sont montés dans la voiture.

> (ii) **Although** he doesn't like the rain, he agreed to go for a walk.
> He was about to go to bed **when** he heard the noise of an aircraft.

> **Bien qu'**il n'aime pas la pluie, il a accepté de faire une promenade.
> Il était sur le point de se coucher, **quand** il a entendu le bruit d'un avion.

Determiner (16) A determiner is used before a noun in order to identify more precisely what is being referred to. Here are some examples of determiners in English: **a** car, **the** car, **my** car, **this** car, **these** cars, **some** cars. Examples of French determiners are: **une** voiture, **la** voiture, **ma** voiture, **cette** voiture, **ces** voitures, **certaines** voitures.

Exclamation An exclamation is a word or phrase conveying a reaction such as surprise, shock, disapproval, indignation, amusement etc. In both English and French, it is usually followed by an exclamation mark.

> Well, well!
> What!

> Ça alors!
> Quoi!

Feminine (10, 13, 19) ▶ Gender

Gender (2, 10, 13, 19) You will see when using the French–English half of this dictionary that some French words are marked (*noun, masculine*) or (*noun, feminine*). Unlike English nouns, every French noun has a gender—it is either masculine or feminine. For example, the French words for *office, pen, tree, roof* are masculine (**un** bureau, **un** stylo, **un** arbre, **un** toit), and the words for *car, table, house, photo* are feminine (**une** voiture, **une** table, **une** maison, **une** photo). When looking up a noun in the dictionary, it is important to note whether the French word is masculine or feminine, because this will determine the form of most adjectives and determiners which go with it—**un grand** arbre, but **une grande** maison.

Imperative The imperative is the form of the verb which we use when we want to order someone to do something. In English, there are two imperatives: for example, *leave* and *let's leave*. In French, there are three in order to allow for the *tu* and *vous* forms of the verb: for example, *pars* (*tu* form), *partons, partez* (*vous* form).

Indicative ▶ Subjunctive

Infinitive The infinitive is a form of the verb which has no indication of person or tense. In English, it is often preceded by *to*: *to walk, to run, to read, to receive*. In French, the infinitive ends in *-er, -ir, -re* or *-oir*: *marcher, courir, écrire, recevoir*. The infinitive is the form you will find at the beginning of verb entries in this and other dictionaries.

Masculine (10) ▶ Gender

Noun (1, 16, 17) A noun is used to identify a person, an animal, an object, an idea or an emotion—*farmer, cat, book, suggestion, happiness* are all nouns. It can also be the name of an individual, a company or an institution—*Emma, Peter, Robertson's, Parliament* are nouns. Equivalent French nouns are *fermier, chat, livre, suggestion, bonheur, Sophie, Pierre, Boulangerie Fauré, Conseil d'État.*

Number (16) As in English, most nouns in French may be singular or plural and change their ending accordingly (usually by adding '-s' in the plural: *a tree, two tree***s***; *un arbre, deux arbre***s**). Unlike English, however, adjectives in French may also be singular or plural and in most cases change their ending in order to agree with the noun they describe: *un grand arbre, deux grand***s** *arbre***s**.

In the French–English half of this dictionary, when a noun has an irregular plural, the plural form is given after the noun. A noun which doesn't change in the plural has the warning (**!** *never changes*).

Object (6) The object of a sentence is the word or group of words which is immediately affected by the action indicated by the verb. So, in the sentence *The dog chewed the bone, dog* is the subject, *chewed* is the verb and **bone** is the object. Similarly, in the sentence *Le chien a rongé l'os, chien* is the subject, *a rongé* is the verb and **os** is the object.

There may be two kinds of object in a sentence, a direct object and an indirect object. In the examples above, *bone* and *os* are strictly direct objects. However, in the sentence *John gave the dog a bone, John* is the subject, *gave* is the verb, *bone* is the direct object and *dog* is the indirect object. Similarly, in the French sentence *Jean a donné un os au chien, Jean* is the subject, *a donné* is the verb, *os* is the direct object and *chien* is the indirect object. So, in general, the indirect object indicates the person or thing which 'benefits' from the action of the verb upon the direct object.

Phrasal verb (15) A phrasal verb is a verb combined with a preposition or an adverb and having a particular meaning. For example, *to* **run away**, meaning to flee, or *to* **see to** *something*, meaning to ensure that something is done.

Phrasal verbs don't exist in French and you therefore need to use your dictionary carefully in order to select the correct translation. If you look up *to run away* for example, you will see that phrasal verbs are

listed after all the other meanings of the word *run*, and in alphabetical order of the following adverb or preposition.

Plural ▶ Number

Preposition (11) A preposition is a word, such as *under, beside, across, in*, which is usually followed by a noun: *under the table, beside the road, in the garden;* **sous** *la table,* **au bord de** *la route,* **dans** *le jardin.* Most preposition + noun groups indicate movement

> *he ran* **towards the house**
> *il a couru* **vers la maison**

position

> *your books are* **on the table**
> *vos livres sont* **sur la table**

or time

> *I'll be there* **at 4 o'clock**
> *je serai là* **à six heures***.*

Pronoun (3, 14) A pronoun is used instead of a noun in order to avoid repeating it unnecessarily. English pronouns are *I, me, you, he, him, she, her, it, we, us, they, them, mine, yours, his, hers, ours, theirs, this, that, these* and *those.* Equivalent French pronouns are: *je, me, tu, te, il, le, elle, la, nous, vous, ils, les, elles, leur, lui, le mien, la mienne, les miens, les miennes* etc, *ceci, cela, celui, celle, ceux, celles.* All of these are labelled as pronouns in this dictionary. However, some of the English pronouns (but *not* their French equivalents) can also be used as determiners and you must be careful not to confuse them. Compare these sentences:

> *He lent me* **his** *book.* (determiner)
> *He lent me* **his***.* (pronoun)

> **These** *ideas are important.* (determiner)
> **These** *are important.* (pronoun)

> **Those** *people have just arrived.* (determiner)
> **Those** *have just arrived.* (pronoun)

Now look at the French equivalents:

> *Il m'a prêté* **son** *livre.* (determiner)
> *Il m'a prêté* **le sien***.* (pronoun)

> **Ces** *idées-ci sont importantes.* (determiner)
> **Celles**-ci sont importantes. (pronoun)

> **Ces** *gens-là viennent d'arriver.* (determiner)
> **Ceux**-là viennent d'arriver. (pronoun)

Reflexive verb (24) A reflexive verb is one whose action is 'reflected back' upon the subject of the verb. In English, this is indicated by the use of reflexive pronouns such as *myself, yourself, herself, themselves, each other* etc. For example:

> *When he hurts* **himself***, he cries.*
> *We speak to* **each other** *every day.*

In French, this reflexive action is conveyed by the use of the pronouns *me, te, se, nous* or *vous*:

*Quand il **se** fait mal, il pleure.*
*Nous **nous** parlons tous les jours.*

Here are the full present tense forms of the reflexive verb *se baigner* (*to go for a swim*):

je **me** baigne	nous **nous** baignons
tu **te** baignes	vous **vous** baignez
il **se** baigne	ils **se** baignent
elle **se** baigne	elles **se** baignent

Remember that many reflexive verbs in French have English equivalents which are not reflexive. Other examples are *se souvenir de* (*to remember*), *se laver* (*to wash*).

Singular ▶ Number

Subject (6) The subject of a sentence is the word or group of words which performs the action indicated by the verb. So, in the sentence *John coughed*, John is the subject of the verb *coughed*. Of course, the verb doesn't necessarily express an action as such. For example, in the sentence *John is tall*, John is the subject of the verb *is*. In the French sentence *Jean a toussé*, *Jean* is similarly the subject of the verb *a toussé*, and in the sentence *Jean est grand*, *Jean* is the subject of the verb *est*.

Subjunctive The subjunctive is a special form of some tenses of the verb, which in French is mostly used to express doubt and possibility, rather than fact or certainty. It is also used when expressing an emotional reaction to something. This form of the verb is much more widely used in French than in English, where it has almost disappeared, and you will find a fuller explanation and examples on p. 291. Note that the usual form of the various tenses of a verb is known as the indicative because it 'indicates' fact or certainty.

Superlative The superlative is the form of the adjective or adverb which is used to express the highest or lowest degree. In English, the adjective or adverb is usually preceded by *most* or *least*, **most** *important*, **least** *important*, **most** *carefully*, **least** *carefully*. Some adjectives and adverbs (usually of one syllable) have their own form: *best, worst, biggest, smallest, fastest, slowest* etc. In French, the superlative adjective (which must agree with its noun) is usually formed by putting *le plus, la plus, les plus, le moins, la moins* or *les moins* before the adjective: *le livre **le plus** long, le livre **le moins** long, la question **la plus** importante, la question **la moins** importante, les avions **les plus** rapides, les avions **les moins** rapides*. The superlative adverb is usually preceded by *le plus* or *le moins*: **le plus** *vite*, **le moins** *vite*, **le plus** *soigneusement*, **le moins** *soigneusement*.

Some French adjectives and adverbs have their own form of the superlative, for example:

bon/bonne	**le meilleur/la meilleure**
mauvais/mauvaise	**le pire/la pire**
bien	**le mieux**
mal	**le plus mal**

Tense The tense is the particular form of the verb which tells us the approximate time when the action of the verb takes place:

Present tense
He **is telephoning** all his friends.
Il téléphone à tous ses amis.

Future tense
He **will telephone** all his friends.
Il téléphonera à tous ses amis.

The main past and future tenses used in French are:

Past tenses	(i) Imperfect
	(ii) Present perfect (or Perfect)
	(iii) Past perfect (or Pluperfect)
Future tenses	(iv) Future (simple)
	(v) Future perfect

For example:

(i) *Il **téléphonait** souvent à tous ses amis.*
(He often used to telephone all his friends.)

(ii) *Hier, il **a téléphoné** à tous ses amis.*
(Yesterday he telephoned all his friends.)

(iii) *Il **avait** déjà **téléphoné** à tous ses amis.*
(He had already telephoned all his friends.)

(iv) *Demain, il **téléphonera** à tous ses amis.*
(Tomorrow he will telephone all his friends.)

(v) *Avant 6 heures il **aura téléphoné** à tous ses amis.*
(By 6 o'clock he will have telephoned all his friends.)

Verb (4, 12, 16) The verb propels the sentence along, telling us what is happening. Look at these examples:

*Paul **carried** the boxes upstairs to the attic.*
*The storm **did** a lot of damage.*

*Paul **a monté** les cartons au grenier.*
*La tempête **a fait** beaucoup de dégâts.*

Sometimes, of course, the verb doesn't describe an action, but rather a state of affairs:

*Paul **has** a back problem.*
*He **is** often ill.*
*The damage **appears** less serious than we expected.*

*Paul **a** un problème de dos.*
*Il **est** souvent malade.*
*Les dégâts **semblent** moins importants que prévu.*